3rd Edition

THE
TOOLS
AND
TECHNIQUES
OF

Employee Benefit And Retirement Planning

• Stephan R. Leimberg

• John J. McFadden

NATIONAL
UNDERWRITER

The National Underwriter Co. • 505 Gest St. • Cincinnati, OH 45203

Library of Congress Catalog Card Number: 93-84916

ISBN 0-87218-115-4

published by

NULAW SERVICES

a department of

THE NATIONAL UNDERWRITER COMPANY

Copyright © 1989, 1990, 1993
The National Underwriter Company
505 Gest Street
Cincinnati, Ohio 45203

Third Printing

Third Edition

Printed in the United States of America

DEDICATION

Stephan R. Leimberg

*To Dan Hoellering, my 85-years-young friend
who always found the time to
do so much for so many*

John J. McFadden

To Rhoda, Susanna, and Diana

ABOUT THE AUTHORS

Stephan R. Leimberg

Stephan R. Leimberg is Professor of Taxation and Estate Planning at The American College. He has been granted the B.A. degree by Temple University, a J.D. by the Temple University School of Law, and holds the CLU designation. Mr. Leimberg is a Lecturer in Law in the Tax Masters Program of Temple University School of Law.

Professor Leimberg is on the Board of Advisors of the Bureau of National Affairs—Tax Management—Financial Planning. He also serves on the Personal Financial Planning Risk Management Task Force of the American Institute of Certified Public Accountants and was co-author of their *Risk Management and Insurance in Personal Financial Planning* text.

Professor Leimberg is the author of over 40 books including *The Tools and Techniques of Estate Planning* and *The Tools and Techniques of Financial Planning*. Leimberg is co-creator, with Dr. Robert T. LeClair, of financial, estate planning and business valuation software: TOOLKIT, NumberCruncher, and BizKit.

Mr. Leimberg is the Editor and Publisher of *Think About It,* a monthly newsletter on income, estate, and gift taxes relating to Insurance, Business, Financial, and Estate Planning, published by many Associations of Life Underwriters, CLU Chapters, and insurance companies, and financial institutions.

Professor Leimberg has been a main platform speaker at both the Million Dollar Round Table annual meeting and the Top of the Table and has appeared before numerous estate planning councils, Life Underwriters Associations, life insurance companies, and study groups. He has also addressed the Advanced Planners meeting of the International Association for Financial Planning, the State Bars of Texas, Wisconsin and Oklahoma, the Pennsylvania Bar Institute Basic Legal Practice Course, numerous CPA societies, and has been a featured speaker at three workshops of the National Aeronautics and Space Administration. He appeared as an expert witness on IRAs before a subcommittee of the House Ways and Means Committee of the United States House of Representatives.

Professor Leimberg has also spoken at the N.Y.U. Tax Institute, The Southern California Tax and Estate Planning Forum, the Duke University Estate Planning Conference and at the Annual Meeting of the National Association of Estate Planning Councils.

Leimberg serves on the Board of Directors of the Philadelphia CLU chapter, has served on the Board of the Philadelphia Estate Planning Council, and was a Director of the Delaware Valley Chapter of the International Association for Financial Planning, Inc.

John J. McFadden

John J. McFadden is Professor of Taxation at The American College in Bryn Mawr, PA. His undergraduate degree is from Lehigh University, with a master's degree from the University of Rochester, and a J.D. from Harvard Law School. He has been admitted to the Pennsylvania Bar and the United States Tax Court.

At the American College Mr. McFadden, a tax and compensation planning specialist, is responsible for the College's graduate courses in Advanced Pension and Retirement Planning and Executive Compensation.

Mr. McFadden is the author of articles in tax and professional journals on such subjects as professional corporations, accumulated earnings, retirement plan distributions, and nonqualified deferred compensation. He is author of *Retirement Plans for Employees* and coauthor of *Employee Benefits*, 3rd edition, published by Dearborn Financial Publishing, Inc. in 1992.

Mr. McFadden also speaks and consults on tax and compensation matters and conducts seminars for financial planners active in those areas.

PREFACE

The Tools and Techniques of Employee Benefit and Retirement Planning, 3rd edition, is intended to serve as an easily accessible, up-to-date guide to creative employee benefit and retirement planning for use by practicing financial planners, insurance agents, accountants, attorneys and other financial services professionals, as well as company managers, personnel departments, and law and graduate school students. It is designed to meet these professionals' needs for timely and accurate introductory, overview, or review information in this area. Such needs are increasing for two reasons. First, the high direct and indirect expenses involved with recruiting, retaining and ultimately retiring employees mandates a careful search for the benefit and compensation package that will accomplish an employer's objectives in the most cost effective way. Second, in recent years, there has been a tremendous growth in federal legislation and regulatory activity in the compensation area; this increases the difficulty of designing benefit packages and also the cost (in taxes and penalties to employer and employee) of mistakes in benefit planning.

This book covers all major types of employee benefit arrangements. Although special consideration is given to employee benefit arrangements as applied to smaller, closely held businesses, most of the benefits described here are used by both small and large companies, and the same tax and other rules apply to both.

As is the case with our companion books, *The Tools and Techniques of Estate Planning*, 9th edition, and *The Tools and Techniques of Financial Planning*, 4th edition, in this book each individual tool or technique of benefit or retirement planning is discussed in an easy-to-use format that is aimed at answering the planner's major questions:

WHAT IS IT? provides a brief description of the benefit planning tool or technique.

WHEN IS IT INDICATED? summarizes the client situations where the particular technique is most often beneficial.

ADVANTAGES and DISADVANTAGES provides a summary of the advantages and disadvantages of each technique.

DESIGN FEATURES summarizes the characteristic features of the technique and the planning options that are available.

TAX IMPLICATIONS describes the federal income, estate and payroll tax implications of the technique to both employer and employee; some state tax aspects are also noted where appropriate.

ERISA AND OTHER IMPLICATIONS summarizes the ERISA reporting and disclosure, funding, and other non-tax federal regulatory requirements.

HOW TO INSTALL THE PLAN provides a summary of the steps that must be taken for an employer to adopt and implement the plan.

WHERE CAN I FIND OUT MORE ABOUT IT? provides a list of references for further study and information.

QUESTIONS AND ANSWERS discusses some specific problems (and their solutions) that are often encountered by planners in connection with the benefit plan.

Where appropriate, some chapters may deviate somewhat from this format in order to provide the best approach to understanding the material.

The authors wish to acknowledge many members of the benefit planning community for discussions and critiques that over the years have contributed to the perspective taken in this book. Also, in particular the authors are fortunate to have received substantial technical copy editing assistance from the following editors: Deborah A. Miner, J.D., CLU, ChFC; Darlene K. Chandler, J.D., CLU, ChFC; April A. Kestel, J.D., CLU, ChFC; William J. Wagner, J.D., LL.M., CLU; Peter A. Fossett, J.D.; Terry A. Shumate, J.D.; and Edward A. Lyon, J.D.

CONTENTS

Contents

Appendices   Page

Chapter 1

THE PROCESS OF EMPLOYEE BENEFIT PLANNING

The tools and techniques of employee benefit and retirement planning described in this book are aimed at and should be used to solve general and specific financial planning problems for employers and their employees. This chapter is about the broad *process* by which the employer-client's needs are determined and "matched-up" with the appropriate benefit arrangements.

WHAT BENEFIT PLANS CAN DO

As with any kind of financial planning, the starting point must be a full appreciation of what the tools and techniques at hand can actually accomplish for clients. In the case of employee benefit plans, here are the two fundamental results that can be achieved:

1. *Help employees meet needs that otherwise cannot be met.* This is the fundamental reason for employee benefit plans, and planners should always keep it in focus. Employee benefits have primarily been developed to help employees meet fundamental needs. For example—

   • health care costs for a serious illness are too great for people other than the very wealthy to meet "out of pocket." Insurance is a necessity—and the least expensive and simplest form of health insurance or health plan is usually a group plan provided by an employer for a group of employees.

   • retirement saving is difficult for most people; employer-sponsored plans not only promote retirement saving but provide tax "leverage" for such saving that the employee cannot obtain personally.

   • family protection in the event of an employee's untimely death can be promoted by employer-sponsored plans that are an attractive supplement to private life insurance—and for some employees, are the *only* form of life insurance reasonably available.

2. *Provide unique tax benefits.* Even if an employee is able to meet health care, retirement and other needs without the employer's help—which is a rare situation, there's a dollars-and-cents reason why an employee benefit plan is the best way to provide for these needs. In many benefit plans, the employer's dollar is "leveraged" by what amounts to an additional contribution by the U.S. Treasury through tax benefits provided for employee benefit plans. This makes the employer's benefit dollar go further than a dollar expended for cash compensation. Specifically:

   • for qualified retirement plans, employers get an up front deduction for funding the plan and providing a full guarantee of the retirement benefit, but employees do not pay taxes on the benefits until they receive them. This tax *deferral* available under an employer plan substantially increases the benefits available at retirement, compared with equal amounts of non tax-deferred private savings by the employee.

   • employer costs for employee health care plans are fully deductible *and* the benefits are *completely tax-free* to employees, regardless of amount. Without the employer plan, employees would have to pay for insurance or health care with after-tax dollars, with a tax deduction available only if (1) the taxpayer itemizes deductions and (2) the medical expense for the year exceeds the substantial "floor" for medical expense deductions.

   • other plans with substantial tax benefits include group-term life insurance plans, dependent care assistance plans, flexible spending accounts, incentive stock options, disability plans, and others discussed in this book.

STEPS IN THE PLANNING PROCESS

The process of employee benefit planning can be broken down into six identifiable steps:

1. *Meet the client and gather data.*

2. *Identify the employer's objectives; quantify and prioritize them.*

3. *Analyze existing plans to identify weaknesses and needs for revision.*

4. *Formulate a new overall employee compensation plan.*

5. *Communicate the new plan effectively.*

6. *Develop a program for periodic review of the plan's effectiveness.*

STEP 1: Meet the client and gather data.

The planning process begins with fact finding. Only a thorough knowledge of the client's personal and business financial picture can provide the right analysis of benefit plan needs.

Some of the most important information will include:

- an employee census; this should include a list of all current employees with their ages, current compensation levels (both anticipated total (Form W-2) income as well as stated salaries), employment status (full or part time), ownership in the business if any, and dates of employment. Data for the current year is mandatory. Similar data for at least five prior years and the employer's projections for the future are extremely useful to the planner.

- financial information about the employer. Current balance sheets and income statements are mandatory, as well as historical data to give an indication of what level of expenditure the business can sustain for compensation programs.

- full information about all existing employee plans— their coverage, funding costs, contract expiration dates, and the like.

- if executive benefit planning for top executives or business owners is a significant consideration—and it usually is—the planner needs information about the executives' individual financial and estate planning situations and needs.

Benefit planners should develop a "fact finder" to record and document the data gathering process. Appendix C includes a data gathering form developed by The American College for its courses in Advanced Pension Planning; this form should help give some idea of documentation needs.

Planners should remember that formalizing the data gathering process in a fact finder not only provides the information for current planning, but it also documents the *fact* that the planner went through this process of "due diligence" should any question about the design process ever arise in the future.

STEP 2: Identify the employer's objectives; quantify and prioritize them.

Clients may have conflicting objectives for their benefit plans, unrealistic expectations as to what the plans can accom-

plish, or an inaccurate idea of the cost of achieving certain objectives. The planner must formulate realistic objectives for the client's compensation planning and must establish an order of priorities. Realistic, achievable goals then become the basis for plan design.

Some benefit plan objectives that clients may formulate include:

- meeting employee needs for health care, retirement income, and protection against disability and premature death

- maintaining a program that complements (without duplicating) social security and each employee's own efforts in providing for health care, retirement income, and other needs

- meeting the "4-R" needs of the employer: recruiting, retaining, rewarding, and ultimately retiring employees

- maintaining a program that helps resist unionization or matches benefits for nonunion employees with those of union employees

- providing employee benefits that are comparable to those of other employers in the industry or in the same geographical area

- meeting cost targets; providing the most effective benefit package within cost limitations

- compensating key employees competitively while minimizing costs for non-key employees

- maximizing benefits for shareholder or owner-employees

STEP 3: Analyze existing plans to identify weaknesses or needs for revision.

To what extent do existing plans fail to meet client needs? Here's a checklist:

- Who is covered under the existing plan?

- What benefits are provided?

- What documentation exists? What documentation have employees received—that is, what have they been promised?

- What are the plan's annual costs and in what direction are these costs headed?

The Tools and Techniques of Employee Benefit and Retirement Planning

- How is the plan funded or financed?

- Who administers the plan—the employer or a third party?

- What are the expiration dates of existing plan contracts?

STEP 4: Formulate a new overall employee compensation plan.

A planner does not necessarily have to overhaul an employer's entire compensation package in order to serve the employer well, but it is important that whatever the planner recommends, it should be based on a comprehensive view of the employer's compensation planning needs, and should contribute to the employer's overall goals.

Individual chapters of this book provide detailed information about the advantages and disadvantages of each individual type of benefit plan, with an indication of situations in which that benefit plan will be most useful. But there is no simple formula by which the right "mix" of benefit plans can be designed to meet an employer's goals. That is an area where the planner's diligence and judgment will make a difference.

STEP 5: Communicate the new plan effectively.

From the earlier discussion of employer objectives, note that a large part of an employer's goals in instituting employee benefit programs depend on the employees' *subjective reaction* to the plan—how it improves morale, helps recruit and retain employees, complements employee efforts, and the like. Also, from other chapters in this book the planner will note that many types of benefit plans require informed choices by employees in order to be effective.

No matter how well the plan is designed, it will *fail* to meet those types of goals if it is not *communicated* effectively to employees. Thus effective communication is a great deal more than a "soft" aspect of plan design; it is just as much a hard, dollars-and-cents matter as drafting documents correctly.

In today's benefit climate, communication with employees is a sophisticated process. First, although employers and planners should try to simplify benefit provisions as much as possible, government regulation and the complexity of the financial environment for benefit plans often make the plans very complicated. (See Appendix A for specific ERISA disclosure requirements.) Second, employees invariably have some degree of skepticism about the value of employer-instituted programs that must be overcome by appropriate types of communication. Finally, the often-noted decline in reading, writing, and speaking skills among the public in general means that planners can no longer assume that normal means of communicating information within a business will be adequate. Special efforts must be made.

Employers traditionally have provided a "benefits booklet" for employees that they can keep for reference concerning benefit plan provisions. With the advent of ERISA, "summary plan descriptions" are mandatory for many types of plans (see Appendix A). Employers should not view this as purely a paperwork requirement. On the contrary, a special effort should be made to provide summary plan descriptions that are part of a "benefits booklet" approach. The booklet should not only meet legal requirements but should also provide information about the employer's benefit plans that is clear and really useful to employees.

Another ERISA requirement that can be turned to advantage is the requirement to provide an "individual benefit statement" to employees on request. Again, instead of providing only the minimum individual information required by law, the statement can be used as a way for the employer to show the employee the full value of the employer's benefit program. Many employers provide individual benefit statements annually, whether or not the employee requests one. An example of such a benefit statement is included at the end of this chapter.

STEP 6: Develop a program for periodic review of the plan's effectiveness.

Benefit plans exist in a dynamic business and government regulatory climate. A business can change drastically in a short time due to new ownership or external or internal business changes. Benefit plans are heavily affected by federal tax laws and Congress, driven by revenue needs in an era of federal deficits, changes the tax laws all too frequently. Thus, no tool or technique of benefit planning is likely to be effective indefinitely without revision.

As part of the planning process, a schedule should be established for reviewing and monitoring plan effectiveness and plan costs. Revision procedures must be developed to assure continuing achievement of the client's objectives.

Figure 1.1

INDIVIDUAL BENEFIT STATEMENT

This Individual Benefit Statement lists the benefits that both protect you and your family now and provide security for your future. We know you will find this statement informative, and we hope it will be useful in your personal planning.

HEALTH-CARE BENEFITS

You have elected coverage for
☐ yourself   ☐ your family   ☐ You have not elected coverage.
The highlights of your Comprehensive Medical Plan are summarized in the following table. See your employee handbook for further details.

In-Hospital Benefits	*Out-of-Hospital Benefits*	*Special Benefits*
$100 deductible per person each calendar year (3-deductible maximum per family)		100% of outpatient emergency treatment of accidental injury (no deductible).
100% of covered expenses, including maternity care, after the deductible is met.	80% of first $3,000 of covered expenses, then 100% of remaining covered expenses. 50% of psychiatric treatment up to $1,000 a year ($20-a-visit maximum benefit).	80% of diagnostic X-ray and laboratory tests (deductible applies).
OVERALL PLAN MAXIMUM: $1 million per person		

DISABILITY INCOME BENEFITS

Salary Continuation Plan
- Your full salary continues for _____ weeks, then $^3/_4$ of your salary continues for _____ weeks.

Long-term Disability Income Plan
- If disabled over 26 weeks, you will receive _____ a month. This is 60% of your base pay and includes benefits under the corporation's plan and any social security benefits, other than family benefits, for which you are eligible.
- If you have eligible dependents you can receive additional family benefits under social security up to _____ a month.
- If total long-term disability income from the above sources exceeds 80% of your base pay, disability benefits under the corporation's plan will be reduced to bring the total to the 70% level.

SURVIVOR'S BENEFITS

Group Life Insurance
- If you die from any cause your survivors will receive _____ from the corporation's group life insurance plan.

Supplemental Life Insurance
- If you participate in the corporation's supplemental life insurance plan, your survivors will receive an additional _____ upon your death from any cause.

Travel Accident Insurance
- An additional benefit of _____ will be paid to your survivors if your death results from an accident while traveling on corporate business.

Figure 1.1 (continued)

Social Security
- Social security will provide a monthly income of up to _____ a month if you have an eligible spouse with 2 or more children.

Medical Coverage
- Dependent's coverage can continue on a contributory basis.

RETIREMENT BENEFITS

Normal Retirement
- At age 65, you will receive an estimated _____ a month from the corporation's retirement plan and social security. Additional social security benefits are payable for an eligible spouse age 62 or older.
- Your spouse will receive an estimated _____ a month from the corporation's retirement plan and social security if your spouse is age 65 or older at your death.
- If you leave the corporation before retirement, you will be eligible to receive a pension amounting to the vested portion of your accrued benefit. The pension is payable at age 65, but reduced benefits are available as early as age 55. Your current accrued benefit is approximately _____ a month. Your vested benefit is _____ a month.

Early Retirement
- You may retire as early as age 55 with five years' service and receive a reduced benefit. For example at age 62, your retirement income from the corporation's plan and social security would be approximately _____.

Other Retirement Benefits
- Medical coverage continues after retirement and is coordinated with medicare.
- Group life insurance coverage continues in the amount of $5,000.

BENEFIT STATEMENT REVIEW

FOR

_____

Many of us forget that there is more to our paycheck than the amount we take home. The following are the "extras" that were provided in 19___ and their value as determined by the cost to your employer.

	Annual Value	Value per Hour
(1) Social Security (employer's contribution)	$_____	$_____
(2) Workers' Compensation Insurance Premium	_____	_____
(3) State Unemployment Insurance Premium	_____	_____
(4) Paid Holidays	_____	_____
(5) Vacation Days	_____	_____
(6) Pension	_____	_____
(7) Salary Continuation	_____	_____
(8) Long-Term Disability Income Insurance	_____	_____
(9) Life Insurance	_____	_____
(10) Medical Expense Insurance (employer's contribution)	_____	_____
(11) Others	_____	_____
_____	_____	_____
_____	_____	_____

The $_____ value of those sometimes forgotten benefits is equal to _____% of the $_____ you received as salary or wages in 19___. These benefits are provided to protect you and your family from certain financial risks and help provide for your future retirement.

Chapter 2

DESIGNING THE RIGHT PENSION PLAN

This chapter is an overview of the process of designing a pension plan for a business client. It is intended to provide a framework for the detailed discussions of *each* type of plan provided in Part A of this book, "Pensions and Deferred Compensation."

Designing the "right" pension plan for a business can be divided into three broad steps:

Step 1: Gather the relevant facts. The most important factual information is (1) an employee census (i.e., a list of all employees with their compensation levels, ages, and years of service for the employer); and (2) information about existing and past pension programs, if any, that the employer has maintained. These are essential; but many other details about an employer's business may be important in various cases. Appendix C of this book contains a detailed Fact Finder developed by The American College for its Advanced Pension Planning courses.

Step 2: Identify employer objectives. In addition to factual information, the planner must develop with the client a list of objectives (objectives that can be promoted by a pension plan) and their priorities with the employer.

Step 3: Choose plan features that promote the employer objectives. This chapter is a preliminary guide to matching objectives with plan design features. Once the design process has zeroed-in on specific plans or design features, later chapters will provide the necessary details.

WHAT CAN A PENSION PLAN DO FOR THE EMPLOYER?

The pension planner must begin with an overall idea of what employer objectives can be promoted by a pension plan. A pension plan—in the broad sense of retirement, deferred compensation, or savings plan of any type—can, if properly designed and implemented, promote many employer and employee objectives, the most important of which are listed here. While not every one of these objectives can be met with a single plan—in fact, some are conflicting—it is useful to begin this chapter by noting what pension plans *can* do.

1. *Help Employees With Retirement Saving.* This is the most fundamental reason for pension plans and it should not be overlooked. Most employees, even highly compensated

employees, find personal savings difficult. It is difficult not merely for psychological reasons, but also because our tax system and economy are oriented toward consumption rather than savings.

For example, the federal income tax system imposes tax on income from savings (even if it is not used for consumption) with only three major exceptions: (1) deferral of tax on capital gains until realized; (2) benefits for investment in a personal residence; and (3) deferral of tax and other benefits for qualified retirement plans and IRAs. In other words, a qualified retirement plan is one of only three ways our government encourages savings through the tax system—but it is available only if an employer adopts the plan. (IRA benefits are very limited.)

2. *Tax Deferral for Owners and Highly Compensated Employees.* While many employees in all compensation categories can benefit from pension plans, owners and other key employees have more money available for saving, have higher compensation, have longer service with the employer, and often are older than regular employees; thus they can benefit more from pension plans. When designing a plan for a business owner, a typical objective is to maximize the benefits for the owner (or, in some cases, to minimize the discrimination *against* the highly compensated that is built into some of the qualified pension plan rules.)

3. *Help Recruit, Reward, Retain, and Retire Employees.* These "four R's" of compensation policy are an important objective in designing pension plans. The plan can help *recruit* employees by matching or bettering pension benefit packages offered by competing employers; it can *reward* employees by tying benefits to compensation; it can help *retain* employees by tying maximum pension benefits to long service; and it can help *retire* employees by allowing them to retire with dignity—without a drastic drop in living standard—when their productivity has begun to decline and the organization needs new members.

4. *Encourage Productivity.* Certain types of plan design can act as employee incentives; this is particularly true of plans whose contributions are profit-based or those providing employee accounts invested in stock of the employer.

5. *Discourage Collective Bargaining.* An attractive pension package—as good as or better than labor union-sponsored plans in the area—can help to keep employees from organizing into a collective bargaining unit. Collective bargaining often poses major business problems for some employers.

QUALIFIED VERSUS NONQUALIFIED PENSION PLANS

All pension plans are plans in which part of an employee's compensation for performing services for the employer is deferred. Deferred compensation is compensation that is not paid currently—in the year services are performed or shortly thereafter.[1] Pension plans are either *qualified* or *nonqualified.* Qualified plans receive more favorable tax benefits, but are subject to very stringent government regulation.

The following chart (Figure 2.1) from The American College's Executive Compensation graduate course summarizes differences between qualified and nonqualified plans.

When is A Nonqualified Plan Indicated? Chapter 16 discusses in detail when and how nonqualified plans are used. Some highlights:

Figure 2.1

COMPARISON OF VARIOUS ITEMS OF QUALIFIED RETIREMENT PLANS WITH UNFUNDED NONQUALIFIED DEFERRED COMPENSATION PLANS		
Item	**Qualified Retirement Plan**	**Unfunded Nonqualified Deferred Compensation Plan**
a. Timing of corporation's income tax deduction	Corporation receives a deduction when contributions are made to the plan.	Corporation receives a deduction when benefits are received by employees.
b. Who must be covered by plan	70 percent of nonhighly compensated employees, or alternative test under Code section 410.	Corporation free to discriminate as it sees fit if plan covers only independent contractors or members of management or highly compensated employees.
c. Extent to which benefits may be forfeitable	Must meet 5-year or 3-to-7-year vesting test; faster vesting for top-heavy plans.	The qualified plan vesting rules apply if plan covers rank-and-file employees. If plan covers only independent contractors or members of management or highly compensated employees, benefits may be forfeitable in full at all times.
d. Tax treatment of earnings on amount set aside to fund plan.	These earnings accumulate tax free but will be taxable to employee along with other plan assets when distributed to employee; no income tax deduction for employer.	These earnings will be taxed currently to the employer and will be taxable to the employee when distributed as benefits; however, employer will be entitled to an income tax deduction at that time.
e. Coverage of independent contractors and directors	Only employees are eligible for coverage.	Independent contractors and directors may be covered in the same manner as an employee.
f. Balance sheet impact	Satisfactory if plan is not underfunded.	Can be adverse (see Appendix E).

- nonqualified plans can be designed for key employees without the sometimes prohibitive cost of covering a broader group of employees.

- nonqualified plans can provide benefits to executives beyond the limits allowed in qualified plans.

- nonqualified plans can provide "customized" retirement or savings benefits for selected executives.

QUALIFIED PLANS—WHAT THEY ARE AND WHAT THEY CAN DO

A qualified plan receives tax benefits that are not available for a nonqualified plan. These tax benefits are:

- Amounts paid into the plan—employer contributions and also employee salary reduction contributions—are deductible by the employer (or tax-excludable by the employee) in the year for which they are paid.

- Employees are not taxed in the year that the employer contributes to the plan, even if they are fully vested in their plan benefits at that time.

- Certain lump-sum benefits are eligible for a special 5-year or 10-year averaging tax computation that reduces tax rates on the benefit.

- The plan itself is a tax-exempt fund. Earnings on plan investments accumulate tax free in the plan and are not taxed currently to the employer or the employee. This significantly increases the effective investment return on plan assets.

These tax benefits add up to a substantial, quantifiable amount of tax "leverage," as will be shown later in this chapter.

Types of Qualified Plans

Qualified plans are either defined contribution or defined benefit plans. As the names imply, this depends on whether the plan specifies an employer contribution rate on the one hand, or guarantees a specified benefit level on the other.

Defined Contribution Plans

In a defined contribution plan, the employer establishes and maintains an individual account for each plan participant. When the participant becomes eligible to receive benefit payments—usually at retirement or termination of employment—the benefit is based on the total amount in the participant's account. The account balance includes employer contributions, employee contributions in some cases, and earnings on the account over all the years of deferral.

The employer does not guarantee the amount of the benefit a participant will ultimately receive in a defined contribution plan. Instead, the employer must make contributions under a formula specified in the plan. There are three principal types of defined contribution plan formulas:

- *Money purchase pension plan.* Under a money purchase plan, the employer must contribute each year to each participant's account a stated percentage of the participant's compensation. This percentage is usually about 10 percent, although percentages up to 25 are possible. The money purchase plan is probably the simplest of all types of plans and is one of the most common.

- *Target benefit pension plan.* A target plan is similar to a money purchase plan in that the employer must make annual contributions to each participant's account under a formula based on compensation. In a target plan, however, the participant's age at plan entry is also taken into account in determining the contribution percentage. This is done on an actuarial basis so that older entrants can build up retirement accounts faster. The objective—the target—is to provide approximately the same benefit level (as a percentage of compensation) for each participant at retirement. The employer does not guarantee this level, however, and the employee bears the risk as well as reaps the benefit of varying investment results.

- *Profit-sharing plan.* A profit-sharing plan is a defined contribution plan under which the employer determines the amount of the contribution each year, rather than having a stated contribution obligation. In a profit-sharing plan, the employer can decide not to contribute to the plan at all in certain cases. Typically, plan contributions are based on the employer's profits in some manner. If a contribution is made, the total amount must be allocated to each participant's account using a nondiscriminatory formula. Such formulas are usually based on compensation, but service can be taken into account. Under proposed qualified plan regulations, the allocation formula can be weighted in favor of plan participants who entered the plan at older ages—an "age-weighted profit-sharing plan." This produces results similar to those of a target plan, but with the greater simplicity and flexibility of a profit-sharing plan.

Profit-sharing plans often feature employee contributions, typically with an employer match. For example, the plan could provide that employees may contribute to the plan up to 6 percent of their compensation, with the employer contributing 50 cents for every $1 of employee contribution. This type of plan is referred to as a *thrift* or *savings* plan.

Another variation on the profit-sharing plan design is the *cash or deferred* or *Section 401(k)* plan. Under this type of plan, employees can make tax deferred contributions by electing salary reductions, which are permitted up to $7,000 annually per employee, as indexed for inflation ($8,994 in 1993). Employers often match employee salary reductions in order to encourage employee participation in these plans.

All these types of plans are discussed in more detail in separate chapters of this book.

Defined Benefit Plans

Defined benefit plans provide a specific amount of benefit to the employee at normal retirement age. There are many different types of formula for determining this benefit, as discussed in Chapter 9 of this book. These formulas are typically based on the employee's earnings averaged over a number of years of service. The formula also can be based on the employee's service.

These plans are funded actuarially, which means that, for a given benefit level, the annual funding amount is greater for employees who are older at entry into the plan, since the time to fund the benefit is less in the case of an older entrant. This makes defined benefit plans attractive to professionals and closely held business owners; they tend to adopt retirement plans for their businesses when they are relatively older than their regular employees. A large percentage of the total cost for a defined benefit plan in this situation funds these key employees' benefits, as discussed further in Chapter 9.

WHY A QUALIFIED PLAN IS—OR IS NOT—BETTER THAN CASH

The tax advantages of qualified plans mean that an employer's dollar spent on qualified plan benefits is "bigger" than a dollar spent on cash compensation. This is because while the employer gets a current deduction for the cost of the plan, benefits are not taxable to employees until paid. The taxes that are not paid currently can be thought of as an "interest free loan" from the U.S. Treasury. The time value of money "leverages" the value of each employer dollar; the income earned on deferred taxes directly benefits the employee but costs the employer nothing extra.

So why doesn't every employer immediately maximize the qualified plan benefits for every employee, since qualified plan benefits are "cheaper" than cash compensation? The problem is that not every employee *perceives* the same value for qualified plan benefits.

Employees who value retirement benefits most highly include:

- older employees nearing retirement

- long-term employees with substantial vested benefits

- highly compensated employees who can afford to forego substantial cash compensation for retirement benefits

- employees who do not depend on their compensation for basic living expenses—for example, the "supplemental" earner in a two-income family

Employees not in these four categories often do not value and do not want deferred plan benefits—they would rather have immediate cash:

- younger employees view retirement as a distant prospect and therefore psychologically "discount" the value of retirement benefits

- transitory employees do not expect to stay with an employer long enough to fully vest or accrue substantial benefits

- low-paid employees cannot afford to forego any substantial amount of cash compensation in return for retirement benefits.

In other words, pension plan design for most employers requires more sophistication than simply "loading up" on benefits. Money spent on plan benefits for employees who do not value these benefits is, in effect, a "pure cost" of the plan. Such costs must not outweigh the value of benefits for those who do want them; otherwise the employer's compensation policy is inefficient and may even be counterproductive.

In designing the plan, a designer must attempt to both (1) maximize the benefits for those who want them and (2) choose a plan design that will be perceived as valuable by the maximum number of employees.

Is a qualified plan cost-effective? An example: For a given client, the threshold question raised by the issues just discussed must be: "Does *any* qualified plan make any sense at all in the client's business?"

To illustrate, let's look at what might be viewed as a "worst case" scenario—the small professional corporation. It is a worst-case situation because the owner or owners are generally much older and higher paid than the rest of the employees; and there is often high turnover among the younger employees. So, the owners want the maximum pension benefits but the rest of the employees probably do not value these benefits much. Thus, the cost of benefits for nonowner employees is about as close to a "pure cost" of providing the owners' benefits as the planner commonly runs into.

Suppose your client, Doctor Leberkrank, age 41, and two office employees are the only employees of the Doctor's professional corporation. The Doctor wants to establish a qualified profit-sharing plan that will enable him to contribute the $30,000 annual maximum (as indexed). A preliminary plan design analysis indicates that in order to do this, a total of $3,000 will have to be contributed annually on behalf of the two office employees, in order to meet the qualified plan nondiscrimination rules. Thus, the Doctor's choice is between $33,000 annually of private savings outside the plan or a $30,000 annual contribution to the plan with its accompanying tax deferral benefits.

Let's use the following worksheet (Figure 2.2) from The American College's Advanced Pension Planning courses. The worksheet records these facts and other inputs and assumptions necessary to make a preliminary calculation.

The worksheet shows that, based on these facts and assumptions, the qualified plan will provide more financial security for the client than a private savings program. The plan will provide an annual net income at retirement of $137,000, as compared with only $97,000 under the private savings program.

You'll note that the advantage of the qualified plan depends to a considerable extent on minimizing contributions on behalf of nonowner employees. Obviously, this will be difficult where there are many employees in the business. In this example, the qualified plan worked out well, but it might not have had the required contribution for office employees been higher.

High required contributions for nonowner employees does not necessarily mean that the plan is not viable. The next step for the planner is then to consider refinements and alternatives:

- Contributions for employees are not really "wasted"—they're a valuable form of additional compensation for employees. The planner should try to design a plan where these contributions have maximum perceived value for the employees and, thus, contribute posi-

tively to the employer's "recruiting, retaining, rewarding, and retiring" goals.

- The plan can be redesigned to maximize contributions for the owners and minimize contributions for other employees.

Planning options that can get these results are discussed in the next section.

MATCHING EMPLOYER OBJECTIVES WITH THE RIGHT PLAN DESIGN

Each type of qualified plan typically meets certain planning objectives better than others. Plan design consists of getting the right match between employer objectives and the qualified plan "menu." Some common employer objectives, and the matching plan design features that are available for customizing the plan to the employer's objectives, will be summarized here.

OBJECTIVE: *Maximize the proportion of plan costs that benefit highly-compensated employees.*

Many employers, particularly small, closely held companies, view retirement plans as worthwhile only if they provide substantial, tax-sheltered retirement benefits for key employees. The following are the commonly used techniques for doing this:

1. *Defined benefit plans.* Defined benefit plans typically provide the maximum possible proportionate benefits for key employees when key employees, as a group, are older than rank and file employees. This age distribution exists in the majority of small businesses.

    A defined contribution plan allows a contribution of no more than $30,000 (indexed) annually for an employee—but for a defined benefit plan there is *no* dollar limit on the amount of contributions. Instead, the projected *benefit* (not the contribution) is subject to a limit of the lesser of 100 percent of high three-year average compensation or $90,000 annually (as indexed, $115,641 for 1993). Funding the maximum annual benefit for a younger employee generally requires a deductible employer contribution that is less than $30,000 annually, while for an employee who enters the plan at an age greater than approximately 45, the deductible contribution for the maximum benefit is considerably more than $30,000 annually. For a given set of actuarial assumptions, there is a "crossover" age at which the defined benefit plan is more favorable to adopt.[2] (See Figure 2.3.)

Figure 2.2

WORKSHEET
Qualified Plan vs. Private Savings

for <u>Dr. Leberkrank, P.C.</u>

Inputs and assumptions

1.	Assumed pre-tax rate of return	<u>8</u> %
2.	Annual plan contribution for owner	<u>$30,000</u>
3.	Cost for employees if plan provides line 2 contribution for owner	<u>$ 3,000</u>
4.	Total cost (line 2 plus line 3)	<u>$33,000</u>
5.	Pre-retirement tax rate	<u>28</u> %
6.	Assumed post-retirement tax rate	<u>33</u> %
7.	Years until retirement	<u>24</u> %
8.	Desired number of years of annuity payout (generally no more than single/joint life expectancy at retirement)	<u>20</u>

Calculations	Qualified Plan	Private Savings
9. Accumulation at retirement (future value (FV of [line 7] years of payments)	<u>$2,002,943</u> • Annual payment = line 2 • Interest rate = line 1	<u>$1,169,253</u> • Annual payment = line 4 - (line 5)% of line 4 • Interest rate = line 1 - (line 5)% of line 1
10. Annual annuity available (amortization [PMT] of line 9 over [line 8] years)	<u>$204,004</u> • Principal = line 9 • Interest = line 1	<u>$96,709</u> • Principal - line 9 • Interest = line 1 - (line 6)% of line 1
11. Income tax* on annuity payment	<u>$67,321</u> (line 6)% of line 10	-0-
12. Net annuity (line 10 - line 11)	<u>$136,683</u>	<u>$96,709</u>

* The 15% excess distribution tax on annual amounts over $150,000 (or $112,500 as indexed) should also be taken into account.

Defined benefit plans can be made even more favorable to key employees by appropriate choices of actuarial assumptions, retirement age and late retirement provisions, form of benefits, and level of Social Security integration. All of these design aspects of defined benefit plans are discussed further in Chapter 9.

2. *Service-based contribution or benefit formulas.* A plan's contribution or benefit formula can be based on an employee's years of service with the employer. This generally benefits the owners and key employees who typically have longer service. Such formulas can be used in defined contribution plans, but are even more effective in defined benefit plans. Defined benefit plans can even provide benefits for *past* service—service prior to establishment of the plan. Of course, the Code's nondiscrimination requirements discussed in Chapter 23 must be satisfied.

3. *Age-weighting.* The age-weighting aspect of a defined benefit plan, which provides favorable funding of benefits for older plan entrants, can also be provided in a

Figure 2.3

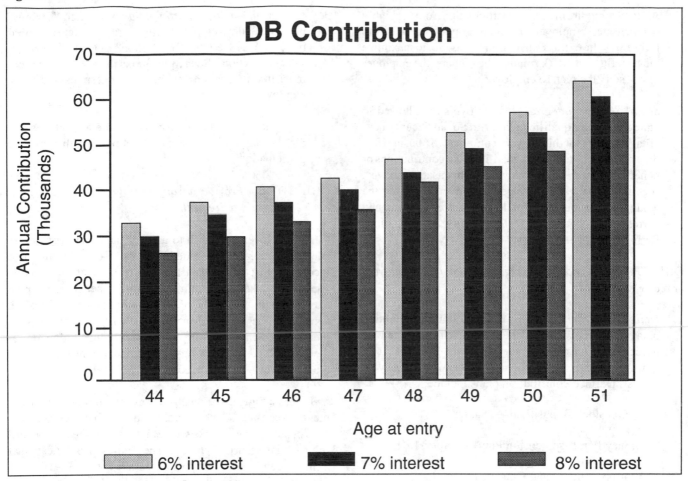

defined contribution plan. Where the employer wants to avoid the complexity of the defined benefit approach, age-weighted defined contribution plans should be considered.

The traditional plan of this type is the target benefit plan, described earlier in this chapter and also in Chapter 21. In addition, proposed nondiscrimination regulations recently introduced by the IRS (and scheduled to be finalized for plan years beginning in 1994) allow even profit-sharing plans to provide an age-weighted allocation formula.[3] This is discussed further in Chapter 17.

4. *Combinations of defined benefit and defined contribution plans.* Is it possible to cover an employee under *both* a maximum defined benefit plan *and* a maximum defined contribution plan? No—Congress eliminated that possible loophole right from the start. Where an employee is covered under both types of plans, there is a combined limit.[4]

For example, if an employee receives a $30,000 annual allocation under a defined contribution plan of an employer and is also covered under a defined benefit plan

of the employer, then the maximum defined benefit limit ($90,000, as indexed, or 100% of compensation) is cut back. Alternatively (and more commonly), the employee can receive the maximum defined benefit, but the defined contribution limit is reduced.

The important thing to note here about the combined limit, however, is that in many cases the combined limit *still* allows a considerable increase in benefits for employees covered under both plans. What is more, the extra benefits are often distributed in a way that is favorable to key employees. Whether this technique will work in a given case can only be determined by "crunching the numbers." The analysis involved is too complicated to give any simple rules of thumb, but any conscientious pension planner should give consideration to combination plan techniques.

5. *401(k) plans.* Section 401(k) plans are extremely popular with employees, but designers should not overlook the fact that these plans can be favorable to highly compensated employees as well. The nondiscrimination rules—the ADP tests[5]—inherently allow a higher rate of contribution for highly compensated employees. However, the

ADP rules require maximum participation from nonhighly compensated employees for the highly compensated to fully enjoy the extra contribution levels. So, to maximize the benefits of a 401(k) plan to the owners, the employer must "sell" the plan to employees.

6. *Social Security integration.* Employers are allowed to "integrate" their qualified plan with Social Security benefits. The rules for this are very complicated,[6] but in effect they allow a higher rate of qualified plan contributions or benefits for each employee with compensation above a specified level. This reduces employer costs for the qualified plan benefits for lower-paid employees and correspondingly allows greater benefits or contributions for higher-paid employees.

OBJECTIVE: *Provide a savings medium that employees perceive as valuable.*

1. *Defined contribution plans.* Every defined contribution plan has an "individual account" for each employee who participates. As a result, the employee knows exactly how much his or her personal benefit is worth from year to year. Defined contribution plans include:

   ESOP/Stock Bonus Plan—Chapter 10

   Money Purchase Pension Plan—Chapter 15

   Profit Sharing Plan—Chapter 17

   Savings Plan—Chapter 18

   Section 401(k) Plan—Chapter 19

   Simplified Employee Pension (SEP)—Chapter 20[7]

   Target Benefit Pension Plan—Chapter 21

   Tax Deferred Annuity—Chapter 22[8]

   The "savings account" feature of defined contribution plans is often popular with younger employees, who may not expect to stay with the employer until they reach age 65—which in any event seems like a remote contingency to them.

2. *Cash balance plans.* These plans are a type of defined benefit plan that operates very much like a defined contribution plan of the money purchase type. The employer guarantees the principal and interest rate, so the employee assumes no investment risk. Cash balance plans tend to provide greater benefits to younger employees and those with shorter service, as compared to other defined benefit plans.[9]

3. *Plans with employee participation.* Qualified "savings" plans can allow employees to make after-tax contributions and a Section 401(k) plan[10] permits *before-tax* salary reductions. Such a plan looks to the employee very much like a tax-favored savings account sponsored by the employer.

Figure 2.4 is a chart comparing the advantages and disadvantages of different types of plans with employee participation.

OBJECTIVE: *Provide adequate replacement income for each employee's retirement.*

An employer may wish to adopt a plan that provides an adequate "replacement ratio"—the ratio of postretirement income to that received just before retirement. What is an adequate replacement ratio? Generally speaking, no plan attempts to provide 100% of preretirement income, because, apart from the high cost of such a plan (1) an employee's income needs are generally somewhat reduced after retirement and (2) personal savings are deemed to contribute part of the employee's income needs.

Figure 2.5 gives the results of several studies of replacement income needs. These studies indicate that a replacement ratio of about 50% to 70% is a useful target for the plan benefit (plus Social Security benefits). The studies also indicate that a higher replacement ratio is necessary for lower-paid employees than for the higher-paid, since fixed costs dominate at lower income levels.

If adequate replacement income is an employer's objective, a defined benefit plan is the best vehicle for the following reasons:

• A defined benefit plan can provide a benefit based on final average compensation, regardless of the employee's years of service (or a full benefit can be earned after only limited service such as 25 years). Defined contribution plans provide benefits that are directly related to service, and a short service employee cannot accumulate a substantial retirement account.

• There is no investment risk taken by the employee in a defined benefit plan—the employer guarantees the benefit (and there is also a limited federal government guarantee of benefits through the Pension Benefit Guaranty Corporation).

• Employer funding of the benefit is mandatory, subject to underfunding penalties, even if the employer's profits drop.

Figure 2.4

A COMPARISON OF RETIREMENT SAVINGS ALTERNATIVES

Savings Alternative	Major Advantages	Major Disadvantages
• After-tax Savings	1. No employer action necessary 2. Complete flexibility for employee	No tax benefits
• IRA	1. No employer action necessary 2. Contribution tax-deductible	1. Limitation if covered under qualified plan 2. Ten percent penalty for withdrawal before age 59½; no loans 3. $2,000/year maximum 4. No 5-year averaging on distribution 5. Cannot invest in life insurance
• SEP (Simplified Employee Pension) with salary reduction feature	1. Employee can choose amount of saving 2. Amounts contributed are non-taxable to employee 3. Tax-free accumulation 4. Simple for employer to adopt	1. Less flexibility for employer than qualified plan 2. $7,000 (as indexed: $8,994 for 1993) limit on salary reduction 3. Relatively cmplex administration 4. No forfeitures available for reallocation to long-term cmployccs 5. No loans permitted 6. Ten percent penalty for pre-age 59½ withdrawal 7. Employer deduction limited to 15% 8. Cannot invcst in lifc insurance
• Thrift (Savings) Plan	1. Employee can choose amount of saving 2. Employer contribution non-taxable to employee 3. Tax-free accumulation 4. Employer matching is attractive incentive feature 5. Liberal loan and withdrawal provisions 6. 5-year averaging on distributions	1. Qualified plan cost and complexity 2. Employer has fixed, nondiscretionary contribution obligation 3. Ten percent penalty on pre-age 59½ withdrawal 4. Must meet Section 401(m) tests
• Section 401(k) Profit-Sharing Plan	1. Employee can choose amount of savings 2. All or part of contributions can be salary reduction 3. Amounts contributed are non-taxable to employee 4. Tax-free accumulation 5. Hardship withdrawals and loans available 6. 5-year averaging on distributions	1. Qualified plan cost and complexity 2. $7,000 (as indexed: $8,994 for 1993) annual limit on salary reductions 3. 401(k) provisions add administrative costs 4. No forfeitures available for reallocation to long-term employees 5. Withdrawals limited to hardship 6. Ten percent penalty on pre-age 59½ withdrawal 7. Employer deduction limited to 15% of payroll

Figure 2.5

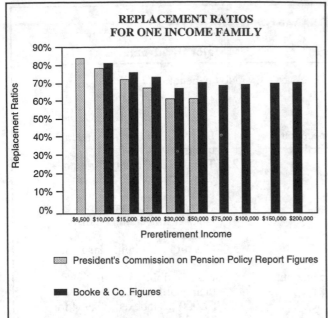

REPLACEMENT RATIOS
FOR ONE INCOME FAMILY

Replacement Ratios (y-axis)
Preretirement Income (x-axis): $6,500 $10,000 $15,000 $20,000 $30,000 $50,000 $75,000 $100,000 $150,000 $200,000

▨ President's Commission on Pension Policy Report Figures

■ Booke & Co. Figures

This figure displays the percentage of preretirement income needed to maintain the same standard of living after retirement.

Assumptions:
- For married couple, age 65, with one income
- 1988 tax rates and exemptions
- Preretirement deductions are the larger of 15% of income or 1988 standard deduction.
- After retirement, 1988 standard deduction
- State taxes computed using same deductions as for federal
- State taxes were between 5% and 6½% of income after federal deductions.
- Preretirement savings between 0% and 20% of after tax income.

Source: England, "How Much Retirement Income Do Employees Need," *Benefits Quarterly*, 1st Quarter, 1988.

- Maximum life insurance can be provided through a defined benefit plan, providing the fullest protection for beneficiaries even if the employee dies after only a few years of service.

OBJECTIVE: *Create an incentive for employees to maximize performance.*

1. *Profit-sharing plan.* Although a "profit sharing" plan is not technically required to make contributions out of profits, most plans are designed to do so. The profit sharing element provides extra, bonus compensation to participating employees when the business does well and that acts as an incentive.

2. *ESOP/stock bonus plan.* A plan providing that the employee's account balance is partially or totally invested in stock of the employer has substantial incentive features, paralleling the "equity-based" compensation arrangements often used for executives. The participant's account goes up and down in value with company stock. So its value depends almost entirely on good performance by the business. If the employee believes that his or her performance has an effect on business results, the plan can be a powerful performance incentive.

3. *Any other defined contribution plan or cash balance plan.* In these plans, employees have an account that begins to grow as soon as they enter the plan. Because of this high visibility, these plans tend to have a better psychological incentive value than defined benefit plans.

OBJECTIVE: *Minimize turnover.*

1. *Defined benefit plan.* In defined benefit plans, employees are encouraged to stay until retirement because (1) benefits can be based on years of service; and (2) benefits are generally based on the employee's highest annual compensation. However, defined contribution benefits also continue to grow with each year of service. In many cases, there is no clear type of plan that minimizes turnover, and other features of the compensation and work environment may be dominant.

2. *Graduated vesting.* Plans are often designed with graduated vesting schedules—that is, an employee is not entitled to the full benefit earned until a minimum period of service has passed. Under current law, the longest wait permitted for full vesting is 7 years (under the graduated 3- to 7-year vesting schedule).[11] Thus, vesting has only limited effect on employee turnover, and should probably be better viewed as a way for the employer to minimize the cost of covering short-service employees.

OBJECTIVE: *Encourage retirement.*

Any retirement plan acts as an incentive to retirement to some degree, since it makes it possible for the employee to support himself and his dependents after retirement.

However, a defined benefit plan works best to encourage retirement because:

- The plan can be designed to allow full benefits to accrue after a specified period such as 25 years, with no further benefits accruing thereafter. Thus, no further benefits can be earned by working for more years thereafter.

- It is relatively easy to design a "subsidized" early retirement benefit in a defined benefit plan by providing a benefit at age 62 (or other early retirement age) that is more than the actuarial equivalent of what the retiree would get at age 65. This provides an economic incentive to retire early.

OBJECTIVE: *Maximize employer contribution flexibility.*

The most flexible plans from a contribution standpoint are qualified profit-sharing plans and SEPs. In these plans, the amount contributed each year can be entirely at the employer's discretion. Contributions can be omitted entirely for a given year without affecting the plan's qualified status. (However, for a profit-sharing plan, contributions must be "substantial and recurring" or the IRS may claim that the plan has been terminated.)

Other types of plan are inflexible to one degree or another:

1. Defined benefit plans are subject to the minimum funding requirements of the Internal Revenue Code, and the required annual minimum contribution must be made or the employer is subject to penalty.

   However, if the employer is in economic distress it may request from the IRS *in advance* a waiver from the minimum funding rules. It should also be noted that the rules for actuarial funding of qualified plans permit some year-to-year variation in the amount that the employer can or must contribute. Thus, in a good year, the employer may contribute the maximum deductible amount, which may tend to reduce the minimum amount that has to be contributed in later years.

2. Defined contribution pension plans (money purchase and target) must have fixed contribution formulas that require

a contribution each year based on a percentage of payroll. Failure to make this contribution subjects the employer to minimum funding penalties. The only relief for this is to apply to the IRS for a minimum funding waiver, or to make a timely amendment to the plan to reduce the contribution level.

3. "Matching" plans (e.g., 401(k), savings, and 403(b)) that require the employer to match employee contributions involve a legally binding commitment by the employer to make the promised matching contributions. Thus, the employer's costs are dependent on employee decisions and out of the employer's control.

FOOTNOTES

1. For tax purposes, compensation is considered current when it is paid no later than 2½ months after the year in which it is earned. Any compensation paid later than this is considered *deferred*, which means that the employer's tax deduction is deferred also unless the plan is a qualified plan. For a *controlling* employee—one who owns more than 50% of the employer—even the 2½ month rule does not apply, i.e., the compensation must be paid within the year earned for the employer to get a tax deduction for that year.

2. This is discussed further in the "Question and Answers" for Chapter 9.

3. Prop. Reg. §1.401(a)(4)-9(c).

4. IRC Sec. 415(e). See Chapter 23 of this book.

5. IRC Sec. 401(k)(3). See Chapter 19 of this book.

6. IRC Sec. 401(l). See Chapter 23 of this book.

7. A SEP is not technically a qualified defined contribution plan, but from the employee perspective it works the same way.

8. A tax deferred annuity is not technically a qualified defined contribution plan, but from the employee perspective it works the same way.

9. See Chapter 8. The fact that a cash balance plan is technically a defined benefit plan has no bearing on the planning objectives discussed here.

10. Tax-exempt employers are generally not allowed to adopt Section 401(k) plans, but for them a Section 403(b) tax deferred annuity plan provides much the same advantages.

11. The vesting rules are covered in Chapter 23.

Chapter 3

DESIGNING THE RIGHT LIFE INSURANCE PLAN

Life insurance planning for executives ranks in importance with retirement and health benefit planning. This chapter summarizes the steps in designing a life insurance plan for executives that will meet identified employer and employee objectives. The design of plans for selected executives, rather than broad groups of employees, is stressed here. For the broad employee group, insurance planning generally emphasizes the group-term plans discussed in Chapter 36.

STEP 1: IDENTIFY INSURANCE/CAPITAL ACCUMULATION NEEDS

Do executives have specific identifiable needs for death benefits or capital accumulation programs that can be financed with life insurance? The business's dollars for executive benefits should be focused toward actual and perceived needs.

Insurance and capital accumulation needs are widespread; the two most common situations involve

- needs for family protection for the younger executive to cover family support needs in the event of premature death

- needs for accumulation of liquid funds in the executive's estate to cover taxes and expenses, or to carry out the transfer of a closely held business interest.

STEP 2: ANALYZE EXISTING PLANS

The employer's existing plans must be analyzed to determine whether and to what extent these plans meet the needs identified. To the extent possible, it is also advisable to take the executive's personally-owned insurance into consideration.

Employer plans that can provide death benefits or capital accumulation include

- group-term life insurance

- pension, profit-sharing and other qualified plans. These plans almost always provide some form of death benefit, even if there is no specific life insurance

benefit in the plan. Benefits from these plans are discussed in Chapter 24.

- nonqualified deferred compensation plans. What benefits are provided if the employee dies—before or after retirement? How is the plan financed? Are specific assets set aside to meet the employer's obligation?

- other insurance plans of the employer such as split-dollar, death benefit only, or other similar arrangements.

STEP 3: IDENTIFY OBJECTIVES

What are the employee and/or the employer intending to accomplish with the plan—and how are the objectives prioritized? Some common objectives in designing life insurance plans include

- provide life insurance protection at the lowest possible cost

- provide the maximum feasible death benefits

- design a plan with the lowest tax cost (or the maximum tax "leverage")

- maximize the employee's federal estate tax marital deduction

- enhance cost effectiveness of the plan by giving the employer (or in some cases the employee) control of policy cash values

- portability or nonportability. The executive generally wants maximum portability, while the employer might want to use the plan as a way of tying a key person to the company—the "golden handcuffs" concept.

STEP 4: DESIGN THE PLAN

When needs and objectives have been analyzed, the planner can then match these needs and objectives with the right type of plan(s). This book covers the major tools of life insurance planning in detail:

Designing the Right Life Insurance Plan

- Bonus or "Section 162" life insurance—Chapter 26
- Split-dollar life insurance—Chapter 49
- Insurance financing of nonqualified deferred compensation plans—Chapter 16

- Death-benefit-only plans—Chapter 30
- Life insurance in qualified plans—Chapter 14

The following chart compares some major characteristics of these plans.

Figure 3.1

	Split Dollar	Bonus Insurance	Insurance in Qualified Plan	Insurance Financing of Nonqualified Deferred Compensation Plan	DBO
Tax deduction for employer outlay	None	Yes (deductible compensation)	Yes (within "incidental" limits)	Deduction deferred to year paid*	Deduction deferred to year paid*
Current taxable income to employee	P.S. 58 cost** less employee contribution	Bonus amount fully taxable	P.S. 58 cost** less employee contribution	None	None
Recovery of employer outlay	Yes	No	No	No	No
Amount of death benefit for employee	Amount at risk (standard plan)	Full death proceeds	Full death proceeds	Full death proceeds "leveraged" by employer's tax deduction	Full death proceeds "leveraged" by employer's tax deduction
Income taxation of death benefit to employee's beneficiary	Tax free	Tax free	Amount at risk is tax free	Fully taxable as received	Fully taxable as received
Federal estate tax treatment	Includible to extent of incidents of ownership	Includible to extent of incidents of ownership	May be excluded by subtrust technique	Value of deferred comp. benefits included	Excluded (noncontrol employee)

*Note, however, that the deduction is based, not on what the employer paid into the plan, but on the much larger amount the employer pays out.

**or one year term cost if lower.

Chapter 4

DESIGNING THE RIGHT HEALTH BENEFIT PLAN

Health care plans are among the most popular and important employee benefits, and are expected to remain so, particularly in view of the aging of the population toward the end of the 20th century. However, the design of these plans is in a state of great change if not crisis. Employers are faced with problems associated with both the rising costs of medical procedures and an aging work force.

The purpose of this chapter is to provide a broad outline for the design of an appropriate health care plan, based on the planning tools discussed in detail in later chapters.

1. WHAT HEALTH BENEFITS DO EMPLOYEES WANT?

The first step in adopting a new benefit design or changing an existing design is to make a preliminary determination of the types of health benefits that will be most valued by employees. In smaller firms, this can often be done by personal interviews and management's personal knowledge of the company's employees. Larger firms often use questionnaires designed by benefit consultants.

The make-up of the employee group may provide some typical responses. For example, a younger work force will typically want to maximize benefits for childbirth and pediatric care, while an older work force will want adequate coverage for major medical expenses. However, employers should not simply accept generalizations but should make an effort to determine what employees actually want.

Where there is a wide variety in the health care needs perceived by the employees, designers should consider making use of two major tools that allow employees to choose the benefits provided by the employer's dollars:

- Cafeteria Plans—Chapter 27

- Flexible Spending Accounts—Chapter 33

2. PLAN DESIGN FEATURES

In designing a health insurance plan to provide appropriate benefits, three aspects are vitally important:

- Efficient *delivery* of the benefits.

- Meeting the employer's *cost* constraints.

- Positive employee *perception* of the plan.

Designers should consider plans designed along the lines of traditional health insurance as discussed in Chapter 37 as well as alternatives such as Health Maintenance Organizations which are addressed in Chapter 38. But modern benefit design requires consideration of a much broader range of options.

For many years, health care costs have increased faster than the rate of inflation. It is expected that this trend will continue although perhaps not at the current rapid rate. While employees expect health care coverage as a standard employee benefit, they are naturally resistant to accepting less cash compensation in return for health benefits. Thus, employers are coming under increasing cost pressures in this area.

Traditional health insurance plans (discussed in Chapter 37) are *postpaid* plans—plans which reimburse (or pay directly) *after* the employee has independently chosen a physician or other provider and undergone the medical or other procedure. Although there are methods for designing cost controls into such plans, with traditional health insurance the fundamental "levers" of cost control are outside the employer's control.

In recent years there has been increased interest in the concept of *managed health care*. Managed health care is a broad concept, aimed at getting the basic cost management into the hands of employers—the people who pay for the product. Managed health care includes the use of "prepaid" health care plans such as HMOs (discussed in Chapter 38). But the concept is a broader one that can utilize a variety of delivery methods for health care services.

In designing health care plans, employers and benefit specialists must consider managed health care concepts. There is no one type of plan that can be described as a "managed health care plan." Managed health care is a set of tools and techniques that can be used to design a health care plan to meet employer—and also employee—needs and cost requirements.

Managed Health Care—Tools and Techniques

Designers of modern health care plans for employers should consider one or more of the following recognized health care management tools and techniques:

1. *Prospective pricing.* A prospective price for health care services is one that is negotiated by the employer (or by a provider or consultant on behalf of the employer) *before* the year in which the health services will be provided to covered employees.

   An HMO is an example of this type of pricing. However, prospective pricing can be used in other types of health care arrangements such as a Preferred Provider Organization (PPO). A PPO is a group of providers with whom an employer negotiates per-unit charges for various types of health services. Employees covered under the employer's health plan are "channeled" or "steered" toward these providers, usually by providing a lower employee cost share if the employee uses the PPO members.

   Why would a health care provider be willing to agree to prospective pricing? Apart from cost pressures that are causing consumers to increasingly demand such arrangements, there is a potential benefit to the doctor, hospital, medical group, or other provider in prospective pricing. While prospective pricing requires the health care provider to assume the risk of cost overruns, the provider also gets the benefit of cost savings not anticipated. And since prospective pricing creates incentives to keep costs down, it can contribute to reducing or slowing health care cost inflation in the long run.

2. *Negotiated discounts.* As either a supplement or an alternative to prospective pricing, employers can negotiate to obtain health services at discounted prices. For example, a hospital might agree to charge the covered employees 75% of the hospital's "usual and customary" rate for hospitalization. However, if the hospital raises its usual and customary rates over the period of the agreement, the amount charged under the plan also goes up, with the discount in effect, so costs are not absolutely controlled.

3. *Channeling.* In order to maximize the benefit of negotiated and prepaid rates, employees must be encouraged as much as possible to utilize providers who operate under these rate agreements. HMOs and PPOs are examples of health care delivery systems that involve channeling. Channeling can also be provided in plan design by providing more favorable cost sharing for utilization of the preferred providers.

4. *Bundling of services.* If a health plan agrees to a per-diem room and board rate with a hospital and the hospital becomes dissatisfied with its revenues during the term of the agreement, there is an incentive for the hospital to try to make up its losses on room charges by increasing pharmacy, laboratory, and other ancillary charges. *Bundling* is a concept designed to avoid this type of "end run" in a pricing agreement. The price negotiated with a provider for a given type of services is arranged to cover the broadest possible range of services connected with a hospital stay or other covered medical event. For example, the agreement would provide a specified price for all hospital charges for a patient whose gall bladder is removed, etc.

5. *Capitation payment.* Under traditional contracts, health care providers have a built-in incentive to maximize utilization since they get paid only when a procedure is actually done. One cost-saving answer is a *capitation* payment—a flat monthly or periodic fee to the provider per plan participant, regardless of the number of procedures the provider actually does. This helps remove the financial incentive to order tests and procedures that are of relatively little benefit to the patient. Moreover, a simple capitation payment agreement can eliminate the need for complicated fee negotiations in many situations.

6. *Peer review.* Peer review is a concept in health services under which a decision to perform medical or surgical procedures on a patient is reviewed by professional colleagues of the physician or provider who first sees the patient. Peer review is built into group practice systems such as HMOs and clinics. Its importance in health benefit plan design lies in the recognition that a large number of medical and surgical procedures currently being performed are unnecessary—unnecessary, that is, in the view of the medical profession itself. Peer review helps to avoid unnecessary procedures and thus plays an important role in controlling costs.

7. *Utilization review.* Utilization review is similar to peer review but is more specifically targeted. An example of utilization review is a requirement in an employer's health benefit plan that covered employees must obtain a second surgeon's opinion in order to be covered for (or to receive full coverage for) specified surgical procedures. These specified procedures are typically those most likely to be recommended unnecessarily.

8. *Quality review.* The quality review concept attempts to insure that health services provided to employees meet minimum quality levels, and thus do not simply lead to further medical costs. With quality review, the employer's health plan provides full coverage only for facilities that

meet minimum requirements, professional groups with minimum credentials, or procedures that follow established medical norms.

9. *Cost sharing.* Cost sharing by requiring deductibles and copayment is a familiar method of holding down an employer's health insurance costs. Currently, good plan design involves creative use of these devices to actually *encourage* employees to use alternative, lower cost methods of providing equivalent health care. For example, the plan should provide an equal or higher employer share for outpatient services than for equivalent inpatient hospital services, so that the plan does not discourage utilization of less costly outpatient alternatives.

10. *Lifestyle management.* The employer should develop programs that encourage employees to stay healthy—an obvious way to reduce health care costs. Exercise programs, weight-loss and no-smoking programs, in addition to many others can be considered.

3. HEALTH BENEFITS FOR EXECUTIVES

Does the employer want to provide health benefits for selected executives over and above benefits provided for employees in general? Congress has indicated its intention to impose "nondiscrimination" rules that would limit special executive benefits in this area. But its first attempt to impose these rules—Section 89 as enacted in 1986—proved unworkable and was repealed in 1989. Current law is relatively flexible. The options for executive health plans are discussed in Chapter 44, Medical Reimbursement Plans.

4. THE PROCESS OF DESIGN AND MAINTENANCE

Designing and maintaining a health benefit plan has the following components:

• Plan design

• Communication with employees

• Financing the plan

• Claim administration

• Claim payment

• Periodic plan review and updating

There are many ways to split responsibilities for these various plan components. To take two extremes, a very large corporation may perform all of these responsibilities; at the other extreme, an employer might delegate all of them to a traditional health insurer.

Increasingly, however, specialized organizations have become available to carry out specific responsibilities in the most cost-effective manner. For example, there are many independent firms that contract to do claims administration for employers or insurers. Similarly, plan design is often done by specialized benefit consulting firms that do not take on any of the other responsibilities, although often they recommend organizations for this purpose.

For the employer, finding the right people and organizations for these responsibilities can be as important to the cost, effective delivery, and positive perception of benefits as plan design itself.

Chapter 5

BENEFIT PLANS FOR PROPRIETORSHIPS, PARTNERSHIPS AND S CORPORATIONS

For benefit plan purposes, proprietorships and partnerships have one significant difference from corporations—the owners of these businesses are not technically *employees* of the business. By contrast, in a corporation an owner, even a 100% shareholder, who works in the business is technically an employee of the corporation. For S corporations, the Internal Revenue Code requires that shareholder employees (those holding more than 2 percent of the S corporation's stock) are to be treated for employee benefit purposes as partners.[1]

Proprietorships, partnerships, and S corporations can have benefit plans for their employees that are exactly the same as those of regular or "C" corporations. Deductibility of benefit costs is the same, and tax treatment to these regular employees is also the same.

But—when the plan attempts to cover the business owners, some differences arise that are covered in this chapter and throughout the book. Many sections of the Code providing favorable tax treatment of employee benefits apply only to employees. Thus, the benefit package for these organizations involves less favorable benefits for owners than if the organization was incorporated. If the situation is seriously adverse to the owners, the planner might even consider incorporating the organization (or, in the case of an S corporation, terminating the S corporation election).

Qualified retirement plans are a very significant exception to the unfavorable treatment of business owners in these organizations. Qualified plans can cover owners of unincorporated businesses or S corporations on much the same basis as regular employees. The differences are discussed in Chapter 12—HR 10 (Keogh) Plans. These differences are so small that it seldom pays to incorporate a business or terminate an S corporation election for qualified plan benefits alone.

PARTNERSHIPS AND PROPRIETORSHIPS

For federal income tax purposes, a proprietorship—an unincorporated business with one owner—is considered simply an extension of the owner. The proprietorship's profit or loss is computed on Schedule C of the owner's federal income tax return. The net income or loss from the business is added to the owner's adjusted gross income from other sources. As a result, business profits are added to other income, while losses are subtracted directly from other income.

This treatment allows all business expenses to be deducted "off the top" so they are available regardless of whether the taxpayer itemizes deductions. Proprietorship expense deductions are also available without any "floor" requirement that may be applicable to itemized deductions. For example, a proprietor can deduct all expenses for business use of an automobile, while an employee must itemize deductions and is subject to a 2% of adjusted gross income floor for employee business expenses.

The tax rates applicable to the business profits of a proprietorship are the same as those applicable to any other kind of individual income, and the income is taxed only once. By comparison, business income of a corporation is taxed at corporate rates, which are different from (and rise to higher levels than) individual rates. Corporate income is taxed at the corporate level and then again at the shareholder level when it is paid out as dividends.

With the exception of contributions to qualified plans, benefits and compensation paid to a proprietor are *not* deductible business expenses. Put another way, expenditures for employee benefits of a proprietor are treated the same as cash taken out by the proprietor. For example, health insurance premiums, life insurance premiums, direct medical reimbursements, or any other form of benefit provided to the proprietor is nondeductible to the business and thus appears directly as income on the proprietor's Schedule C. The owner's benefits are nondeductible even if the business maintains the benefit plan for other, nonowner employees of the business as well as for the owner.

Partnerships, in principle, are treated for tax purposes the same as proprietorships. That is, the partners, not the partnership, are the taxable entities. However, because more than one taxpayer is involved, the tax rules for partnerships are complicated. In fact, they are among the most complex provisions of the tax law, but fortunately for benefit purposes most of the complexities can be overlooked.

A partnership typically pays no federal income taxes. All the taxes on the partnership's income are paid by the partners. However, a partnership must file a federal income tax return; the return is an information return that reports the partners' shares of income, losses, and other tax items.

Each partner must report and pay taxes on his "distributive share" of the partnership's income for the taxable year. A partner's distributive share is the amount of income that he is entitled to receive under the partnership agreement, even if it is not actually distributed to him during the taxable year. If the partnership has losses, each partner may deduct his share of the losses on his own tax return, subject to various limitations on "passive loss" deductions designed to deter "tax shelter" partnerships.

Employee benefits for partners are treated as follows:

- For qualified retirement plans (1) contributions for partners are deductible by the partnership along with those for regular employees, and (2) partners are taxed on qualified plan contributions and benefits much the same as regular employees. (See Chapter 12.)

- Costs for fringe benefits of any other type are deductible by the partnership in computing its taxable income—they are deductible under Section 162 as "guaranteed payments" to partners as defined in Code section 707(c). (This is the same way that guaranteed "salary" payments to partners are treated.) Alternatively, the partnership can treat the premium payment or other fringe benefit cost as a reduction in cash distributions to the partner.[2]

- Partners must then report as taxable income the value of all fringe benefits (other than qualified plans) provided for them by the partnership.[3]

S CORPORATIONS

The S corporation is a corporation that has elected (under Subchapter S of the Internal Revenue Code) to be taxed like a partnership for federal income tax purposes. (Most state income tax laws also recognize S corporations). "Like a partnership" is an oversimplification, of course—this will not come as any surprise to students of federal tax law. However, for fringe benefit purposes it is generally a close enough description.

In order to elect S corporation status, the corporation must comply with certain "don'ts"—it must *not*[4]:

- have more than 35 shareholders

- have a shareholder that is not an individual or a decedent's estate, with some exceptions designed to facilitate estate planning

- be organized in a foreign country or have a nonresident alien shareholder

- have more than one "class of stock" (some differences in voting rights are allowed)

- be a member of an affiliated group of corporations or one of several specified ineligible types of corporation.

Some of these restrictions can have relevance in benefit planning that involves the use of employer stock. Such plans cannot violate the 35-shareholder rule, or use a nonindividual as a shareholder. This effectively rules out the use of stock bonus plans or ESOPs in an S corporation (see Chapter 10). Also, benefit plans using stock must be designed so as not to violate the "one class of stock" requirement.[5]

The Code provides that if an employee of an S corporation owns more than two percent of the stock (an MTTPSE—*more-than-two-percent shareholder-employee*—for purposes of this chapter), the MTTPSE is treated as a partner for fringe benefit purposes.[6] The Congressional committee reports on this provision[7] list the following specific fringe benefits (1) the $5,000 employee death benefit exclusion under Section 101(b); (2) the tax exclusion for *benefits* under a health and accident plan, Section 105; (3) the tax exclusion for *coverage* under a health and accident plan, Section 106; (4) the tax benefits for group-term life insurance, Section 79; and (5) the exclusion for meals and lodging furnished for the convenience of the employer, Section 119. Qualified retirement plans are *not* covered by this provision; MTTPSEs are treated much like regular employees for qualified plan purposes.

Fringe benefits provided to MTTPSEs are treated as follows for tax purposes:

- The S corporation can deduct the cost of fringe benefits for MTTPSEs in determining its taxable income.[8]

- MTTPSEs must report—as compensation income—the value of any fringe benefits provided to them. These items must be included on the Form W-2 provided by the employer to the MTTPSE. Note that in the case of health and accident premiums, the amount of the premium is includable in full, but the MTTPSE is eligible for the 25% deduction under Code section 162(l), (to the extent that this deduction is available in the future — see Chapter 37).

- For FICA (social security) purposes, these fringe benefit amounts may or may not be includable, depending on the FICA rules for the type of plan involved. For example, health and accident premiums are not includable in the FICA tax base if there is a "plan or system" of health benefits for employees and dependents generally, or a class of employees. However, if the premiums are paid for a single employee or a few executives, the amounts may be includable in the FICA base.[9]

- Qualified retirement plans for MTTPSEs present some additional technical problems that are discussed in Chapter 12. The principal issue is, "What constitutes the MTTPSE's compensation for plan purposes?"

SPECIFIC FRINGE BENEFITS

The chart in Figure 5.1 summarizes the treatment of specific fringe benefits for proprietors, partners, and MTTPSEs.

A "yes" in the chart indicates that the plan can be provided for these people with full tax benefits. A "no" indicates that the plan will provide no tax benefits for these key people. Note that some fringe benefit provisions of the Code such as dependent care (Section 129) do provide tax benefits for proprietors, partners, and MTTPSEs, despite the provisions discussed in this chapter.

The term "partial" in the chart referring to group health plans reflects the limited deduction under Code section 162(l) equal to 25% of the cost of health insurance for a self-

employed individual, to the extent that this deduction is available in the future. This is discussed in Chapter 37.

Finally, in reviewing this chart, note that it reflects the treatment only of partners, proprietors, and MTTPSEs. All business organizations can adopt benefit plans providing full tax benefits for rank and file employees.

FOOTNOTES

1. IRC Section 1372.
2. Rev. Rul. 91-26, 1991-1 CB 184.
3. Under IRC Section 61(a), all fringe benefits are currently taxable unless there is a specific provision of the Code that exempts or defers taxation of the benefit. Since most benefit exemptions or deferrals in the Code apply only to employees, partners are currently taxable on virtually all fringe benefits.
4. IRC Section 1361.
5. IRC Sec. 1361(b)(1)(D). See Blau et al, "Planning for Noncash Executive Compensation in S Corporations," *Journal of Taxation*, November 1988, p. 338.
6. IRC Section 1372.
7. Committee Reports, Subchapter S Revision Act of 1982, P.L. 97-354, enacted October 19, 1982.
8. Rev. Rul. 91-26, 1991-1 CB 184.
9. Announcement 92-16, 1992-5 IRB 53.

Figure 5.1

Comparison of Fringe Benefits by Entity Type				
Benefit	**Sole Prop.**	**Partnership**	**S Corp**	**C Corp**
Qualified plan	Yes	Yes	Yes	Yes
Deferred compensation	No	No	No	Yes
Salary continuation	No	Yes	Yes	Yes
Group life	No	No	No	Yes
Group health	Partial	Partial	Partial	Yes
Group disability	No	No	No	Yes
Medical reimb. plans	No	No	No	Yes
Accidental death	No	No	No	Yes
Disability income plan	No	No	No	Yes
Employee death benefit				
-Employer provided	No	No	No	Yes
-Qualified plan	Yes	Yes	Yes	Yes
Group legal plan	Yes	Yes	Yes	Yes
Educ. assistance plan	Yes	Yes	Yes	Yes
Dependent care	Yes	Yes	Yes	Yes
Meals & lodging	No	Yes	Yes	Yes
Cafeteria plan	No	No	No	Yes

Source: Adapted from Jenkins, Gary E., "The Impact of Choice of Entity Selection upon Compensation and Fringe Benefit Planning after Tax Reform," *Journal of American Society of CLU and ChFC*, March 1988.

Chapter 6

THE RETIREMENT PLANNING PROCESS

Retirement planning is an increasingly important part of the financial services industry. The "baby boom" generation is approaching middle age, so the number of individuals with significant savings and retirement planning needs is increasing. At the same time, the economic and tax complexity of all types of retirement-related financial planning has also increased.

Retirement planning is "interdisciplinary." It combines the skills of the traditional estate planner, the financial planner, and the benefit/compensation planner. The broad range of issues that must be addressed makes this one of the most challenging of the financial services disciplines now emerging.

Retirement planning is also multifaceted because of the broad range of clients that must be served. For example it encompasses advice to clients many years in advance of retirement, as well as to clients just at retirement and thereafter. Clients may also range from business owners who are able to use their businesses to help provide retirement benefits, to key executives who can bargain effectively with their employers regarding retirement benefits, to employees who have no significant say in their employee benefit package. All these different types of clients may have needs for retirement planning as well as sufficient assets to enable the payment of adequate fees or commissions to the planner.

Perhaps no single individual should attempt to handle all aspects of retirement planning. Any person giving advice in these situations should know when it is appropriate to call in an employee benefits expert, a lawyer specializing in estate planning, an expert portfolio manager, or whatever other specialist is required. However, all financial planners should understand the basics of retirement planning—the broad general approaches, the tools and techniques—and where they fit in.

This chapter is designed to provide the beginnings of an understanding of the *process* of retirement planning—some broad guidelines with an indication of where individual financial planning tools and techniques fit into this process. In particular, the employee benefit aspects covered in this book will be highlighted here.

I. THE RETIREMENT PLANNING PROCESS—LONG RANGE

Serious retirement planning should begin well in advance of actual retirement. Nobody would expect a person in their twenties to make firm financial plans for retirement, other than very general plans such as establishing the basics of a savings and investment program and participating in employer retirement plans such as 401(k) plans. However, beginning 15 to 20 years in advance of retirement, clients become aware that they should begin definite and detailed plans.

While detailed planning is appropriate at this point, planners and clients should not expect exactness in the financial planning targets. There are too many imponderables—future investment return rates, future tax rates, the client's life expectancy. Nevertheless, the targets for retirement planning are near enough at this point to try to quantify plans and make sure they are systematically carried out.

Step 1: Where is the client now?

As with estate planning, a worthwhile retirement plan cannot be provided unless the planner has detailed and precise financial information about the client. In fact, "due diligence" in retirement planning *requires* the planner to make every effort to obtain accurate and complete financial information. The planner should be wary of clients who are reluctant to provide such information. (See Appendix H, Malpractice.)

Retirement planning practitioners should develop a "fact finder" for clients that will systematize this process. Some key elements:

A. *Benefit plan information.* Retirement planning requires complete information about all employee benefit plans in which the client *and* the client's spouse are currently participating *or have ever participated.* Not only retirement plans (qualified or nonqualified) but other benefit plans such as health insurance, life insurance, or even such fringe benefits as membership in company athletic or health clubs after retirement may be significant in the retirement planning process.

   In addition to private employer benefit plans, government benefits also should be estimated—Social Security, veterans' benefits, and the like.

   In order to accurately forecast the level of employee benefits available, the planner needs to see actual benefit plan documents; it is not enough to rely simply on the client's informal impression of what his benefit programs provide. Generally, if a plan provides a Summary Plan Description (SPD), as do most ERISA-affected plans (see Appendix A), the SPD should be sufficient. For qualified plans, employers are required also to provide an individual benefit statement at least once annually. In some cases, the planner might wish to look at the actual underlying plan documents, which under ERISA the client has the right to do. (Companies can charge a reasonable copying fee for providing copies.)

For non-ERISA plans, there often are no formal documentation requirements, so it may be difficult to obtain adequate written information about such benefits. However, most companies provide a "benefits manual" or other literature covering these benefits.

In general, in examining benefit plans, focus on

- What vested benefits at retirement does the plan *now* provide—that is, even if the employee terminated employment today?

- What will the plan provide at retirement, if the employee continues working? If the benefits are based on salary, what is a reasonable salary forecast?

- How solid are predictions of future benefits? For example, health benefit plans are currently in constant flux. Can a planner have any confidence that health benefit plans available at retirement 15 years from now will have any resemblance to current benefits? The employer's financial stability also has a bearing on this issue.

- To what extent can the employee control the employee benefits available at retirement? Do employer plans have options available to the employee to change or increase benefits, possibly on a contributory basis? (See the chapters on FSAs (Chapter 33) and Cafeteria Plans (Chapter 27), for example.) Can the employee individually negotiate better or different benefits? At the extreme, an owner or majority shareholder can—and generally should—arrange the company's benefit plans to be consistent with his or her individual retirement planning.

B. *Detailed current asset information.* The planner must have detailed information about the client's current assets and sources of income. Completeness is a must—it is not optional. Develop asset fact finders; a sample Retirement Planning Asset Worksheet (see Figure 6.1) is included at the end of this chapter.

Assets must be valued—book value is of little use in developing a financial or retirement plan. Some assets are easy to value; others may be impossible to value with certainty. Asset valuation is discussed in *Tools and Techniques of Estate Planning.*

Owners of closely held businesses are in a special category. It is difficult to value an interest in a small business, of course. But retirement planning requires more than this. What is important about a small business interest is not what it is worth now, but what will happen to it in the future—how (and if) it will continue as a source of income in retirement. In other words, retirement planning for closely held business owners is inextricable from planning for business succession through buy-sell agreements, gifts or sales to successors, or whatever mechanism is set up for continuation of the business or retrieving its value for the owner's benefit.

In obtaining asset information, do not overlook *liability* information. This includes not only traditional debts outstanding, but also legal obligations such as future alimony or child support that involves a recurring obligation; property settlement payments that are outstanding; state or federal tax liabilities outstanding; or fines or judgments not yet fully paid. Many of these are things that clients understandably would rather not think about and they may not be volunteered.

C. *Other information.* As with estate and financial planning, retirement planning requires the development of a complete profile of the client's financial status. For example, does the client have major financial needs coming up *before* retirement—perhaps a child's college or graduate school expenses, or long term care for a dependent? Or, on the plus side, does the client expect a future windfall—an inheritance, for example? These contingencies can be very difficult to value. In extreme cases they can render a financial or retirement plan virtually worthless. The planner must deal with these issues as well as possible, but must also be willing to "caveat" the ultimate retirement plan—that is, state clearly that the plan *does not* take into account certain contingencies that potentially exist but are impossible to predict.

Step 2—Determine Retirement Needs

Although a client far from retirement cannot foresee what his or her life will actually be like after retirement, a good approximation of retirement needs—at least a good starting point—is to make an estimate of what it costs *now* for a standard of living that the client considers acceptable. By adjusting these amounts for inflation, a reasonable estimate of the total capital needs—the lump sum amount needed at retirement—can be made.

A Retirement Needs Worksheet outlining the steps in this process is included at the end of this chapter (see Figure 6.2). As an illustration of this worksheet, suppose that your client provides information for lines 1 through 9 that indicates he will need $60,000 annually (in current dollars). If the client is 10 years from retirement, assuming a 4 percent rate of inflation, this translates to a need for $88,814 (line 14) at retirement 10 years from now. Assuming continued 4 percent inflation, a 20-year payout after retirement, and after-tax investment return of 7 percent, this requires a total capital at retirement (line 21) of $1,374,059.

This worksheet converts everything to a capital equivalent. For example, if the client in the preceding paragraph expects to receive a monthly pension benefit at retirement, it should be converted to its then lump-sum equivalent. If the benefit is worth $300,000, for example, then the client's capital need is reduced to $1,074,059 ($1,374,059 less $300,000).

Step 3—Getting there.

The retirement planner's critical contribution is, after identifying the needs and the current assets, to develop a plan for reaching the client's targeted capital needs. All the tools and techniques of financial planning for capital accumulation should be brought to bear on this problem.

Planning requires not only reaching the capital needs targets, but also making sure that the capital is translated appropriately into living expense needs. For example, a client's personal residence may have a considerable market value on paper, but how will this value contribute to living standards in retirement? Questions like this emphasize the need for planning for liquidity and diversification—here as in all investment planning, but with a focus on retirement needs.

II. PLANNING AT OR NEAR RETIREMENT

As retirement approaches, the focus changes from accumulation planning toward the need to make the right decisions about assets the client already has. These issues include:

- Housing—what should be done with the client's primary residence? What are the client's long range plans for housing?

- Health care—What options are available under the client's employee health plans? (See Chapter 37.) What private insurance is necessary to supplement employee benefits and government benefits?

- Pensions and Social Security. Here there are often many possible choices and options; issues include:

    1. How much current income does the client need?

    2. Does the client want to maximize current income or provide for beneficiaries after his (or his and his spouse's) death?

    3. What options are available under the client's benefit plans?

    4. What are the tax consequences of different distribution options—federal income tax, the 15 percent excess distribution/accumulation tax, and federal estate and gift taxes, as well as state taxes?

    5. Does the client want to explore possibilities of moving money out of current qualified plans (through a rollover or other option) and investing it in another way—annuities, life insurance, or other investments?

Issues concerning distributions from qualified plans, tax deferred annuities, and IRAs are discussed in Chapter 24 in greater detail.

Figure 6.1

RETIREMENT PLANNING ASSET WORKSHEET

DATE _____

Client's Name: _____

Address: _____

Telephone: (home) _____ (office)_____

Business Address: _____

Spouse's name: _____

Business Address: _____ telephone _____

Figure 6.1 (continued)

RETIREMENT PLANNING ASSET WORKSHEET

ASSETS

Valuation as of date prepared unless otherwise indicated.

1. Cash and cash equivalents

	Value	Current Return (pretax)
a. checking accounts	_____	_____
b. savings accounts	_____	_____
c. money market accounts	_____	_____
d. life insurance cash values	_____	_____
Total Cash/Cash Equivalents	_____	_____

2. Retirement Plans
(Do not include defined benefit plans)

	Current balance	Current Return (pretax)
a. IRA	_____	_____
b. Keogh	_____	_____
c. Section 401(k)	_____	_____
d. Section 403(b)	_____	_____
e. Other defined contribution	_____	_____
Total Retirement Plans	_____	_____

Figure 6.1 (continued)

3. **Investments**
   (Do not include amounts
   included in 2 above)

	Fair Market Value	Adjusted Basis	Current return (pretax)
a. Portfolio Investments			
(1) *money market instruments*			
certificates of deposit	_____	_____	_____
T bills	_____	_____	_____
commercial paper	_____	_____	_____
(2) *fixed-income securities*			
U.S. government	_____	_____	_____
U.S. agencies	_____	_____	_____
municipal bonds	_____	_____	_____
preferred stock	_____	_____	_____
corporate bonds	_____	_____	_____
notes receivable	_____	_____	_____
(3) *common stocks*			
listed	_____	_____	_____
OTC	_____	_____	_____
restricted stock	_____	_____	_____
(4) *other portfolio assets*			
options	_____	_____	_____
mutual funds	_____	_____	_____
physical assets (collectibles)	_____	_____	_____
b. Passive Investments			
(1) direct participation investments	_____	_____	_____
(2) real estate (passive)	_____	_____	_____

Figure 6.1 (continued)

3. Investments (continued)

	Fair Market Value	Adjusted Basis	Current return (pretax)
c. Active Businesses			
(1) value of business owned and operated	_____	_____	_____
(2) real estate (active participation)	_____	_____	_____
Total Investments	_____	_____	_____

4. Personal Assets

	Fair Market Value	Adjusted Basis
a. primary residence	_____	_____
b. other real estate	_____	_____
c. household contents	_____	_____
d. automobiles	_____	_____
e. other	_____	_____
Total Personal Assets	_____	_____

LIABILITIES

1. Short-Term Liabilities
(12 months or less)

	Balance Outstanding	Interest Rate	Monthly Payment	Maturity Date
Consumer credit (credit cards & open charge accounts)	_____	_____	_____	_____
Personal notes payable	_____	_____	_____	_____
Loans from life insurance policies	_____	_____	_____	_____
Notes guaranteed	_____	_____	_____	_____
Other	_____	_____	_____	_____
Total	_____	_____	_____	_____

Figure 6.1 (continued)

2. Long-Term Liabilities

	Balance Outstanding	Interest Rate	Monthly Payment	Maturity Date
Mortgages on personal residences	_____	_____	_____	_____
Loans against investment assets	_____	_____	_____	_____
Loans against personal residences	_____	_____	_____	_____
Total	_____			

3. Other

	Balance Outstanding	Interest Rate	Monthly Payment	Maturity Date
Deferred Taxes	_____	_____	_____	_____
Alimony, child support, etc.	_____	_____	_____	_____
Judgments, etc.	_____	_____	_____	_____
Total	_____			

SUMMARY

Assets (fair market value)

Total cash and cash equivalents	_____
Total investment plans	_____
Total investments	_____
Total Personal assets	_____
Total Assets	_____

Liabilities (outstanding balances)

Short-term	_____
Long-term	_____
Other	_____
Total Liabilities:	_____

Figure 6.2

Retirement Needs Work Sheet
Estimated Retirement Living Expenses and Required Capital (in current dollars)

	Per Month x 12 =	Per Year
1. Food	_____	_____
2. Housing:		
a. Rent/mortgage payment	_____	_____
b. Insurance (if not included in a.)	_____	_____
c. Property taxes (if not included in a.)	_____	_____
d. Utilities	_____	_____
e. Maintenance (if you own)	_____	_____
f. Management fee (if a condominium)	_____	_____
3. Clothing and Personal Care:		
a. Wife	_____	_____
b. Husband	_____	_____
c. Dependents	_____	_____
4. Medical Expenses:		
a. Doctor	_____	_____
b. Dentist	_____	_____
c. Medicines	_____	_____
d. Medical insurance to supplement medicare	_____	_____
5. Transportation:		
a. Car payments	_____	_____
b. Gas	_____	_____
c. Insurance	_____	_____
d. License	_____	_____
e. Car Maintenance (tires and repairs)	_____	_____
f. Other transportation	_____	_____
6. Recurring Expenses:		
a. Entertainment	_____	_____
b. Travel	_____	_____
c. Hobbies	_____	_____
d. Club fees and dues	_____	_____
e. Other	_____	_____
7. Insurance	_____	_____
8. Gifts and Contributions	_____	_____
9. Income Taxes (if any)	_____	_____

Figure 6.2 (continued)

10. Total Annual Expenses (current dollars) _____ $ _____

11. Inflation Rate until Retirement (I) _____

12. Total Years until Retirement (N) _____

13. Inflation Adjustment Factor $(1 + I)^N$ x _____

14. Total Annual Expenses (future dollars) = _____

15. Inflation Rate Postretirement (i) _____

16. Aftertax Rate of Return (r) _____

17. Anticipated Duration of Retirement (n) _____

18. Inflation-Adjusted Discount Factor _____

$$a = \frac{1 + i}{1 + r}$$

19. Capital Required at Retirement to Fund Retirement

    Living Expenses

    Amt line 14 $x \dfrac{1 - a^n}{1 - a}$ $ _____

20. One-Time Expenses +$ _____

21. Total Capital Need at Retirement =$ _____

Source: Robert J. Doyle, Jr., *Retirement Planning Handbook*, The American College, Bryn Mawr, PA.

The Tools and Techniques of Employee Benefit and Retirement Planning

Chapter 7

KNOWING THE RULES: GOVERNMENT REGULATIONS AND HOW TO FIND THEM

An employer can pay its top executives as much as it wants to; the federal government does not regulate this except for very general "reasonableness" limits on the amount of salary payments that can be deducted. By contrast, federal tax law specifically limits the maximum pension benefit that an employer can provide to an employee.

There are innumerable other detailed federal laws and regulations effective in the employee benefits area; just to pick another one at random, the government specifies, to the day, when an employer must allow an employee to begin participating in the employer's pension plan.

Why does the federal government "micromanage" an employer's benefit programs? What is the impact of this extensive regulation on the employee benefit planner, and how can the planner keep up with the rules? That's the subject of this chapter.

WHY THE RULES EXIST

Maintaining income of individuals when they cannot support themselves has been a major governmental concern. Governments are not always happy at being handed this responsibility but usually end up with it if it is not picked up somewhere else in society. So, governments have always tried to encourage private organizations to act in this area. This is one reason why charitable institutions are exempt from tax.

When the American economy started to become mainly industrial around the beginning of the 20th century, the need for retirement plans increased, since the industrial economy tended to break up the traditional supportive, extended farm family, and industry provides less work for the aged than farming. The government became involved in retirement plans in a twofold way.

First, in the 1920s the federal government began encouraging private, employer-sponsored retirement plans by providing two kinds of tax benefits: (1) pension funds were made tax exempt[1] and (2) employer contributions to plan funds were made currently deductible even though benefits were not paid until later years.[2] The second big federal initiative in the

retirement plan area was, of course, the adoption of the Social Security system in the 1930s at a time when private pension plans were in great decline.

Since the 1940s, private pension plans have revived to an enormous degree; assets in these plans now amount to more than 1.5 *trillion* dollars—a pot of money constituting as much as 10 percent of the nation's *total capital.*

However, something else has grown as fast or faster than the dollars in pension funds: the words, paragraphs, pages, and volumes of federal statutes, court cases, rulings, and regulations based on the simple, original 1920s tax benefit arrangements for private pension plans. How does the government justify the sometimes almost unbelievable complexity of this regulatory scheme? Three reasons are generally given; two are respectable, while the third is questionable:

- the government loses substantial revenue by providing tax benefits for retirement and other benefit plans. So, it has to make sure that benefits go where they are most needed so that the tax "expenditure" is cost effective.

- private saving for retirement should be encouraged so that individuals do not become dependent on the government. But such saving should not fail to help those who really need the retirement benefit. There have to be rules so that plans do not simply benefit highly compensated employees who have other sources of retirement income.

- the government can gain a lot of tax revenue—without the political pain of "raising taxes"—by fine-tuning the employee benefit law to reduce tax benefits for certain plan participants. Fine-tuning adds page after page to federal laws and regulations, year after year. Last year's fine-tuning scheme is seldom repealed— it's just added to or amended.

What's the significance of all this history and government policy to the benefit planner? Just two points have to be made:

- It is a lot easier to understand the rules if you know where they come from. For example, can you adopt a plan provision that gives extra benefits to one or more employees who are not "highly compensated"? You can search the federal law until doomsday and you will not find the answer to this in so many words. But if you understand what the law is trying to do, you will understand immediately that this kind of provision usually will not violate the law.

- If you know what kinds of concerns motivate our Congress, you can give your clients useful advice about potential future changes in the law. While nobody can predict tax law changes in detail, it's pretty safe to say, for example, that until the federal deficit problem is resolved, the limits on pension plan benefits and contributions will not be raised in the near future by any meaningful amount.

THE RULES

Planners need to understand where the employee benefit plan rules are and how to find them. They also must understand the significance of the rules; for example, some rules are binding on everybody, while certain other authorities are merely sources of information about the government's position on a certain issue in case the issue should get into court.

Government regulation is expressed through the following, in order of importance: (1) the statutory law; (2) the law as expressed in court cases; (3) regulations of government agencies; (4) rulings and other information issued by government agencies.

The law (statutory).

The "law" as expressed by statutes passed by the U.S. Congress is the highest level of authority and is the basis of all regulation; the court cases, rulings, and regulations are simply interpretations of the statute. If the statute was detailed enough to cover every possible case, there theoretically would not be any need for anything else. But despite the best efforts of Congressional drafting staffs, the statutes cannot cover every situation.

Benefit planners should become as familiar as possible with the statutory law since it is the basis for all other rules, regulations, and court cases. One of the main causes for confusion among non-experts is a lack of understanding of the relative status of sources of information. That is, while a rule found in the Internal Revenue Code is controlling, a statement in an IRS ruling or instructions to IRS forms may be merely

a matter of interpretation that is relatively easy to "plan around."

In the benefits area, the sources of statutory law are:

- *Internal Revenue Code (the Code).* The tax laws governing the deductibility and taxation of pension and employee benefit programs are controlling. These are found primarily in Sections 401-425, with important provisions also in Sections 72, 83, and other sections.

- *Employee Retirement Income Security Act of 1974 (ERISA), as amended, and other labor law provisions.* Labor law provisions such as ERISA govern the non-tax aspects of federal regulation. These involve plan participation requirements, notice to participants, reporting to the federal government, and a variety of rules designed to safeguard any funds that are set aside to pay benefits in the future. There is some overlap between ERISA and the Code in the areas of plan participation, vesting, prohibited transactions, and others.

- *Pension Benefit Guaranty Corporation (PBGC).* The PBGC is a government corporation set up under ERISA in 1974 to provide termination insurance for participants in qualified defined benefit plans up to certain limits. In carrying out this responsibility, the PBGC regulates plan terminations and imposes certain reporting requirements on covered plans that are in financial difficulty or in a state of contraction.

- *Securities laws.* The federal securities laws are designed to protect investors. Benefit plans may involve an element of investing the employee's money. While qualified plans are generally exempt from the full impact of the securities laws, if the plan holds employer stock, a federal registration statement may be required and certain securities regulations may apply.

- *Civil Rights laws.* Benefit plans are part of an employer's compensation policies, and these plans are therefore subject to the Civil Rights Act of 1964 prohibiting employment discrimination on the basis of race, religion, sex, or national origin.

- *Age Discrimination.* The Age Discrimination in Employment Act of 1978, as amended, has specific provisions aimed at benefit plans.

- *State legislation.* ERISA contains a broad "preemption" provision under which the provisions of ERISA supersede any state laws relating to employee benefit plans. If ERISA does not deal with a particular issue, however, there may be room for state legislation. For example, there is considerable state legislation and regulation governing the types of group-term life insurance contracts that can be offered as part of an employer plan. There are also certain areas where states continue to assert authority even though ERISA also has an impact—for example in the area of creditors' rights to pension fund assets.

Court cases.

The courts enter this picture primarily when a specific taxpayer decides to appeal a tax assessment made by the IRS. The courts do not act on their own to resolve tax or other legal issues. Consequently, the law as expressed in court cases is a crazy-quilt affair that offers some answers but often raises more questions than it answers. However, after statutes, court cases are the most authoritative source of law. Courts can and do overturn regulations and rulings of the IRS and other regulatory agencies.

A taxpayer wishing to contest a tax assessment has three choices: (1) the Federal District Court in the taxpayer's district; (2) the United States Tax Court; or (3) the United States Court of Federal Claims.[3] So, tax law can be found in decisions of any of these three courts.

All three courts are equally authoritative. Most tax cases, however, are decided by the U.S. Tax Court, because it offers a powerful advantage: the taxpayer can bring the case before the Tax Court without paying the disputed tax. The other courts require payment of the tax followed by a suit for refund.

Decisions of these three courts can be appealed to the Federal Circuit Court of Appeals for the applicable federal "judicial circuit"—the U.S. is divided into eleven of these circuits. The circuit courts sometimes differ on certain points of tax law; as a result tax and benefit planning may depend on what judicial circuit the taxpayer is located in. Where these differences exist, one or more taxpayers will eventually appeal a decision by the Court of Appeals to the United States Supreme Court to resolve differences of interpretation among various judicial circuits. However, this process takes many years and the Supreme Court may ultimately choose not to hear the case. Congress also sometimes amends the Code or other statute to resolve these interpretive differences.

Regulations.

Regulations are interpretations of statutory law that are published by a government agency; in the benefits area, the most significant regulations are those published by the Trea-

sury Department (the parent of the IRS), the Labor Department, and the PBGC.

Regulations are structured as abstract rules, like the statutory law itself. They are not related to a particular factual situation, although they often contain useful examples that illustrate the application of the rules. Treasury regulations currently are often issued in question-and-answer form.

The numbering system for regulations is supposed to make them more accessible by including an internal reference to the underlying statutory provision. For example, Treasury Regulation Section 1.401(k)-2 is a regulation relating to Section 401(k) of the Internal Revenue Code. Labor Regulation Section 2550.408b-3 relates to Section 408(b) of ERISA.

Issuance of regulations follows a prescribed procedure involving an initial issuance of *proposed regulations*, followed by hearings and public comment, then *final regulations*. The process often takes years. Where taxpayers have an urgent need to know answers, the agency will issue *regulations* that are both *temporary* and proposed. Technically, temporary regulations are binding while regulations issued only in proposed form are not. However, if a taxpayer takes a position contrary to such a proposed regulation, the taxpayer is taking the risk that the regulation will ultimately be finalized and be enforced against him.

Rulings and other information.

IRS Rulings. IRS rulings are responses by the IRS to requests by taxpayers to interpret the law in light of their particular fact situations. A *Technical Advice Memorandum (TAM)* is similar to a ruling except that the request for clarification and guidance is initiated from an IRS agent in the field during a taxpayer audit, rather than directly from the taxpayer.

There are two types of IRS rulings—*Revenue Rulings*, which are published by the IRS as general guidance to all taxpayers, and *Private Letter Rulings (Let. Ruls.)*, which are addressed only to the specific taxpayers who requested the rulings. The IRS publishes its Revenue Rulings in IRS Bulletins (collected in Cumulative Bulletins—CB—each year). Revenue rulings are binding on IRS personnel on the issues covered in them, but often IRS agents will try to make a distinction between a taxpayer's factual situation and a similar one covered in a ruling if the ruling appears to favor the taxpayer.

Private letter rulings are not published by the IRS, but are available to the public with taxpayer identification deleted. These "anonymous" letter rulings are published for tax professionals by various private publishers. They are not binding interpretations of tax law except for the taxpayer who requested the ruling, and even then they apply only to the exact situation described in the ruling request and do not apply to even a slightly different fact pattern involving the same taxpayer. Nevertheless, letter rulings are very important in research since they are often the only source of information about the IRS position on various issues.

A *General Counsel Memorandum (GCM)* is an internal IRS document prepared by the General Counsel of the Service for its own staff's guidance in administering the Code. GCMs also give an indication of the probable approach the Service will take in a particular area.

Because of frequent changes in the tax law, the IRS has been unable to promulgate regulations and rulings on a timely basis, and has increasingly used less formal approaches to inform taxpayers of its position. These include various types of published *Notices* and even speeches by IRS personnel. Finally, many important IRS positions are found only in *IRS Publications* (pamphlets available free to taxpayers) and *instructions* for filling out IRS forms. The IRS also maintains telephone question-answering services, but the value of these for information on complicated issues is minimal.

Other rulings. The Department of Labor and the PBGC issue some rulings in areas of employee benefit regulation under their jurisdiction. DOL rulings include the *Prohibited Transaction Exemptions (PTEs)* which rule on types of transactions that can avoid the prohibited transaction penalties—for example, sale of life insurance contracts to qualified plans.

HOW TO FIND THE ANSWERS

Tax experts find it difficult to get answers to employee benefit tax questions, so non-experts should not be surprised if they also have trouble. The following approach is used by many successful financial planning professionals:

1. Investigate secondary sources, choose several that you find helpful, and keep them handy. Secondary sources are overviews of the law that give you a general understanding and direct you toward more detailed information. The *Tools and Techniques* series of books are examples of secondary sources of information that provide rapid access to an overview and general explanation of the law.

2. When a tax or other benefit issue arises, review the secondary sources to get a general idea of the law in that area and where additional information can be found.

3. Review the statutory provisions and regulations (if any) relating to the issue—particularly the Internal Revenue Code and ERISA and the related regulations.

4. Review court cases and rulings dealing with the issue and compare their factual situations with the one you are dealing with.

At this point, non-lawyer professionals must confront the problem of *unauthorized practice of law.* While the concept of "practice of law" is too complex to define here, in general a non-lawyer may not express an opinion to a client as to the specific law applicable to, and the legal implications of, the client's factual situation. A professional can, however, discuss the legal background of the client's situation in general and can advise the client to obtain an opinion of counsel as to the law's specific impact on the client. That should be the non-lawyer professional's role in a benefit planning situation involving complex or unsettled legal issues. See Appendix F.

WHAT HAPPENS IF THE LAW IS NOT FOLLOWED?

There are both *criminal* and civil penalties that can apply if a taxpayer fails to abide by the tax law by taking too large a deduction or under-reporting items of income. Criminal penalties are those that can result in imprisonment.[4] Nothing will be said further here about criminal penalties except this: if a client discovers that the IRS is considering criminal tax sanctions against him, that client is in very serious trouble and needs immediate legal help from an expert in criminal tax law.

Most IRS audits that end unfavorably to the taxpayer do not result in penalties; the taxpayer merely has to pay back taxes plus interest—which can be substantial. However, certain penalties can also be assessed. These include penalties for:

- failure to file return or pay the tax indicated on the return. *Penalty*—5% of the underpayment per month, up to 25%.[5]

- substantial understatement of income tax (understatement of the greater of $5000 or 10 percent of tax). *Penalty*—20 percent of the understatement.[6]

- negligence, imposed if a taxpayer fails to make a reasonable attempt to comply with the tax law. *Penalty*—20% of the underpayment.[7]

- fraud. *Penalty*—75% of the underpayment.[8]

- substantial valuation overstatement (for example, an overstatement of pension liabilities to inflate pension plan deductions). *Penalty*—20 to 40% of the under-payment.[9]

Legal opinion letters. Can a taxpayer rely on a legal opinion as to the tax consequences of a transaction—that is, will the taxpayer at least avoid the negligence or fraud penalties by doing so? Yes, generally speaking; however, there are some things the client should watch for:

- many legal opinion letters avoid expressing an opinion on certain aspects of a transaction, so the client must read the opinion letter carefully.

- the client should be sure the legal opinion applies to the taxpayer and transaction in question, and is not aimed at some other, similar transaction; a "borrowed" opinion letter may provide useful information but taxpayer reliance on it is risky since the author of the opinion did not focus on the facts of the actual situation.

- if the transaction involves a "tax shelter," which is broadly defined, the substantial underpayment pen-

alty can be avoided only if the taxpayer reasonably believes that his tax treatment was "more likely than not" the proper treatment.[10] Therefore, the opinion letter should provide a basis for the "more likely than not" standard in these cases.

FOOTNOTES

1. Revenue Acts of 1921 and 1926.
2. Revenue Act of 1928.
3. Prior to October 30, 1992, the U.S. Court of Federal Claims was known as the U.S. Claims Court.
4. A complete discussion of both criminal and civil penalties is contained in Saltzman, *IRS Practice and Procedure*: Warren, Gorham and Lamont.
5. IRC Section 6651.
6. IRC Sections 6662(b)(2), 6662(d).
7. IRC Sections 6662(b)(1), 6662(c).
8. IRC Section 6663.
9. IRC Sections 6662(b)(4), 6662(f), 6662(h).
10. IRC Section 6662(d)(2)(C).

CASH BALANCE PENSION PLAN

WHAT IS IT?

A cash balance pension plan is a qualified employer pension plan that provides for annual employer contributions at a specified rate to hypothetical individual accounts that are set up for each plan participant. The employer guarantees not only the contribution level but also a minimum rate of return on each participant's account. A cash balance plan works somewhat like a money purchase pension plan discussed in a later chapter, but money purchase plans do not involve employer guarantees of rate of return.

WHEN IS IT INDICATED?

1. When the employees are relatively young and have substantial time to accumulate retirement savings.

2. When employees are concerned with security of retirement income.

3. When the work force is large and the bulk of the employees are middle-income. (Banks and similar financial institutions find this type of plan particularly appealing.)

4. When the employer is able to spread administrative costs over a relatively large group of plan participants.

ADVANTAGES

1. As with all qualified plans, the cash balance plan provides a tax-deferred savings medium for employees.

2. Plan distributions are eligible for the special 5-year (or 10-year) averaging tax computation available for qualified plans.

3. The employer guarantee removes investment risk from the employee.

4. Plan benefits are guaranteed by the federal Pension Benefit Guaranty Corporation (PBGC).

5. The benefits of the plan are easily communicated to and appreciated by employees.

DISADVANTAGES

1. The retirement benefit may be inadequate for older plan entrants—see Figures 8.1 and 8.2.

2. Because of actuarial and PBGC aspects, the plan is more complex administratively than qualified defined contribution plans.

Figure 8.1

CASH BALANCE PLAN ACCUMULATIONS

Pay credit: 10 percent of compensation
Interest credit: 7 percent annually guaranteed rate

Age at plan entry	Annual compensation	Account balance at age 65
25	$30,000	$640,827
30	30,000	443,739
40	30,000	203,028
50	30,000	80,664
55	30,000	44,349
60	30,000	18,459

Figure 8.2

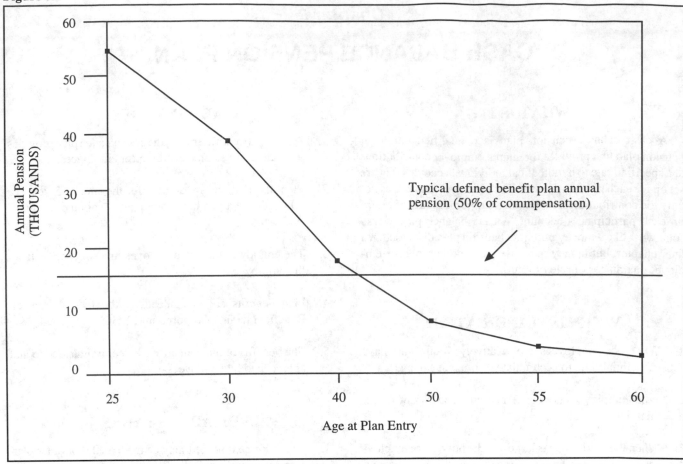

Typical defined benefit plan annual pension (50% of commpensation)

3. The shift of investment risk to the employer increases employer costs.

DESIGN FEATURES OF THESE PLANS

A cash balance plan sets up hypothetical individual accounts for each participant. These hypothetical accounts are credited by the employer at least once a year with two types of credit—the "pay credit" and the "interest credit."

The pay credit uses a formula based on compensation. For example, the plan might require the employer to credit each employee's account annually with a pay credit of 6 percent of compensation. The pay credit formula may also be "integrated" with Social Security. With Social Security integration, employee pay below a level specified in the plan—the "integration level"—receives a lesser credit than compensation above the integration level. This reflects the fact that the employer pays Social Security taxes to provide retirement benefits through Social Security. Social Security integration for qualified plans is discussed in Chapter 23 of this book.[1]

The interest credit is an amount of employer-guaranteed investment earnings that is credited annually to each employee's account. The interest credit must follow a formula in the plan and cannot merely be discretionary on the employer's part. For example, the interest credit formula in the plan might provide for each employee's account to be credited annually with a rate of earnings defined as the lesser of (a) the increase in the Consumer Price Index over the preceding year or (b) the one-year rate for U.S. Treasury securities. The plan can allow the employer to credit accounts with actual plan earnings, if these are higher.

In a cash balance plan there are no actual individual accounts, as there are in true defined contribution plans. All amounts are pooled in a single fund. Any plan participant has a legal claim on the entire fund to satisfy his or her claim to plan benefits.

The employer's annual cost for the plan is determined on an actuarial basis because of the employer guarantee feature. Investment risk lies with the employer; if actual plan earnings fall below total interest credits for the year, the employer must make up the difference. Employer costs can be controlled primarily by choosing the right kind of formula for the interest credit, one that does not risk uncontrollable and unforeseeable employer obligations. However, the interest credit formula should not be excessively conservative—if actual plan earnings year after year are more than interest credits, plan participants may resent the employer's enrichment and the positive employee relations value of the plan may be lost.

Investment discretion by participants (earmarking) is not available in a cash balance plan, because the plan is not technically an individual account plan under ERISA section 404(c). Loans from the plan can be made available, but most employers will not want a loan provision because of the administrative problems resulting from the plan's status as a defined benefit plan without separate participant accounts. Life insurance can be purchased by the plan as an incidental benefit to participants or as a plan investment, under the limitations discussed in Chapter 14.

TAX IMPLICATIONS

1. Employer contributions to the plan are deductible when made.[2]

2. Code section 415(b) limits the benefits provided under the plan to the lesser of $90,000 annually (as indexed, $115,641 for 1993) or 100% of the participant's high 3-year average compensation. This is the *defined benefit* plan limit. This limit may be more or less favorable than the defined contribution limit applicable to a comparable money purchase plan.

3. Taxation of the employee on employer contributions is deferred.[3] Both contributions and earnings on plan assets are nontaxable to plan participants until withdrawn assuming the plan remains "qualified." A plan is qualified if it meets the eligibility, vesting, funding and other requirements explained in Chapter 23.

4. Distributions from the plan must follow the rules for qualified plan distributions. Certain premature or excessive distributions are subject to penalties. These distribution rules are discussed in Chapter 24.

5. Lump sum distributions made after age 59½ are subject to a limited election to use a special 5-year averaging tax calculation. Not all distributions are eligible. Chapter 24 has complete coverage of these rules, including IRS forms.

6. The plan is subject to the minimum funding rules of section 412 of the Internal Revenue Code.[4] This requires minimum contributions, subject to a penalty if less than the minimum amount is contributed in any year. Such contributions must be made on at least an estimated quarterly basis.[5]

7. A cash balance plan is considered a defined benefit plan and is subject to mandatory insurance coverage by the Pension Benefit Guaranty Corporation (PBGC). The PBGC is a government corporation funded through a mandatory premium paid by employer-sponsors of covered plans. The current premium flat rate is $19 annually per participant.[6] An additional annual premium of up to $53 per participant may be required, depending on the amount of the plan's unfunded vested benefit.[7] If the plan is terminated by the employer, PBGC termination procedures must be followed.

8. The plan is subject to the ERISA reporting and disclosure rules outlined in Appendix A.

ALTERNATIVES

1. Money purchase pension plans and profit-sharing plans build up similar qualified retirement accounts for employees, but without the employer guaranteed minimum investment return. (See the comparison chart in Figure 8.3.)

2. Traditional defined benefit plans provide guaranteed benefits for employees, but are more complex in design and administration. (See the comparison chart in Figure 8.3.)

3. Individual retirement saving is always an alternative or supplement to any qualified plan, but there is no tax deferral except in the case of IRAs.

HOW TO INSTALL A CASH BALANCE PLAN

A cash balance plan follows the qualified plan installation procedure discussed in Chapter 25 of this book.

WHERE CAN I FIND OUT MORE ABOUT THESE PLANS?

1. McFadden, John J., *Retirement Plans For Employees*, Homewood, IL: Richard D. Irwin, 1988.

2. Graduate course: Advanced Pension and Retirement Planning II (GS 843), The American College, Bryn Mawr, PA.

Figure 8.3

CASH BALANCE vs. CONVENTIONAL PLANS

	Cash Balance Plan	Typical defined contribution plan	Typical defined benefit plan
Contribution rate	percentage of salary (with actuarial aspects)	percentage of salary	actuarially determined
Investment risk	employer	employee	employer
Investment earmarking	not available	available	not available
Social Security integration	available	available	available
PBGC cost/ coverage	yes	no	yes
401(k) feature	not available	available in profit-sharing plan	not available
Adequate benefit for older entrants	no	no	yes
Administrative cost	higher	lower (unless 401(k) or earmarking)	higher

FOOTNOTES

1. A safe harbor provided for cash balance plans in nondiscrimination regulations under Section 401(a) permits a cash balance plan to satisfy the permitted disparity rules on the basis of the defined contribution rules. See Reg. §1.401(a)(4)-8(c)(3)(iii)(B).

2. IRC Section 404(a).

3. IRC Section 402(a).

4. Actuaries differ as to the correct approach in applying the minimum funding rules. For discussion, see Grubbs, "The Cash Balance Plan—A Closer Look," *Journal of Pension Planning and Compliance*, Vol. 15, No. 3 (1989).

5. IRC Section 412(m).

6. ERISA Section 4006(a)(3)(A)(i).

7. ERISA Section 4006(a)(3)(E).

Chapter 9

DEFINED BENEFIT PENSION PLAN

WHAT IS IT?

A defined benefit pension plan is a qualified employer pension plan that guarantees a specified benefit level at retirement.

WHEN IS IT INDICATED?

1. When the employer's plan design objective is to provide an adequate level of retirement income to employees regardless of their age at plan entry.

2. When the employer wants to allocate plan costs to the maximum extent to older employees—often key or controlling employees in a closely held business.

3. When an older controlling employee in a small business—for example a doctor or dentist in a professional corporation—wants to maximize tax-deferred retirement savings.

ADVANTAGES

1. As with all qualified plans, employees obtain a tax-deferred retirement savings medium.

2. Retirement benefits at adequate levels can be provided for all employees regardless of age at plan entry.

3. Benefit levels are guaranteed both by the employer and by the Pension Benefit Guaranty Corporation (PBGC).

4. For an older highly compensated employee, a defined benefit plan generally will allow the maximum amount of tax-deferred retirement saving.

DISADVANTAGES

1. Actuarial and PBGC aspects of defined benefit plans result in higher installation and administration costs than for defined contribution plans.

2. Defined benefit plans are complex to design and difficult to explain to employees.

3. Employees who leave before retirement may receive relatively little benefit from the plan.

4. The employer is subject to a recurring annual funding obligation (that must be paid in quarterly or more frequent installments) regardless of whether, in a given year, it has made a profit or incurred a loss.

5. The employer assumes the risk of bad investment results in the plan fund.

DESIGN FEATURES

Defined benefit plans provide a specified amount of benefit to the plan participant at the plan's specified retirement age—the "normal retirement age."

There are many types of formulas for determining this benefit. The most common formulas can be summarized as the "flat amount," the "flat percentage" and the "unit credit" types.

Flat amount formula. A flat amount formula provides simply a stated dollar amount to each plan participant. For example, the plan might provide a pension of $500 per month for life, beginning at age 65, for each plan participant. Such a plan might require some minimum service to obtain the full amount—perhaps 10 or 15 years of service with the employer—with the benefit scaled back for fewer years of service.

A flat amount formula does not differentiate among employees with different compensation levels, so it would be appropriate only when there is relatively little difference in compensation among the group of employees covered under the plan.

Flat percentage formula. Flat percentage formulas are very common; they provide a retirement benefit that is a percentage of the employee's average earnings. For example, the formula might provide a retirement benefit at age 65 equal to 50 percent of the employee's average earnings prior to retirement. Under this formula, a participant whose average earnings was $100,000 prior to retirement would receive an annual pension of $50,000.

Typically a plan will require certain minimum service—such as 10 or 15 years—to obtain the full percentage benefit, with the percentage scaled back for fewer years of service. For example, if the plan provides a benefit of 50 percent of average compensation for an employee who retires with at least 10 years of service, it might provide a benefit of only 25 percent of average compensation for an employee who retires at age 65 with only 5 years of service for the employer.

Unit credit formula. A unit credit formula is based on the employee's service with the employer. For example, the formula might provide 1.5 percent of earnings for each of the employee's years of service, with the total percentage applied to the employee's average earnings. Under this formula, a participant with average annual compensation of $100,000 who retired after 30 years of service would receive an annual pension of $45,000 (that is, 1.5 times 30, or 45 percent of $100,000).

There are two methods generally used to compute average earnings for these formulas, the "career-average" and the "final average" methods.

Under the *career average* method, the formula uses earnings averaged over the employee's entire career with the employer. The career-average method takes early and often low-earning years into account, and thus the total benefit may not fully reflect the employee's earning power at retirement.

Under the *final average* method, earnings are averaged over a number of years—usually the 3 to 5 years immediately prior to retirement. The final average method usually produces a retirement benefit that is better matched to the employee's income just prior to retirement.

In either a career average or final average formula, only the first $200,000 (as indexed, $235,840 for 1993) of each employee's compensation is taken into account. In other words, an employee earning $275,000 in 1993 is treated as if compensation was $235,840.

In most plans, these formulas are further modified by "integrating" them with Social Security benefits. Integrating the formula gives the employer some credit for paying the cost of employee Social Security benefits. It helps to provide a reasonable level of retirement income for all employees by taking Social Security benefits into account. The rules for integrating defined benefit formulas are complex; they are discussed in more detail in Chapter 23.

Employers must fund defined benefit plans with periodic deposits determined actuarially to insure that the plan fund will be sufficient to pay the promised benefit as each participant retires. The objective is to accumulate a fund at the employee's retirement age that is sufficient to "buy an annuity" equal to the retirement benefit. (In some plans, annuities are actually purchased at retirement age, but this is not required.)

For example, suppose the actuary hired by the employer estimates that a pension of $50,000 per year beginning at age

65 is equivalent to a lump sum of $475,000 at age 65. In other words, for a given interest rate and other assumptions, the amount of $475,000 deposited at age 65 will produce an annuity of $50,000 per year for the life of an individual aged 65. For a participant aged 45 at plan entry, the employer has 20 years to fund this benefit—that is, to build up a fund totaling $475,000 at age 65.

The actuary will use various methods and assumptions to determine how much must be deposited periodically. As an illustration, a "level annual premiums" method (equal annual payment method) with a 6 percent interest assumption would require the employer to deposit $12,180 annually for 20 years in order to build up a fund of $475,000. (As discussed below, the law actually requires deposits to be made at least quarterly; annual deposit illustrations are used here for simplicity.) This shows how investment return works for the benefit of the employer; the 20 deposits of $12,180 total only $243,600, but at age 65 the fund will actually total $475,000 if all annual deposits are made and the fund actually earns a 6 percent investment return annually.

Actuarial methods and assumptions are chosen to provide the desired pattern for spreading the plan's cost over the years it will be in effect. The actuarial method and assumptions often have to be adjusted over the years to make sure that the fund is adequate. It is even possible for a defined benefit plan to become overfunded, in which case employer contributions must be suspended for a period of time.

The actuarial funding approach for defined benefit plans means that, for a given benefit level, the annual funding amount is greater for employees who are older at entry into the plan (see table below), since the time to fund the benefit is less in the case of an older entrant.

AGE/CONTRIBUTION LEVEL FOR DEFINED BENEFIT PLAN

Age at Plan Entry	Annual Benefit at Age 65	Years to fund	Annual Employer Contribution
30	$25,000	35	$ 1,971
40	25,000	25	4,309
50	25,000	15	10,847

This set of calculations assumes (1) that money deposited before retirement will earn a 7 percent investment return (2) no mortality (no discount for the possibility that some plan participants may die before retirement) and (3) a unisex annuity purchase rate of $1,400 per $10 monthly at age 65 (i.e., it will take a deposit of $1,400 at age 65 to purchase a lifetime annuity of $10 per month beginning at age 65, for any plan participant, male or female).

This makes defined benefit plans attractive to professionals and closely held business owners; they tend to adopt retirement plans for their businesses when they are relatively older than their regular employees. A large percentage of the total cost for a defined benefit plan in this situation goes to fund these key employees' benefits.

Example: Doctor Retractor, aged 48, is a sole practitioner with two office employees, a nurse aged 35 and a receptionist aged 25. The doctor earns $200,000 annually and the nurse and receptionist earn $30,000 and $20,000 respectively. Compare the 1993 cost allocation for a maximum defined benefit plan for the doctor with that for a maximum defined contribution plan (annual contribution of 15% of salary for all employees—an annual contribution of $30,000 for the doctor). The maximum defined benefit pension for the doctor is $115,641, which is 57.8% of his compensation; because the doctor has only 18 years to retirement at age 66 (his Social Security retirement age—see item 3 under "Tax Implications," below), the other participants must receive a benefit percentage that is 25/18 of this, or 80% of compensation (for explanation of this see the discussion of proposed Section 401(a)(4) regulations in the "Questions and Answers" at the end of this chapter).

	Annual cost for Defined Benefit Plan	Annual cost for Defined Contribution Plan
Doctor	$35,907	$30,000
Nurse	2,306	4,500
Receptionist	735	3,000
Total	$38,950	$37,500
Percent for Doctor	92%	80%

Assumptions: 7 percent of pre-retirement investment return, no pre-retirement mortality, unisex annuity purchase rate of $1,400 per $10 monthly at age 66 (equivalent to a lump sum of $1,306,269 at age 65 for a benefit of $115,641 per year).

To back up the employer's funding obligation and safeguard employees, defined benefit plans are insured by the federal Pension Benefit Guaranty Corporation (PBGC) up to specified limits. The employer must pay annual premiums to the PBGC to fund this insurance. Furthermore, the employer is liable for reimbursement to the PBGC for any guaranteed payments the PBGC must make to employees.

TAX IMPLICATIONS

1. Employer contributions to the plan are deductible when made.[1]

2. Taxation of the employee on employer contributions is deferred. Contributions and earnings on plan assets are nontaxable to plan participants until withdrawn, assum-

ing the plan remains "qualified."[2] A plan is qualified if it meets the eligibility, vesting, funding and other requirements explained in Chapter 23.

3. Under Code section 415, there is a maximum limit on the projected annual benefit that the plan can provide. For a benefit beginning at age 65 (or the social security retirement age, which is later than 65 for persons born after 1938), the maximum life annuity or joint and survivor benefit is the lesser of (a) $90,000, as indexed for inflation ($115,641 in 1993), or (b) 100% of the participant's compensation averaged over his three highest-earning consecutive years.

For example, if Foxx retires in 1993 at age 65, and his high three-year average compensation was $60,000, his employer's defined benefit plan cannot provide a life or joint and survivor annuity of more than $60,000 per year. For employee Sharp, who retires in 1993 at age 65 with high 3-year average compensation of $250,000, the limit is $115,641 annually.

4. Distributions from the plan must follow the rules for qualified plan distributions. Certain premature or excessive distributions are subject to penalty taxes. The distribution rules and reporting forms are discussed in Chapter 24. Lump sum distributions made after age 59½ are subject to a limited election to use a special 5-year averaging tax calculation. Not all distributions are eligible.

5. The plan is subject to the "minimum funding" rules of section 412 of the Code. This requires minimum periodic contributions by the employer, with a penalty if less than the minimum amount is contributed. The employer must make plan contributions at least quarterly. Chapter 23 discusses the minimum funding rules further.

6. A defined benefit plan is subject to mandatory insurance coverage by the Pension Benefit Guaranty Corporation (PBGC). The PBGC is a government corporation funded through a mandatory premium paid by employer-sponsors of covered plans. The current premium flat rate is $19 annually per participant.[3] An additional annual premium of up to $53 per participant may be required, depending on the amount of the plan's unfunded vested benefits.[4] If the employer wants to terminate the plan, the PBGC must be notified in advance and must approve any distribution of plan assets to participants.[5]

ERISA REQUIREMENTS

The plan is subject to all the ERISA requirements for qualified plans (participation, funding, vesting, etc.) described in Chapter 23 and the ERISA reporting and disclosure requirements outlined in Appendix A.

ALTERNATIVES

1. Money purchase pension plans provide retirement benefits, but without employer guarantees of benefit levels, and with adequate benefits only for younger plan entrants.

2. Target benefit pension plans may provide adequate benefits to older entrants, but without an employer guarantee of the benefit level.

3. Cash balance pension plans provide an employer guarantee of principal and investment earnings on the plan fund, but provide adequate benefits only to younger plan entrants.

4. Profit-sharing plans, simplified employee pensions (SEPs), stock bonus plans, and ESOPs provide a qualified, tax-deferred retirement savings medium, but the benefit adequacy is tied closely to the financial success of the employer.

5. Section 401(k) plans and savings plans provide a qualified, tax-deferred savings medium in which the amount saved is subject to some control by employees themselves.

6. Private retirement savings without a qualified plan does not have the same tax benefits as a qualified plan, except to the extent that IRAs can be used.

See Chapter 2 for a further discussion of planning alternatives.

HOW TO INSTALL A PLAN

Defined benefit plans are installed according to the qualified plan installation procedure outlined in Chapter 25.

WHERE CAN I FIND OUT MORE ABOUT IT?

1. Gee, Judith Boyers, *Pensions in Perspective*, 4th ed. Cincinnati, OH: The National Underwriter Co., Fall 1993.

2. McFadden, John J., *Retirement Plans for Employees*, Homewood, IL: Richard D. Irwin, 1988.

3. Scott, Elaine A., *Simple Defined Benefit Plans: Methods of Actuarial Funding*, Homewood, IL: Dow Jones-Irwin, 1989.

4. Graduate Course: Advanced Pension and Retirement Planning II (GS 843), The American College, Bryn Mawr, PA.

5. CLU/ChFC Course: Pensions and Other Retirement Plans (HS 326), The American College, Bryn Mawr, PA.

6. CFP Course: Retirement Planning and Executive Benefits (CFP V), College for Financial Planning, Denver, CO.

QUESTIONS AND ANSWERS

Question — At what age is a defined benefit plan more advantageous than a defined contribution plan for tax-deferring the maximum amount of retirement savings?

Answer — Somewhere between age 45 and 50 approximately, depending on the actuarial method and assumptions used in the defined benefit plan.

For example, suppose a doctor, a sole practitioner, aged 42, wants to adopt a plan providing maximum deductible contributions. Under Code section 415, the maximum contribution to a defined contribution plan is $30,000 annually (or 25 percent of compensation up to $200,000—as indexed, $235,840 for 1993—if this is less than $30,000). Can the doctor put more into a defined benefit plan with the maximum benefit allowed by Section 415 ($90,000 annually at age 65, as indexed for inflation—$115,641 in 1993)? That depends on the actuarial assumptions. The following table shows the annual contribution level for a maximum defined benefit plan for a given set of actuarial assumptions and method, varying only the assumed investment return.

Age at Entry	Level funding amount at		
	6%	7%	8%
41	$26,550	$23,190	$20,207
42	28,708	25,248	22,156
43	31,092	27,530	24,328
44	33,735	30,071	26,757
45	36,676	32,910	29,482
46	39,963	36,094	32,552
47	43,654	39,682	36,025
48	47,820	43,746	39,974

Assumptions: $115,641 annual benefit at age 65, equivalent to lump sum at age 65 of $1,349,145. No mortality assumption. These figures can be converted to their post-1993 values by multiplying them by

<u>Current Section 415 dollar limit</u>
$115,641

This indicates that at age 42, based on the assumptions in this table, a defined contribution plan would allow a larger contribution, unless an investment return assumption lower than 6% can be used. Of course, this example is oversimplified; in actual cases a careful study of all the possible actuarial methods and assumptions should be made. Also, the maximum allowable contribution may depend on the doctor's coverage under other qualified plans in the past (see the next question).

Question — Can an employee be covered under both a defined benefit plan and a defined contribution plan of the same employer?

Answer — Yes, but the Section 415 limitations for one or both plans must be cut back. It is not possible for an employer to contribute $30,000 annually to a defined contribution plan for an employee and at the same time provide a defined benefit plan with a retirement age benefit of $90,000 per year, as indexed for inflation ($115,641 in 1993). The maximum allowed benefit under one or both plans must be cut back, under a complex formula in section 415 of the Code.[6]

The combined plan formula requires a cutback even if one of the plans has been terminated, so long as a benefit is still due to the employee from the terminated plan. So, in designing qualified plans, all past plans must be taken into account.

Question — If the retirement age is less than 65 in a defined benefit plan, can the annual funding level be increased because of the shorter time left to fund the benefit?

Answer — Yes. However, the tax benefits of this for highly compensated employees are minimized by the fact that the maximum Section 415 limitation on benefits is cut back for retirement earlier than 65 (or the Social Security retirement age, if that is greater).[7] The maximum annual benefit for various retirement ages (1993 figures) is

Retirement age	Maximum annual benefit
55	$ 54,480
60	78,917
62	92,513
65	115,641

This cutback limits the deductible annual funding and thus the amount of extra tax deferral available through an accelerated retirement age.

Another factor that has to be taken into account if accelerating the funding is desired is that the maximum benefit limit is also cut back proportionately if a participant has participated in the plan for less than 10 years.[8] For example, suppose Dr. Drill, a self-employed dentist, aged 57 wants to start a defined benefit plan. If the retirement age is 65 in the plan, Dr. Drill will have only 8 years of participation at retirement. Assuming that the maximum benefit would be $115,641 for 10 years of participation, the benefit for Dr. Drill will be cut back to 8/10 of that amount, or $92,513 annually.

Question — Suppose an employer can afford to make substantial contributions to a defined benefit plan. Can a plan be designed with a very low actuarial interest assumption so that the annual deductible contributions will be maximized?

Answer — In designing a plan for a "cash rich" employer an actuary will generally use the lowest reasonable actuarial interest assumption in order to maximize deductible contributions in the early years of the plan, thus maximizing tax deferral. However, Congress and the IRS have in recent years severely restricted the discretion of actuaries to choose relatively low interest assumptions.

Current law requires all actuarial assumptions *individually* to be reasonable.[9] This means that an actuary cannot justify an aggressively low interest rate on the ground that other actuarial assumptions are less aggressive. In addition, the IRS is auditing small defined benefit plans and is actively challenging interest rate assumptions lower than 8 percent and retirement ages lower than 65.[10]

A possible alternative for the "cash rich" employer is to use *fully insured* funding for the defined benefit plan. A fully insured plan is not subject to many of the restrictions on deductible funding and may permit larger plan contributions in the initial years of the plan. Fully insured plans are discussed further in Chapter 14 (Life Insurance in a Qualified Plan).

Question — What is the impact of the proposed "nondiscrimination in benefits" regulations on defined benefit design, particularly for older owner-employees of closely held businesses?

Answer — The proposed regulations under Code section 401(a)(4) have rules requiring nondiscrimination in benefits that will restrict the design possibilities for defined benefit plans, particularly for business owners who are less than 25 years from retirement.

Under the proposed regulations, there is a *general* test for nondiscrimination, with three "safe harbors" available if the plan does not meet the general test.[11]

General test. Although the general test is complex, in effect it requires that highly compensated employees covered under the plan must not accrue benefits faster than nonhighly compensated employees. For example, suppose a plan is adopted for an employer with two employees: one is aged 55 and is highly compensated and the other, nonhighly compensated employee is aged 30. If the plan provides both participants with a benefit equal to 50 percent of final average compensation, it will not meet the general test because the older, highly compensated employee will accrue full benefits in ten years (at age 65) whereas it will take the younger employee 35 years to accrue the same benefit.

Safe harbors. The safe harbor exceptions are as follows. A plan is deemed to be nondiscriminatory if one is satisfied:

1. For a unit credit plan, if the plan calculates benefits for each year of service as a percentage of compensation or a fixed dollar amount per year, it will be considered nondiscriminatory if the unit credit formula is uniform for all employees in the plan and the plan meets the "133⅓ percent" accrual rule of ERISA. Under this rule, the annual accrual rate for any year of service cannot be more than 133⅓ percent of the accrual rate for any prior year of service.

2. A plan satisfies the second safe harbor if it satisfies the "fractional accrual" rule of ERISA (parallel section 411(b)(1(C) of the Internal Revenue Code). (Under the fractional rule, the benefit accrued at any given time must be no more than the fraction of years served to total years from plan entry to retirement. For example, if an employee enters the plan at age 40, with 25 years to retirement, his benefit after 10 years of service cannot be more than 10/25 of the total under

the fractional rule.) In addition, one of several alternative tests for accrual must be met; for example, if the plan uses a flat benefit formula, the total accrual period used must be at least 25 years. The example for "Doctor Retractor" earlier in this chapter illustrates the use of this safe harbor provision. As the example indicates, using this safe harbor limits but does not eliminate the favorable aspects of defined benefit plans for older business owners.

3. The third safe harbor applies to a fully insured insurance contract plan under Code section 412(i) (discussed above) that meets certain benefit accrual requirements.

These proposed regulations are scheduled to go into effect for plan years beginning on or after January 1, 1994.[12]

FOOTNOTES

1. IRC Section 404(a).
2. IRC Sections 402(a), 403(a).
3. ERISA Section 4006(a)(3)(A)(i).
4. ERISA Section 4006(a)(3)(E).
5. ERISA Section 4041.
6. IRC Section 415(e).
7. IRC Section 415(b)(2)(C).
8. IRC Section 415(b)(5).
9. IRC Section 412(c)(3). Under pre-1988 law, actuarial assumptions only had to be reasonable in the aggregate.
10. For taxpayer victories over the IRS' assault on low interest rate and retirement age assumptions, see *Vinson & Elkins v. Comm.*, 99 TC No.2 (1992); *Wachtell, Lipton, Rosen & Katz v. Comm.*, TC Memo 1992-392.
11. Prop. Reg. §1.401(a)(4)-3.
12. Prop. Reg. §1.401(a)(4)-13. Until such time, plans must be operated in accordance with a reasonable, good faith interpretation of the requirements of Section 401(a)(4). A plan operated in accordance with the proposed regulations will be deemed in reasonable, good faith compliance.

Chapter 10

ESOP/STOCK BONUS PLAN

WHAT IS IT?

A stock bonus plan is a qualified employer plan—similar to a profit-sharing plan—in which participants' accounts are invested in stock of the employer company. An ESOP is a stock bonus plan that the employer can use as a conduit for borrowing money from a bank or other financial institution.

WHEN IS IT INDICATED?

1. To provide a tax-advantaged means for employees to acquire company stock at low cost to the employer.

2. When estate and financial planning for shareholders would benefit from the additional market for company stock. An ESOP not only creates a market but provides estate tax benefits for sale of stock to the ESOP.

3. In the case of an ESOP, to provide an advantageous vehicle for the company to borrow money for business needs.

4. When a company wants to broaden its ownership—for example, to help prevent a hostile takeover of the company.

5. When the business is a regular or "C" corporation. Partnerships do not have stock, and S corporations are not permitted to own stock in an ESOP.[1]

ADVANTAGES

1. Employees receive an ownership interest in the employer company, which may provide a performance incentive.

2. A market is created for employer stock, which helps improve liquidity of existing shareholders' assets or estates and helps in business continuity planning.

3. Employees are not taxed until shares are distributed. Furthermore, unrealized appreciation of stock held in the plan may not be taxed to employees at receipt of a distribution from the plan. Taxation of the unrealized appreciation may be deferred until shares are sold by the employee.

4. The employer receives a deduction either for a cash contribution to the plan or a noncash plan contribution in the form of shares of stock.

5. The cost of corporate borrowing can be reduced by using an ESOP.

6. A shareholder can obtain tax benefits by selling stock to the plan.

DISADVANTAGES

1. Since the plan is qualified, all the qualified plan requirements apply—coverage, vesting, funding, reporting and disclosure, and others.

2. Issuing shares of stock to employees "dilutes" (reduces the relative value of) existing shareholders' stock and their control of the company.

3. Company stock may be a very speculative investment. This can create employee ill will either because the plan is not considered very valuable by employees or because employees expect too much from the plan.

DESIGN FEATURES

ESOPs and stock bonus plans are qualified defined contribution plans similar to profit-sharing plans. However, participants' accounts are stated in terms of shares of employer stock. Benefits are generally distributable in the form of employer stock.[2] Dividends on shares can be used to increase participants' accounts or can be paid directly in cash to participants. If dividends are paid directly in cash, the employer gets a tax deduction (see below) and the dividends are currently taxable to the employees.

Employer contributions are either shares of stock, or cash that the plan uses to buy stock.

Plan allocation formulas must not discriminate in favor of highly compensated employees and are typically based on employee compensation. For example, if total payroll of participating employees is $500,000 and the employer contributes stock worth $50,000, an employee earning $10,000

Figure 10.1

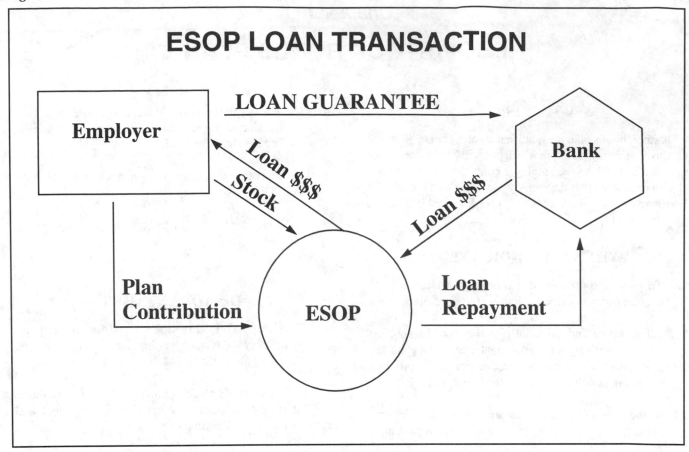

ESOP LOAN TRANSACTION

Employer

LOAN GUARANTEE

Bank

Loan $$$

Stock

Loan $$$

Plan Contribution

ESOP

Loan Repayment

is allocated $1,000 worth of stock under a compensation-based allocation formula. As with all qualified plans, only the first $200,000 of compensation (as indexed, $235,840 in 1993) can be used in the plan's allocation formula. The formula for a stock bonus plan can be integrated with Social Security, but this is rarely done. An ESOP formula cannot be integrated.[3]

If shares of the employer company are closely held—that is, not publicly traded on an established securities market—then plan participants must be given the right to vote on certain specific corporate issues: (a) approval or disapproval of any corporate merger or consolidation, recapitalization, reclassification, liquidation, or dissolution; (b) sale of substantially all assets of the trade or business; or (c) a similar transaction as prescribed in IRS regulations.[4]

If employer stock is publicly traded, plan participants must be allowed to vote the stock on all issues.[5]

Distributions from stock bonus plans and ESOPs are subject to the same rules applicable to all qualified plans, as described in Chapter 24. For example, distributions prior to age 59½, death, or disability are subject to a 10 percent penalty, with some exceptions. Note, however, that a stock bonus plan or ESOP is generally not required to provide a joint and survivor annuity or other spousal death benefit.[6]

Distributions from a stock bonus plan or ESOP must generally be made in the form of employer stock. However, if the participant receives stock that is not traded on an established market, the participant has a right to require the employer to repurchase the stock under a fair valuation formula. This requirement is referred to as the "put option."[7]

To protect employees against unrealistic expectations of stock value, if the stock or securities used in the plan are not traded on an established market, stock valuations used for all plan purposes must be made by an independent appraiser.[8]

Another protective feature is a requirement that participants in ESOPs who have reached age 55 and have at least 10 years of participation are entitled to an annual election to diversify investments in their accounts. For a 6-year period after becoming eligible for this election, the participant can elect annually to diversify 25 percent of the account balance. In the last year, diversification of 50 percent of the account balance can be elected. (A plan may offer higher percentages of diversification, if desired.) The plan must offer at least three options other than employer stock for diversification.[9]

ESOP Loans

An ESOP is distinguished from a regular stock bonus plan primarily by the "leveraging" feature of an ESOP that enables the employer company to borrow money on a favorable basis.[10] The transaction works like this (see Figure 10.1):

(a) The ESOP trustee borrows money from a lending institution such as a bank (with the loan guaranteed by the employer corporation).

(b) The trustee uses the loan proceeds to purchase stock of the employer from the employer corporation (or from principal shareholders of the corporation).

(c) The employer makes tax deductible contributions to the ESOP in amounts sufficient to enable the trustee to pay off the principal and interest of the loan to the bank or other lender.

The net effect of this is that the corporation receives the loan proceeds and repays the loan, both principal and interest, with tax deductible dollars.

The Code allows an even further advantage—the lending institution is permitted to exclude from tax 50 percent of the interest income from a loan to an ESOP used to acquire employer securities. However, for this exclusion to apply, the ESOP must own more than 50 percent of the outstanding stock of the employer corporation.[11]

TAX IMPLICATIONS

1. Employer contributions to the plan are deductible when made, up to an annual limit. For a stock bonus plan, the limit is 15 percent of payroll of employees covered under the plan.[12] For an ESOP, higher limits apply—up to 25 percent of covered payroll for amounts used to repay loan principal, with no limit on amounts used to pay interest.[13]

2. The regular annual additions limit for defined contribution plans applies to ESOPs and stock bonus plans: the annual addition to each participant's account cannot exceed the lesser of (a) 25 percent of the participant's compensation or (b) $30,000 (as indexed, $30,000 in 1993).[14] Deductible employer contributions applied by the plan to the payment of interest on certain loans incurred to acquire employer stock and forfeitures of

employer stock acquired with such loans are excluded from this limit if no more than one-third of the employer contributions applied to the repayment of such loans are allocated to highly compensated employees.[15]

3. Within certain limitations, a corporation can deduct dividends paid on stock acquired with an ESOP loan. The dividends must be paid in cash to plan participants or beneficiaries or used to make payments on certain loans incurred to acquire employer stock.[16]

4. Taxation to the employee on employer contributions is deferred, as with any qualified plan.[17] An additional tax benefit to employees with a stock bonus plan or ESOP is deferral of tax on unrealized appreciation of stock received in a lump sum distribution.[18] For example, suppose an ESOP buys stock for $1,000 and allocates it to participant Farley's account. At retirement 20 years later, the stock is worth $5,000. If Farley receives this stock in a lump sum distribution from the plan, he pays tax only on $1,000. The $4,000 of unrealized appreciation is not taxed until Farley sells the stock. Farley could, however, elect out of this deferred treatment.

The taxable amount of any lump sum distribution from a stock bonus plan or ESOP may be eligible for the special 5-year (or 10-year) averaging tax treatment for qualified plans.[19]

5. The plan is subject to the eligibility and vesting rules applicable to all qualified plans (see Chapter 23).

ERISA AND OTHER REGULATORY REQUIREMENTS

The plan is subject to the usual ERISA eligibility, vesting, and funding requirements for qualified plans discussed in Chapter 23 and the reporting and disclosure requirements summarized in Appendix A.

Certain directors and policy-making officers with ESOP or stock bonus accounts may be subject to "insider trading" restrictions under federal securities laws.[20]

HOW TO INSTALL THE PLAN

Plan installation follows the qualified plan installation procedure described in Chapter 25. In addition, if the employer's stock is subject to securities regulation requirements and the employer issues new stock for the plan, a registration statement may have to be filed with federal or state securities regulatory agencies.

WHERE CAN I FIND OUT MORE ABOUT IT?

1. Leimberg, Stephan R., et al. *Tools and Techniques of Estate Planning*, 9th ed. Cincinnati, OH: The National Underwriter Company, 1992.

2. Kalish, Gerald, *ESOPs, The Handbook of Employee Stock Ownership Plans*, Probus Publishing Company, Chicago, IL, 1989.

3. Frisch, Robert A., *ESOP: The Ultimate Instrument of Corporate Finance*, Margate Associates, Los Angeles, CA, 1990.

4. Blasi, Joseph R., *Employee Ownership*, Ballinger Publishing Company (a subsidiary of Harper & Row Publishers, NY), 1988.

QUESTIONS AND ANSWERS

Question — How is an ESOP or stock bonus plan used for estate planning for shareholders of closely held businesses?

Answer — The existence of the ESOP or stock bonus plan as a potential buyer for stock can be very valuable in planning the estate of a shareholder of a closely held business. Such estates are often illiquid because of a lack of a market for the stock, while at the same time the estate may be liable for substantial death taxes because of the inherent value of the stock.

In most small companies, owners typically expect the company to buy stock from their estate at the shareholder's death. However, for a number of reasons this plan may be difficult to carry out:

(a) Accumulation of corporate funds can be difficult. Funds to purchase stock must be accumulated by the corporation out of after-tax income, which is particularly burdensome since current corporate tax rates may be higher than individual rates.

(b) The corporation can purchase life insurance to provide assured funding, but the premiums are not deductible to the corporation, so this is also an accumulation from after-tax income.

(c) An accumulation of funds at the corporate level may result in exposure to the accumulated earnings tax, particularly if the shareholder is a majority shareholder.

(d) Receipt by the corporation of otherwise income-tax-free life insurance proceeds may trigger the corporate alternative minimum tax (AMT).

(e) If insurance is owned by the corporation to fund a buy out, corporate value is increased, which in turn increases the federal estate tax.

Use of an ESOP or stock bonus plan as the purchaser avoids these problems. The corporation gets a deduction for amounts contributed to the plan, and the plan is a tax-exempt entity so its income is not taxed. Thus, funds accumulate in the plan on a before-tax basis. And, the plan is not subject to the accumulated earnings tax or the alternative minimum tax. Furthermore, life insurance held in the ESOP will not increase corporate value for purposes of the federal estate tax.

While it may be difficult to accumulate a large amount of cash in the plan, particularly in a short time, the plan can purchase insurance on the shareholder's life as an investment that will provide funds to purchase stock from a shareholder at the shareholder's death.

Should there be a formal plan to carry out this type of stock purchase? Probably not. A shareholder can give the ESOP or stock bonus plan an option to buy his or her shares, but requiring the plan to do so would probably violate the ERISA fiduciary requirements.

One potentially serious tax problem with this type of plan should be noted—the possibility that the IRS will treat the sale of stock as a dividend paid to the estate by the corporation rather than a sale to the ESOP. Taxwise, this would greatly increase the cost of the transaction. As a sale, little or no capital gain would be realized by the estate because its basis for the stock would be stepped up to the date of death value. However, if the proceeds from the sale were treated as a dividend, all of it would be taxable.

Dividend treatment on a sale of stock to an ESOP is not a serious possibility unless the decedent was a major shareholder. However, the IRS will probably consider all stock held by the decedent and related family members together in determining whether the decedent was a controlling shareholder. In such cases, despite the apparent policy of Congress to encourage stock sales to ESOPs, the IRS may ignore the ESOP and treat the transaction as a dividend paid directly from the corporation to the shareholder, the decedent's estate.

It is advisable in doubtful situations to apply to the IRS for a ruling that the transaction is not a dividend. The IRS has announced, however, that it will not issue such a ruling unless the combined beneficial interest of the selling shareholder and all related persons in the stock held in the plan does not exceed 20 percent and certain other representations are made.[21] It may be possible to meet this condition in certain cases by amending the ESOP or stock bonus plan to reduce the stock in the selling stockholder's account below this 20 percent limit.

A final and important incentive for the use of ESOPs in estate planning relates to the tax benefit provided for sales of stock to these plans (see the following question).

Question — What special tax benefit is provided for sales of stock to an ESOP?

Answer — The major tax benefit allows nonrecognition of gain for income tax purposes when a shareholder sells nonpublicly traded employer stock to an ESOP.[22] To qualify for this treatment, the shareholder must use the proceeds from the sale to purchase "replacement securities"—that is, stock or securities of another corporation. The replacement securities take the same basis as the stock sold to the ESOP, and the shareholder does not pay tax until the replacement securities are sold. Many requirements apply; in particular, after the sale, the ESOP must own at least 30% of the employer corporation. Special holding period rules also apply.[23]

Question — Are there any problems in a shareholder's selling stock to an ESOP or stock bonus plan during the shareholder's lifetime as a means of obtaining cash?

Answer — This is often a good planning technique.

The dividend problem mentioned in the first question also applies to a lifetime sale of stock to an ESOP. However, it may be a less important factor in a lifetime sale. If the shareholder's stock has a low basis—as is often the case in closely held companies—then the capital gain under a "sale" treatment will cost almost as much in taxes as dividend treatment. For example, if a shareholder sells stock with a basis of $20,000 to an ESOP for $500,000, the taxable capital gain is $480,000. Dividend treatment would result in taxable ordinary income of $500,000, a relatively small difference so long as capital gain tax rates are not significantly lower than those for ordinary income.

Question — Can any type of stock or securities be used in an ESOP?

Answer — Stock used in an ESOP must be either (a) common stock traded regularly on an established market or (b) common stock having a combination of voting power and dividend rights equal to or greater than that of the employer's class of common stock having the greatest voting rights and the class of stock having the greatest dividend rates.[24] If there is only one class of stock, as is often the case with closely held companies, the second test is met.

Question — Can any type of business organization have an ESOP or stock bonus plan?

Answer — Only a regular, or "C," corporation can adopt a stock bonus plan or ESOP. In an S corporation, transferring stock to the plan would cause the Subchapter S election to terminate, because the plan is not a permitted shareholder in an S corporation.[25] Unincorporated businesses—partnerships or proprietorships—cannot have ESOPs or stock bonus plans because they have no stock.

Finally, a professional corporation may not be able to establish an ESOP or stock bonus plan because state corporate law may require all shareholders of a professional corporation to be licensed professionals.

Question — How can an ESOP or stock bonus plan be used to carry out a corporate buy-sell agreement among shareholders?

Answer — For illustration, take a very simple situation with only two major shareholders, Alf and Ben, each owning about half of the corporation's stock, with a relatively small amount held in a stock bonus plan for participants other than Alf and Ben.

The simplest type of arrangement is for the plan trustee to purchase insurance on the lives of Alf and Ben. This insurance is held as key person insurance, since the trust has an insurable interest in the lives of the two business principals. On the death of one shareholder—suppose it is Alf—the trustee collects the insurance proceeds and uses that money to purchase stock from Alf's estate. The stock is reallocated to plan participants. Ben's account will probably receive most of this stock eventually and Ben will retain majority ownership. However, some stock may also be allocated to other participants.

Another arrangement, slightly more formal, makes use of "participant investment direction" or "earmarking," which is permitted under ERISA. With participant investment direction in a qualified plan, a participant is given the right to direct the trustee to invest his or her plan account in specified property. In this case, Alf directs the trustee to invest in insurance on Ben's life. Ben directs investment in insurance on Alf's life. The insurance proceeds on the death of one owner are therefore used to purchase stock directly for the account of the other owner, with no allocation of stock to other plan participants.

Question — Can a stock bonus plan or ESOP hold life insurance or investments other than employer stock?

Answer — A stock bonus plan is apparently flexible in its investments and can hold the same types and diversity of investments as a regular profit-sharing plan.

An ESOP, however, must meet a requirement that it be invested "primarily in employer securities."[26] Neither the IRS nor the Labor Department has issued an official interpretation of this "primarily" requirement, so investments other than employer securities should be very limited.

Stock bonus plans and ESOPs can invest in insurance contracts, within the limitations discussed here. However, if the plan participant has the right to name the beneficiary of the death benefit, the amount of insurance is subject to the same "incidental" limitations that apply to qualified profit-sharing plans (see Chapter 14).

FOOTNOTES

1. IRC Section 1361(b)(1)(B).
2. Regs. §1.401-1(a)(2)(iii); 1.401-1(b)(1)(iii). See also, Rev. Rul. 69-65, 1969-1 CB 114.
3. Reg. §54.4975-11(a)(7)(ii).
4. IRC Sections 401(a)(22), 409(e)(3). However, if the employer stock was acquired pursuant to a "securities acquisition loan," plan participants must be allowed to vote the stock on *all* issues. IRC Section 133(b)(7).
5. IRC Section 409(e)(2).
6. IRC Section 401(a)(11)(c).
7. IRC Sections 401(a)(23), 409(h).
8. IRC Section 401(a)(28)(C).
9. IRC Section 401(a)(28)(B).
10. The prohibited transaction exemption required for ESOP loans is in Code sections 4975(d) and (e), with further conditions in Section 409(e).
11. IRC Section 133.
12. IRC Section 404(a)(3).
13. IRC Section 404(a)(9).
14. IRC Section 415(c). The $30,000 limit will not increase until the defined benefit dollar limit exceeds $120,000. The defined benefit dollar limit for 1993 is $115,641.
15. IRC Section 415(c)(6).
16. IRC Section 404(k).
17. IRC Sections 402(a), 403(a).
18. IRC Section 402(e)(4). If employer securities are distributed in other than a lump sum distribution, the net unrealized appreciation is excludable only to the extent attributable to nondeductible employee contributions. IRC Section 402(e)(4)(A).
19. IRC Section 402(d)(4)(D).
20. See Blair, "Insider Reporting and Short Swing Trading Rules for Qualified Defined Contribution Plans," *Benefits Quarterly*, 1st Quarter 1992.
21. See Rev. Proc. 87-22, 1987-1 CB 718.
22. IRC Section 1042.
23. IRC Sections 1042(b)(4), 4978(b)(1).
24. IRC Sections 4975(e)(8), 409(e).
25. IRC Section 1361(b)(1)(B).
26. IRC Section 4975(e)(7)(A).

Chapter 11

GOVERNMENTAL EMPLOYER DEFERRED COMPENSATION (SECTION 457) PLAN

WHAT IS IT?

Section 457 of the Code provides rules governing all nonqualified deferred compensation plans of governmental units, governmental agencies, and also non-church controlled tax-exempt organizations. A plan designed to comply with these rules is referred to as a Section 457 plan.

WHEN IS IT INDICATED?

If the employer is an affected organization, Section 457 is mandatory. Any nonqualified deferred compensation plan adopted by such an employer generally must comply with the rules discussed here.

DESIGN FEATURES

What Employers Are Covered by Section 457?

Section 457 applies to nonqualified deferred compensation plans of:

(a) a state, a political subdivision of a state (such as a city, township, etc.), and any agency or instrumentality of a state or political subdivision of a state (for example, a school district or a sewage authority), and

(b) any organization exempt from federal income tax, except for a church or synagogue or an organization controlled by a church or synagogue.[1]

Limit on Amount Deferred

The amount deferred annually by an employee under a plan covered by Section 457 cannot exceed the lesser of $7,500 or one-third of the employee's compensation currently includable in gross income. However, see the "Questions and Answers," below, as to how this limit may be exceeded for executive-type deferred compensation plans.

The $7,500 limit is applied on a per-individual not a per-plan basis. For example, if an individual is employed by two

different governmental employers, the individual's total annual deferral from both employers cannot exceed $7,500. The one-third of compensation limit applies on a per-plan basis; thus, an individual employed by two different governmental employers may defer more than one-third of his includable compensation so long as the total deferred under any one plan does not exceed the one-third limit and the total deferred under both plans does not exceed $7,500.[2]

The $7,500 limit is not indexed for inflation. By comparison, various limits for qualified plans (such as the $7,000 limit for salary reductions under Section 401(k) plans) are subject to indexing.

If an employee is covered under a Section 403(b) tax deferred annuity plan or a simplified employee pension (SEP), then any 403(b) or SEP salary reductions will reduce the $7,500 limit.[3] For example, if an individual employed by a tax-exempt college elects a salary reduction of $7,500 for 1993 under the college's 403(b) plan, then for 1993, the $7,500 limit under Section 457 is reduced to zero for that individual. Deferrals to certain cash or deferred arrangements adopted generally before 1986 may also reduce the $7,500 limit.[4]

For employees nearing retirement there is a "catch-up" provision. The $7,500 ceiling can be increased in each of the last three years before normal retirement age to the lesser of:

(a) $15,000 or

(b) the regular limit of the lesser of $7,500 or one-third of taxable compensation plus the total amount of deferral not used in prior years.[5]

Catch-up Example:
Lew Sludge begins working at age 60 as a part-time engineer for the Effluent City, PA, Sewage Authority. His compensation is $30,000 annually. The authority has a Section 457 plan with a normal retirement age of 65. Lew makes contributions of $5,000 annually to the plan until his last year of service, for which he wants to make the maximum contribution. This maximum is $15,000, as shown by the following table:

Year	Max Deferral	Actual Deferral	Difference
1	$ 7,500	$ 5,000	$ 2,500
2	7,500	5,000	2,500
3	12,500	5,000	7,500
4	15,000	5,000	10,000
5	15,000	15,000	

Year 3 is the beginning of the last 3 years prior to retirement. The maximum deferral amount in Year 3 is the lesser of $15,000 or the regular ceiling of $7,500 plus the potential deferral of $2,500 not used in Year 1 and the $2,500 not used in Year 2—a total of $5,000. Thus the maximum deferral in Year 3 is $7,500 plus $5,000 or $12,500. The maximums for Years 4 and 5 are computed in the same manner. In Year 4 Lew can contribute $15,000. This consists of the $7,500 he could have contributed (but did not) in prior years, plus the $7,500 regular limit. In Year 5, his last year, Lew's regular limit of $7,500 plus his unused prior years' amount totals $17,500, but the $15,000 maximum holds his contribution to $15,000 for that year.

Timing of Salary Reduction Elections

Employee elections to defer compensation monthly under Section 457 must be made under an agreement entered into before the beginning of the month.[6]

Distribution Requirements

Plan distributions cannot be made before[7]:

(a) the calendar year in which the participant attains age 70½,

(b) separation from service, or

(c) an "unforeseeable emergency" as defined in regulations. The definition of unforeseeable emergency is discussed in the "Questions and Answers," below.

Distributions must begin no later than April 1 of the calendar year after the year in which the plan participant attains age 70½. Minimum distributions must be made under the rules of Code section 401(a)(9).[8] This Code section applies to qualified plans as well, and the minimum distribution rules are discussed in more detail in Chapter 24.

There are special rules governing death or survivorship benefits under Section 457 plans.[9]

1. If a plan distribution begins before the death of the participant, (a) the amount payable with respect to the participant must be paid at times not later than those determined under Section 401(a)(9)(G) relating to incidental death benefits; and (b) any amount distributed to the beneficiary after the participant's death must be distributed at least as rapidly as it would have been if the participant survived.

2. If the plan distribution begins after the participant's death, the entire amount must be paid out over no more than 15 years (or if a surviving spouse is the beneficiary over the life expectancy of the spouse).

Coverage and Eligibility

There are no specific coverage requirements for Section 457 plans. For a governmental organization, the plan can be offered to all employees, or to any group of employees, even a single employee.

However, most private non-governmental tax-exempt organizations are subject to ERISA. Therefore, the ERISA eligibility rules may apply to the Section 457 plan of the tax-exempt organization. The eligibility requirements would be the same as those applicable to a nonqualified deferred compensation plan for a taxable employer, as discussed in Chapter 16. Such plans can avoid the ERISA rules only if they are unfunded and cover only a select group of management and highly compensated employees—the "top-hat" group.

Funding

A Section 457 plan may not be funded. However, "financing" the plan with insurance or annuity contracts is allowed and is almost always appropriate, as discussed in the "Questions and Answers."

For a tax-exempt organization, the "no funding" requirement of Section 457 may conflict directly with the ERISA funding requirements if the plan covers more than the "top-hat" group; this issue has not yet been resolved.[10]

TAX IMPLICATIONS

1. Since the employer in a Section 457 plan does not pay federal income taxes, deductibility is not an issue.

2. Employees or their beneficiaries include Section 457 plan distributions in income when they are actually paid or otherwise made available.[11]

However, if a nonqualified deferred compensation plan of a governmental or tax-exempt employer does not comply with Section 457, compensation deferred is included in the employee's income in the first taxable year in which there is no substantial risk of forfeiture of the rights to the compensation. Any distributions from an ineligible plan are treated in the same manner as annuity distributions under Section 72.[12] The implications of this are discussed in the "Questions and Answers," below.

3. Section 457 plan distributions are not eligible for the favorable lump sum 5-year averaging treatment available for qualified plans.

4. Section 457 plan distributions are not eligible for tax-free rollover to an individual retirement account or annuity plan (IRA). However, a total distribution from a Section 457 plan can be rolled over tax-free to another Section 457 plan.[13]

ERISA REQUIREMENTS

Governmental employers and church-related organizations are not subject to ERISA. However, tax-exempt private employers will encounter the ERISA compliance problems discussed above.

ALTERNATIVES

Tax-exempt employers can adopt qualified pension and profit-sharing plans for employees. In addition, tax-exempts can adopt Section 403(b) plans that provide as good or better benefits for employees as a Section 457 plan.

Governmental employers can also adopt governmental pension plans similar to qualified private plans. However, since the 403(b) type of plan is not available to governmental employers such employers are more likely to use Section 457 plans to supplement a pension plan.

The design of nonqualified deferred compensation plans for top management employees of governmental and tax-exempt employers is discussed in the "Questions and Answers," below.

HOW TO INSTALL A PLAN

A written plan containing the provisions described above should be adopted. Also, forms must be furnished to employees to carry out the required monthly salary reduction elections. For tax-exempt private employers subject to ERISA, the

same ERISA requirements applicable to nonqualified deferred compensation will apply. These are discussed in Chapter 16.

WHERE CAN I FIND OUT MORE ABOUT IT?

1. *Fundamentals of Employee Benefit Programs*, 3rd ed. Washington, DC: Employee Benefit Research Institute, 1987.

2. *Tax Facts 1*, Cincinnati, OH: The National Underwriter Company, (revised annually).

QUESTIONS AND ANSWERS

Question — How can a governmental or tax-exempt employer provide a substantial deferred compensation benefit for an executive or key employee for whom the $7,500 limit would be inadequate?

Answer — There are three statutory provisions that would allow deferred compensation beyond the $7,500 limit, and planners should investigate these where executive compensation plans are desired.

Grandfathered plans. A grandfather provision in Section 457 may preserve some existing executive deferred compensation plans. Under that provision, Section 457 does not apply to "nonelective" deferred compensation that was deferred either before or after July 14, 1988 under a written agreement covering the individual in question that was in effect on July 14, 1988 and provided for deferral of a fixed amount or deferral under a fixed formula. A nonelective plan is one that does not provide for salary reductions—essentially the type of plan that would be provided for top management employees who negotiate individual employment contracts.[14]

Nonemployee plans. Nonelective deferred compensation plans for nonemployees—for example, doctors working for hospitals as independent contractors—are not subject to Section 457. However, for this exception to apply, all such nonemployees must be treated the same under the plan, with no individual variations.[15]

Nonforfeitable plans. The most general provision that allows escape from the $7,500 limit is Section 457(f). Under this section, if an employee defers more than the $7,500 limit, the deferred amount is not necessarily taxed immediately; it is taxed in the first taxable year in which there is *no substantial risk of forfeiture*. Thus, if a deferred compensation plan has forfeiture provisions, amounts greater than the $7,500 annual limit can be deferred until the year in which the forfeiture provision lapses.

For example, an employer subject to Section 457 might provide supplemental deferred compensation to selected executives, in amounts greater than $7,500 annually, with a provision that the amount deferred would not be payable unless the executive served a full term under a multi-year contract. Taxation on the amount deferred would not occur until the year in which each executive served the full term and the deferred amounts became nonforfeitable.

The IRS has approved forfeitable deferred compensation plans of this type for employers subject to Section 457,[16] and this should be considered an appropriate technique of executive compensation for governmental and nonprofit employers.

A major problem in designing such plans is to develop forfeiture provisions that are substantial enough to defer taxes (see the Regulations under Code section 83) but are nevertheless acceptable to the executive. Another major design problem occurs at retirement. In general, it is very difficult to design a bona fide, substantial forfeiture provision that extends past the executive's retirement. Consequently, Section 457(f) amounts generally are taxable in full no later than the year of the executive's retirement. If deferral past retirement is essential, other techniques such as equity-type split dollar plans might be investigated.

Question — What constitutes an "unforeseeable emergency" that permits distributions from a Section 457 plan?

Answer — The current regulations under Section 457 define unforeseeable emergency as severe financial hardship to the participant resulting from a sudden and unexpected illness or accident of the participant or a dependent, a loss of property due to casualty, or other similar extraordinary and unforeseeable circumstances arising as a result of events beyond the control of the participant.[17]

The regulations specifically mention that the purchase of a residence or college education of children is not considered an unforeseeable emergency. Any amount distributed from the plan as the result of an emergency cannot exceed the amount reasonably needed to satisfy the emergency.

Question — How is a Section 457 plan informally funded or "financed" through the purchase of insurance or annuities?

Answer — Although a Section 457 plan cannot be funded in the same sense as a qualified plan, that is with an irrevocable trust fund for the exclusive benefit of employees, the employer can, and in most cases should, finance its obligations under the plan by setting aside assets in advance of the time when payments will be made. Life insurance or annuity contracts are often used for this purpose.

If the employer purchases life insurance contracts to finance the plan, there is no current life insurance cost to employees as long as the employer retains all incidents of ownership in the policies, is the sole beneficiary under the policies, and is under no obligation to transfer the policies or pass through the proceeds of the policies. This favorable result applies even if the contracts are purchased at the option of participants.[18]

FOOTNOTES

1. IRC Sections 457(e)(1), 457(e)(13).
2. IRC Sections 457(b)(2), 457(c)(1).
3. IRC Section 457(c)(2)(A).
4. IRC Section 457(c)(2)(B).
5. IRC Section 457(b)(3).
6. IRC Section 457(b)(4).
7. IRC Sections 457(b)(5), 457(d)(1).
8. IRC Sections 457(b)(5), 457(d)(2)(A).
9. IRC Section 457(d)(2)(B).
10. Both the IRS (Notice 87-13, 1987-1 CB 432, Q&A-25) and The Department of Labor (DOL News Release 86-527) have confirmed that this "catch 22" exists. Both organizations have ruled that in order to comply with both Section 457 and ERISA, a deferred compensation plan of a tax-exempt organization must be limited to the "top hat" group.
11. IRC Section 457(a).
12. IRC Section 457(f).
13. IRC Section 457(e)(10).
14. Technical and Miscellaneous Revenue Act of 1988, Section 6064(d)(3).
15. IRC Section 457(e)(12).
16. Let. Ruls. 8831022, 9008059. The latter ruling involved a nonprofit (Section 501(c)) employer that had *two* Section 457 plans, both maintained only for a select group of management and highly compensated employees (the top hat group). Plan 1 provided benefits within the $7,500 limits (and had graduated vesting) while Plan 2 provided supplemental additional benefits that were forfeited if employment was terminated prior to normal retirement age for reasons other than death or disability.
17. Reg. §1.457-2(h)(4).
18. Let. Rul. 9008043.

Chapter 12

HR 10 (KEOGH) PLAN

WHAT IS IT?

A Keogh plan, sometimes referred to as an HR 10 plan, is a qualified retirement plan that covers one or more self-employed individuals. A self-employed individual is a sole proprietor or partner who works in his or her unincorporated business. Like all qualified plans, a Keogh plan enables those covered under the plan to accumulate a private retirement fund that will supplement their other pension and Social Security benefits.

A Keogh plan works much like any qualified plan; the details of the various types of qualified plans such as defined benefit, money purchase, or profit-sharing plans are discussed in separate chapters of this book. This chapter focuses on the special features of a qualified plan that covers self-employed individuals.

WHEN IS IT INDICATED?

1. When long-term capital accumulation, particularly for retirement purposes, is an important objective of a self-employed business owner.

2. When an owner of an unincorporated business wishes to adopt a plan providing retirement benefits for regular employees as an incentive and employee benefit, as well as retirement savings for the business owner.

3. When a self-employed person has a need to shelter some current earnings from federal income tax.

4. When an employee has self-employment income as well as income from employment, and wishes to invest as much as possible of the self-employment income and defer taxes on it.

ADVANTAGES

1. Keogh contributions are deducted from taxable income and the tax is deferred until funds are withdrawn from the plan at a later date.

2. Income generated by the investments in a Keogh plan is also free of income taxes until it is withdrawn from the

plan. This reinvestment of income and build-up of tax deferred earnings is one of the main features that make Keogh plans attractive.

For example, the following table shows the results of investing $7,500 annually in a Keogh plan where the rate of return is 8 percent, compounded daily:

Number of Years	Total Contribution	Tax Deferred Interest	Total Value
5	$ 37,500	$ 10,645	$ 48,145
10	75,000	45,365	120,365
15	112,500	116,201	228,701
20	150,000	241,213	391,213
25	187,500	447,490	634,990

As can be seen, the tax-deferred earnings portion of the program will eventually exceed the amount of personal annual contributions. This is a strong incentive to start early and continue to make the largest possible contribution to such a plan.

3. Certain lump sum distributions from Keogh plans may be eligible for favorable 5-year (or 10-year) averaging income tax treatment.

4. The limits on Keogh plan contributions are more liberal than those applied to IRAs (individual retirement accounts). IRAs have an annual contribution limit of $2,000 ($2,250 for spousal IRAs) as compared with the maximum contribution of $30,000 permitted under a defined contribution Keogh plan. Thus, a self-employed person may contribute up to 15 times as much to a Keogh plan as a person may contribute to an IRA. In addition, deductions for IRA contributions may be limited if the individual (or his spouse) is an active participant in a qualified retirement plan (see Chapter 13).

5. From the viewpoint of an employee of an unincorporated business, Keogh plans are advantageous because employees of the business must participate in the plan (within the limits of the coverage requirements for qualified plans described in Chapter 23).

DISADVANTAGES

1. Keogh plans involve all the costs and complexity associated with qualified plans. However, for a small plan, particularly one covering only one self-employed individual, it is relatively easy to minimize these factors by using prototype plans offered by insurance companies, mutual funds, banks, and other financial institutions.

2. If a self-employed person has a significant number of employees, the qualified plan coverage requirements, which require nondiscriminatory plan coverage (see Chapter 23), may increase the cost of the plan substantially.

3. As with all qualified plans, there is a 10% penalty, in addition to regular federal income tax, for withdrawal of plan funds generally before age 59 ½, death, or disability (see Chapter 24).

4. Again as with regular qualified plans, benefit payments from the plan generally must begin by April 1 of the year after the plan participant attains age 70 ½, even if the participant is not retired. There is a penalty for noncompliance (see Chapter 24). Thus, Keogh plans, like all qualified plans, can not be viewed as a means of avoiding income tax and passing assets to succeeding generations tax free.

5. Loans from the plan to a plan participant who is an owner-employee (a self-employed person owning more than 10% of the business) are "prohibited transactions" subject to penalty. Thus, owner-employees cannot make use of plan loans which are permitted (generally up to $50,000 or half the vested benefit) for regular employees. (However, a loan to an owner-employee is permitted if the Department of Labor grants an administrative exemption from the prohibited transaction rules with respect to such a loan.)

6. Life insurance in a qualified plan for a self-employed person, described below, is treated somewhat less favorably than for regular employees.

TYPES OF KEOGH PLANS

In general any type of qualified plan can be designed to cover self-employed persons. However, the typical Keogh plan covering one self-employed person, and possibly the spouse of the self-employed person, as well as a few employees, is usually designed as either (a) a profit-sharing plan or (b) a money purchase plan.

In a *profit-sharing plan* the annual contribution can be any amount up to 15% of the total payroll of plan participants. Plan contributions can be omitted entirely in a bad year. However, the IRS requires "substantial and recurring" contributions or the plan may be deemed terminated.[1] This contribution flexibility is very advantageous for a small business whose income typically may fluctuate substantially from year to year.

For a self-employed person with earned income of $200,000 or more—not unusual for a successful professional—the 15% profit-sharing limit permits the maximum possible plan contribution available under any kind of defined contribution plan. Under Code section 415, annual contributions to a defined contribution plan can never be more than $30,000 annually (as indexed for inflation—see Chapter 23). Fifteen percent of $200,000 of earned income produces the maximum annual contribution of $30,000 for this successful professional, so there is no reason for a person at this income level to adopt any defined contribution plan other than a profit-sharing plan. (See below for a discussion of the special definition of "earned income" of self-employed persons.)

A *money purchase plan* permits annual contributions for each self-employed person of 25% of earned income (25% of compensation for any regular employees covered under the plan) up to the $30,000 dollar limit. However, a money purchase plan is subject to the Code's minimum funding requirements (see Chapter 23). These require the employer to make contributions to each employee's and self-employed person's account each year equal to the percentage of compensation stated in the plan. Such contributions must be made regardless of good or bad business results for the year.

A self-employed person can adopt other types of qualified plans as well. A *defined benefit* plan (see Chapter 9) is attractive to the older self-employed person who is just starting a plan, because the actuarial funding approach allows a greater relative contribution for older plan participants. Often considerably more can be contributed annually to a defined benefit plan than the $30,000 maximum for defined contribution plans.

A target plan (see Chapter 21) permits funding based on age like a defined benefit plan, but with annual funding limited to the lesser of $30,000 or 25% of earned income or compensation. The target plan is attractive because of its simplicity, and the 25%/$30,000 limit permits adequate contribution levels for self-employed persons earning relatively lower amounts.

HOW ARE KEOGHS DIFFERENT FROM OTHER QUALIFIED PLANS?

The unique feature of a Keogh plan, as compared with qualified plans adopted by corporations, is that the Keogh plan covers self-employed individuals, who are not technically considered "employees." This leads to some significant special rules for self-employed individuals covered under the plan.

Earned Income

The most important special rule is the definition of earned income. For a self-employed individual, "earned income" takes the place of "compensation" in applying the qualified plan rules. Earned income is defined as the self-employed individual's net income from the business after all deductions *including the deduction for Keogh plan contributions.*[2] In addition, the IRS has ruled that the self-employment tax must be computed and a deduction of one-half of the self-employment tax must be taken *before* determining the Keogh deduction.[3]

To resolve the potential complexity of this computation, *IRS Publication 560* imposes the following steps in determining the Keogh deduction: (1) determine net income from Schedule C income; (2) subtract one-half of the actual amount of the self-employment tax; and (3) multiply the result by the "net" contribution rate from the rate table below.

Example: Len earns $100,000 of Schedule C income in 1993. His self-employment tax is $9,820.55. (The net income amount of $100,000 is first reduced by 7.65%, leaving $92,350 net earnings subject to the self-employment tax—$57,600 x 12.4% (OASDI) + $92,350 x 2.9% (HI) = $9,820.55.) The deduction for one-half of the self-employment tax then is $4,910.28 ($9,820.55 ÷ 2). The Keogh contribution base is thus $100,000 less $4,910.28, or $95,089.72. If the nominal plan contribution rate is 15%, the net contribution rate is 13.0435%. This rate is applied to the Keogh contribution base and results in a contribution of $12,403.03. (Note that this amount is 15% of "earned income," which is equal to $82,686.69 (i.e., the Keogh contribution base of $95,089.72 less the Keogh contribution of $12,403.03).)

The IRS table of "net" contribution rates is as follows:

Self-Employed Person's Rate Table

Column A	Column B
If the Plan Contribution Rate is: (shown as a %)	The Self-Employed Person's Rate is: (shown as a decimal)
1	.009901
2	.019608
3	.029126
4	.038462
5	.047619
6	.056604
7	.065421
8	.074074
9	.082569
10	.090909
11	.099099
12	.107143
13	.115044
14	.122807
15*	.130435*
16	.137931
17	.145299
18	.152542
19	.159664
20	.166667
21	.173554
22	.180328
23	.186992
24	.193548
25	.200000

*The deduction for annual employer contributions to a SEP or profit-sharing plan cannot exceed 15% of the common-law employee participants' compensation, or 13.0435% of your compensation (figured without deducting contributions for yourself) from the business that has the plan.

Life Insurance

Life insurance can be used as an incidental benefit in a plan covering self-employed individuals, but the tax treatment for the self-employed individuals is different from that applicable to regular employees in a qualified plan.

The entire cost of life insurance for regular employees is deductible as a plan contribution. Employees then pick up the value of the pure life insurance element as extra taxable compensation valued under the "P.S. 58" table (see Chapter 14).

By contrast, for a self-employed individual, the pure life insurance element of an insurance premium is *not* deductible.[4] Only the portion of the premium that exceeds the pure protection value of the insurance is deductible. The pure protection value of the insurance is determined using the P.S. 58 table. Since all income and deductions flow automatically to the owners in an unincorporated business, the nondeductible life insurance element in effect becomes additional taxable income to the self-employed individual.

Example: Leo, a self-employed individual, has a Keogh plan providing incidental insurance through a cash value life insurance contract. This year's premium is $3,000, of which $1,200 is for pure life insurance protection and the remainder is used to increase the cash value. Leo can deduct $1,800 of the premium as a plan contribution. The remaining $1,200 is nondeductible. Leo therefore must pay tax on the $1,200 used for pure life insurance protection.

Another difference in the treatment of life insurance comes when benefits are paid from the plan. Regular employees have a "cost basis" (a nontaxable recovery element) in a plan equal to any P.S. 58 costs they have included in income in the past, so long as the plan distribution is made from the same life insurance contract on which the P.S. 58 costs were paid (see Chapter 14). For a self-employed individual, however, the P.S. 58 costs, although effectively included in income since they were nondeductible, are not includable in cost basis.[5]

Loans

Qualified plans can make loans to regular employees, within a $50,000 maximum and certain other limits (see Chapter 24). However, loans to an "owner-employee" are prohibited transactions under the Internal Revenue Code.[6] An owner-employee is a self-employed person who is either a sole proprietor or a partner owning more than 10% of the business.

A prohibited transaction does not cause a plan to become disqualified and lose all tax benefits. However, there is a two-level penalty tax on prohibited transactions. The initial tax is five percent of the amount involved, with an additional tax of 100% of the amount involved if the transaction is not rescinded.[7]

Because this rule arbitrarily penalizes owner-employees, as compared with business owners who incorporate their businesses, Congress changed the law to permit a plan to make a loan to an owner-employee if the Department of Labor grants an administrative exemption from the prohibited transaction rules with respect to such a loan.[8]

TAX AND ERISA IMPLICATIONS

Except for the differences described just above, Keogh plans generally have the same tax and ERISA implications as regular qualified plans. For example, see Chapter 17 for the tax treatment of Keogh profit-sharing plans, etc.

The annual reporting requirement for qualified plans has been simplified for many Keogh plans and other small plans. If a plan covers only the business owner or partners, or the owner or partners and their spouses, the reporting requirement is satisfied by filing Form 5500EZ instead of the longer Form 5500C/R. A sample Form 5500EZ is included at the end of this chapter.

ALTERNATIVES

1. The disadvantages, if any, of Keogh status of any qualified plan can be eliminated if the business owner incorporates the business and adopts a corporate plan. The owner is then a shareholder and employee of the corporation. Generally under current law it is not advantageous to incorporate a business simply to obtain corporate treatment for qualified plans. Incorporation may result in higher taxes overall and the advantages of corporate plans over Keogh plans are minimal in most cases.

2. A simplified employee pension (SEP) may be even simpler to adopt than a Keogh plan, particularly if only one self-employed individual is covered. In addition, SEPs can be adopted as late as the individual's tax return filing date, when it is too late to adopt a new Keogh plan. SEP contributions, however, are limited to 15% of earned income. See Chapter 20 for more discussion of SEPs.

3. Tax deductible IRAs are available up to $2,000 annually, if the individual (or his spouse) is not an active participant in a qualified plan. The $2,000 deduction is subject to cutbacks based on adjusted gross income if the individual (or his spouse) is an active participant in a qualified plan (see Chapter 13). Because of these limitations, a Keogh plan often permits much greater levels of tax-deferred savings.

HOW TO INSTALL A PLAN

A Keogh plan follows the installation procedure for qualified plans described in Chapter 25. However, in adopting a Keogh plan it is customary to use a "prototype" plan designed by a bank, insurance company, mutual fund, or other financial institution. With a prototype, the sponsoring institution does most of the paperwork involved in installing the plan, at low or nominal cost to the self-employed individual. In return, the self-employed individual must keep most or all of the plan funds invested with that institution.

WHERE CAN I FIND OUT MORE ABOUT IT?

1. Banks, insurance companies, and other financial institutions actively market Keogh plans and will usually provide extensive information about their services.

2. IRS Publication 560, *Self-Employed Retirement Plans*, covers Keogh plans in detail. It is revised annually and available free from the IRS.

3. *Tax Facts 1*, Cincinnati, OH, The National Underwriter Co. (revised annually).

QUESTIONS AND ANSWERS

Question — Who can establish a Keogh retirement plan?

Answer — Any sole proprietor or partnership, whether or not the business has employees—for example, doctors, lawyers, accountants, writers, etc. Generally, employees of the business must be included as participants in the plan on the same general basis as the key employees.

Question — Can I collect benefits if I become disabled?

Answer — In the event that any participant in the plan becomes so disabled as to render him or her unable to engage in any substantial gainful activity, all contributed amounts plus earnings may be paid immediately without being subject to a premature distribution penalty.

Question — What happens to my plan if I die?

Answer — In the event that any participant dies, all contributed amounts plus earnings may be immediately paid to the participant's designated beneficiary or estate.

Question — May I set up a Keogh plan in addition to an IRA?

Answer — Yes. If you are eligible to set up a Keogh plan you may also create an IRA as well. Remember, though, that the general limit on IRA contributions is $2,000 ($2,250 for an individual and spousal IRA). Also, because you are an active participant in the Keogh plan, IRA contributions will not be tax deductible if your income is above certain limits (see Chapter 13).

Question — Can a Keogh plan be established if the self employed person is covered under a corporate retirement plan of an employer?

Answer — Yes. An individual who works for a regular employer, and is covered under that employer's qualified plan, can establish a separate Keogh plan for an additional business carried on separately as a self-employed individual. For example, an engineering professor at a university may have additional income earned as a consulting engineer for outside clients. A Keogh plan will shelter some of that income from taxation and provide increased retirement savings on a tax-favored basis. The deduction limits for Keogh contributions are not affected unless the individual also controls or owns the regular employer.

For example, suppose the engineer earns $60,000 this year from his university position and is covered under the university's qualified pension plan. The engineer earns an additional $40,000 in consulting fees from outside clients. If he adopts a Keogh money purchase plan for this year, he can contribute and deduct up to 25% of earned income to the Keogh plan.

Question — Can a Keogh plan fund be reached by the owner's creditors?

Answer — Assets in a qualified pension plan may have protection under federal law against diversion for any purpose other than providing benefits for the plan participant and his or her beneficiary, including an ERISA prohibition against "assignment or alienation" of benefits.[9] This generally protects pension assets from creditors,[10] and even spouses have only the limited rights provided under the QDRO provisions (see Chapter 24).

FOOTNOTES

1. Reg. §1.401(b)(2).
2. IRC Section 401(c)(2).
3. GCM 39807.
4. IRC Section 404(e); Reg. §1.404(e)-1A(g).
5. Reg. §1.72-16(b)(4).
6. IRC Section 4975(d)(1), last paragraph.
7. IRC Sections 4975(a), 4975(b).
8. ERISA Section 408(d).
9. IRC Sections 401(a)(1), 401(a)(13); ERISA Section 206(d)(1).
10. The U.S. Supreme Court held that assets in a plan that is qualified under section 401(a) of the Internal Revenue Code and subject to ERISA are protected in bankruptcy. *Patterson v. Shumate*, 112 S. Ct. 1662 (1992). However, it is unclear if assets in a Keogh plan which covers only sole proprietors or partners are protected since such plans are not subject to Title I of ERISA.

Form **5500EZ**

Department of the Treasury
Internal Revenue Service

Please type or
machine print

Annual Return of One-Participant
(Owners and Their Spouses) Pension Benefit Plan
▶ Instructions are separate.

For the calendar year 1992 or fiscal plan year beginning ⬚ , 19 ⬚ ,

and ending ⬚ , 19 ⬚ .

OMB No. 1545-0956

1992

This Form Is Open
to Public Inspection

This return is: *(i)* ☐ the first return filed　*(ii)* ☐ an amended return　*(iii)* ☐ the final return　*(iv)* ☐ a short plan year (less than 12 mos.)

Use IRS label. Other-wise, please type or machine print.	**1a** Name of employer

1b Employer identification number

1c Telephone number of employer

Number, street, and room or suite no. (If a P.O. box, see instructions for line 1a.)

City or town, state, and ZIP code

1d If plan year has changed since last return, check here . . ▶ ☐

2a Is the employer also the plan administrator? ☐ Yes　☐ No (If "No," see instructions.)

2b *(i)* Name of plan ▶ ....

....

(ii) ☐ Check if name of plan has changed since last return

2c Date plan first became effective

Month　Day　Year

2d Enter three-digit plan number ▶ ⬚ ⬚ ⬚

		Yes	No
3a Enter the date the most recent plan amendment was adopted . . . . . Month ⬚ Year ⬚			
b Enter the date of the most recent IRS determination letter . . . . . Month ⬚ Year ⬚			
c Is a determination letter request pending with IRS? . . . . ▶			

4a Enter the number of other qualified pension benefit plans maintained by the employer ▶ _____

b If you have more than one pension plan and the total assets of all plans are more than $100,000, check this box . . . . ▶ ☐

5 Type of plan: *a* ☐ Defined benefit pension plan (attach Schedule B (Form 5500)) *b* ☐ Money purchase plan
c ☐ Profit-sharing plan　*d* ☐ Stock bonus plan　*e* ☐ ESOP plan (attach Schedule E (Form 5500))

6 Were there any noncash contributions made to the plan during the plan year? . . . . ▶

7 Enter the number of participants in each category listed below:

Number

a Under age 59½ at the end of the plan year	**7a**	
b Age 59½ or older at the end of the plan year, but under age 70½ at the beginning of the plan year	**7b**	
c Age 70½ or older at the beginning of the plan year	**7c**	

8a A fully insured plan with no trust and which is funded entirely by allocated insurance contracts that fully guarantee the amount of benefit payments should check the box at the right and not complete 8c through 10d . . . . ▶ ☐

b Contributions received for this plan year	**8b**	
c Net plan income other than from contributions	**8c**	
d Plan distributions	**8d**	
e Plan expenses other than distributions	**8e**	
9a Total plan assets at the end of the year	**9a**	
b Total plan liabilities at the end of the year	**9b**	

10 During the plan year, if any of the following transactions took place between the plan and a party-in-interest (see instructions), check "Yes" and enter amount. Otherwise, check "No."

	Yes		Amount	No
a Sale, exchange, or lease of property	**10a**			
b Loan or extension of credit	**10b**			
c Acquisition or holding of employer securities	**10c**			
d Payment by the plan for services	**10d**			

	Yes	No
11a Does your business have any employees other than you and your spouse (and your partners and their spouses)? ▶		

If "No," do NOT complete the rest of this question; go to question 12.

b Total number of employees (including you and your spouse and your partners and their spouses) ▶ _____

c Does this plan meet the coverage test of Code section 410(b)? . . . . ▶
See the specific instructions for line 11c.

12 Answer these questions only if there was a benefit payment, loan, or distribution of an annuity contract made during the plan year and the plan is subject to the spousal consent requirements (see instructions).

a Was there consent of the participant's spouse to any benefit payment or loan within the 90-day period prior to such payment or loan? ▶

b If "No," check the reason for no consent: *(i)* ☐ the participant was not married
(ii) ☐ the benefit payment made was part of a qualified joint and survivor annuity　*(iii)* ☐ other

c Were any annuity contracts purchased by the plan and distributed to the participants? . . . . ▶

Under penalties of perjury and other penalties set forth in the instructions, I declare that I have examined this return, including accompanying schedules and statements, and to the best of my knowledge and belief, it is true, correct, and complete.

Signature of employer/plan sponsor ▶ _____　Date ▶ _____

For Paperwork Reduction Act Notice, see page 1 of the instructions.　　Cat. No. 63263R　　Form **5500EZ** (1992)

★U.S.GPO:1992-0-315-365

Chapter 13

INDIVIDUAL RETIREMENT ACCOUNT (IRA)

WHAT IS IT?

An IRA (which stands for either individual retirement account or individual retirement annuity) is a type of retirement savings arrangement under which IRA contributions, up to certain limits, and investment earnings are tax-deferred. That is, interest earned and gains received inside the IRA are free of federal income tax until withdrawn from the IRA.

IRAs are primarily plans of individual savings, rather than employee benefits. However, their features should be understood since they fit into an employee's plan of retirement savings and therefore they influence the form of employer retirement plans to some degree.

Employers can sponsor IRAs for employees, as a limited alternative to an employer-sponsored qualified retirement plan. Employer-sponsored IRAs are discussed in the "Questions and Answers" at the end of this chapter. An arrangement similar to the employer-sponsored IRA which allows greater annual employer contributions is the SEP (simplified employee pension) discussed in Chapter 20.

WHEN IS IT INDICATED?

1. When there is a need to shelter current compensation or earned income from taxation.

2. When it is desirable to defer taxes on investment income.

3. When long-term accumulation, especially for retirement purposes, is an important objective.

4. When a supplement or alternative to a qualified pension or profit-sharing plan is needed.

ADVANTAGES

1. Eligible individuals may contribute up to $2,000 to an IRA ($2,250 if a spousal IRA is available) and deduct this amount from their current taxable income.

2. Investment income earned on the assets held in an IRA is not taxed until it is withdrawn from the account. This deferral applies no matter what the nature of the investment income. It may be in the form of interest, dividends,

rents, capital gain, or any other form of income. Such income will be taxed only when it is withdrawn from the account and received as ordinary income.

DISADVANTAGES

1. The IRA deduction is limited to $2,000 maximum each year ($2,250 if a spousal IRA is available), with even more stringent limits, or a complete unavailability of the deduction, if the individual (or his spouse) is an active participant in a tax-favored employer retirement plan, as discussed below.

2. IRA withdrawals are subject to the 10% penalty on premature withdrawals applicable to all tax-favored retirement plans.

3. IRA withdrawals are not eligible for the 5-year (or 10-year) averaging tax computation that applies to certain lump sum distributions from qualified plans.

4. IRAs cannot be established once an individual reaches age 70½ (except in the case of rollover-IRAs) and withdrawals from the account are required by April 1 of the year after the year in which the individual reaches age 70½. For additional information on required distributions, see the section on "Tax Implications," below.

TAX IMPLICATIONS

Contribution Rules

1. The maximum deductible IRA contribution for an individual is the lesser of (a) $2,000 or (b) 100% of the individual's earned income—that is, income from employment or self-employment; investment income cannot be counted.[1] If the individual has a spouse with no earned income (or one who elects to be treated as having no earned income), then a spousal IRA (SPIRA) can be set up and the maximum contribution for both spouses is $2,250.[2]

   If both spouses have earned income, each can have an IRA. The deduction limit for each spouse with earned income is the $2,000/100% limit.

2. Current law imposes income limitations on the deductibility of IRA contributions for those persons who are "active participants" in an employer retirement plan that is tax-favored—a qualified retirement plan, simplified employee pension (SEP), or Section 403(b) tax deferred annuity plan.[3]

Single individuals who are active participants may make a deductible contribution up to the full $2,000 if their adjusted gross income (AGI) is less than $25,000.

- Single active participants can make a partial deductible contribution (less than $2,000) if their income is between $25,000 and $35,000.

- Single active participants cannot make any deductible contribution if their AGI exceeds $35,000.

A similar structure exists for married couples where *either spouse*, or both spouses, are active participants in a qualified plan. The income limitations are higher than for single individuals, as follows:

- Married couples, where one or both are active participants can each make up to a $2,000 deductible contribution if their combined AGI is less than $40,000.

- Partial contributions are allowed if their combined AGI is between $40,000 and $50,000.

- No deductible contributions can be made if their combined AGI exceeds $50,000.

Both single and married persons can make nondeductible contributions up to $2,000 even though their incomes exceed the $35,000 or $50,000 maximums (see number 5(c), below).

A reduction formula determines the amount of any IRA contribution which will not be tax deductible if AGI falls into the $25,000-$35,000 range for singles or $40,000-$50,000 for married couples. This formula reduces the deductible contribution by the percentage of "excess" AGI, or the amount of AGI over the figures of $25,000 and $40,000, respectively.

The "nondeduction" formula is

$$\$2,000 \ \times \ \frac{\text{Excess AGI}}{\$10,000} \ = \ \text{Nondeductible Amount}$$

Example: A single person with AGI of $30,000 who is an active participant in a qualified retirement plan can contribute $2,000 to his or her IRA but only $1,000 of the contribution can be taken as a current tax deduction. The reduction amount is [$2,000 x ($5,000/$10,000)].

There is a $200 "floor" under the reduction formula. As long as the taxpayer is below the AGI level where deductions cut off entirely, at least $200 can be contributed and deducted.[4] For example, if married taxpayers have AGI of $49,900, they can contribute and deduct $200, even though the reduction formula would produce a lesser deduction.

3. An individual or married couple can also make *nondeductible* IRA contributions, within limits.[5] The limit is the same regardless of income level; it is the difference between (a) the overall contribution limit ($2,000, or $2,250 for SPIRAs) *and* (b) the amount of deductible contributions made for the year. If the individual or couple make no deductible contributions, they can therefore contribute up to $2,000/$2,250 on a nondeductible basis. Nondeductible contributions will be free of tax when they are distributed, but income earned on such contributions will be taxed. If nondeductible contributions are made to an IRA, amounts withdrawn will be treated as partly tax free and partly taxable.

4. Eligible persons may establish an IRA account and claim the appropriate tax deduction any time prior to the due date of their tax return, *without* extensions, even if the taxpayer actually receives an extension of the filing date.[6] For most individuals or married couples the contribution cutoff date is April 15th. However, since earnings on an IRA account accumulate tax-free, taxpayers may want to make contributions as early as possible in the tax year. The advantage of making an IRA contribution at the beginning of the year can be seen in the following table which assumes $2,000 annual contributions and a rate of return of eight percent.

YEARS OF GROWTH	BEGINNING OF YEAR JANUARY 1	END OF YEAR DECEMBER 31	ADVANTAGE OF EARLY CONTRIBUTIONS
5	$ 12,572	$ 11,733	$ 939
10	31,291	28,973	2,318
15	58,649	54,304	4,344
20	98,846	91,524	7,322
25	157,909	146,212	11,697
30	244,692	226,566	18,125
35	372,204	344,634	27,571
40	559,562	518,113	41,449
45	834,852	773,011	61,841

Distribution and Rollover Rules

1. The government penalizes certain early withdrawals from IRAs. The premature distribution penalty is 10 percent of the taxable amount withdrawn from the IRA.[7] Therefore,

IRA contributions should be made from funds that can be left in the account until one of the "non-penalty" events listed below occurs.

The premature distribution penalty (discussed further in Chapter 24) does *not* apply to IRA distributions

- made on or after attainment of age 59½.

- made to the IRA participant's beneficiary or estate on or after the participant's death.

- attributable to the participant's disability.

- that are part of a series of substantially equal periodic payments made at least annually over the life or life expectancy of the participant, or the participant and a designated beneficiary.

This last exception—the *periodic payment* exception—provides some flexibility and can be very favorable in some cases. For example, suppose Ira Participant decides at age 52 to take some money out of his IRA. Ira can do so without penalty, as long as the amount taken out annually is substantially what the annual payment would be under a life annuity (or joint life annuity) purchased with his IRA account balance. No actual annuity purchase is required.[8] Then, when Ira reaches age 59½, he can withdraw all the rest of the money in his IRA account. Ira doesn't have to continue the annuity payments since he is now relying on a different penalty exception, the exception for payments after age 59½.

However, if the series of payments is changed before the participant reaches age 59½ or, if after age 59½, within five years of the date of the first payment, the tax which would have been imposed, but for the periodic exception, is imposed with interest in the year the change occurs. In the example above, if Ira Participant had begun receiving payments under the periodic payment exception when he was 57, he would have to continue the annuity payments for at least five years to avoid the penalty.[9]

2. Distributions must begin by April 1 of the year after the year in which age 70½ is reached.[10] The IRA owner can receive the entire IRA balance in a lump sum or, if preferred, choose some other payment option. Typical permissible payment options include (a) periodic payments over the IRA owner's life and the life of a designated beneficiary, (b) periodic payments over a fixed period not longer than the IRA owner's life expectancy, or a fixed period not longer than the life expectancy of the owner and a designated beneficiary. Life expectancy for this purpose is determined from tables provided in IRS regulations.

The Financial Planning TOOLKIT illustration (see below) indicates that a person age 71, with an IRA account of $500,000, would have to begin making withdrawals of at least $32,680, based on his remaining life expectancy of 15.3 years.

If, after distributions are required to begin, sufficient amounts are not withdrawn from an IRA in a tax year, there is a 50 percent excise tax on the under-distribution. An under-distribution is the difference between the minimum payout required for the tax year and the amount actually paid.[11]

3. An additional penalty tax of 15% will be imposed if aggregate "retirement" distributions to an individual in a calendar year exceed the greater of (1) $150,000, or (2) $112,500 as adjusted for inflation ($144,551 in 1993). This tax is in addition to any regular income taxes due and applies only to the excess portion of the distribution. All qualified plans and individual retirement plans are aggregated for this additional tax.[12]

4. An IRA can be used to receive a "rollover" of certain distributions of benefits from employer-sponsored retirement plans. The distribution must be directly transferred or rolled over to the rollover IRA within 60 days after it is received. It is advisable to create a special IRA for a rollover and not make further contributions to it; the right to roll these amounts back into a qualified plan (which is often a possibility) is lost if the funds in the special IRA are mixed with funds from other sources.[13]

IRA rollovers are usually straightforward, but there are some complicated rules in special situations. These are discussed further in Chapter 24.

5. When an IRA owner dies, a somewhat complex pattern of tax rules applies. Planners need to understand the tax treatment of this common situation in order to prevent unnecessary tax penalties for their clients. These rules are generally designed to prevent IRA distributions from being "stretched out" unduly to increase tax deferral.[14]

(a) If the owner dies after payments under the IRA have begun, payments must continue to the beneficiary or heir to the IRA at least as rapidly as under the method of distribution in effect during the owner's life. The only exception to this is if the beneficiary or heir is the owner's spouse (see (c), below).

(b) If the owner had *not* begun receiving payments and the heir or beneficiary is not the owner's spouse, there are two possible options for distribution:

Figure 13.1

IRA WITHDRAWAL — REQUIRED MINIMUM

INPUT: INDIVIDUAL'S CURRENT AGE 71   Years
          (Ages 71 and over)

          REMAINING LIFE EXPECTANCY ....15.3   Years
          (Males and Females)

INPUT: Remaining IRA Balance $500,000

          Required Withdrawal in Current Year .... $ 32,680

Reprinted with permission from *Financial Planning* TOOLKIT, Financial Data Corporation.

---

(1) the entire amount must be distributed within five years, or

(2) the benefit can be paid (annuitized) over the life expectancy of that beneficiary; distributions under this option must begin within one year of the decedent's death.

(c) If the heir or beneficiary is the owner's spouse, distributions do not have to begin until December 31 of the later of (1) the year immediately following the year in which the owner died or (2) the year in which the owner would have attained age 70½. However, the recipient spouse can elect to treat the inherited IRA as his or her own. This means that distributions do not have to begin until April 1 of the year following the year in which the *recipient spouse* reaches age 70½. This election is permitted whether or not the decedent had begun receiving distributions from the IRA prior to death. The election is made simply by *not* withdrawing money until the spouse attains age 70½ and thus deferring the reporting of the income until such time.[15] As an alternative to making this election, the recipient spouse can roll the decedent's IRA over to the recipient spouse's own IRA, which accomplishes the same result.

WHERE CAN I FIND OUT MORE ABOUT IT?

1. Most banks, savings and loans, insurance companies, and brokerage firms actively market IRAs, and can provide brochures describing their IRA plans. These firms will indicate the types of investments available as well as any charges that may be applied to such accounts.

2. IRS Publication 590, *Individual Retirement Arrangements (IRAs)*, is available without charge from the IRS or the U.S. Government Printing Office.

QUESTIONS AND ANSWERS

Question — If neither an individual nor his or her spouse is covered by a tax-favored retirement plan, are there any limitations on the deductibility of IRA contributions?

Answer — No. If neither the individual nor the spouse is covered by a qualified retirement plan, simplified employee pension (SEP), or Section 403(b) annuity plan, they may contribute up to the full deduction limit (the lesser of $2,000 or 100 percent of earned income for each spouse with earned income, or a total of $2,250 if only one spouse has earned income) and deduct the full amount of the contribution regardless of the level of AGI.

Examples:

1. Minnie and Bill, a married couple, each earn $75,000 annually. Neither is an active participant in any qualified plan, SEP or Section 403(b) plan. Minnie and Bill can each contribute and deduct up to $2,000 to their own IRA plan (a total of $4,000 for both).

2. Mabel earns $75,000 annually. Her husband, Alf, has no earned income (although he has investment income over $100,000 annually). Neither spouse is an active participant in a tax-favored plan. Mabel can contribute and deduct a total of $2,250 to an IRA for herself and an IRA for her spouse.

3. Stan earns $75,000 annually, and his wife Fran has earned income of $1,200. Neither is an active participant in a tax-favored retirement plan. Stan can contribute and deduct up to $2,000 to his IRA, and Fran can contribute and deduct up to $1,200 to her IRA (she is limited by 100 percent of her earned income).

Question — What does it mean to be an "active" participant in a qualified plan, SEP, or TDA plan?

Answer — A person is an active participant in an employer's retirement plan only if the participant actually receives an employer contribution for that year or accrues a benefit under an employer's defined benefit plan.

For example, in a qualified profit-sharing plan it is possible for an employer to omit making a plan contribution in a given year. For such a year, an employee is *not* considered an active plan participant even though covered under the plan, so long as there was no contribution made to the employee's account under the plan.

Note, however, that an employee is considered an active participant if a contribution is made for him by the employer but the employee is not vested in the amount in his account. If the employee stays long enough to become vested, he will acquire full rights to that amount, so he is considered an active participant for the year in which the contribution was made.

Question — If only one spouse is an active participant, can the other spouse receive a full IRA deduction by filing a separate return?

Answer — The reduced deduction limit can be avoided by the non-active participant spouse only if a separate return is filed *and* the spouses lived apart at all times during the taxable year.

Question — Is there any minimum contribution required each year?

Answer — No, there is no required minimum contribution to an IRA. An individual can put aside relatively small amounts each year and still see them grow into a considerable sum for retirement. Also, a contribution does not have to be made every year. It is possible to skip a year or any number of years without jeopardizing the tax-deferred status of the account. However, failure to make contributions reduces the value of the account for tax-shelter purposes and limits the amount of earnings that will build up on a tax-free basis.

Question — What kind of income is eligible to be contributed to an IRA account?

Answer — The income must be produced from personal services which would include wages, salaries, professional fees, sales commissions, tips, and bonuses.

Unearned income such as dividends, interest, or rent cannot be used in determining the amount of the IRA contribution.

Question — Do married couples with two incomes contribute to one or two regular IRAs?

Answer — Two. Each should establish a separate IRA account. Contributions are based on each separate income and each contribution is a separate tax deduction. This is true even though a couple may live in a community property state.

Question — How are IRA benefits paid?

Answer — Benefits must be paid in one of two ways — (a) a single lump-sum payment, or (b) payments over a period which is not longer than a period equal to the life expectancy of the contributor or the joint life expectancies of the contributor and his designated beneficiary. Special rules apply if the spouse is the beneficiary.

Payments to a beneficiary must only be "incidental" under IRS regulations. These regulations in general require a payment schedule under which more of the expected benefit will be paid to the original IRA owner than is paid to the beneficiary. See Chapter 24.

Question — Are IRA contributions locked into any one particular investment?

Answer — No. First, the IRA participant may select more than one organization which sponsors IRA programs, as long as the total of all deductible investments made each year is within the contribution limit. For example, part of the contribution could be placed in a savings account and the remainder in a mutual fund plan. Second, at any time the IRA participant may request an IRA sponsor to transfer IRA assets directly from one sponsoring organization to another; not all IRA sponsors will agree to do this, however. Alternatively, assets may be taken out of an IRA and reinvested with another IRA sponsor within 60 days without any tax consequences. However, the IRA participant is allowed to make this type of transaction—a "rollover"—only once every 12 months.[16]

Question — If an IRA participant becomes disabled, can an early withdrawal be made from the IRA account?

Answer — Yes. In order to avoid the 10 percent early distribution penalty, a person under age 59½ must have a total and permanent physical or mental disability which prevents gainful employment and which is determined by a physician to be terminal or expected to continue for at least one year.

Question — When are taxes paid on IRA plans?

Answer — If IRA funds are taken out in a lump sum, the entire account, including principal and earnings is ordinary income in the year of receipt. However, if nondeductible contributions have been made to the account, they are recovered tax-free. If money is withdrawn periodically in installments or an annuity, only the amount received each year is taxable. If nondeductible contributions have been made, a portion of each payment is received tax-free.

Question — What happens if too much is contributed to an IRA account in any one year?

Answer — If more than the maximum allowable amount is contributed in any year, a 6 percent excise tax will be imposed on the excess contribution. However, the 6 percent tax can be avoided by withdrawing the excess contribution and earnings prior to the filing date for the federal income tax return (normally April 15). If the excess contribution plus earnings is not withdrawn by the tax return filing date, the 6 percent excise tax will be imposed in each succeeding year until the excess is eliminated.[17]

Question — How can an employer sponsor IRAs for employees?

Answer — An employer (or a labor union) can sponsor IRAs for its employees as an alternative to a pension plan. There is no requirement of nondiscrimination in coverage. The IRAs can be made available to any employee or a discriminatory group of employees.

Contributions to the IRA can be made either as additional compensation from the employer or as a salary reduction elected by the employee. If the employer contributes extra compensation, it is taxable to the employee, but the employee is eligible for the IRA deduction.

The deduction limit for an employer-sponsored IRA is the same as for regular individual IRAs (the lesser of $2,000 or 100 percent of compensation).

An arrangement similar to the employer-sponsored IRA is the SEP (simplified employee pension) discussed in Chapter 20. SEPs allow greater annual employer contributions—up to a limit of 15% of compensation, or $30,000 (as indexed for inflation), whichever is greater. However, SEPs require nondiscriminatory coverage of employees.

Question — In what types of assets may IRA funds be invested?

Answer—IRA funds can be invested in any type of asset, with three specific limitations:

(1) An IRA cannot be invested in a "collectible" as defined in Code section 408(m). A collectible is any work of art, rug, antique, metal or gem, stamp, coin, alcoholic beverage, or any other item designated as a collectible by the IRS. The IRA can, however, invest in certain state or federally-issued coins.[18]

(2) IRAs cannot be invested in life insurance contracts.[19]

(3) Since IRAs cannot make loans to an IRA participant,[20] the participant's note is in effect another type of property the IRA cannot invest in. That is, an IRA owner cannot lend IRA funds to himself or to a related person or business. IRAs can, however, make loans to individuals or companies that are not "disqualified persons" under the prohibited transaction rules. For example, Letter Ruling 8723082 states that an IRA owner could make loans from the IRA to an unrelated company that was in the business of owning and managing shopping centers.

Question — How can an IRA owner make use of IRA funds prior to reaching age 59½?

Answer — While there is a 10% tax penalty for withdrawals from IRAs prior to age 59½, there are exceptions to the penalty: funds can be withdrawn without penalty if the owner is disabled (the owner must, however, meet the stringent "total and permanent" definition of disability provided under Social Security law). Funds are also available without penalty to the owner's beneficiaries if the owner dies. Finally, an IRA owner may begin "annuity" type withdrawals from an IRA at any time without penalty; the annuity amount must be based on a life annuity for the owner (or joint life annuity for the owner and beneficiary), so the amount that can be withdrawn in any one year is limited. There is no exception to the penalty for any kind of "hardship" withdrawal from an IRA.

Loans from IRAs to the IRA owner or a related party are prohibited transactions subject to penalty. However, an IRA owner can use the 60-day IRA rollover provision to, in effect, make a 60-day interest free loan from an IRA.[21] The owner simply takes the money out, uses it during the 60-day period, and then deposits it in the same or another IRA on or before the 60th day after withdrawal. This type of transaction may be helpful as part of a "swing loan" when selling one residence and buying another, or for similar financial needs.

Question — How are IRAs treated for state tax law purposes?

Answer — State tax laws vary, and not every state accords IRAs the same favorable tax treatment as does federal law. Three issues can arise:

The Tools and Techniques of Employee Benefit and Retirement Planning

1. Is the IRA contribution deductible for state (or local) income tax purposes?

2. Are IRA withdrawals taxable under state income tax law?

3. If an IRA owner takes a deduction for an IRA contribution in State A and then moves to State B, does the owner owe income tax to State A when making an IRA withdrawal? Some states apparently take the position that taxes are due in that situation. If State B has no income tax law, there would be no tax credit available against the State A tax liability.

Question — If a participant's spouse is the beneficiary of the participant's IRA, is the amount eligible for the marital deduction for federal estate tax purposes?

Answer — In general, amounts transferred to a spouse at death are eligible for the marital deduction. There is no problem with this if the spouse receives the IRA directly. However, if a trust for the spouse's benefit receives the IRA assets, the trust must qualify as a "QTIP" (qualified terminable interest property) trust in order to be eligible for the marital deduction.

In Revenue Ruling 89-89,[22] the IRS indicated the requirements that must be met for an IRA-beneficiary trust to qualify as a QTIP trust. Generally, the IRA must distribute all its income for the calendar year plus the annual installment of its principal balance to the trust. Income must then be distributed currently to the spousal beneficiary. If an IRA participant wishes to use a QTIP trust in estate planning for the IRA assets, a beneficiary designation meeting the requirements of Revenue Ruling

89-89 should be adopted in advance of the participant's death.

FOOTNOTES

1. IRC Section 219(a), (b).
2. IRC Section 219(c).
3. IRC Section 219(g).
4. IRC Section 219(g)(2)(B).
5. IRC Section 408(o).
6. IRC Section 219(f)(3).
7. IRC Section 72(t).
8. Rules for calculating the annual annuity payment are provided by the IRS in IRS Notice 89-25, 1989-1 CB 662, Question 12. Three methods of calculating payments are listed with approval: (1) use of the minimum distribution rules of Section 401(a)(9); (2) amortizing the account balance over single or joint life expectancies of owner and beneficiary; (3) using an annuity factor using a "reasonable" interest rate and mortality table; 8 percent and the UP-1984 table are used in the IRS' example. See also IRS Publication 590.
9. IRC Section 72(t)(4).
10. IRC Sections 408(a)(6), 408(b)(3), 401(a)(9).
11. IRC Section 4974.
12. IRC Section 4980A.
13. IRC Section 408(d)(3)(A)(ii).
14. Prop. Regs. §§1.408-8, A-1, 1.401(a)(9)-1, C-1 to C-5.
15. Prop. Reg. §1.408-8, A-4.
16. Prop. Reg. §1.408-4(b)(4)(ii).
17. IRC Sections 4973, 408(d)(4).
18. IRC Section 408(m)(3).
19. IRC Section 408(a)(3).
20. It is a prohibited transaction under IRC Section 4975(c)(1)(B).
21. Let. Rul. 9010008.
22. Rev. Rul. 89-89, 1989-2 CB 231.

Chapter 14

LIFE INSURANCE IN A QUALIFIED PLAN

WHAT IS IT?

Life insurance for employees covered under a qualified plan can often be provided favorably by having the insurance purchased and owned by the plan, using deductible employer contributions to the plan as a source of funds. This chapter deals with the advantages and methods of doing this, as well as the limitations.

WHEN IS IT INDICATED?

1. When a substantial number of employees covered under a qualified plan have an otherwise unmet life insurance need, either for family protection or estate liquidity.

2. When there are gaps and limitations in other company plans providing death benefits, such as Section 79 group-term life insurance plans, nonqualified deferred compensation plans, and split dollar plans. Planners should consider using life insurance in a qualified plan to fill those gaps or supplement those plans.

3. When a qualified plan for a closely held business or professional corporation is overfunded or close to the full funding limitation for regular trusteed plans, the addition of an incidental life insurance benefit, or a change to fully insured funding, may permit future deductible contributions at a higher rate than before.

4. When highly compensated plan participants are potentially subject to the 15% excess accumulation tax on plan death benefits or substantial estate taxes on death benefits.

   • Life insurance in the plan can reduce the exposure to the excess accumulation tax since, as discussed below, pure life insurance is not subject to the tax.

   • Insured plan death benefits can (potentially) be structured to avoid estate taxes.

   • Life insurance in a plan can provide funds to pay estate taxes and excess accumulation taxes, if any, thereby enhancing the ability of plan proceeds to provide financial security for the participant's survivors.

5. When life insurance would be attractive to plan participants as an additional option for investing their plan accounts. This technique is most often used in a profit-sharing or 401(k) plan, but can be used in other types of defined contribution plans as well.

6. When an employer wants an extremely secure funding vehicle for a plan, with the best available guarantees as to future plan costs and benefits.

ADVANTAGES

1. The tax treatment of life insurance in a qualified plan, as discussed below, usually provides an overall cost advantage, as compared with individual life policies provided by the employer outside the qualified plan or those personally-owned by plan participants. Recent tax changes have reduced this advantage but have not (in most cases) eliminated it.

2. Life insurance provides one of the safest available investments for a qualified plan.

3. Using appropriate life insurance products for funding a qualified plan can provide extremely predictable plan costs for the employer.

4. Life insurance products in a qualified plan can provide employees with retirement benefits guaranteed by an insurance company as well as by the employer.

5. The "pure insurance" portion of a qualified plan death benefit (basically, the death proceeds less any policy cash values) is not subject either to regular income tax or to the 15% tax on excess accumulations. This makes it, dollar for dollar, a more effective means of transferring wealth than any other type of plan asset.

6. Some authorities believe that insured plan death benefits can be structured to keep them out of the plan participant's estate for federal estate tax purposes. (See "Questions and Answers," below.)

7. A fully insured plan (one holding only life insurance policies or annuity contracts) is exempt from the minimum funding standards and the actuarial certification requirement of Code section 412. This can reduce the administrative cost and complexity of a defined benefit plan. A fully insured plan can also allow a higher initial

level of deductible plan contributions than a regular trusteed plan.

8. Some life insurance companies provide low cost installation and administrative services for plans using their investment products. This also reduces the employer's cost for the plan.

DISADVANTAGES

1. Some life insurance policies may provide a rate of return on their cash values which, as compared with alternative plan investments, may be relatively low. However, rates of return should be compared on investments of similar risk.

2. Policy expenses and commissions on life insurance products may be greater than for comparable investments.

HOW IS IT USED?

Insurance Coverage

Insurance coverage should be provided for all plan participants under a nondiscriminatory formula related to the retirement benefit or plan contribution formula. For example, the amount of insurance for each employee might be specified as 100 times the expected monthly pension under the plan.

Insurance coverage can be conditioned on taking a medical exam if this does not result in discrimination in favor of highly compensated employees. For employees who do not "pass" the medical exam, insurance is typically limited to the amount, if any, that can be purchased for them using the amount of premium dollars that would be available if they were insurable. For example, if the plan's insurance formula provides insurance of 100 times the monthly benefit for standard risks (employees who pass the medical exam), the insurance provided for a medically "rated" employee might be only 50 times the monthly benefit, since a 50 times benefit for that employee would cost as much to provide as a 100 times benefit for a standard risk.

Turnover costs involved in buying cash value insurance policies can be minimized by having a longer waiting period for insurance than the plan's waiting period for entry. In the interim period, the death benefit for participants not covered by cash value policies can be provided by term insurance. In the past, many plans did not provide insurance for employees who were beyond a specified cutoff age. Under current age discrimination law, this probably is no longer allowed. (See Appendix I.)

How Much Insurance—The "Incidental" Test

Life insurance can be used to provide an "incidental" death benefit to participants in a qualified retirement plan, either a defined contribution or defined benefit plan. The IRS considers any nonretirement benefit in a qualified plan to be incidental so long as the cost of that benefit is less than 25% of the total cost of the plan. Since this standard by itself is difficult to apply, the IRS has developed two practical tests for life insurance in a qualified plan.[1] If the amount of insurance meets either of the following tests, it is considered incidental:

1. The participant's insured death benefit must be no more than 100 times the expected monthly benefit, or

2. The aggregate premiums paid (premiums paid over the entire life of the plan) for a participant's insured death benefit are at all times less than the following percentages of the plan cost for that participant:

"ordinary life" insurance	50%
term insurance	25%
universal life	25%

Traditionally, defined contribution plans such as profit-sharing plans have used the "percentage limits" in determining how much insurance to provide. Defined benefit plans have typically used the "100 times" limit. However, any type of plan can use either limit. It is becoming more common for defined benefit plans to use the percentage limits since the necessary calculations are easily computerized.

Life Insurance in Defined Benefit Plans

Life insurance is particularly advantageous in defined benefit plans because it *adds to* the limit on deductible contributions. This add-on feature allows greater tax-deferred funding of the plan. That is, a defined benefit plan can be funded to provide the maximum tax-deductible contribution for retirement benefits for each participant. The cost for life insurance can then be added to this amount and deducted.

By comparison, in a defined contribution plan, the costs of the life insurance must be part of the contributions to each participant's account. Using life insurance does not increase the Section 415 annual additions limit for participants' accounts in defined contribution plans. That limit is the lesser of (a) 25% of compensation or (b) the greater of $30,000 or ¼ of the dollar limitation for defined benefit plans (see Chapter 23), whether or not life insurance is provided.

Life insurance can be used in defined benefit plans in many ways. Three common approaches will be discussed here: the "combination plan," the "envelope funding" approach, and the fully insured plan.

Combination Plan

In a combination plan, retirement benefits are funded with a combination of (1) whole life policies and (2) assets in a separate trust fund called the "side fund" or "conversion fund." At each participant's retirement, the policies for that participant are cashed in. The participant's retirement benefit is then funded through a combination of the policy cash values and an amount withdrawn from the side fund. (Since whole life policies have a relatively slow cash value buildup, the cash values alone are not usually adequate at age 65 to fund the retirement benefit; this is the reason for the side fund.)

This type of funding combines the advantages of (1) an insured death benefit and the investment security of policy cash values, together with (2) an opportunity to invest more aggressively using side fund assets.

Combination plans are very appropriate for funding smaller pension plans—fewer than about 25 employees—but can be administratively costly for larger plans due to the number of insurance policies necessary for funding.

The amount of death benefit provided for each employee is usually determined using the 100-to-1 test. The annual cost for the plan each year then consists of the insurance premiums required, plus an amount deposited in the side fund that is determined on an actuarial basis. Actuarial methods and assumptions for the side fund can be varied within reasonable limits, providing some flexibility in funding.

The following example shows how a combination plan works and how it differs from an uninsured plan providing the same retirement benefit:

Example: Dr. X, a sole practitioner physician, adopts a pension plan at age 45. His annual compensation is $200,000.

	Insured Plan	Uninsured Plan
Monthly pension at age 65	$ 7,500	$ 7,500
Insured death benefit	750,000	0
Amount required at age 65	900,000	900,000
Less: cash value at age 65	258,750	0
Side fund at 65	641,250	900,000
Level annual deposit at 6% from age 45 to age 65	16,446	23,082
Life insurance premium (not considering dividends)	16,343	0
Total annual contribution	32,789	23,082

Note: Future dividends on the life insurance contract can be applied to reduce the annual premium, and typically will reduce it substantially after a number of years.

Envelope Funding

At the opposite pole from the combination plan, where the entire plan is structured around the insurance policies, is the envelope funding approach, where insurance policies are simply considered as plan assets like any other asset. In funding, the actuary determines total annual contributions (that must be paid in quarterly or more frequent installments in the case of defined benefit plans) to the plan to provide both retirement and death benefits provided under the plan. The employer makes the contributions as determined by the actuary. Assets, including insurance policies, are purchased by the plan trustee to fund the costs of both the death benefits and the retirement benefits.

The amount of insured death benefit in this approach is kept within the incidental limits either by providing a death benefit of no more than 100 times each participant's projected monthly pension, or by keeping the amount of insurance premiums within the appropriate percentage limits (50 percent of aggregate costs for whole life insurance, 25% for term insurance, and so on).

The envelope funding approach tends to require lower initial contributions to the plan than a combination plan approach, since the actuary's assumptions are usually less conservative than the assumptions used to determine life insurance premiums. Long-term costs, however, will depend on actual investment results, policy dividends, and benefit and administrative costs of the plan.

Fully Insured Pension Plans

A fully insured pension plan is one that is funded exclusively by life insurance or annuity contracts (and meets other requirements discussed below.) There is no trusteed side fund. Such plans were once common, but the high investment returns of the late 1970s lured many pension investors away from traditional insured pension products. Today, however, the advantages of fully insured plans are coming into their own, and life insurance agents and pension sponsors should take another look at these products. The immediate reason is that recent changes in the pension law have made many noninsured plans "overfunded," and fully insured plans may offer a solution to this widespread problem. But even where the overfunding problem is not a factor, the fully insured plan may offer advantages.

The Overfunding Problem

Qualified defined benefit plans are subject to minimum funding standards requiring a minimum annual employer contribution, with penalties for noncompliance. The minimum funding amount is determined actuarially, and there is a "full funding limitation" which when reached prevents further deductible contributions.[2]

For many defined benefit plans, two recent changes in these rules have resulted in a severe reduction or outright elimination of plan contributions for the current year and often future years as well:

1. The full funding limitation of Code section 412(c) and ERISA section 302(c) was amended, effective for plan years beginning after 1987, in a way that reduces this funding "lid" considerably for many plans.

2. In addition, the law now limits interest rates that can be used in determining plan liabilities. Code section 412(b)(5) requires that the interest rate in general must be within 10 percent of the average rate for 30-year Treasury bonds for the prior 4-year period. This rule currently requires interest rates considerably higher than actuaries have used in the past. For example, for the calendar 1993 plan year, the permissible range of interest rates is 7.27 percent to 8.88 percent.[3] Many actuaries used interest rates much lower than this in prior years to maximize current contributions.

A Solution—Fully Insured Plans

"Fully insured plans" have always been exempt from the minimum funding rules.[4] And, exemption from the minimum funding rules in effect exempts fully insured plans from the impact of the unfavorable changes discussed above, since they are part of the minimum funding rules.

A plan is considered fully insured for the plan year if it meets the following requirements:

- the plan is funded exclusively by the purchase of individual insurance contracts. Under the regulations, such contracts can be either individual or group, and can be life insurance or annuity contracts or a combination of both.[5]

- the contracts provide for level annual (or more frequent) premiums extending to retirement age for each individual. However, the employer's cost need not be level, since the regulations permit experience gains and dividends to reduce premiums.[6]

- plan benefits are equal to the contract benefits and are guaranteed by a licensed insurance company.

- premiums have been paid without lapse (or the policy has been reinstated after a lapse).

- no rights under the contracts have been subject to a security interest during the plan year.

- no policy loans are outstanding at any time during the plan year.

Proposed nondiscrimination regulations provide a safe harbor for fully insured plans meeting certain requirements; the benefit formulas of plans satisfying the safe harbor and specified uniformity requirements will be considered to be nondiscriminatory.[7]

Other Advantages

In addition to exemption from minimum funding, a fully insured plan is eligible for a simplification of the ERISA reporting requirements (Form 5500 series). An insured plan need not file Schedule B, Actuarial Information with its Form 5500 (or 5500-C/R) and thus does not need a certification by an enrolled actuary.[8] This reduces the cost and complexity of plan administration to some degree. Finally, a fully insured plan is exempt from the requirement of quarterly pension deposits[9] since that is also tied together with the minimum funding requirements. Fully insured plans are, however, subject to Pension Benefit Guaranty (PBGC) coverage and annual premium requirements.

How Does It Work?

Fully insured funding can be used either with a new plan or an existing plan.[10] The employer can be a corporation or an unincorporated business. Typically, a group type of contract is used, with individual accounts for each participant. All benefits are guaranteed by the insurance company. The premium is based on the guaranteed interest and annuity rates, which are typically conservative, resulting in larger initial annual deposits than in a typical uninsured plan. However, excess earnings beyond the guaranteed level are used to reduce future premiums.

Using excess earnings to reduce future premiums results in a funding pattern that is the opposite of that found in a trusteed (uninsured) plan. In the insured plan, (for a given group of plan participants) the funding level is higher at the beginning of the plan (or the fully insured funding arrangements) and drops as participants move toward retirement. This allows maximization of the overall tax deduction by allowing more of it to be taken earlier. It also often permits deductions for an existing plan that has reached the full funding limitation with uninsured funding. By comparison, a traditional trusteed plan starts with a relatively low level of funding, which increases as each participant nears retirement.

Life Insurance in Defined Contribution Plans

In defined contribution plans, a part of each participant's account is used to purchase insurance on the participant's life. This plan can provide (a) that insurance purchases are voluntary by participants (using a *directed account* or *earmarking* provision), (b) the insurance is provided automatically as a plan benefit, or (c) that insurance is provided at the plan administrator's option (on a nondiscriminatory basis).

The amount of insurance must be kept within the incidental limits already discussed. Usually, defined contribution plans rely on the percentage limits applicable to the type of insurance purchased. For example, if whole life insurance is purchased, aggregate premiums paid from each participant's account must be kept below 50% of aggregate contributions to that account.

If a plan has been in existence for a number of years, it may be possible to purchase a considerable amount of insurance in a later year, because the tests are computed in the aggregate.

For example, suppose a money purchase pension plan has existed for ten years and the employer has contributed $10,000 annually to employee Clyde's account. In the eleventh year, suppose the employer contributes another $10,000 to Clyde's account in the plan. In that eleventh year, an insurance premium amounting to just under $55,000 (50% of aggregate contributions of $110,000) can be paid out of Clyde's account to purchase whole life insurance. In some cases, such large purchases of insurance may be justified for planning purposes. For example, Clyde may be facing a potential excess accumulation tax on plan benefits in his estate that can be reduced by providing a large insured plan death benefit, as discussed below. The planner must be sure, however, that application of the percentage limits in the future will not prevent the deductible payment of required periodic premiums under the policy.

Profit-sharing plans have an additional feature that may allow large insurance purchases. Since profit-sharing plans potentially allow in-service cash distributions prior to termination of employment (see Chapter 17), the amount available for an in-service distribution can be used without limit to purchase life insurance. Based on IRS rulings,[11] this means that any employer contribution that has been in the profit-

sharing plan for at least two years can be used up to 100% for insurance purchases of any type as long as the plan specifies that the insurance will be purchased only with such funds.

TAX IMPLICATIONS

1. Employer contributions to the plan, including those used to purchase life insurance, are deductible if the amount of life insurance is within the incidental limits discussed earlier.

2. The economic value of pure life insurance coverage on a participant's life is taxed annually to the participant at the lower of the IRS "P.S. 58" table (see Figure 14.1) or the life insurance company's actual term rates for standard risks.[12] Any amount actually contributed to the plan by the participant is subtracted from this amount. (If the participant is an owner-employee in a "Keogh" plan, the taxation is slightly different, as discussed in Chapter 12.)

   Example: Participant Lemm, aged 45, is covered under a defined benefit plan that provides an insured death benefit in addition to retirement benefits. The death benefit is provided under a whole life policy with a face amount of $100,000. At the end of 1993 the policy's cash value is $40,000. The plan is noncontributory (that is, Lemm does not contribute to the plan).

   For 1993 Lemm must report an additional $378 of taxable income on his tax returns (60 times the P.S. 58 rate of $6.30 per thousand for a participant aged 45, to reflect the amount of pure insurance coverage in 1993). The employer is required to report the insurance coverage on Lemm's Form W-2 for the year.

   This computation is shown in more detail in the NumberCruncher software which is illustrated in Figure 14.2.

3. Taxation of an insured death benefit received by a beneficiary can be summarized in the following points:

   - The pure insurance element of an insured plan death benefit (the death benefit less any cash value) is income tax free to a participant's beneficiary.[13]

   - An additional $5,000 may qualify for the employer death benefit exclusion of Code section 101(b).

   - The total of all P.S. 58 costs paid by the participant can be recovered tax free from the plan death benefit (if it is paid from the same insurance contracts that gave rise to the P.S. 58 costs).[14]

Figure 14.1

"P.S. 58" Rates

The following rates are used in computing the "cost" of pure life insurance protection that is taxable to the employee under: qualified pension and profit sharing plans; split-dollar plans; and tax-sheltered annuities. Rev. Rul. 55-747, 1955-2 CB 228; Rev. Rul. 66-110, 1966-1 CB 12.

The rate at insured's attained age is applied to the excess of the amount payable at death over the cash value of the policy at the end of the year.

One Year Term Premiums for $1,000 of Life Insurance Protection (One Life)

Age	Premium	Age	Premium	Age	Premium
0	$ 42.10*	35	$ 3.21	70	$ 48.06
1	4.49*	36	3.41	71	52.29
2	2.37*	37	3.63	72	56.89
3	1.72*	38	3.87	73	61.89
4	1.38*	39	4.14	74	67.33
5	1.21*	40	4.42	75	73.23
6	1.07*	41	4.73	76	79.63
7	.98*	42	5.07	77	86.57
8	.90*	43	5.44	78	94.09
9	.85*	44	5.85	79	102.23
10	.83*	45	6.30	80	111.04
11	.91*	46	6.78	81	120.57
12	1.00*	47	7.32	82	130.86*
13	1.08*	48	7.89	83	141.95*
14	1.17*	49	8.53	84	153.91*
15	1.27	50	9.22	85	166.77*
16	1.38	51	9.97	86	180.60*
17	1.48	52	10.79	87	195.43*
18	1.52	53	11.69	88	211.33*
19	1.56	54	12.67	89	228.31*
20	1.61	55	13.74	90	246.45*
21	1.67	56	14.91	91	265.75*
22	1.73	57	16.18	92	286.25*
23	1.79	58	17.56	93	307.98*
24	1.86	59	19.08	94	330.94*
25	1.93	60	20.73	95	355.11*
26	2.02	61	22.53	96	380.50*
27	2.11	62	24.50	97	407.03*
28	2.20	63	26.63	98	434.68*
29	2.31	64	28.98	99	463.35*
30	2.43	65	31.51	100	492.93*
31	2.57	66	34.28	101	523.30*
32	2.70	67	37.31	102	554.30*
33	2.86	68	40.59	103	585.75*
34	3.02	69	44.17	104	617.42*

* Rates are derived by the editor of *Tax Facts 1* from U.S. Life Table 38, and are based on the underlying actuarial assumptions of the PS 58 rates.

• The remainder of the distribution is taxed as a qualified plan distribution.[15] This taxable portion of the distribution may be eligible for 5-year averaging if the plan participant is over 59½ at death. If the decedent participated in the plan before 1987, there are also some favorable "grandfather" tax provisions that may apply.

Chapter 24 contains a detailed discussion of the tax treatment and planning options available for an insured death benefit from a qualified plan.

4. As compared with the tax treatment of life insurance personally owned or provided by the employer outside

the plan, there is usually an economic advantage to insurance in the plan, all other things being equal. Insurance outside the plan is paid for entirely with after-tax dollars, so there is no tax deferral. The death benefit of non-plan insurance may be entirely instead of partially tax-free; however, the deferral of tax with plan-provided insurance potentially results in a measurable net tax benefit.

Recent tax law trends have reduced the potential value of this deferral of taxes. Current personal tax rates have been reduced (though on a broader tax base) and there is an expectation that future tax rates may be higher. On the other hand, the relative increase in corporate tax rates has increased the value of any employee benefit that can be paid for with deductible corporate dollars. Some alternatives to plan-provided life insurance (split-dollar plans, for example—see Chapter 49) involve nondeductible corporate premium payments.

5. The pure insurance amount of a qualified plan death benefit is not subject to the 15% excess accumulation tax

of Code section 4980A.[16] Also, P.S. 58 costs can be recovered free of the excess accumulation tax.

6. Qualified plan death benefits are, in general, included in a decedent's estate for federal estate tax purposes. However, it may be possible to exclude the insured portion of the death benefit if the decedent had no "incidents of ownership" in the policy. This planning technique is discussed further in the "Questions and Answers," below.

ALTERNATIVES

1. Personally-owned life insurance

2. Group-term life insurance

3. Life insurance financing in a nonqualified deferred compensation plan

4. Split-dollar life insurance

Figure 14.2

P.S. 58 COMPUTATION
(INSERT CO'S STANDARD INDIVIDUAL 1 YR TERM RATES AT B1 IF LOWER)
PART A

INPUT: EMPLOYEE'S AGE	45
INPUT: FACE AMOUNT OF DEATH BENEFIT	$100,000
INPUT: CASH VALUE TO EMPLOYER	-$40,000
NET AMOUNT AT RISK	$60,000
P.S. 58 CHARGE	$6.30
GROSS AMOUNT INCLUDIBLE	$378.00
INPUT: EMPLOYEE'S CONTRIBUTION	$.00

PART B

INPUT: AMOUNT OF DIVIDEND PAID IN CASH TO EMPLOYEE	$.00
INPUT: AMT OF DIV USED TO REDUCE EE'S PREM CONTRIBUTION	$.00
INPUT: AMOUNT OF DIVIDEND HELD AT INTEREST FOR EMPLOYEE	$.00
INPUT: AMOUNT OF DIVIDEND — IF CASH VALUE & DEATH BENEFIT OF PAID UP ADDITIONS ARE CONTROLLED BY EMPLOYEE	$.00
INPUT: AMOUNT OF DIVIDEND — IF DIVIDENDS WERE USED TO BUY ONE YEAR TERM INSURANCE FOR THE EMPLOYEE	$.00
INPUT: P.S. 58 COST OR, IF LOWER, PUBLISHED YEARLY RENEWABLE TERM COST — IF EMPLOYER GETS CASH VALUE OF PAID UP ADDITIONAL INSURANCE AND EMPLOYEE'S BENEFICIARY RECEIVES ANY BALANCE	$.00
REPORTABLE P.S. 58 COST	$378.00

QUESTIONS AND ANSWERS

Question — Can life insurance be used in a Keogh (HR 10) plan?

Answer — A Keogh plan is a qualified plan covering a proprietor or one or more partners of an unincorporated business. Life insurance can be used to provide a death benefit for regular employees covered under the plan, and the rules discussed in this chapter apply. Life insurance can also be provided under the plan for a proprietor or partners. However, slightly less favorable rules apply; these are discussed in detail in Chapter 12.

Question — Can life insurance be used in a Section 403(b) tax deferred annuity plan?

Answer — Life insurance can be provided as an incidental benefit under a tax deferred annuity plan. It is provided on much the same basis as in a qualified profit-sharing plan. Covered employees will have P.S. 58 costs to report as taxable income, as in a regular qualified plan.

Question — Can universal life insurance be used to provide an insured death benefit under a qualified plan?

Answer — Universal life and similar products may be used. However, even though universal life has an investment element like that in a whole life policy, the IRS has taken the view that the "incidental" limits applicable to universal life premiums are the same as those that apply to term insurance. So, if the percentage test is used, aggregate universal life premiums must be less than 25% of aggregate plan contributions. This appears to be an overly conservative rule, and may eventually be subject to a court challenge.

Question — Is it possible for an insured death benefit to be excluded from the decedent participant's estate for federal estate tax purposes?

Answer — Although there have not yet been any decisive court cases or IRS rulings on the issue, some planners believe that an insured death benefit in a qualified plan is governed by the estate tax rules relating to insurance policies (Code section 2042) and, therefore, can be kept out of a participant's estate by avoiding "incidents of ownership" in the policies.

For insurance in a qualified plan, this probably requires at least the following steps: (1) having life insurance policies owned by separate "subtrusts" under the plan; (2) appointing the subtrustee and successors (who should be independent parties such as a bank) irrevocably; (3) having all incidents of ownership exercised by the subtrustee, including owning the policy, receiving the proceeds, and selecting the beneficiary; and (4) designing plan provisions so that the participant has no lifetime right to receive policy cash values (policy cash values can be assigned to fund the required spousal survivor annuity).

Question — If a plan participant is uninsurable but already owns insurance policies, can these policies be sold to the plan to fund the plan death benefit?

Answer — Yes. Although the sale of property from a participant to a qualified plan would ordinarily be a prohibited transaction, the Department of Labor has issued an exemption that allows such sales for this purpose.[17] The opportunity to sell personally owned insurance to the plan must be offered to all participants on a nondiscriminatory basis in order to use this exemption.

Question — How can insurance coverage be continued by a qualified plan after a plan participant has retired or accrued the maximum benefit under the plan?

Answer — If a plan participant's full retirement benefit has accrued, the employer can no longer make deductible contributions to the plan. Several alternatives are available for continuing insurance coverage: (1) the policy can be put on a reduced, paid-up basis; (2) the policy can be sold to the participant for its cash surrender value (possibly financed using a policy loan); (3) the participant can continue to pay premiums (they are nondeductible); or (4) the plan trustee can continue to pay premiums out of fund earnings (P.S. 58 costs to the participant continue under this alternative).

Question — What types of employer should consider using fully insured plans?

Answer — Fully insured plans should be considered if contributions to an employer's existing, conventionally funded defined benefit plan have been severely reduced by the current actuarial restrictions or the full funding limitation. Also, consider fully insured plans for an employer that wants to maximize its initial rate of contribution to a new defined benefit plan, because of particularly good current financial condition or because substantial early funding is preferable for any reason, including maximum current tax sheltering.

One caution: if any of the conditions under Section 412(i) that are listed above is not met for a plan year, the plan ceases to be a fully insured plan and must meet the minimum funding requirements for that year. In particular, a failure to make a regular premium payment will terminate fully insured status. Therefore, a fully insured plan is not appropriate for an employer if there is any doubt about its financial ability to make regular premium payments now and in the foreseeable future. A stable business, rather than a boom and bust enterprise, is the best prospect for fully insured funding.

Question — What are the considerations in determining whether fully insured funding is advisable from an economic, investment point of view?

Answer — Employers are likely to wonder if the accelerated tax deduction permitted under fully insured plans is outweighed by an increased overall cost for the plan over the years in which it is in effect. This is not an easy question to answer. In theory, the excess earnings credited to the employer under the contract could provide as good a return on investment as the employer might obtain in a trusteed plan. However, there is no reliable method to predict future earnings, either under the contract or in a trust. Selling a fully insured plan requires "selling the company" so that the employer has confidence that the rate of return will be reasonable. The guarantee features of the contract must be paid for, which implies a lower rate of return in the contract. However, these features are valuable to the employer, since they reduce the downside risk of large losses. Lower administrative costs for fully insured plans must also be factored into the analysis.

Question — Can a participant in a qualified plan have the plan purchase life insurance on the life of another person—a spouse or a business partner, for example?

Answer — Yes; some of the applications of this technique are (1) the purchase of life insurance on a co-shareholder to help fund a buy-sell agreement; or (2) to provide for a beneficiary and avoid estate taxes on the death of the employee-participant.

These "third-party" insurance techniques are primarily used in qualified profit-sharing or stock bonus plans because of the need for an "earmarked" or "directed investment" account, as well as rulings prohibiting pen-sion plans from providing third-party insurance.[18] They are discussed further in Chapter 10 and Chapter 17.

A profit-sharing plan can also hold "second-to-die" life insurance on the lives of the participant and his or her spouse. This technique is also discussed in the questions and answers in Chapter 17.

Question — Can a qualified plan trustee borrow against the cash value of life insurance policies held in the plan?

Answer — Yes, but borrowing by the plan creates "unrelated business taxable income" from any reinvestment of the loan proceeds. For example, if the loan proceeds are reinvested in certificates of deposit, the plan must pay tax on interest income from those certificates.[19]

FOOTNOTES

1. See e.g., Rev. Rul. 68-453, 1968-2 CB 163; Rev. Rul. 74-307, 1974-2 CB 126.
2. IRC Section 412(h). In addition, note Code section 6662(f) imposes a *penalty* for the substantial overstatement of pension liabilities.
3. IRS Notice 93-10, 1993-5 IRB 13.
4. IRC Sections 412(h), 412(i).
5. Regs. §§1.412(i)-1(b), 1.412(i)-1(c).
6. Reg. §1.412(i)-1(b)(2)(ii).
7. Prop. Reg. §1.401(a)(4)-3(b).
8. Labor Reg. §2520.104-44; Instructions for Schedule B (Form 5500).
9. IRC Section 412(c)(10).
10. See Rev. Rul. 81-196, 1981-2 CB 107, which allowed an existing split-funded plan to be converted into a fully insured plan.
11. See e.g., Rev. Rul. 61-164, 1961-2 CB 99; Rev. Rul. 66-143, 1966-1 CB 79.
12. IRC Section 72(m)(3); Reg. §1.72-16(b).
13. Reg. §1.72-16(c)(4).
14. Ibid; see also, Let. Rul. 8539066.
15. IRC Section 72(m)(3); Reg. §1.72-16(c).
16. IRC Section 4980A(d)(4); Temp. Reg. §54.4981A-1T, c-8.
17. PTE 92-6, 57 FR 5189, revising and extending prior PTE 77-8, 1977-2 CB 425, to include self-employed persons and shareholder-employees in S corporations.
18. Rev. Rul. 69-523, 1969-2 CB 90.
19. TAM 8445006, citing *Dean v. Simpson*, 35 TC 1038 (1961).

Chapter 15

MONEY PURCHASE PENSION PLAN

WHAT IS IT?

A money purchase plan is a qualified employer retirement plan that is, in many ways, the simplest of all qualified plans:

- Each employee has an individual account in the plan. The employer makes annual contributions to each employee's account under a nondiscriminatory contribution formula. Usually the formula requires a contribution of a specified percentage (up to 25%) of each employee's annual compensation. Annual employer contributions to the employee's account generally cannot be more than $30,000 (see below).

- Plan benefits consist of the amount accumulated in each participant's account at retirement or termination of employment. This is the total of employer contributions, interest or other investment return on plan assets, and capital gains realized by the plan on sales of assets in the employee's account.

- The plan may provide that the employee's account balance is payable in one or more forms of annuities equivalent in value to the account balance.

WHEN IS IT INDICATED?

1. When an employer wants to install a qualified retirement plan that is simple to administer and explain to employees.

2. When employees are relatively young and have substantial time to accumulate retirement savings.

3. When employees are willing to accept a degree of investment risk in their plan accounts, in return for the potential benefits of good investment results.

4. When some degree of retirement income security in the plan is desired. (While accounts are not guaranteed, annual employer contributions are required. This provides a degree of retirement security that is intermediate between a defined benefit plan and a profit-sharing plan.)

5. When an employer seeks to reward long-term employee relationships.

ADVANTAGES

1. As with all qualified plans, a money purchase plan provides a tax-deferred retirement savings medium for employees.

2. The plan is relatively simple and inexpensive to design, administer, and explain to employees.

3. The plan formula can provide a deductible annual employer contribution of up to 25% of each employee's compensation, as compared with the 15% of payroll limit on deductible contributions to profit-sharing plans.[1]

4. Plan distributions may be eligible for the special 5-year (or 10-year) averaging tax computation available for qualified plans.

5. Individual participant accounts allow participants to benefit from good investment results in the plan fund.

DISADVANTAGES

1. Retirement benefits may be inadequate for employees who enter the plan at older ages. For example, if an employer contributes 10% of compensation annually to each employee's account, the accumulation at age 65 for employees with varying entry ages will be as follows, assuming the plan fund earns 9% interest on the average (a very good return by current standards):

Age at plan entry	Annual compensation	Account balance at age 65
25	$35,000	$1,289,022
30	35,000	822,937
40	35,000	323,134
50	35,000	112,012
55	35,000	57,961
60	35,000	22,832

This illustration shows that the "time factor" works rapidly to increase account balances. If a closely held corporation that has been in business for many years adopts a money purchase plan, key employees often will be among the older plan entrants. The money purchase plan's failure to provide adequately for such employees, even with their high compensation levels, can be a serious disadvantage.

However, this is not the whole story—there's another factor in realistic situations that reduces the apparent disparity between long-service and short-service employees. Because salaries increase over time, the long service/short service disparity in the annual pension from a money-purchase plan—as a percentage of final average compensation—is much less than if you assume salaries do not increase. Figure 15.1 shows that, if all salaries increase at 7% annually, a 15-year employee receives a pension of 19% of final average salary while the 35-year employee gets 48% of final average salary. This is much less than the disparity resulting if salaries increase at only 3% annually, or do not increase at all. In short, in actual practice a money purchase plan may not be as disadvantageous to shorter service employees as might appear.

2. The annual addition to each employee's account in a money purchase plan is limited to the lesser of (a) 25% of compensation or (b) the greater of $30,000 or ¼ of the defined benefit dollar limitation.[2] (The dollar limitation for defined benefit plans is $115,641 for 1993.) This limits the relative amount of funding available for highly compensated employees. For example, if an employee earns $200,000, no more than $30,000 annually can be contributed for that employee; but that $30,000 is only 15% of the employee's compensation. So for this employee, the money purchase plan offers no advantage over a profit-sharing plan.

3. Employees bear investment risk under the plan. The ultimate amount that can be accumulated under a money purchase plan is very sensitive to investment return, even for an employee who entered the plan at an early age. Figure 15.2 shows this by comparing the ultimate account balance resulting from $1,000 of annual contribution at two different return rates.

Figure 15.1

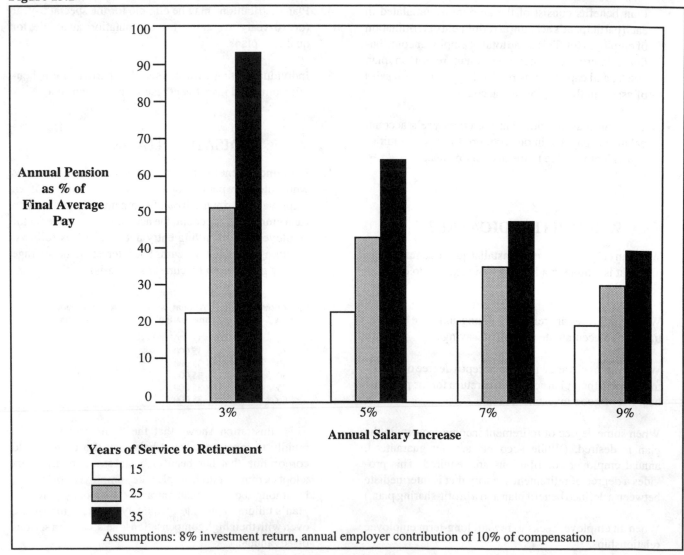

Annual Pension as % of Final Average Pay

Annual Salary Increase

Years of Service to Retirement
- 15
- 25
- 35

Assumptions: 8% investment return, annual employer contribution of 10% of compensation.

Figure 15.2

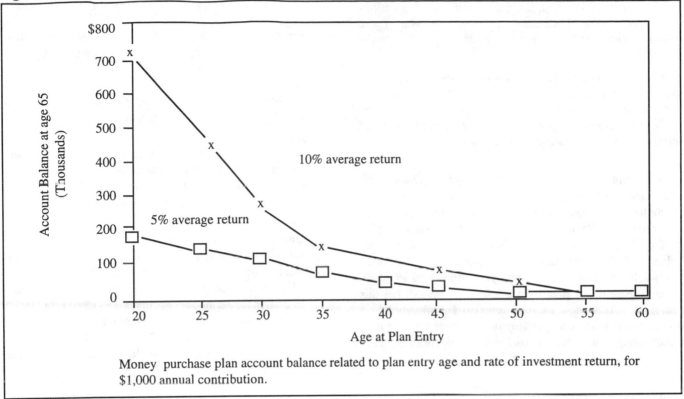

Money purchase plan account balance related to plan entry age and rate of investment return, for $1,000 annual contribution.

While bearing investment risk is a potential disadvantage to employees, it does tend to reduce employer costs as compared with a defined benefit plan.

4. The plan is subject to the Code's minimum funding requirements. Employers are obligated to make the plan contribution each year or be subject to minimum funding penalties.

DESIGN FEATURES

Most money purchase plans use a benefit formula requiring an employer contribution that is a flat percentage of each employee's compensation. Percentages up to 25 percent may be used. Only the first $200,000 (as indexed, $235,840 in 1993) of each employee's compensation can be taken into account in the plan formula.

Some money purchase formulas also use a factor related to the employee's service. Service-related factors generally favor owners and key employees. In small, closely held businesses or professional corporations, the use of a service-related factor might result in prohibited discrimination in favor of highly compensated employees. Plan designers generally avoid service-related contribution formulas in these situations.

Proposed nondiscrimination regulations under Code section 401(a)(4) provide safe harbors for money purchase plans with uniform allocation formulas; alternative methods for satisfying nondiscrimination requirements include satisfying a general nondiscrimination test, restructuring or cross-testing (testing defined contribution plans on the basis of benefits).[3]

A plan benefit formula can be "integrated" with Social Security (also referred to as "permitted disparity"). This avoids duplicating Social Security benefits already provided to the employee and reduces employer costs for the plan. An integrated formula defines a level of compensation known as the "integration level." The plan then provides a higher rate of employer contributions for compensation above that integration level than the rate for compensation below that integration level.

Example: A money purchase plan specifies an integration level of $20,000 and provides for employer contributions of 14% of compensation above the $20,000 integration level and 10% below the $20,000 integration level. Employee Art Rambo earns $30,000 this year. The employer contribution to Art's account this year totals $3,400—14% of $10,000 (Art's compensation in excess of the $20,000 integration level) plus 10% of the first $20,000 of Art's compensation.

The Internal Revenue Code and proposed regulations specify the degree of integration permitted in a plan. These rules are discussed further in Chapter 23.

Any of the Code's permitted vesting provisions can be used in a money purchase plan. Since money purchase plans tend to be oriented toward longer service employees, the five year "cliff vesting" provision (that is, no vesting until 5 years of service, then 100% vesting) is often used.

If an employee leaves before becoming fully vested in his or her account balance, an unvested amount referred to as a "forfeiture" is left behind in the plan. Forfeitures can be used either to reduce future employer contributions under the plan or they can be added to remaining participants' account balances. Adding forfeitures to participants' account balances tends to be favorable to key employees, since they are likely to participate in the plan over a long time period. For this reason, the IRS requires forfeitures to be allocated in a nondiscriminatory manner. This usually requires forfeiture allocation in proportion to participants' compensation, rather than in proportion to their existing account balances.

Benefits in a money purchase plan are usually payable at termination of employment or at the plan's stated normal retirement age. Money purchase plans traditionally provide that the participant's account balance is converted to an equivalent annuity at retirement, based on annuity rates provided in the plan. This is the origin of the term "money purchase." It is becoming more common to provide for a lump sum or installment payment from the plan as an alternative to an annuity. However, a money purchase plan, as a condition of qualification, must provide a joint and survivor annuity as the automatic form of benefit. The participant, with the consent of the spouse, may elect a different benefit option. This is discussed further in Chapter 24.

The IRS generally does not allow money purchase plans to provide for "in-service distributions"—that is, benefits payable before termination of employment. Distributions of employer contributions or earnings from pension plans are not permitted prior to death, retirement, disability, severance of employment or termination of the plan.[4] However, plan loan provisions are allowable, although relatively uncommon.

Money purchase plan funds are generally invested in a pooled account managed (through a trustee or insurance company) by the employer or a fund manager designated by the employer. Either a trust fund or group or individual insurance contracts can be used. Chapter 14 discusses how life insurance can be used in the plan.

TAX IMPLICATIONS

1. Employer contributions to the plan are deductible when made, so long as the plan remains "qualified."[5] A plan is qualified if it meets eligibility, vesting, funding and other requirements discussed in Chapter 23. In addition, the plan must designate that it is a money purchase pension plan.[6]

2. Assuming the plan remains qualified, taxation of the employee on plan contributions is deferred. Both employer contributions and earnings on plan assets are nontaxable to plan participants until withdrawn.[7]

3. Under Code section 415, annual additions to each participant's account are limited to the lesser of (a) 25% of the participant's compensation or (b) the greater of $30,000 or ¼ of the defined benefit limit. (The dollar limitation for defined benefit plans is $115,641 for 1993.) Annual additions include (1) employer contributions to the participant's account; (2) forfeitures from other participants' accounts; and (3) employee contributions to the account.

4. Distributions from the plan must follow the rules for qualified plan distributions. Certain premature or excessive distributions are subject to penalties. The distribution rules are discussed in Chapter 24.

5. Lump sum distributions made after age 59½ are subject to a limited election to use a special 5-year averaging tax calculation. Certain older participants may also be eligible for a 10-year averaging tax calculation for lump sum distributions. Not all distributions are eligible for these special tax calculations. Chapter 24 covers these rules, including IRS forms.

6. The plan is subject to the minimum funding rules of section 412 of the Code.[8] This requires minimum annual contributions, subject to a penalty imposed on the employer if less than the minimum amount is contributed.[9] For a money purchase plan, the minimum contribution is generally the amount required under the plan's contribution formula. For example, if the plan formula requires a contribution of 20% of each participant's compensation, this is generally the amount required to meet the minimum funding rules. Chapter 23 discusses these rules further.

7. The plan is subject to the ERISA reporting and disclosure rules outlined in Appendix D.

ALTERNATIVES

1. Target benefit plans are much like money purchase plans, but the employer contribution percentage can be based on age at plan entry—higher for older entrants. Such a plan may be more favorable where the employer wants to provide adequate benefits for older employees.

2. Profit-sharing plans provide more employer flexibility in contributions, but deductible contributions are limited to 15% of payroll.

3. Defined benefit plans provide more security of retirement benefits and proportionately greater contributions for older plan entrants, but are much more complex to design and administer.

4. Nonqualified deferred compensation plans can be provided exclusively for selected executives, but the employer's tax deduction is generally deferred until benefit payments are made. This can be as much as 20 or 30 years after the employer's contribution is made.

5. Individual retirement saving is available as an alternative or supplement to an employer plan, but except for an IRA there is no tax deferral.

See also the discussion in Chapter 2, "Designing the Right Pension Plan."

HOW TO INSTALL A PLAN

Installation of a money purchase plan follows the qualified plan installation procedure described in Chapter 25.

WHERE CAN I FIND OUT MORE ABOUT IT?

1. McFadden, John J., *Retirement Plans for Employees*, Homewood, IL: Richard D. Irwin, 1988.

2. Gee, Judith Boyers, *Pensions in Perspective*, 4th ed. Cincinnati, OH: The National Underwriter Co., Fall 1993.

3. Graduate Course: Advanced Pension and Retirement Planning I (GS 814), The American College, Bryn Mawr, PA.

QUESTIONS AND ANSWERS

Question — Can a self-employed person adopt a money purchase plan?

Answer — A self-employed person can adopt a money purchase plan covering not only his or her regular employees, if any, but also covering the self-employed person(s). Such plans are sometimes referred to as "Keogh" or "HR 10" plans. The self-employed person is treated much the same as the regular employees covered, but there are some special rules and planning considerations that are covered in Chapter 12 of this book.

Question — What special issues are involved in money purchase plans covering shareholder-employees in an S corporation?

Answer—S corporations can have money purchase plans that cover shareholder-employees as well as regular employees. However, the plan contribution formula generally cannot provide an employer contribution for all of the shareholder-employee's income from the corporation. The employer contribution formula can be based only on the shareholder's compensation for services rendered to the corporation. Any portion of the shareholder's income that represents dividends must be excluded from the plan formula.

A shareholder-employee who holds more than 5 percent of the S corporation's stock is subject to the same restriction on plan loans that applies to an owner-employee of an unincorporated business; this is discussed in Chapter 12 of this book.

Question — Can an employer fund a money purchase plan using employee salary reductions?

Answer — Salary reductions by employees allowing employee contributions on a before-tax basis are allowed only in (1) a profit-sharing (Section 401(k) type) plan, (2) a salary reduction SEP (simplified employee pension) or (3) a Section 403(b) tax deferred annuity plan (tax-exempt employers only). Thus, this kind of funding for a money purchase plan is not available except for a plan "grandfathered" under pre-1974 law.

However, money purchase plans can allow after-tax contributions by employees to increase account balances (permitting greater tax-sheltered investment accumulation) and ultimate retirement benefits. Such after-tax contribution provisions must meet the administratively complex nondiscrimination rules of Code section 401(m). (These are discussed in Chapter 18.) As a result of these rules, after-tax contribution provisions in money purchase plans are less common than in the past.

FOOTNOTES

1. But the employer's deduction to a money purchase pension plan cannot exceed the 415 limits for a defined contribution plan. IRC Section 404(j)(1).

2. IRC Section 415(c).
3. See Prop. Reg. §1.401(a)(4)-2.
4. See Rev. Rul. 69-277, 1969-1 CB 116; Rev. Rul. 74-417, 1974-2 CB 131.
5. IRC Section 404(a).
6. IRC Section 401(a)(27)(B).
7. IRC Section 402(a).
8. IRC Secs. 412(a), 412(h).
9. IRC Section 4971.

Chapter 16

NONQUALIFIED DEFERRED COMPENSATION

WHAT IS IT?

A nonqualified deferred compensation plan is any employer retirement, savings, or deferred compensation plan for employees that does not meet the tax and labor law (ERISA) requirements applicable to qualified pension and profit-sharing plans.

Nonqualified plans are usually used to provide retirement benefits to a select group of executives or to provide such a select group with supplemental benefits beyond those provided in the company's qualified retirement plans.

Nonqualified plans do not provide the same type of tax benefit as qualified plans because in the nonqualified plan the employer's income tax deduction generally cannot be taken "up front." The employer must wait until the year in which the employee reports income from the deferred compensation plan to take its deduction. However, a nonqualified plan can provide tax deferral for the employee, as well as meet employer and employee compensation and financial planning objectives. Informal financing of the plan through life insurance or some other type of employer-held asset reserve can increase the security of the plan to the employee almost to the level of a qualified plan.

WHEN IS IT INDICATED?

1. When an employer wants to provide a deferred compensation benefit to an executive or group of executives but the cost of a qualified plan would be prohibitive because of the large number of non-executive employees who would have to be covered. A nonqualified plan is ideal for many companies that do not have or cannot afford qualified plans but want to provide key employees with retirement income.

2. When an employer wants to provide additional deferred compensation benefits to an executive who is already receiving the maximum benefits or contributions under the company's qualified retirement plan.

3. When the business wants to provide certain key employees with tax deferred compensation under terms or conditions different from those applicable to other employees.

4. When an executive or key employee wants to use the employer to, in essence, create a forced, automatic, and relatively painless investment program that uses the employer's tax savings to "leverage" the future benefits. Since amounts paid by the employer in the future will be tax deductible, the after-tax cost of the deferred compensation will be favorable. For example, if the employer is in a combined federal and state tax bracket of 40 percent, it can pay $50,000 to a retired executive at a net after-tax cost of only $30,000, because its tax deduction saves it $20,000 (40% of $50,000).

5. When an employer needs to solve the "4R" (recruit, retain, reward, or retire) problem. These plans are a fundamental tool in designing executive compensation plans to meet these issues.

6. When a closely-held corporation wants something to attract and hold nonshareholder employees. For such employees, an attractive deferred compensation package can be a substitute for the equity-based compensation packages—company stock and stock options—that these employees would expect to receive if they were employed by a publicly-held company.

ADVANTAGES

1. The design of nonqualified plans is much more flexible than that of qualified plans. A nonqualified plan

   - allows coverage of any group of employees or even a single employee, without any nondiscrimination requirements;

   - can provide an unlimited benefit to any one employee (subject to the "reasonable compensation" requirement for deductibility);

   - allows the employer to provide different benefit amounts for different employees, on different terms and conditions.

2. A nonqualified plan involves minimal IRS, ERISA, and other governmental regulatory requirements, such as reporting and disclosure, fiduciary, and funding requirements.

3. A nonqualified plan can provide deferral of taxes to employees (but the employer's deduction is also deferred). The advantage of deferral as such is currently being debated since current income tax rates are relatively low and there is some expectation of higher rates in the future. However, if dollars otherwise paid currently in taxes can be put to work over the period of deferral, planners can show advantages in nonqualified plans even if future tax rates are higher.

4. A nonqualified plan can be used by an employer as a form of "golden handcuffs" that help to bind the employee to the company. Since the qualified plan vesting rules do not apply if the plan is properly designed (as discussed below), the plan can provide forfeiture of benefits according to almost any vesting schedule the employer desires and for almost any contingency such as terminating employment before retirement or misconduct such as going to work for a competitor.

5. Although the plan generally involves only the employer's unsecured promise to pay benefits, security to the executive can be provided through informal financing arrangements such as corporate-owned life insurance or a "rabbi trust" (defined below).

6. Assets set aside in some types of informal financing arrangements are available to use for corporate purposes at all times.

DISADVANTAGES

1. The company's tax deduction is generally not available for the year in which compensation is earned; it must be deferred until the year in which income is taxable to the employee. This can be a substantial period of time—ten, twenty or even thirty or more years in the future.

2. From the executive's point of view, the principal problem is lack of security as a result of depending only on the company's unsecured promise to pay. In addition, most of the protections of federal tax and labor law (ERISA) that apply to qualified plans— for example the vesting, fiduciary, and funding requirements—are not applicable to the typical nonqualified plan.

3. While accounting treatment is not entirely clear (see Appendix E, below), some disclosure of executive nonqualified plans on financial statements may be required. This would reduce the confidentiality of the arrangement, which could be considered undesirable by both employer and employee.

4. Not all employers are equally suited to take advantage of nonqualified plans.

- Because of their pass through tax structure, S corporations and partnerships cannot take full advantage of nonqualified plans.

- The employer must be one that is likely to last long enough to make the payments promised under the plan. Although funds can be set aside to secure payment even if the employer disappears, the full tax benefits of the plan cannot be provided unless the employer exists at the time of payment so it can take its tax deduction. Many closely-held businesses, family businesses, and professional corporations do not meet this criterion.

- Special problems exist when nonprofit corporations or governmental organizations enter into nonqualified plans. See Chapter 11.

OBJECTIVES IN PLAN DESIGN

Through its considerable flexibility, a nonqualified deferred compensation plan can help both the employer and the employee achieve their planning objectives. The plan should be designed to achieve these objectives to the maximum extent possible. Figure 16.1 provides a design worksheet that can be used to illustrate the design process.

Employer Objectives

Employers usually adopt nonqualified deferred compensation plans to provide an incentive to hire key employees, to keep key employees, and to provide performance incentives—in other words, the typical employer compensation policy objectives that apply to other forms of compensation planning.

Plans reflecting employer objectives will typically consider the following types of design:

- Eligibility will be confined to key executives or technical employees that the employer wants to recruit and keep.

- Plan eligibility can be part of a predetermined company policy or the plan can simply be adopted for specific individuals as the need arises.

- Performance incentive features will be included. The features may include benefits or contributions based on salary, increases if specific profits or sales goals are achieved, or benefits related to the value of the employer's stock.

- Termination of employment will typically cause loss or forfeiture of benefits, particularly for terminations resulting in undesirable conduct such as competing with the employer.

- The plan often will not provide immediate vesting of benefits, but vesting will occur over a period of time to help retain employees.

- It is generally not in the employer's interest to fund the plan in advance or set aside funds for the plan prior to the commencement of benefit payments.

Employee Objectives

An employee's personal financial planning objective is primarily to obtain additional forms of compensation for which income tax is deferred as long as possible, preferably until the money is actually received. Usually it is only highly compensated employees who wish to (or can afford to) defer compensation to a substantial extent, since only they have enough discretionary income to support substantial saving. From the employee's point of view, the tax deferral, and therefore the compounding of dollars that otherwise would be paid currently in taxes, is a major benefit of the plan. In addition, it is possible that plan benefits may be paid when the employee is in a lower marginal tax bracket. (However, due to frequent changes in the tax laws this factor is difficult to predict.)

An employee who has enough bargaining power to influence the design of a nonqualified deferred compensation plan will favor the following types of provisions:

- Benefit certainty is usually more important than incentive provisions; employees rarely seek contingent features unless the company is definitely growing and the employee wants a benefit based on company growth.

- Employees will want a benefit that is immediately 100 percent vested without forfeiture provisions for cause or otherwise.

- Concern for benefit security is significant and employees will want to explore some of the financing (informal funding) arrangements described later, such as corporate-owned life insurance, the rabbi trust, or a surety bond.

Types of Benefit and Contribution Formulas

Nonqualified deferred compensation plans generally use either a "*salary continuation*" or "*salary reduction*" approach.

- The salary continuation approach provides a specified deferred amount payable in the future without any stated reduction of current salary. The benefit is in the form of a continuation of salary at a specified level at retirement, disability, or other termination of employment.

- The salary reduction design provides for the deferral of a specified amount of the compensation of the employee otherwise payable. Salary reduction plans are sometimes simply called "deferred compensation," but this term will not be used here to avoid confusion. The employer contribution (or deemed contribution) to this type of plan can also be in the form of a "bonus" without actual reduction of salary.

Economically, both the salary continuation and the salary reduction approach amount to the same thing, but represent significantly different underlying compensation philosophies. Employer-instituted plans often use the salary continuation approach rather than salary reduction, but this is not universal.

A salary continuation plan generally uses a defined-benefit type of formula to calculate the benefit amount. The salary reduction approach typically resembles a defined-contribution plan, with individual "accounts" that usually have an investment element for each participant.

Salary Continuation (Defined Benefit) Formulas. The salary continuation or defined-benefit approach usually specifies plan benefits as a percentage of compensation. Compensation for this purpose is typically measured over a three to five year period of the employee's highest earnings, as in a qualified defined-benefit plan. The benefit payable can also be dependent on the employee's years of service.

The salary continuation benefit can be integrated with social security, usually using a 100 percent offset. For example, the nonqualified plan might provide an annual retirement benefit of 60 percent of the employee's final average (or highest three year average) compensation less the actual social security benefit paid to the employee. The complex social security integration rules applicable to qualified plans do not apply so any suitable type of integration formula can be used. An offset for other types of benefits can also be used in the formula; for example, the nonqualified salary continuation payments could be offset by any other retirement or disability payable to the employee under qualified or other plans.

Two common types of salary continuation plan formulas are the "supplemental executive retirement plan" (SERP) and the "excess benefit plan."

A SERP is a plan similar to a qualified defined benefit plan in that it focuses on providing adequate retirement income to executives. Benefit formulas and other provisions are similar to those for qualified defined benefit plans. The term SERP is usually used to refer to a plan covering a relatively broad group of executives. A company may also refer to its entire collection of special retirement benefits for executives as a "SERP."

An excess benefit plan is one that makes up the qualified plan benefits lost by highly compensated employees as the result of Code section 415's benefit limitations. Section 415 limits an employee's annual pension to no more than $90,000, as indexed ($115,641 in 1993).

For example, suppose Blarp Corporation provides a qualified defined benefit plan with an annual retirement benefit equal to 60% of final average compensation. Executive Frank Blarp retires in 1993 with final three year average compensation of $230,000. The qualified plan benefit can provide him with a pension of only $115,641 (about ½ of his preretirement income) because of the Section 415 limit, even though the 60% benefit formula applied to other employees provides an annual pension equal to almost ⅔ of their preretirement income. If Blarp Corporation has a nonqualified excess benefit plan, the excess benefit plan can "make up the difference" by providing additional retirement benefits so that Frank receives a full $138,000 annually.

Salary Reduction (Defined Contribution) Formula. With a defined contribution approach, a specified amount (the salary reduction or employer "bonus") is periodically added to a participant's "account," which can be either a real accumulation of funds or simply a bookkeeping account. The benefit payable at retirement or termination of service represents the accumulation in the participant's account. This is similar to the money purchase approach for qualified plans. Nonqualified plans of this type are sometimes referred to as money purchase plans.

Contributions typically are a specified percentage of the employee's current compensation each year. However, the contribution level can also be an amount determined as the annual funding required to meet a "target" benefit level at retirement. (Chapter 21 discusses the "target" type of benefit formula.)

If the employee's account is only a bookkeeping account, the employer can guarantee a specified minimum interest rate on the account in order for the employee to avoid losing the benefit of investment earnings on the deferred compensation. Alternatively, the employer can make an annual allocation to the account based on an interest formula or index specified in the plan (usually an index beyond the employer's control such as Moody's Bond Index). Sometimes the rate of return that is guaranteed is tied to the value of the company's stock.

Form of Benefits. Nonqualified deferred compensation plans usually provide payments at retirement in a lump sum or a series of annual payments. Life annuities or joint and survivor annuities for the participant and spouse can also be provided. Since the elaborate restrictions on qualified plan payouts do not apply, considerable design flexibility is available.

Payout options must avoid the triggering of the constructive receipt doctrine—that is, the taxation of benefits before they are actually received by the employee. Constructive receipt problems are discussed further in "Tax Implications," below.

Termination of Employment

If the plan emphasizes employer objectives, termination provisions will be designed to maximize incentive features and noncompetition and similar provisions. At the extreme, an employer-instituted plan may even provide a complete forfeiture of nonqualified benefits if the employee terminates employment before retirement. Most employer-instituted plans will at least have a vesting schedule under which benefits do not become vested until a specified number of years of service has been attained. Graduated vesting can also be used. As discussed below, if the plan is unfunded the ERISA vesting provisions generally do not apply and any type of vesting schedule generally can be used.

If an executive's termination of employment results from disability, special benefits may be provided, particularly if the employee has some bargaining power in designing the plan. An employee will generally want benefits paid immediately upon disability. For this purpose, the employee will also want to use a definition of disability that is somewhat less than the "total and permanent" disability required for social security disability benefits. A typical disability provision based on employee objectives would provide for disability payments if the employee is no longer able to continue working in his specific profession or executive position. Disability determinations can be shifted to a third party such as an insurer, or a physician chosen by the employer and employee, in order to minimize possible disputes.

Figure 16.1
(pg. 1)

NONQUALIFIED DEFERRED COMPENSATION

Design Worksheet

A. EMPLOYER AND EMPLOYEE DATA

Employer _____

Employer's address _____

_____

_____ Zip _____

Telephone No. (   ) _____

Employer I.D. No. _____

S corporation election? Yes _____ No _____

Date of S election _____

Accounting year _____

Company contact (name and title) _____

Telephone No. (   ) _____

Employee _____

Title _____

Employee address _____

_____ Zip _____

Telephone No. (   ) _____

Social Security No. _____

Percent ownership of employer _____

Effective date of deferred compensation arrangement _____

B. PLAN FORMULA

Formula type (check)

_____ Salary reduction

_____ Salary continuation

_____ Other

Figure 16.1
(pg. 2)

Salary reduction formula (if applicable)

    Reduction amount   _____

    Per (month, year, other)   _____

    Date of initial election   _____

    Annual election date thereafter   _____

    Other election date (specify)   _____

    Company contribution, if any   _____

    Conditions on company contribution   _____

    Company guarantee of interest on account balance (check one)

    _____fixed rate of _____ percent

    _____rate based on

    _____ adjusted (how often)_____

Salary continuation formula (if applicable)

    Benefits payable at (check)

    _____age 65

    _____other specified age _____

    Benefit formula

    _____ percent of compensation monthly

    (times years of service)(up to _____ years)

    Compensation means

    _____Annual compensation over highest _____ years

    _____Other (specify)_____

    _____

    Offset for other benefits

    _____ percent of social security benefits actually received

    _____ percent of qualified retirement plan benefits

    Other (describe — e.g., workers compensation, disability)

    _____

    _____

Benefit payable at termination of employment prior to retirement

    _____ No benefit

    _____ Account balance

    _____ Vested accrued benefit determined as follows _____

    _____

    _____

Figure 16.1
(pg. 3)

C.   VESTING

Vesting Schedule

_____Immediate 100 percent vesting

_____Graduated schedule (specify) _____

_____

Forfeiture provisions

_____None

_____Forfeiture for _____

_____

D.   DISABILITY BENEFIT

_____Disability treated like other termination of employment

or

_____Special disability provisions

_____ Full Vesting

_____ Special benefit computation (specify) _____

_____

_____ Service continues to accrue for purposes of this plan

Definition of disability _____

_____

E.   BENEFIT PAYMENT

Options

_____Lump sum (actuarially equivalent to _____)

_____Periodic payment options (specify) _____

_____

Optional forms must be elected before _____

_____

After benefits commence, payment option (cannot be changed) (can be changed or modified) (annually)

(other _____) by election prior to _____

After benefits commence, future benefits are forfeited if _____

_____

Figure 16.1
(pg. 4)

F.   DEATH BENEFITS

_____Benefits forfeited at death

_____Death benefit payable to named beneficiary or estate if no named beneficiary

_____Other _____

_____

Amount of Benefit

_____Amount that would have been paid to employee at termination of employment

_____Face amount of insurance contracts (describe contracts) _____

_____

_____Other _____

_____

_____

Payment Form

_____Lump sum only

_____Beneficiary has same options employee would have had if terminated employment on date of death.

Describe how beneficiary makes elections _____

_____

_____Other _____

_____

G.   FINANCING

_____Formal funding (specify) _____

_____

_____Informal financing

_____ Insurance contracts (specify) _____

_____

_____ Rabbi trust (describe) _____

_____

_____ Third party guarantees, surety bonds, etc.

(describe) _____

_____

_____

_____ No financing arrangement

Funded versus Unfunded Plans

In the employee benefit area, the term *funded plan* has a very specialized meaning. In the tax and ERISA sense, a plan is formally funded if the employer has set aside money or property to the employee's account in an irrevocable trust, or through some other means that restricts access to the fund by the employer and the employer's creditors.

Assets to informally fund or "finance" the employer's obligation under a nonqualified plan can (and almost always should) be set aside, but if this fund is accessible to the employer and its creditors, providing no explicit security to the employee ahead of other employer creditors, the plan is deemed to be unfunded for tax and ERISA purposes.

Most nonqualified deferred compensation plans are unfunded because of significant tax and ERISA considerations:

- In a funded plan, amounts in the fund are taxable to the employee at the time the employee's rights to the fund become "substantially vested."[1] As discussed in Chapter 46, under the rules of Code section 83 substantial vesting can occur before funds are actually received by the employee.

- Funded plans are generally subject to the ERISA vesting and fiduciary requirements, which create design inflexibility.[2] Under the ERISA vesting rules, the plan must have a vesting schedule that is at least as fast as either the five year schedule (no vesting up to five years of service, 100 percent vesting after five years) or the three to seven year schedule:

Years of Service	Vested Percentage
3	20%
4	40%
5	60%
6	80%
7 or more	100%

The vesting and fiduciary rules for funded nonqualified plans are the same as those for qualified plans, as discussed in Chapter 23.

Financing Approaches

Since almost all nonqualified deferred compensation plans are unfunded in the formal sense, employees initiating deferred compensation arrangements are likely to seek ways to increase benefit security. The following approaches are commonly used:

- *Reserve account maintained by employer.* The employer maintains an actual account invested in securi-

ties of various types. There is no trust. Funds are fully accessible to the employer and its creditors. The plan is considered unfunded for tax and ERISA purposes.

- *Employer reserve account with employee investment direction.* With this variation, the employee obtains greater security by having the right to "direct" (select) investments in the account. This right must be limited to a choice of broad types of investment (equity, bonds, family of mutual funds, etc.); the ability to choose specific investments may lead to constructive receipt by the employee.[3]

- *Corporate-owned life insurance.* Life insurance policies on the employee's life, owned by and payable to the employer corporation, can provide financing for the employer's obligation under nonqualified deferred compensation plans. With life insurance financing, the plan can provide a substantial death benefit even in the early years of the plan. This is of significant value to younger employees.

- *Rabbi trust.* A rabbi trust is a trust set up to hold property used for financing a deferred compensation plan, where the funds set aside are subject to the employer's creditors. The IRS has ruled that trusts designed this way do not constitute formal funding in the tax sense. These trusts are referred to as rabbi trusts because an early IRS letter ruling involved an arrangement between a rabbi and the employing congregation. The design of rabbi trusts is discussed in the "Questions and Answers," below.

- *Third-party guarantees.* In these arrangements, the employer obtains a guarantee from a third party to pay the employee if the employer defaults. The guarantor may be a shareholder, a related corporation, or a "letter of credit" from a bank. Employer involvement raises the possibility that the guarantee will cause the plan to be deemed formally funded for tax purposes. However, it appears that if the employee, independently of the employer, obtains a third-party guarantee, the IRS will not necessarily view the plan as formally funded.[4]

TAX IMPLICATIONS

Constructive Receipt

Under the constructive receipt doctrine (Code section 451), an amount is treated as received for income tax purposes, even if it is not actually received, if it is "credited to the employee's account, set aside, or otherwise made available."

Constructive receipt does not occur if the employee's control over the receipt is subject to a "substantial limitation or restriction." A requirement of a passage of time until money can be received by the employee is usually considered a substantial limitation or restriction.[5] In a typical deferred compensation plan, for example, if the plan provides that an amount is not payable for five years or not payable until the employee terminates employment or retires, it will not be constructively received before that time.

If a nonqualified plan uses salary reductions to fund the plan, the employee's election to reduce salary generally must be made before rendering the services for which the compensation is paid. In order to defer compensation *after* services have already been performed, the IRS view is that the plan must have a substantial risk of forfeiture of the benefits.[6]

Plan distribution provisions must also be designed to avoid constructive receipt. For example, if the plan provides for distribution in ten equal annual installments, if the employee can elect at any time to accelerate payments, under the constructive receipt doctrine the employee would have to include in income each year any amount that the employee could have elected to receive. As another example, if the plan provides for a payout in ten annual installments with an election at any time to spread payments out further, the constructive receipt doctrine may require taxation under the original ten payment schedule, regardless of any election to further defer payments, unless the election to further defer also involved a substantial risk of forfeiture.[7] A typical forfeiture provision found in nonqualified plan distribution provisions of this type is a requirement that the employee be available for consulting and refrain from competing with the employer. As discussed in Chapter 46 the question of whether this constitutes a substantial risk of forfeiture depends on the specific facts and circumstances of the situation.

Economic Benefit

A compensation arrangement that provides a current "economic benefit" to an employee can result in current taxation to the employee even though the employee has no current right to receive cash or property. For example, suppose that an employee is covered under a funded nonqualified deferred compensation plan that has an irrevocable trust for the benefit of the employee. Under the economic benefit doctrine, the employee will be taxed as soon as the employee is vested in contributions made to the fund, even though the employee does not at that time have a right to withdraw cash.[8] This factor makes funded plans extremely unattractive.

The economic benefit doctrine does not generally affect unfunded plans, and as discussed earlier, almost all nonqualified deferred compensation plans are unfunded. It is possible that some incidental benefits in the plan could create an economic benefit. This issue has sometimes been raised where the plan includes an insured death benefit. However, currently the IRS does not claim that there is an economic benefit resulting from the insured death benefit in a properly designed nonqualified plan.

Income Taxation of Benefits and Contributions

Employees must pay ordinary income tax on benefits from unfunded nonqualified deferred compensation plans in the first year in which the benefit is actually or constructively received. The 5-year (or 10-year) averaging provisions available for qualified plan lump sum distributions do not apply to payments from nonqualified plans.

Death benefits from nonqualified plans that are payable to a beneficiary are taxable as income in respect of a decedent to the recipient. However, up to $5,000 can be excluded as an employee death benefit under Code section 101(b) if the employee did not have vested rights to the benefit immediately before death.

Social Security (FICA) and Federal Unemployment (FUTA) Taxes

Amounts deferred under nonqualified deferred compensation plans are not subject to social security taxes until the year in which the employee no longer has any substantial risk of forfeiting the amount.[9] In other words, as soon as the covered executive cannot lose his interest in the plan, he will be subject to social security taxes. Conceivably, this could be earlier than the year of actual receipt.

For example, if the plan provides that benefits are payable at retirement, but the benefits become vested five years after they are earned, then the amounts deferred will enter into the social security tax base five years after they are earned. Note that this is neither the year they are earned nor the year they are paid, a circumstance that complicates tax compliance in this situation.

If the executive's taxable current compensation is above the Medicare taxable wage base ($135,000 for 1993), inclusion of deferred compensation for FICA purposes in that year will not increase the executive's FICA taxes. (If compensation is above the OASDI limit but below the Medicare limit, any included deferred compensation will be taxed only at the Medicare rate.) Most highly-paid executives will generally not be greatly affected by these rules for inclusion, except for the additional administrative burden of determining the FICA and FUTA wage bases.

Federal Estate Tax Treatment

The amount of any death benefit payable to a beneficiary under a nonqualified deferred compensation plan is generally included in the deceased employee's estate for federal estate tax purposes, at its then present value. In other words, the commuted value of payments made to the employee's beneficiary will be included in the employee's gross estate. But such payments will be considered "income in respect of a decedent" (Code section 691 income) and an income tax deduction will be allocated to the recipient of that income for the additional estate tax the inclusion generated. To the extent payments are made to the employee's spouse in a qualifying manner, the unlimited marital deduction will eliminate any federal estate tax.

A plan can be designed so that the decedent did not have a right to receive the benefit prior to death. A plan designed to provide only death benefits is referred to as a death benefit only (DBO) plan. For employees potentially liable for substantial federal estate taxes, the DBO plan may be an appropriate design. DBO plans are covered in Chapter 30.

Taxation of the Employer

For a nonqualified deferred compensation plan, the employer does not receive a tax deduction until its tax year that includes the year in which the employee includes the compensation in taxable income.[10] If the plan is unfunded, the year of inclusion is the year in which the compensation is actually or constructively received. For a formally funded plan, compensation is included in income in the year in which it becomes substantially vested, as discussed earlier.

Payments under a deferred compensation plan, like other forms of compensation, are not deductible unless the amounts meet the reasonableness test discussed in Chapter 28. The same issues can arise with deferred compensation as with regular cash compensation or bonus arrangements.

The reasonableness issue is raised by the IRS in the year in which an employer attempts to take a deduction. For nonqualified deferred compensation, this is generally the year in which the employee includes the amount in income—that is, a year that is later than the year in which the services were rendered. Compensation can be deemed reasonable on the basis of prior service; however, it is possible that a combination of deferred compensation and current compensation

received in a given year could raise reasonableness issues, particularly if the deferred amount is very large.

If assets are set aside in a reserve used to informally finance the employer's obligation under the plan, income on these assets is currently taxable to the employer. Consequently, the use of assets providing a deferral of taxation can be advantageous. Life insurance policies are often used because their cash value build-up from year to year is not currently taxed. Death proceeds from the policy are also free of tax, except for a possible alternative minimum tax (AMT) liability (see Chapter 40 for discussion).

If assets to finance the plan are held in a rabbi trust, the employer's tax consequences are much the same as if assets were held directly by the employer. For tax purposes, the rabbi trust is a "grantor trust." A grantor trust's income, deductions, and tax credits are attributed to the grantor (the employer) for tax purposes.

ERISA REQUIREMENTS

Two types of nonqualified deferred compensation plans are eligible for at least partial exemptions from the ERISA requirements. The first exemption is for an unfunded excess benefit plan. This type of nonqualified deferred compensation plan, designed to supplement the qualified retirement benefits limited in amount by Code section 415, is not subject to any ERISA requirements.[11] The second exemption deals with a type of plan often referred to as a "top-hat" plan. Under ERISA, if a nonqualified plan is unfunded and maintained by an employer primarily for the purpose of providing deferred compensation for a "select group of management or highly compensated employees," the plan is exempt from all provisions of ERISA except for a simple reporting requirement of notifying the Department of Labor concerning some basic plan data, and ERISA's administrative and enforcement provisions.[12] Figure 16.2 is an example of the simple reporting notice.

The term "highly compensated" for this purpose is not as clearly defined as it is for qualified and other plans (see Chapter 23). The Department of Labor is responsible for interpreting this provision of ERISA and it has not yet issued clear guidelines. However, a plan that covers only a few highly paid executives probably will meet this ERISA exemption.

If a plan does not meet one of these ERISA exemptions, it must generally comply with most of the ERISA provisions applicable to qualified pension plans, including the vesting, fiduciary, minimum funding, and reporting and disclosure provisions.

As a result of these ERISA aspects, almost all nonqualified deferred compensation plans are limited to management or highly compensated employees and are formally unfunded, even though they may utilize some informal financing methods as discussed earlier.

WHERE CAN I FIND OUT MORE ABOUT IT?

1. Graduate Course: Executive Compensation (GS 842), The American College, Bryn Mawr, PA.

2. Leimberg et al., *The Tools and Techniques of Estate Planning*, 9th ed. Cincinnati, OH: The National Underwriter Co., 1992.

QUESTIONS AND ANSWERS

Question — How is life insurance used to finance an employer's obligation under a nonqualified deferred compensation plan?

Answer — Life insurance can be used in many ways, much like any other asset set aside to finance the plan. Life insurance has several advantages such as its tax-free build-up of cash values and the availability of substantial death benefits even in early years of the plan.

Because of the particular advantages of life insurance, many deferred compensation plans are designed specifically to make use of life insurance financing.

For example, suppose Crood Petroleum Corporation enters into a deferred compensation agreement with its executive Frank Furness under which Frank agrees to defer an anticipated $10,000 annual salary increase in return for the following specified benefits: (a) If Frank dies before retirement, $10,000 a year will be paid to his widow for a period equal to the number of years he was covered under the plan; (b) If Frank remains employed by Crood until retirement at age 65, he will receive $20,000 per year for ten years, in addition to other company retirement benefits.

Frank's deferred $10,000 per year of compensation would have had an after-tax cost of $6,600 to the corporation if paid currently (assuming a 34 percent marginal corporate tax bracket). The corporation can use this $6,600 instead to finance Frank's benefits by purchasing a life insurance policy on Frank's life. If Frank is age 45, about $150,000 of cash value insurance (paid up at 65) can be purchased with this $6,600 annually. The corpo-

ration would be the policyowner, the policy beneficiary, and would pay the premiums, which would be nondeductible. (The tax implications of corporate-owned insurance are discussed in detail in Chapter 40.)

If Frank died at age 50, the corporation would receive $150,000 of tax free policy proceeds (in addition to policy dividends and perhaps interest, but reduced by any corporate AMT liability). It would have paid about $33,000 in premiums over the past five years. It is obligated to pay a total of $50,000 ($10,000 a year for five years) to Frank's widow, but since these payments are deductible their after-tax cost is only $33,000 (66% of $50,000). This results in a net gain to the corporation of approximately $84,000 ($150,000 insurance proceeds less $33,000 of premiums and less $33,000 of after-tax cost of benefit payments). (This example does not take into account the time value of money, but to do so does not change the result significantly since the corporation's loss of the use of five annual premium payments is balanced by being reimbursed in advance for the five years of benefit payments due Frank's widow.)

If Frank had retired before his death, policy cash values and the corporation's current cash flow could be used to finance Frank's annual benefit payments. However, a better solution in most cases is to keep the policy intact and use current corporate cash to make benefit payments. Then when the employee dies, policy proceeds will reimburse the employer and often add to the company's surplus. This approach is often referred to as "cost recovery" nonqualified deferred compensation.

The employer should purchase enough insurance to offset any corporate AMT liability on the proceeds. Although the AMT should be no more than about 15 percent of policy proceeds, to be on the safe side it is suggested that the employer obtain about 17 or 18 percent more than the amount targeted to meet nonqualified deferred compensation needs.

Question — When should a benefit planner recommend using a rabbi trust?

Answer — Factors indicating that a rabbi trust might be advantageous include (a) a fear that the ownership or management of the business might change before deferred compensation benefits are paid; (b) a situation where new management might be hostile to the key employee in the future and fail to honor its contractual obligation to pay deferred compensation; and (c) situations where litigation to enforce payment of deferred compensation in the future would likely be too costly to be practical.

Figure 16.2

ALTERNATIVE REPORTING AND DISCLOSURE STATEMENT
FOR UNFUNDED NONQUALIFIED DEFERRED COMPENSATION PLANS
FOR CERTAIN SELECTED EMPLOYEES

To: Top Hat Plan Exemption
    Pension and Welfare Benefits Administration
    Room N-5644
    U.S. Department of Labor
    200 Constitution Avenue, N.W.
    Washington, D.C. 20210

In compliance with the requirements of the alternative method of reporting and disclosure under Part 1 of Title I of the Employee Retirement Income Security Act of 1974 for unfunded or insured pension plans for a select group of management or highly compensated employees, specified in Department of Labor Regulations, 29 C.F.R. Sec. 2520.104-23, the following information is provided by the undersigned employer.

Name and Address of Employer: _____

_____

_____

Employer Identification Number: _____

(Name of employer) maintains a plan (or plans) primarily for the purpose of providing deferred compensation for a select group of management or highly compensated employees.

Number of Plans and Participants in Each Plan:

_____ Plan covering _____ employees (or)

_____ Plans covering _____, _____, and

_____ employees; respectively)

Dated _____, 19____

(Name of Employer)

By _____
                           Plan Administrator

Question — What costs or risks are involved in the use of a rabbi trust-type of financing arrangement for deferred compensation?

Answer — Costs and risks include (a) the legal and administrative costs of setting up the rabbi trust agreement in a manner that will meet IRS requirements; (b) the loss of use of plan assets by the employer corporation (since they must be put in trust for the employee) except in bankruptcy or liquidation; (c) the rate of return on plan assets is limited by trust investments (assets might get a higher return invested in the employer's business); (d) from the employee's standpoint, the employee is not protected against the employer's insolvency.

Question — What provisions should (or should not) be included in a "rabbi trust" agreement?

Answer — A rabbi trust can be valid without obtaining a specific IRS ruling. However, most clients will either want to obtain a ruling or, at a minimum, will want to use a form of rabbi trust that conforms with IRS' known ruling requirements.

Revenue Procedures 92-64 and 92-65, 1992-33 IRB 11 and 16, contain the IRS' ruling position for rabbi trusts. The IRS will generally rule on a nonqualified deferred compensation arrangement using a rabbi trust *only* if the IRS' model rabbi trust (Revenue Procedure 92-64, reproduced at the end of this chapter) is used. If a rabbi trust does not conform with the model, a ruling will be issued only in "rare and unusual circumstances."

The model trust generally conforms with IRS guidelines already well-known from its prior private letter rulings. Optional paragraphs are provided to allow some degree of customization. The model contains some relatively favorable provisions. For example, it allows the use of "springing" irrevocability—that is, a triggering event, like a change of ownership of the employer, can cause the trust to become irrevocable or can obligate the employer to make an irrevocable contribution sufficient to cover its obligations as of the time of the triggering event. Also, the model permits the rabbi trust to own employer stock. However, the model does not contain trigger provisions to allow acceleration of payments if the employer moves toward insolvency; the employee's rights must never be better than those of the employer's general, unsecured creditors. The model rabbi trust also has no provision giving employees investment authority over rabbi trust assets.

Question — Can a corporation provide a nonqualified deferred compensation plan to an executive who is a controlling shareholder (more than 50%) in the corporation?

Answer — In principle, a deferred compensation arrangement can be provided for a controlling shareholder under the rules discussed in this chapter. However, the IRS generally will not issue an advance private letter ruling on the tax effect of such a plan.[13] The IRS will carefully scrutinize such an arrangement because of the controlling shareholder's legal right to require corporate distributions at any time. Here are seven ways to cut down the IRS' odds:

(1) Research key cases on point. In particular, see *Casale v. Comm., Moline Properties, Inc. v. Comm.*, and Revenue Ruling 59-184,[14] which support the proposition that a corporation is a separate entity from its stockholders as long as the corporation is carrying on a valid business activity and is not a sham. See also *Commerce Union Bank v. U.S., First Trust Company of St. Paul v. U.S.*, and Revenue Ruling 77-139,[15] which suggest that mere stock ownership by a plan participant is insufficient to invoke the doctrine of constructive receipt.

(2) Separate the financing of the employer's obligation from the plan itself. For example, if a life insurance policy is to be used, do not match the policy benefit to the promises made. When benefits under the financing vehicle are identical to and directly keyed into the benefits promised under the plan, the IRS will likely deny favorable tax treatment.[16] If the life insurance is maintained by the employer as key employee coverage and is kept totally separate from the agreement, there should be no constructive receipt (or economic benefit) problem.

(3) Include at least one highly compensated person other than a shareholder employee in the plan. The participation of a nonshareholder employee greatly enhances the argument that the plan is for corporate rather than shareholder purposes and will be of great help in justifying a corporate income tax deduction when benefits are to be paid.

(4) Create full documentation in the corporate minutes and in the agreement itself detailing the advantages to the corporation and the business purpose of the plan. Use wording that indicates that other successful competitive companies are providing similar supplemental compensation in their benefit programs. Incorporate wording from trade journals that shows that this type of plan is often used in the industry as a form of compensation helpful in recruiting, retaining, or retiring employees.

(5) A rabbi trust (discussed above) can be implemented to substantially limit even a controlling shareholder's

ability to reach deferred amounts until the occurrence of specific events. The trust should have an independent trustee with the fiduciary responsibility, under state law, to deny access to anyone until the covered person satisfies the plan's triggering criterion (e.g., disability, death, or reaching the specified retirement age). Thus, the rabbi trust negates any "raw power" that a controlling shareholder may have.

(6) Establish an independent compensation review committee with the power to deny benefits to participants who do not meet plan criteria. The committee should actually meet and review the operation of the plan and police its provisions.

(7) Be sure the plan benefits do not fail the "HOG" test[17] by providing overgenerous benefit amounts that would not be provided to nonshareholder employees. Provide that contributions or benefits on behalf of shareholder employees cannot be proportionately greater than those provided to key employees who are not shareholders. In other words, base the plan benefit formula on a reasonable and uniform percentage of salary.

Question — How can an executive determine whether it is better to defer compensation and pay the taxes later or to receive the compensation currently and pay taxes at relatively low income tax rates?

Answer — Because of the uncertainty of future tax rates and investment return, there can never be a certain answer to this question. However, some simple computations can provide a "handle" on the question. Figure 16.3 shows the "break-even" point or the number of years of deferral required to make deferral pay, given a higher estimated rate of tax in future years.

As an example of the use of Figure 16.3, suppose an executive is currently in the 28 percent marginal income tax bracket. If the marginal tax rate is assumed to be 40 percent in future years, and investments can earn 9 percent before taxes, then it will take 4.14 years of deferral for deferred compensation to be better than current taxable compensation. Figure 16.3 indicates that deferred compensation is generally still a good idea for a relatively wide range of assumptions and reasonably short periods of deferral.

This computation does not take into account the effect of a corporate tax bracket that is higher than the individual employee's. This situation increases the value of a current tax deduction and accordingly decreases the overall tax value of deferral to the corporation and employee

together. "Secular trust" plans, discussed in the following question, are responsive to this situation.

For a comprehensive look at deferral break-even analysis, see Doyle, "Creative Wealth Planning Techniques," in the *Financial Services Professional's Guide to the State of the Art*, Second Edition, 1991, The American College, Bryn Mawr, PA 19010.

Question — What is a "secular trust?"

Answer — The secular trust (so named to contrast it with a rabbi trust) is an arrangement that meets two current employee objections to deferred compensation plans: the fear that tax savings will disappear because future tax rates will be very high, and the lack of security to the employee in relying on a formally unfunded plan.

A secular trust is an irrevocable trust for the benefit of the employee, with funds placed beyond the reach of the employer's creditors. This is generally thought to result in taxation to the employee in the year in which assets are placed in the trust, with a corresponding deduction to the employer in that year. The amounts already taxed can be distributed tax free to the employee at retirement, even if tax rates have gone up considerably.

The secular trust arrangement provides considerable security of benefits to the employee, as well as the ability to take advantage of currently low income tax rates. In addition, since corporate tax rates are higher than individual rates in some cases, the acceleration of the employer's tax deduction may provide more tax benefit than is lost by the employee in paying tax currently instead of deferring.

Secular trust designers try to structure secular trusts as "grantor" trusts in order to avoid possible double taxation. A grantor trust is generally ignored for tax purposes, with its income and tax reportable directly by the grantor. The IRS has previously ruled favorably on "employee-grantor" secular trusts, but employers are often more interested in the "employer-grantor" arrangement because this allows employers to maintain more control of the trust assets, a major objective in the "golden handcuffs" type of plan.

However, recent letter rulings reached strongly negative results on employer-funded secular trusts.[18] In a complex technical analysis applying Code sections 402(b) and 404(a)(5), the IRS held that an employer-funded secular trust can not be taxed as an employer-grantor trust. Moreover, the rulings held that employer-funded secular trust earnings can be taxed twice, once to the trust and again to the employees.

Figure 16.3

YEARS UNTIL BREAK EVEN FOR DEFERRED COMPENSATION ASSUMING TAX RATES WILL INCREASE AND CURRENT RATE IS 28 PERCENT

Current Tax Rate		28%	28%	28%	28%	28%
Projected Tax Rate		35%	40%	45%	50%	55%
			Number of Years to Break Even*			
	3%	7.55	12.07	16.05	19.62	22.84
	4%	5.69	9.09	12.10	14.78	17.21
	5%	4.57	7.31	9.72	11.88	13.84
	6%	3.83	6.12	8.14	9.95	11.59
Before-tax	7%	3.30	5.27	7.01	8.57	9.98
Return on Plan	8%	2.90	4.63	6.16	7.53	8.77
Investments	9%	2.59	4.14	5.51	6.73	7.83
	10%	2.34	3.74	4.98	6.08	7.08
	11%	2.14	3.42	4.55	5.56	6.47
	12%	1.97	3.15	4.19	5.12	5.96
	13%	1.83	2.92	3.88	4.74	5.52

YEARS UNTIL BREAK EVEN FOR DEFERRED COMPENSATION ASSUMING TAX RATES WILL INCREASE AND CURRENT RATE IS 33 PERCENT

Current Tax Rate		33%	33%	33%	33%	33%
Projected Tax Rate		35%	40%	45%	50%	55%
			Number of Years to Break Even			
	3%	1.99	6.51	10.49	14.06	17.28
	4%	1.50	4.90	7.91	10.59	13.02
	5%	1.21	3.94	6.36	8.52	10.47
	6%	1.01	3.30	5.32	7.13	8.77
Before-tax	7%	0.87	2.84	4.58	6.14	7.55
Return on Plan	8%	0.76	2.50	4.03	5.40	6.64
Investments	9%	0.68	2.23	3.60	4.82	5.93
	10%	0.62	2.02	3.25	4.36	5.36
	11%	0.56	1.84	2.97	3.98	4.89
	12%	0.52	1.70	2.74	3.67	4.51
	13%	0.48	1.57	2.54	3.40	4.18

$$*\text{number of years} = \frac{\text{natural log of (new tax rate/current tax rate)}}{\text{natural log of (1 + interest rate)}}$$

Source: *Financial Services Professional's Guide to the State of the Art 1989*, The American College, Bryn Mawr, PA 19010, 1-800-841-8000, ext. 19.

At best, these rulings create confusion and uncertainty; a pessimistic view might be that without changes in the Internal Revenue Code the employer-funded secular trust is not viable for compensation planning.

FOOTNOTES

1. Reg. §1.83-1(a).
2. ERISA Sections 201, 401(a).
3. See Rev. Rul. 82-54, 1982-1 CD 11 and rulings cited therein. See Let. Rul. 8648011 for an IRS-approved reserve account with investment direction by the employee. See also Let. Rul. 8804057.
4. See Let. Rul. 8406012.
5. Reg. §1.451-2(a).
6. Rev. Rul. 60-31, 1960-1 CB 174; Rev. Proc. 71-19, 1971-1 CB 698, as amplified by Rev. Proc. 92-65, 1992-33 IRB 16.
7. But see *Martin v. Comm.*, 96 TC 814 (1991); *Veit v. Comm.*, 8 TCM 919 (1949).
8. *Sproull v. Comm.*, 16 TC 244 (1951), aff'd per curiam, 194 F.2d 541 (6th Cir. 1952); Rev. Rul. 72-25, 1972-1 CB 127; Rev. Rul. 68-99, 1968-1 CB 193; Rev. Rul. 60-31, 1960-1 CB 174.
9. IRC Sections 3121(v)(2) [FICA] and 3306(r)(2) [FUTA].
10. IRC Section 404(a)(5); Reg. §1.404(a)-12(b)(1).
11. ERISA Sections 4(b)(5), 4021(b)(8).
12. ERISA Sections 201(2), 301(a)(3), 401(a)(1), 503, 4021(b)(6); Labor Regs. §§2520.104-23, 2560.503-1(a), 2560.503-1(b).
13. Rev. Proc. 93-3, Sec. 3.01(32), 1993-1 IRB 71, at 76. This item has been on the IRS' annually revised list of "no ruling" items for many years. Active hostility to controlling shareholder-employee deferred compensation was expressed in a side discussion, or "dictum," in Let. Rul. 8607029, a ruling otherwise favorable to the taxpayer. See also TAM 8828004.
14. *Casale v. Comm.*, 247 F.2d 440 (2nd Cir. 1957); *Moline Properties, Inc. v. Comm.*, 319 U.S. 436, 63 S.Ct. 1132 (1943); Rev. Rul. 59-184 1959-1 CB 65.
15. *Commerce Union Bank v. U.S.*, 76-2 USTC ¶13,157 (M.D. Tenn. 1976); *First Trust Company of St. Paul v. U.S.*, 321 F. Supp. 1025 (D. Minn. 1970); Rev. Rul. 77-139, 1977-1 CB 278.
16. See *Casale v. Comm.*, above, note 14; *Goldsmith v. U. S.*, 78-1 USTC ¶9312 (Ct. Cl. Tr. Div. 1978), no appeal (adopted by full court), 586 F.2d 810 (Ct. Cl. 1978). But see Let. Ruls. 8103089 and 7940017.
17. See, e.g., *Willmark Service System, Inc. v. Comm.*, TC Memo 1965-294, aff'd, 368 F.2d 359 (2nd Cir. 1966).
18. See Let. Ruls. 9212024, 9212019, 9207010, 9206009.

IRS Model Rabbi Trust

TRUST UNDER_____PLAN

OPTIONAL
(a) This Agreement made this_____day of,_____by and between_____(Company) and_____(Trustee);

OPTIONAL
(b) WHEREAS, Company has adopted the nonqualified deferred compensation Plan(s) as listed in Appendix_____.

OPTIONAL
(c) WHEREAS, Company has incurred or expects to incur liability under the terms of such Plan(s) with respect to the individuals participating in such Plan(s);

(d) WHEREAS, Company wishes to establish a trust (hereinafter called "Trust") and to contribute to the Trust assets that shall be held therein, subject to the claims of Company's creditors in the event of Company's Insolvency, as herein defined, until paid to Plan participants and their beneficiaries in such manner and at such times as specified in the Plan(s);

(e) WHEREAS, it is the intention of the parties that this Trust shall constitute an unfunded arrangement and shall not affect the status of the Plan(s) as an unfunded plan maintained for the purpose of providing deferred compensation for a select group of management or highly compensated employees for purposes of Title I of the Employee Retirement Income Security Act of 1974;

(f) WHEREAS, it is the intention of Company to make contributions to the Trust to provide itself with a source of funds to assist it in the meeting of its liabilities under the Plan(s);

NOW, THEREFORE, the parties do hereby establish the Trust and agree that the Trust shall be comprised, held and disposed of as follows:

Section 1. *Establishment Of Trust*

(a) Company hereby deposits with Trustee in trust_____[insert amount deposited], which shall become the principal of the Trust to be held, administered and disposed of by Trustee as provided in this Trust Agreement.

ALTERNATIVES—Select one provision.

(b) The Trust hereby established shall be revocable by Company.

(b) The Trust hereby established shall be irrevocable.

(b) The Trust hereby established is revocable by Company; it shall become irrevocable upon a Change of Control, as defined herein.

(b) The Trust shall become irrevocable_____[insert number] days following the issuance of a favorable private letter ruling regarding the Trust from the Internal Revenue Service.

(b) The Trust shall become irrevocable upon approval by the Board of Directors.

(c) The Trust is intended to be a grantor trust, of which Company is the grantor, within the meaning of subpart E, part I, subchapter J, chapter 1, subtitle A of the Internal Revenue Code of 1986, as amended, and shall be construed accordingly.

(d) The principal of the Trust, and any earnings thereon shall be held separate and apart from other funds of Company and shall be used exclusively for the uses and purposes of Plan participants and general creditors as herein set forth. Plan participants and their beneficiaries shall have no preferred claim on, or any beneficial ownership interest in, any assets of the Trust. Any rights created under the Plan(s) and this Trust Agreement shall be mere unsecured contractual rights of Plan participants and their beneficiaries against Company. Any assets held by the Trust will be subject to the claims of Company's general creditors under federal and state law in the event Of Insolvency, as defined in Section 3(a) herein.

ALTERNATIVES—Select one or more provisions as appropriate.

(e) Company, in its sole discretion, may at any time, or from time to time, make additional deposits of cash or other property in trust with Trustee to augment the principal to be held, administered and disposed of by Trustee as provided in this Trust Agreement. Neither Trustee nor any Plan participant or beneficiary shall have any right to compel such additional deposits.

(e) Upon a Change of Control, Company shall, as soon as possible, but in no event longer than_____ [fill in blank] days following the Change of Control, as defined herein, make an irrevocable contribution to the Trust in an amount that is sufficient to pay each Plan participant or beneficiary the benefits to which Plan participants or their beneficiaries would be entitled pursuant to the terms of the Plan(s) as of the date on which the Change of Control occurred.

(e) Within_____ [fill in blank] days following the end of the Plan years, ending after the Trust has become irrevocable pursuant to Section 1(b) hereof, Company shall be required to irrevocably deposit additional cash or other property to the Trust in an amount sufficient to pay each Plan participant or beneficiary the benefits payable pursuant to the terms of the Plan(s) as of the close of the Plan year(s).

Section 2. *Payments to Plan Participants and Their Beneficiaries.*

(a) Company shall deliver to Trustee a schedule (the "Payment Schedule") that indicates the amounts payable in respect of each Plan participant (and his or her beneficiaries), that provides a formula or other instructions acceptable to Trustee for determining the amounts so payable, the form in which such amount is to be paid (as provided for or available under the Plan(s)), and the time of commencement for payment of such amounts. Except as otherwise provided herein, Trustee shall make payments to the Plan participants and their beneficiaries in accordance with such Payment Schedule. The Trustee shall make provision for the reporting and withholding of any federal, state or local taxes that may be required to be withheld with respect to the payment of benefits pursuant to the terms of the Plan(s) and shall pay amounts withheld to the appropriate taxing authorities or determine that such amounts have been reported, withheld and paid by Company.

(b) The entitlement of a Plan participant or his or her beneficiaries to benefits under the Plan(s) shall be determined by Company or such party as it shall designate under the Plan(s), and any claim for such benefits shall be considered and reviewed under the procedures set out in the Plan(s).

(c) Company may make payment of benefits directly to Plan participants or their beneficiaries as they become due under the terms of the Plan(s). Company shall notify Trustee of its decision to make payment of benefits directly prior to the time amounts are payable to participants or their beneficiaries. In addition, if the principal of the Trust, and any earnings thereon, are not sufficient to make payments of benefits in accordance with the terms of the Plan(s), Company shall make the balance of each such payment as it falls due. Trustee shall notify Company where principal and earnings are not sufficient.

Section 3. *Trustee Responsibility Regarding Payments to Trust Beneficiary When Company Is Insolvent.*

(a) Trustee shall cease payment of benefits to Plan participants and their beneficiaries if the Company is Insolvent. Company shall be considered "Insolvent" for purposes of this Trust Agreement if (1) Company is unable to pay its debts as they become due, or (ii) Company is subject to a pending proceeding as a debtor under the United States Bankruptcy Code.

OPTIONAL
*, or (iii) Company is determined to be insolvent by*_____*[insert names of applicable federal and/or state regulatory agency].*

(b) At all times during the continuance of this Trust, as provided in Section l(d) hereof, the principal and income of the Trust shall be subject to claims of general creditors of Company under federal and state law as set forth below.

(1) The Board of Directors and the Chief Executive Officer [or substitute the title of the highest ranking officer of the Company] of Company shall have the duty to inform Trustee in writing of Company's Insolvency. If a person claiming to be a creditor of Company alleges in writing to Trustee that Company has become Insolvent, Trustee shall determine whether Company is Insolvent and, pending such determination, Trustee shall discontinue payment of benefits to Plan participants or their beneficiaries.

(2) Unless Trustee has actual knowledge of Company's Insolvency, or has received notice from Company or a person claiming to be a creditor alleging that Company is Insolvent, Trustee shall have no duty to inquire whether Company is Insolvent. Trustee may in all events rely on such evidence concerning Company's solvency as may be furnished to Trustee and that provides Trustee with a reasonable basis for making a determination concerning Company's solvency.

(3) If at any time Trustee has determined that Company is Insolvent, Trustee shall discontinue payments to Plan participants or their beneficiaries and shall hold the assets of the Trust for the benefit of Company's general creditors. Nothing in this Trust Agreement shall in any way diminish any rights of Plan participants or their beneficiaries to pursue their rights as general creditors of Company with respect to benefits due under the Plan(s) or otherwise.

(4) Trustee shall resume the payment of benefits to Plan participants or their beneficiaries in accordance with Section 2 of this Trust Agreement only after Trustee has determined that Company is not Insolvent (or is no longer Insolvent).

(c) Provided that there are sufficient assets, if Trustee discontinues the payment of benefits from the Trust pursuant to Section 3(b) hereof and subsequently resumes such payments, the first payment following such discontinuance shall include the aggregate amount of all payments due to Plan participants or their beneficiaries under the terms of the Plan(s) for the period of such discontinuance, less the aggregate amount of any payments made to Plan participants or their beneficiaries by Company in lieu of the payments provided for hereunder during any such period of discontinuance.

Section 4. *Payments to Company.*
[The following need not be included if the first alternative under l(b) is selected.]

Except as provided in Section 3 hereof, after the Trust has become irrevocable, Company shall have no right or power to direct Trustee to return to Company or to divert to others any of the Trust assets before all payment of benefits have [*sic*] been made to Plan participants and their beneficiaries pursuant to the terms of the Plan(s).

Section 5. *Investment Authority.*

ALTERNATIVES—Select one provision, as appropriate[.]

(a) In no event may Trustee invest in securities (including stock or rights to acquire stock) or obligations issued by Company, other than a de minimis amount held in common investment vehicles in which Trustee invests. All rights associated with assets of the Trust shall be exercised by Trustee or the person designated by Trustee, and shall in no event be exercisable by or rest with Plan participants.

(a) Trustee may invest in securities (including stock or rights to acquire stock) or obligations issued by Company. All rights associated with assets of the Trust shall be exercised by Trustee or the person designated by Trustee, and shall in no event be exercisable by or rest with Plan participants.

OPTIONAL

,except that voting rights with respect to Trust assets will be exercised by Company.

OPTIONAL

,except that dividend rights with respect to Trust assets will rest with Company.

OPTIONAL

Company shall have the right, at anytime, and from time to time in its sole discretion, to substitute assets of equal fair market value for any asset held by the Trust.

[If the second Alternative 5(a) is selected, the trust must provide either (1) that the trust is revocable under Alternative l(b), or (2) the following provision must by included in the Trust]:

> *"Company shall have the right at anytime, and from time to time in its sole discretion, to substitute assets of equal fair market value for any asset held by the Trust. This right is exercisable by Company in a nonfiduciary capacity without the approval or consent of any person in a fiduciary capacity."*

Section 6. *Disposition of Income.*

ALTERNATIVES—*Select one provision.*

(a) During the term of this Trust, all income received by the Trust, net of expenses and taxes, shall be accumulated and reinvested.

(a) During the term of this Trust, all, or_____[insert amount] part of the income received by the Trust, net of expenses and taxes, shall be returned to Company.

Section 7. *Accounting by Trustee.*

OPTIONAL

Trustee shall keep accurate and detailed records of all investments, receipts, disbursements, and all other transactions required to be made, including such specific records as shall be agreed upon in writing between Company and Trustee. Within_____ [insert number] days following the close of each calendar year and within_____[insert number] days after the removal or resignation of Trustee, Trustee shall deliver to Company a written account of its administration of the Trust during such year or during the period from the close of the last preceding year to the date of such removal or resignation, setting forth all investments, receipts, disbursements and other transactions effected by it, including a description of all securities and investments purchased and sold with the cost or net proceeds of such purchases or sales (accrued interest paid or receivable being shown separately), and showing all cash, securities and other property held in the Trust at the end of such year or as of the date of such removal or resignation, as the case may be.

Section 8. *Responsibility of Trustee.*

OPTIONAL

(a) Trustee shall act with the care, skill, prudence and diligence under the circumstances then prevailing that a prudent person acting in like capacity and familiar with such matters would use in the conduct of an enterprise of a like character and with like aims, provided, however, that Trustee shall incur no liability to any person for any action taken pursuant to a direction, request or approval given by Company which is contemplated by, and in conformity with, the terms of the Plan(s) or this Trust and is given in writing by Company. In the event of a dispute between Company and a party, Trustee may apply to a court of competent jurisdiction to resolve the dispute.

OPTIONAL

(b) If Trustee undertakes or defends any litigation arising in connection with this Trust, Company agrees to indemnify Trustee against Trustee's costs, expenses and liabilities (including, without limitation, attorneys' fees and expenses) relating thereto and to be primarily liable for such payments. If Company does not pay such costs, expenses and liabilities in a reasonably timely manner, Trustee may obtain payment from the Trust.

OPTIONAL

(c) Trustee may consult with legal counsel (who may also be counsel for Company generally) with respect to any of its duties or obligations hereunder.

OPTIONAL

(d) Trustee may hire agents, accountants, actuaries, investment advisors, financial consultants or other professionals to assist it in performing any of its duties or obligations hereunder.

(e) Trustee shall have, without exclusion, all powers conferred on Trustees by applicable law, unless expressly provided otherwise herein, provided, however, that if an insurance policy is held as an asset of the Trust, Trustee shall have no power to name a beneficiary of the policy other than the Trust, to assign the policy (as distinct from conversion of the policy to a different form) other than to a successor Trustee, or to loan to any person the proceeds of any borrowing against such policy.

OPTIONAL

(f) However, notwithstanding the provisions of Section 8(e) above, Trustee may loan to Company the proceeds of any borrowing against an insurance policy held as an asset of the Trust.

(g) Notwithstanding any powers granted to Trustee pursuant to this Trust Agreement or to applicable law, Trustee shall not have any power that could give this Trust the objective of carrying on a business and dividing the gains therefrom, within the meaning of section 301.7701-2 of the Procedure and Administrative Regulations promulgated pursuant to the Internal Revenue Code.

Section 9. *Compensation and Expenses of Trustee.*

OPTIONAL

Company shall pay all administrative and Trustee's fees and expenses. If not so paid, the fees and expenses shall be paid from the Trust.

Section 10. *Resignation and Removal of Trustee.*

(a) Trustee may resign at any time by written notice to Company, which shall be effective_____[insert number] days after receipt of such notice unless Company and Trustee agree otherwise.

OPTIONAL

(b) Trustee may be removed by Company on____[insert number] days notice or upon shorter notice accepted by Trustee.

OPTIONAL

(c) Upon a Change of Control, as defined herein, Trustee may not be removed by Company for_____[insert number] year(s).

OPTIONAL

(d) If Trustee resigns within_____[insert number] year(s) after a Change of Control, as defined herein, Company shall apply to a court of competent jurisdiction for the appointment of a successor Trustee or for instructions.

OPTIONAL

(e) If Trustee resigns or is removed within_____[insert number] year(s) or a Change of Control, as defined herein, Trustee shall select a successor Trustee in accordance with the provisions of Section 11(b) hereof prior to the effective date of Trustee's resignation or removal.

(f) Upon resignation or removal of Trustee and appointment of a successor Trustee, all assets shall subsequently be transferred to the successor Trustee. The transfer shall be completed within_____[insert number] days after receipt of notice of resignation, removal or transfer, unless Company extends the time limit.

(g) If Trustee resigns or is removed, a successor shall be appointed, in accordance with Section 11 hereof, by the effective date of resignation or removal under paragraph(s) (a) [or (b)] of this section. If no such appointment has been made, Trustee may apply to a court of competent jurisdiction for appointment of a successor or for instructions. All expenses of Trustee in connection with the proceeding shall be allowed as administrative expenses of the Trust.

Section 11. *Appointment of Successor.*

OPTIONAL

(a) If Trustee resigns or is removed in accordance with Section 10(a) [or (b)] hereof, Company may appoint any third party, such as a bank trust department or other party that may be granted corporate trustee powers under state law, as a successor to replace Trustee upon resignation or removal. The appointment shall be effective when accepted in writing by the new Trustee, who shall have all of the rights and powers of the former Trustee, including ownership rights in the Trust assets. The former Trustee shall execute any instrument necessary or reasonably requested by Company or the successor Trustee to evidence the transfer.

OPTIONAL

(b) If Trustee resigns or is removed pursuant to the provisions of Section 10(e) hereof and selects a successor Trustee, Trustee may appoint any third party such as a bank trust department or other party that may be granted corporate trustee powers under state law. The appointment of a successor Trustee shall be effective when accepted in writing by the new Trustee. The new Trustee shall have all the rights and powers of the former Trustee, including ownership rights in Trust assets. The former Trustee shall execute any instrument necessary or reasonably requested by the successor Trustee to evidence the transfer.

OPTIONAL

(c) The successor Trustee need not examine the records and acts of any prior Trustee and may retain or dispose of existing Trust assets, subject to Sections 7 and 8 hereof. The successor Trustee shall not be responsible for and Company shall indemnify and defend the successor Trustee from any claim or liability resulting from any action or inaction of any prior Trustee or from any other past event, or any condition existing at the time it becomes successor Trustee.

Section 12. *Amendment or Termination.*

(a) This Trust Agreement may be amended by a written instrument executed by Trustee and Company. [Unless the first alternative under 1(b) is selected, the following sentence must be included.] Notwithstanding the foregoing, no such amendment shall conflict with the terms of the Plan(s) or shall make the Trust revocable after it has become irrevocable in accordance with Section 1(b) hereof.

(b) The Trust shall not terminate until the date on which Plan participants and their beneficiaries are no longer entitled to benefits pursuant to the terms of the Plan(s) [unless the second alternative under 1(b) is selected, the following must be included:], "unless sooner revoked in accordance with Section 1(b) hereof." [*Sic*] Upon termination of the Trust any assets remaining in the Trust shall be returned to Company.

OPTIONAL

(c) Upon written approval of participants or beneficiaries entitled to payment of benefits pursuant to the terms of the Plan(s), Company may terminate this Trust prior to the time all benefit payments under the Plan(s) have been made. All assets in the Trust at termination shall be returned to Company.

OPTIONAL

(d) Section(s)_____[insert number(s)] of this Trust Agreement may not be amended by Company for_____[insert number] year(s) following a Change of Control, as defined herein.

Section 13. *Miscellaneous.*

(a) Any provision of this Trust Agreement prohibited by law shall be ineffective to the extent of any such prohibition, without invalidating the remaining provisions hereof.

(b) Benefits payable to Plan participants and their beneficiaries under this Trust Agreement may not be anticipated, assigned (either at law or in equity), alienated, pledged, encumbered or subjected to attachment, garnishment, levy, execution or other legal or equitable process.

(c) This Trust Agreement shall be governed by and construed in accordance with the laws of_____.

OPTIONAL

(d) For purposes of this Trust, Change of Control shall mean: [insert objective definition such as: "the purchase or other acquisition by any person, entity or group of persons, within the meaning of section 13(d) or 14(d) of the Securities Exchange Act of 1934 ("Act"), or any comparable successor provisions, of beneficial ownership within the meaning of Rule 13d-3 promulgated under the Act) of 30 percent or more of either the outstanding shares of common stock or the combined voting power of Company's then outstanding voting securities entitled to vote generally, or the approval by the stockholders of Company of a reorganization, merger, or consolidation, in each case, with respect to which persons who were stockholders of Company immediately prior to such reorganization, merger or consolidation do not, immediately thereafter, own more than 50 percent of the combined voting power entitled to vote generally in the election of directors of the reorganized, merged or consolidated Company's then outstanding securities, or a liquidation or dissolution of Company or of the sale of all or substantially all of Company's assets"].

Section 14. *Effective Date.*

The effective date of this Trust Agreement shall be_____, 19[___].

Chapter 17

PROFIT-SHARING PLAN

WHAT IS IT?

A profit-sharing plan is a qualified, defined contribution plan featuring a flexible employer contribution provision. The major characteristics are:

- The employer's contribution to the plan each year can be either a purely discretionary amount (or nothing at all, if the employer wishes) or can be based on some type of formula, usually relating to the employer's annual profits.

- Each participant has an individual account in the plan. The employer's contribution is allocated to the individual participant accounts on the basis of a nondiscriminatory formula. The formula usually allocates employer contributions in proportion to each employee's compensation for the year. (Age-weighted formulas can also be used—see Chapter 21.)

- Plan benefits consist of the amount accumulated in each participant's account at retirement or termination of employment. This is the total of (a) employer contributions, (b) forfeitures from other employees' accounts (discussed below), and (c) the interest, capital gains, and other investment return realized over the years on plan assets.

- The plan usually distributes the employee's account balance in a lump sum at termination of employment, although other forms of payout may be available or, in the case of certain plans, may be required.

WHEN IS IT INDICATED?

1. When an employer's profits, or financial ability to contribute to the plan, varies from year to year. A profit-sharing plan is particularly useful as an alternative to a qualified pension plan where the employer anticipates that there may be years in which no contribution can be made.

2. When the employer wants to adopt a qualified plan with an incentive feature by which employee accounts increase with the employer's profits.

3. When the employee group has the following characteristics:

   - many employees are relatively young and have substantial time to accumulate retirement savings

   - employees can and are willing to accept a degree of investment risk in their accounts, in return for the potential benefits of good investment results.

4. When the employer wants to supplement an existing defined benefit plan. The advantages of a profit-sharing plan tend to provide exactly what is missing in a defined benefit plan—and vice versa—so that the two together provide an ideal balanced tax-deferred savings and retirement program.

ADVANTAGES

1. A profit-sharing plan provides the maximum contribution flexibility from the employer's viewpoint.

2. Contributions can be made even if there are no current or accumulated profits.[1] Even a nonprofit organization can have a qualified profit-sharing plan.

3. As with all qualified plans, a profit-sharing plan provides a tax-deferred retirement savings medium for employees.

4. The plan is relatively simple and inexpensive to design, administer, and explain to employees.

5. Plan distributions may be eligible for the special 5-year or (10-year) averaging tax computation available for qualified plans.

6. Individual participant accounts allow participants to benefit from good investment results in the plan fund.

DISADVANTAGES

1. Deductible annual contributions to a profit-sharing plan are limited to 15 percent of total payroll of covered employees; other types of qualified plans permit higher annual contributions. For example, a money purchase

plan allows an employer contribution of up to 25 percent of each employee's compensation.

2. Retirement benefits may be inadequate for employees who enter the plan at older ages. This is discussed, with some illustrations, in Chapter 15 relating to money purchase plans. The problem of adequate benefits is even worse in a profit-sharing plan than in a money purchase plan because a profit-sharing plan does not involve any required minimum annual contribution by the employer. Thus, ultimate retirement benefits in a profit-sharing plan are quite speculative. Some planners argue that a profit-sharing plan should be considered primarily as a supplemental form of incentive-based deferred compensation and not as a retirement plan. Note that this disadvantage can be reduced by using an age-weighted formula, as discussed in Chapter 21.

3. The annual addition to each employee's account in a profit-sharing plan is limited to the *lesser of* (a) 25 percent of compensation or (b) the greater of $30,000 or ¼ of the defined benefit dollar limitation. (The defined benefit dollar limitation is $115,641 in 1993.) This limits the relative amount of plan funding available for highly compensated employees. For highly paid employees (those earning more than $120,000 annually), the "$30,000" limit represents a smaller percentage of their compensation than can be contributed for lower-paid employees.

4. Employees bear investment risk under the plan. While bearing investment risk is a potential disadvantage to employees, from the employer's viewpoint it is an advantage compared with a defined benefit plan. The employer's risk and costs tend to be lower for a profit-sharing plan.

5. From the employee's standpoint, profit-sharing plans are disadvantageous because there is no predictable level of employer funding under the plan. However, employees have a right to expect that employer contributions will be "substantial and recurring," as discussed below.

DESIGN FEATURES

Employer Contribution Arrangements

Employer contribution provisions in a profit-sharing plan can be either (a) discretionary or (b) formula type.

Under a *discretionary* provision, the employer can determine each year the amount to be contributed. A contribution can be made to a profit-sharing plan even if there are no current or accumulated profits. If the employer desires to make a contribution, any amount up to the maximum deductible limit can be contributed.

An employer can omit a contribution under a discretionary provision, but IRS regulations require "recurring and substantial" contributions.[2] There are no clear guidelines from the IRS as to how often contributions can be omitted. If too many years go by without contributions, the IRS will likely claim that the plan has been terminated. When a qualified plan is terminated, all nonvested amounts in participants' accounts become 100 percent vested. This is usually an undesirable result from the employer's viewpoint.

Under a *formula* provision, a specified amount must be contributed to the plan whenever the employer has profits. For example, a formula might provide that the employer will contribute 10 percent of all company profits in excess of $100,000 (but not to exceed the deduction limit discussed below under "Tax Implications"). The IRS does not dictate how to define profits for this purpose, so the employer can specify any appropriate formula. The most common approach is to define profits as determined on a before-tax basis under generally accepted accounting principles. As mentioned earlier, even a nonprofit corporation can adopt a profit-sharing plan with contributions based on some appropriately defined surplus account.

Once a formula approach has been adopted, the employer is legally obligated to contribute the amount determined under the formula. However, formulas can be drafted that allow an omitted contribution if certain adverse financial contingencies occur. A suitable "fail-safe" provision of this type will avoid the necessity of amending the plan in the future if financial difficulties arise.

Allocation to Participant Accounts

All profit-sharing plans, regardless of how the total amount of employer contributions are determined, must have a formula under which the employer's contribution is allocated to employee accounts. This allocation formula must not discriminate in favor of highly compensated employees.

Most formulas make allocation to participants on the basis of their compensation as compared with the compensation of all participants.

Example: Participant Fred earns $50,000 this year. Total payroll for all plan participants this year is $500,000. For this year, the employer contributes $100,000 to the plan and the amount allocated to Fred's account is determined as follows:

$$\text{Total employer contribution} \quad X \quad \frac{\text{Fred's Compensation}}{\text{Compensation of All Participants}}$$

$$\$100,000 \quad X \quad \frac{\$50,000}{\$500,000} \quad = \quad \$10,000$$

Allocation to Fred's account equals 1/10 of $100,000, or $10,000.

The plan must define the term "compensation" in a nondiscriminatory way.[3] For example, if compensation is defined to include bonuses and exclude overtime pay, and only highly compensated employees receive bonuses and only lower paid employees receive overtime pay, the formula would likely be found discriminatory.

It is important for planners to note that only the first $200,000 (as indexed for inflation, $235,840 for 1993) of each employee's compensation can be taken into account in the allocation formula, as well as for the 15% deduction limit discussed below under "Tax Implications."[4]

Some profit-sharing allocation formulas also take into account the years of service of each employee. Such a formula can satisfy the nondiscrimination requirements by falling within one of the safe harbors provided in the regulations.[5]

The allocation formula can be "integrated" with Social Security. This helps the employer avoid duplicating Social Security benefits that are already provided to the employee. It also reduces the employer's cost for the plan.

An integrated formula defines a level of compensation known as the "integration level." The plan then provides a higher rate of allocation of the employer contribution for compensation above that integration level than the rate for compensation below that integration level.

Example: For the year 1993, a profit-sharing plan has two participants with compensation as shown below. For 1993, the employer contributes $15,000 to the plan. The plan's integration level is $20,000. Under the plan's allocation formula, each participant's account is to receive the maximum permitted percent allocation for compensation above $20,000. (As discussed in the "Questions and Answers," below, this is 4.3%.) The remaining amount of the employer contribution is allocated in proportion to total compensation. Plan allocations would then be as follows:

Employee	1993 Compensation	Compensation above $20,000	4.3% of Excess	Allocation of Remainder	Total Allocation
Al	$100,000	$80,000	$3,440	$10,052	$13,492
Betty	15,000	0	0	1,508	1,508
					$15,000

The amount in column 4 is arrived at by (a) taking the difference between the excess allocations (total of column 3) and the $15,000 employer contribution; this is $11,560; (b) for each participant, this difference ($11,560) is then multiplied by a fraction, the numerator of which is the participant's total compensation and the denominator of which is the total payroll of $115,000. This allocation meets the current IRS integration rules.

Proposed regulations specify the degree of integration permitted in a plan—the integration levels and the percentages allowed. Choosing the best integration level within the limits of these rules is discussed in the "Questions and Answers," below.

Vesting

Any vesting (nonforfeiture) provision permitted by the Code can be used in a profit-sharing plan. Vesting tends to be relatively generous in a profit-sharing plan since it is designed as an employee incentive.

Usually the graded "3- to 7-year" vesting provision is used. This provides 20 percent vesting after 3 years of service. Vesting increases by 20 percent for each subsequent year of service and reaches 100 percent after 7 years of service. (See Chapter 23.)

If an employee leaves before becoming fully vested in his or her account balance, the nonvested amount, referred to as a "forfeiture," is left behind in the plan. In profit-sharing plans, forfeitures are usually added to remaining participants' account balances. Adding forfeitures to participants' account balances tends to favor key employees, since they are more likely to participate in the plan over a long time period. For this reason, forfeitures must be allocated in a nondiscriminatory manner.[6] This usually requires forfeiture allocation in proportion to participants' compensation rather than in proportion to their existing account balances. In profit-sharing plans, the formula for allocating forfeitures is usually the same as the formula for allocating employer contributions to participants' accounts.

Benefits from a profit-sharing plan are usually payable at termination of employment or at the plan's stated normal retirement age. Profit-sharing plans usually provide payment in the form of either a lump sum or a series of installment payments. The minimum installment payment must meet the minimum distribution rules discussed in Chapter 24. Some profit-sharing plans also offer annuity options with a life contingency, but this is relatively uncommon. (Note, however, that certain plans are subject to the joint and survivor annuity requirements discussed in Chapter 24.)

Profit-sharing plans typically allow "in service distributions"—that is, benefits payable before termination of employment. Many plans allow such distributions only in the event of "hardship" as specified in the plan. Typical hardship situations might include medical emergencies, home repair, or educational expenses. Employers traditionally administer such hardship provisions fairly liberally for the benefit of employees. The strict hardship definition applicable to Section 401(k) plans (see the "Questions and Answers" in Chapter 19) does not apply to profit-sharing plans.

The amount that a participant can withdraw before retirement or termination of employment cannot exceed the participant's vested account balance. In addition, the IRS has generally required that employer contributions cannot be withdrawn from the plan before termination of employment unless they have been in the plan for at least a 2-year period.[7] In some cases, the 2-year period can be waived if the participant has a minimum specified number of years of service, such as 5.[8] In order to control and limit withdrawals to prevent depletion of plan funds, many plans impose a "plan penalty" for withdrawals, such as suspending an employee from the plan for a period of 6 months after a withdrawal. No plan penalty, however, can take away any of the participant's vested benefits.

In addition to any plan penalties that may apply, there is a 10 percent early distribution penalty for many distributions to participants before age 59½. This penalty is discussed further in Chapter 24.

Because of the impact of the 10 percent early distribution penalty, it is very much in plan participants' interests to have a loan provision in a profit-sharing plan. Loan provisions allow participants access to plan funds for emergencies and other financial needs without incurring the tax penalty of an early withdrawal. Plan loans are discussed further in Chapter 24.

Profit-sharing plan funds are generally invested in a pooled account managed (through a trustee or insurance company) by the employer or a fund manager designated by the employer. Either a trust fund or group or individual insurance contract can be used. Chapter 14 discusses how life insurance can be used in the plan.

In a profit-sharing plan, it is common to use "participant investment direction" or "earmarking" of participants' accounts. Earmarked accounts can be invested at the participant's direction. Usually, the plan limits the number of possible investments to reduce administrative costs. If the participant-directed account provision meets Department of Labor (DOL) regulations,[9] the plan trustee is relieved from any fiduciary responsibility for the success or failure of an investment

chosen by the participant. Typically, the plan will offer the participant a choice of investments from a family of mutual funds. Under the DOL regulations, at least three diversified choices must be permitted.[10]

TAX IMPLICATIONS

1. Employer contributions to the plan are deductible when made, so long as the plan remains "qualified." A plan is qualified if it meets eligibility, vesting, funding, and other requirements discussed in Chapter 23. In addition, the plan must designate that it is a profit-sharing plan.[11]

   The maximum total employer contribution to the plan cannot exceed 15 percent of the payroll of all employees covered under the plan.[12] Any excess over this amount is not only nondeductible, but is also subject to a 10 percent penalty.[13] Only the first $200,000 (as indexed for inflation, $235,840 for 1993) of each employee's compensation can be taken into account for purposes of this limit.

   If, in addition to the profit-sharing plan, an employer maintains a defined benefit plan covering some of the same employees, the total contribution for both plans is limited to 25 percent of compensation of the covered employees (or, if greater, the amount necessary to meet the minimum funding standard for the defined benefit plan; in which case the contribution to the profit-sharing plan is not deductible).[14]

2. Assuming the plan remains qualified, taxation of the employee is deferred. That is, (1) employer contributions, (2) forfeitures added to the participant's account, (3) investment earnings on the account and (4) capital gains realized in the account, are all nontaxable to a plan participant until withdrawn.[15]

3. Under Code section 415, annual additions to each participant's account are limited to the *lesser of* (a) 25 percent of the participant's compensation or (b) the greater of $30,000 or ¼ of the defined benefit dollar limitation. (The defined benefit dollar limitation is $115,641 in 1993.) Annual additions include (1) employer contributions to the participant's account; (2) forfeitures from other participants' accounts; and (3) employee contributions to the account.

4. Distributions from a plan must follow the rules for qualified plan distributions. These distribution rules are discussed in Chapter 24.

5. Lump sum distributions made after age 59½ are subject to a limited election to use a special 5-year averaging tax

calculation. Certain older participants may also be eligible for a 10-year averaging tax calculation for lump sum distributions. Not all distributions are eligible for these special tax calculations. Chapter 24 covers the applicable rules and includes the appropriate IRS forms for making the calculation.

6. The plan is subject to the ERISA reporting and disclosure rules outlined in Appendix A.

ALTERNATIVES

1. Money purchase plans are defined contribution plans similar to profit-sharing plans except that the employer contribution percentage can be up to 25 percent of each participant's compensation. However, unlike a profit-sharing plan, the employer is required to make a contribution to a money purchase plan each year. (See Chapter 15.)

2. Target and other age-weighted plans are a defined contribution alternative similar to defined benefit plans. With age-weighted plans, the employer contribution percentage can be based on age at plan entry—higher for older entrants. An age-weighted plan may be favorable where the employer wants to provide adequate benefits for older (often key) employees. (See Chapter 21.)

3. Defined benefit plans provide more security of retirement benefits and proportionately greater contributions for older plan entrants, but are much more complex to design and administer. (See Chapter 9.)

4. Nonqualified deferred-compensation plans can be provided exclusively for selected executives. But the employer's tax deduction when a nonqualified plan is used is generally deferred until benefit payments are made. This can be as much as 20 or 30 years after the employer's contribution is made. (See Chapter 16.)

5. Individual retirement saving is an alternative or a supplement to an employer plan. But there is generally no tax deduction and tax deferral available except for the limited IRA provisions.

See also the discussion in Chapter 2, "Designing the Right Pension Plan."

HOW TO INSTALL A PLAN

Installation of a profit-sharing plan follows the qualified plan installation procedure described in Chapter 25.

WHERE CAN I FIND OUT MORE ABOUT IT?

1. McFadden, John J., *Retirement Plans for Employees*. Homewood, IL: Richard D. Irwin, 1988.

2. Gee, Judith Boyers, *Pensions in Perspective*, 4th ed. Cincinnati, OH: The National Underwriter Co., Fall 1993.

3. Graduate Course: Advanced Pension and Retirement Planning I (GS 814), The American College, Bryn Mawr, PA.

QUESTIONS AND ANSWERS

Question — Can a self-employed person adopt a profit-sharing plan?

Answer — A self-employed person (sole proprietor or partner in a partnership) can adopt a profit-sharing plan covering not only his or her regular employees, if any, but also covering the self-employed person(s). Such a plan is one type of "Keogh" or "HR 10" plan discussed in Chapter 12. Generally the self-employed person is treated the same as regular employees in a profit-sharing plan, but there are some special rules that apply.

Question — Can employees make contributions to a profit-sharing plan?

Answer — Employees can contribute to the plan only on an after-tax basis. If employees want to contribute on a before-tax (salary reduction) basis, the plan must meet the additional requirements of Section 401(k); these are discussed in Chapter 19. Furthermore, if the plan allows employee after-tax contributions, an additional set of nondiscrimination requirements must be met, the "Section 401(m)" rules. These are discussed in Chapter 18.

Question — How can an employer decide when a profit-sharing plan should be integrated with Social Security, and what are the factors involved in choosing the integration level?

Answer — A "stand alone" profit-sharing plan—where the employer has no qualified defined benefit or other plan—is almost always integrated with Social Security because (1) employer costs are reduced and (2) the employer contribution in an integrated plan is disproportionately allocated to higher paid key employees.

If an employer has two or more qualified plans covering even one employee in common, IRS integration rules do not allow both plans to be fully integrated; the degree of integration in one or all plans must be cut back under complex guidelines. Planners generally find that if an employer has both a defined benefit plan and a profit-sharing plan covering a common group of employees, it is most favorable to the employer and key employees to maximize the integration in the defined benefit plan and not to integrate the profit-sharing plan at all.

The current integration rules for defined contribution plans are as follows:

A defined contribution plan is integrated by providing a higher rate of contributions for compensation *above* a specified earnings level (excess-contribution percentage) than for compensation below a specified earnings level (base-contribution percentage).[16]

The maximum difference (permitted disparity) between the excess contribution percentage and the base-contribution percentage depends on the earnings level (integration level) chosen. If the integration level is the taxable wage base (TWB) used for Social Security purposes ($57,600 in 1993), the permitted disparity cannot exceed the lesser of (a) double the base percentage or (b) the base percentage plus 5.7 percent.[17] For example, if the employer contributes 5 percent for the first $57,600 of compensation, a 10 percent contribution can be made for compensation above that level. If, however, the base contribution percentage is 6 percent of the first $57,600, only an 11.7 percent contribution (not a 12 percent contribution) can be made for compensation above that level.

The law does not permit an integration level greater than the TWB for a defined contribution plan.[18] An integration level *below* the TWB can be used, however. If an integration level below the TWB is chosen, then the permitted disparity is reduced depending on the amount of the integration level.[19]

- The maximum excess contribution percentage used in a plan where the integration level is $46,080 to $57,599 (80% or more of the TWB) is the lesser of (a) double the base percentage or (b) the base percentage plus 5.4 percent.

- The maximum excess contribution percentage used in a plan where the integration level is $11,520 to $46,079 (20-79% of the TWB) is the lesser of (a) double the base percentage or (b) the base percentage plus 4.3 percent.

Question — What "integration level" should an employer choose?

Answer — Most small business owners will want to set the integration level at a point that will maximize contributions for owners and key employees. This can be accomplished by carefully looking at the employee census and assessing where a proper cutoff level would be.

Under prior law, the "optimum" integration level for a small business was just above the compensation level of the highest paid nonowner employee. This level gave *only* the owners the benefit of the extra percentage—the permitted disparity—under the integration rules.

Under the new integration regulations, choosing an optimum integration level is *much more complicated*. Because of the stepwise nature of the reduction in permitted disparity, a reduction in the integration level sometimes increases the owner's benefit from the permitted disparity and in some cases it does not.

In deciding on a reduced integration level, in most cases it will not pay to reduce the integration level if the reduction reduces the owner's benefit level, so certain integration levels are unfavorable.

Example: Rodin Industries has the following employee census:

Employee	Compensation
A. Rodin	$100,000
S. Q. Earl	30,000
Chip Munch	25,000

Rodin has a qualified integrated profit-sharing plan. What integration level will provide the maximum percentage of employer contributions for A. Rodin? Assuming a base percentage contribution of 6% of all compensation, calculations show:

Integration Level	Percent of Total Contributions for A. Rodin
$57,600	71.84%
46,080	72.98
45,000	71.71
30,000	73.19
20,000	70.53

The optimum integration level happens in this case to be $30,000 which produces 73.19% of the total contribution for Rodin.

While in some cases the difference between the optimum integration level and simply using the TWB of $57,600 may be relatively small, can a financial planner afford not to point it out to a client before somebody else does?

Question — Can a participant in a qualified profit-sharing plan use his profit-sharing account to purchase insurance on the life of his spouse (or the joint lives of himself and his spouse)?

Answer — Yes. IRS rulings have permitted a participant in a profit-sharing account to direct the plan trustee to purchase life insurance on the life of a person in whom he has an insurable interest.[20] Note that the plan must (a) include a "directed investment" (earmarking) provision and (b) must permit the purchase of such life insurance. If the plan does not have these two provisions, it cannot be used for this purpose unless it is amended to include these provisions.

The amount of the insurance on the participant's life is governed by the "incidental" limits discussed in Chapter 14. Note that for a profit-sharing plan, these rules allow all amounts that have been in the plan for at least two years to be used for insurance. Therefore, profit-sharing plans offer an opportunity to provide substantial amounts of insurance using tax-sheltered plan funds.

When an individual and his or her spouse have potentially large estates subject to federal estate tax, the tax becomes payable primarily at the death of the second, not the first to die. The advantage of a survivorship policy on an individual and spouse is that it provides substantial liquid funds when they are actually needed, and at an annual premium cost substantially lower than that for first-death insurance. If an individual in this situation has a substantial profit-sharing account, that account provides a source of funds to pay premiums for this insurance.

As with insurance for the participant alone under a qualified plan, survivorship insurance results in current, annual taxable income to the participant. Some advisers maintain that this income is not measurable under the P.S. 58 table rates, but rather using a lower annual cost reflecting the second-death feature—the "Table 38" cost.[21]

If the participant spouse dies first under this arrangement, the policy should be continued outside the plan.

The participant (while living) should direct that at his death the policy (which is part of his profit-sharing account balance) should be transferred to an irrevocable life insurance trust for the benefit of his family. If the nonparticipant spouse is the first to die, the participant should consider purchasing the policy from the plan, then contributing it to a life insurance trust.

It should be noted that there are no rulings (official or otherwise) which specifically sanction the use of survivorship policies in profit-sharing plans.

FOOTNOTES

1. IRC Section 401(a)(27)(A).
2. Reg. §1.401-1(b)(2).
3. IRC Section 414(s). See Prop. Reg. §1.414(s)-1.
4. IRC Section 401(a)(17).
5. Alternative methods for satisfying nondiscrimination requirements include satisfying a general nondiscrimination test, restructuring or cross-testing (testing defined contribution plans on the basis of benefits). See Prop. Reg. §1.401(a)(4)-2.
6. Prop. Reg. §1.401(a)(4)-1(b)(2)(ii).
7. Reg. §1.401-1(b)(1)(ii); Rev. Rul. 73-553, 1973-2 CB 130; Rev. Rul. 71-295, 1971-1 CB 184; Rev. Rul. 80-155, 1980-1 CB 84.
8. Rev. Rul. 68-24, 1968-1 CB 150.
9. DOL Reg. §2550.404c-1.
10. DOL Reg. §2550.404c-1(b)(3).
11. IRC Section 401(a)(27)(B).
12. IRC Section 404(a)(3).
13. IRC Section 4972.
14. IRC Section 404(a)(7).
15. IRC Section 402(a).
16. IRC Section 401(l)(2). See also, Regs. §§1.401(l)-1, -2, -4
17. IRC Section 401(l)(2)(A).
18. IRC Section 401(l)(5)(A)(ii).
19. Reg. §1.401(l)-2(d).
20. Let Ruls. 8445095, 8108110 (co-shareholder).
21. Where the spouse or dependent coverage is only available through the purchase of a rider to the policy on the life of the participant, the cost of the insurance currently includable in the participant's income may not be measured by the actual cost of the rider, but must be measured using the P.S. 58 rate. See Let. Rul. 9023044.

Chapter 18

SAVINGS PLAN

WHAT IS IT?

A savings plan (or "thrift plan") is a qualified defined contribution plan that is similar to a profit-sharing plan, with features that provide for and encourage after-tax employee contributions to the plan.

A typical savings plan provides after-tax employee contributions with matching employer contributions. Each employee elects to contribute a certain percentage of his or her compensation, and these employee contributions are matched—either dollar for dollar or under some other formula—by employer contributions to the plan. Employee contributions are not deductible—the employee pays tax on the money before contributing it to the plan.

In recent years, "pure" savings plans featuring only after-tax employee contributions have generally been replaced by the 401(k) type of plan described in Chapter 19. However, a savings plan with after-tax employee contributions is often added to a Section 401(k) plan.

WHEN IS IT INDICATED?

1. As an add-on feature to a Section 401(k) plan to allow employees to increase contributions beyond the $7,000 annual limit on salary reductions under Section 401(k) plans. (The $7,000 limit is indexed for inflation and is $8,994 in 1993.) However, after-tax contributions are subject to their own complex limitations as discussed under "Tax Implications," below.

2. When the employee group has the following characteristics:

   • Many employees are relatively young and have substantial time to accumulate retirement savings.

   • Many employees are willing to accept a degree of investment risk in their plan accounts in return for the potential benefits of good investment results.

   • There is a wide variation among employees in the need or desire for retirement savings.

3. When the employer wants to supplement the company's defined benefit pension plan with a plan that features

individual participant accounts and the opportunity for participants to save on a tax-deferred basis. The use of a combination of plans provides a balanced retirement program. The defined benefit plan appeals to older employees with a desire for secure retirement benefits, while the savings plan (or other defined contribution plan such as a profit-sharing or Section 401(k) plan) generally appeals to younger employees who prefer to see their savings build up year-by-year rather than anticipating a projected benefit when they retire.

ADVANTAGES

1. As with all qualified plans, a savings plan provides a tax-deferred retirement savings medium for employees. The tax on the after-tax employee contribution itself is not deferred. However, subsequent investment earnings on after-tax employee contributions are generally not subject to tax until distributions are made to employees from the plan.

2. The plan allows employees to control the amount of their savings. Employees have the option of taking all their compensation in cash and not contributing to the plan. (However, if they do so, they generally lose any employer matching contributions under the plan.)

3. Plan distributions may be eligible for the special 5-year (or 10-year) averaging tax computation available for qualified plans.

4. Individual participant accounts allow participants to benefit from good results in the plan fund.

DISADVANTAGES

1. The plan cannot be counted on by employees to provide an adequate benefit. First, benefits will not be significant unless employees make substantial contributions to the plan on a regular basis. Furthermore, employees who enter the plan at older ages may not be able to make sufficient contributions to the plan, even if they wish to do so, because of (a) the limits on annual contributions discussed under "Tax Implications," below, and (b) the limited number of years remaining for plan contributions prior to retirement.

2. Employees bear investment risk under the plan. Bearing the investment risk is a potential disadvantage to employees, but from the employer's perspective the shift of risk is a positive feature. Employer costs are lower for a defined contribution plan such as a savings plan, as compared with a defined benefit plan.

3. Since employee accounts and matching amounts must be individually accounted for in the plan, the administrative costs for a savings plan are greater than those for a money purchase or simple profit-sharing plan without employee contributions.

4. The annual addition to each employee's account in a savings plan is limited to the *lesser of* (a) 25 percent of compensation or (b) the greater of $30,000 or ¼ of the defined benefit dollar limitation.[1] (The defined benefit dollar limitation is $115,641 in 1993.) This limits the relative tax advantage available to highly compensated employees under a savings plan or any other defined contribution plan.

DESIGN FEATURES

Typical savings plans provide after-tax employee contributions with employer matching contributions. Participation in the plan is voluntary; each employee elects to contribute a chosen percentage of compensation up to a maximum percentage specified in the plan. The employee receives no tax deduction for this contribution and the contribution is fully subject to income tax as if it were in the employee's hands.

The employer makes a matching contribution to the savings plan. The employer match can be dollar-for-dollar, or the employer may put in some percentage of the employee contribution. A typical plan might permit an employee to contribute annually any whole percentage of compensation from one to six percent, with the employer contributing at the rate of half the chosen employee percentage. In this example then, if the employee elected to contribute 4 percent of compensation, the employer would be obligated to contribute an additional 2 percent.

In general, higher paid employees are in a position to contribute considerably more to this type of plan than lower paid employees. To prevent discrimination in savings plans, there is a numerical limit on the contributions by highly compensated employees (discussed under "Tax Implications," below). One of the principal administrative burdens in a savings plan is a need to monitor employee contribution levels to be sure the Section 401(m) nondiscrimination tests are met.

Apart from the employee contribution features, savings plans have features similar to profit-sharing plans. Emphasis is usually put on the "savings account-like" features of the plan. Usually there are generous provisions for employee withdrawal of funds and for plan loans. Savings plans often feature participant-investment direction or earmarking. Earmarking is usually provided by allowing employees a choice among several specified pooled investment funds (such as mutual funds). However, it is possible, although administratively burdensome, to allow participants to direct virtually any type of investment for their account. If certain Department of Labor regulations are satisfied, the use of a participant-directed investment provision relieves the plan trustee and the employer from fiduciary liability for investments chosen by the participant.[2] The regulations include the requirement that at least 3 different diversified investment alternatives be made available to the employee. Life insurance can be used in the plan, as discussed in Chapter 14.

Although savings plans with only after-tax employee contributions and employer matching contributions were very popular in the past, the after-tax employee contribution approach is currently used primarily as an add-on to a Section 401(k) plan. Employers often adopt a plan that combines all the features of a regular profit-sharing plan, a savings plan, and Section 401(k) salary reductions. These combined plans can have one or more of the following features:

• employee after-tax contributions

• employer matching of employee after-tax contributions

• employee (before-tax) salary reductions (Section 401(k) amounts)

• employer matching of Section 401(k) amounts

• employer contribution based on a formula

• discretionary employer contribution

These are discussed further in Chapter 19.

TAX IMPLICATIONS

1. Employer contributions to the plan are deductible when made so long as the plan remains "qualified" and separate accounts are maintained for all participants in the plan.[3] A plan is qualified if it meets eligibility, vesting, funding and other requirements discussed in Chapter 23.

2. Employee contributions to the plan, whether or not matched, are not tax deductible. (Before-tax employee salary reductions must meet the rules of Section 401(k) discussed in Chapter 19.)

3. Assuming a plan remains qualified, taxation of the employee is deferred with respect to (a) employer contributions to the plan and (b) investment earnings on both employer and employee contributions. These amounts are nontaxable to plan participants until a distribution is made from the plan.[4]

4. In order to prevent discrimination in favor of highly compensated employees, the plan must meet a special test under Code section 401(m). Under Section 401(m), the plan is not deemed discriminatory for a plan year if, for highly compensated employees, the average ratio (expressed as a percentage) *of* employee contributions (both matched and non-matched) plus employer matching contributions *to* compensation does not exceed the greater of

- 125 percent of the contribution percentage (i.e., ratio) for all other eligible employees, or

- the lesser of (a) 200 percent of the contribution percentage for all other eligible employees, or (b) such percentage plus 2 percentage points.

For example, if employee contributions and employer matching contributions for nonhighly compensated employees are 6 percent of compensation, those for highly compensated employees can be up to 8 percent (6 percent plus 2 percent).

Administratively, the employer must monitor the level of contributions made by nonhighly compensated employees, and then make sure that highly compensated employees do not exceed this level in order for the plan to remain qualified.

Under the Code and regulations, in meeting this test the employer may take into account certain 401(k) salary reduction contributions and certain employer plan contributions may be considered.[5] The definition of highly compensated employee is the same as that applicable to all benefit plans (and is discussed in detail in Chapter 23).

5. Distributions from the plan must follow the rules for qualified plan distributions. Certain premature or excessive distributions are subject to penalties. The distribution rules are discussed in Chapter 24.

6. Lump sum distributions made after age 59½ are subject to a limited election to use a special 5-year averaging tax calculation. Certain older participants may also be eligible for a 10-year averaging tax calculation for lump sum distributions. Not all distributions are eligible for these special tax calculations. The rules are discussed in detail in Chapter 24.

7. The plan is subject to the ERISA reporting and disclosure rules outlined in Appendix A.

HOW TO INSTALL A PLAN

Installation of a savings plan follows the qualified plan installation procedures described in Chapter 25.

WHERE CAN I FIND OUT MORE ABOUT IT?

1. McFadden, John J., *Retirement Plans for Employees.* Homewood, IL: Richard D. Irwin, 1988.

2. Gee, Judith Boyers, *Pensions in Perspective*, 4th ed. Cincinnati, OH: The National Underwriter Co., Fall 1993.

FOOTNOTES

1. IRC Section 415(c).
2. DOL Reg. §2550.404c-1.
3. IRC Section 404(a)(3).
4. IRC Section 402(a).
5. IRC Section 401(m)(3); Reg. §1.401(m)-1(b)(5).

Chapter 19

SECTION 401(k) PLAN

WHAT IS IT?

A Section 401(k) plan (also known as a "qualified cash or deferred plan") is a qualified profit-sharing or stock bonus plan under which plan participants have an option to put money in the plan (up to $7,000 annually, as indexed for inflation—$8,994 in 1993) or receive the same amount as taxable cash compensation. Amounts contributed to the plan under this option are not taxable to the participants until withdrawn. Aside from features related to the cash or deferred option, a Section 401(k) plan is much like a regular qualified profit-sharing plan described in Chapter 17.

WHEN IS IT INDICATED?

1. When an employer wants to provide a qualified retirement plan for employees but can afford only minimal extra expense beyond existing salary and benefit costs. A Section 401(k) plan can be funded entirely from employee salary reductions, except for installation and administration costs. In most plans, however, additional direct employer contribution to the plan can enhance its effectiveness.

2. When the employee group has one or more of the following characteristics:

    • Many would like some choice as to the level of savings—that is, a choice between various levels of current cash compensation and tax deferred savings. A younger, more mobile work force often prefers this option.

    • Many employees are relatively young and have substantial time to accumulate retirement savings.

    • Many employees are willing to accept a degree of investment risk in their plan accounts in return for the potential benefits of good investment results.

3. When an employer wants an attractive, "savings-type" supplement to its existing defined benefit or other qualified retirement plan. Such a supplement can make the employer's retirement benefit program attractive to both younger and older employees by providing both security of retirement benefits and the opportunity to increase savings and investment on a tax-deferred basis.

ADVANTAGES

1. As with all qualified plans, a Section 401(k) plan provides a tax-deferred retirement savings medium for employees.

2. A Section 401(k) plan allows employees a degree of choice in the amount they wish to save under the plan.

3. Section 401(k) plans can be funded entirely through salary reductions by employees. As a result, an employer can adopt the plan with no additional cost for employee compensation; the only extra cost is plan installation and administration. The plan may actually result in some savings as a result of lower state or local (but not federal) payroll taxes.

4. Plan distributions may be eligible for the special 5-year (or 10-year) averaging tax computation available for qualified plans.

5. In-service withdrawals by employees for "hardship" are permitted; these are not available in qualified pension plans.

DISADVANTAGES

1. As with all defined contribution plans (except target plans), account balances at retirement age may not provide adequate retirement savings for employees who entered the plan at later ages.

2. The annual employee salary reduction under the plan is limited to $8,994 (as indexed for 1993). However, this amount can be supplemented by direct employer contributions to provide additional tax-deferred savings.

    Furthermore, $8,994 (as indexed) annually is a substantial amount of savings for most employees. A Section 401(k) plan must limit salary reductions to about 15% of compensation in any event, because of the employer deduction limit (see "Tax Implications" below). Thus, the $8,994 limit, as indexed, is not really a limiting factor for employees with compensation below about $60,000 annually.

    Moreover, saving $8,994 (as indexed) annually provides a substantial amount of retirement savings, especially for those who enter a Section 401(k) plan at earlier ages. For illustration, the ultimate account balances for plan participants who enter the plan in 1993 and who save the maximum amount each year until retirement are as follows, assuming (a) an inflation rate (and corresponding increase in the $8,994 limit) of 3% annually and (b) investment return of 7% annually on the plan account balance:

Age at Plan Entry	Account Balance at age 65	Account Balance at age 65 (1993 dollars)
25	$ 2,794,458	$ 856,661
35	1,237,084	509,662
45	492,347	272,601
55	148,697	110,644

3. Employer deductions for plan contributions (including employee salary reductions as well as direct employer contributions) cannot exceed 15% of the total payroll of employees covered under the plan. This contrasts with a limit of 25% of compensation for a money purchase or target plan—and no percentage limit for a defined benefit plan. These other types of plans can provide greater tax-deferred savings than a Section 401(k) plan. (Many employers combine a Section 401(k) plan with a pension plan to provide maximum benefits for employees.)

4. Because of the "actual deferral percentage" (ADP) non-discrimination tests described below, a Section 401(k) plan can be relatively costly and complex to administer.

5. Employees bear investment risk under the plan. (However, they can also potentially benefit from good investment results.)

DESIGN FEATURES

Salary Reductions

Virtually all Section 401(k) plans are funded entirely or in part through salary reductions elected by employees. An alternative sometimes used is for the employer to provide all employees with an annual "bonus" that employees can either receive in cash or contribute to the plan. In substance both approaches are the same, but the salary reduction approach is more popular because it uses existing salary scales as a starting point.

Salary reductions must be elected by employees before compensation is earned—that is, before they render the services for which compensation is paid. Salary reductions

elected after compensation is earned are ineffective as a result of the tax doctrine of "constructive receipt."

The usual practice is to provide plan participants with a salary reduction election form that they must complete before the end of each calendar year. The election specifies how much will be contributed to the plan from each paycheck received for the forthcoming year. The amount cannot be increased later in the year. But usually the employee can reduce or entirely withdraw the election for pay not yet earned, if circumstances dictate. The plan must restrict each participant's salary reductions to no more than the annual limit, as indexed for inflation ($8,994 in 1993).

The participant is always 100% vested in any salary reductions contributed to the plan and any plan earnings on those salary reductions. Even if a participant leaves employment after a short time, his plan account based on salary reductions cannot be forfeited. Usually plan account balances are distributed in a lump sum when a participant terminates employment.

Salary reductions, as well as any other plan contribution if the employee has the option to receive the amount in cash (referred to as "elective deferrals"), are subject to an annual limit. The employee must add together each year all elective deferrals from (1) Section 401(k) plans, (2) salary reduction SEPs (see Chapter 20) and (3) Section 403(b) tax deferred annuity plans (see Chapter 22). All elective deferrals from all employer plans that cover the employee must be aggregated. The total must not exceed $8,994 (as indexed). (As discussed in Chapter 22, a higher $9,500 limit may apply for a Section 403(b) tax deferred annuity plan. Salary reductions under a Section 457 deferred compensation plan (see Chapter 11) maintained by a government or non-profit employer must also be coordinated with these elective deferrals.) Any excess elective deferrals over this limit are taxable income to the employee.[1]

Employer Contributions

Many Section 401(k) plans provide direct employer contributions in order to encourage employee participation and make the plan more valuable to employees. Plans typically use one or more of the following types of employer contributions:

• Formula matching contributions. The employer matches employee salary reductions, either dollar for dollar or under another formula. For example, the plan might provide that the employer contributes an amount equal to 50% of the amount the employee elects as a salary reduction. So, if an employee elects a salary reduction of $6,000, the employer puts an additional $3,000 into the employee's plan account.

- Discretionary matching contributions. Under this approach, the employer has discretion to make a contribution to the plan each year; the employer contribution is allocated to each participant's plan account in proportion to the amount elected by the participant as a salary reduction during that year. For example, at the end of a year the employer might decide to make a discretionary matching contribution of 40% of each participant's salary reduction for the year. Thus, if a participant had salary reductions of $5,000 for that year, the employer would contribute another $2,000 to that participant's account.

- Pure discretionary or "profit-sharing" contribution. The employer makes a discretionary contribution to the plan that is allocated simply on the basis of each employee's compensation, without regard to the amount of salary reductions elected by that employee. For example, at the end of a year the employer might decide to contribute another $100,000 to the plan. This contribution would be allocated to plan participants' accounts in the same manner as a discretionary profit-sharing contribution, as described in Chapter 17.

- Formula contribution. For example, the plan might provide that the employer will contribute 3 percent of compensation to the plan for employees whose annual compensation is less than $50,000. So, for an employee who earned $30,000, the employer would contribute 3 percent, or $900, to that employee's plan account.

Direct (nonelective) employer contribution provisions in Section 401(k) plans are usually intended to help the plan meet the ADP tests discussed below. The plan designer will use whatever contribution provision is most likely to be helpful for this purpose, given the group of employees covered under the plan. Note that nonelective employer contributions can be used to help meet the ADP tests only if they are immediately 100% vested and are subject to the same withdrawal restrictions applicable to elective deferrals (discussed below).[2]

Section 401(k) plans can also include nonelective employer contributions that are not intended to be counted in the ADP tests. The advantage of this is that such employer contributions need not be 100% vested. Graded vesting under the 3-to-7-year provision is usually used (see Chapter 23). Graded vesting reduces employer cost for the plan since employees who leave employment before they are fully vested forfeit the nonvested part of their account balances. These "forfeitures" can then be used to reduce future employer contributions or, more commonly, redistributed to remaining participants' accounts in the plan. (Forfeitures cannot be repaid to the employer in cash in any qualified plan.)

Plan Distributions

Distributions from Section 401(k) plans are subject to the qualified plan distribution rules detailed in Chapter 24. Most plans provide for distributions in a lump sum at termination of employment.

Section 401(k) plans often allow participants to make in-service withdrawals (withdrawals before termination of employment). However, there are a variety of restrictions that reduce the attractiveness of such provisions to employees. First, there is a special rule that Section 401(k) accounts based on elective deferrals cannot be distributed prior to occurrence of one of the following:

- retirement

- death

- disability

- separation from service with the employer

- attainment of age 59½ by the participant

- plan termination (if the employer has no other defined contribution plan other than an ESOP)

- hardship[3]

"Hardship" is defined more restrictively than many participants may think, as discussed in the "Questions and Answers," below.

Note also that many pre-retirement distributions will not only be taxable, but will also be subject to the 10% early withdrawal penalty tax discussed in Chapter 24. To summarize, a 10% penalty tax applies to the taxable amount (amount subject to regular income tax) of any qualified plan distribution, except for distributions

- after age 59½

- on the employee's death

- upon the employee's disability

- that are part of a joint or life annuity payout following separation from service

- that are paid after separation from service after attaining age 55, or

- that do not exceed the amount of medical expenses deductible as an itemized deduction for the year.[4]

From this list, it is evident that many "hardship" distributions from a Section 401(k) plan, though permitted by the terms of the plan, will be subject to the 10% penalty tax.

Many Section 401(k) plans have provisions for plan loans to participants. A plan loan provision may be extremely valuable to employees because it allows them access to their plan funds without the "hardship" restriction or the 10% penalty tax. Plan loans are discussed in detail in Chapter 24.

TAX IMPLICATIONS

1. Employee elective deferrals (including salary reductions) are not currently income taxable to the employee, within the annual limit discussed earlier ($8,994 in 1993).[5] However, elective deferrals are subject to Social Security tax (both employer and employee).[6] In other words, even though salary has been deferred for income tax purposes, it is treated as received for Social Security purposes.

2. Nonelective employer contributions to the plan and employee elective deferrals are deductible by the employer for federal income tax purposes up to a limit of 15% of the total taxable payroll of all employees covered under the plan.[7] Elective deferrals, but not nonelective employer contributions, are subject to Social Security (FICA) and federal unemployment (FUTA) payroll taxes. The impact of state payroll taxes depends on the particular state's law. Both elective deferrals and nonelective employer contributions may be exempt from state payroll taxes in some states.

3. Elective deferrals must meet a special test for nondiscrimination—the "actual deferral percentage" or ADP test.[8] The plan must meet one of the following two tests in actual operation:

   Test 1 — The ADP for eligible highly compensated employees must not be more than the ADP of all other eligible employees multiplied by 1.25.

   Test 2 — The ADP for eligible highly compensated employees must not exceed the ADP for other eligible employees by more than 2 percent *and* the ADP for eligible highly compensated employees must not be more than the ADP of all other eligible employees multiplied by 2.

For example, if the ADP for nonhighly compensated employees is 6 percent, the ADP for highly compensated employees can be as high as 8 percent (6 percent plus 2 percent). This meets Test 2.

"Highly compensated employee" is defined as it is for all qualified plan purposes.[9] In summary (more details are in Chapter 23), a highly compensated employee is an employee who:

- was at any time, during the current or preceding plan year, a more-than-5 percent owner of the employer,

- received compensation from the employer over $75,000, as indexed for inflation ($96,368 in 1993),

- received compensation over $50,000, as indexed ($64,245 in 1993) and was in the highest-paid 20% of the employer's employees, or

- was an officer and received compensation in excess of 50% of the defined benefit dollar limitation (in excess of $57,820.50 in 1993).

4. As with any defined contribution plan, annual additions to each participant's account are limited to the *lesser of* (a) 25 percent of compensation or (b) the greater of $30,000 or ¼ of the defined benefit dollar limitation.[10] (The defined benefit dollar limitation is $115,641 in 1993.) Annual additions include the total of (1) nonelective employer contributions to the participant's account, (2) salary reductions or other elective deferrals contributed to the account, (3) forfeitures from other participants' accounts, and (4) after-tax employee contributions to the account.[11]

5. Distributions from the plan to employees are subject to income tax when received. Lump sum distributions made after age 59½ are subject to a limited election to use a special 5-year averaging tax calculation. Certain older participants may also be eligible for a 10-year averaging tax calculation. Not all distributions are eligible for these special tax calculations. The details of taxation of distributions are discussed in Chapter 24.

HOW TO INSTALL A PLAN

Installation of a Section 401(k) plan follows the qualified plan installation procedure described in Chapter 25.

In addition, elective deferral or salary reduction forms must be completed by plan participants before the plan's effective date so that salary reduction elections will be immediately effective.

The success of a Section 401(k) plan in meeting the employer's objectives and the ADP tests depends on effective communication with employees. Effective employer-employee communication is always important in employee benefit plans, but it is particularly essential for a Section 401(k) plan because of the active role of employees in the plan.

WHERE CAN I FIND OUT MORE ABOUT IT?

1. McFadden, John J., *Retirement Plans for Employees.* Homewood, IL: Richard D. Irwin, 1988.

2. Gee, Judith Boyers, *Pensions in Perspective*, 4th ed. Cincinnati, OH: The National Underwriter Co., Fall 1993.

3. Graduate Course: Advanced Pension and Retirement Planning I (GS 814), The American College, Bryn Mawr, PA.

QUESTIONS AND ANSWERS

Question — What kinds of organizations can adopt Section 401(k) plans?

Answer — Any incorporated or unincorporated business can adopt a Section 401(k) plan for its employees. The plan of an unincorporated business can cover partners or a sole proprietor as well as regular employees.

Non-profit organizations and governmental (federal, state, or local) organizations are generally not eligible to maintain a Section 401(k) plan.[12] (However, such employers who maintained pre-1987 plans that were "grandfathered" under the Tax Reform Act of 1986 and certain rural cooperative organizations are exempt from this prohibition.[13]) Non-profit organizations should investigate adoption of a Section 403(b) tax deferred annuity plan (see Chapter 22) as an alternative. Both non-profit and governmental organizations can also adopt Section 457 plans (see Chapter 11), which provide some features similar to a Section 401(k) plan.

Question — Can a Section 401(k) plan participant make deductible IRA contributions as well as salary reductions under a Section 401(k) plan?

Answer — Yes, but only within the reduced deductible IRA limits allowed for active qualified plan participants—see Chapter 13. No deduction is allowed for a year in which adjusted gross income is $50,000 or more for a married couple filing jointly ($35,000 for a single person), with reduced deductions for adjusted gross income between $40,000 and $50,000 joint ($25,000 to $35,000 single).

Question — What is a "hardship" that permits a Section 401(k) plan participant to make withdrawals?

Answer — The IRS regulations require that a hardship distribution must meet two conditions: (a) The distribution must be necessary in light of immediate and heavy financial needs of the employee, and (2) funds must not be reasonably available from other resources of the employee.

As guidance in interpreting the first requirement, the regulations[14] list the following as meeting the "immediate and heavy" requirement:

- Medical expenses incurred by the participant or the participant's spouse or dependents.

- Purchase of a principal residence for the participant (mortgage payments do not typically constitute a hardship).

- Payment of tuition for the next 12 months of post-secondary education for a participant or his spouse, children, or dependents.

- Payments of amounts necessary to prevent the eviction of the participant from his principal residence or from foreclosure on the mortgage.

The second issue—the existence of other resources—is determined on the basis of individual facts and circumstances. To simplify plan administration, there is a "safe harbor" test for this—the requirement will be deemed met if the following circumstances exist:

(1) The distribution does not exceed the amount of the immediate and heavy financial need,

(2) the employee must obtain all distributions other than hardship distributions and all nontaxable loans available under all plans maintained by the employer, and

(3) the plan must provide that the employee's elective deferral contributions and nondeductible contributions will be suspended for 12 months after the distribution and that the maximum contribution in the year following the suspension will be reduced by the amount contributed in the prior year.

Question — What types of investments are appropriate for Section 401(k) plans?

Answer — Generally, investments traditionally used in qualified profit-sharing plans are also used in Section 401(k) plans. Employee accounts in the plan fund are usually pooled for investment purposes. Investment tends toward bonds, money market, and liquid, cash-type media. Smaller plans often use a "family" of mutual funds for plan investments. The level of equity investment (common stocks) in Section 401(k) plans is usually lower than in defined benefit plans.

Many plans use a "directed investment" or "earmarking" provision that allows participants some degree of choice in the investment of their plan accounts. Directed investment provisions increase administrative costs of the plan. But they are attractive to employees and, if the directed investment provision meets the standards of Labor Department regulations,[15] the employer is relieved of fiduciary responsibility for any investment directed by the participant.

Life insurance is often provided in Section 401(k) plans in much the same way as it is used in a regular profit-sharing plan. The use of life insurance in a qualified plan is discussed in Chapter 14.

FOOTNOTES

1. IRC Section 402(g)(1); Reg. §1.402(g)-1.
2. IRC Section 401(k)(3)(D); Regs. §§1.401(k)-1(b)(5), 1.401(k)-1(g)(13).
3. IRC Section 401(k)(2)(B).
4. IRC Section 72(t).
5. IRC Section 402(g).
6. IRC Section 3121(v)(1).
7. IRC Section 404(a)(3).
8. IRC Section 401(k)(3)(A).
9. IRC Section 414(q).
10. IRC Section 415(c).
11. IRC Section 415(c)(2).
12. IRC Section 401(k)(4)(B).
13. See TRA '86, Section 1116(f)(2)(B); TAMRA '88, Section 1101(k)(8).
14. Reg. §1.401(k)-1(d)(2).
15. DOL Reg. §2550.404c-1.

Chapter 20

SIMPLIFIED EMPLOYEE PENSION (SEP)

WHAT IS IT?

A simplified employee pension (SEP) is an employer-sponsored retirement/deferred compensation arrangement that is similar to a qualified profit-sharing plan. Congress enacted the SEP provisions of the Code to provide employers with a "simplified" alternative to a qualified plan.

Like a qualified profit-sharing plan, a SEP combines simplicity of design with a high degree of flexibility from the employer's viewpoint. In substance, a SEP is merely an employer agreement to contribute on a nondiscriminatory basis to IRAs maintained by employees. The limits for SEP contributions are much higher than those for individually-owned IRAs, however—up to the lesser of (a) 15 percent of compensation or (b) $30,000 (as indexed for inflation— see Chapter 23).

WHEN IS IT INDICATED?

1. When the employer is looking for an alternative to a qualified profit-sharing plan that is easier and less expensive to install and administer. For very small employers, a SEP is probably the simplest type of tax-deferred employee retirement plan available. For larger employers (more than about 10 employees) the cost of installing and administering a regular qualified plan can be spread over enough employees that the advantages of a SEP are less significant.

2. When an employer wants to install a tax-deferred plan and it is too late to adopt a qualified plan for the year in question. (Qualified plans must be adopted before the end of the year in which they are to be effective. SEPs can be adopted as late as the tax return filing date for the year in which they are to be effective.)

3. When an employer has 25 or fewer employees and wants a simple plan funded through employee salary reductions (before-tax contributions); see #2 under "Tax Implications," below.

ADVANTAGES

1. A SEP can be adopted by completing a simple IRS form (Forms 5305-SEP or 5305A-SEP, reproduced at the end

of this chapter) rather than by the complex procedure required for qualified plans (described in Chapter 25). However, if the employer adopts a master or prototype qualified plan, the installation costs and complexity may not actually be much greater than that for a SEP, even though the documentation is more voluminous

2. Benefits of a SEP are totally portable by employees since funding consists entirely of IRAs for each employee and employees are always 100 percent vested in their benefits. Employees own and control their SEP-IRA accounts, even after they terminate employment with the original employer.

3. A SEP provides as much or more flexibility in the amount and timing of contributions as a qualified profit-sharing plan. The employer is free at its discretion to make no contribution to the plan in any given year.

4. Individual IRA accounts allow participants to benefit from good investment results (as well as run the risk of bad results).

5. A SEP can be funded through salary reductions by employees (sometimes referred to as a "SARSEP"), if conditions described in "Tax Implications," below, are met.

DISADVANTAGES

1. Employees cannot rely upon a SEP to provide an adequate retirement benefit. First, benefits are not significant unless the employer makes substantial, regular contributions to the SEP. The employer has no obligation to do this under the plan. Furthermore, employees who enter the plan at older ages have only a limited number of years remaining prior to retirement to build up their SEP accounts.

2. Employees bear investment risk under the plan.

3. The annual contribution to each employee's account in a SEP is limited to the lesser of (a) 15 percent of compensation or (b) the greater of $30,000 or ¼ of the dollar limitation for defined benefit plans. (The dollar limitation for defined benefit plans is $115,641 for 1993.) This

limits the relative tax advantage available to highly compensated employees under a SEP.

4. Distributions from SEPs are not eligible for the 5-year (or 10-year) averaging provisions available for certain qualified plan distributions.

TAX IMPLICATIONS

1. An employer may deduct contributions to a SEP, up to the 15%/$30,000 limit, if they are made under a written formula that meets various requirements of the Internal Revenue Code. These requirements are somewhat similar to those for qualified plans. The "qualified plan rules," as such, do not apply to SEPs.

The major SEP requirements are[1]:

• A SEP must cover all employees who are at least 21 years of age and who have worked for the employer during 3 out of the preceding 5 calendar years. Part-time employment counts in determining years of service.

• Contributions need not be made on behalf of employees whose compensation for the calendar year was less than $300, as indexed for inflation ($385 in 1993).

• The plan can exclude employees who are members of collective bargaining units if retirement benefits have been the subject of good-faith bargaining; nonresident aliens can also be excluded.

The employer need not contribute any particular amount to a SEP or make any contribution at all. The "recurring and substantial contributions" requirement applicable to qualified profit-sharing plans (as discussed in Chapter 17) has no effect on SEPs, so a SEP is more flexible contribution-wise than a qualified plan. An employer can freely omit many year's contributions to a SEP without any concern about adverse tax consequences. The employer contribution, if made, must be allocated to plan participants under a written formula that does not discriminate in favor of highly compensated employees. The definition of "highly compensated" is that used for most employee benefit purposes, as discussed in Chapter 23.

SEP formulas usually provide allocations as a uniform percentage of total compensation of each employee. In the allocation formula, only the first $200,000 (as indexed—$235,840 in 1993) of each employee's compensation can be taken into account.

SEP allocation formulas can be integrated with Social Security under the integration rules applicable to qualified defined contribution plans; these are discussed in Chapter 23. A salary reduction SEP (see below) may not be integrated.

2. If an employer has 25 or fewer eligible employees during the preceding year, SEPs can be funded through employee salary reductions. With a salary reduction plan, employees have an election to receive cash or have amounts contributed to the SEP. The arrangement works very much like a Section 401(k) salary reduction arrangement described in Chapter 19. The $7,000 limit as indexed ($8,994 in 1993) on elective deferrals applies to the total of salary reduction SEP and 401(k) salary reductions, if any.[2]

An employer cannot use a salary reduction SEP unless 50 percent or more of the employees eligible to participate elect to make SEP contributions. In addition, "average deferral percentage" (ADP) rules similar to the 401(k) rules apply to a salary reduction SEP.

The deferral percentage for each highly compensated eligible employee who participates must be no more than 1.25 times the ADP of nonhighly compensated eligible employees. For example, if nonhighly compensated employees elect salary reductions averaging 6 percent of compensation, no highly compensated employee can elect more than a 7.5 percent salary reduction.

3. If an employer maintains a SEP and also maintains a regular qualified plan, contributions to the SEP reduce the amount that can be deducted for contributions to the regular plan.

4. In a SEP plan, each participating employee maintains an IRA. Employer contributions are made directly to the employee's IRA, as are any employee salary reduction contributions. Employer contributions and employee salary reductions, within the limits discussed above, are not included in the employee's taxable income.

5. Salary reductions, but not direct employer contributions, are subject to Social Security (FICA) and federal unemployment (FUTA) taxes.[3] The impact of state payroll taxes depends on the particular state's law. Both salary reductions and employer contributions may be exempt from state payroll taxes in some states.

6. Distributions to employees from the plan are treated as distributions from an IRA. All the restrictions on IRA

distributions apply and the distributions are taxed the same. The taxation of IRA distributions is discussed in Chapter 13. In particular, note that the 5-year (or 10-year) averaging provisions are not available for either IRA or SEP distributions.

HOW TO INSTALL A PLAN

Installation of a SEP can be very simple. The employer merely completes Form 5305-SEP. For a salary reduction SEP, Form 5305A-SEP is used. Copies of these forms and instructions are reproduced at the end of this chapter. To adopt the SEP, the relevant form is completed and signed by the employer prior to the tax filing date for the year in which the SEP is to take effect.[4] The form does not have to be sent to the IRS or other government agency.

A SEP adopted by filling out Form 5305-SEP or Form 5305A-SEP is somewhat inflexible since it must follow the provisions set out on those IRS forms. Some of the provisions in these forms are more stringent than are actually required by the SEP rules; in particular

1. The plan set out on Form 5305-SEP is not integrated with Social Security.

2. By their terms, Forms 5305-SEP and 5305A-SEP cannot be used if the employer (1) currently maintains a qualified plan or (2) maintained a qualified defined benefit plan at any time in the past covering one or more of the employees to be covered under the SEP.

3. Form 5305A-SEP includes a formula that automatically requires top-heavy contributions (see Chapter 23) even if the plan is not actually top-heavy.

If the employer wants to adopt a SEP plan that avoids the limitations of the IRS forms, the plan must be custom designed. Costs for custom designing and installing a SEP are comparable to those for a qualified profit-sharing plan.

ERISA REQUIREMENTS

The reporting and disclosure requirements for SEPs are simplified if the employer uses the IRS form of SEP contained on Form 5305-SEP or 5305A-SEP. The annual report form (5500 series) need not be filed if these forms are used. In other cases, reporting and disclosure requirements are similar to those for a qualified profit-sharing plan.

WHERE CAN I FIND OUT MORE ABOUT IT?

1. IRS Publication 334, *Tax Guide for Small Business,* and Publication 535, *Business Expense Deductions*, available free from the IRS; revised annually.

2. Gee, Judith Boyers, *Pensions in Perspective*, 4th ed. Cincinnati, OH: The National Underwriter Co., Fall 1993.

QUESTIONS AND ANSWERS

Question—How does the "last minute" adoption feature of a SEP operate?

Answer — Suppose an employer reviews financial results shortly after the close of the employer's tax year—say it's a calendar year—and decides that the company should have a qualified plan for the year just ended. It is not possible to adopt a qualified plan after the close of the taxable year, as discussed in Chapter 25. However, a SEP can be adopted at any time up to the tax return filing date for the year, including extensions. For example, if an incorporated employer uses the calendar year, the tax return filing date for the year 1992 is March 15, 1993, with extensions possible to September 15, 1993. Therefore a SEP could be adopted for 1992 as late as September 15, 1993.

Note, however, that a SARSEP arrangement must be adopted prior to the time employees begin salary reductions.

Question — Can an unincorporated business adopt a SEP covering partners or a sole proprietor?

Answer — Yes. Partners and proprietors can be covered under the SEP of an unincorporated employer, as well as regular employees. As discussed in Chapter 12 (relating to HR 10 plans), for a partner or proprietor, "earned income" is used in place of compensation in computing SEP contributions.

Question—Can an employer make contributions to a SEP for employees who are over age 70½?

Answer — An individual cannot make contributions to his or her own IRA after attaining age 70½. However, employers can make contributions to SEPs for employees who are over age 70½. In fact, the age discrimination law, if applicable, would generally require such contributions to be made.

Question — Can a family business adopt a salary reduction SEP?

Answer — If family members are the only employees of the business, it is possible that all of the employees would be considered "highly compensated" under the Code definition (Chapter 23). Technically, the ADP test could not be met. However, the IRS has acknowledged in its regulations under Section 401(k) that a Section 401(k) plan does not fail to qualify just because all eligible employees are highly compensated.[5] This reasoning should also apply to a SEP. Note, however, that Form 5305A-SEP cannot be used if the employer has only highly compensated employees.

Question — Can an employee participating in a SEP also make deductible contributions to his or her own IRA?

Answer — For individual IRA purposes, a SEP participant is treated the same as a participant in a regular qualified plan. That is, if the individual is an "active participant" in the plan, individual IRA contributions can be made and deducted, but the $2,000/$2,250 deduction limit is reduced for individuals with adjusted gross income (AGI) of more than $25,000 or married couples with AGI of more than $40,000. If the individual is not an active participant in the plan, the full IRA deduction is available. These rules are discussed in detail in Chapter 13.

An employee covered under a SEP would be considered an active participant in any year in which salary reductions or employer contributions were allocated to his or her SEP account. However, in a year in which no allocation was made to the individual's SEP account, the individual would have a full individual IRA deduction available (up to the $2,000/$2,250 limit).[6] The higher SEP limit is not available for individual IRA contributions, only for employer contributions or salary reductions under a SEP arrangement.

FOOTNOTES

1. The rules described in this chapter for SEPs are contained in Code Section 408(k) unless otherwise indicated in the footnotes.
2. IRC Section 402(g), (h).
3. IRC Sections 3121(a)(5)(C), 3306(b)(5)(C).
4. Prop. Reg. §1.408-7(b).
5. Reg. §1.401(k)-1(b)(2)(i).
6. Notice 87-16, 1987-1 CB 446, I.

Form **5305-SEP**	**Simplified Employee Pension-Individual**	OMB No. 1545-0499
(Rev. June 1991)	**Retirement Accounts Contribution Agreement**	Expires 4-30-94
Department of the Treasury Internal Revenue Service	(Under Section 408(k) of the Internal Revenue Code)	**Do NOT File with Internal Revenue Service**

_____ makes the following agreement under the terms of section 408(k) of

(Business name—employer)

the Internal Revenue Code and the instructions to this form.

The employer agrees to provide for discretionary contributions in each calendar year to the Individual Retirement Accounts or Individual Annuities (IRA's) of all eligible employees who are at least _____ years old (not over 21 years old) (see instruction "Who May Participate") and worked in at least _____ years (enter 1, 2, or 3 years) of the immediately preceding 5 years (see instruction "Who May Participate"). This ☐ includes ☐ does not include employees covered under a collective bargaining agreement and ☐ includes ☐ does not include employees whose total compensation during the year is less than $363*.

The employer agrees that contributions made on behalf of each eligible employee will:

- Be made only on the first $222,220* of compensation.
- Be made in an amount that is the same percentage of total compensation for every employee.
- Be limited to the smaller of $30,000 or 15% of compensation.
- Be paid to the employee's IRA trustee, custodian, or insurance company (for an annuity contract).

_____   _____

Signature of employer   Date

_____

By

Instructions for the Employer

(Section references are to the Internal Revenue Code, unless otherwise noted.)

Paperwork Reduction Act Notice.— We ask for the information on this form to carry out the Internal Revenue laws of the United States. You are required to give us the information. We need it to determine if you are entitled to a deduction for contributions made to a Simplified Employee Pension (SEP). Complete this form only if you want to establish a Model SEP.

The time needed to complete this form will vary depending on individual circumstances. The estimated average time is:

Recordkeeping	7 min.
Learning about the law or the form	24 min.
Preparing the form	18 min.

If you have comments concerning the accuracy of these time estimates or suggestions for making this form more simple, we would be happy to hear from you. You can write to both the **Internal Revenue Service**, Washington, DC 20224, Attention: IRS Reports Clearance Officer, T:FP; and the **Office of Management and Budget**, Paperwork Reduction Project (1545-0499), Washington, DC 20503. This form is NOT to be sent to either of these offices. The Form 5305-SEP is only to be kept for your records.

Purpose of Form.—Form 5305-SEP (Model SEP) is used by an employer to make an agreement to provide benefits to all employees under a SEP described in section 408(k). This form is NOT to be filed with IRS.

What Is a SEP Plan?—A SEP provides an employer with a simplified way to make contributions toward an employee's retirement income. Under a SEP, the employer is permitted to contribute a certain amount (see below) to an employee's Individual Retirement Account or Individual Retirement Annuity (IRAs). The employer makes contributions directly to an IRA set up

by an employee with a bank, insurance company, or other qualified financial institution. When using this form to establish a SEP, the IRA must be a model IRA established on an IRS form or a master or prototype IRA for which IRS has issued a favorable opinion letter. Making the agreement on Form 5305-SEP does not establish an employer IRA as described under section 408(c).

This form may not be used by an employer who:

- Currently maintains any other qualified retirement plan.
- Has maintained in the past a defined benefit plan, even if now terminated.
- Has any eligible employees for whom IRAs have not been established.
- Uses the services of leased employees (as described in section 414(n)).
- Is a member of an affiliated service group (as described in section 414(m)), a controlled group of corporations (as described in section 414(b)), or trades or businesses under common control (as described in section 414(c)), UNLESS all eligible employees of all the members of such groups, trades, or businesses, participate under the SEP.
- This form should only be used if the employer will pay the cost of the SEP contributions. This form is not suitable for a SEP that provides for contributions at the election of the employee whether or not made pursuant to a salary reduction agreement.

Who May Participate.—Any employee who is at least 21 years old and has performed "service" for you in at least 3 years of the immediately preceding 5 years must be permitted to participate in the SEP. However, you may establish less restrictive eligibility requirements if you choose. "Service" is any work performed for you for any period of time, however short. If you are a member of an affiliated service group, a controlled group of corporations, or trades or businesses under common control, "service" includes

any work performed for any period of time for any other member of such group, trades, or businesses. Generally, to make the agreement, all eligible employees (including all eligible employees, if any, of other members of an affiliated service group, a controlled group of corporations, or trades or businesses under common control) must participate in the plan. However, employees covered under a collective bargaining agreement and certain nonresident aliens may be excluded if section 410(b)(3)(A) or 410(b)(3)(C) applies to them. Employees whose total compensation for the year is less than $363* may be excluded.

Amount of Contributions.—You are not required to make any contributions to an employee's SEP-IRA in a given year. However, if you do make contributions, you must make them to the IRAs of all eligible employees, whether or not they are still employed at the time contributions are made. The contributions made must be the same percentage of each employee's total compensation (up to a maximum compensation base of $222,220*). The contributions you make in a year for any one employee may not be more than the smaller of $30,000 or 15% of that employee's total compensation (figured without considering the SEP-IRA contributions).

For this purpose, compensation includes:

- Amounts received for personal services actually performed (see Regulations section 1.219-1(c)); and
- Earned income as defined under section 401(c)(2).

You may not discriminate in favor of any employee who is highly compensated if you use Form 5305-SEP.

Under this form you may not integrate your SEP contributions with, or offset them by, contributions made under the Federal Insurance Contributions Act (FICA).

Currently, employers who have established a SEP using this agreement and have provided each participant with a copy

---

*This amount reflects the cost-of-living increase under section 408(k)(8) effective 1-1-91. This amount is adjusted annually. Each January, IRS announces the increase, if any, in the Internal Revenue Bulletin.   Cat. No. 11825J   Form **5305-SEP** (Rev. 6-91)

Simplified Employee Pension (SEP)

of this form, including the questions and answers below. are not required to file the annual information returns, Forms 5500, 5500-C/R, or 5500EZ for the SEP.

Deducting Contributions.—You may deduct all contributions to a SEP subject to the limitations of section 404(h). This SEP is maintained on a calendar year basis and contributions to the SEP are deductible for your taxable year with or within which the calendar year ends. Contributions made for a particular taxable year and contributed by the due date of your income tax return (including extensions) shall be deemed made in that taxable year.

Making the Agreement.—This agreement is considered made when (1) IRAs have been established for all of your eligible employees, (2) you have completed all blanks on the agreement form without modification, and (3) you have given all of your eligible employees copies of the agreement form. instructions, and questions and answers.

Keep the agreement form with your records; do not file it with IRS.

Information for the Employee

The information provided below explains what a SEP is, how contributions are made, and how to treat your employer's contributions for tax purposes.

Please read the questions and answers carefully. For more specific information, also see the agreement form and instructions on page 1 of this form.

Questions and Answers

1. Q. What is a Simplified Employee Pension, or SEP?

A. A SEP is a retirement income arrangement under which your employer may contribute any amount each year up to the smaller of $30,000 or 15% of your compensation into your own Individual Retirement Account/Annuity (IRA).

Your employer will provide you with a copy of the agreement containing participation requirements and a description of the basis upon which employer contributions may be made to your IRA.

All amounts contributed to your IRA by your employer belong to you, even after you separate from service with that employer.

2. Q. Must my employer contribute to my IRA under the SEP?

A. Whether or not your employer makes a contribution to the SEP is entirely within the employer's discretion. If a contribution is made under the SEP, it must be allocated to all the eligible employees according to the SEP agreement. The Model SEP specifies that the contribution on behalf of each eligible employee will be the same percentage of compensation (excluding compensation higher than $222,220*) for all employees.

3. Q. How much may my employer contribute to my SEP-IRA in any year?

A. Under the Model SEP **(Form 5305-SEP)** that your employer has adopted, your employer will determine the amount of contribution to be made to your IRA each year. However, the contribution for any year is limited to the smaller of $30,000 or 15% of your compensation for that year. The compensation used to determine this limit does not include any amount which is contributed by your employer to your IRA under the SEP. The agreement does not require an employer to maintain a particular level of contributions. It is possible that for a given year no employer contribution will be made on an employee's behalf.

Also see Question 5.

4. Q. How do I treat my employer's SEP contributions for my taxes?

A. The amount your employer contributes for years beginning after 1986 is excludable from your gross income subject to certain limitations including the lesser of $30,000 or 15% of compensation mentioned in 1.A. above and is not includible as taxable wages on your Form W-2.

5. Q. May I also contribute to my IRA if I am a participant in a SEP?

A. Yes. You may still contribute the lesser of $2,000 or 100% of your compensation to an IRA. However, the amount which is deductible is subject to various limitations.

Also see Question 11.

6. Q. Are there any restrictions on the IRA I select to deposit my SEP contributions in?

A. Under the Model SEP that is approved by IRS, contributions must be made to either a Model IRA which is executed on an IRS form or a master or prototype IRA for which IRS has issued a favorable opinion letter.

7. Q. What if I don't want a SEP-IRA?

A. Your employer may require that you become a participant in such an arrangement as a condition of employment. However, if the employer does not require all eligible employees to become participants and an eligible employee elects not to participate, all other employees of the same employer may be prohibited from entering into a SEP-IRA arrangement with that employer. If one or more eligible employees do not participate and the employer attempts to establish a SEP-IRA agreement with the remaining employees, the resulting arrangement may result in adverse tax consequences to the participating employees.

8. Q. Can I move funds from my SEP-IRA to another tax-sheltered IRA?

A. Yes. it is permissible for you to withdraw, or receive, funds from your SEP-IRA, and no more than 60 days later, place such funds in another IRA, or SEP-IRA. This is called a "rollover" and may not be done without penalty more frequently than at one-year intervals. However, there are no restrictions on the number of times you may make "transfers" if you arrange to have such funds transferred between the trustees, so that you never have possession.

9. Q. What happens if I withdraw my employer's contribution from my IRA?

A. If you don't want to leave the employer's contribution in your IRA, you may withdraw it at any time, but any amount withdrawn is includible in your income. Also, if withdrawals occur before attainment of age 59½, and not on account of death or disability, you may be subject to a penalty tax.

10. Q. May I participate in a SEP even though I'm covered by another plan?

A. An employer may not adopt this IRS Model SEP **(Form 5305-SEP)** if the employer maintains another qualified retirement plan or has ever maintained a qualified defined benefit plan. However, if you work for several employers you may be covered by a SEP of one employer and a different SEP or pension or profit-sharing plan of another employer.

Also see Questions 11 and 12.

11. Q. What happens if too much is contributed to my SEP-IRA in one year?

A. Any contribution that is more than the yearly limitations may be withdrawn without penalty by the due date (plus extensions) for filing your tax return (normally April 15th), but is includible in your gross income. Excess contributions left in your SEP-IRA account after that time may have adverse tax consequences. Withdrawals of those contributions may be taxed as premature withdrawals.

Also see Question 10.

12. Q. Do I need to file any additional forms with IRS because I participate in a SEP?

A. No.

13. Q. Is my employer required to provide me with information about SEP-IRAs and the SEP agreement?

A. Yes, your employer must provide you with a copy of the executed SEP agreement (Form 5305-SEP), these Questions and Answers, and provide a statement each year showing any contribution to your IRA.

Also see Question 4.

14. Q. Is the financial institution where I establish my IRA also required to provide me with information?

A. Yes, it must provide you with a disclosure statement which contains the following items of information in plain, nontechnical language:

(1) the statutory requirements which relate to your IRA;

(2) the tax consequences which follow the exercise of various options and what those options are;

(3) participation eligibility rules, and rules on the deductibility and nondeductibility of retirement savings;

(4) the circumstances and procedures under which you may revoke your IRA, including the name, address, and telephone number of the person designated to receive notice of revocation **(this explanation must be prominently displayed at the beginning of the disclosure statement);**

(5) explanations of when penalties may be assessed against you because of specified prohibited or penalized activities concerning your IRA; and

(6) financial disclosure information which:

(a) either projects value growth rates of your IRA under various contribution and retirement schedules, or describes the method of computing and allocating annual earnings and charges which may be assessed;

(b) describes whether, and for what period, the growth projections for the plan are guaranteed, or a statement of the earnings rate and terms on which the projection is based;

(c) states the sales commission to be charged in each year expressed as a percentage of $1,000; and

(d) states the proportional amount of any nondeductible life insurance which may be a feature of your IRA.

In addition to this disclosure statement, the financial institution is required to provide you with a financial statement each year. It may be necessary to retain and refer to statements for more than one year in order to evaluate the investment performance of the IRA and for information on how to report IRA distributions for tax purposes.

This amount reflects the cost-of-living increase under section 408(k)(8) effective 1-1-91. This amount is adjusted annually. Each January, IRS announces the increase, if any, in the Internal Revenue Bulletin.

☆U.S. GPO: 1992-312-699/60114

Form **5305A-SEP** (Rev. September 1990) Department of the Treasury Internal Revenue Service	**Salary Reduction and Other Elective Simplified Employee Pension-Individual Retirement Accounts Contribution Agreement** (Under Section 408(k) of the Internal Revenue Code)	OMB No. 1545-1012 Expires: 3-31-93 **Do NOT File with Internal Revenue Service**

Caution: *This form may only be used if the three conditions found at Article III, items E, F, and G are met.*

_____ establishes the following arrangement under the terms of section

(Business name—employer)

408(k) of The Internal Revenue Code and the instructions to this form.

Article I—Eligibility Requirements

Provided the requirements of Article III are met, the employer agrees to permit elective deferrals to be made in each calendar year to the Individual Retirement Accounts or Individual Retirement Annuities (IRA), established by or on behalf of all employees who are at least _____ years old (see instructions) and have performed services for the employer in at least _____ years (see instructions) of the immediately preceding 5 years. This ☐ includes ☐ does not include employees covered under a collective bargaining agreement and ☐ includes ☐ does not include employees whose total compensation during the year is less than $300 (as adjusted annually per section 408(k)(8)).

Article II—Elective Deferrals

A. Salary Reduction Option. A participant may elect to have his or her compensation reduced by the following percentage or amount per pay period, as designated in writing to the employer (check appropriate box, or boxes, and fill in the blanks):

1. ☐ An amount not in excess of _____ % (enter a specified percent of 15% or less) of a participant's compensation.
2. ☐ An amount not in excess of $ _____ (not to exceed $7,000 per year as adjusted per Code section 415(d)).

B. Cash Bonus Option. A participant may base elective deferrals on bonuses that, at the participant's election, may be contributed to the SEP or received by the participant in cash during the calendar year. Check here ☐ if such elective deferrals may be made to this SEP.

Article III—SEP Requirements

The employer agrees that each employee's elective deferrals to this SEP will:

A. Be based only on the first $200,000 of compensation (as adjusted annually per Code section 408(k)(8)).

B. Be limited annually to the lesser of:

1. 15% of compensation (see instructions for Article III); **or**
2. $7,000 (as adjusted annually per Code section 415(d)).

Amounts in excess of these limits will be treated as excess SEP deferrals.

C. Be further reduced, as necessary in accordance with Code section 415, if the employer also maintains a SEP to which non-elective SEP employer contributions are made for a calendar year.

D. Be paid to the employee's IRA trustee, custodian, or insurance company (for an annuity contract) or, if necessary, an IRA established for an employee by an employer.

E. Be made only if at least 50% of the employer's employees eligible to participate elect to have amounts contributed to the SEP.

F. Be made only if the employer had 25 or fewer employees eligible to participate at all times during the prior calendar year.

G. Be adjusted only if deferrals to this SEP for any calendar year do not meet the "ADP" requirements described in the instructions on page 3.

Article IV—Excess SEP Contributions

The employer agrees to notify each employee by March 15 of each year of any excess SEP contributions to the employee's SEP-IRA for the preceding calendar year.

Article V—Top-heavy Requirements

A. Unless paragraph B below is checked, the minimum top-heavy contribution for each year must be allocated to the SEP-IRA of each non-key employee eligible to participate in this SEP in accordance with Code section 416. This allocation may not be less than the smaller of: **(1)** 3% of the non-key employee's compensation; **or (2)** the largest percentage of elective deferrals, as a percentage of the first $200,000 of the key employee's compensation, deferred by any key employee for that year.

B. ☐ The top-heavy requirements of section 416 will be satisfied through contributions to this employer's non-elective SEP-IRA.

_____   _____
Signature of employer   Date

_____
By

Form **5305A-SEP** (Rev. 9-90)

Simplified Employee Pension (SEP)

Instructions for the Employer

(Section references are to the Internal Revenue Code, unless otherwise noted.)

Paperwork Reduction Act Notice.—The Paperwork Reduction Act of 1980 says we must tell you why we are collecting this information, how it is to be used, and whether you must give it to us. The information is used to determine if you are entitled to a deduction for contributions made to a SEP. Completion of this form is required only if you want to establish a Model Elective SEP.

The time needed to complete and file this form will vary depending on individual circumstances. The estimated average time is:

Recordkeeping	40 min.
Learning about the law or the form	54 min.
Preparing the form, copying, assembling, and sending the form to IRS	20 min.

If you have comments concerning the accuracy of these time estimates or suggestions for making this form more simple, we would be happy to hear from you. You can write to both the **Internal Revenue Service,** Washington, DC 20224, Attention: IRS Reports Clearance Officer, T:FP; and the **Office of Management and Budget,** Paperwork Reduction Project (1545-1012), Washington, DC 20503.

Purpose of Form.—Form 5305A-SEP (model elective SEP) is used by an employer to permit employees to make elective deferrals to a Simplified Employee Pension (SEP) described in section 408(k). This form is NOT to be filed with IRS.

What is a SEP?—A SEP is a plan that provides an employer with a simplified way to enhance the employee's retirement income. Under an elective SEP, employees may choose whether or not to make elective deferrals to the SEP. The employer puts the amounts deferred by employees directly into an IRA set up by or on behalf of the employee with a bank, insurance company, or other qualified financial institution. When using this form to establish a SEP, the IRA established by or on behalf of an employee must be a model IRA or a master or prototype IRA for which IRS has issued a favorable opinion letter. Making the agreement on Form 5305A-SEP does not establish an employer IRA as described under section 408(c).

This form may NOT be used by an employer who:

1. Currently maintains any other qualified retirement plan. This does not prevent an employer from also maintaining a Model SEP (Form 5305-SEP) or other SEP to which either elective or non-elective contributions are made.

2. Has maintained in the past a defined benefit plan, even if now terminated.

3. Has any eligible employees by or for whom IRAs have not been established.

4. Has only highly compensated employees.

5. Is a member of one of the groups described in the Specific Instructions for Article III, G, 2 below, UNLESS all eligible employees of all the members of such groups, trades, or businesses are eligible to make elective deferrals to this SEP, and PROVIDED that in the prior calendar year there were never more than 25 employees eligible to participate in this SEP, in total, of all the members of such groups, trades, or businesses.

6. Is a state or local government or a tax-exempt organization.

This form should be used only if the employer intends to permit elective deferrals to a SEP. If the employer wishes to establish a SEP to which non-elective employer contributions may be made, Form 5305-SEP or a non-model SEP should be used instead of, or in addition to, this form.

Making the Agreement.—This agreement is considered made when:

1. IRAs have been established by or for all of your eligible employees;

2. You have completed all blanks on the agreement form without modification; **and**

3. You have given all your eligible employees copies of the agreement form, instructions, and questions and answers.

Keep the agreement form with your records; do NOT file it with IRS.

Currently, employers who have established a SEP using this agreement and have provided each participant with a copy of this form, including the questions and answers, are not required to file the annual information returns, Form 5500, 5500-C/R, or 5500EZ for the SEP.

Deducting Contributions.—You may deduct contributions made by the due date of the employer's tax return, and extensions thereof, to a SEP subject to the limitations of section 404(h). This SEP is maintained on a calendar year basis, and contributions to the SEP are deductible for your taxable year with or within which the calendar year ends.

However, please see the Actual Deferral Percentage worksheet on page 6.

Specific Instructions

Article I.—Eligibility Requirements

Any employee who is at least 21 years old and has performed "service" for you in at least 3 years of the immediately preceding 5 years must be permitted to participate in the SEP. However, you may establish less restrictive eligibility requirements if you choose. Service is any work performed for you for any period of time, however short. Further, if you are a member of one of the groups described in Article III, G, 2 below, service includes any work performed for any period of time for any other member of such group, trades, or businesses. Generally, to make the agreement, all eligible employees, including leased employees within the meaning of section 414(n), of the affiliated employer must be permitted to make elective deferrals to the SEP. However, employees covered under a collective bargaining agreement and certain nonresident aliens may be excluded if section 410(b)(3)(A) or 410(b)(3)(C) applies to them. Employees whose total compensation for the year is less than $300 also may be excluded.

Article II.—Elective Deferrals

You may permit your employees to make elective deferrals through salary reduction or on the basis of bonuses that, at the participant's option, may be contributed to the SEP or received by the participant in cash during the calendar year.

You are responsible for telling your employees how they may make, change, or terminate elective deferrals based on either salary reduction or cash bonuses. You must also provide a form on which they may make their deferral elections. (This requirement may be satisfied by use of the model form provided on page 5 or by use of a form setting forth, in a manner calculated to be understood by the average plan participant, the information contained in the "Model SEP Deferral Form.") No deferral election may be made with respect to compensation already received.

Article III.—SEP Requirements

A. Elective deferrals may not be based on more than $200,000 of compensation, as adjusted per section 408(k)(8) for cost of living changes. Compensation is the employee's compensation from the employer (figured without including the SEP-IRA contributions) and includes:

● Amounts received for personal services actually performed (see section 1.219-1(c) of the Income Tax Regulations), **and**

● Earned income defined under section 401(c)(2).

Note: *The deferral limit of 15% of compensation (less employer SEP-IRA contributions) is computed using the following formula: (compensation including employer SEP-IRA contribution ÷ 115%) × .15 = 15% of compensation limitation.*

B. The maximum limit on the amount of compensation an employee may elect to defer under a SEP for a calendar year is the lesser of:

● 15% of the employee's compensation; or

● $7,000, adjusted as explained below.

Amounts deferred for a year in excess of $7,000 as adjusted are considered excess deferrals and are subject to the consequences described below.

The $7,000 limit on the amount an employee may elect to defer in each year applies to the total elective deferrals the employee makes for the year under the following arrangements:

1. Elective SEPs under section 408(k)(6);

2. Cash or deferred arrangements under section 401(k); and

3. Salary reduction arrangements under section 403(b).

Thus, the employee may have excess deferrals even if the amount deferred under this SEP does not exceed $7,000.

The $7,000 limit will be indexed according to the cost of living. In addition, the limit may be increased to $9,500 if the employee makes elective deferrals to a salary reduction arrangement under section 403(b).

If an employee who elects to defer compensation under this SEP has made excess deferrals for a year, he or she must withdraw those excess deferrals by April 15 following the year of the deferral. Excess

The Tools and Techniques of Employee Benefit and Retirement Planning

Simplified Employee Pension (SEP)

deferrals not withdrawn by April 15 following the year of the deferral may also be subject, when withdrawn, to the 10% tax on early distributions under section 72(t).

C. If you also maintain a Model SEP or any other SEP to which you make non-elective contributions, contributions to the two SEPs together may not exceed the lesser of $30,000 or 15% of compensation for any employee. If these limits are exceeded on behalf of any employee for a particular calendar year, that employee's elective deferrals for that year must be reduced to the extent of the excess.

E. and F. Each of these calculations is made after first excluding employees who do not meet the eligibility requirements of Article I, including employees covered under a collective bargaining agreement and nonresident aliens.

F. New employers who had no employees during the prior calendar year will meet this requirement if they have 25 or fewer employees throughout the first 30 days that the employer is in existence.

G. Actual Deferral Percentage (ADP) Requirements. An excess SEP contribution for the calendar year is the amount of each highly compensated employee's elective deferrals that exceeds the ADP for a calendar year. To meet the ADP requirements for a calendar year, the following test must be satisfied. The ADP of any "highly compensated employee" eligible to participate in this SEP may not be more than the product obtained by multiplying the average of the ADPs for that year of all non-highly compensated employees eligible to participate by 1.25. Only elective deferrals count for this test; non-elective SEP contributions may not be included.

For purposes of making this computation, the calculation of a highly compensated employee's ADP is made on the basis of the entire "affiliated employer." The determination of the number and identity of highly compensated employees is also made on the basis of the affiliated employer.

In addition, for purposes of determining the ADP of a highly compensated individual, the elective deferrals and compensation of the employee will also include the elective deferrals and compensation of any "family member." This special rule applies, however, only if the highly compensated employee is a 5% owner and is one of a group of the ten most highly compensated employees. The elective deferrals and compensation of family members used in this special rule do not count in computing the ADP of individuals who do not fall into this group.

The following definitions apply for purposes of this ADP computation:

1. ADP—the ratio of an employee's elective deferrals for a calendar year to the employee's compensation (as defined in III A. above) for that year. The ADP of an employee who is eligible to make an elective deferral, but who does not make a deferral during the year, is zero.

2. Affiliated employer—the employer and any member of an affiliated service group (as described in section 414(m)), a controlled group of corporations (as described in section 414(b)) or trades or businesses as described in section 414(c),

or any other entity required to be aggregated with the employer under section 414(o).

3. Family member—an individual who is related to a highly compensated individual as a spouse, or as a lineal ascendant, such as a parent or grandparent, or a descendent such as a child or grandchild, or spouse of either of those.

4. Highly compensated individual—an individual who (as described in section 414(q)) during the current or preceding calendar year:

(i) was a 5% or more owner;

(ii) received compensation in excess of $75,000;

(iii) received compensation in excess of $50,000 and was in the top-paid group (the top 20% of employees, by compensation); **or**

(iv) was an officer and received compensation in excess of 50% of the section 415 dollar limit for defined contribution plans. (No more than 3 employees need be taken into account under this rule. At least one officer, the highest-paid officer if no one else meets this test, however, must be taken into account.)

A worksheet to calculate the ADP test and excess SEP contributions is provided on page 6

Article IV.—Excess SEP Contributions

A. As stated above, a worksheet to calculate excess SEP contributions is provided on page 6 of this booklet. This worksheet should be used to determine the amount of excess SEP contributions to be reported to employees with respect to a calendar year. The employer is responsible for notifying each employee by March 15 of the amount, if any, of any excess SEP contributions to that employee's SEP-IRA for the preceding calendar year. If you do not notify any of your employees by March 15, you must pay a tax equal to 10% of the excess SEP contributions for the preceding calendar year. If you fail to notify your employees by December 31 of the calendar year following the year of the excess SEP contributions, your SEP no longer will be considered to meet the requirements of section 408(k)(6). This means that the earnings on the SEP are subject to tax immediately, that no more deferrals can be made under the SEP, and that deferrals of all employees in the uncorrected excess are includible in their income in that year.

Your notification to each affected employee of the excess SEP contributions must specifically state in a manner calculated to be understood by the average plan participant: (i) the amount of the excess contributions attributable to that employee's elective deferrals; (ii) the calendar year for which the excess contributions were made; (iii) that the excess contributions are includible in the affected employee's gross income for the specified calendar year; and (iv) that failure to withdraw the excess contributions and income attributable thereto by the due date (plus extensions) for filing the affected employee's tax return for the preceding

calendar year may result in significant penalties, with a reference to Question 6 of Form 5305A-SEP for further information concerning possible penalties. If you wish, you may use the model form we have included for this purpose on page 5 following the "Model Elective SEP Deferral Form." If you already have issued W-2s to your employees by the time of the notification of the excess SEP contributions, you must also issue to the affected employees any required forms that reflect the fact that excess SEP contributions must be included in an employee's taxable income.

Example: Employee "A," a highly-compensated employee of employer "X," elects to defer $4,000 for calendar year 1987 to his SEP-IRA. A's compensation for 1987, excluding his SEP contribution, was $60,000. On January 15, 1988, X issues to A a W-2 stating that A's taxable income for 1987 was $60,000.

In February of 1988, X calculates the ADP test for 1987 for the SEP and discovers that A's maximum permissible SEP-IRA contribution for 1987 was $3,500. A is the only employee of X with excess SEP contributions. Therefore, on February 20, 1988, X notifies A that A had an excess SEP contribution of $500 for 1987. In addition, X issues the required form to A on that date that specifies that A's corrected taxable income for 1987 was $60,500. X is not liable for the 10% tax on excess SEP-IRA contributions because he notified A of the excess SEP-IRA contributions by March 15, 1988.

To avoid excess SEP contributions with respect to which you must notify employees you may want to institute a mechanism that would monitor elective deferrals on a continuing basis throughout the calendar year to insure that the deferrals comply with the limits as they are paid into each employee's SEP-IRA.

Article V.—Top-heavy Requirements

A. For purposes of determining whether a plan is top-heavy under section 416, elective deferrals are considered employer contributions. Elective deferrals may not be used, however, to satisfy the minimum contribution requirement under section 416. Thus, in any year in which a key employee makes an elective deferral, this Model SEP is deemed top-heavy for purposes of section 416 and the employer is required to make the minimum contribution to the SEP-IRA of each non-key employee eligible to participate in the SEP.

A key employee under section 416(i)(1) is any employee or former employee (and the beneficiaries of these employees) who, at any time during the "determination period," was:

1. an officer of the employer (if the employee's compensation exceeds 50% of the limit under section 415(c)(1)(A));

2. an owner of one of the ten largest interests in the employer (if the employee's compensation exceeds 100% of the limit under section 415(c)(1)(A));

3. a 5% or more owner of the employer; **or**

Simplified Employee Pension (SEP)

4. a 1% owner of the employer (if the employee has compensation in excess of $150,000).

The "determination period" is the current calendar year and the four preceding years.

B. The employer may satisfy the minimum contribution requirement of section 416 by making the required contributions through a non-elective SEP.

Information for the Employee

The following information explains what a Simplified Employee Pension plan is, how contributions are made, and how to treat these contributions for tax purposes.

Please read the questions and answers carefully. For more specific information, also see the agreement form and instructions to your employer on this form.

Questions and Answers

1. Q. What is a Simplified Employee Pension, or SEP?

A. A SEP is a retirement income arrangement. In this particular "elective" SEP, you may choose to defer compensation to your own Individual Retirement Account/Annuity (IRA). These elective deferrals may be based either on a salary reduction arrangement or on bonuses that, at your election, may be contributed to your IRA or received by you in cash. This type of elective SEP is available only to an employer with 25 or fewer eligible employees.

Your employer will provide you with a copy of the agreement containing eligibility requirements and a description of the basis upon which contributions may be made to your IRA.

All amounts contributed to your IRA belong to you, even after you separate from service with that employer.

2. Q. Must I make elective deferrals to an IRA?

A. No. However, if more than half of the eligible employees choose not to make elective deferrals in a particular year, then no employee may participate in an elective SEP of that employer for the year.

3. Q. How much may I elect to defer to my SEP-IRA in a particular year?

A. The amount that may be deferred to this SEP for any year is limited to the lesser of:

(1) 15% of compensation; **or**

(2) $7,000 (as adjusted for increases in the cost of living).

These limits may be reduced if your employer also maintains a SEP to which non-elective contributions are made. In that case, total contributions on your behalf to both SEPs may not exceed the lesser of $30,000 or 15% of your compensation. If these limits are exceeded, the amount you may elect to contribute to this SEP for the year will be correspondingly reduced.

The $7,000 is an overall cap on the maximum amount you may defer in each calendar year to all elective SEPs and cash-or-deferred arrangements under section 401(k), regardless of how many employers you may have worked for during the year.

The $7,000 will be indexed according to the cost of living and is increased to $9,500 (more in some cases) if you make salary reduction contributions under a section 403(b) arrangement of another employer.

If you are a highly compensated employee there may be a further limit on the amount you may contribute to a SEP-IRA for a particular year. This limit is calculated by your employer and is based on a special kind of non-discrimination test known as an ADP test. This test is based on a mathematical formula that limits the percentage of pay that highly compensated employees may elect to defer to a SEP-IRA. As discussed below, your employer will notify you if you have exceeded the ADP limits.

4. Q. How do I treat elective deferrals for tax purposes?

A. The amount you elect to defer to your SEP-IRA is excludible from your gross income, subject to the limitations discussed above, and is not includible as taxable wages on your Form W-2. These amounts are treated as amounts subject to FICA taxes.

5. Q. How will I know if too much is contributed to my SEP-IRA in one year?

A. There are two different ways in which you may contribute too much to your SEP-IRA. One way is to make "excess elective deferrals," i.e., exceed the $7,000 limitation described above. The second way is to make "excess SEP contributions," i.e., violate the "ADP" test, as discussed above. You are responsible for calculating whether or not you have exceeded the $7,000 limitation. Your employer is responsible for determining whether you have made any excess SEP contributions.

Your employer is required to notify you by March 15 if you have made any excess SEP contributions for the preceding calendar year. Your employer will notify you of an excess SEP contribution by providing you with any required form for the preceding calendar year.

6. Q. What must I do about excess deferrals to avoid adverse tax consequences?

A. Excess deferrals are includible in your gross income in the year of the deferral. You should withdraw excess deferrals under this SEP and any income allocable to the excess deferrals from your SEP-IRA by April 15. These amounts cannot be transferred or rolled over to another SEP-IRA.

If you fail to withdraw your excess deferrals and any income allocable thereto by April 15 of the following year, your excess deferrals will be subject to a 6% excise tax for each year they remain in the SEP-IRA.

If you have both excess deferrals and excess SEP contributions (as described in 6a below), the amount of excess deferrals you withdraw by April 15 will reduce your excess SEP contributions.

6a. Q: What must I do about excess SEP contributions to avoid adverse tax consequences?

A. Excess SEP contributions are includible in your gross income in the year of the deferral. You should withdraw excess SEP contributions for a calendar year and

any income allocable to the excess SEP contributions by the due date (including extensions) for filing your income tax return for the year. These amounts cannot be transferred or rolled over to another SEP-IRA.

If you fail to withdraw your excess SEP contributions and income allocable thereto by the due date (including extensions) for filing your income tax return, your excess SEP contributions will be subject to a 6% excise tax for each year they remain in the SEP-IRA.

7. Q. Can I reduce excess elective deferrals or excess SEP contributions by rolling over or transferring amounts from my SEP-IRA to another IRA?

A. No. Excess elective deferrals or excess SEP contributions may be reduced only by a distribution to you. Excess amounts rolled over or transferred to another IRA will be includible in income and subject to the penalties discussed above.

8. Q. How do I know how much income is allocable to my excess elective deferrals or any excess SEP contributions?

A. The rules for determining and allocating income to excess elective deferrals or SEP contributions are the same as those governing regular IRA contributions. The trustee or custodian of your SEP-IRA may be able to inform you of the amount of income allocable to your excess amounts.

9. Q. May I also contribute to my IRA if I am a participant in a SEP?

A. Yes. You may still contribute the lesser of $2,000 or 100% of compensation to an IRA. However, the amount that is deductible is subject to various limitations. See Publication 590 for more specific information.

10. Q. Are there any restrictions on the IRA I select to deposit my SEP contributions in?

A. Under the Model Elective SEP that is approved by IRS, contributions must be made either to a Model IRA that is executed on an IRS form or a master or prototype IRA for which IRS has issued a favorable opinion letter.

11. Q. Can I move funds from my SEP-IRA to another tax-sheltered IRA?

A. Yes but see below. It is permissible for you to withdraw, or receive, funds from your SEP-IRA, and no more than 60 days later, place such funds in another IRA or SEP-IRA. This is called a "rollover" and may not be done without penalty more frequently than at one-year intervals. However, there are no restrictions on the number of times you may make "transfers" if you arrange to have such funds transferred between the trustees, so that you never have possession.

12. Q. What happens if I withdraw my elective deferrals to my SEP-IRA?

A. If you don't want to leave the money in the IRA, you may withdraw it at any time, but any amount withdrawn is includible in your income. Also, if withdrawals occur before you are 59½, and not on account of death or disability, you may be subject to a 10% penalty tax. (As discussed above, different rules apply to the removal of excess amounts contributed to your SEP-IRA.)

Simplified Employee Pension (SEP)

13. Q. What happens if I transfer or distribute contributions from my SEP before the ADP test described in Question 3 has been satisfied.

A. If you make a transfer or a distribution from your SEP before the nondiscrimination test has been satisfied, the distribution will be subject to regular income tax as provided in section 72 and the additional 10% tax on early distributions in section 72(t).

14. Q. May I participate in a SEP even though I'm covered by another plan?

A. An employer may adopt this IRS Model Elective SEP (Form 5305A-SEP) and at the same time maintain an IRS Model SEP (Form 5305-SEP) or other non-elective SEP. However, an employer may not adopt this IRS Model Elective SEP if the employer maintains any qualified retirement plan or has ever maintained a qualified defined benefit plan. If you work for several employers, however, you may be covered by a SEP of one employer and a different SEP or pension or profit-sharing plan of another employer.

You should remember, however, as discussed in Question 3 above, that your elective deferrals to all plans or arrangements, even if maintained by unrelated employers, are subject to a $7,000 limit (more if one is a section 403(b) annuity). If you participate in two arrangements that permit elective deferrals, you should take care that this limit is not exceeded for any calendar year.

15. Q. Do I need to file any additional forms with IRS because I participate in a SEP?

A. No.

16. Q. Is my employer required to provide me with information about SEP-IRAs and the SEP agreement?

A. Yes. Your employer must provide you with a copy of the executed SEP agreement (Form 5305A-SEP), these Questions and Answers, the form used by the employee to defer amounts to the SEP, the notice of excess SEP contributions, if applicable, and a statement each year showing any contribution to your SEP-IRA.

17. Q. Is the financial institution where my IRA is established also required to provide me with information?

A. Yes. It must provide you with a disclosure statement that contains the following items of information in plain, nontechnical language:

(1) the statutory requirements that relate to your IRA;

(2) the tax consequences that follow the exercise of various options and what those options are;

(3) participation eligibility rules, and rules on the deductibility and nondeductibility of retirement savings;

(4) the circumstances and procedures under which you may revoke your IRA, including the name, address, and telephone number of the person designated to receive notice of revocation (this explanation must be prominently displayed at the beginning of the disclosure statement);

(5) explanations of when penalties may be assessed against you because of specified prohibited or penalized activities concerning your IRA; and

(6) financial disclosure information which:

(a) either projects value growth rates of your IRA under various contribution and retirement schedules, or describes the method of computing and allocating annual earnings and charges which may be assessed;

(b) describes whether, and for what period, the growth projections for the plan are guaranteed, or a statement of earnings rate and terms on which these projections are based; and

(c) states the sales commission to be charged in each year expressed as a percentage of $1,000.

See **Publication 590**, Individual Retirement Arrangements (IRAs), available at most IRS offices, for a more complete explanation of the disclosure requirements.

In addition to this disclosure statement, the financial institution is required to provide you with a financial statement each year. It may be necessary to retain and refer to statements for more than one year to evaluate the investment performance of the IRA and in order that you will know how to report IRA distributions for tax purposes.

Model Elective SEP Deferral Form

I. Salary reduction deferral

Subject to the requirements of the Model Elective SEP of _____ , I authorize the following amount or percentage of my
(insert name of employer)
compensation to be withheld from each of my paychecks and contributed to my SEP-IRA:

(a) _____ percent of my salary (not in excess of 15%): or **(b)** _____ dollar amount.

This salary reduction authorization shall remain in effect until I give a written modification or termination of its terms to my employer.

II. Cash bonus deferral

Subject to the requirements of the Model Elective SEP of _____ , I authorize the following amount to be contributed to my
(insert name of employer)

SEP-IRA rather than being paid to me in cash: _____ dollar amount.

III. Amount of deferral

I understand that the total amount I defer in any calendar year to this SEP may not exceed the lesser of: **(a)** 15% of my compensation: or **(b)** $7,000 (as adjusted per Code section 415(d)).

IV. Commencement of deferral

The deferral election specified in either I. or II. above shall not become effective before: _____
(Specify a date no earlier than the next payday beginning after this authorization.)   (Month, Day, Year)

Signature ▶   Date ▶

Notification of Excess SEP Contributions

To: _____
(Name of employee)

Our calculations indicate that the elective deferrals you made to your SEP-IRA for calendar year _____ exceed the maximum permissible limits under section 408(k)(6) of the Internal Revenue Code. You made excess SEP contributions of $_____ for that year.

These excess SEP contributions are includible in your gross income for the calendar year specified above.

These excess SEP contributions must be distributed from your IRA by the due date (plus extensions) for filing your tax return for the preceding calendar year (normally April 15th) in order to avoid significant penalties. Income allocable to the excess amounts must be withdrawn at the same time and is includible in income along with the excess contributions. Excess contributions left in your SEP-IRA account after that time are subject to a 6% excise tax.

Signature ▶   Date ▶

Simplified Employee Pension (SEP)

Elective SEP Actual Deferred Percentage Worksheet

a Employee Name	b Status H = Highly compensated F = Family 0 = Other	c Compensation (Including compensation from related employers and compensation of family.)	d Deferrals (Add all SEP defer- rals; add deferrals of family to HCE*)	e Ratio (if family member enter N.A. - otherwise d ÷ c)	f Permitted ratio (for HCE* only from below)	g Permitted amount (for HCE* only) c X f	h Excess (for HCE* only) d minus g
1.							
2.							
3.							
4.							
5.							
6.							
7.							
8.							
9.							
10.							
11.							
12.							
13.							
14.							
15.							
16.							
17.							
18.							
19.							
20.							
21.							
22.							
23.							
24.							
25.							

Permitted Ratio Computation for column f:

A. Enter the total of all the ratios of the employees marked as "-0-" in column b _____

B. Divide line A by the number of employees marked as "-0-" in column b _____

C. Permitted ratio—Multiply line B by 1.25 and enter the permitted ratio here _____

* Highly compensated employee

☆ U.S. Government Printing Office: 1990-262-151/00162

The Tools and Techniques of Employee Benefit and Retirement Planning

Chapter 21

TARGET/AGE-WEIGHTED PLAN

WHAT IS IT?

A target or other age-weighted formula for a defined contribution plan allows higher contribution levels (as a percentage of compensation) for older plan entrants. That is, the formula for annual employer contributions or allocations to participant accounts is based not only on the participant's compensation but also the participant's *age* on entering the plan.

Age-weighting permits adequate account balances to build up in the relatively short time available to older entrants before retirement. In addition, with an age-weighted formula the employer's plan contributions tend to be weighted toward owners and key employees since in many businesses these employees will be older than rank-and-file employees when the plan is adopted.

Three broad types of age-weighted plans can be identified:

(1) The traditional *target plan* is an age-weighted money purchase pension plan. The employer must make regular annual contributions at the rate specified in the plan. In some ways, a traditional target plan is a hybrid between a defined contribution pension plan and a defined benefit plan, since the funding of each participant's account is aimed at producing a *target* amount at retirement, like a defined benefit plan. However, since the plan is a defined contribution plan, the actual benefit is the amount in each participant's account at retirement. The plan participant assumes the investment risk.

(2) The *age-weighted profit-sharing plan* is a profit-sharing plan with an age-weighted factor in the allocation formula. Like all profit-sharing plans, the employer's annual contribution can be discretionary, so the participants have no assurance of a specific annual funding level. However, since the plan allocations are age-weighted, older plan entrants are favored.

(3) The new *comparability plan* (discussed in the "Questions and Answers," below) represents an attempt to push age-weighting to its maximum limit under the "cross-testing" provisions of the proposed nondiscrimination regulations under Code section 401(a)(4).

WHEN IS IT INDICATED?

1. When the features of a regular defined contribution plan would be attractive to the employer, except that there are older employees whose retirement benefits would be inadequate because of the relatively few years remaining for participation in the plan. The age-weighted formula allows proportionately greater employer contributions for these older employees (greater percentages of their compensation).

2. When the employer is looking for an alternative to a defined benefit plan that provides adequate retirement benefits to older employees but has the lower cost and simplicity of a defined contribution plan.

3. When an employer wants to terminate an existing defined benefit plan in order to avoid the increasing cost and regulatory burdens associated with these plans under recent changes in the law. If an age-weighted plan is substituted for the defined benefit plan, in many cases the new plan will provide approximately the same benefits to most employees, and it will be relatively easy to obtain IRS approval for the defined benefit plan termination.

4. When a closely held business or professional corporation has a relatively large number of key employees who are approximately age 50 or older and who generally want to contribute $30,000 or less annually to the plan. The age-weighted plan is generally the ideal qualified plan to adopt in this situation, because its benefit level is just as high as would be available in a defined benefit plan (given the $30,000 annual restriction), but is much simpler and less expensive to install and administer.

ADVANTAGES

1. Retirement benefits can be made adequate for employees who enter the plan at older ages. The following comparison of a target plan with a money purchase plan illustrates this. The illustration shows how the annual contribution and retirement benefit vary for three employees, each earning $30,000 annually:

	Annual Contribution		Accumulation at 65 (5½% return)	
Employee age at entry	Money Purchase (14%)	Target	Money Purchase	Target
30	$4,200	$1,655	$444,214	$175,000
40	4,200	3,243	226,657	175,000
50	4,200	7,402	99,292	175,000

2. From the viewpoint of a business owner, particularly in a small, closely held business, the feature illustrated in the paragraph above also means that in an age-weighted plan, more of the total employer contributions in the age-weighted plan will likely be allocated to owners and key employees, as compared with a money purchase or other defined contribution plan. This will be the case if the owners and key employees are older than the average of all employees when the plan is adopted.

3. As with all qualified plans, an age-weighted plan provides a tax-deferred retirement savings medium for employees.

4. The age-weighted plan is relatively simple and inexpensive to design, administer, and explain to employees. An age-weighted plan is especially simple compared to a defined benefit plan because actuarial valuations and an enrolled actuary's certification are not required. Yet the plan's benefits can be much the same as those from a defined benefit plan.

5. Plan distributions may be eligible for the special 5-year (or 10-year) averaging tax computation available for certain qualified plan distributions.

6. Individual accounts for participants allow participants to benefit from good investment results in the plan fund.

DISADVANTAGES

1. As with any defined contribution plan, the annual addition to each employee's account is limited to the lesser of (a) 25% of compensation or (b) the greater of $30,000 or ¼ of the defined benefit dollar limit under Code section 415. This limits the relative amount of funding for highly compensated employees. For older employees, a defined benefit plan may allow a much higher level of employer contributions to the plan, as discussed further under "Design Features," below.

2. Employees bear investment risk under the plan. While this is a disadvantage to employees, it also tends to reduce employer costs compared to a defined benefit plan. This

is because the employer bears the investment risk in a defined benefit plan.

3. A target pension plan is subject to the Code's minimum funding requirements. Employers are obligated to make minimum contributions each year under the plan's contribution formula or be subject to minimum funding penalties. While an age-weighted profit-sharing plan is not subject to the minimum funding requirements, contributions must be recurring and substantial as discussed in Chapter 17.

4. If the age-weighted plan is a profit-sharing plan, the ultimate benefits to participants are particularly uncertain since the employer is not necessarily committed to any specific funding level and may even omit funding in some years.

DESIGN FEATURES

While the concept of age-weighting is an old one, the design of current age-weighted plans is dictated by the need to meet the proposed nondiscrimination requirements under Code section 401(a)(4), scheduled to go into effect in 1994. Since there are many potential ways to meet these requirements, it is difficult to present a simple discussion of age-weighted formula design. In this section, we will simply illustrate some formulas that presumably satisfy the regulations, without implying that these are the only types of formulas that are permitted.

Target Pension Plan

The formula for employer contributions to a target plan requires the employer to contribute annually to each plan participant's account. The annual contribution is a percentage of each employee's annual compensation, with the percentage varying according to the age of the employee when that employee first entered the plan.

Compensation must be defined in the plan in a manner that does not discriminate in favor of highly compensated employees.[1] Only the first $200,000 (as indexed, $235,840 in 1993) of each employee's compensation can be taken into account.[2]

There are two basic steps in designing the formula that specifies the percentage of each participant's contribution that the employer will contribute annually:

(1) The employer chooses a "target" level of retirement benefits as a percentage of annual compensation. For example, the employer might want the plan to aim for

an annual retirement benefit of 50% of preretirement compensation for all participants.

(2) The plan designer chooses actuarial assumptions to determine how much must be contributed for each participant in order to provide the targeted level of benefit. Actuarial assumptions include (a) rate of investment return on plan assets, (b) cost of an annuity at age 65 (involving post-retirement mortality and investment return), and (c) the form of the benefit (straight life annuity, joint and survivor annuity, etc.) These actuarial assumptions are developed into a table of contribution percentages that are incorporated into the target plan.

Contribution percentages derived from the table are then applied to each employee's annual compensation to determine the annual employer contribution. The percentage for each employee is determined when the employee enters the plan and remains the same thereafter; it does not increase each year. Also, the percentages remain the same even if investment results are higher or lower than the initial assumptions. Unlike a defined benefit plan, there are no periodic actuarial valuations. The participant gets the benefit of good investment results and bears the risk of poor results.

An illustrative contribution table is set out in Figure 21.1; this is not the only possible table, since different actuarial assumptions can be used. There are some limits on possible actuarial assumptions:

- The table must be a "unisex" table—the same for both males and females. Current law (see Appendix I) prohibits plan contribution rates based on sex, since this would result in different benefits at retirement for males and females. (Sex-based actuarial assumptions can be used in defined benefit plans because there they do not affect the amount of benefit a participant receives, only the amount of the employer's cost.)

- Actuarial assumptions must be reasonable.

- The investment return assumption must not be less than 7.5% or more than 8.5%.[3] Under proposed regulations, a target benefit plan will be deemed to meet the nondiscrimination requirements if it satisfies a specified safe harbor and certain other conditions are met.[4]

Example: Archer Co. adopts a target plan with a target benefit of 50% of compensation. Using this table, and based on the employee data below, annual employer contributions are as follows. (The contribution percentages for a target of 50% of compensation are just five times those provided in the table for a target of 10% of compensation. Thus the table can be used for any target level by "scaling" the percentages up or down proportionately.)

Employee	Age at entry	Compensation	Annual contribution
A	30	$30,000	$ 840
B	50	30,000	5,310
C	30	60,000	1,680
D	50	60,000	10,620

For Employee A, the annual contribution percentage is 5 times .56 percent, or 2.8 percent of compensation. This is multiplied by $30,000, A's annual compensation, to arrive at the annual contribution of $840. The others are computed the same way.

Section 415 Limit

A very important limitation on target contributions must be kept in mind: the Section 415 "annual additions limit." This limit, which applies to all defined contribution plans, restricts annual additions to each participant's account to the lesser of (a) 25 percent of compensation or (b) the greater of $30,000 or ¼ of the dollar limitation for defined benefit plans. (The dollar limitation for defined benefit plans is $115,641 for 1993.) If the target percentage from the table calls for a larger contribution than this, the contribution must be cut back to the Section 415 limit.

For example, suppose Archer Co. in the example above employs Hood, who enters the plan at age 55 and earns $80,000 annually. The compensation percentage specified from the table for Archer Co.'s 50% target benefit is 33.15% (5 times 6.63%). This would dictate an annual contribution of $26,520. In fact, however, the company can contribute only $20,000 annually to Hood's account; this is the applicable annual additions limit of 25% of Hood's compensation (the lesser of 25% or $30,000 as indexed).

In effect, an employee in a situation like Hood's is "losing" benefits because the plan is a defined contribution plan subject to the annual additions limit. If the plan were a defined benefit plan, it could provide a 50% of compensation retirement benefit that could be fully funded by the employer, because the annual additions limit would not apply (see Chapter 9).

Hood's situation in the example may be typical of owners or key employees in many closely held businesses. This illustrates the major "tradeoff" in adopting a target benefit plan instead of a defined benefit plan. The target plan is simpler and less expensive, but the upper limit available for tax deferred retirement savings is reduced.

Figure 21.1

TARGET BENEFIT TABLE

Target benefit: 10 percent of compensation
Normal retirement age: 65
Benefit form: Straight life annuity
Assumed investment return: 8% preretirement, 6% postretirement
Postretirement mortality: UP 84 unixes contribution made on last day of year

Years to retirement	Annual employer contribution (percentage of compensation)	Years to retirement	Annual employer contribution (percentage of compensation)
1	96.01	19	2.32
2	46.16	20	2.10
3	29.57	21	1.90
4	21.31	22	1.73
5	16.37	23	1.58
6	13.09	24	1.44
7	10.76	25	1.31
8	9.03	26	1.20
9	7.69	27	1.10
10	6.63	28	1.01
11	5.77	29	0.92
12	5.06	30	0.85
13	4.47	31	0.78
14	3.96	32	0.72
15	3.54	33	0.66
16	3.17	34	0.61
17	2.84	35	0.56
18	2.56		

Benefit Payments

Although the target in a target plan is a retirement benefit similar to that provided in a defined benefit plan, a target plan actually provides a benefit like other types of defined contribution plans, particularly a money purchase plan. For example, suppose a participant retires from a company having a target plan with a target of 50% of compensation. The purpose of the target was only to determine the level of employer contributions. The benefit this retiree receives actually has no direct relation to his compensation. As with any other defined contribution plan, his benefit is equal to the amount built up in his account as a result of (a) employer contributions, (b) after-tax employee contributions (rare in target plans), (c) forfeitures from other employees' accounts, and (d) interest, capital gains, and other investment returns realized over the years on plan assets.

As a condition of qualification, a target benefit plan must provide for a qualified joint and survivor annuity as its automatic benefit unless waived by the participant, with the consent of his spouse.[5] If the automatic form of benefit is waived, account balances may be paid at retirement in installments over a period of years, in a lump sum, or other annuity options may be provided whereby the retiree can convert the amount in his or her account to an equivalent life or refund (period certain) annuity.

Other Provisions

Vesting and investment features of target plans are similar to those for money purchase plans discussed in Chapter 15. Integration of target plans with Social Security is discussed in the "Questions and Answers," below.

Age-Weighted Profit-Sharing Plans

An age-weighted profit-sharing plan is one that relates allocation percentages to age—a higher allocation for a participant who enters the plan at a later age. According to the cross-testing concept (see "Questions and Answers," below), if the age-weighting is done properly, benefits at retirement age will be nondiscriminatory as a percentage of compensation because the older entrant has fewer years to accumulate allocations.

To see how this works, consider a simple case study. Suppose Dot Matrix, aged 55, owns a software consulting business with profits that vary greatly from year to year. However, she wants to save at least $30,000 annually, preferably sheltered in a retirement plan. She has one employee, Arthur Data, aged 25.

This year Dot's compensation (all the net income of the corporate business) is $200,000. Data's salary is $40,000.

As a planner, you rule out a defined benefit plan or target plan because of the variability of annual income. You suggest the age-weighted profit-sharing plan because of (1) the ability to vary contributions from year to year or skip contributions in a bad year, and (2) the weighting of the allocation in favor of Dot because of her age.

The maximum annual contribution of $30,000 will be made by Dot; this is 15% of her compensation. Based on an "age-weighting" table,[6] the corresponding percentage contribution for Data is only 1.31 percent, because Data is so much younger. This is actually less than the top heavy minimum contribution of 3%; therefore, the allocation for Data is 3% of compensation or $1,200.

A comparison of the age-weighted plan with some alternatives shows its advantages:

Employee	Salary	Regular profit-sharing plan	Integrated profit-sharing plan	Age weighted plan
Dot	$200,000	$30,000	$30,000	$30,000
Data	40,000	6,000	4,360	1,200
% for Dot		83.3%	87.3%	96.15%

TAX IMPLICATIONS

1. Employer contributions to an age-weighted plan are deductible when made, so long as the plan remains "qualified." A plan is qualified if it meets the eligibility, vesting, funding and other requirements discussed in Chapter 23.

2. Assuming the plan remains qualified, taxation of the employee on plan contributions is deferred. Both employer contributions and earnings on plan assets are nontaxable to plan participants until withdrawn.[7]

3. Annual additions to each participant's account are limited to the lesser of (a) 25% of the participant's compen-

sation or (b) the greater of $30,000 or ¼ of the dollar limitation for defined benefit plans.[8] (The dollar limitation for defined benefit plans is $115,641 for 1993.) Annual additions include (1) employer contributions to participants' accounts; (2) forfeitures from other participants' accounts; and (3) employee contributions to the account.[9]

4. Distributions from the plan must follow the rules for qualified plan distributions. Certain premature or excessive distributions are subject to penalties. The distribution rules are discussed in Chapter 24.

5. Lump sum distributions made after age 59½ are subject to a limited election to use a special 5-year averaging tax calculation. Certain older participants may also be eligible for a 10-year averaging tax calculation for lump sum distributions. Not all distributions are eligible for these special tax calculations. Chapter 24 covers these rules and includes IRS forms.

6. A target pension plan, but not an age-weighted profit-sharing plan, is subject to the minimum funding rules of section 412 of the Code. This requires minimum annual contributions,[10] subject to a penalty imposed on the employer if less than the minimum amount is contributed. For a target plan, the minimum funding requirement is generally the amount required under the plan's contribution formula. The minimum funding requirements therefore will be satisfied so long as the employer contributes to each participant's account the percentage of compensation required by the plan. Chapter 23 discusses the minimum funding rules further.

7. The plan is subject to the ERISA reporting and disclosure rules outlined in Appendix A.

ALTERNATIVES

1. Defined benefit plans provide more benefit security because of the employer and government guarantee of benefit levels. Defined benefit plans also allow greater tax deductible employer contributions for older plan entrants who are highly compensated because the 25%/$30,000 annual additions limit does not apply. However, defined benefit plans are more complex and costly to design and administer.

2. Money purchase plans offer an alternative similar to target plans, but without the age-related contribution feature.

3. Nonqualified deferred compensation plans can be provided exclusively for selected executives. But with those plans the employer's tax deduction is generally deferred until benefit payments are made. This can be as much as 20 or 30 years after the employer's contribution is made.

4. Individual retirement savings is available as an alternative or supplement to an employer plan, but except for the limited provision for deductible IRAs there is no tax deferral.

HOW TO INSTALL THE PLAN

Installation of an age-weighted plan follows the qualified plan installation procedure described in Chapter 25.

WHERE CAN I FIND OUT MORE ABOUT IT?

1. McFadden, John J., *Retirement Plans for Employees*. Homewood, IL: Richard D. Irwin, 1988.

2. Gee, Judith Boyers, *Pensions in Perspective*, 4th ed. Cincinnati, OH: The National Underwriter Co., Fall 1993.

3. Graduate Course: Advanced Pension and Retirement Planning I (GS 814), The American College, Bryn Mawr, PA.

QUESTIONS AND ANSWERS

Question — How is the contribution formula in a target benefit plan integrated with Social Security?

Answer — Target benefit contribution formulas can be integrated with Social Security. In the past, this was frequently done. The applicable rules were a combination of those applicable to defined benefit and money purchase plans.

Under the proposed nondiscrimination regulations, target plans generally must apply the rules for defined benefit plans to the target formula.[11]

Question — Can a self-employed person adopt a target plan?

Answer — Yes. The plan can cover not only regular employees of the business, but also the self-employed person(s) who own the business—the sole proprietor or partners. Plans covering self-employed persons are known as "Keogh" or "HR 10" plans. These plans are basically the same as regular qualified plans, but some of the special rules that apply are covered in Chapter 12 of this book.

The contribution or allocation formula applied to self-employed individuals must be based on their "earned income" as contrasted with the "compensation" base for regular employees. The definition of earned income is covered in Chapter 12.

Question — How is an age-weighted plan applied where shareholder-employees of an S corporation are covered?

Answer — For an S corporation, the plan contribution or allocation formula cannot provide an employer contribution for all of the shareholder-employee's income from the corporation. The formula must be based only on the shareholder's compensation for services rendered to the corporation. Any portion of the shareholder's income that represents dividends from the S corporation must be excluded from the plan formula.

Question — What is "cross-testing" and how does it provide opportunities for creative plan design?

Answer — Under the proposed nondiscrimination regulations, a defined contribution plan can be tested on the basis of its projected *benefits* at retirement, and a defined benefit plan can be tested on the basis of annual employer *contributions*. This concept is referred to as "cross-testing."[12] In effect, it is cross-testing that makes age-weighted defined contribution plans permissible. Such plans are discriminatory on the basis of their annual contribution levels, but they are designed to be cross-tested. If projected benefit levels in an age-weighted plan are not discriminatory, the plan meets the nondiscrimination tests of the proposed regulations.

Cross-testing can be used to design a defined contribution plan that has the *maximum permissible* level of discrimination. The planner's actuarial consultant "works backward" from the projected benefit levels that just meet the cross-testing requirements and then computes the annual employer contribution required to support those projected benefit levels. Such plans often permit startlingly low contribution levels for younger, lower-paid participants. These plans are described by various names such as cross-tested plan, new comparability plans, etc.

FOOTNOTES

1. IRC Section 414(s); Reg. §1.414(s)-1T.
2. IRC Section 401(a)(17).

3. See definition of "standard interest rate," Prop. Reg. §1.401(a)(4)-12.

4. See Prop. Reg. §1.401(a)(4)-8(b)(3).

5. IRC Section 401(a)(11)(B)(ii).

6. No IRS approved age-weighting table exists as of this writing; however, for a table based on the proposed regulations, see Phillips, *The Pension Actuary*, November 1990.

7. IRC Section 402(a).

8. IRC Section 415(c).

9. IRC Section 415(c)(2).

10. Estimated quarterly required contributions of Section 412(m) apply only to defined benefit pension plans, not defined contribution pension plans. See IRC Section 412(m).

11. Prop. Reg. §1.401(a)(4)-8(b)(3)(i)(C).

12. Prop. Reg. §1.401(a)(4)-8.

Chapter 22

TAX DEFERRED ANNUITY

WHAT IS IT?

A tax deferred annuity plan (also called a "TDA" plan or Section 403(b) plan) is a tax deferred employee retirement plan that can be adopted only by certain tax-exempt private organizations and certain public schools and colleges. Employees have accounts in a TDA plan to which employers contribute (or employees contribute through salary reductions).

The benefits of a TDA plan to employees are similar to those of a qualified profit-sharing plan, particularly the Section 401(k) type of plan (see Chapter 19): (1) the TDA contribution is, within limits, not currently taxable to employees; (2) plan account balances accumulate tax free, and (3) tax on plan contributions and account earnings is deferred until the employee actually withdraws amounts from the plan.

Because of recent tax law changes, TDA plans have become much more like qualified plans—Section 401(k) plans in particular. In addition to imposing nondiscrimination rules on TDA plans, current law generally forbids tax-exempt and governmental organizations from adopting Section 401(k) plans. Thus, in effect the TDA plan is the "Section 401(k) substitute" for a tax-exempt organization or public school.

WHEN IS IT INDICATED?

1. When (and only when) the employer organization is eligible under the TDA provisions of the Code. An organization must be one of the following in order to adopt a TDA plan:

   (a) A tax-exempt employer described in Section 501(c)(3) of the Code. This means that

      (1) The employer must be "organized and operated exclusively for religious, charitable, scientific, testing for public safety, literary, or educational purposes, or to foster national or international amateur sport competition...or for the prevention of cruelty to children or animals."

      (2) The organization must benefit the public, rather than a private shareholder or individual.

      (3) The organization further must refrain from political campaigning or propaganda intended to in-

fluence legislation. In other words, most familiar non-profit institutions such as churches, hospitals, private schools and colleges, and charitable institutions are eligible to adopt a TDA.

   (b) An educational organization with (1) a regular faculty and curriculum and (2) a resident student body, that is operated by a state or municipal agency. In other words, most public schools and colleges may adopt a TDA plan.

2. Assuming the employer organization is eligible, the positive indications for a TDA plan are similar to those for a taxable organization that is considering the adoption of a Section 401(k) plan. A TDA plan is indicated:

   (a) When the employer wants to provide a tax deferred retirement plan for employees but can afford only minimal extra expense beyond existing salary and benefit costs. A TDA plan can be funded entirely from employee salary reductions (except for installation and administration costs, which must be paid for by the employer). In most plans, however, some additional employer contribution to the plan can enhance its effectiveness.

   (b) When the employee group has one or more of the following characteristics:

      • many would like some choice as to the level of savings—that is, a choice between various levels of current cash compensation and tax deferred savings. A younger, more mobile work force often prefers this option.

      • many employees are relatively young and have substantial time to accumulate retirement savings.

      • many employees are willing to accept a degree of investment risk in their plan accounts in return for the potential benefits of good investment results.

   (c) When an employer wants an attractive, "savings-type" supplement to its existing defined benefit or other qualified plan. Such a supplement can make the employer's retirement benefit program attractive to both younger and older employees by providing both security of retirement benefits and the opportunity to increase savings and investment on a tax deferred basis.

ADVANTAGES

1. As with qualified plans, a TDA plan provides a tax-deferred retirement savings medium for employees.

2. A salary reduction-type TDA plan allows employees a degree of choice in the amount they wish to save under the plan.

3. TDA plans can be funded entirely through salary reductions by employees. As a result, an employer can adopt the plan with no additional cost for employee compensation; the only extra cost is plan installation and administration. The plan may actually result in some savings as a result of lower state or local (but not federal) payroll taxes.

4. In-service withdrawals by employees are permitted; these are not available in qualified pension plans.

DISADVANTAGES

1. As with qualified defined contribution plans, account balances at retirement age may not provide adequate retirement savings for employees who entered the plan at later ages.

2. For each employee the annual salary reduction under the plan is limited to $9,500. However, this amount can be supplemented by employer contributions to provide additional tax deferred savings.

3. Because of the nondiscrimination tests described below, a TDA plan can be relatively costly and complex to administer.

4. Employees bear investment risk under the plan. However, TDA funds are in large part invested in low risk annuity contracts. Only the mutual fund (custodial account—see below) type of TDA investment (and possibly some variable annuity contracts) involve significant investment risk, and employees usually are given a choice of mutual fund investments so they can control the degree of risk.

DESIGN FEATURES

In the past, employers had great freedom and discretion in designing TDA plans; they could be provided to any group of employees desired, or even a single employee, and employer contributions could vary from employee to employee on a discriminatory basis. However, TDA plans are now subject to nondiscrimination rules. The rules applicable to plans other than pure salary reduction plans are similar to those for qualified plans. The current nondiscrimination rules are discussed further in the "Questions and Answers," below.

However, there are some important differences between TDA plans and qualified plans and this chapter will focus on these differences:

- The annual limit on contributions for a TDA plan is computed in a different and much more complicated way.

- Salary reductions in a TDA plan are currently subject to a higher ($9,500) limit than Section 401(k) plans, and there are "catch up" provisions that allow employees with 15 or more years of service to contribute in excess of this limit.

- Distributions from a TDA plan are not eligible for the 5-year or (10-year) averaging provisions for qualified plans.

- Plan investments are limited to annuity contracts or custodial accounts invested in mutual funds; incidental life insurance is also permitted.

Salary Reductions

Most TDA plans are funded entirely or in part through salary reductions elected by employees. To prevent discrimination, there is a requirement that if the plan permits salary reductions of more than $200 (not indexed) by any participant, then all employees must be given the same option (except for employees covered under a Section 401(k) or Section 457 plan, students employed by the school in which they are enrolled, or employees who normally work less than 20 hours per week).[1]

Salary reductions must be elected by employees before compensation is earned—that is, before they render the services for which compensation is paid. Salary reductions elected after compensation is earned are ineffective as a result of the tax doctrine of "constructive receipt."

The usual practice is to provide plan participants with a salary reduction election form that they must complete before the end of each calendar year. The election specifies how much will be contributed to the plan from each paycheck received for the forthcoming year. The amount cannot be increased later in the year. But usually the employee can reduce or entirely withdraw the election for pay not yet earned if circumstances dictate.

Salary reductions in TDA plans are subject to an annual limit. The employee must add together each year all of his or her salary reductions from:

(1) TDA plans,

(2) Section 401(k) plans, and

(3) salary reduction SEPs.

The total must not exceed $9,500.[2] This $9,500 limit will remain unchanged until the $7,000 limit for Section 401(k) plans, as indexed for inflation, reaches $9,500. (The $7,000 limit reached $8,994 as of 1993.) From then on, there will be a single indexed limit for all salary reduction plans.

If the employee has completed 15 years of service for the employer, and the employer is (1) an educational organization, (2) a hospital, (3) a home health care agency, (4) a health and welfare service agency, or (5) a church, synagogue or related organization, the $9,500 salary reduction limit is increased by an additional sum equal to the lesser of:

• $3,000 per year, up to a total of $15,000, or

• $5,000 times the employee's years of service with the employer, less all prior salary reductions with that employer.[3]

The $9,500 salary reduction limit (as indexed), plus the "salary reduction catch up" provision described in the preceding paragraph, is the *absolute* limit on the amount of annual salary reductions for any employee. Some (usually relatively lower paid) employees may not be able to reduce salary by this much, since the "exclusion allowance" for them may be less than this. The exclusion allowance is discussed below under "Tax Implications." (See also Figure 22.1, "The Five-Step Procedure.")

Vesting

The participant is always 100% vested in all amounts contributed to the TDA plan and in any plan earnings on those amounts. Unlike a regular qualified plan, graded vesting is not permitted. Even if a participant leaves employment after a short time, his or her plan account cannot be forfeited. Often plan account balances are distributed in a single sum when a participant terminates employment.

Employer Contributions

Many TDA plans provide for employer contributions, either in addition to or instead of salary reduction contributions, in order to encourage employee participation and make the plan more valuable to employees. TDA plans most often use a "formula matching contribution." Under this approach the employer matches employee salary reductions, either dollar for dollar or under another formula. For example, the plan might provide that the employer contributes an amount equal to 50% of the amount the employee elects as a salary reduction. So if an employee elects a salary reduction of $6,000, the employer puts an additional $3,000 into the employee's plan account. Other employer contribution approaches can be used similar to those used in Section 401(k) plans, as discussed in Chapter 19.

As with a qualified plan, employer contributions to the plan must not discriminate in favor of highly compensated employees. "Highly compensated" is defined as for qualified plans (see Chapter 23). Furthermore, only the first $200,000 (as indexed, $235,840 in 1993) of each employee's compensation can be taken into account in any contribution formula; this rule is the same as that for qualified plans.

Plan Investments

All plan funds in TDA plans must be invested in either (1) annuity contracts purchased by the employer from an insurance company, or (2) mutual fund (regulated investment company) shares held in custodial accounts. Many plans provide both types of investments and allow participants full discretion to divide their accounts between the two investment media.

Annuities used in TDA plans can be either group or individual contracts, level or flexible premium annuities, or fixed dollar or variable annuities. Face amount certificates providing a fixed maturity value and a schedule of redemptions are also permitted. Annuity contracts can give participants a degree of choice as to investment strategy. For example, the participant can be given a choice of investment mix between equity funds and fixed investment funds.

"Incidental life insurance" protection under annuity contracts is also permitted. The amount of life insurance is limited by the "incidental" tests discussed in Chapter 14—i.e., the limits are the same as those for qualified plans. As with qualified plans, the value of the life insurance protection is taxed annually to the employee using the P.S. 58 table reproduced in Chapter 14, and the P.S. 58 costs may be recovered tax free on a subsequent plan distribution.

Plan Distributions

Distributions from TDA plans are subject to the qualified plan distribution rules detailed in Chapter 24. Many plans provide for distributions in a lump sum at termination of employment. However, a plan subject to ERISA must either provide for a qualified joint and survivor annuity as its automatic benefit or provide that if the participant dies, 100% of his nonforfeitable benefit will be paid to his surviving spouse unless the spouse is deceased or has consented to another beneficiary.[4]

TDA plans often allow participants to make in-service withdrawals (i.e., withdrawals before termination of employment). Withdrawals are not permitted from a TDA custodial account (mutual funds) before (1) attainment of age 59½, (2) death, disability or separation from service, or (3) (with respect to amounts attributable to salary reduction contributions) financial hardship. Similar restrictions apply to TDAs other than custodial accounts with respect to distributions of amounts attributable to salary reduction, but the restrictions do not apply to amounts held in the account at the close of the last year beginning before January 1, 1989. Distributions may also be made to former spouses under qualified domestic relations orders (QDROs).

All withdrawals are subject to income tax. In addition, many in-service distributions will be subject to the 10% early withdrawal penalty tax discussed in Chapter 24, even if the distribution is permitted under the terms of the TDA plan. To summarize, a 10% penalty tax applies to the taxable amount (i.e., amount subject to regular income tax) of any qualified plan or TDA distribution, except for distributions

- after age 59½

- on the employee's death

- upon the employee's disability

- that are part of a joint or life annuity payout following separation from service

- that are paid after separation from service after age 55

- that do not exceed the amount of medical expenses deductible as an itemized deduction for the year.[5]

Many TDA plans have provisions for plan loans to participants. A plan loan provision is extremely valuable to employees because it allows them access to their plan funds without the 10% penalty tax. Plan loans are discussed in detail in Chapter 24.

TAX IMPLICATIONS

1. Employees are not taxed currently on either salary reductions or employer contributions under a TDA plan, so long as these in total do not exceed any of three limits. The first limit is the "exclusion allowance" provided under section 403(b) of the Code.

The formula for the annual exclusion allowance is:

(1) 20 percent of the participant's "includable compensation" from the employer $_____

multiplied by

(2) the participant's total years of service for the employer _____(years)

minus

(3) amounts contributed to the plan in prior years that were excluded from the participant's income $_____

equals

(4) annual exclusion allowance $_____

The third item in the formula—prior contributions—must include not only prior TDA contributions but also prior year contributions to regular qualified plans on behalf of the employee.

Example: Doctor Vanderslice has been employed by Staph Hospital for 10 years, including this year. Her includable compensation from the hospital this year is $60,000. Prior TDA contributions by the hospital on her behalf total $110,000.

Her exclusion allowance for this year is (1) 20 percent of taxable income this year—$12,000—times (2) 10 years of service—$120,000—minus (3) prior contributions of $110,000—a result of $10,000. Because this is not a salary reduction contribution, the hospital can contribute $10,000 to Doctor Vanderslice's TDA account this year, unless the limit explained in 2 below is lower.

Where the TDA plan is funded through salary reductions—as most plans are—the computation has another wrinkle to it. The 20% limit is applied to the participant's "includable compensation." This means the compensation that is includable in the participant's taxable income. Since salary reductions are *not* includable in income, the 20% limit must be applied to the amount of compensation *after* the salary reduction is taken into account.

Example: TDA participant Hal earns $30,000 this year and has no prior service (i.e., one year of total service) and no prior TDA contributions. Hal's maximum exclusion allowance for salary reduction contributions is $5,000. This is because Hal's salary *after* the salary reduction is $25,000. Twenty percent of the reduced salary of $25,000 is $5,000.

A general formula for the maximum salary reduction permitted under the exclusion allowance is:

$$\text{Maximum salary reduction} = \frac{(S \times T) - 5B}{T + 5}$$

where

S = unreduced salary

T = total years of service including current year

B = prior years' excludable contributions.

2. A TDA plan is subject to the "annual additions limit" of Code section 415. Annual additions to each participant's account are limited to the lesser of (a) 25% of the participant's includable compensation or (b) the greater of $30,000 or ¼ of the dollar limitation for defined benefit plans. (The dollar limitation for defined benefit plans is $115,641 for 1993—see Chapter 23.) Annual additions include the total of (1) employer contributions to the participant's account; (2) salary reductions or other elective deferrals contributed to the account; and (3) after-tax employee contributions to the account. (If the employee participates in other retirement plans, contributions to those plans may have to be considered in determining how much may be contributed under this limit.)

Section 415 acts as an upper limit on the exclusion allowance described in the preceding section. Annual additions to a participant's account cannot exceed the Section 415 limit even if the exclusion allowance works out to a higher figure.

Example. Doctor Finster is an employee of Staph Hospital with a total of five years of service. His current annual includable compensation is $200,000.

The hospital has made prior TDA contributions of $50,000 to Finster's account.

Doctor Finster's exclusion allowance for this year is 20% of $200,000, or $40,000, times 5 years of service ($200,000), minus prior contributions of $50,000—a net of $150,000. However, the Section 415 annual additions limit for this year is $30,000 (the lesser of 25% of Finster's compensation or $30,000). Thus, the hospital may contribute no more than $30,000 to Doctor Finster's TDA account this year.

3. There is yet a further complication to the TDA limit. The Section 415 limit and exclusion allowance discussed in the preceding two sections can, in the case of TDA plans for certain employers only, be increased under "catch-up alternatives" that are aimed at long service participants in TDA plans.[6]

These catch up provisions are available only if the employer is (1) an educational organization, (2) a hospital, (3) a home health care agency, (4) a health and welfare service agency, or (5) a church, synagogue or related organization.

There are three alternative catch up provisions. An employee must affirmatively elect one of these (on his or her income tax return) in order to use it. Only one of these alternatives can ever be elected by an employee and, once made, the election is irrevocable. However, the alternative elected may be used as many times thereafter as the employee chooses (except that the first, or A, alternative may be used only once). The alternatives are:

(A) the "last year of service" alternative. In the employee's last year of service only, he can elect to use the regular exclusion allowance (using no more than 10 years of service) instead of the 25% limit under Section 415. The $30,000 limit still applies, however. In other words, this alternative allows a contribution of more than 25% of compensation, but not more than $30,000.

(B) the "any year" alternative. Instead of the 25% of compensation limit under Section 415, the employee can elect to apply a limit equal to the lesser of

—$4,000 plus 25% of includable compensation for the year;

—the regular exclusion allowance for the year; or

—$15,000.

(C) the "overall" alternative. Instead of the regular exclusion allowance, the participant can elect simply to use the 25%/$30,000 Section 415 limit.

There are in addition some special rules for employees of churches, synagogues, and related organizations only.

The effect of all these overlapping limitations is to make it extremely difficult for employees to understand just exactly how much they can put in a TDA plan. In addition, the administrative cost and complexity to the employer can be considerable. Figure 22.1 summarizes the procedure for determining an employee's maximum allowable salary reduction.

4. Salary reductions, but not employer contributions, are subject to Social Security (FICA) and federal unemployment (FUTA) payroll taxes.[7] The impact of state payroll taxes depends on the particular state's law. Both elective deferrals and employer contributions may be exempt from state payroll taxes in some states.

5. If the plan provides employer matching contributions or employee after-tax contributions, it must meet the nondiscrimination tests of Code section 401(m). Under these tests, the ratio of employer matching contributions and employee after-tax contributions (as a percentage of each eligible employee's compensation) is computed. The average of these ratios for highly compensated employ-

ees cannot exceed the average of these ratios for all other eligible employees by more than the greater of:

• 125 percent, or

• the lesser of (a) 200 percent, or (b) the percentage of all other eligible employees plus 2 percentage points.

For example, if the average of employee after-tax contributions and employer matching contributions to compensation for nonhighly compensated employees is 6 percent of compensation, the average for highly compensated employees can be up to 8 percent (6 percent plus 2 percent).

Administratively the employer must monitor the level of contributions made by nonhighly compensated employees, and then make sure that highly compensated employees do not exceed this level in order for the plan to remain qualified.

To meet this test, the employer may take into account 401(k) contributions to a plan maintained by the employer, or employer contributions to which the 401(k) vesting and withdrawal restrictions apply.[8]

"Highly compensated employee" is defined as it is for qualified plan purposes. In summary (the details are in

Figure 22.1

THE FIVE STEP PROCEDURE

A summary of the procedure for determining an employee's
maximum salary reduction in a salary reduction-only TDA plan

1. Compute the employee's regular exclusion allowance under the procedure described in (1) under Tax Implications.
2. Compute the employee's Section 415 limit as described in (2) under Tax Implications.
3. Work out any catch up alternatives available to the employee. These are described in (3) under Tax Implications. If any of these provides a greater contribution than the lesser of the amount determined in Steps 1 and 2, the employee may want to make an election to use that alternative.
4. The limit so far is the greater of (i) Step 3 or (ii) the lesser of Steps 1 or 2. Compare this result with the $9,500 annual salary reduction limitation. If the result of the first 3 steps is more than $9,500, only $9,500 can be contributed, unless —
5. Determine if the "salary reduction catch up" described in Design Features above applies. If the employee has the required service and is employed by the right type of employer, the $9,500 limit can be raised to $12,500 or more (but never more than $15,000).

This five step procedure is just a simplified, schematic illustration of the computation procedure to show how the various limits interact. The actual annual calculation for each participant in a TDA plan is a complex, costly burden for the employer, and one that is full of possibilities for error. The planner who can develop a way to deliver this administrative service to client tax exempt organizations can get a considerable edge on the competition for selling investment products to the plan.

Chapter 23) a highly compensated employee is an employee who:

- was at any time a more than 5 percent owner of the employer

- received compensation from the employer over $75,000 (as indexed, $96,368 for 1993)

- received compensation over $50,000 (as indexed, $64,245 for 1993) and was in the highest-paid 20% of the employer's employees

- was an officer and received compensation over 50% of the defined benefit dollar limitation (i.e., over $57,820.50 for 1993)

6. Distributions from the plan must follow the rules for qualified plan distributions. Certain premature or excessive distributions are subject to penalties. The distribution rules are discussed in Chapter 24.

7. Distributions from the plan to employees are subject to income tax when received. Single sum distributions are *not* eligible for the special 5-year or 10-year averaging computations applicable to qualified plan distributions.

ERISA REQUIREMENTS

In general, ERISA applies to a TDA plan to the same extent it applies to a qualified plan. The reporting and disclosure requirements discussed in Appendix A therefore apply to a TDA in most cases. In addition, a plan subject to ERISA must observe its other requirements, including fiduciary requirements and plan requirements protecting spousal benefits. However, TDAs of certain employers may be subject to the ERISA exemption applicable to governmental and church plans (see Appendix A). In addition, an ERISA exemption under Labor Department regulations applies to plans that are (1) funded purely through voluntary salary reductions by employees, and (2) not considered "established or maintained by the employer."[9] This exemption permits only minimal employer involvement with the plan.

HOW TO INSTALL A PLAN

Installation of a TDA plan is not subject to the qualified plan rules. Furthermore, some employers having TDA plans are not subject to any provisions of ERISA (e.g., church or governmental organizations.) Government approval of a TDA plan is not necessary and is not now generally sought by plan installers (although the IRS reportedly is considering a deter-

mination letter program for TDAs similar to that for qualified plans). However, a written plan document similar to a qualified plan document is required if ERISA applies to the plan, and should be adopted as a matter of good policy even where not required by law.

In addition, salary reduction forms must be completed by plan participants before the plan's effective date so that salary reduction elections will be immediately effective.

The success of a TDA plan in meeting the employer's objectives and the nondiscrimination tests depends on effective communication with employees. Effective employer-employee communication is always important in employee benefit plans. But it is particularly essential for a TDA plan because of the active role of employees in the plan.

WHERE CAN I FIND OUT MORE ABOUT IT?

1. McFadden, John J., *Retirement Plans for Employees*. Homewood, IL.: Richard D. Irwin, 1988.

2. Gee, Judith Boyers, *Pensions in Perspective*, 4th ed. Cincinnati, OH: The National Underwriter Co., Fall 1993.

3. Graduate Course: Advanced Pension and Retirement Planning I (GS 814), The American College, Bryn Mawr, PA.

4. *Advanced Sales Reference Service*, Section 61, The National Underwriter Co.

QUESTIONS AND ANSWERS

Question — How can a planner determine if an employer organization meets the technical eligibility requirements in the Code?

Answer — Most organizations that are tax exempt under Section 501(c)(3) have obtained a government ruling letter to that effect. Also, organizations that have been ruled tax exempt are listed in a government publication available at libraries. Planners should ask the prospective TDA client for a copy of the ruling letter, if any, and keep it in their files. If there is no ruling letter, or if the organization is not a Section 501(c)(3) organization, the planner should at minimum obtain an attorney's or accountant's written opinion that the organization meets the TDA criteria. In large or questionable cases, an IRS ruling should be sought.

Question — Can TDA plans cover "independent contractors"—for example, anesthesiologists or radiologists associated with, but not formally employed by, hospitals?

Answer — No. TDA plan participants must be employees of the plan sponsor. The best way for a planner to verify this is to ask the sponsor how these individuals are treated by the sponsor for employment tax purposes—Social Security (FICA) and federal unemployment (FUTA). Employees and independent contractors are treated differently under these taxes (the employer pays no employment taxes for independent contractors) and the treatment of these individuals in the TDA plan should be consistent.

Question — Can a TDA plan participant make deductible IRA contributions as well as salary reductions under the TDA plan?

Answer — Yes. However, in a year in which an individual makes salary reduction contributions to a TDA plan or the employer contributes to his TDA account, the individual is considered an "active participant" under the IRA rules. IRA contributions are deductible only within the reduced deductible IRA limits allowed for active plan participants—see Chapter 13. No deduction is allowed for a year in which adjusted gross income on a joint basis is $50,000 or more ($35,000 for a single person), with reduced deductions for adjusted gross income between $40,000 and $50,000 joint ($25,000-$35,000 single).

Question — Can a TDA participant transfer funds from one annuity contract or mutual fund investment to another without adverse tax effect?

Answer — Yes; such a transfer is not a taxable event. The transfer can be structured as a "direct rollover" or "rollover" as described in Chapter 24. However, for TDAs it is also possible to make a direct transfer. As approved by the IRS in Rev. Rul. 90-24,[10] the plan participant simply directs the insurance company or mutual fund now holding the participant's account to transfer part or all of it directly to the new insurance company contract or mutual fund designated by the participant. No distribution to the participant should be made.

There is no income tax or early distribution penalty on a direct transfer. However, some annuity contracts may have a penalty provision for withdrawals that will reduce the net amount available for withdrawal.

Question — What nondiscrimination rules currently apply to TDA plans providing employer contributions?

Answer — The IRS has not issued final guidance on these rules. IRS Notice 89-23[11] provides "safe harbors" that employers can use until final rules are established.[12] In applying the safe harbors, an employer can aggregate its TDA and qualified plans. If any one of the following three safe harbors is met, the aggregated arrangement is deemed to comply with the nondiscrimination rules:

1. The *maximum disparity* safe harbor is satisfied if (a) the highest percentage of compensation contributed on behalf of any highly compensated employee (HCE) who is earning benefits under the aggregated arrangement does not exceed 180% of the lowest percentage of compensation contributed on behalf of any nonhighly compensated employee (NHCE) who is earning benefits, (b) at least 50% of the NHCEs are earning benefits under the aggregated arrangement, and (c) the percentage of NHCEs who are earning benefits under the aggregated arrangement is at least 70%.

2. The *lesser disparity* safe harbor is satisfied if (a) the highest percentage of compensation contributed on behalf of any HCE who is earning benefits under the aggregated arrangement does not exceed 140% of the lowest percentage of compensation contributed on behalf of any NHCE who is earning benefits, (b) at least 30% of the NHCEs are earning benefits under the aggregated arrangement, and (c) the percentage of NHCEs who are earning benefits under the aggregated plans is at least 50%.

3. The *no disparity* safe harbor is satisfied if (a) the highest percentage of compensation contributed on behalf of any HCE who is earning benefits under a plan or plans in the aggregated arrangement does not exceed the percentage of compensation contributed on behalf of any NHCE who is earning benefits and (b) either of the following tests is satisfied: (i) At least 20% of the NHCEs must be earning benefits and the percentage of NHCEs who are earning benefits under the aggregated arrangement must be at least 70%; or (ii) At least 80% of the NHCEs must be earning benefits and the percentage of NHCEs who are earning benefits under the aggregated arrangement must be at least 30%.

In applying these tests, employees who have not met the plan's minimum age and service requirements may be excluded. If a plan fails to meet these safe harbors, it is still possible to comply with the general nondiscrimination rules as discussed in Chapter 23. A plan will be deemed to be in compliance if the employer operates the plan in accordance with a reasonable, good faith interpretation of the rules.

FOOTNOTES

1. Unless other references are provided, the rules in this chapter are found in IRC Section 403(b).
2. IRC Sections 402(g)(3), 402(g)(4).
3. IRC Section 402(g)(8). Deferrals under a Section 457 plan (see Chapter 11) must also be taken into account in determining "all prior salary reductions with that employer." IRC Section 457(c)(2).
4. ERISA Section 205.
5. IRC Section 72(t).
6. IRC Section 415(c)(4).
7. IRC Sections 3121(a)(5) [FICA], 3306(b)(5) [FUTA].
8. IRC Section 401(m); Reg. §1.401(m)-1(b)(5).
9. DOL Reg. §2510.3-2(f).
10. 1990-1 CB 97.
11. 1989-1 CB 654.
12. Subsequent notices have extended the use of the safe harbors and the "good faith" compliance standard until specific guidance is issued under Section 403(b). Notice 90-73, 1990-2 CB 353; Notice 92-36, 1992-2 CB 364.

QUALIFIED PLANS: GENERAL RULES FOR QUALIFICATION

The design of qualified pension and profit-sharing plans is a very complex subject, and the complete details are beyond the scope of this book. However, because of the great importance of these plans in an employer's benefit program and for individual financial and retirement planning, every planner should have a basic understanding of how these plans are structured, what they can do, and the rules for "qualifying" these plans.

In order to obtain the tax advantages of qualified plans, complex Internal Revenue Code and IRS regulatory requirements must be met. The following will summarize these requirements as briefly as possible. These rules have many exceptions and qualifications that will not be covered in detail.

ELIGIBILITY AND COVERAGE

A qualified plan must cover a broad group of employees, not just key employees and business owners. Two types of rules must be satisfied: the "age and service" ("waiting period") requirements, and the "overall coverage" and "participation" requirements.

Minimum waiting period and age requirements are often used in plans to avoid burdening the plan with employees who terminate after short periods of service. However, the plan cannot require more than one year of service for eligibility, and any employee who has attained the age of 21 must be allowed to enter the plan upon meeting the plan's waiting period requirement. As an alternative, the plan waiting period can be up to 2 years if the plan provides immediate 100 percent vesting upon entry. No plan can impose a maximum age for entry. For eligibility purposes, a year of service means a 12-month period during which the employee has at least 1,000 hours of service.[1]

In addition to the rules restricting age- and service-related eligibility provisions, qualified plan coverage is further regulated through two alternative overall coverage tests. A qualified plan must satisfy one of the two following tests:[2]

1. *Ratio percentage test.* The plan must cover a percentage of nonhighly compensated employees that is at least 70 percent of the percentage of highly compensated employees covered.

2. *Average benefit test.* The plan must benefit a nondiscriminatory classification of employees, and the average benefit, as a percentage of compensation, for all nonhighly compensated employees of the employer must be at least 70 percent of that for highly compensated employees.

"Highly compensated" is a concept defined in detail in Code section 414(q) (see below).

In addition, no plan can be qualified unless it covers, on each day of the plan year, the lesser of (1) 50 employees of the employer or (2) 40 percent or more of all employees of the employer (i.e., the 50/40 test).[3]

The average benefit test is a two-pronged test—it requires (1) a *nondiscriminatory classification* and (2) the *70 percent average benefit* requirement.[4]

The nondiscriminatory classification test is expanded upon in some detail in the regulations under Section 410(b). First, the regulations provide a "safe harbor" table (Figure 23.1) under which certain plans are deemed to meet the nondiscriminatory classification requirement automatically. The safe harbor test is best explained through an example using the table.

Example: Suppose Average Co. has 700 salaried office employees, including 100 highly compensated employees, and 9,300 production employees, of whom 300 are highly compensated. Average Co. would like to maintain a qualified plan just for the office employees. The office plan will not meet the ratio percentage test since its ratio percentage is 25% [(600/9,600)/(100/400)]. Does it meet the average benefit test under the regulations? Its nonhighly compensated concentration percentage is 9,600/10,000 or 96%. From the table, the "safe harbor" ratio percentage is 23 percent. Since the plan has an actual ratio percentage of 25%, it is deemed to meet the nondiscriminatory classification test without actually looking at the classification itself. (Of course, the plan also has to meet the average benefit percentage portion of the average benefit test.)

Figure 23.1

Nonhighly compensated employee concentration percentage	Safe harbor percentage	Unsafe habor percentage	Nonhighly compensated employee concentration percentage	Safe harbor percentage	Unsafe harbor percentage
0-60	50.00	40.00	80	35.00	25.00
61	49.25	39.25	81	34.25	24.25
62	48.50	38.50	82	33.50	23.50
63	47.75	37.75	83	32.75	22.75
64	47.00	37.00	84	32.00	22.00
65	46.25	36.25	85	31.25	21.25
66	45.50	35.50	86	30.50	20.50
67	44.75	34.75	87	29.75	20.00
68	44.00	34.00	88	29.00	20.00
69	43.25	33.25	89	28.25	20.00
70	42.50	32.50	90	27.50	20.00
71	41.75	31.75	91	26.75	20.00
72	41.00	31.00	92	26.00	20.00
73	40.25	30.25	93	25.25	20.00
74	39.50	29.50	94	24.50	20.00
75	38.75	28.75	95	23.75	20.00
76	38.00	28.00	96	23.00	20.00
77	37.25	27.25	97	22.25	20.00
78	36.50	26.50	98	21.50	20.00
79	35.75	25.75	99	20.75	20.00

If a plan's ratio percentage falls between the safe and "unsafe harbor" percentages in the table, the IRS will examine the facts and circumstances of the classification to determine whether it is in fact discriminatory. If the ratio percentage is *below* the unsafe harbor percentage, the plan is considered automatically discriminatory.[5]

In applying the above coverage tests, certain employees are not counted, which means that they can effectively be excluded from the plan. In particular, employees included in a collective bargaining unit can be excluded if there was good faith bargaining on retirement benefits.[6]

When the coverage rules are applied, all related employers must be treated as a single employer. Thus, an employer generally cannot break up its business into a number of corporations or other separate units to avoid covering rank-and-file employees. Appendix B discusses these complex rules in further detail.

However, if the employer actually has bona fide "separate lines of business," it is possible to apply the coverage test and the 50/40 test separately to employees in each line of business. This allows plans to be provided only to one line of business, or several different plans tailored to different lines of business.[7]

Highly Compensated—Definition for Employee Benefit Purposes

A *highly compensated employee* is any employee who, during the year or the preceding year:

(a) was at any time a 5-percent owner (as defined for top-heavy purposes);

(b) received compensation from the employer in excess of $75,000, as indexed for inflation ($96,368 in 1993);

(c) received compensation from the employer in excess of $50,000, as indexed for inflation ($64,245 in 1993), and was in the "top-paid group" for the year; or

(d) was at any time an officer and received compensation greater than 50 percent of the defined benefit plan dollar limit in effect for that year (50% of $115,641 in 1993).[8]

An employee described in (b), (c), or (d) will not be treated as a highly compensated employee for the current year unless he also was described in (b), (c), or (d) for the prior year, or if he is also one of the 100 highest paid employees for the current year.

For purposes of these rules, the "top-paid group" of employees for a year is the group of employees in the top 20 percent, ranked on the basis of compensation paid for the year. For the purpose of determining the top-paid group, the following employees may be excluded: (1) employees with less than 6 months of service, (2) employees who normally work less than 17½ hours per week, (3) employees who normally work during not more than 6 months in any year, (4) employees under the age of 21, (5) except as provided by regulations, employees covered by a collective bargaining agreement, and (6) nonresident aliens with no U.S. earned income. At the employer's election, a shorter period of service, smaller number of hours or months, or lower age than those specified in (1) through (4) may be used.[9] (A simplified alternative definition of "highly compensated" may be elected by an employer who maintained significant business operations in at least 2 significantly separate geographic areas. Such an employer may elect to treat an employee earning $50,000 (as indexed) as highly compensated without regard to whether he was a member of the top 20% of employees.[10])

No more than 50 employees (or, if fewer, the greater of 3 employees or 10 percent of the employees) need be treated as officers; however, at least one officer must be treated as such. If no officer of an employer has received compensation greater than 50 percent of the defined benefit plan dollar limit, the highest paid officer will, nevertheless, be treated as "highly compensated."[11]

Any compensation paid to an employee who is a member of the family of a 5-percent owner, or of one of the 10 highly compensated employees paid the greatest compensation during the year, will be treated as paid to the 5-percent owner or highly compensated employee. Family members include the spouse of an employee, the employee's lineal ascendants and descendants, and their spouses.[12]

Former employees are treated as highly compensated employees if (1) they were highly compensated employees when they separated from service, or (2) they were highly compensated employees at any time after attaining age 55.[13]

The controlled group, common control, affiliated service group, and employee leasing provisions of Section 414 (see Appendix B) are to be applied before applying the highly compensated employee rules.

NONDISCRIMINATION IN BENEFITS AND CONTRIBUTIONS

Qualified plans may not discriminate in favor of highly compensated employees either in terms of benefits or in terms of employer contributions to the plan.[14] Some nondiscrimina-tory formulas will, however, provide a higher benefit for highly compensated employees. Contributions or benefits can be based on compensation or years of service, for example.

The IRS issued final regulations in 1991 and then in January of 1993 issued new proposed regulations relating to nondiscrimination in compensation and benefits under Code section 401(a)(4). Under these regulations, a plan must be nondiscriminatory in either contributions or benefits. A defined contribution plan will generally be tested under the "contributions" test,[15] although the plan accounts can be converted to benefits and tested under the "benefits" test.[16] However, ESOPs (see Chapter 10), Section 401(k) plans (see Chapter 19), and plans with after-tax employee contributions and/or employer matching contributions (see Chapter 18) may not be tested on a benefits basis.[17] Section 401(k) plans and plans with after-tax employee contributions/and or employer matching contributions must continue to meet the special nondiscrimination tests for those plans, as discussed in the chapters referenced.

Under the new proposed regulations, a defined benefit plan will be nondiscriminatory if it meets a *general* test or a uniformity requirement and one of three "safe harbors."[18] These nondiscrimination rules for defined benefit plans relate to the rate at which benefits accrued for highly compensated employees compare with benefits accrued for other employees. The implications of these rules for defined benefit plans are discussed in the "Questions and Answers" in Chapter 9.

Integration with Social Security

Qualified plan benefit or contribution formulas can be "integrated" with Social Security.[19] In an integrated plan, greater contributions or benefits generally are provided for higher paid employees whose compensation is greater than an amount based on the Social Security taxable wage base.

Since most employees will receive Social Security benefits when they retire, a calculation of an employee's retirement needs must take these into account. Since Social Security benefits are effectively paid out of employer compensation costs, it is appropriate, and permitted by law, to reflect Social Security benefits by "integrating" a qualified plan's benefit formula with Social Security benefits. However, the rules for doing so are quite complex. The details will not be discussed here, but the financial planner should be familiar with the basic rules for Social Security integration.

Social Security integration benefits employers from a cost point of view since it effectively reduces the cost of the qualified plan. Also, since Social Security provides a higher retirement income, relatively speaking, for lower paid employees, Social Security integration of qualified plans permits such plans to provide relatively greater benefits for highly compensated employees, which is often an employer objective.

Defined Benefit Plans

There are two methods for integrating defined benefit formulas with Social Security: the "excess" method and the "offset" method.

Under the excess method of integration with Social Security, the plan defines a level of compensation called the integration level. The plan then provides a higher rate of benefits for compensation above the integration level. A plan's integration level is an amount of compensation specified under the plan by a dollar amount or formula. Benefits under the plan expressed as a percentage of compensation are lower for compensation below the integration level than they are for compensation above the integration level.[20]

Example: Plan A's integrated formula provides an annual benefit of 30 percent of final average annual compensation plus 25 percent of compensation above the plan's integration level. Labelle, born in 1928, is a participant in plan A. He retires in 1993. Labelle's final average compensation is $40,000. The integration level (covered compensation—see below) is $22,716. Labelle's annual retirement benefit is determined as follows:

— 30 percent of final average compensation of $40,000, or $12,000, plus

— 25 percent of $17,284 ($40,000 - $22,716) or $4,321.

The total benefit is $16,321 ($12,000 plus $4,321).

The Code and regulations provide various rules specifying what maximum integration level a plan can use, and how big the percentage spread above and below the integration level can be. As a general rule, a plan's integration level cannot exceed an amount known as "covered compensation," which is specified by the IRS in a table. Covered compensation is the average of the contribution and benefit base under the Social Security Act for each year during the 35-year period ending with the year in which an employee attains Social Security retirement age.[21] Therefore, the covered compensation amount for each employee depends upon the year when the employee retires (see Figure 23.2). Under the regulations, a plan may determine an employee's covered compensation by use of a different IRS table that is developed by rounding the actual

amounts of covered compensation for different years of birth (see Figure 23.2).[22]

The Code and IRS regulations also restrict the percentage spread between the benefit as a percentage of compensation above and below the integration level. The "base benefit percentage" is the percentage of compensation that the plan provides for compensation below the integration level, and the "excess benefit percentage" is the percentage of compensation above the integration level.

The excess benefit percentage cannot exceed the base benefit percentage by more than ¾ of one percentage point for any year of service, or participant's years of service up to 35.[23]

For example, if a defined benefit plan provides a benefit of 1 percent of compensation below the integration level for each year of service, then it can provide not more than 1.75 percent of compensation above the integration level for each year of service. Or, for a participant with 35 years of service, if the plan provides a benefit of 30 percent of final average compensation below the integration level, it cannot provide more than 56.25 percent of compensation above the integration level. (The spread of 26.25 percent is ¾ of one percentage point multiplied by 35 years of service.) The difference between the base and excess benefit percentages—the *maximum excess allowance*—can be no greater than the base percentage. Thus if a plan provides 10 percent of final average compensation below the integration level, it can provide no more than 20 percent of compensation above the integration level.[24]

Under the offset method of integration, the plan formula is reduced by a fixed amount or a formula amount that is designed to represent the existence of Social Security benefits.[25] There is no integration level in an offset plan. The Code and regulations provide limits on the extent of an offset for Social Security. In particular, the rules provide that no more than half of the benefit provided under the formula without the offset may be taken away by an offset. For example, if a plan formula provides 50 percent of final average compensation with an offset, even the lowest paid employee must receive at least 25 percent of final average compensation from the plan.

Defined Contribution Plans

Defined contribution plans can be integrated only under the excess method. Generally, if the integration level is equal to the Social Security taxable wage base in effect at the beginning of the plan year ($57,600 for plan years beginning in 1993), the difference in the allocation percentages above

Figure 23.2

1993 COVERED COMPENSATION TABLE

Calendar Year of Birth	Calendar Year of Social Security Retirement	1993 Covered Compensation	Calendar Year of Birth	Calendar Year of Social Security Retirement	1993 Covered Compensation
1907	1972	$4,488	1946	2012	$49,500
1908	1973	4,704	1947	2013	50,640
1909	1974	5,004	1948	2014	51,636
1910	1975	5,316	1949	2015	52,536
1911	1976	5,664	1950	2016	53,340
1912	1977	6,060	1951	2017	54,060
1913	1978	6,480	1952	2018	54,684
1914	1979	7,044	1953	2019	55,248
1915	1980	7,692	1954	2020	55,764
1916	1981	8,460	1955	2022	56,604
1917	1982	9,300	1956	2023	56,964
1918	1983	10,236	1957	2024	57,240
1919	1984	11,232	1958	2025	57,420
1920	1985	12,276	1959	2026	57,540
1921	1986	13,368	1960	2027	57,600
1922	1987	14,520	1961	2028	57,600
1923	1988	15,708	1962	2029	57,600
1924	1989	16,968	1963 or later	2030	57,600
1925	1990	18,312			
1926	1991	19,728			
1927	1992	21,192			
1928	1993	22,716			
1929	1994	24,228			
1930	1995	25,728			
1931	1996	27,240			
1932	1997	28,752			
1933	1998	30,252			
1934	1999	31,764			
1935	2000	33,276			
1936	2001	34,728			
1937	2002	36,192			
1938	2004	39,036			
1939	2005	40,452			
1940	2006	41,880			
1941	2007	43,272			
1942	2008	44,604			
1943	2009	45,876			
1944	2010	47,112			
1945	2011	48,324			

1993 Rounded Table

Year of Birth	Covered Compensation
1924 - 1925	$18,000
1926 - 1927	21,000
1928 - 1929	24,000
1930 - 1931	27,000
1932 - 1933	30,000
1934 - 1935	33,000
1936 - 1937	36,000
1938 - 1939	39,000
1940 - 1941	42,000
1942 - 1943	45,000
1944 - 1945	48,000
1946 - 1948	51,000
1949 - 1953	54,000
1954 - 1959	57,000
1960 or later	57,600

and below the integration level can be no more than the lesser of:

(1) the percentage contribution below the integration level or

(2) the greater of (a) 5.7% or (b) the old age portion of the Social Security tax rate.[26]

Thus, for a plan year beginning in 1993, if an integrated plan has an integration level of $57,600 and the plan allocates employer contributions plus forfeitures at the rate of 15.7 percent of compensation above the integration level, then it would have to provide at least a 10 percent allocation for compensation below the integration level (making the difference 5.7 percent).

Further rules, and considerations in choosing an "optimum" integration level for a defined contribution plan, are discussed in the "Questions and Answers" in Chapter 17.

VESTING

If a qualified plan provides for employee contributions, the portion of the benefit or account balance attributable to employee contributions must at all times be 100 percent vested (nonforfeitable).[27] The portion attributable to employer contributions must be vested under a specified vesting schedule that is at least as favorable as one of two alternative minimum standards[28]:

1. *5-year vesting*. A plan's vesting schedule satisfies this minimum requirement if an employee with at least 5 years of service is 100 percent vested. No vesting at all is required before 5 years of service.

2. *3- to 7-year vesting*. The plan must provide vesting that is at least as fast as the following schedule:

Years of Service	Vested Percentage
3	20%
4	40
5	60
6	80
7 or more	100

Top-heavy plans (discussed below) are required to provide a faster vesting schedule.

FUNDING REQUIREMENTS

Employer and employee contributions to a qualified plan must be deposited into an irrevocable trust fund or insurance contract that is for the "exclusive benefit" of plan participants and their beneficiaries.[29] The *minimum funding standard* of federal law provides a mathematical calculation of the minimum amount that must be contributed to a qualified pension plan.[30] Pension plans, both defined benefit and defined contribution, must meet these annual minimum funding standards or be subject to penalty. Profit-sharing plans are not subject to the minimum funding standards as such, but contributions must be "recurring and substantial" or the IRS can deem the plan to be terminated. Substantial and recurring is not clearly defined in the law so that there is always some risk in repeatedly omitting contributions.[31]

The minimum funding standards applicable to defined benefit plans are related to the method by which an annual cost for these plans is determined. As discussed below, this annual cost must be paid in quarterly or more frequent installments. The annual cost is based on an *actuarial cost method*.

Actuarial Cost Methods

An actuarial cost method determines the employer's annual cost for a defined benefit plan. Actuaries use a number of different actuarial cost methods, which can be relatively complex mathematically. However, these methods are based on simple principles that should be understood by financial planners even though the computational complexities are left to the actuary. An actuarial cost method develops a series of annual deposits to the plan fund that will grow to the point where as each employee retires the fund is sufficient to fully fund the employee's retirement benefit. There are two basic ways of spreading these costs over future working careers of employees. Under the *projected benefit* or level funding method, the total cost is divided into equal deposits for each employee's benefit spread over the period remaining until the employee's retirement. With the *accrued benefit* method the annual deposit is based on the benefit accrued each year. The accrued benefit method produces a generally rising series of deposits for a given employee, because as retirement approaches there is less time to fund each additional piece of accrued benefit. The overall plan cost does not necessarily rise, however, with the accrued benefit method, because employees may enter and leave the plan from time to time.

If a defined benefit plan provides past service benefits, the cost of these can be made part of the annual cost using a projected benefit or accrued benefit method. Alternatively, the past service benefit can be funded separately by developing what is known as an unfunded past service liability or a *supplemental liability*. The supplemental liability is paid off through deposits to the plan fund over a fixed period of years, up to 30, regardless of actual retirement dates for employees. The use of a supplemental liability can provide additional funding flexibility in many cases.

Projected benefit actuarial cost methods can be either individual or aggregate. With the individual methods, a separate cost is determined for each employee, with the total employer deposit being the sum of all the separate pieces. With the aggregate method, the cost is developed for the employer's payroll as a whole and is expressed as a percentage of payroll.

Because there are so many different approaches in determining the annual cost using an actuarial cost method, there is no one single annual cost applicable to a given defined benefit plan for a given group of employees. Different actuarial methods should be developed giving a variety of annual cost approaches as part of the design stage for a defined benefit plan.

Actuarial Assumptions

Actuarial cost methods depend on making assumptions about various cost factors, since actual results cannot be known in advance. The annual cost developed under an actuarial cost method depends significantly on these assumptions, and there is some flexibility in choosing assumptions. Under the Code, each assumption must be reasonable, within guidelines in the Code and regulations.[32] Actuarial assumptions include:

- investment return on the plan fund

- salary scale—an assumption about increases in future salaries; this is particularly significant if the plan uses a final average type of formula

- mortality—the extent to which some benefit will not be paid because of the death of employees before retirement

- annuity purchase rate—this determines the funds needed at retirement to provide annuities in the amount designated by the plan formula

- the annuity purchase rate in turn depends on assumptions about future investment return and post-retirement mortality

- turnover—the extent to which employees will terminate employment before retirement and thereby receive limited or no benefit

Deduction Limits

The minimum funding standards require *minimum* annual (or, in some cases, quarterly) contributions to the plan to maintain the plan fund soundness from an actuarial viewpoint. However, the opposite issue also exists; some employers would like to overfund their plans in order to accelerate tax deductions. This is prevented by a series of deduction limits which disallow deductions above specified levels (determined actuarially in the case of defined benefit plans).[33] Between the minimum funding requirements and the deduction limit, there may be comfortable levels of funding for the plan that can be varied to meet employer cost objectives.

Timing of Contributions

Under the minimum funding rules, plan contributions to a defined benefit plan must be paid at least quarterly. For a calendar year taxpayer, contributions are due April 15, July 15, October 15 and January 15 of the following year; corresponding dates apply to fiscal year taxpayers. A failure to make timely payments subjects the taxpayer to interest on the missed installment.[34]

Each quarterly payment must be 25% of the lesser of (a) 90% of the annual minimum funding amount or (b) 100% of the preceding year's minimum funding amount.[35]

Fiduciary Rules

There are strict limits on the extent to which an employer can exercise control over the plan fund.[36] The plan trustee can be a corporation or an individual, even a company president or shareholder, but plan trustees are subject to stringent federal fiduciary rules requiring them to manage the fund solely in the interest of plan participants and beneficiaries. Loans to employees are permitted within limits (see Chapter 24), but the employer is penalized for borrowing from the plan.

LIMITATIONS ON BENEFITS AND CONTRIBUTIONS

To prevent a qualified plan from being used primarily as a tax shelter for highly compensated employees, there is a limitation on plan benefits or employer contributions.

Defined Benefit Limits

Under a defined benefit plan, the benefit at age 65 or the Social Security retirement age, if later, cannot exceed the lesser of:

- 100 percent of the participant's compensation averaged over the 3 years of highest compensation, or

- $90,000 as indexed for inflation[37]

The $90,000 limit is adjusted under a cost-of-living indexing formula. (For 1993, the amount is $115,641.)

The $90,000 limit (as indexed) is adjusted actuarially for retirement ages earlier or later than the Social Security retirement age. The table below indicates Social Security retirement ages under current law. For a participant born before 1938 whose Social Security retirement age is 65, the following is the maximum dollar benefit available (the figures should be indexed upward for years after 1993):

Retirement Age	Maximum Dollar Benefit LImit
55	$ 54,480
60	78,917
62	92,513
65	115,641
70	200,243

SOCIAL SECURITY RETIREMENT AGE

Born in	Can Retire with Full Social Security Benefits at
1937 or earlier	65 years
1938	65 years, 2 months
1939	65 years, 4 months
1940	65 years, 6 months
1941	65 years, 8 months
1942	65 years, 10 months
1943 to 1954	66 years
1955	66 years, 2 months
1956	66 years, 4 months
1957	66 years, 6 months
1958	66 years, 8 months
1959	66 years, 10 months
1960 or later	67 years

Defined Contribution Limits

For a defined contribution plan, the "annual additions" (employer contributions, employee salary reductions, employee contributions, and plan forfeitures reallocated from other participants' accounts) to each participant's account is limited. This annual additions limit cannot exceed the lesser of:

- 25 percent of the participant's annual compensation, or

- $30,000[38]

The $30,000 limit is subject to indexing. This limit will be adjusted when the adjusted defined benefit dollar limit reaches $120,000. Thereafter, the defined contribution dollar limit will be set at one-fourth of the defined benefit limit.

Combined Limit

Where the same employee is covered under both a defined benefit plan and a defined contribution plan, there is a combined limit applicable. This limit prevents the employee from maximizing coverage under both types of plans.

The maximum amount of benefit or contribution under a combination defined benefit plan and defined contribution plan is determined as follows: The benefit or contribution is permitted as long as the total of two "fractions" or percentages does not exceed 1 (or 100%, expressed as a percentage).[39] These fractions are:

Defined benefit fraction:

$$\frac{\text{Projected annual benefit}}{\text{the lesser of}}$$
1.25 x dollar limit, or
1.4 x 3-yr. high avg. compensation

Defined contribution fraction:

$$\frac{\text{Sum of annual additions}}{\text{sum of the lesser of}}$$
(for each year of service)
1.25 x dollar limit, or
1.4 x 25% of compensation

For example, suppose your client Chet Gall currently earns $40,000 per year and is covered under a defined benefit plan that will provide an annual pension for him at age 65 equal to $20,000. The $20,000 pension is 50 percent of the maximum defined benefit allowable (see above—the maximum is the lesser of $115,641—in 1993—or 100 percent of his average salary of $40,000; the lesser of these is $40,000). In addition, suppose Chet is covered under a defined contribution plan that contributes $4,000 to his account this year. Assuming no prior service with the employer (prior service complicates the defined contribution fraction):

DB fraction:

$$\frac{\$20,000 \text{ (Chet's projected benefit)}}{\text{lesser of}}$$
1.25 x $115,641 = $144,551.25 or
1.4 x $40,000 = $56,000

Result: $\dfrac{\$20,000}{\$56,000} = 36\%$

DC fraction:

$$\frac{\$4,000 \text{ (annual addition)}}{\text{lesser of}}$$
1.25 x $30,000 = $37,500 or
1.4 x $10,000 = $14,000

Result: $\dfrac{\$4,000}{\$14,000} = 29\%$

Total combined fraction: 36% + 29% = 65% (0.65)

Thus, Chet's contributions and benefits produce a combined fraction that is less than 1—and the plan, therefore, meets the combined Section 415 limit.

Combined fraction for top-heavy plans. If a plan is top-heavy (see below), the DB and DC fractions are modified by substituting "1" for "1.25" as the multiplier of the dollar limits. The result of this modification is to make the fraction more restrictive for higher paid employees who are governed by the dollar limit in the "lesser of" denominators of the DB and DC fractions. In other words, higher paid employees can get less benefits by having a combination of plans. This result can be *avoided* if the top-heavy minimums are increased by one percentage point: the 2 and 3 percent minimums are increased to 3 and 4 percent for defined benefit and defined contribution plans respectively.[40]

However, if the plan is *super top-heavy*, the fractions are modified regardless—it does not matter if the minimums are increased to 3 and 4 percent, the 1.25 multiplier is still reduced to 1.[41] A plan is super top-heavy if *more than 90 percent* (rather than 60 percent) of accrued benefits or account balances belong to key employees. This rule severely restricts the benefits of combined plans for certain types of clients—for example, the typical doctor or dentist in a small professional corporation. Such plans are almost always super top-heavy, so the combined plan fraction must meet the more restrictive rule.

$200,000 Compensation Limit

A further limitation on plan benefits or contributions is that only the first $200,000 of each employee's annual compensation (as indexed for inflation, $235,840 in 1993) can be taken into account in the plan's benefit or contribution formula. For example, if an employee earns $300,000 annually and the employer has a 10 percent money purchase plan, the maximum contribution for that employee is $23,584 (10% of $235,840). Any compensation paid to an employee who is a member of the family of a 5 percent owner, or of one of the 10 highly compensated employees paid the greatest compensation during the year, will be treated as paid to the 5-percent owner or highly compensated employee. For this purpose, family members include the spouse of an employee and the employee's lineal descendants who have not attained age 19 by the close of the year.[42]

TOP-HEAVY REQUIREMENTS

A *top-heavy* plan is one that provides more than 60 percent of its aggregate accrued benefits or account balances to *key employees*, as defined below. Such plans must meet certain additional qualification rules.[43]

If a plan is top-heavy for a given year, it must provide more rapid vesting than generally required.[44] The plan can either provide 100 percent vesting after 3 years of service, or 6-year graded vesting as follows:

Years of Service	Vested Percentage
2	20%
3	40
4	60
5	80
6 or more	100

In addition, a top-heavy plan must provide minimum benefits or contributions for non-key employees.[45]

For defined benefit plans the benefit for each non-key employee during a top-heavy year must be at least 2 percent of compensation multiplied by the employee's years of service, up to 20 percent. The average compensation used for this formula is based on the highest 5 years of compensation.

For a defined contribution plan, employer contributions during a top-heavy year must be at least 3 percent of compensation.

Even more stringent rules apply if the plan is deemed to be *super top-heavy*—that is, provides more than 90 percent of its accrued benefits or account balances for key employees.

A *key employee* for purposes of the top-heavy rules is an employee who, at any time during the plan year or any of the 4 preceding plan years, is:

- an officer of the employer having annual compensation greater than 50 percent of the Section 415 defined benefit dollar limit (50% of $115,641, or $57,820.50, for 1993),

- 1 of 10 employees having annual compensation from the employer of more than the Section 415 defined contribution dollar limit ($30,000 for 1993) and owning (with ownership attribution rules) the largest interests in the employer.

- a more-than-5 percent owner of the employer, or

- a more-than-1 percent owner of the employer having annual compensation from the employer of more than $150,000.[46]

For these purposes, no more than 50 employees (or, if lesser, the greater of 3 or 10 percent of the employees) are treated as officers.

FOOTNOTES

1. IRC Section 410(a).
2. IRC Section 410(b); Reg. §1.410(b)-2.
3. IRC Section 401(a)(26).
4. See Reg. §1.410(b)-2(b)(3).
5. Reg. §1.410(b)-4.
6. IRC Section 410(b)(3).
7. IRC Sections 410(b)(5), 401(a)(26)(G).
8. IRC Section 414(q).
9. IRC Section 414(q)(8).
10. IRC Section 414(q)(12).
11. IRC Section 414(q)(5).
12. IRC Section 414(q)(6).

13. IRC Section 414(q)(9).

14. IRC Section 401(a)(4).

15. Prop. Reg. §1.401(a)(4)-2.

16. Prop. Reg. §1.401(a)(4)-8.

17. Prop. Reg. §1.401(a)(4)-2(b)(3).

18. Prop. Reg. §1.401(a)(4)-3.

19. IRC Section 401(l).

20. IRC Section 401(l)(3)(A).

21. Reg. §1.401(l)-1(c)(7). For plan years beginning prior to 1995, plans may use the 35 calendar years ending with the year *preceding* the calendar year an individual attains Social Security retirement age. Reg. §1.401(l)-1(c)(7)(ii)(B).

22. Reg. §1.401(l)-1(c)(7)(ii)(A).

23. IRC Section 401(l)(4)(A).

24. IRC Section 401(l)(4)(A), flush language.

25. IRC Section 401(l)(3)(B).

26. IRC Section 401(l)(2). The IRS will publish the percentage rate of the portion attributable to old age insurance when it exceeds 5.7%.

27. IRC Section 411(a)(1).

28. IRC Section 411(a)(2).

29. IRC Section 401(a)(2).

30. IRC Section 412. For penalties for noncompliance, see IRC Section 4971.

31. See Chapter 17.

32. IRC Section 412(c)(3).

33. IRC Section 404(a)(1).

34. IRC Section 412(m).

35. IRC Section 412(m)(4).

36. ERISA, Part 4 (section 401, et seq.). The "prohibited transaction" rules are reiterated in IRC Section 4975.

37. IRC Section 415(b).

38. IRC Section 415(c).

39. IRC Section 415(e).

40. IRC Section 416(h)(2).

41. IRC Section 416(h)(1).

42. IRC Section 401(a)(17).

43. IRC Section 416(a).

44. IRC Section 416(b).

45. IRC Section 416(c).

46. IRC Section 416(i).

Chapter 24

QUALIFIED PLANS: DISTRIBUTIONS AND LOANS

CONTENTS OF THIS CHAPTER

I. PLANNING RETIREMENT DISTRIBUTIONS

Distributions from qualified pension, profit-sharing, and employer stock plans and Section 403(b) tax deferred annuity plans are subject to numerous special rules and distinctive federal income tax treatment. Advance consideration of all the potential implications of plan distributions is an important part of overall plan design.

Furthermore, in advising clients who are plan participants, a clear understanding of the qualified plan rules is important. A qualified or Section 403(b) plan can allow employees to accumulate substantial retirement benefits. Even a middle-level employee may have an account balance of hundreds of thousands of dollars available at retirement or termination of employment. Careful planning is important in order to make the right choices of payment options and tax treatment for a plan distribution, in order to obtain the right result in financial planning for retirement, and also to avoid adverse tax results or even a tax disaster.

The retirement plan distribution rules are astonishingly complicated. They are a maze full of tax traps that have developed in the law over many years, with Congress and the IRS adding new twists and turns almost every year. This chapter is only a basic outline of these rules, but even this basic outline is quite complex.

One way to thread the maze and give some structure to the subject is to look at the issue from the standpoint of advice to a plan participant who is about to retire. What questions need to be asked and what decisions must be made? Typically, the process might proceed by asking and answering these questions—

1. What kinds of distributions does the plan itself allow? The retiree's advisor should review plan documents, particularly the summary plan description (SPD), to determine what options are available. Sections II and III of this chapter discuss the issues that arise here.

2. Should the distribution be in a lump sum or in a periodic payout? Section V of this chapter discusses the basic tax tradeoffs. Can or should the distribution be rolled over? (Section IX.)

3. If a periodic payment is chosen, what kind of payment schedule is best?

    —Note the requirement of spousal consent for a payment option that "cuts out" the spouse. (Section II.)

    —Are the minimum distribution requirements satisfied? (Section VIII.)

    —Is the payment subject to a 10% early distribution penalty? (Section VIII.)

    —Is the payment subject to the 15% excess distribution penalty? (Section VIII.)

    —How will the payments be taxed? (Section IV A and B.)

4. If a lump sum payment is chosen—

    —Is it eligible for 5-year or 10-year averaging? (Section IV A, C, and D.)

—If eligible for 10-year averaging, is the election of 10-year averaging beneficial? (Section IV E.)

—If the participant was in the plan before 1974, is election of capital gain treatment beneficial? (Section IV E.)

—How much tax is payable? (Section IV C, D, and E.)

—Is the distribution subject to the 15% excess distribution penalty tax? (Section VIII.)

5. What are the potential future estate tax and excess accumulation tax consequences of the form of distribution chosen? (Sections IV G and VIII.)

II. PLAN PROVISIONS—REQUIRED SPOUSAL BENEFITS

All qualified pension plans must provide two forms of survivorship benefits for spouses: (1) the *"qualified pre-retirement survivor annuity"* and (2) the *"qualified joint and survivor annuity."* Stock bonus plans, profit-sharing plans, and ESOPs generally need not provide these survivorship benefits for the spouse if the participant's nonforfeitable account balance is payable as a death benefit to that spouse.[1]

Pre-retirement Survivor Annuity

Once a participant in a plan requiring these spousal benefits is vested, the nonparticipant spouse acquires the right to a pre-retirement survivor annuity, payable to the spouse in the event of the participant's death before retirement. This right is an actual property right created by federal law.

In a defined benefit plan, the survivor annuity payable under this provision of law is the amount that would have been paid under a qualified joint and survivor annuity if the participant had either (1) in the case of the participant dying after attaining the earliest retirement age under the plan, retired on the day before his or her death, or (2) in the case of the participant dying before attaining such age, separated from service on the earlier of the actual time of separation or death and survived to the plan's earliest retirement age, then retired with an immediate joint and survivor annuity.[2] (The calculation of joint and survivor annuity amounts is discussed below.)

If the plan is a defined contribution plan, the qualified pre-retirement survivor annuity is an annuity for the life of the surviving spouse that is the actuarial equivalent of at least 50 percent of the participant's vested account balance as of the date of death.[3]

The pre-retirement survivor annuity is an automatic benefit. If no other election is made, a pre-retirement survivor annuity is provided. If the plan permits, a participant can elect to receive some other form of retirement survivorship benefit, including no pre-retirement survivorship benefit at all, or survivorship benefits payable to a beneficiary other than the spouse. However, the spouse must understand the rights given up and must consent in writing to the participant's choice of another form of benefit.[4]

The right to make an election of a benefit other than the pre-retirement survivor annuity must be communicated to all participants with a vested benefit who have attained age 32 or older.[5] The participant can elect to receive some other benefit than the pre-retirement survivor annuity at any time after age 35.[6] The participant can also change this election at any time before retirement.

Consideration of "electing out" of the pre-retirement survivorship benefit becomes more important as a participant nears retirement age. Electing out of the pre-retirement survivorship benefit will generally increase the participant's benefit after retirement, unless the plan specifically subsidizes the retirement benefit. Thus, a participant may want to elect out of the benefit to increase the size of the monthly check received during the post-retirement period. Alternatively, the participant may wish to provide a pre-retirement survivorship benefit for a beneficiary other than the surviving spouse.

Such elections must be considered very carefully, particularly by the nonparticipant spouse. Generally a nonparticipant spouse would (and should) not agree to waive this benefit unless the couple's overall retirement planning provided some compensating benefit to the spouse. The existence and amount of any such compensating benefit to the spouse should be documented in connection with the spouse's benefit waiver.

Any benefit waiver is potentially subject to contest by the deprived spouse at some later time. For this reason, full disclosure—in writing—to the nonparticipant spouse must be made, and that spouse should be advised to obtain an independent legal (and possibly also financial) advisor in connection with the waiver. Any consent of the nonparticipant spouse to an optional benefit form selected by the participant should be notarized. For large benefits, this advice to the spouse is an extremely important consideration.

Qualified Joint and Survivor Annuity

A qualified joint and survivor annuity is a post-retirement death benefit for the plan participant's spouse. If the plan is subject to these requirements, it must automatically provide, as a retirement benefit, an annuity for the life of the participant with a survivor annuity for the life of the participant's spouse. The survivor annuity must be (1) not less than 50 percent of nor (2) greater than 100 percent of, the annuity payable during the joint lives of the participant and spouse.[7] For example, if $1,000 per month is payable during the joint lives, the annuity to the surviving spouse can be any specified amount from $500 per month to $1,000 per month. The spouse's annuity must be continued even if the spouse remarries.[8]

As with the pre-retirement survivor annuity, a participant may elect to receive another form of benefit if the plan permits. However, as with a qualified pre-retirement survivor annuity, the spouse must consent in writing to the election.[9] An election to waive the joint and survivor form must be made during the 90-day period ending on the "annuity starting date"—the date on which benefit payments should have begun to the participant, not necessarily the actual date of payment.[10] The waiver can be revoked—that is, the participant can change the election during the 90-day period. Administrators of affected plans must provide participants with a notice of the election period and an explanation of the consequences of the election within a reasonable period before the annuity starting date.[11]

Since the joint and survivor annuity must be the actuarial equivalent of other forms of benefit, the participant may wish to increase the monthly pension by waiving the joint and survivor annuity and receiving a straight life annuity or some other form of benefit. Because of the spouse's right to the benefit, as discussed earlier, it is extremely important that spouses are made aware of what they are giving up if they consent to some other benefit form. Communication of the consequences of a waiver must be made in writing, the spouse should be advised by independent counsel, and any waiver should be notarized.

III. PLAN PROVISIONS—OTHER BENEFIT OPTIONS

A qualified plan can offer a wide range of distribution options. Participants benefit from having the widest possible range of options, because this increases their flexibility in personal retirement planning. However, a wide range of options increases administrative costs. Also, the IRS makes it difficult to withdraw a benefit option once it has been established.[12] Consequently, most employers provide only a relatively limited "menu" of benefit forms for participants to choose from.

In addition, generally, for distributions after 1992, a qualified plan must provide for "direct rollovers" of certain distributions.[13] Failure to elect a "direct rollover" will subject the

distribution to mandatory 20% withholding. Plan administrators must provide a written explanation to the distributee of his right to elect a "direct rollover" and the withholding consequences of not making the election.[14] See "Tax Treatment of Rollovers," under Section IX.

Defined Benefit Plan Distribution Provisions

Defined benefit plans must provide a married participant with a *joint and survivor annuity* as the automatic form of benefit, as described earlier. For an unmarried participant, the plan's automatic form of benefit is usually a *life annuity*—typically monthly payments to the participant for life, with no further payments after the participant's death.

Many plans allow participants to elect to receive some other form of benefit from a list of options in the plan. However, to elect any option that eliminates the benefit for a married participant's spouse, the spouse must consent on a notarized written form to waive the spousal right to the joint and survivor annuity. As discussed earlier, this is not just a legal formality; in consenting to another form of benefit, the spouse gives up important and often sizable property rights in the participant's qualified plan that are guaranteed under federal law.

Typically plans offer, as an option to the joint or single life annuity, a *period-certain* annuity. A period-certain annuity provides payments for a specified period of time—usually 10 to 20 years—even if the participant, or the participant and spouse, both die before the end of that period. Thus, the period-certain annuity makes it certain that periodic (usually monthly) benefits will continue for the participant's heirs even if the participant and spouse die early. Because of this guarantee feature, the annual or monthly payments under a period-certain option are less than they would be under an option where payments end at death (see table below).

MONTHLY PAYMENTS — VARIOUS ANNUITY FORMS

Assumptions: plan participant aged 65, spouse aged 62, lump sum equivalent at age 65 of $200,000

Form of annuity	Monthly benefit
Life	$1,818
Life — 10 years certain	1,710
Life — 20 years certain	1,560
Joint and survivor — 50 percent	1,696
Joint and survivor — 66 ⅔ percent	1,626
Joint and survivor — 100 percent	1,504

As the above comparison indicates, a period-certain option should be chosen if the participant wants to make sure that his heirs are provided for in case both he and his spouse die shortly after retirement. The reduction in monthly income is relatively small, since it is based on the average life expectancy of all annuitants and assumes that the average annuitant (male or female) lives about 20 years after attaining age 65. Thus, the participant and spouse should consider a period-certain option if they are both in poor health, or if they want to make sure that children (or other heirs) with large financial needs are provided for in the event of their deaths. On the other hand, if the participant wants the largest possible monthly income from the plan, a life annuity should be chosen.

Defined benefit plans may allow a participant to choose a joint annuity with a beneficiary other than a spouse—for example, an annuity for the life of a participant with payments continuing after the parent-participant's death to a son or daughter. Proposed tax regulations limit the amount of annuity payable to a much younger beneficiary in order to ensure that the participant personally receives (and therefore is taxed on) at least a minimum portion of the total value of the plan benefit and that plan payments are not unduly deferred beyond the participant's death. (See the minimum distribution rules discussed below in Section VIII.) Thus, a much younger beneficiary (except for a spouse) generally would not be allowed to receive a 100 percent survivor annuity benefit.

Defined Contribution Plan Distribution Provisions

Defined contribution plans include such plans as profit-sharing, 401(k), and money purchase plans. Section 403(b) tax-deferred annuity plans also have distribution provisions similar to defined contribution plans. Some defined contribution plans provide annuity benefits like those in defined benefit plans. In fact, money purchase plans, target benefit plans and Section 403(b) tax deferred annuity plans subject to ERISA must meet the pre-retirement and joint and survivor annuity rules discussed above. Other defined contribution plans do not have to meet these rules if (1) there is no annuity option and (2) the plan participant's account balance is payable to the participant's spouse in the event of the participant's death.[15] Avoiding the required joint and survivor provisions simplifies plan administration and therefore reduces the plan's cost.

Annuity benefits are computed by converting the participant's account balance in the defined contribution plan into an equivalent annuity. The TIAA/CREF plan for college teachers, for example, is a defined contribution plan that primarily offers annuity options. In some plans the participant can elect to have his account balance used to purchase an annuity from an insurance company. The same considerations in choosing annuity options then apply as have already been discussed. If the plan offers annuity options, the required joint and survivor provisions apply, as discussed earlier.

Defined contribution plans often provide a lump sum benefit at retirement or termination of employment. Defined contribution plans often also allow the option of taking out non-annuity distributions over the retirement years. That is, the participant simply takes out money as it is needed, subject to the minimum distribution requirements discussed later. Such distribution provisions provide much flexibility in planning.

IV. TAX IMPACT

For many plan participants retirement income adequacy is more important than minimizing taxes to the last dollar. Nevertheless, taxes on both the federal and state levels must never be ignored since they reduce the participant's "bottom line" financial security. The greater the tax on the distribution, the less financial security the participant has.

A qualified plan distribution may be subject to federal, state, and local taxes, in whole or in part. This section will focus only on the federal tax treatment. The federal tax treatment is generally the most significant because federal tax rates are usually higher than state and local rates. Also, many state and local income tax laws provide a full or partial exemption or specially favorable tax treatment for distributions from qualified retirement plans.

Nontaxable and Taxable Amounts

Qualified plans often contain after-tax employee money—that is, contributions that have already been taxed. These amounts can be received by the employee free of Federal income taxes, although the order in which they are recovered for tax purposes depends on the kind of distribution.

The first step in determining the tax on any distribution, then, is to determine the participant's cost basis in the plan benefit.

The participant's cost basis can include[16]:

- the total after-tax contributions made by the employee to a contributory plan

- the total cost of life insurance actually reported as taxable income on federal income tax returns by the participant (the P.S. 58 costs) if the plan distribution is received under the same contract that provides the life insurance protection. (If the plan trustee cashes in the life insurance contract before distribution, this cost basis amount is not available. For a person who is now or was self-employed, no P.S. 58 costs are available.)

- any employer contributions previously taxed to the employee—for example, where a nonqualified plan later becomes qualified

- certain employer contributions attributable to foreign services performed before 1963

- the amount of any policy loans included in income as a taxable distribution (see VI, below)

In-service (Partial) Distributions. If a participant takes out a partial plan distribution before termination of employment (as is provided for in many savings or thrift plans), the distribution is deemed to include both nontaxable and taxable amounts; the nontaxable amount will be in proportion to the ratio of total after-tax contributions (i.e., the employee's cost basis) to the plan account balance (similar to the computation of the annuity exclusion ratio discussed below).[17] Expressed as a formula it looks like this:

$$\text{nontaxable amount} = \text{distribution} \times \frac{\text{employee's cost basis}}{\text{total account balance}}$$

However, there is a "grandfather" rule for pre-1987 after-tax contributions to the plan. If certain previously existing plans include contributions made before 1987, it is possible to withdraw after-tax money first. That is, if a distribution from the plan is made (at any time, even after 1987) that is *less* than the total amount of pre-1987 after-tax contributions, the entire distribution is received tax free. Once a participant's pre-1987 amount (if any) has been used up, the regular rule applies.[18]

A taxable in-service distribution may also be subject to the early distribution penalty discussed later. In addition, in-service distributions made after 1992 generally will be subject to mandatory withholding at 20% unless the distribution is transferred to an eligible retirement plan by means of a "direct rollover" (see "Retirement Plan Rollovers," below).[19]

Total Distributions. If the participant begins annuity payments based on the entire account balance, the nontaxable amount will be in proportion to the ratio of total after-tax contributions (i.e., the employee's cost basis) in the plan to the total annuity payments expected to be received (see below). If the participant withdraws his or her entire account balance, the distribution may be eligible for the lump sum distribution treatment discussed below. Total distributions may also be subject to the early distribution penalty discussed below. In addition, certain distributions may be subject to mandatory withholding at 20% unless such distributions are rolled over by means of a "direct rollover" (see "Retirement Plan Rollovers," below).

Taxation of Annuity Payments

The annuity rules of Code section 72 apply to periodic plan distributions made over more than one taxable year of the employee in a systematic liquidation of the participant's benefit. Amounts distributed are taxable in the year received, except for a proportionate recovery of the cost basis. The cost basis is recovered as part of each benefit payment through the calculation of an *exclusion ratio* that is applied to each payment to determine the nontaxable amount.

The exclusion ratio is:

$$\frac{\text{investment in the contract}}{\text{expected return}}$$

Basically, the "investment in the contract" is the participant's cost basis. In the case of a life annuity, the "expected return" is determined by multiplying the total annual payment by the participant's life expectancy. Life expectancies are determined under tables found in Treasury regulations. One of these tables, shown in Figure 24.1, is a unisex table of life expectancies which can be used for single life annuities.

Example: Fred Retiree retires at age 65 with a pension of $500 per month for his life. Fred's cost basis in the plan is $20,000. Fred's exclusion ratio will be

$$\frac{\$20,000}{\$120,000} = \frac{1}{6}$$

The numerator ($20,000) is Fred's cost basis; the denominator ($120,000) is Fred's annual pension of $6,000 multiplied by his life expectancy of 20 years from Table V (see Figure 24.1). Therefore, 1/6 of each payment Fred receives will be nontaxable. The remaining 5/6 of each payment is taxable as ordinary income.

Once the exclusion ratio is determined, it will continue to apply until the cost basis is fully recovered. Payments received subsequently are taxable in full.[20] If the participant dies before the cost basis is fully recovered, the participant's estate is allowed an income tax deduction for the unrecovered basis.[21]

Other tables are used for joint life expectancies and special computations may be necessary to determine expected return in some situations, e.g., where there is a period-certain guarantee.

IRS Notice 88-118[22] provides a simplified "safe harbor" method of computing the amount of each payment excluded from tax. The safe harbor applies only to payments from a

Figure 24.1

Table V - Ordinary Life Annuities
One Life - Expected Return Multiples
(from Reg. Sec. 1.72-9)

Age	Multiple	Age	Multiple	Age	Multiple
5	76.6	42	40.6	79	10.0
6	75.6	43	39.6	80	9.5
7	74.7	44	38.7	81	8.9
8	73.7	45	37.7	82	8.4
9	72.7	46	36.8	83	7.9
10	71.7	47	35.9	84	7.4
11	70.7	48	34.9	85	6.9
12	69.7	49	34.0	86	6.5
13	68.8	50	33.1	87	6.1
14	67.8	51	32.2	88	5.7
15	66.8	52	31.3	89	5.3
16	65.8	53	30.4	90	5.0
17	64.8	54	29.5	91	4.7
18	63.9	55	28.6	92	4.4
19	62.9	56	27.7	93	4.1
20	61.9	57	26.8	94	3.9
21	60.9	58	25.9	95	3.7
22	59.9	59	25.0	96	3.4
23	59.0	60	24.2	97	3.2
24	58.0	61	23.3	98	3.0
25	57.0	62	22.5	99	2.8
26	56.0	63	21.6	100	2.7
27	55.1	64	20.8	101	2.5
28	54.1	65	20.0	102	2.3
29	53.1	66	19.2	103	2.1
30	52.2	67	18.4	104	1.9
31	51.2	68	17.6	105	1.8
32	50.2	69	16.8	106	1.6
33	49.3	70	16.0	107	1.4
34	48.3	71	15.3	108	1.3
35	47.3	72	14.6	109	1.1
36	46.4	73	13.9	110	1.0
37	45.4	74	13.2	111	.9
38	44.4	75	12.5	112	.8
39	43.5	76	11.9	113	.7
40	42.5	77	11.2	114	.6
41	41.5	78	10.6	115	.5

qualified plan or Section 403(b) tax-deferred annuity plan which are to be paid for the life of the employee or the joint lives of the employee and beneficiary. Under this method, the employee's investment in the contract is divided by the number of expected monthly payments set out in the IRS table below. The number of payments is based on the employee's age at the annuity starting date and the same table is used for both single life and joint and survivor annuity payments. The resulting dollar amount is excluded from each payment until the cost basis is fully recovered.

Age	# of payments
55 and under	300
56-60	260
61-65	240
66-70	170
71 and over	120

Lump Sum Distributions

A lump sum distribution may be desirable for retirement planning purposes, but the participant may not want a lump sum if it is taxed in high tax brackets. However, certain lump sums are eligible for a special, favorable tax calculation.

For qualified plans only (total distributions from IRAs, SEPs, or TDA (Section 403(b)) plans are not technically "lump sum distributions") there is a special one-time 5-year averaging tax computation that a participant may elect if (a) the lump sum distribution is received after age 59½ *and* (b) meets the following 4 requirements[23].

• it is made in one taxable year of the recipient,

• it represents the entire amount of the employee's benefit in the plan,

• It is payable on account of the participant's death, attainment of age 59½, separation from service (non-self-employed person) or disability (self-employed person only), and

• the employee participated in the plan for at least 5 taxable years prior to the tax year of distribution (a death benefit is exempted from this requirement)

In determining whether the distribution is a "total" distribution, all pension plans maintained by the same employer are treated as a single plan, all profit-sharing plans are treated as a single plan, and all stock bonus plans are treated as one plan.[24]

If the distribution meets all of these qualifications, the taxable amount is eligible for 5-year averaging. The participant must elect this treatment; it is not automatic. Only one election is permitted and the election is available only if the distribution is received on or after the employee attained age 59½. In addition, the participant must elect to treat all lump sum distributions received during the year in the same manner.[25]

Five-year averaging is not available to a recipient of a death benefit unless the deceased plan participant had attained age 59½. (If the recipient is a spouse, the distribution can be rolled over to an IRA—see "Rollovers," below.)

Five-year averaging is available to a spouse or former spouse of a participant who receives a total distribution of a plan interest under a qualified domestic relations order (QDRO) pursuant to a divorce or separation, if a total distribution would be eligible for five-year averaging if paid to the participant.[26]

For participants who had attained age 50 by January 1, 1986, some of the more liberal rules of prior law for averaging and capital gains treatment are preserved (see "Grandfather Rules," below).

In determining the tax on a lump sum distribution, the first step is to calculate the taxable amount of the distribution. The taxable amount consists of (a) the total value of the distribution less (b) after-tax contributions and other items constituting the employee's cost basis (see "Nontaxable and Taxable Amounts," above). If employer securities are included in the distribution, the net unrealized appreciation of the stock is generally subtracted from the value of a lump sum distribution (see Chapter 10).

Five-year averaging works as follows: (1) A "minimum distribution allowance" is subtracted from the taxable amount. The minimum distribution allowance is the *lesser* of $10,000 or one-half of the total taxable amount *reduced by* 20 percent of the total taxable amount in excess of $20,000. In other words, if the taxable amount is $70,000 or more the minimum distribution allowance disappears. (2) The remaining taxable amount after the minimum distribution allowance is divided by 5 and a separate tax is determined on this portion. The separate tax is based on the single taxpayer rate without any deductions or exclusions. The tax determined in this manner is multiplied by 5.[27]

Example: (Using 1993 tax rates)

1.	Total taxable amount	$ 40,000
2.	Minimum distribution allowance	
	$10,000 - [20% x ($40,000 - $20,000)]	-6,000
3.	Balance	34,000
4.	⅕ of the balance	6,800
5.	Tax on line 4	1,020
6.	Total tax	$ 5,100

Figure 24.2 shows the federal income tax on lump sum distributions using 5-year averaging for 1993 distributions and *taking steps (1) and (2), above,* into account; thus, enter the table using the total taxable amount (i.e., not 1/5 of the total).

The taxpayer elects and reports this calculation on Form 4972 reproduced at the end of this chapter, which is filed with the tax return for the year. Form 4972 includes detailed instructions and a worksheet for making the calculation. The plan administrator of a plan making a distribution must report it on Form 1099-R.

Lump sum distributions may be subject to the early distribution penalty and/or the excess distribution penalty (see Section VIII). In addition, lump sum distributions made after

Figure 24.2

5-Year Averaging (1993 Tax Rates)				
If the total taxable amount is				
at least	but not over	the separate tax is	plus this %	of the excess over
...	20,000	0	7.5	0
20,000	70,000	1,500	18.0	20,000
70,000	110,500	10,500	15.0	70,000
110,500	267,500	16,580	28.0	110,500
267,500	...	60,540	31.0	267,500

1992 generally will be subject to mandatory withholding at 20%.[28]

"Grandfather" Rules

The tax break for lump sum distributions was 10-year averaging instead of 5-year averaging from 1974 through 1986. For an individual who attained age 50 before January 1, 1986, the 10-year averaging provision is "grandfathered" to a certain extent and can be elected even if the participant is not age 59½ or older at the time of the distribution. Such an individual who receives a distribution in 1987 or later may elect to use 10-year averaging using the 1986 tax rates (taking into account the prior law zero bracket amount) instead of 5-year averaging with current rates.[29] This grandfathering provision will normally be elected if it produces a lower tax than using 5-year averaging.

A further grandfather rule retains the capital gain rate of 20% for the capital gain portion of distributions (the portion attributable to pre-1974 accumulations, if any) to participants who attained age 50 before January 1, 1986 and elect capital gain treatment.[30] The capital gain treatment is not mandatory; distributees should elect it only if it produces a lower overall tax, as it generally will.

When to Elect 10-year Averaging or Capital Gain

10-year Averaging. A plan participant is eligible to elect the 10-year averaging provision instead of 5-year averaging if he or she attained age 50 before January 1, 1986 (i.e., was born on or before January 1, 1936).

If the tax on distributions of various amounts is computed under both 5-year and 10-year averaging, assuming 1993 tax rates, 10-year averaging provides the lowest tax as long as the adjusted total taxable amount is less than $385,800. Above $385,800 of taxable income, the 5-year averaging is preferable. Thus, clients who are eligible for 10-year averaging and have distributions of less than $385,800 will benefit from 10-year averaging.

It should also be noted that for a participant who attained age 50 before January 1, 1986, not only the 10-year averaging calculation but the other favorable lump sum rules of earlier law were grandfathered. Thus, 10-year averaging (but not 5-year averaging) can be elected for a distribution on separation from service prior to age 59½, if the participant attained age 50 before January 1, 1986. In cases where these favorable provisions can be used, electing 10-year averaging will almost always be advantageous.

Capital Gains. As mentioned earlier, a plan participant who attained age 50 before January 1, 1986 (was born on or before January 1, 1936) can elect to treat pre-1974 plan accruals as long term capital gain (under pre-1987 law). Any amount taxed as capital gain is taxed at a rate no greater than 20 percent. Therefore, as a general rule, an eligible participant will save taxes by electing the capital gain treatment whenever the adjusted total taxable amount of a lump sum distribution, after subtracting the capital gain portion, is taxed at an effective rate of more than 20 percent.

For example, suppose a participant receives a taxable distribution of $160,000, of which $20,000 is capital gain. The participant is eligible to elect 10-year averaging. Under the applicable tax computation, any amount over $137,100 is taxed at a rate of 23 percent or higher. Thus, the participant should elect capital gain treatment. With capital gain treatment, the last $20,000 of the distribution—the capital gain amount—will be taxed at a rate of only 20 percent, instead of 23 percent or more.

Taxation of Death Benefits

In general, the same income tax treatment applies to death benefits paid to beneficiaries as to lifetime benefits payable to participants. The special lump sum provision can be used by the beneficiary. However, 5-year averaging is available only if the distribution is received on or after the decedent employee attained age 59½. If the employee had attained age 50 before January 1, 1986, the beneficiary may elect 10-year averaging even if the participant was not 59½ or older at his or her death.[31] For an annuity distribution, the beneficiary uses the same annuity rules described earlier.

There are also some additional income tax benefits available.

First, up to $5,000 of the death benefit may be excludable as an employer-paid death benefit. If the benefit is a lump sum distribution, the full exclusion is available. If the benefit is in the form of periodic payments, the $5,000 exclusion is available only to the extent the employee's benefit was nonforfeitable prior to the employee's death.[32]

Second, if the death benefit is payable under a life insurance contract held by the qualified plan, the pure insurance amount of the death benefit is excludable from income taxation.[33] The pure insurance amount is the difference between the policy's face amount and its cash value at the date of death.

Example: Ellen Employee, aged 62, dies in 1993 before retirement. Her beneficiary receives a lump sum death benefit of $100,000 from the plan. The $100,000 is the proceeds of a cash value life insurance contract; the contract's cash value at Ellen's death was $60,000. Ellen reported a total of $10,000 of P.S. 58 insurance costs for this contract on her income tax returns during her lifetime. The taxable amount of the $100,000 distribution to the beneficiary is $100,000 less the following items:

- the pure insurance amount of $40,000 ($100,000 less the cash value of $60,000),

- the $5,000 employee death benefit exclusion, and

- Ellen's cost basis of $10,000 of P.S. 58 costs.

The taxable amount of this benefit is therefore $45,000. The beneficiary is eligible for 5-year (or 10-year) averaging on this taxable amount, or capital gain treatment for at least a portion of any pre-1974 amounts.

A third factor in the treatment of death benefits involves rollovers to an IRA. A spouse can roll over the death benefit received from a participant to the spouse's IRA.[34] However, a nonspouse beneficiary is not allowed to roll over the benefit.

Federal Estate Tax

The entire value of a qualified plan death benefit is subject to inclusion in the decedent's gross estate for federal estate tax purposes. However, only high-income plan participants will actually be subject to estate tax. First, there is a high minimum

tax credit applicable to the estate tax which essentially eliminates estate taxes for gross estates of less than $600,000. In addition, the unlimited marital deduction for federal estate tax purposes defers federal estate tax on property transferred at death to a spouse in a qualifying manner until the death of the second spouse.

In some cases, however, avoiding federal estate tax can be significant. For example, the estate may be relatively large and the participant may be single or for whatever reason unwilling to pay the death benefit to the spouse. Therefore, the marital deduction would not be available. Also, even when the death benefit is payable to a spouse, federal estate tax is merely delayed and is not really avoided; a spouse is often about the same age as the decedent, and thus within a few years much of the property transferred to the spouse is potentially subject to federal estate tax at the surviving spouse's death.

Some authorities believe it is possible to design a qualified plan so that death benefits can be excluded from the participant's estate. Here is the rationale: The federal estate tax law provides that all of a decedent's property is includable in the estate unless there is a specific exclusionary provision. Qualified plan death benefits are not subject to any specific exclusion, so they are generally includable. There is, however, a specific provision in the estate tax law for life insurance—Section 2042. Life insurance proceeds are includable in a decedent's estate only if the decedent had "incidents of ownership" (some valuable property right) in the insurance policies (or if proceeds are payable to the decedent's estate).

An incident of ownership includes the right to designate the beneficiary as well as similar rights under the policy. Some planners have attempted to design qualified plan death benefits using life insurance policies in which the decedent has no incidents of ownership. Some methods for doing this include the use of separate trusts or subtrusts under the plan for holding insurance policies, together with irrevocable beneficiary designations.

At this point the law is not entirely clear on whether these provisions will in fact avoid incidents of ownership. A conservative view is that they will not. However, if the amount is large enough so that the participant is willing to incur the costs of drafting the subtrust arrangement and the potential court costs if the arrangement is challenged by the IRS, there may be little to lose in the use of this technique, since estate inclusion is certain without it.

V. LUMP SUM VS. DEFERRED PAYMENTS—THE TRADEOFFS

Often plan participants have a choice between a single lump sum plan distribution and a series of deferred payments. This requires a choice between competing advantages.

Advantages of a lump sum distribution include:

- 5-year (or 10-year) averaging tax treatment, if the distribution is eligible

- freedom to invest plan proceeds at the participant's— not the plan administrator's—discretion

The contrasting advantages of a deferred payout are:

- deferral of taxes until money is actually distributed

- continued tax shelter of income on the plan account while money remains in the plan

- security of retirement income

There is not one single favored alternative but rather competing advantages. In a given situation, a lump sum distribution may save more taxes, and in others the deferred payment may be a better tax choice. And, taxes are not the only factor to consider.

A full analysis for an individual may be complex, considering all the factors involved. A complete analysis should certainly be done where very large sums are involved. In other cases, it may be adequate to make a good estimate of the result.

The factors involved in determining which alternative to choose include:

- the age of the participant (or the participant and beneficiary, if a survivorship annuity is involved). This affects the expected number of years of payout.

- the health of the participant (and beneficiary), which also affects the expected number of payout years.

- the expected return on investment.

- the current and future expected tax rates for the participant. This involves estimating not only what the rates will be, but also what tax bracket the participant will be in—i.e., the amount of total taxable income the participant will have.

- the nontax aspects—the amounts of income needed and when it will be needed.

- the total amount of the benefit; if the amount is large enough, the effect of the 15% excess distribution/accumulation penalty tax must be taken into account (see below).

In a sense, it is impossible to make an exact determination of this issue; for example, we can never know exactly what future tax rates will be or the amount of investment earnings actually received in the future. However, by making reasonable assumptions in a given case, some conclusions can usually be drawn.

VI. LOANS

Because of the 10% penalty tax on "early" distributions from qualified plans (see below), a plan provision allowing loans to employees may be attractive. This allows employees access to plan funds without extra tax cost. However, a loan provision increases administrative costs for the plan and may deplete plan funds available for pooled investments.

For participants to borrow from a plan, the plan must specifically permit such loans. Any type of qualified plan or Section 403(b) annuity plan may permit loans. Loan provisions are most common in defined contribution plans, particularly profit-sharing plans. There are considerable administrative difficulties connected with loans from defined benefit plans because of the actuarial approach to plan funding. Loans from IRAs and SEPs are not permitted.

Loans from a qualified plan to the following types of employees are prohibited transactions subject to penalties[35]:

- an owner-employee—a proprietor or more-than-10 percent partner in an unincorporated business

- an S corporation employee who is a more-than-5 percent shareholder in the corporation.

However, a plan may make a loan to such employees if the Secretary of Labor grants an administrative exemption from prohibited transaction treatment for such loans.[36]

Loans to regular employees are prohibited transactions subject to penalties unless such loans (1) are exempted from the prohibited transaction rules by an administrative exemption or (2) meet the requirements set out in Code section 4975(d)(1). That section requires that:

(1) loans made by the plan are available to all participants and beneficiaries on a reasonably equivalent basis;

(2) they are not made available to highly compensated employees in an amount greater than the amounts made available to other employees;

(3) loans are made in accordance with specific provisions regarding such loans set forth in the plan;

(4) the loans bear reasonable rates of interest; and

(5) the loans are adequately secured.

Security for the loan is usually the participant's plan account balance, but a participant can and may want to offer other security instead.

A loan from a qualified plan (or a Section 403(b) tax deferred annuity) will be treated as a taxable distribution if it does not meet the requirements of Code section 72(p). Section 72(p) provides that aggregate loans from qualified plans to any individual plan participant cannot exceed the *lesser* of:

- $50,000 reduced by the excess of the highest outstanding loan balance during the preceding one-year period over the outstanding balance on the date the loan is made, or

- one-half the present value of the participant's vested account balance (or accrued benefit, in the case of a defined benefit plan).

A loan of up to $10,000 can be made, even if this is more than one-half the participant's vested benefit.[37] For example, a participant having a vested account balance of $17,000 could borrow up to $10,000.

Loans must be repayable by their terms within 5 years, except for loans used to acquire a principal residence of the participant.

Interest on a plan loan in most cases will be consumer interest that is not deductible by the employee as an itemized deduction unless the loan is secured by a home mortgage. Interest deductions, however, are specifically prohibited in two situations: (1) if the loan is to a key employee as defined in the Code's rules for top-heavy plans (Section 416), or (2) if the loan is secured by a Section 401(k) or Section 403(b) plan account based on salary reductions.[38]

VII. QUALIFIED DOMESTIC RELATIONS ORDERS (QDROs)

In general, a qualified plan benefit cannot be assigned or "alienated" by a participant, voluntarily or involuntarily.[39] The idea behind this rule is to protect the participant's retirement fund from attachment by creditors. However, after a series of conflicting state court cases, an exception to this rule was added to deal with the claims of spouses and dependents in domestic relations situations.

This exception permits an assignment of a qualified plan benefit under a *qualified domestic relations order* (QDRO) as defined in Code section 414(p). A QDRO is a decree, order, or property settlement under state law relating to child support, alimony, or marital property rights that assigns part or all of a participant's plan benefits to a spouse, former spouse, child, or other dependent of the participant. Consequently, a participant's plan benefits now are generally part of the negotiable assets in domestic disputes. The pension law does not indicate how such benefits are to be divided; this is still a matter of state domestic relations law and the negotiation of the parties. The QDRO provisions of the Code simply provide a means by which state court orders in domestic relations issues can be enforced against plan trustees.

To protect plan administrators and trustees from conflicting claims, a QDRO cannot assign a benefit that the plan does not provide. Also, a QDRO cannot assign a benefit that is already assigned under a previous order.[40]

If, under the plan, a participant has no right to an immediate cash payment from the plan, a QDRO cannot require the trustees to make such a cash payment. If an immediate cash settlement is desired, the parties will generally agree to allow the participant to keep the entire plan benefit and pay compensating cash to the nonparticipant spouse. (Such compensating cash payments are not, however, treated as qualified plan distributions to the nonparticipant spouse.) If compensating cash payments are not possible, QDROs have been used to segregate plan assets into a subtrust for the benefit of the spouse making the claim, with cash distributions made at the earliest time they would be permitted under plan provisions.

VIII. PENALTY TAXES

In addition to the complicated regular tax rules, distributions must be planned so that recipients avoid—or at least are not surprised by—four types of tax penalties. These are summarized as follows.

Early Distribution Penalty

This is in effect a penalty for making distributions "too soon." Early distributions from qualified plans, 403(b) tax deferred annuity plans, IRAs and SEPs are subject to a penalty of 10% of the taxable portion of the distribution.[41]

The penalty does *not* apply to distributions:

- made on or after attainment of age 59½,

- made to the plan participant's beneficiary or estate on or after the participant's death,

- attributable to the participant's disability,

- that are part of a series of substantially equal periodic payments made at least annually over the life or life expectancy of the participant, or the participant and a designated beneficiary (separation from the employer's service is required, except for IRAs),

- made after separation from service after attainment of age 55 (not applicable to IRAs),

- made to a former spouse, child or other dependent of the participant under a qualified domestic relations order (not applicable to IRAs),

- distributions to the extent of medical expenses deductible for the year under Code section 213, whether or not actually deducted (not applicable to IRAs).

In the case of the periodic payment exception, if the series of payments is changed before the participant reaches age 59½ or, if after age 59½, within 5 years of the date of the first payment, the tax which would have been imposed, but for the periodic exception, is imposed with interest in the year the change occurs.[42]

Minimum Distribution Requirements and Penalty

Distributions from qualified plans, 403(b) tax deferred annuity plans, IRAs, SEPs, and Section 457 governmental deferred compensation plans must generally begin by April 1 of the calendar year after the participant attains age 70½.[43]

- There is an annual *minimum* distribution required; if the distribution is less than the minimum amount required there is a penalty of 50 percent of the amount not distributed that should have been.[44]

- The minimum initial annual distribution is determined by dividing the participant's account balance (as of the last plan valuation date prior to the year of attaining age 70½) by the participant's life expectancy (or the participant and designated beneficiary's joint life expectancy from IRS regulations). Payments can be stretched out by re-calculating life expectancy annually. (Other minimum limits may also apply.)

- If the beneficiary is not a spouse, the minimum distribution may be further increased (using a factor—the "incidental benefit factor"—in proposed IRS regulations) to insure that the participant's share of the benefit is at least a minimum amount of the expected total.[45] This factor will come into effect where the

nonspouse beneficiary is more than 10 years younger than the participant.

Excess Distribution Penalty

In addition to regular income tax, there is a penalty tax of 15 percent on annual distributions exceeding the greater of (a) $112,500 as indexed for inflation ($144,551 in 1993), or (b) $150,000.[46]

- This penalty applies to the total (aggregate) of all distributions to the individual in a year from all qualified plans, 403(b) tax deferred annuities, IRAs and SEPs.

- If the recipient elects lump sum treatment on the distribution, the limit is increased to five times the above limit, i.e., $562,500 as indexed ($722,755 in 1993) or $750,000.

- There were potentially favorable "grandfather" provisions for participants whose accrued plan benefit on August 1, 1986 exceeded $562,500. To take advantage of these provisions, an election had to have been made on the participant's 1987 or 1988 tax return, before the due date of the return, including extensions.

Excess Accumulation Penalty

At a participant's death, remaining balances in qualified plans, 403(b) tax deferred annuities, IRAs and SEPs are aggregated; there is a 15 percent penalty on any excess of this total over the present value (at date of death) of an annuity of $150,000 per year over the participant's life expectancy at death. (The $150,000 will be replaced by the excess distribution amount of $112,500 when that amount, as indexed, is more than $150,000.)

For individuals who had accrued plan benefits or account balances on August 1, 1986, a potentially favorable "grandfather" rule was available if an election was made on their tax return for 1988 or earlier.

This 15 percent tax penalty is *in addition* to any regular federal estate tax and cannot be reduced by the marital deduction, charitable deduction, or the estate tax unified credit (although the tax is deductible from the gross estate). To the extent that the excise tax reduces estate taxes, the effective rate of the excise tax is reduced. For example, if the 15 percent excise tax reduces a portion of the estate otherwise taxable at 50%, the effective rate of the excise tax is only 7.5% (15% x 50%).

If the participant's surviving spouse is the sole beneficiary (or beneficiary of all but a minimal amount) of the plan benefit, the spouse can elect to have the excise tax on excess accumulations not apply at the participant spouse's death and, instead, to treat the plan benefit as his or her own for purposes of the application of the excess distribution and excess accumulation tax.[47]

IX. RETIREMENT PLAN ROLLOVERS

Tax-free "rollovers" of distributions from qualified plans, IRAs and SEPs, and Section 403(b) tax deferred annuity plans are specifically allowed by the Internal Revenue Code. With a rollover, a distribution of money or property from a retirement plan can be transferred or "rolled over" to a special type of IRA—the rollover IRA. Alternatively, in some cases the distribution can be rolled over to another plan of the same type—for example, from a qualified plan of one employer to another employer's qualified plan.

If the rollover is made within 60 days of receipt of the distribution and follows statutory rules, the tax on the distribution is deferred, i.e., the receipt is not a taxable event to the participant. However, "eligible rollover distributions" made after 1992 from qualified plans and Section 403(b) tax deferred annuities are subject to mandatory withholding at 20% unless the rollover is effected by means of a "direct rollover" (see "Tax Treatment of Rollovers," below.)

When Are Rollovers Used?

1. When a retirement plan participant receives a plan distribution and wants to defer taxes (and avoid any early distribution penalties) on part or all of the distribution.

2. When an individual participates in a qualified retirement plan or a 403(b) annuity plan that is being terminated by the employer, will receive a large termination distribution from the plan, has no current need for the income, and wishes to defer taxes on it.

3. When a participant in a qualified plan, 403(b) annuity plan, or IRA would like to continue to defer taxes on the money in the plan, but wants to change the form of the investment or gain greater control over it.

Tax Treatment of Rollovers

1. Any distribution from a qualified plan or Section 403(b) tax deferred annuity plan is eligible for rollover except the following:

- a required minimum distribution (generally beginning at age 70½), or

- a distribution that is one of a series of substantially equal periodic payments payable (a) for a period of ten years or more, or (b) for the life or life expectancy of the employee or the employee and a designated beneficiary.[48]

2. Eligible rollover distributions received from the qualified plan (or Section 403(b) deferred annuity) must be either transferred to the rollover IRA by means of a "direct rollover," pursuant to the employee's election, or transferred by the participant to the rollover IRA not later than the 60th day after the distribution from the plan. A "direct rollover" is defined as an eligible rollover distribution that is paid directly to another qualified plan or rollover IRA for the benefit of the distributee. It can be accomplished by any reasonable means of direct payment including the use of a wire transfer or a check that is negotiable only by the trustee of the new plan.[49] (In the case of a Section 403(b) tax deferred annuity, the distribution must be paid directly to another Section 403(b) annuity or a rollover IRA.) If the "direct rollover" method is not chosen, the distribution is subject to mandatory withholding at 20%.[50]

Failure to roll over the distribution within 60 days subjects it to income taxes (although the employee may be eligible to elect special 5-year or 10-year averaging to cushion the blow if the distribution qualifies for averaging).

3. Distributions from a rollover IRA are not eligible for 5-year (or 10-year) averaging tax treatment.

4. Distributions from the rollover IRA are subject to the same rules and limitations as all IRA distributions, discussed in Chapter 13. To summarize, distributions must: (a) begin no later than April 1 of the year after the participant attains age 70½, and (b) be made in minimum amounts based on a life or joint life payout. Distributions are taxable as ordinary income, without 5-year (or 10-year) averaging. Distributions prior to age 59½ are subject to the 10 percent early withdrawal penalty, with the exceptions discussed earlier in this chapter. Also certain excess distributions may be subject to the 15% excise tax discussed earlier.

5. Loans from a rollover IRA, like loans from any other IRA, are not permitted.

6. If a participant dies before withdrawing all of the rollover IRA account, the death benefit is includable in the de-

ceased participant's estate for federal estate tax purposes. If payable to the participant's surviving spouse in a qualifying manner, the marital deduction will defer estate taxes. However, if the amount from the plan included in the estate—together with all other amounts includable in the estate from qualified plans, TDA plans, or IRAs—exceeds a specified amount (see above), the 15 percent excess accumulation penalty tax may apply. This tax cannot be reduced by the marital deduction or any other estate tax deduction or credit. (See the discussion of the excess accumulation penalty above.)

7. An IRA can be used as a conduit to hold qualified plan funds for transfer from one qualified plan to another when an employee changes employers. The initial transfer from the qualified plan to the IRA is tax-free if the amount is transferred within 60 days. (Although the distribution will be subject to 20% mandatory withholding unless transferred by means of a "direct rollover"—see #2 above.) If the IRA contains no assets other than those attributable to the distribution from the qualified plan, then the amount in the IRA may subsequently be transferred tax free to another qualified plan if that plan allows such transfers. Thus an existing IRA should not be used for conduit rollovers; a new one should be established.[51] (An IRA can also be used as a conduit between two Section 403(b) annuity plans. However, conduit rollovers are not permitted between a qualified plan and a Section 403(b) annuity plan.)

As an alternative to a conduit IRA, a qualified plan distribution can be rolled over directly within 60 days to another qualified plan covering the employee, without using an IRA. However, the second qualified plan must be in existence and must permit such rollovers.

Alternatives to Rollovers

In cases where the rollover IRA is an alternative to leaving the money in the existing qualified plan, it may be better—or no worse—to leave the money in the plan if the participant is satisfied with the qualified plan's investment performance and the payout options available under that plan meet the participant's needs.

Results similar to a rollover IRA can be achieved if the qualified plan distributes an annuity contract to a participant in lieu of a cash distribution. The annuity contract does not have to meet the requirements of an IRA, but the tax implications and distribution restrictions are generally similar.

If a participant's objective is to absorb an existing Keogh or other qualified pension or profit-sharing plan account to

avoid continuing administrative requirements, there is an alternative to the rollover IRA or direct rollover from old plan to new plan. Simply transfer all the assets directly from the trustee of the old Keogh plan to the trustee of the new transferee plan. This can be advantageous because a distribution from the plan is then eligible for the 5-year (or 10-year) lump sum provision. However, there are potential tax traps in a trustee-to-trustee transfer, and it should be done only under the guidance of an experienced tax advisor.

WHERE CAN I FIND OUT MORE ABOUT RETIREMENT PLAN DISTRIBUTIONS?

1. *Tax Facts 1*, National Underwriter Co., Cincinnati, OH; revised annually.

2. IRS Publications 575, *Pension and Annuity Income,* and 590, *Rollover IRAs,* available from local IRS offices.

3. Doyle, Robert J., Jr. and Ivers, James F., "Planning for Minimum Distributions From Qualified Plans and IRAs," *Benefits Quarterly*, 3rd Quarter, 1988.

FOOTNOTES

1.   IRC Section 401(a)(11).
2.   IRC Section 417(c)(1).
3.   IRC Section 417(c)(2).
4.   IRC Section 417(a).
5.   IRC Section 417(a)(3)(B).
6.   IRC Section 417(a)(6)(B).
7.   IRC Section 417(b).
8.   Reg. §1.401(a)-11(b)(2). See also Reg. §1.401(a)-11(g).
9.   IRC Section 417(a)(2).
10. IRC Section 417(a)(6)(A).
11. IRC Section 417(a)(3)(A).
12. IRC Section 411(d)(6)(B)(ii); Reg. §1.411(d)(4), Q&A 1, Q&A 2.
13. IRC Section 401(a)(31).
14. IRC Section 402(f).
15. IRC Section 401(a)(11)(B)(iii).
16. IRC Section 72(f); Regs. §§1.72-8, 1.72-16(b)(4), 1.402(a)-1(a)(6), 1.403(a)-2; Rev. Rul. 72-149, 1972-1 CB 218.
17. IRC Section 72(e)(8).
18. IRC Section 72(e)(8)(D).
19. IRC Section 3405(c)(1).
20. IRC Section 72(b)(2).
21. IRC Section 72(b)(3).
22. 1988-2 CB 450.
23. IRC Section 402(d)(4).

24. IRC Section 402(d)(4)(C).

25. IRC Section 402(d)(4)(B).

26. IRC Section 402(d)(4)(J).

27. IRC Section 402(d)(1).

28. Tax Reform Act of 1986, Section 1122(h)(5).

29. Tax Reform Act of 1986, Section 1122(h)(3).

30. IRC Section 3405(c)(1).

31. Tax Reform Act of 1986, Section 1122(h)(5).

32. IRC Section 101(b).

33. Reg. §1.72-16(c)(4).

34. IRC Section 402(c)(9). Generally, after 1992, a surviving spouse also must elect the "direct rollover" method or the distribution will be subject to mandatory withholding at 20%.

35. IRC Section 4975(d), last paragraph. Loans from Section 403(b) tax deferred annuity plans are subject to the prohibited transactions rules and penalties if the plan is subject to ERISA. ERISA Sections 408(b), 502(i); Labor Reg. §2550-408b-1.

36. ERISA Section 408(d).

37. IRC Section 72(p)(2). However, additional security may be required in order to insure that such a loan meets the "adequate security" requirement. See Labor Reg. §2550-408b-1(f)(2).

38. IRC Section 72(p)(3).

39. IRC Section 401(a)(13).

40. IRC Section 414(p)(3).

41. IRC Section 72(t).

42. IRC Section 72(t)(4).

43. IRC Sections 401(a)(9), 408(a)(6), 408(b)(3), 403(b)(10), 457(d)(2).

44. IRC Section 4974.

45. See Prop. Reg. §1.401(a)(9)-2.

46. IRC Section 4980A.

47. IRC Section 4980A(d)(5).

48. IRC Section 402(c)(4).

49. Temp. Reg. §1.401(a)(31)-1T, A-3.

50. IRC Section 3405(c)(1).

51. IRC Section 408(d)(3).

Form 4972

Department of the Treasury
Internal Revenue Service

Tax on Lump-Sum Distributions

(Use This Form Only for Lump-Sum Distributions From Qualified Retirement Plans)

▶ Attach to Form 1040 or Form 1041. ▶ See separate instructions.

OMB No 1545-0193

1992

Attachment Sequence No **28**

Name of recipient of distribution

Identifying number

Part I	Complete this part to see if you qualify to use Form 4972.			
			Yes	No
1	Did you roll over any part of the distribution? If "Yes," do not complete the rest of this form	1		
2	Was the retirement plan participant born before 1936? If "No," do not complete the rest of this form . .	2		
3	Was this a lump-sum distribution from a qualified pension, profit-sharing, or stock bonus plan? (See **Distributions That Qualify for the 20% Capital Gain Election or for 5- or 10-Year Averaging** in the instructions.) If "No," do not complete the rest of this form	3		
4	Was the participant in the plan for at least 5 years before the year of the distribution?	4		
5	Was this distribution paid to you as a beneficiary of a plan participant who died?	5		
	If you answered "No" to both questions 4 **and** 5, do not complete the rest of this form.			
6	Was the plan participant:			
a	An employee who received the distribution because he or she quit, retired, was laid off, or was fired? . .	6a		
b	Self-employed or an owner-employee who became permanently and totally disabled before the distribution?	6b		
c	Age 59½ or older at the time of the distribution?	6c		
	If you answered "No" to question 5 and **all** parts of question 6, do not complete the rest of this form.			
7	Did you use Form 4972 in a prior year for any distribution received after 1986 for the same plan participant, including you, for whom the 1992 distribution was made? If "Yes," do not complete the rest of this form	7		

If you qualify to use this form, you may choose to use Part II, Part III, or Part IV; **or** Part II and Part III; **or** Part II and Part IV.

Part II	Complete this part to choose the 20% capital gain election. (See instructions.)		
8	Capital gain part from box 3 of Form 1099-R. (See instructions.)	8	
9	Multiply line 8 by 20% (.20) and enter here. If you do not choose to use Part III or Part IV, also enter the amount on Form 1040, line 39, or Form 1041, Schedule G, line 1b	9	

Part III	Complete this part to choose the 5-year averaging method. (See instructions.)		
10	Ordinary income from Form 1099-R, box 2a minus box 3. If you did not complete Part II, enter the taxable amount from box 2a of Form 1099-R. (See instructions.)	10	
11	Death benefit exclusion. (See instructions.)	11	
12	Total taxable amount—Subtract line 11 from line 10	12	
13	Current actuarial value of annuity, if applicable (from Form 1099-R, box 8)	13	
14	Adjusted total taxable amount—Add lines 12 and 13. If this amount is $70,000 or more, skip lines 15 through 18, and enter this amount on line 19	14	
15	Multiply line 14 by 50% (.50), but **do not** enter more than $10,000 . [15]		
16	Subtract $20,000 from line 14. If line 14 is $20,000 or less, enter -0- . . . . . [16]		
17	Multiply line 16 by 20% (.20) . . . . [17]		
18	Minimum distribution allowance—Subtract line 17 from line 15	18	
19	Subtract line 18 from line 14	19	
20	Federal estate tax attributable to lump-sum distribution. Do not deduct on Form 1040 or Form 1041 the amount attributable to the ordinary income entered on line 10. (See instructions.) . .	20	
21	Subtract line 20 from line 19	21	
22	Multiply line 21 by 20% (.20)	22	
23	Tax on amount on line 22. See instructions for Tax Rate Schedule	23	
24	Multiply line 23 by five (5). If line 13 is blank, skip lines 25 through 30, and enter this amount on line 31	24	
25	Divide line 13 by line 14 and enter the result as a decimal. (See instructions.)	25	
26	Multiply line 18 by the decimal amount on line 25	26	
27	Subtract line 26 from line 13	27	
28	Multiply line 27 by 20% (.20)	28	
29	Tax on amount on line 28. See instructions for Tax Rate Schedule	29	
30	Multiply line 29 by five (5)	30	
31	Subtract line 30 from line 24. (Multiple recipients, see instructions.)	31	
32	Tax on lump-sum distribution—Add Part II, line 9, and Part III, line 31. Enter on Form 1040, line 39, or Form 1041, Schedule G, line 1b . . . . ▶	32	

For Paperwork Reduction Act Notice, see separate instructions. Cat. No. 13187U Form **4972** (1992)

Qualified Plans: Distributions and Loans

Part IV   Complete this part to choose the 10-year averaging method. (See instructions.)

33	Ordinary income part from Form 1099-R, box 2a minus box 3. If you did not complete Part II, enter the taxable amount from box 2a of Form 1099-R. (See instructions.)	**33**		
34	Death benefit exclusion. (See instructions.)	**34**		
35	Total taxable amount—Subtract line 34 from line 33	**35**		
36	Current actuarial value of annuity, if applicable (from Form 1099-R, box 8)	**36**		
37	Adjusted total taxable amount—Add lines 35 and 36. If this amount is $70,000 or more, skip lines 38 through 41, and enter this amount on line 42	**37**		
38	Multiply line 37 by 50% (.50), but **do not** enter more than $10,000 .	**38**		
39	Subtract $20,000 from line 37. If line 37 is $20,000 or less, enter -0-	**39**		
40	Multiply line 39 by 20% (.20)	**40**		
41	Minimum distribution allowance—Subtract line 40 from line 38	**41**		
42	Subtract line 41 from line 37	**42**		
43	Federal estate tax attributable to lump-sum distribution. Do not deduct on Form 1040 or Form 1041 the amount attributable to the ordinary income entered on line 33. (See instructions.) . .	**43**		
44	Subtract line 43 from line 42	**44**		
45	Multiply line 44 by 10% (.10)	**45**		
46	Tax on amount on line 45. See instructions for Tax Rate Schedule	**46**		
47	Multiply line 46 by ten (10). If line 36 is blank, skip lines 48 through 53, and enter this amount on line 54	**47**		
48	Divide line 36 by line 37 and enter the result as a decimal. (See instructions.)	**48**		
49	Multiply line 41 by the decimal amount on line 48	**49**		
50	Subtract line 49 from line 36	**50**		
51	Multiply line 50 by 10% (.10)	**51**		
52	Tax on amount on line 51. See instructions for Tax Rate Schedule	**52**		
53	Multiply line 52 by ten (10)	**53**		
54	Subtract line 53 from line 47. (Multiple recipients, see instructions.)	**54**		
55	Tax on lump-sum distribution—Add Part II, line 9, and Part IV, line 54. Enter on Form 1040, line 39, or Form 1041, Schedule G, line 1b . . . . ▶	**55**		

9898 ☐ VOID ☐ CORRECTED

PAYER'S name, street address, city, state, and ZIP code		1 Gross distribution $	OMB No. 1545-0119 19**93**	Distributions From Pensions, Annuities, Retirement or Profit-Sharing Plans, IRAs, Insurance Contracts, etc.
		2a Taxable amount $		
		2b Taxable amount not determined ☐	Total distribution ☐	**Copy A** For **Internal Revenue Service Center**
PAYER'S Federal identification number	RECIPIENT'S identification number	3 Capital gain (included in box 2a) $	4 Federal income tax withheld $	File with Form 1096.
RECIPIENT'S name		5 Employee contributions or insurance premiums $	6 Net unrealized appreciation in employer's securities $	For Paperwork Reduction Act Notice and instructions for completing this form, see **Instructions for Forms 1099, 1098, 5498, and W-2G.**
Street address (including apt. no.)		7 Distribution code	IRA/ SEP ☐	8 Other $ %	
City, state, and ZIP code		9 Your percentage of total distribution %		
Account number (optional)		10 State income tax withheld $	11 State/Payer's state number	12 State distribution $
		13 Local income tax withheld $	14 Name of locality	15 Local distribution $

Form **1099-R**   Cat. No. 14436Q   Department of the Treasury - Internal Revenue Service

Do NOT Cut or Separate Forms on This Page

☐ VOID ☐ CORRECTED

PAYER'S name, street address, city, state, and ZIP code		1 Gross distribution $	OMB No. 1545-0119 19**93**	Distributions From Pensions, Annuities, Retirement or Profit-Sharing Plans, IRAs, Insurance Contracts, etc.
		2a Taxable amount $		
		2b Taxable amount not determined ☐	Total distribution ☐	**Copy 1** For **State, City, or Local Tax Department**
PAYER'S Federal identification number	RECIPIENT'S identification number	3 Capital gain (included in box 2a) $	4 Federal income tax withheld $	
RECIPIENT'S name		5 Employee contributions or insurance premiums $	6 Net unrealized appreciation in employer's securities $	
Street address (including apt. no.)		7 Distribution code	IRA/ SEP ☐	8 Other $ %	
City, state, and ZIP code		9 Your percentage of total distribution %		
Account number (optional)		10 State income tax withheld $	11 State/Payer's state number	12 State distribution $
		13 Local income tax withheld $	14 Name of locality	15 Local distribution $

Form **1099-R**   Department of the Treasury - Internal Revenue Service

19**93** Form W-4P

Department of the Treasury
Internal Revenue Service

What Is Form W-4P? This form is for recipients of income from annuity, pension, and certain other deferred compensation plans to tell payers whether income tax is to be withheld and on what basis. The options available to the recipient depend on whether the payment is periodic or nonperiodic (including an eligible rollover distribution) as explained on page 3.

Recipients can use this form to choose to have no income tax withheld from the payment (except for eligible rollover distributions or payments to U.S. citizens delivered outside the United States or its possessions) or to have an additional amount of tax withheld.

What Do You Need To Do? Recipients who want no tax to be withheld can skip the worksheet below and go directly to the form at the bottom of this page. All others should complete lines A through F of the worksheet. Many recipients can stop at line F.

Other Income? If you have a large amount of income from other sources not subject to withholding (such as interest, dividends, or taxable social security), you should consider making estimated tax payments using **Form 1040-ES,** Estimated Tax for Individuals. Call 1-800-829-3676 for copies of Form 1040-ES, and **Pub. 505,** Tax Withholding and Estimated Tax.

When Should I File? File as soon as possible to avoid underwithholding problems.

Multiple Pensions? More Than One Income? To figure the number of allowances you may claim, combine allowances and income subject to withholding from all sources on one worksheet. You can file a Form W-4P with each pension payer, but do not claim the same allowances more than once. Your withholding will usually be more accurate if you claim all allowances on the largest source of income subject to withholding.

Personal Allowances Worksheet For 1993, the value of your personal exemption(s) is reduced if your income is over $108,450 ($162,700 if married filing jointly, $135,600 if head of household, or $81,350 if married filing separately). Get Pub. 919, Is My Withholding Correct for 1993? for details. Call 1-800-829-3676 to order this publication.

A Enter "1" for **yourself** if no one else can claim you as a dependent . . . . **A** _____

B Enter "1" if: {
- You are single and have only one pension; or
- You are married, have only one pension, and your spouse has no income subject to withholding; or
- Your income from a second pension or a job, or your spouse's pension or wages (or the total of all) is $1,000 or less.
} **B** _____

C Enter "1" for your **spouse.** You may choose to enter -0- if you are married and have either a spouse who has income subject to withholding or you have more than one source of income subject to withholding. (This may help you avoid having too little tax withheld.) . . . . **C** _____

D Enter number of **dependents** (other than your spouse or yourself) you will claim on your return . . . . **D** _____

E Enter "1" if you will file as a **head of household** on your tax return . . . . **E** _____

F Add lines A through E and enter total here . . . . ▶ **F** _____

For accuracy, do all worksheets that apply.
- If you plan to itemize or claim other deductions and want to reduce your withholding, see the **Deductions and Adjustments Worksheet** on page 2.
- If you have more than one source of income subject to withholding or a spouse with income subject to withholding AND your combined earnings from all sources exceed $30,000, or $50,000 if you are married filing a joint return, see the **Multiple Pensions/More Than One Income Worksheet** on page 2 if you want to avoid having too little tax withheld.
- If **neither** of the above situations applies to you, **stop here** and enter the number from line F on line 2 of Form W-4P below.

············· **Cut here and give the certificate to the payer of your pension or annuity. Keep the top portion for your records.** ·············

Form **W-4P**

Department of the Treasury
Internal Revenue Service

Withholding Certificate for
Pension or Annuity Payments

OMB No. 1545-0415

19**93**

Type or print your full name	Your social security number
Home address (number and street or rural route)	Claim or identification number (if any) of your pension or annuity contract
City or town, state, and ZIP code	

Complete the following applicable lines:

1 I elect not to have income tax withheld from my pension or annuity. (Do not complete lines 2 or 3.) . . . . . ▶ ☐

2 I want my withholding from each **periodic** pension or annuity payment to be figured using the number of allowances and marital status shown. (You may also designate an amount on line 3.) . . . . ▶ _____ (Enter number of allowances.)

Marital status: ☐ Single ☐ Married ☐ Married, but withhold at higher Single rate

3 I want the following additional amount withheld from each pension or annuity payment. **Note:** For periodic payments, you cannot enter an amount here without entering the number (including zero) of allowances on line 2 . . . . ▶ $ _____

Your signature ▶ _____ Date ▶ _____

Cat. No. 10225T

Deductions and Adjustments Worksheet

NOTE: *Use this Worksheet only if you plan to itemize deductions or claim adjustments to income on your 1993 tax return.*

1. Enter an estimate of your 1993 itemized deductions. These include: qualifying home mortgage interest, charitable contributions, state and local taxes (but not sales taxes), medical expenses in excess of 7.5% of your income, and miscellaneous deductions in excess of 2% of your income. (For 1993, you may have to reduce your itemized deductions if your income is over $108,450 ($54,225 if married filing separately). Get Pub. 919 for details.). **1** $ _____

2. Enter: { $6,200 if married filing jointly or qualifying widow(er)
    $5,450 if head of household
    $3,700 if single
    $3,100 if married filing separately } **2** $ _____

3. **Subtract** line 2 from line 1. If line 2 is greater than line 1, enter -0- **3** $ _____
4. Enter estimate of your 1993 adjustments to income. These include alimony paid and deductible IRA contributions. **4** $ _____
5. **Add** lines 3 and 4 and enter the total **5** $ _____
6. Enter an estimate of your 1993 income not subject to withholding (such as dividends or interest income) **6** $ _____
7. **Subtract** line 6 from line 5. Enter the result, but not less than zero. **7** $ _____
8. **Divide** the amount on line 7 by $2,500 and enter the result here. Drop any fraction **8** _____
9. Enter the number from **Personal Allowances Worksheet,** line F, on page 1 **9** _____
10. **Add** lines 8 and 9 and enter the total here. If you plan to use the **Multiple Pensions/More Than One Income Worksheet,** also enter the total on line 1 below. Otherwise **stop here** and enter this total on Form W-4P, line 2 on page 1 **10** _____

Multiple Pensions/More Than One Income Worksheet

NOTE: *Use this Worksheet only if the instructions under line F on page 1 direct you here. This applies if you (and your spouse if married filing a joint return) have more than one source of income subject to withholding (such as more than one pension, or a pension and a job, or you have a pension and your spouse works).*

1. Enter the number from line F on page 1 (or from line 10 above if you used the **Deductions and Adjustments Worksheet**) **1** _____
2. Find the number in **Table 1** below that applies to the **LOWEST** paying pension or job and enter it here **2** _____
3. If line 1 is **GREATER THAN OR EQUAL TO** line 2, subtract line 2 from line 1. Enter the result here (if zero, enter -0-) and on Form W-4P, line 2, page 1. **Do not** use the rest of this worksheet **3** _____
4. If line 1 is **LESS THAN** line 2, enter -0- on Form W-4P, line 2, page 1, and enter the number from line 2 of this worksheet here **4** _____
5. Enter the number from line 1 of this worksheet **5** _____
6. **Subtract** line 5 from line 4 and enter the result here **6** _____
7. Find the amount in **Table 2** below that applies to the **HIGHEST** paying pension or job and enter it here **7** $ _____
8. **Multiply** line 7 by line 6 and enter the result here **8** $ _____
9. **Divide** line 8 by the number of pay periods in each year. (For example, divide by 12 if you are paid every month.) Enter the result here and on Form W-4P, line 3, page 1. This is the additional amount to be withheld from each payment **9** $ _____

Table 1: Multiple Pensions/More Than One Income Worksheet

Married Filing Jointly		All Others	
If amount from **LOWEST** paying pension or job is—	Enter on line 2, above	If amount from **LOWEST** paying pension or job is—	Enter on line 2, above
0 - $3,000	0	0 - $6,000	0
3,001 - 8,000	1	6,001 - 11,000	1
8,001 - 13,000	2	11,001 - 15,000	2
13,001 - 18,000	3	15,001 - 19,000	3
18,001 - 22,000	4	19,001 - 24,000	4
22,001 - 27,000	5	24,001 - 50,000	5
27,001 - 31,000	6	50,001 and over	6
31,001 - 35,000	7		
35,001 - 40,000	8		
40,001 - 60,000	9		
60,001 - 85,000	10		
85,001 and over	11		

Table 2: Multiple Pensions/More Than One Income Worksheet

Married Filing Jointly		All Others	
If amount from **HIGHEST** paying pension or job is—	Enter on line 7, above	If amount from **HIGHEST** paying pension or job is—	Enter on line 7, above
0 - $50,000	$350	0 - $30,000	$350
50,001 - 100,000	660	30,001 - 60,000	660
100,001 and over	730	60,001 and over	730

Paperwork Reduction Act Notice.—We ask for the information on this form to carry out the Internal Revenue laws of the United States. The Internal Revenue Code requires this information under sections 3405 and 6109 and their regulations. Failure to provide this information may result in inaccurate withholding on your payment(s).

The time needed to complete this form will vary depending on individual circumstances. The estimated average time is:

Recordkeeping	40 min.
Learning about the law or the form	20 min.
Preparing the form	49 min.

If you have comments concerning the accuracy of these time estimates or suggestions for making this form more simple, we would be happy to hear from you. You can write to both the **Internal Revenue Service,** Washington, DC 20224, Attention: IRS Reports Clearance Officer, T:FP; and the **Office of Management and Budget,** Paperwork Reduction Project (1545-0415), Washington, DC 20503. **DO NOT** send the tax form to either of these offices. Instead, give it to your payer.

Changes for 1993

Beginning on January 1, 1993, you will no longer have the option of claiming exemption from withholding for eligible rollover distributions from qualified pension or annuity plans (e.g., 401(k) pension plans) or tax sheltered annuity plans. See Pub. 505 for more details. Plan payers will be required to withhold 20% from all such distributions from qualified pension or tax sheltered annuity plans.

Exception. The only way to avoid this 20% withholding is to have the plan administrator transfer your distribution amount to an IRA or qualified pension or annuity plan in a **direct rollover.** See Pub. 505 for more information on how to make a direct rollover.

If you receive an eligible rollover distribution and roll over the entire amount within 60 days, it will not be taxable. However, because the plan payer must withhold 20% of the distribution, you would have to add this 20% from your own funds to the amount you received to roll over the entire amount of the distribution. For example, if you had a $100,000 eligible rollover distribution, the plan administrator would withhold $20,000 and you would receive $80,000. To roll over the entire $100,000 distribution, you would have to reinvest the $80,000 you received plus $20,000 from your own funds in an IRA or qualified pension plan within 60 days. You would recover the withheld $20,000 when you file your next tax return.

If you rolled over only the amount received from the distribution, the remaining 20% ($20,000 in the above example) would be taxable. In addition, you would be liable for an additional 10% excise tax on the taxable amount if you are under age 59½.

Withholding From Pensions and Annuities

Generally, withholding applies to payments made from pension, profit-sharing, stock bonus, annuity, and certain deferred compensation plans; from individual retirement arrangements (IRAs); and from commercial annuities. The method and rate of withholding depends upon the kind of payment you receive.

Periodic payments from all of the items above are treated as wages for the purpose of withholding. A periodic payment is one that is includible in your income for tax purposes and that you receive in installments at regular intervals over a period of more than 1 full year from the starting date of the pension or annuity. The intervals can be annual, quarterly, monthly, etc.

You can use Form W-4P to change the amount of tax to be withheld by using lines 2 and 3 of the form or to exempt the payments from withholding by using line 1 of the form. This exemption from withholding does not apply to certain recipients who have payments delivered outside the United States or its possessions. See **Exemption From Income Tax Withholding** later.

Caution: *Remember that there are penalties for not paying enough tax during the year, either through withholding or estimated tax payments. New retirees, especially, should see Pub. 505. It explains the estimated tax requirements and penalties in detail. You may be able to avoid quarterly estimated tax payments by having enough tax withheld from your pension or annuity using Form W-4P.*

Unless you tell your payer otherwise, tax must be withheld on **periodic** payments if your pension or annuity is more than $1,104 a month ($13,250 a year).

There are some kinds of periodic payments for which you **cannot** use Form W-4P since they are already defined as wages subject to income tax withholding. Retirement pay for service in the Armed Forces of the United States generally falls into this category. Certain nonqualified deferred compensation plans and state and local deferred compensation plans described in section 457 also fall into this category. Your payer should be able to tell you whether Form W-4P will apply. Social security payments are not subject to withholding but may be includible in income.

For periodic payments, your certificate stays in effect until you change or revoke it. Your payer must notify you each year of your right to elect to have no tax withheld or to revoke your election.

Nonperiodic payments will have income tax withheld at a flat 10% rate unless the payment is an eligible rollover distribution.

Tax will be withheld from an eligible rollover distribution at a flat 20% rate, unless the entire distribution is transferred by the plan administrator in a direct rollover to an IRA or qualified pension plan. (See the **Changes for 1993** section above for more details.)

Distributions from an IRA that are payable upon demand are treated as nonperiodic payments. You can elect to have no income tax withheld from a nonperiodic payment, except for an eligible rollover distribution as discussed above, by filing Form W-4P with the payer and checking the box on line 1. Generally, your election to have no tax withheld will apply to any later payment from the same plan. You cannot use line 2 to change the way tax is withheld. But you may use line 3 to specify that an additional amount be withheld.

Exemption From Income Tax Withholding

The election to be exempt from income tax withholding does not apply to any periodic payment or nonperiodic distribution that is delivered outside the United States or its possessions to a U.S. citizen or resident alien.

Other recipients who have these payments delivered outside the United States or its possessions can elect exemption only if an individual certifies to the payer that the individual is not: (1) a U.S. citizen or resident alien or (2) an individual to whom section 877 of the Internal Revenue Code applies (concerning expatriation to avoid tax). The certification must be made in a statement to the payer under the penalties of perjury. A nonresident alien who elects exemption from withholding under section 3405 is subject to withholding under section 1441.

Revoking the Exemption From Withholding

If you want to revoke your previously filed exemption from withholding for periodic payments, file another Form W-4P with the payer. If you want tax withheld at the rate set by law, write "Revoked" by the checkbox on line 1 of the form. If you want tax withheld at any different rate, complete line 2 on the form.

If you want to revoke your previously filed exemption for nonperiodic payments, write "Revoked" by the checkbox on line 1 and file Form W-4P with the payer.

Statement of Income Tax Withheld From Your Pension or Annuity

By January 31 of next year, you will receive a statement from your payer showing the total amount of your pension or annuity payments and the total income tax withheld during the year.

☆ **U.S. GOVERNMENT PRINTING OFFICE: 1992 315-084**

Chapter 25

INSTALLING A QUALIFIED RETIREMENT PLAN

This chapter covers the complicated and distinctive steps involved in installing a qualified retirement plan. Qualified plans comprise the following plans covered in this book:

Cash Balance Pension Plan	Chapter 8
Defined Benefit Pension Plan	Chapter 9
ESOP/Stock Bonus Plan	Chapter 10
HR 10 (Keogh) Plan	Chapter 12
Money Purchase Pension Plan	Chapter 15
Profit-Sharing Plan	Chapter 17
Savings Plan	Chapter 18
Section 401(k) Plan	Chapter 19
Target/Age-Weighted Plan	Chapter 21

Installing a plan involves various steps, some of which must comply with a fairly strict legal timetable. To help focus this discussion, an installation checklist for a typical qualified plan is set out in Figure 25.1 for reference.

Plan Adoption

An employer must legally "adopt" a qualified plan during the employer's taxable year in which it is to be effective.[1] (By contrast, a simplified employee pension (SEP) can be adopted as late as the tax filing date for the year—see Chapter 20.) The plan sponsor should adopt (and document the adoption of) the plan before the end of the year in which the plan is to become effective. The plan can be made effective to the beginning of the year of adoption. An adoption that is made later and reflected in "backdated" documents is not legally effective for purposes of the tax treatment of a qualified plan.

The reason for this requirement is basically one of tax accounting. An employer cannot obtain a deduction for an expense accrued during a year unless it meets the "all events" test for accrual. That is, all events that make the accrual a legally binding obligation of the employer must have occurred by the end of the tax year. Thus, a qualified plan must have been legally adopted by the end of a particular tax year if the employer wishes to take a tax deduction for contributions to the plan for that year.

A corporation adopts a plan by a formal action of the corporation's board of directors. An unincorporated business should adopt a written resolution in a form similar to a corporate resolution. The plan does not have to be in final form in order to be legally adopted; the corporate resolution can simply set out the principal terms of the plan such as coverage, benefit formula, vesting, etc.

If the plan will use a trust for funding, a trust must be established before the end of the year of adoption that is valid under the law of the state in which it is established. A nominal plan contribution may be required for that purpose. If the plan is to be funded through an insurance contract, the insurer must accept the application for the contract before the end of the year, but the contract need not be formally adopted in final form at that time.

Advance Determination Letter

Because of the complexity of the qualified provisions, and the tax cost of having a plan considered "disqualified" by the IRS, most plan sponsors apply to the IRS for a ruling that the plan provisions meet Code requirements for favorable tax treatment as a qualified plan. This letter is generally referred to as a "determination letter."

Technically, a plan does not have to receive a favorable determination letter in order to be qualified. If the plan provisions in letter and in operation meet Code requirements, the plan is qualified and entitled to the appropriate tax benefits. However, without a determination letter, the issue of plan qualification for a given year does not arise until the IRS audits the employer's tax returns for that year. By that time, it is generally too late for the employer to amend the plan to correct any disqualifying provisions. So if the plan has a disqualifying provision or lacks an essential provision, the employer's tax deduction for the year being audited is lost. (In addition, the plan fund will lose its tax-exempt status and employees will become taxable on their vested benefits—a true all-around tax disaster.) A determination letter helps to avoid this problem since auditing agents generally will not raise the issue of plan qualification if the employer has a current determination letter—that is, one that shows the plan complies with current law.

Plans generally must be amended periodically to conform to changes in the law. Each time there is a significant amendment to the plan a new determination letter should be obtained.

It is always possible for the IRS to raise the issue that a plan is discriminatory *in operation*—as opposed to merely having discriminatory provisions on paper. A determination letter

Figure 25.1

PLAN INSTALLATION CHECKLIST AND TIMETABLE

Assumptions: 1. Employer uses calendar year for tax reporting.
2. Plan is to be effective January 1, 1993.

Before December 31, 1993
1. Corporate board must pass a resolution adopting the plan. Plan document does not have to be in final form.
2. Trust agreement must be signed and trust established under state law; or application for group pension contract must be made and accepted by insurance company.
3. Plan must be "communicated to employees." This can be done orally at employee meetings or through a written communication. The summary plan description (SPD) can be used for this purpose simply by distributing it earlier than its regular due date (see below).

Before Employer's Tax Filing Date (March 15, 1994, with extensions to September 15, 1994 if applied for)
1. Plan should be drafted in final form and signed by plan sponsor and trustee.
2. Employer must make the 1993 contribution to the plan by this date in order for it to be deductible on the 1993 tax return.
3. Application for IRS determination letter should be filed before this date in order to extend the retroactive amendment period. However, there is no specific deadline for filing the application for determination.

Within 120 Days After Plan is Adopted (i.e., Board of Directors' resolution)
1. Furnish SPD to participants (see Appendix A of this book).
2. File SPD with Department of Labor.

Before Filing Application For Determination With IRS
1. Provide "Notice to Interested Parties" to employees as required by IRS regulations. This is a prescribed formal notice to employees of their rights in connection with the determination letter process. The notice must be provided 10 to 24 days before filing if the notice is mailed, and 7 to 20 days before filing if the notice is posted.

On or Before July 31, 1994 (and each July 31 thereafter)
1. File Annual Report (Form 5500 series) — see Appendix A.

On or Before September 30, 1994 (and each September 30 thereafter)
1. Furnish Summary Annual Report to participants (see Appendix A).

---

cannot prevent this. Fortunately such IRS attacks are relatively rare.

The Code contains a "retroactive amendment" procedure that allows plan sponsors to amend a plan retroactively to eliminate certain disqualifying provisions.[2] Retroactive plan amendments may be made up to the employer's tax filing date for the year in question, including extensions. For example, if a corporate employer uses a calendar tax year, the tax filing date for the year 1993 is March 15, 1994, with possible extensions to September 15, 1994. A plan effective January 1, 1993 can be retroactively amended as late as September 15, 1994 under this provision.

An additional advantage of the determination letter procedure is that it can extend the time for retroactive amendments.

If the determination letter request is filed before the tax filing date, retroactive amendments can be made as long as the determination letter request is still pending.

Determination letter requests are made on IRS forms. Copies of Form 5300, used for custom designed plans, and Form 5307, used for master or prototype plans (see below) are reproduced at the end of this chapter. A "short form," Form 6406, is available for determination letter requests involving plan amendments only (not a new plan).

The IRS once provided determination letters as a free service, but a fee schedule is now in effect. For a smaller employer, this fee can be a substantial factor in the cost of installing a plan. The fee currently is $700 for a custom designed plan with fewer than 100 participants, $825 for a plan with 100 or more participants, and $125 for a master or prototype plan.[3] Form 8717 is filed along with the fee and the form from the appropriate member of the 5300 family.

Master and Prototype Plans

Custom design of a qualified plan can be costly because the plan document must be very lengthy to reflect all of the complex requirements of current law. The pension industry has developed methods to reduce the cost of plan drafting; these are particularly important to smaller employers, since the cost of installation must be spread over relatively few employees.

One of the most common methods of reducing drafting costs is to use a "master" or "prototype" plan offered by a financial institution as an inducement to use that institution's investment products to fund the plan. Insurance companies, banks, and mutual funds frequently offer master or prototype plans. These plans are standardized plans of various types—for example prototype profit-sharing or prototype money purchase—that use standardized language approved by the IRS. The plan sponsor has some degree of choice in basic provisions of the plan such as the vesting schedule, the contribution or benefit formula, etc.

A master plan is distinguished from a prototype in that a master plan usually refers to a plan under which various employers use a single financial institution for funding, while a prototype plan generally does not commit the plan sponsor to use any particular funding institution or medium.

The use of master or prototype plans greatly simplifies plan installation in many cases. The fee for adopting a master or prototype plan is usually much less than the cost of drafting a custom designed plan. The determination letter procedure is also simplified, because the "boilerplate" provisions of the plan have already been approved by the IRS. All the IRS has to do is determine whether the basic vesting schedule, contribution or benefit formula, etc., as applied to the employer in question, is nondiscriminatory.

The cost of drafting a custom designed plan has also been addressed by the pension industry. There are "document preparation services" that will generate documents from their central word processors based on a checklist of plan provisions submitted by the plan installer. Usually, the use of a document preparation service will speed IRS approval of a plan, because the IRS becomes familiar with the standard language used by various document preparers.

FOOTNOTES

1. Reg. §1.401-1(a)(2). See also, *Engineered Timber Sales, Inc. v. Comm.*, 74 TC 808 (1980).
2. IRC Section 401(b).
3. See Rev. Proc. 92-23, Section 6(09), 1993-19 IRB 6, 14.

| < | 5300 | > |
| < | Rev 2/90 | > |

Department of the Treasury
Internal Revenue Service

**Application for
Determination for Employee Benefit Plan**

(Under sections 401(a) and 501(a) of the Internal Revenue Code)

OMB No. 1545-0197
Expires 1-31-93

For IRS Use Only
File folder number ▶
Case number ▶

File page 1 of Form 5300 in duplicate.

Note: *User fee must be attached to this application. (See Instruction B—What To File).*

The information provided herein will be read by computer. Therefore page 1 must be typed (except the signature). Please enter information exactly as requested and only in the space provided. Do not type in areas that are shaded.

Review the Procedural Requirements Checklist before submitting this application.

1a Name of plan sponsor (employer if single-employer plan)

<   >

Address (number and street)

<   >

City   State   ZIP code

<   > <   > <   >

1b Employer identification number

<   >

1c Employer's tax year ends-Enter N/A or (MM)

1d Telephone number

(   )

2 Person to be contacted if more information is needed. (See Specific Instructions.)
(If same as 1a, leave blank.) (Complete even if Power of Attorney is attached):

Name

<   >

Address (number and street)

<   >

City   State   ZIP code   Telephone number

<   > <   > <   > (   )

3a Determination requested for (enter applicable number(s) at left and fill in required information). (See Specific Instructions.)

< > Enter 1 for Initial Qualification—Date plan signed . . . . _____

< > Enter 2 for Amendment after initial qualification—Is plan restated? . . . Yes < > No < >
Date amendment signed_____ Date amendment effective _____

< > Enter 3 for Affiliated Service Group status (section 414(m))—Date effective _____

< > Enter 4 for Leased Employee Status

< > Enter 5 for Partial termination—Date effective _____

b Has the plan received a determination letter? If "Yes," submit a copy of the latest letter . . . Yes < > No < >

c Have interested parties (as defined in Treasury Regulation section 1.7476-1) been given the required notification of this application? . . . . Yes < > No < >

d Does the plan have a cash or deferred arrangement, or employee or matching contributions (section 401(k) or (m))? . . . . Yes < > No < >

Name of Plan:

4a <   >

< > **b** Enter plan number (3 digits) _____ **d** Enter date plan effective (MMDDYY)

< > **c** Enter date plan year ends (MMDD) <   > **e** Enter number of participants in plan

5a If this is a defined benefit plan, enter the appropriate number in box at left.

<   >   Enter 1 for unit benefit   Enter 3 for flat benefit

       Enter 2 for fixed benefit   Enter 4 for other (Specify) _____

b If this is a defined contribution plan, enter the appropriate number in box at left.

<   >   Enter 1 for profit sharing   Enter 4 for target benefit

       Enter 2 for stock bonus   Enter 5 for other (Specify) _____

       Enter 3 for money purchase

6a Is the employer a member of an affiliated service group?

<   >   Enter 1 if "Yes"   Enter 2 if "No"   Enter 3 if "Not Certain"

b Is the employer a member of a controlled group of corporations or a group of trades or businesses under common control?

<   >   Enter 1 if "Yes"   Enter 2 if "No"

7 Enter type of plan:

<   >   Enter 1 if governmental plan or church plan not subject to ERISA

       Enter 2 if multiple employer plan (described in section 413(c)). Enter number of participating employers. _____

       Enter 3 if other

Under penalties of perjury, I declare that I have examined this application, including accompanying statements, and to the best of my knowledge and belief, it is true, correct, and complete. **Both copies of this page must be signed.**

Signature ▶ _____ Title ▶ _____ Date ▶ _____

Instructions are separate. See page 1 for Paperwork Reduction Act Notice.

Form **5300** (Rev. 2-90)

Installing a Qualified Retirement Plan

8a Do you maintain any other qualified plan(s)? (See Specific Instructions.) . . . . ☐ Yes   ☐ No
    If "Yes," complete 8b and 8c.

  b If this is a defined contribution plan and you also maintain a defined benefit plan, or if this is a
    defined benefit plan and if you also maintain a defined contribution plan, when the plan is
    top-heavy, do non-key employees covered under both plans receive:

    (i) the top-heavy minimum benefit under the defined benefit plan? . . . . ☐ N/A   ☐ Yes   ☐ No
    (ii) at least a 5% minimum contribution under the defined contribution plan? . . . . . . ☐ N/A   ☐ Yes   ☐ No
    (iii) the minimum benefit offset by benefits provided by the defined contribution plan? . . . . . ☐ N/A   ☐ Yes   ☐ No
    (iv) benefits under both plans that, using a comparability analysis, are at least equal to the
         minimum benefit? (See Specific Instructions.) . . . . ☐ N/A   ☐ Yes   ☐ No

  c Do the provisions of the plan preclude the possibility that the section 415 limitations will be
    exceeded with respect to any employee who is or has been a participant in this plan and any other
    qualified plan of the employer? . . . . ☐ Yes   ☐ No

9 COVERAGE (See Specific Instructions.):

  a Is the employer applying the separate line of business rules of section 414(r)? . . . . ☐ Yes   ☐ No
    (If "Yes," see Specific Instructions.)

  b Does the employer receive services from any leased employees within the meaning of section 414(n)? . . . . . ☐ Yes   ☐ No

  c Coverage of plan at (give date) _____

  d Enter the percentage of nonhighly compensated employees who benefit under the plan, excluding
    employees who benefit only under a part of the plan containing a CODA or employee or matching
    contributions. (If 70 percent or more, proceed to f.) . . . . ☐ N/A   _____ %

  e Divide the percentage of nonhighly compensated employees who benefit under the plan (9d) by the
    percentage of highly compensated employees who benefit under the plan, excluding employees
    who only benefit under a part of the plan containing a CODA or employee or matching contributions ☐ N/A   _____

  f If the plan contains a CODA. compute the ratio in line e above on the basis of employees eligible
    to make elective deferrals under the CODA portion of the plan . . . . ☐ N/A   _____

  g If the plan provides for employee or matching contributions, compute ratio in line e above on the
    basis of employees eligible to make employee contributions or to receive matching contributions
    under the plan . . . . ☐ N/A   _____

  h Are the results in line e, f, or g based on the aggregated coverage of more than one plan? . . . . ☐ Yes   ☐ No
    (If "Yes," see Specific Instructions.)

  i If line e, f, or g is less than .7, does the plan pass the average benefit test? . . . ☐ N/A   ☐ Yes   ☐ No
    (i) Enter the safe harbor percentage . . . . _____
    (ii) Enter the average benefit percentage . . . . _____
    (See Specific Instructions.)

10 PARTICIPATION (See Specific Instructions.):

  a Is a determination requested as to whether the plan satisfies the participation test under section
    401(a)(26) with respect to each of the plan's current benefit structures? . . . . ☐ Yes   ☐ No

  b (For defined benefit plans only) Do at least the lesser of 50 employer's employees or 40 percent of
    the employer's employees accrue the minimum current accrual under the plan? . . . . . . ☐ N/A   ☐ Yes   ☐ No

  c (For defined benefit plans only) If the answer to b is "No," does the plan satisfy section 401(a)(26)
    with respect to its prior benefit structure under one of the other tests in the Proposed Regulations
    under section 401(a)(26)? (See Specific Instructions.) . . . . ☐ N/A   ☐ Yes   ☐ No

11 Is a determination requested as to whether the plan satisfies the coverage or participation tests with
    respect to former employees benefiting under the plan? . . . . ☐ Yes   ☐ No
    If "Yes," has a demonstration been attached showing how the plan satisfies sections 410(b) and
    401(a)(26) with respect to former employees? . . . . ☐ N/A   ☐ Yes   ☐ No

Form 5300 (Rev. 2-90)   Page **3**

	N/A	Yes	No

12 PERMITTED DISPARITY:

a If the plan provides for disparity in contributions or benefits, is the plan intended to meet the requirements of section 401(l)? . . . .

If N/A, do not complete lines b through f. If "Yes" or "No," complete lines b through f, and also see the Specific Instructions.

b In the case of a defined contribution plan, does the excess contribution percentage exceed the base contribution percentage by a uniform amount that does not exceed the maximum excess allowance? . . . .

Base Contribution Percentage _____ Excess Contribution Percentage _____

c In the case of a defined benefit excess plan, does the excess benefit percentage exceed the base benefit percentage by a uniform amount no greater than the maximum excess allowance? . . . .

Base Benefit Percentage _____ Excess Benefit Percentage _____

d In the case of a defined benefit offset plan, is the offset uniform and is it less than the maximum offset allowance?

Benefit formula _____ Offset _____

e What is the plan's integration level? _____

f In the case of a defined benefit plan, does the plan reduce the 3/4 percent factor by 1/15th for the first five years, 1/30th for the next five years and actuarially thereafter for benefits beginning before social security retirement age?

13 General eligibility requirements —Complete a, b, and c below.

a Check one box:

(i) ☐ All employees

(ii) ☐ Hourly rate employees only

(iii) ☐ Salaried employees only

(iv) ☐ Other (Specify) _____

b Length of service (number of years) _____ ☐ **N/A**

c Minimum age (Specify) _____ ☐ **N/A**

14 Vesting:

Check one box to indicate the vesting provisions of the plan:

a ☐ Full and immediate.

b ☐ Full vesting after two years of service.

c ☐ Full vesting after three years of service.

d ☐ Full vesting after five years of service.

e ☐ Six year graded vesting.

f ☐ Three to seven year graded vesting.

g ☐ Other (Specify—see Specific Instructions and attach a schedule)

15 Benefits and requirements for benefits:

a For defined benefit plans—Method for determining accrued benefit: _____

(i) Benefit formula at normal retirement age is _____

(ii) Benefit formula at early retirement age is _____

(iii) Normal form of retirement benefit is _____

b For defined contribution plans—Employer contributions:

(i) Profit-sharing or stock bonus plan contributions are determined under:

☐ A definite formula   ☐ An indefinite formula   ☐ Both

(ii) Money purchase—Enter rate of contribution _____

(iii) State target benefit formula

	N/A	Yes	No

16 Miscellaneous Provisions:

a Does any amendment to the plan reduce or eliminate any section 411(d)(6) protected benefit? (See Specific Instructions.)

b Are contributions or benefits allocated on the basis of total compensation within the meaning of section 414(s)? If "No," explain. (See Specific Instructions) . . . .

c Are forfeitures allocated, in the case of a defined contribution plan, on the basis of total compensation? If "No," explain .

d Are trust earnings and losses allocated on the basis of account balances in a defined contribution plan?

e Is this plan or trust currently under examination or is any issue related to this plan or trust currently pending before the Internal Revenue Service, the Department of Labor, the Pension Benefit Guaranty Corporation, or any court? If "Yes," attach explanation . . . .

f Is this application also expected to satisfy the notice requirement for this plan for merger, consolidation, or transfer of plan assets or liabilities involving another plan? (See Specific Instructions) . . . .

Procedural Requirements Checklist

This checklist identifies certain basic data required to process your application. The checklist identifies items that MUST be included with your application. Completion of this checklist is optional and is for the benefit of the plan sponsor.

		Yes	No
a	Have you attached **Form 5302**, Employee Census?		
b	Have you attached the appropriate user fee and **Form 8717**, User Fee for Employee Plan Determination Letter Request? .		
c	Have you attached a copy of the plan? (Initial applications and Restated plans only)		
d	Have you attached a copy of the plan's latest determination letter? (Previously approved plans only)		
e	Have you submitted page one in duplicate (at least one must be an original)?		
f	Have you signed both copies of page one of the application?		
g	Have you entered the plan sponsor's 9-digit employer identification number in line 1b?		
h	If appropriate, have you attached **Form 2848**, Power of Attorney and Declaration of Representative, or **Form 2848-D**, Tax Information Authorization and Declaration of Representative (see General Information)?		
i	Have you entered the effective date of the plan in line 4d?		
j	**Affiliated Service Groups, Controlled Groups or Entities Under Common Control**—Have you attached the information requested in General Instructions B, "What To File," and line 6 of the Specific Instructions?		
k	**Multiple-Employer Plans**—Have you attached the information required by General Instruction B.II.g.?		

ALL APPLICATIONS ARE SCREENED BY COMPUTER. FAILURE TO INCLUDE A REQUIRED ITEM WILL RESULT IN THE RETURN OF THIS APPLICATION TO YOU.

Employee Census

Form **5302**
(Rev. February 1990)
Department of the Treasury
Internal Revenue Service

▲ **Attach to application for determination—defined benefit and defined contribution plans.** (Round off to nearest dollar)

Schedule of 25 highest paid participating employees for 12-month period ended ▲

OMB No. 1545-0416

This Form is NOT Open to Public Inspection

Name of employer

Date business incorporated

Employer identification number

Line no.	Participant's last name and initials (See instructions) (a)	Check		Age (d)	Years of service (e)	Annual Nondeferred Compensation			Employee and matching contributions under the plan (i)	Defined Benefit		Defined Contribution			
		Highly compensated (b)	Percent of business owned (c)			Used in computing benefits or employee's share of contributions (f)	Excluded (g)	Total (h)		Annual benefit expected under this plan (j)	Annual benefit under each other qualified defined benefit plan (k)	Employer contribution allocated (l)	Forfeitures allocated in the year (m)	Amount allocated under each other qualified defined contribution plan (n)	Other deferred compensation (o)
1															
2															
3															
4															
5															
6															
7															
8															
9															
10															
11															
12															
13															
14															
15															
16															
17															
18															
19															
20															
21															
22															
23															
24															
25															
Total for above															
Totals for all others (specify number) ▲	( )														
Total for all participants															

For Paperwork Reduction Act Notice, see back of this form.

See instructions on the back of this form.

Form **5302** (Rev. 2 90)

General Information

(Section references are to the Internal Revenue Code unless otherwise noted.)

Paperwork Reduction Act Notice. — We ask for this information to carry out the Internal Revenue laws of the United States. We need it to determine whether taxpayers meet the legal requirements for plan approval. If you want to have your plan approved by IRS, you are required to give us this information.

The time needed to complete and file this form will vary depending on individual circumstances. The estimated average time is:

Recordkeeping	10 hrs., 31 min.
Learning about the law or the form	42 min.
Preparing, copying, assembling, and sending the form to IRS	54 min.

If you have comments concerning the accuracy of these time estimates or suggestions for making this form more simple, we would be happy to hear from you. You can write to the **Internal Revenue Service**, Washington, DC 20224, Attention: IRS Reports Clearance Officer, T:FP; or the **Office of Management and Budget** (1545-0416), Washington, DC 20503.

Purpose of Form. — This schedule is to be used by the Internal Revenue Service in its analysis of an application for determination as to whether a plan of deferred compensation qualifies under section 401(a).

Public Inspection. — Section 6104(a)(1)(B) provides, generally, that applications filed for the qualification of a pension, profit-sharing, or stock bonus plan will be open to public inspection. However, section 6104(a)(1)(C) provides that information concerning the compensation of any participant will not be open to public inspection. Consequently, the information contained in this schedule will not be open to public inspection, including inspection by plan participants and other employees of the employer who established the plan.

General Instructions

Prepare the employee census for a current 12-month period. Generally the 12-month period should be the plan year. If the actual information is not available, compensation, contributions, etc., may be projected for a 12-month period. However, such projection must be clearly identified.

Who Must File. — Every employer or plan administrator who files an application for determination for a defined benefit plan or a defined contribution plan is required to attach this schedule, complete in all details.

For collectively bargained plans a Form 5302 is required only if the plan benefits any employees who are not included in a unit of employees who are covered under a collective bargaining agreement, or if more than 2 percent of the employees who are included in a unit of employees covered under a collective bargaining agreement are professional employees. If so, a separate Form 5302 is required for each employer of such employees. For a plan, described in section 413(c), other than a collectively bargained plan, maintained by more than one employer where all employers in each affiliated service group, controlled group of corporations, or group of trades or businesses under common control are considered one employer, a separate Form 5302 is required for each such employer.

Specific Instructions

Column (a), first list any participant who at any time during the 5-year period prior to the start of the current 12-month period owned directly or indirectly 5% or more of the voting stock or 5% or more of the business. Next, list the remaining participants in order of current compensation (see Note 2 and instructions for column (h), below) starting with the highest paid, followed by the next highest paid and so on. If there are fewer than 25 participants, list all the participants. Otherwise, only the first 25 who fall under the priorities listed above need be listed on lines 1 through 25.

Note 1: *For purposes of this form, "participant" means any employee who satisfies the participation requirements prescribed by the plan.*

Column (b), enter a check mark or an "X" to indicate that a participant is a highly compensated employee under section 414(q). Enter N/A if the participant is not a highly compensated employee under section 414(q).

Column (c), (i) enter the percentage of total voting power of the stock owned by a participant. For example, participant "P" owns 200 shares of voting stock of the employer's 5,000 shares outstanding. The percentage is 4% (200 ÷ 5,000). If a participant owns any nonvoting stock of the employer, enter the percentage of ownership of all types of stock issued, if greater.

(ii) if an unincorporated business, enter the percentage of the business owned by the participant.

If a participant owns neither of the above, enter N/A.

Column (d), enter the attained age of each participant as of the end of the year for which this schedule applies. For example, if a participant's 47th birthday was on January 7, 1990, and the schedule covers the calendar year 1990, enter 47 for that participant.

Column (e), enter the number of full years of service recognized for plan purposes that each participant has been employed by the employer, and any prior employer.

Column (f), enter the amount of each participant's compensation that is recognized for plan purposes in computing the benefit (for a defined benefit plan) or in computing the amount of employer contribution that is allocated to the account of each participant (for a defined contribution plan). Do not include any portion of the employer contributions to this or any other deferred plan as compensation for any participant.

Column (g), enter the amount of compensation that is not recognized for purposes of column (f). For example, if a participant received $12,500 compensation for the year, $1,000 of which was a bonus and the plan does not recognize bonuses for plan purposes, enter $11,500 in column (f) and $1,000 in column (g).

Note 2: *"Compensation" for purposes of column (h) is defined as all amounts (including bonuses and overtime) paid to the participant for services rendered the employer. Do not enter employer contributions made to this or any other deferred compensation plan.*

Column (h), enter the total amount of compensation for the year for each participant. The amount entered in this column will be the sum of the amounts entered in columns (f) and (g) for each participant.

Column (i), enter the total amount of mandatory and voluntary contributions and matching contributions made by each participant. If the plan does not provide for employee contributions of any kind, enter "N/A."

Column (j), enter the amount of benefit each participant may expect to receive at normal retirement age based on current information, assuming no future compensation increases. For example, under a 30% benefit plan, a participant whose benefit is based on annual compensation of $10,000 may expect an annual benefit of $3,000 ($10,000 × 30%) at retirement. In this case enter $3,000.

Column (k), enter the amount of benefit each participant may expect to receive under another qualified defined benefit plan(s) of the employer.

Column (l), enter the amount of the employer's contribution that is allocated to the account of each participant.

Column (m), enter the amount of the forfeitures that is allocated to each participant, unless forfeitures are allocated to reduce employer contributions.

Column (n), enter the employer's contribution allocated to the account of each participant under all qualified defined contribution plans of the employer other than this plan.

Column (o), enter any other amounts allocated to each employee, including any allocation/deferral to a section 408(k) arrangement or a section 403(b) annuity contract.

Caution: *Before submitting this schedule, be sure that all relevant items are complete. Failure to meet this requirement will result in the return of the schedule for completion.*

< 5307 >

< Rev 2/90 >

Department of the Treasury
Internal Revenue Service

Application for Determination for Adopters of Master or Prototype, Regional Prototype or Volume Submitter Plans
(Other than Collectively Bargained Plans)
(Under sections 401(a) and 501(a) of the Internal Revenue Code)

OMB No. 1545-0200

For IRS Use Only
File folder number ▶
Case number ▶

Note: User fee must be attached to this application. (See Instruction B, "What To File.")
File page 1 of Form 5307 in duplicate.
The information provided herein will be read by computer. Therefore page 1 must be typed (except the signature). Please enter information exactly as requested and only in the space provided. Do not type in areas that are shaded.
Review the Procedural Requirements Checklist before submitting this application.

1a Name of plan sponsor (employer if single employer plan)

< _____ >

Address (number and street)

< _____ >

City   State   ZIP code

< _____ > < _____ > < _____ >

1b Employer identification number

< _____ >

1c Employer's tax year ends—
Enter (MM)

_____

1d Telephone number

( )

2 Person to be contacted if more information is needed. (See Specific Instructions.)
(If same as 1a, leave blank.) (Complete even if Power of Attorney is attached.)

Name

< _____ >

Address (number and street)

< _____ >

City   State   ZIP code   Telephone number

< _____ > < _____ > < _____ >   ( )

3a Determination requested for (enter applicable number(s) at left and fill in required information.) (See Specific Instructions.)

< _____ > Enter 1 for Initial Qualification—Date plan signed . . . . _____

< _____ > Enter 2 for Amendment after Initial Qualification

Date amendment signed _____ Date amendment effective . . . . _____

< _____ > Enter 3 for Standardized Plans (section 401(a)(26) plans and nonpaired plans)

b Has the plan received a determination letter dated after 1/1/84? (Submit a copy of the latest letter if one was **ever** received.) . . . . Yes < > No < >

If 3b is no, were required amendments made retroactively effective? . . . . . . Yes _____ No _____

c Have interested parties (as defined in Treasury Regulation section 1.7476-1) been given the required notification of this application? . . . . Yes < > No < >

d Does the plan have a cash or deferred arrangement, or employee or matching contributions (section 401(k) or (m))? . . . . Yes < > No < >

4a Name of plan:

< _____ >

< _____ > **b** Enter plan number (3 digits) _____ **d** Enter date plan effective (MMDDYY)

< _____ > **c** Enter date plan-year ends (MMDD) < _____ > **e** Enter number of participants in plan

5a If this is a defined benefit plan, enter the appropriate number in box at left.

< _____ > Enter 1 for unit benefit   Enter 3 for flat benefit
Enter 2 for fixed benefit   Enter 4 for other (Specify) _____

b If this is a defined contribution plan, enter the appropriate number in box at left.

< _____ > Enter 1 for profit sharing   Enter 4 for target benefit
Enter 2 for stock bonus   Enter 5 for other (Specify) _____
Enter 3 for money purchase

6a Is the employer a member of an affiliated service group?

< _____ > Enter 1 if "Yes"   Enter 2 if "No"

b Is the employer a member of a controlled group of corporations or a group of trades or businesses under common control?

< _____ > Enter 1 if "Yes"   Enter 2 if "No"

7 Enter type of adopter.

< _____ > Enter 1 if a master or prototype plan   Enter 3 if a District approved volume submitter plan
Enter 2 if a regional prototype plan

8 Enter type of plan.

< _____ > Enter 1 if governmental plan or church plan not subject to ERISA
Enter 2 if other

Under penalties of perjury, I declare that I have examined this application, including accompanying statements, and to the best of my knowledge and belief it is true, correct, and complete. Both copies of this page must be signed.

Signature ▶   Title ▶   Date ▶

Instructions are separate. See page 1 for Paperwork Reduction Act Notice.

Form **5307** (Rev. 2-90)

Installing a Qualified Retirement Plan

9a Do you maintain any other qualified plan(s)? (See Specific Instructions.) . . . . ☐ Yes   ☐ No
    If "Yes," complete 9b and 9c.

b If this is a defined contribution plan and you also maintain a defined benefit plan, or if this is a defined benefit plan and you also maintain a defined contribution plan, when the plan is top-heavy, do non-key employees covered under both plans receive:

   (i) the top-heavy minimum benefit under the defined benefit plan? . . . .☐ N/A ☐ Yes ☐ No

   (ii) at least a 5% minimum contribution under the defined contribution plan? . . . .☐ N/A ☐ Yes ☐ No

   (iii) the minimum benefit offset by benefits provided by the defined contribution plan? . . . .☐ N/A ☐ Yes ☐ No

   (iv) benefits under both plans that, using a comparability analysis, are at least equal to the minimum benefit? (See Specific Instructions.) . . . .☐ N/A ☐ Yes ☐ No

c Do the provisions of the plan preclude the possibility that the section 415 limitations will be exceeded with respect to any employee who is or has been a participant in this plan and any other qualified plan of the employer? . . . . ☐ Yes   ☐ No

---

10 COVERAGE (See Specific Instructions.):

a Is the employer applying the separate line of business rules of section 414(r)? . . . . ☐ Yes   ☐ No
    (If "Yes," see Specific Instructions.)

b Does the employer receive services from any leased employees within the meaning of section 414(n)? . . . ☐ Yes   ☐ No

c Coverage of plan at (give date)   _____

d Enter the percentage of nonhighly compensated employees who benefit under the plan, excluding employees who benefit only under a part of the plan containing a CODA or employee or matching contributions. (If 70 percent or more, proceed to f). . . . .☐ N/A   _____ %

e Divide the percentage of nonhighly compensated employees who benefit under the plan (10d) by the percentage of highly compensated employees who benefit under the plan, excluding employees who only benefit under a part of the plan containing a CODA or employee or matching contributions . . . .☐ N/A   _____

f If the plan contains a CODA, compute the ratio in line **e** above on the basis of employees eligible to make elective deferrals under the CODA portion of the plan . . . .☐ N/A   _____

g If the plan provides for employee or matching contributions, compute ratio in line **e** above on the basis of employees eligible to make employee contributions or to receive matching contributions under the plan. . . . .☐ N/A   _____

h Are the results in lines **e**, **f**, or **g** based on the aggregated coverage of more than one plan? . . . . ☐ Yes   ☐ No
    (If "Yes," see Specific Instructions.)

i If line **e**, **f**, or **g** is less than .7, does the plan pass the average benefit test? . . . .☐ N/A ☐ Yes ☐ No

   (i) Enter the safe harbor percentage . . . . _____

   (ii) Enter the average benefit percentage . . . . _____

---

11 PARTICIPATION (See Specific Instructions.):

a Is a determination requested as to whether the plan satisfies the participation test under section 401(a)(26) with respect to each of the plan's current benefit structures? . . . . ☐ Yes   ☐ No

b (For defined benefit plans only) Do at least the lesser of 50 employer's employees or 40 percent of the employer's employees accrue the minimum current accrual under the plan? . . . . . .☐ N/A ☐ Yes ☐ No

c (For defined benefit plans only) If the answer to **b** is "No," does the plan satisfy section 401(a)(26) with respect to its prior benefit structure under one of the other tests in the Proposed Regulations under section 401(a)(26). (See Specific Instructions.) . . . .☐ N/A ☐ Yes ☐ No

---

12 Is a determination requested as to whether the plan satisfies the coverage or participation tests with respect to former employees benefiting under the plan? . . . . ☐ Yes   ☐ No
    If "Yes," has a demonstration been attached showing how the plan satisfies sections 410(b) and 401(a)(26) with respect to former employees? . . . .☐ N/A ☐ Yes ☐ No

---

Form 5307 (Rev. 2-90) Page **3**

		N/A	Yes	No
13	Miscellaneous provisions:			
a	Does any amendment to the plan reduce or eliminate any section 411(d)(6) protected benefit? (See Specific Instructions.)			
b	Are contributions or benefits allocated on the basis of total compensation within the meaning of section 414(s)? If "No," explain. (See Specific Instructions.)			
c	Is this plan or trust currently under examination or is any issue related to this plan or trust currently pending before the Internal Revenue Service, the Department of Labor, the Pension Benefit Guaranty Corporation, or any court? If "Yes," attach explanation			

Procedural Requirements Checklist

This checklist identifies certain basic data required to process your application. The checklist identifies items that MUST be included with your application. Completion of this checklist is optional and is for the benefit of the plan sponsor.

	Yes	No
a. Have you attached **Form 5302**, Employee Census?		
b. Have you attached the appropriate user fee and **Form 8717**, User Fee for Employee Determination Letter Request? . .		
c. **Master or Prototype or Regional Prototype Plans**—Have you attached a copy of the adoption agreement? (See General Instruction B.5.)		
d. Have you attached a copy of the master or prototype, regional prototype or volume submitter letter? (See General Instruction B.7.)		
e. Have you attached a copy of the plan's latest determination letter? (Previously approved plans only)		
f. Have you submitted page one in duplicate (at least one copy must be an original)?		
g. Have you signed both copies of page one of the application?		
h. Have you entered the plan sponsor's 9-digit employer identification number on line 1b?		
i. If appropriate, have you attached **Form 2848**, Power of Attorney and Declaration of Representative, or **Form 2848-D**, Tax Information Authorization and Declaration of Representative? (See General Information.)		
j. Have you entered the effective date of the plan on line 4d?		
k. **Affiliated Service Groups, Controlled Groups or Entities Under Common Control**—Have you attached the information requested in General Instructions B.II "What To File" and item 6 of the Specific Instructions?		
l. **Volume Submitter Plans**—Have you attached a copy of the plan or trust instrument? (See General Instruction B.I.6.) . .		

ALL APPLICATIONS ARE SCREENED BY COMPUTER. FAILURE TO INCLUDE A REQUIRED ITEM WILL RESULT IN THE RETURN OF THIS APPLICATION TO YOU.

Form **8717** (Rev. May 1993) Department of the Treasury Internal Revenue Service	**User Fee for Employee Plan Determination Letter Request** ▶ Attach to determination letter applications.	**For IRS Use Only** Control number _____ Amount paid _____ User fee screener

1	Sponsor's name	2	Sponsor's employer identification number

3	Plan name	4	Plan number

5 Type of request — Fee

		Fee
a ☐	Form 5300 for plan with fewer than 100 participants	$ 700
b ☐	Form 5300 for plan with 100 or more participants	825
c ☐	Form 5310 (for plan terminations only) with fewer than 100 participants	225
d ☐	Form 5310 (for plan terminations only) with 100 or more participants	375
e ☐	Form 5303	800
f ☐	Form 5307	125
g ☐	Form 6406	125
h	**Multiple employer plans (Form 5300):**	
(1) ☐	2 to 10 employers	700
(2) ☐	11 to 99 employers	1,400
(3) ☐	100 to 499 employers	2,800
(4) ☐	Over 499 employers	5,600
i ☐	Volume submitter specimen plan	1,500
(1) ☐	Non-model amendment (sec. 401(a)(31))	400
j ☐	Form 4461 or Form 4461-A (regional prototype plan)	1,500
(1) ☐	Non-model amendment (sec. 401(a)(31))	400
k ☐	Form 4461-B (adopter of mass submitter regional prototype plan)	100
l ☐	Group trust	750

Instructions

The Omnibus Budget Reconciliation Act of 1990 requires payment of a user fee with each application for a determination letter. The user fees are listed on line 5 above. For more information, see Rev. Proc. 93-23, 1993-19 I.R.B. 6, and Rev. Proc. 93-12, 1993-3 I.R.B 14.

Check the box on line 5 for the type of application you are submitting.

Note: *For lines 5a through 5d, the term "participant" includes active employees participating in the plan, retirees, other former employees, and a beneficiary of a deceased employee who is receiving or will in the future receive benefits under the plan. For details, see the instructions for Form 5300 or 5310.*

Attach to Form 8717 a check or money order payable to the Internal Revenue Service for the full amount of the user fee. If you do not include the full amount, your application will be returned. Attach Form 8717 to your determination letter application. To avoid delays, send the determination letter application and Form 8717 to the applicable IRS address shown

below. If you have multiple plans (e.g., a profit-sharing plan and a money purchase plan), submit a separate determination letter application and Form 8717 for each plan.

Note: *Restated plans and plans amended to comply with the Tax Reform Act of 1986 cannot use Form 6406, Short Form Application for Determination for Amendment of Employee Benefit Plan. These plans should use Form 5300 or Form 5303, whichever applies.*

If the entity is in: ▼	Send fee and request for determination letter or notification letter to: ▼
Connecticut, Maine, Massachusetts, New Hampshire, New York, Rhode Island, Vermont	Internal Revenue Service EP/EO Division P. O. Box 1680, GPO Brooklyn, NY 11202
Delaware, District of Columbia, Maryland, New Jersey, Pennsylvania, Virginia, any U.S. possession or foreign country	Internal Revenue Service EP/EO Division P. O. Box 17288 Baltimore, MD 21203
Indiana, Kentucky, Michigan, Ohio, West Virginia	Internal Revenue Service EP/EO Division P. O. Box 3159 Cincinnati, OH 45201
Arizona, Colorado, Kansas, Oklahoma, New Mexico, Texas, Utah, Wyoming	Internal Revenue Service EP/EO Division Mail Code 4950 DAL 1100 Commerce Street Dallas, TX 75242
Alabama, Arkansas, Florida, Georgia, Louisiana, Mississippi, North Carolina, South Carolina, Tennessee	Internal Revenue Service EP/EO Division P. O. Box 941 Atlanta, GA 30370
Alaska, California, Hawaii, Idaho, Nevada, Oregon, Washington	Internal Revenue Service EP Application EP/EO Division McCaslin Industrial Park 2 Cupania Circle Monterey Park, CA 91754-7406
Illinois, Iowa, Minnesota, Missouri, Montana, Nebraska, North Dakota, South Dakota, Wisconsin	Internal Revenue Service EP/EO Division 230 S. Dearborn DPN 20-6 Chicago, IL 60604

Attach Check or Money Order Here

Cat. No. 64727O

Form **8717** (Rev. 5-93)

Chapter 26

BONUS PLAN

WHAT IS IT?

A bonus is an addition to regular salary or compensation that is provided, usually near year end, to enable employees to share in profits resulting from a successful year. This chapter discusses the tax and other planning considerations that apply.

WHEN IS IT INDICATED?

1. Bonuses are often used in closely held companies to enable shareholder-employees to withdraw the maximum compensation income from the company each year.

2. Bonuses are used for executives of larger companies as an incentive-oriented form of compensation, based on the attainment of profit or other goals during the year.

3. Bonuses may be used to assist executives in funding cross-purchase buy-sell agreements or in contributing their share of the premium to a split dollar arrangement.

ADVANTAGES

1. For executives of larger companies, bonuses represent an incentive-based form of compensation that is very effective because of the close connection between performance and receipt. Often, the executive uses the bonus to purchase a life insurance policy which provides death benefit protection and tax deferred accumulation of cash value.

2. Bonuses allow flexibility in compensation to reflect company performance, both in closely held and larger corporations.

3. Bonus arrangements are flexible and simple to design, within the tax constraints discussed below.

DISADVANTAGES

1. Bonuses generally do not offer an opportunity for the employee to defer taxation of compensation for more than one year.

2. Bonuses are limited by the requirement of "reasonableness" for the deductibility of compensation payments by the employer.

TAX IMPLICATIONS

Bonus payments are deductible under the same rules as other forms of cash compensation. These rules are discussed in detail in Chapter 28, but will be covered in summary here as they apply to bonuses.

A bonus, together with other compensation, cannot be deducted unless it constitutes (a) a reasonable allowance for (b) services actually rendered. Factors indicating reasonableness—the first part of the test—are listed in the general discussion in Chapter 28. Bonuses can be very large if they are based on profits or earnings and the company has a very good year. For example, suppose a sales manager receives a $400,000 bonus in addition to his regular $100,000 base salary, under a sales-target bonus formula. Although $500,000 of compensation might, as a general rule, be considered unreasonably high for this type of sales manager, this arrangement might be sustained by the IRS for two reasons:

- Reasonableness of compensation is often tested in accordance with circumstances existing when the bonus agreement is entered into rather than when the bonus is actually paid.

- In testing the reasonableness of a bonus, both the IRS and the courts will usually take into account the element of risk involved to the employee. That is, an employee presumably had a choice between a relatively lower amount of guaranteed compensation and a higher amount of contingent compensation. So the two should be deemed equivalent for purposes of testing reasonableness. For instance, a sales manager who receives a $100,000 base salary and a bonus of 10% of the gross sales increase in 1994, producing a $400,000 bonus for 1994, probably could not at the beginning of 1994 have negotiated a contract for $500,000 of guaranteed compensation without bonus. The reasonableness of the bonus contract should be based on the reasonableness of the equivalent fixed salary agreement that the sales manager could have negotiated, not on the $500,000 total resulting from taking a chance and then having a good year.

This emphasizes the importance of planning ahead when using bonuses as an employee benefit technique. If reasonableness might become an issue, decide upon a bonus formula well in advance of the time the bonus is paid. (Preferably, in advance of the year in which the bonus will be earned). In other words, a formula for determining a bonus for year end 1994 should be determined in writing before the beginning of 1994 to help support the reasonableness of the amount.

The timing of income to the employee and deductions to the corporation are governed by the rules discussed in detail in Chapter 28 with regard to cash compensation. Since bonuses are often payable after the end of the year in which they are earned, the "2½ month safe-harbor rule" is important for bonus planning. Under this rule an accrual method corporation can deduct a compensation payment that is properly accrued before the end of a given year, so long as the payment is made no later than 2½ months after the end of the corporation's taxable year. For example, for a calendar year accrual method corporation, a bonus earned for services completed in 1994 can be deducted by the corporation for 1994 so long as it is paid on or before March 15, 1995. Note, however, that the 2½ month rule does not apply to payments to employees who own or control (50 percent or more) the corporation under Code section 267(b). For those employees, the corporation must pay the bonus during its taxable year in order to deduct it during that taxable year.

For regular employees who can make use of the 2½ month safe harbor technique, the ability to move taxable income into the employee's next taxable year is a significant advantage of the bonus form of compensation. For example, a bonus might be earned (and deducted by the corporation) in 1994, paid on March 15, 1995, and the employee could defer the payment of tax to April 15, 1996 (the employee's due date for the 1995 tax return.)

ALTERNATIVES

1. As with cash compensation in general, as discussed in Chapter 28, taxation can be avoided or deferred by various types of noncash compensation plans that are discussed throughout this book, including qualified pension and profit-sharing plans, nonqualified deferred compensation plans, and medical benefit plans.

2. A form of deferred compensation with many of the same incentive features as a cash bonus plan is a stock option, incentive stock option (ISO), or restricted stock plan. These are discussed in later chapters.

HOW ARE THESE PLANS SET UP?

Bonus plans can be informal or even oral. There are no tax or other legal requirements for a written plan or for filing anything with the government. However, a written plan is often desirable, and in that case employer and employee might want to consult with an attorney experienced in handling employee compensation matters.

WHERE CAN I FIND OUT MORE ABOUT THESE PLANS?

1. Graduate Course: Executive Compensation (GS 842), The American College, Bryn Mawr, PA.

2. CLU/ChFC Courses: Income Taxation (HS 321) and Planning for Business Owners and Professionals (HS 331), The American College, Bryn Mawr, PA.

3. CFP Course: Retirement Planning and Employee Benefits (CFP V), College for Financial Planning, Denver, CO.

QUESTIONS AND ANSWERS

Question — What are the advantages of a written bonus plan?

Answer — A written agreement has at least two advantages:

First, a written plan, particularly one drafted in advance of the year in which compensation is earned, helps to avoid disallowance of the corporation's deduction on the ground that the amount is unreasonable. Without a written plan, the IRS is likely to claim that a bonus is simply a discretionary payment that is excessive and therefore nondeductible. If this payment is made to a shareholder, the payment may be characterized as a dividend instead of deductible compensation. This means that the corporation will not receive a tax deduction even though the entire distribution will probably be taxable as ordinary income to the shareholder-recipient.

A second reason for a written agreement is that it defines the terms of the bonus and assures the employee of legal grounds to require the corporation to live up to the agreement. The terms of the agreement should be clearly defined for this reason.

Question — If a bonus is based on "profits," is there any specific definition of profits that must be used?

Answer — There is no tax or legal reason for any specific definition of profits in a bonus agreement. The important thing is a clear definition to protect against later misunderstandings. Profits can be defined as the amount shown in financial statements, as taxable income for federal income tax purposes, or some other method of defining profits. If the definition relies on company accounting methods or federal tax laws, the agreement should take possible changes in accounting method or the tax laws into account. Paying a bonus in itself may affect profits. So, the agreement must specify whether profits are determined before or after bonus payments. For a company with more than one division or subsidiary, an executive may want to tie the bonus to profits in one particular unit rather than the company as a whole.

Chapter 27

CAFETERIA PLAN

WHAT IS IT?

A cafeteria plan is one under which employees may, within limits, choose the form of employee benefits from a "cafeteria" of benefit plans provided by their employer. Cafeteria plans must include a "cash option"—an option to receive cash in lieu of noncash benefits of equal value.[1]

WHEN IS IT INDICATED?

1. When employee benefit needs vary within the employee group—for example where the employee mix includes young, unmarried people with minimal life insurance and medical benefit needs as well as older employees with families who need maximum medical and life insurance benefits.

2. When employees want to choose the benefit package most suited to their needs.

3. When an employer seeks to maximize employee satisfaction with the benefit package and thereby maximize the employer's benefit from its compensation expenditures.

4. When the employer is large enough to afford the expense of such a plan. Because of administrative costs and complexity, cafeteria plans, in general, tend to be used by larger employers. However, there is one type of cafeteria plan—the flexible spending account or FSA—that provides very specific tax benefits and is often used even by smaller employers including closely held businesses. FSAs feature benefit funding through salary reductions by employees. FSA plans are discussed in detail in Chapter 33.

ADVANTAGES

1. Cafeteria plans help give employees an appreciation of the value of their benefit package.

2. The flexibility of a cafeteria benefit package helps meet varied employee needs.

3. Cafeteria plans can help control employer costs for the benefit package because provision of benefits that employees do not need is minimized.

DISADVANTAGES

1. Cafeteria plans are more complex and expensive for the employer to design and administer than fixed, standardized benefit packages.

2. Benefit packages usually include some insured benefits—medical and life insurance benefits, for example—and not all insurers will provide these programs on a cafeteria basis.

3. Complex tax requirements apply to the plan under Section 125 of the Internal Revenue Code.

4. Highly compensated employees may lose the tax benefits of the plan if it is discriminatory. Key employees may lose tax benefits if more than 25% of aggregate benefits under the plan are provided to them.

EXAMPLE OF CAFETERIA PLAN

1. All employees receive a "basic benefit package" consisting of

   • Term life insurance equal to 1½ times salary

   • Medical expense insurance for employee and dependents

   • Disability income insurance (long and short term)

2. Each employee receives an additional "credit" based on salary and years of service (3 percent of salary for 0-5 years of service, 4½ percent for 5-10 years of service, and 6 percent for 10 or more years). Each year the employee can elect to apply this credit to one or more of a list of additional benefits specified by the employer. These benefits might include:

   • Cash only

   • Additional term life insurance up to 1 times salary

   • Dental insurance for employee or dependents

   • Up to two weeks additional vacation time

TAX IMPLICATIONS

1. A cafeteria plan must comply with the provisions of section 125 of the Internal Revenue Code. This code section provides an exception for cafeteria plans from the "constructive receipt" doctrine. Under that doctrine, an employee is taxed on money or property that he has a free election to receive, even if he chooses not to receive it. So, if the terms of Section 125 are not met in a cafeteria plan, an employee is taxed on the value of any taxable benefits available from the plan, even if the participant chooses nontaxable benefits such as medical insurance.

2. Under Section 125 and its regulations, only certain benefits—"qualified benefits"—can be made available in a cafeteria plan.[2] Qualifying benefits include cash and most tax-free benefits provided under the Code, except for

    • scholarships and fellowships under Code section 117

    • educational assistance provided under a plan governed by Code section 127

    • employee discounts (for example, those for department store employees), no-additional-cost services (for example, standby airline travel for airline employees) and other fringe benefits provided under Code section 132.[3]

    • retirement benefits such as qualified or nonqualified deferred compensation; however, a 401(k) arrangement can be included.[4]

3. A cafeteria plan must meet certain nondiscrimination requirements:

    Participation. The plan must be made available to a group of employees in a manner that does not discriminate in favor of "highly compensated" employees.[5] The definition of highly compensated is a participant who is an officer, a shareholder owning more than 5 percent of the employer, a highly compensated employee or the spouse or dependent of any of these.[6] The following "safe-harbor" eligibility provision is permitted: the plan will not be considered discriminatory if it benefits a group of employees under a classification that does not discriminate in favor of highly compensated employees *and* it covers all employees with three years of service beginning no later than the first day of the plan year after the three years' service is attained.[7]

    Benefits. The plan must not discriminate in favor of highly compensated employees as to contributions and benefits.[8] Plus, qualified benefits provided to key employees (as defined in the top-heavy plan rules, Code section 416(i) — see Chapter 23) under the plan must not exceed, in value, 25 percent of the aggregate value of plan benefits provided to all employees.[9]

    If these nondiscrimination tests are not met by the plan, the result is that otherwise nontaxable benefits become taxable to highly compensated employees or key employees—but not to regular employees.

    In addition, any type of benefit offered under the plan must meet its own nondiscrimination tests—for example, any group term life insurance offered under the plan would also have to meet the nondiscrimination requirements of Section 79. These requirements are discussed in the chapters of this book covering these plans.

    In many cases it is not difficult to meet the nondiscrimination tests. In other cases, the result of not meeting the tests—some taxation to highly compensated employees only—may not be objectionable in view of the overall advantages of the plan.

ALTERNATIVES

1. The FSA, or flexible spending account is a cafeteria plan funded through salary reductions. It is not just an alternative but a special type of cafeteria plan design that should be thoroughly investigated whenever cafeteria benefits are considered—see Chapter 33.

2. Fixed benefit programs without employee choice may be adequate where most employees have the same benefit needs or where the employer cannot administer a more complex program.

3. Cash compensation as an alternative to benefits gives up tax advantages in favor of maximum employee choice, and assumes that employees will have adequate income to provide benefits on their own.

HOW ARE THESE PLANS SET UP?

1. First, a plan design must be decided upon. This involves a survey of employee needs and employer costs, and a business decision as to the best alternative.

2. A written plan must be drafted and adopted by the employer. IRS or other governmental approval of the plan is generally not necessary, but an IRS ruling can be obtained if there is any doubt about some aspect of the tax treatment of the plan as designed. However, an informa-

tion return (i.e., one of the Form 5500 series) must be filed with the IRS.[10]

3. Employee election (choice of benefit) forms must be designed and distributed to employees. Generally, employees must make benefit choices in advance of the year in which the benefits are earned.[11] For example, for benefits to be earned and used in 1995, employees should complete and file their election forms with the employer before the end of 1994.

4. Skillful communication with employees is the most important element in the success of a cafeteria plan; these plans are often complicated.

HOW DO I FIND OUT
MORE ABOUT THESE PLANS?

1. Beam, Burton T., Jr. and John J. McFadden, *Employee Benefits*, 3rd ed. Chicago, IL: Dearborn Financial Publishing, Inc.

2. Graduate Course: Executive Compensation (GS 842), The American College, Bryn Mawr, PA.

FOOTNOTES

1. IRC Section 125(d)(1).
2. IRC Section 125(d)(1)(B).
3. IRC Section 125(f).
4. IRC Section 125(d)(2).
5. IRC Section 125(b)(1)(A).
6. IRC Section 125(e).
7. IRC Section 125(g)(3).
8. IRC Section 125(b)(1)(B).
9. IRC Section 125(b)(2).
10. IRC Section 6039D. The IRS has exempted cafeteria plans from furnishing information required under Section 6039D concerning highly compensated employees for any plan year beginning prior to the issuance of further guidance. Notice 90-24, 1990-1 CB 335.
11. Prop. Reg. §1.125-1, Q&A 15.

Chapter 28

CASH COMPENSATION PLANNING

WHAT IS IT?

Although cash compensation—the employee's compensation paid currently (during the year in which it is earned)—is not generally thought of as an employee benefit, actually it is the core of any compensation and benefit package. Any proposed employee benefit has to be compared in effectiveness with equivalent cash compensation. In addition, many employee benefit plans such as pension and life insurance plans have benefit or contribution schedules that are based on the employee's cash compensation. Finally, from a tax point of view, cash compensation is not as simple as it might appear. Financial planners must understand the rules to avoid adverse tax results from inappropriate planning.

WHEN IS IT INDICATED?

Opportunities for planning cash compensation primarily arise for employees, including shareholder-employees, of regular or "C" corporations (not "S" corporations). In an unincorporated business or an "S" corporation, all income and losses pass directly through to the owners' tax returns, so there are few compensation planning opportunities.

ADVANTAGES

1. Compared with noncash benefits or deferred payments, cash compensation provides certainty and, therefore, greater security to the employee.

2. Cash compensation tends to set an employee's status in the company and community; the amount of annual salary must be carefully considered for this reason.

3. Cash compensation is an important part of overall financial planning for shareholder-employees of closely held corporations.

4. For employers, cash compensation is preferable to noncash benefits because it is easier to budget, with no unknown or uncontrollable costs.

5. Cash compensation plans rarely involve design and administrative complexities, including ERISA aspects, that may apply to medical benefits, pensions, and other types of noncash or deferred compensation.

DISADVANTAGES

1. Cash compensation paid currently is generally all taxable currently at ordinary income rates.

2. Cash compensation must meet the reasonableness test for deductibility and other tax issues discussed below. In some cases, other forms of compensation can avoid or defer these problems.

TAX IMPLICATIONS

Reasonableness of Compensation

The Internal Revenue Code allows an employer who carries on a trade or business to deduct "a reasonable allowance for salaries or other compensation for personal services actually rendered."[1] This "reasonableness" test is the main tax issue in determining whether an employer's payments for compensating an employee are deductible. If the company's payment does not meet this reasonableness test, its deduction is disallowed.

At a corporate income tax rate of 34 percent, the corporation's deduction saves 34 cents for every deductible dollar. Stated in another manner, the out-of-pocket cost for reasonable (deductible) compensation is $.66 of each $1.00 paid, as opposed to $1.00 for nondeductible payments. Since state income tax deductibility usually follows the federal rules, the true difference between deductibility and nondeductibility can be even more than this.

The IRS does not usually raise the reasonableness issue if salaries are not particularly high. However, as the amount paid and deducted increases, it becomes important for a company to "build a case" that compensation is reasonable. Steps to suggest to a client include:

- Determine compensation levels prior to the beginning of each fiscal year, before salary has been earned, instead of simply determining salaries from year to year on a purely discretionary basis. This avoids the impression that the amount of salary is based simply on the amount that shareholder employees wish to withdraw from the corporation for a given year.

- Written employment contracts should be provided and signed before compensation is earned.

- The company's board of directors should document in the minutes of directors' meetings how the amount of salary was determined.

- Court cases and IRS publications mention many factors in determining what constitutes reasonable compensation. These factors, listed below, should be reviewed in documenting the amount of salary and other compensation.

Factors in Determining Reasonable Compensation

Factors mentioned by the courts in "reasonableness of compensation" cases and by the IRS in its publications include the following:

- Comparison with compensation paid to executives in comparable positions for comparable employers.

- The employee's qualifications for the position.

- The nature and scope of the employee's duties.

- The size and complexity of the business enterprise.

- Comparison of the compensation paid with the company's gross and net income.

- The company's compensation policy for all employees.

- Economic conditions—including the condition of the industry and the local economy as well as the overall national economy.

- Comparison with dividend distributions to shareholders. Abnormally low dividends can create an inference that a so-called salary payment to a shareholder-employee is really a disguised dividend.

Treatment of Disallowed Compensation

A deduction for compensation that is disallowed because it is unreasonable is treated in various ways depending on the circumstances. IRS regulations state that if a corporation makes excessive payments and such payments are made primarily to shareholders, these payments will be treated as dividends.[2] Dividend treatment is the most typical situation for disallowed compensation. Other types of treatment are

possible, depending on the facts. For example, if an employee at some point had transferred property to the corporation, excessive compensation payments could be treated as payments for this property, which would be nondeductible capital expenditures to the corporation.

From the recipient's point of view, in the absence of any other evidence, any excessive payments for salaries or compensation will be taxable as ordinary income to the recipient. In other words, from the employee's point of view, the reasonableness issue may not have much tax effect.

However, if the employee is a shareholder in the corporation, the corporation's tax picture and the possible loss of a compensation deduction at the corporate level can be very important. For example, suppose Larry Sharp owns 100% of Sharp Corporation and is its sole employee. Sharp Corporation earns $400,000 in 1993. If the corporation pays all $400,000 of this to Larry as deductible compensation, the only tax burden on the $400,000 is the individual income tax that Larry pays. But if the IRS disallows $100,000 of the compensation deduction and treats it as a nondeductible dividend, then Larry still has $400,000 of taxable ordinary income, but the corporation also has $100,000 of taxable income. The corporation's tax on this—$22,250—is a direct reduction in Larry's wealth since he is a 100% shareholder.

Reimbursement Agreements

Because of the uncertainty of the reasonable compensation issue, companies often enter into reimbursement agreements with employees under which the employee is required to pay back the excessive portion of the compensation to the corporation if the IRS disallows a deduction for compensation. The employee does not generally have to pay income tax on the amount repaid. These agreements can be useful but they do not necessarily solve the reasonableness problem. In fact they may be a "red flag" to the IRS examiner. The IRS sometimes asserts that such an agreement is evidence that the corporation intended to pay unreasonable compensation. Therefore, such an agreement can make the compensation even more likely to attract a tax audit and more difficult to defend in litigation.

An agreement to reimburse is rarely in the direct financial interest of the employee, since the employee would usually be better off keeping the money rather than returning it. The employee's tax on any excessive portion is treated as a dividend so the tax paid from the employee's perspective is the same as if the entire payment was compensation. Reimbursement agreements are primarily used by shareholder-employees where the corporation's tax status is of indirect financial interest to the employee. In those cases what hurts the corporation hurts the employee as a stockholder.

Timing of Income and Deductions

The tax rules for the timing of a corporation's deduction for compensation are more complicated than one might expect, primarily because the IRS sees potential for abuse in compensation payment situations.

Under the usual tax accounting rules for accrual method taxpayers an item is deductible for an accounting period if that item has been properly accrued, even if not actually paid. Accrual occurs for tax purposes in the taxable year when all events have happened that legally require the corporation to pay the amount—the so-called "all events" test. Usually the all events test is satisfied as soon as the employee has performed all the services required under the terms of the employment contract. Because of the apparent potential for abuse of compensation arrangements, particularly for closely held businesses, there are specific rules for deducting compensation payments that override the usual accrual rules in some cases. These are summarized below.

If the company uses the cash method of accounting, deductions for compensation cannot be taken before the year in which the compensation is actually paid.

No employer, whether using the cash method or the accrual method, can take a deduction for compensation for services that are not rendered before the end of the taxable year for which the deduction is claimed. Any compensation paid in advance must be deducted pro rata over the period during which services are actually rendered.

Timing of Corporate Deductions for Compensation Payments

The tax rules for timing of deductions distinguish between *current compensation* and *deferred compensation*. If the compensation qualifies as current compensation, then the employer can deduct it in the year in which it is properly accrued to the corporation under the tax accounting accrual rules. If the amount qualifies as deferred compensation, then the employer corporation cannot deduct it until the taxable year of the corporation in which, or with which, ends the taxable year of the employee in which the amount is includable in the employee's income.[3] For example, if an employer sets up a deferred compensation arrangement in 1994 for work performed in 1994 with compensation payable in 1996 and taxable to the employee in 1998, the corporation cannot deduct the compensation amount until 1998.

Whether an amount is considered current or deferred compensation depends on the type of employee:

- For a regular employee—an employee who is not a controlling shareholder or otherwise related to the employer corporation—the IRS takes the position that a plan is deferred compensation if the payment is made more than 2½ months after the end of the taxable year of the corporation.[4] In other words, there is a 2½ month *safe harbor rule*. For example, if a calendar year accrual-method corporation declares and accrues a bonus to an employee before the end of 1994, the employer is entitled to a 1994 deduction for the bonus as long as the bonus is paid before March 15, 1995. The employee would include this bonus in income for 1995. However, if the bonus was paid on April 1, 1995—beyond the 2½ month limit—then, although the employee still must include the amount in income for 1995, the employer's deduction would be delayed until 1995.

- If the employee is related to the corporation—owns more than 50 percent of the corporation, directly or indirectly—then the 2½ month safe harbor rule does not apply.[5] Deductions and income are matched in all cases. So, if a calendar year accrual-method corporation declares and accrues a bonus to its controlling shareholder before the end of 1994, but pays it on February 1, 1995, the corporation cannot deduct the bonus until 1995.

ALTERNATIVES

1. Taxation can be avoided or deferred by various types of noncash compensation plans, which are discussed throughout this book. Some examples of plans that defer taxation, usually until cash is actually received by the employee, are:

   • nonqualified deferred compensation plans

   • qualified pension, profit-sharing, ESOP, 401(k) and similar plans

   • stock option and restricted stock plans

   Compensation options that are completely tax free (no taxation either currently or deferred) include such plans as:

   • health and accident plans (provided that certain nondiscrimination and eligibility requirements are met)

   • disability income plans of certain types

   • dependent care and educational assistance plans (subject to certain maximum limits on amounts that may be excluded from income by employees)

• group term life insurance up to $50,000 (unless the plan discriminates in favor of key employees)

• the pure death benefit amount from any life insurance plan, even if the premium is currently taxable

2. Where the employer may lose a deduction for cash compensation due to a reasonableness of compensation problem, part of the compensation might be provided in a form that is both tax-deferred to the employee and deduction-deferred to the employer. This is discussed further under nonqualified deferred compensation plans. The reasonableness of compensation issue does not arise until the year in which the employer takes the deduction, so deferring the deduction can be helpful.

HOW IS THE PLAN SET UP?

Cash compensation planning is simple and is often not even thought of as a form of employee benefit planning. However, for a complex employment agreement involving cash and other forms of compensation, and in situations where reasonableness of compensation may be an issue, a tax accountant, tax attorney, or financial planner specializing in employee benefits and compensation planning can provide useful guidance.

WHERE CAN I FIND OUT MORE ABOUT IT?

1. IRS publication 334, *Tax Guide for Small Business*, has a simple explanation of the IRS position on the employer's tax treatment of employee pay and benefits. IRS Publication 17, *Your Federal Income Tax*, covers the tax treatment from the employee side. Both these publications are available free from the IRS and are revised annually.

2. Graduate Course: Executive Compensation (GS 842), The American College, Bryn Mawr, PA.

3. CLU/ChFC Courses: Income Taxation (HS 321) and Planning for Business Owners and Professionals (HS 331), The American College, Bryn Mawr, PA.

4. CFP Course: Retirement Planning and Employee Benefits (CFP V), College for Financial Planning, Denver, CO.

QUESTIONS AND ANSWERS

Question — If an executive's compensation is based on profits or sales, will it be deemed unreasonable (and therefore nondeductible) if the company has an unusually good year and the payment is therefore very high?

Answer — The reasonableness of salary is typically tested according to the circumstances existing at the time a profit-oriented compensation agreement is entered into rather than when it is actually paid. Thus, if the percentage or formula itself is not unreasonable at the time the agreement becomes binding on the parties, the actual amount may be deemed reasonable, however high. In addition, the issue of reasonableness can also take into account the element of risk involved to the employee. That is, suppose a company agrees to pay an employee $100,000 plus 25 percent of profits for the upcoming year. The company has an extremely good year and the employee receives $600,000. While a $600,000 guaranteed salary might be deemed unreasonable, the fact that the executive took some risk in accepting a contingent type of compensation may bring the $600,000 amount within the limits of reasonableness.

Question — What is the significance of cash compensation planning for an employee of a S corporation?

Answer — An S corporation is a corporation that has made an election under federal tax law to be taxed essentially as a partnership. In an S corporation, all corporate income and losses are passed through to stockholders in proportion to their stock ownership. Corporate income is taxable to shareholders whether or not it is actually distributed as dividends. For S corporation shareholder-employees, there is no opportunity to defer taxation of their share of current income except through a qualified retirement plan, which is discussed in other chapters of this book.

When S corporation shareholders are also employees of the corporation, as is often the case, it is important to distinguish between compensation for services to the shareholder-employees, as opposed to their share of corporate earnings passed through to them from the corporation. This distinction between compensation and dividend income has a significant effect on the various qualified and nonqualified employee benefit plans discussed later in this book. For example, pension plans and group-term life insurance plans often base their benefits on the employee's compensation income, which does not include any element of income from the corporation that is characterized as a dividend.

FOOTNOTES

1. IRC Section 162(a)(1).
2. Reg. §1.162-8.
3. IRC Section 404(a)(5); Reg. §1.404(a)-12(b)(2).
4. Temp. Reg. §1.404(b)-1(T), Q 2.
5. IRC Sections 267(a)(2), 267(b)(2).

Chapter 29

COMPANY CAR OR REIMBURSEMENT PLAN

WHAT IS IT?

Cars are often an essential business tool for employees or the self-employed. Employers often provide cars or reimburse expenses for business use of personally owned vehicles. Company cars or car expense reimbursement plans are not employee benefits as such, since their purpose is not actually to compensate the employee. However, an employer's policy regarding business use of cars is often viewed as part of the employer's fringe benefit package.

There are three possible types of arrangements between employer and employee regarding business use of cars:

(1) *Company car.* The business can provide the car directly to the employee.

(2) *Reimbursement plan.* The business can reimburse the employee for costs incurred in using the employee's car for business.

(3) *No plan.* The employee or self-employed person can assume the costs of business use of the car and deduct them on his or her tax return. (The employee's salary or other compensation implicitly will reflect the fact that the employee assumes this burden.)

For an employee, the first scenario—the company car—generally provides the best tax result, since it can allow all business related car expenses to be excluded from taxable income in all cases. A reimbursement approach, or the unreimbursed use of the employee's car (scenarios two or three) may not allow full deductions since the employee must deduct car expenses as a "miscellaneous expense." These are subject to a 2% of gross income "floor," as discussed below under "Reporting."

For a self-employed person, all business related car expenses are deductible without a 2% floor.

The tax rules for car expense deductions are inordinately complicated, apparently because Congress and the IRS believe that taxpayers often abuse these provisions. This chapter will summarize the rules for handling deductions and reimbursements for car use.

COMPANY CARS

When is it Indicated?

Because of the administrative complexity of company car plans, company cars are provided primarily where employees use them substantially for business or commuting. They are also provided as a fringe benefit for selected executives in high tax brackets.

Advantages of Company Car Programs

1. The "company car" approach can maximize tax benefits for the employee by avoiding the 2% of adjusted gross income floor for miscellaneous itemized deductions.

2. Companies can maintain maximum control over the cars employees use in business (type of car, maintenance, etc.).

Disadvantages

1. Companies must bear the capital investment costs of car ownership. With the termination of the investment credit and less favorable depreciation rules, such an investment has fewer tax benefits than in past years.

2. Companies must bear substantial administrative costs. In particular, if the car is used for personal purposes to a significant extent, the company must bear the burden of determining the value of personal use if the employee is to avoid the 2% floor limitation on miscellaneous itemized deductions (see the rules discussed below).

Tax Treatment of Employer

In a company car plan, the employer is the owner of the car and is entitled to deductions for depreciation, as well as for any other expenses it actually pays.

Employer reporting. The employer must report the value of car availability to affected employees. There are basically three options for reporting:

1. The employer can report the entire value of car availability on the employee's W-2 and the employee can claim a deduction for business use. In this case, the employee is subject to the 2% floor requirement for miscellaneous itemized deductions;

2. The employer can determine the amount of personal or commuting use and report that only; or

3. If the plan meets the requirements for a written plan as discussed below under "Employee Recordkeeping," the employer can report only commuting use for which the employer has not been reimbursed by the employee.

The employer must withhold Social Security (FICA and FUTA) on the amount reported, but the employer can elect not to withhold federal income tax on this amount.[1] If so, the employee may have to increase withholding or estimated tax payments to avoid an underpayment penalty.

The employer can elect a special accounting rule under which fringe benefits, such as company cars, provided during the last two months of a calendar year can be treated as provided during the following calendar year.[2] If the employer elects this treatment, the employee must follow it also.

Valuation of car availability. The taxable value of a car to an employee is the amount an unrelated third party would charge for its use in an arms-length transaction.[3] A comparable lease value can be used.

Alternatively, the employer can elect one of three special valuation rules; if the employer does so, the employee must use either the same rule that the employer elected or the general arms-length rule.[4] The three special rules are:

• A lease value from the IRS's Annual Lease Value Table.[5]

• A mileage rate of 28 cents per mile (in both 1992 and 1993) for all business use. To use the mileage rate the car must be (1) used more than 50% in business; (2) used each weekday in an employer sponsored commuting pool; or (3) driven at least 10,000 miles during the year and used primarily by employees. Also, to use the mileage rate the car's fair market value cannot exceed $13,700 if the car was first made available in 1992. This amount is adjusted annually for inflation.[6]

• A "commuting valuation rule" of $1.50 per one-way commute or $3.00 per round trip. To use this rule, the employer must have (and enforce) a written policy that the employee must commute in the vehicle and cannot

use the vehicle for other than minimal personal use. This election is unavailable to "control employees" (directors and certain officers and owners — see below).[7]

Tax Treatment of Employee

To the extent used for business, providing a car to an employee is a "working condition fringe" under Code section 132 and, thus, its value is not included in income. (See Chapter 34, Fringe Benefits.) If the car is used for commuting or for personal purposes, the amount included in the employee's income for the year is:

$$\frac{\text{personal/commuting miles}}{\text{total miles}} \times \text{value of car availability}$$

See the "Questions and Answers" section at the end of this chapter for a definition of "commuting."

The employee is entitled to a business deduction for any expenses the employee actually pays for business use of the automobile (such as gasoline, etc.). The employee is also entitled to a deduction to the extent of business use if the employer chooses to report 100% of the car's availability value on the employee's W-2. (In that case, the employee's deduction on Form 2106, line 27 is the business use percentage of the total amount reported on the W-2.)

However, if the employee claims a deduction in either situation, it must be reported on Schedule A as a miscellaneous deduction and is therefore subject to the 2% of adjusted gross income limitation for such deductions. In other words, the most advantageous company car plan will be one which minimizes or eliminates the need for the employee to claim any business expense deductions.

Employee recordkeeping. If the car is used partly for business and partly for personal use, the employee must keep records substantiating the business use. These are necessary either to allow the employer to determine the amount of business use, or to allow the employee to claim a business deduction if the employer reports 100% of the car's value on the employee's W-2 (see above).

However, if the car is used only for business and commuting, with minimal personal use, the employee does not have to keep records if

1. The company has a written policy statement (meeting requirements set out in IRS Regulations) of no personal use except for commuting;

2. the employee is not a control employee (director, officer earning $50,000 or more, employee earning $100,000 or more, 1% or more owner);

3. the employer reports the commuting value on the employee's W-2 to the extent the commuting value is not reimbursed to the employer; and

4. the employee is required, for "bona fide noncompensatory business reasons," to travel to or from work in the vehicle.[8]

REIMBURSEMENT PLANS AND "NO PLANS"

The IRS recognizes three types of reimbursement plans:

1. An *accountable plan* is one that requires the employee (a) to adequately account to the employer for expenses and (b) return any excess reimbursement to the employer.

2. A *nonaccountable plan* is one that *either* (a) does not require the employee to adequately account to the employer, or (b) allows the employee to keep excess reimbursements.

3. *No plan*—that is, the employer does not reimburse directly at all, and the employee is responsible for paying expenses and is entitled to any deduction for them. However, the employer can indirectly reimburse the employee in this situation by increasing salary or paying a bonus.

The IRS table shown in Figure 29.1 summarizes the employer and employee reporting treatment under these three situations.[9]

REPORTING

Employer W-2 reporting requirements have been discussed above.

For an *employee* claiming a car expense deduction, Form 2106 must be filed. Form 2106 and instructions are reproduced at the end of this chapter. The deductible amount determined on Form 2106 is entered on the employee's Schedule A, Form 1040, as a miscellaneous deduction. Miscellaneous deductions, in total, are allowable only to the extent that they exceed 2% of the employee's adjusted gross income.

A *self-employed person* does not file Form 2106. Instead, car expenses are computed and entered as a deduction on Schedule C, "Income From Business or Profession." There is no 2% of adjusted gross income limitation on Schedule C deductions.

WHERE CAN I GET ADDITIONAL INFORMATION?

The rules in this area are extremely complex. A summary of these rules is found in IRS Publication 917, *Business Use of a Car*, and IRS Publication 535, *Business Expenses*. IRS regulations under Code sections 61, 132, and 274 also deal with car expenses.

QUESTIONS AND ANSWERS

Question — Is interest on a car loan deductible as a business expense?

Answer — Interest on a car loan is not deductible by most taxpayers. However, if the taxpayer is self-employed, the interest is deductible as a Schedule C deduction, to the extent of business use of the car.

Question — What types of "getting to work" trips are business expenses as opposed to commuting?

Answer — The IRS has persistently attempted to crack down on alleged abuses in this area. Some current IRS positions:

- Using a car telephone for business calls, carrying tools or instruments, or having advertising signs on your car will not cause a commute to be considered a business trip.

- If you work at two different workplaces, the cost of getting from one place to the other is deductible as a business expense. The cost of traveling between an office at home and other work locations is a deductible business expense *if* the home office is the principal place of business. But a commute to and from home to a part-time job is not a deductible expense.

- You can deduct the round trip cost of travel from your home to a temporary work assignment (i.e., where work is performed on an irregular or short term basis).[10]

Question — How does the car expense deduction differ if the car is used 50% or less (as opposed to more than 50%) for business purposes?

Figure 29.1

REPORTING EMPLOYEE BUSINESS EXPENSES AND REIMBURSEMENTS		
Type of Reimbursement (or Other Expense Allowance) Arrangement	**Employer Reports on Form W-2**	**Employee Shows on Form 2106**
Accountable		
Actual expense reimbursement Adequate accounting and excess returned	Not reported	Not shown
Actual expense reimbursement Adequate accounting and return of excess both required but excess not returned	Excess reported as wages in Box 10. Amount adequately accounted for is reported only in Box 17—it is *not* reported in Box 10.	All expenses and reimbursements reported on Form W-2, Box 17, *only* if some or all of the unreturned excess expenses are claimed.* Otherwise, form is not filed.
Per diem or mileage allowance (up to federal rate) Adequate accounting and excess returned	Not reported	All expenses and reimbursements *only* if excess expenses are claimed.* Otherwise, form is not filed.
Per diem or mileage allowance (exceeds federal rate) Adequate accounting up to the federal rate only and excess not returned	Excess reported as wages in Box 10. Amount up to the federal rate is reported only in Box 17—it is *not* reported in Box 10.	All expenses and reimbursements equal to the federal rate *only* if expenses in excess of the federal rate are claimed.* Otherwise, form is not filed.
Nonaccountable		
Either adequate accounting or return of excess, or both, not required by plan	Entire amount is reported as wages in Box 10.	All expenses*
No reimbursement	Normal reporting of wages, etc.	All expenses*
* Any allowable business expense is carried to line 19 of Schedule A and deducted as a miscellaneous itemized deduction.		

Answer — The amount of the deduction allowed for depreciation is computed in a different, less favorable way if the car is used 50% or less for business.

If the car is used 50% or less for business, the taxpayer must compute depreciation on a straight-line basis over a five-year period. Neither accelerated depreciation nor the Section 179 election to expense[11] can be used.

Question — When can the "standard mileage rate" be used to compute car business expenses?

Answer — Generally, whenever a taxpayer wants to deduct car business expenses, there is a choice between determining the actual expenses and using the simpler standard mileage rate. The mileage rate for both 1992 and 1993 is 28 cents per mile for all business use.[12]

In order to use the standard mileage rate the taxpayer must choose the rate for the first year in which the car was placed in service in business. If actual expenses (using certain accelerated depreciation) are used in the first year, the mileage rate cannot be used in later years. But if the

The Tools and Techniques of Employee Benefit and Retirement Planning

mileage rate is used in the first year the taxpayer can change to actual expenses in later years.

FOOTNOTES

1. IRC Secs. 3121(a)(20), 3402(s).
2. Ann. 85-113, 1985-31 IRB 31; see Reg. §1.61-21(c)(7).
3. Reg. §1.61-21(b)(4).
4. Reg. §1.61-21(b)(4).
5. Reg. §1.61-21(d)(2).
6. Reg. §1.61-21(e)(1)(iii)(A); Rev. Proc. 92-43, 1992-1 CB 873; see IRC Section 280F(d)(7)(i). For automobiles placed in service in tax years before 1992 the fair market value limitations were as follows: 1991 — $13,400; 1985 through 1990 — $12,800. (See Rev. Proc. 91-30, 1991-1 CB 563; Rev. Proc. 90-22, 1990-1 CB 504; and Rev. Proc. 89-64, 1989-2 CB 783.)
7. Reg. §1.61-21(f).
8. Regs. §§1.61-21(f), 1.132-5(f), 1.274-6T(c) and (d).
9. This table is found in IRS Pub. 334 (1992), *Tax Guide for Small Business*, p. 65.
10. Rev. Rul. 90-23, 1990-1 CB 28.
11. Reg. §1.179-1(d).
12. Rev. Proc. 92-104, 1992-2 CB 583; Rev. Proc. 91-67, 1991-2 CB 887.

Form **2106**	**Employee Business Expenses**	OMB No. 1545-0139
Department of the Treasury Internal Revenue Service (O)	▶ See separate instructions. ▶ Attach to Form 1040.	**19**92 Attachment Sequence No. **54**

Your name	Social security number	Occupation in which expenses were incurred

---

Part I **Employee Business Expenses and Reimbursements**

STEP 1 Enter Your Expenses

		Column A Other Than Meals and Entertainment		Column B Meals and Entertainment	
1	Vehicle expense from line 22 or line 29	1			
2	Parking fees, tolls, and local transportation, including train, bus, etc.	2			
3	Travel expense while away from home overnight. including lodging, airplane, car rental, etc. **Do not** include meals and entertainment	3			
4	Business expenses not included on lines 1 through 3. **Do not** include meals and entertainment	4			
5	Meals and entertainment expenses (see instructions)	5			
6	**Total expenses.** In Column A, add lines 1 through 4 and enter the result. In Column B, enter the amount from line 5	6			

Note: *If you were not reimbursed for any expenses in Step 1, skip line 7 and enter the amount from line 6 on line 8.*

STEP 2 Enter Amounts Your Employer Gave You for Expenses Listed in STEP 1

7	Enter amounts your employer gave you that were **not** reported to you in box 10 of Form W-2. Include any amount reported under code "L" in box 17 of your Form W-2 (see instructions) . . .	7			

STEP 3 Figure Expenses To Deduct on Schedule A (Form 1040)

8	Subtract line 7 from line 6	8			
	Note: *If **both columns** of line 8 are zero, **stop here.** If Column A is less than zero, report the amount as income and enter -0- on line 10, Column A. See the instructions for how to report.*				
9	Enter 20% (.20) of line 8, Column B	9			
10	Subtract line 9 from line 8	10			
11	Add the amounts on line 10 of both columns and enter the total here. **Also, enter the total on Schedule A (Form 1040), line 19.** (Qualified performing artists and individuals with disabilities, see the instructions for special rules on where to enter the total.) . . . . ▶	11			

For Paperwork Reduction Act Notice, see instructions.   Cat. No. 11700N   Form **2106** (1992)

Part II   Vehicle Expenses (See instructions to find out which sections to complete.)

Section A.—General Information

			(a) Vehicle 1	(b) Vehicle 2
12	Enter the date vehicle was placed in service	12	/ /	/ /
13	Total miles vehicle was driven during 1992	13	miles	miles
14	Business miles included on line 13	14	miles	miles
15	Percent of business use. Divide line 14 by line 13	15	%	%
16	Average daily round trip commuting distance	16	miles	miles
17	Commuting miles included on line 13	17	miles	miles
18	Other personal miles. Add lines 14 and 17 and subtract the total from line 13.	18	miles	miles

19   Do you (or your spouse) have another vehicle available for personal purposes? . . . . ☐ Yes ☐ No

20   If your employer provided you with a vehicle, is personal use during off duty hours permitted? ☐ Yes ☐ No   ☐ Not applicable

21a Do you have evidence to support your deduction? . . . . ☐ Yes ☐ No

21b If "Yes," is the evidence written? . . . . ☐ Yes ☐ No

Section B.—Standard Mileage Rate (Use this section only if you own the vehicle.)

22	Multiply line 14 by 28¢ (.28). Enter the result here and on line 1. (Rural mail carriers, see instructions.)	22	

Section C.—Actual Expenses

			(a) Vehicle 1		(b) Vehicle 2	
23	Gasoline, oil, repairs, vehicle insurance, etc.	23				
24a	Vehicle rentals	24a				
b	Inclusion amount (see instructions)	24b				
c	Subtract line 24b from line 24a	24c				
25	Value of employer-provided vehicle (applies only if 100% of annual lease value was included on Form W-2—see instructions)	25				
26	Add lines 23, 24c, and 25 . .	26				
27	Multiply line 26 by the percentage on line 15 . . .	27				
28	Depreciation. Enter amount from line 38 below	28				
29	Add lines 27 and 28. Enter total here and on line 1.	29				

Section D.—Depreciation of Vehicles (Use this section only if you own the vehicle.)

			(a) Vehicle 1		(b) Vehicle 2	
30	Enter cost or other basis (see instructions)	30				
31	Enter amount of section 179 deduction (see instructions) .	31				
32	Multiply line 30 by line 15 (see instructions if you elected the section 179 deduction)	32				
33	Enter depreciation method and percentage (see instructions) .	33				
34	Multiply line 32 by the percentage on line 33 (see instructions) . .	34				
35	Add lines 31 and 34	35				
36	Enter the limitation amount from the table in the line 36 instructions	36				
37	Multiply line 36 by the percentage on line 15 . . .	37				
38	Enter the smaller of line 35 or line 37. Also, enter this amount on line 28 above	38				

★U.S.GPO:1992-0-315-283

Chapter 30

DEATH BENEFIT ONLY (DBO) PLAN

WHAT IS IT?

A death benefit only plan, or DBO plan, (sometimes referred to as an "employer-paid death benefit" or a "survivor's income benefit plan") is a plan by which an employer defers employee compensation and pays it to the employee's designated beneficiary at the employee's death. No benefit is payable in any form to the employee during his or her lifetime.

WHEN IS IT INDICATED?

1. The DBO type of plan is most valuable in the case of a highly compensated employee who (1) expects to have a large estate and (2) faces significant federal estate tax liability because the estate will be payable to a nonspouse beneficiary (i.e., will not be able to fully use the estate tax marital deduction). If the covered employee owns 50 percent or less of the corporation's stock and the plan is properly designed, the benefit from a DBO plan is not subject to federal estate tax.

2. The plan can be used for selected employees as a supplement to qualified retirement plan benefits. Under current law, maximum qualified plan benefits to highly compensated employees may be significantly limited; moreover, many highly compensated employees may want to limit qualified plan benefits to limit their exposure to the 15% excess distribution penalty under Code Section 4980A. A DBO plan can provide extra benefits not affected by these limitations.

3. The plan can be used to replace a split dollar plan (see Chapter 49) where the cost to the employee (the P.S. 58 table cost) is increasing rapidly because of age—usually after age 60.

4. A DBO plan can be used for deferring compensation of younger employees with families and a need for insurance; the DBO plan can be converted to full nonqualified deferred compensation with lifetime benefits when the employee's value to the employer has increased to the point where this is indicated.

5. A limited employer-paid death benefit plan can be provided to any employee to fully utilize the $5,000 income tax exclusion that is available.

ADVANTAGES

1. If the covered employee is not a controlling (more than 50%) shareholder, properly designed DBO benefits can be kept out of the deceased employee's estate for federal estate tax purposes.

2. The plan's death benefit provides valuable estate liquidity and a source of immediate and continuing cash to the beneficiary upon the employee's death.

3. The benefit is not taxable to the employee during lifetime.

4. The plan can be financed by the employer through the purchase of life insurance, which provides funds to pay the death benefit and avoids current tax on investment returns under the policy. (Some alternative minimum tax—AMT—on the death proceeds may be payable at the corporate level.)

DISADVANTAGES

1. The entire benefit (except for a $5000 exclusion, if applicable) is income taxable to the beneficiary—as ordinary income. This applies even if the benefit is financed using life insurance.

2. Avoiding estate tax requires very careful plan design and avoidance of technical tax traps, thus limiting flexibility in plan design.

3. The employer-corporation's tax deduction for the plan is deferred until the benefit is paid and the beneficiary includes the payments received in income. The employer must wait to take the deduction even if it sets funds aside in advance (such as through the purchase of a life insurance contract).

DESIGN FEATURES

The plan's benefit formula can take many forms:

1. The simplest formula is a fixed dollar amount—for example, $50,000 for each employee covered under the plan or $10,000 a year for 5 years.

2. Benefits can be based on average compensation over a period of years—for example, the death benefit might be equal to a year's salary averaged over the five years prior to death.

3. Benefits are often related loosely to the death benefit under an insurance policy on the employee's life that is owned by and paid for the employer in order to finance the plan. For example, suppose the employer and employee agree that the employee's salary will be reduced by $100 per month—or agree to extra employer payments of $100 per month—that will be used toward the premiums on an insurance policy. If the $1,200 per year will buy approximately a $50,000 life insurance policy for that employee, given his age and health, then the death benefit under the plan will be $50,000. Note, however, that most planners recommend against tying the benefit directly, dollar for dollar, to a life insurance policy. The plan should be designed to avoid any inference that it is simply the purchase of life insurance for the employee.[1]

TAX IMPLICATIONS

1. The death benefit from the plan will not be included in the deceased employee's estate so long as (1) the plan does not provide any benefits payable during the employee's lifetime and (2) the employee does not have the right to change the beneficiary, once the plan is established.[2]

   In determining whether the plan pays lifetime benefits, the IRS will look beyond the DBO plan itself. Another plan that provides benefits during lifetime can be taken into account for this purpose, even if the employee never actually lives to collect those benefits. Thus, a DBO plan will not be excluded from an employee's estate if the employer also maintains a nonqualified deferred compensation plan providing lifetime benefits. The two plans will be linked together for this purpose and the estate tax exclusion will be lost. However, a *qualified* pension or profit-sharing plan is not taken into account for this purpose, so those plans can be provided in addition to DBOs. After several court cases on the issue, the IRS also now agrees that an employer's long-term disability benefit plan will not "taint" a DBO unless the disability plan requires that the employee be "retired on disability" to receive benefits.

2. Benefits paid to the employee's beneficiary are taxable in full to the beneficiary as ordinary income, except for an exclusion of the first $5000 under Code section 101(b) if the benefit was forfeitable by the employee during life-

time—that is, could be lost because of some event such as quitting before retirement.

3. The benefit payments are deductible to the corporation when paid, so long as they constitute "reasonable compensation" for the services of the deceased employee in prior years. See Chapter 28 of this book for a detailed discussion of the "reasonableness" test. The reasonableness issue is most likely to be raised by the IRS when the decedent was a major or controlling stockholder, particularly if the beneficiary is also a stockholder.

The IRS may also question whether the death benefit payment was "for services actually rendered" by the employee, as required for deductibility under Code section 162. This issue is most likely to be raised where (1) the deceased employee was a majority shareholder or (2) where there was no written agreement to pay the benefit prior to the employee's death. If the corporation's deduction is disallowed for this reason, the amount could be treated as a nondeductible dividend, or in unusual cases as a gift by the corporation, with deductibility limited to $25 under Code section 274(b).

ERISA REQUIREMENTS

1. If the plan is limited to a "select group of management or highly compensated employees," it is exempt from all the provisions of ERISA, except that a simple notification of the Department of Labor is required. A form for this notification is provided in Chapter 16, Nonqualified Deferred Compensation.[3]

2. If the plan covers a broader group of employees, the ERISA vesting, funding, and reporting and disclosure requirements applicable to pension plans may apply. The vesting and funding requirements are discussed in Chapter 23 of this book and the reporting and disclosure requirements are summarized in Appendix A.

ALTERNATIVES

1. Group-term life insurance.

2. Life insurance in a qualified plan.

3. Split dollar life insurance.

4. Individually-owned life insurance (perhaps paid for through additional bonus compensation from the employer).

HOW TO INSTALL A PLAN

Except for a "voluntary" plan (see "Questions and Answers," below), there should always be a written plan adopted under a corporate resolution by the board of directors, in advance of the time that payments are to be made under the plan. The plan document can be simple, but it should specify (a) the amount of the benefit, (b) what employee or group of employees is entitled to it, and (c) should indicate that the benefit is intended as compensation for services to be rendered by the employee. Nothing has to be filed with the government, except for the possible ERISA requirements listed earlier.

WHERE CAN I FIND OUT MORE ABOUT IT?

1. Leimberg, Stephan R., et al., *The Tools and Techniques of Estate Planning*, 9th ed. Cincinnati, OH: The National Underwriter Co., 1992.

2. Richey, Louis R., and Brody, Lawrence, *Comprehensive Deferred Compensation*, 2nd ed. Cincinnati, OH: The National Underwriter Co., Fall 1993.

QUESTIONS AND ANSWERS

Question — Should an employer finance its obligations under a death benefit plan in advance?

Answer — These plans, if provided to a select group of management or highly compensated employees, do not come within the funding requirements of ERISA. However, if they are formally funded, many ERISA requirements come into effect. This is discussed in detail in Chapter 16, Nonqualified Deferred Compensation. Therefore "formal" funding—funding where the employee has rights to the fund ahead of corporate creditors—is undesirable.

Many plans are "informally funded"—a better term to use is "financed"—through the corporation's setting aside an asset or combination of assets that is designed to grow to the point where benefit payments can be made from it. The amount, however, must be available to corporate creditors. The IRS and Department of Labor (which administers parts of ERISA) do not consider this type of arrangement a "fund" for either tax or ERISA purposes.

One of the most common types of investment for this type of fund is life insurance, since the insurance guarantees that adequate amounts will be available even if the employee dies at a relatively young age.

Question — How is life insurance used in a DBO plan?

Answer — As an example, suppose the plan provides a $100,000 death benefit to a key executive. If the employer corporation expects to be in a 34% tax bracket when the benefit is paid, it purchases a $66,000 policy on the employee's life. The corporation is owner and beneficiary of the policy and pays the premiums. The corporation's premium payments are nondeductible. If the employee dies, the corporation pays out $100,000 to the beneficiary and it deducts $100,000 as compensation, which saves $34,000 in taxes. The $66,000 death proceeds from the policy are tax-free to the corporation, assuming no AMT tax. These proceeds reimburse the corporation for its out-of-pocket cost.

If the benefit is to be paid to the beneficiary over a period of years rather than in a lump sum, the amount of life insurance needed by the corporation is further reduced. This is because investment earnings received by the corporation on the policy death proceeds are available to help fund the benefit payments.

Question — What mistakes in plan design or other circumstances would cause an employer death benefit to be included in the employee's estate?

Answer — The promise of the employer to pay a death benefit to a specified beneficiary in return for the employee's promise to continue working for the employer is considered a transfer by the employee of a property right. If the agreement gives the employee the right to change the beneficiary, that retention of the power to designate who will enjoy the "transfer" has been held by the IRS to cause estate tax inclusion.[4]

If the beneficiary's right to receive the death benefit is conditioned on surviving the employee and the employee retained a right to direct the disposition of the property (for example, where the death benefit is payable to the employee's spouse, but if the spouse does not survive the employee, the death benefit is payable to the employee's estate), that reversionary interest may cause inclusion.[5]

If the beneficiary is a revocable trust established by the employee, the right to alter, amend, or revoke the transfer by changing the terms of the trust would cause inclusion.[6]

Another problem relates to an employee who is also a controlling shareholder (more than 50 percent). The IRS argues that such an individual, by virtue of his or her voting control, has the right to alter, amend, revoke, or terminate the agreement. Therefore, the benefit should be includable in the estate of such an individual.[7]

If the employee already has postretirement benefits, such as a nonqualified deferred compensation agreement that pays a retirement benefit, the IRS could claim that the preretirement death benefit plan and the postretirement deferred compensation plan should be considered as a single plan. This would cause the present value of the death benefit to be treated for estate tax purposes as if it were a joint and survivor annuity; the present value of the death benefit would be includable in the deceased employee's estate.[8]

If the death benefit is payable to a trust over which the employee had a general power of appointment, the IRS might argue that he had a power of appointment over the death proceeds, which would result in inclusion for estate tax purposes.[9]

If the death benefit is funded with life insurance on the employee's life and the employee owned the policy or had veto rights over any change in the beneficiary, the IRS would probably attempt to include the policy proceeds because of the employee's incidents of ownership.[10]

Question — What is the advantage of a "voluntary" DBO plan?

Answer — A voluntary DBO is a payment not made under a contract or plan, but rather at the employer's discretion, after the employee's death. Such a payment probably will not be included in the employee's estate because neither the employee nor the beneficiary possessed any right to compel the employer to pay the benefit and, therefore, there was no transfer to the employee.[11] However, if the employee owned more than 50% of the company's stock, the IRS is likely to argue for inclusion, for the reasons discussed above, even in this type of plan.

Even though there is no formal contract in this type of plan, it may be satisfactory since the employee can reasonably expect the benefit to be paid in many cases. However, in other situations, this expectation may not be enough. The benefit then will provide the employee no peace of mind or financial security and a written plan should be adopted.

FOOTNOTES

1. See *Dependahl v. Falstaff Brewing Corp.*, 491 F.Supp. 1188 (E.D. Mo. 1980), aff'd in part, 653 F.2d 1208 (8th Cir.), cert. denied; also Labor Dep't Advisory Opinion 81-11A regarding conditions under which life insurance is not considered a "plan asset."

2. See the question and answer above relating to "mistakes in plan design."

3. See the authorities in footnote 1 for conditions required for the ERISA exemption; also see discussion in Chapter 16. A DBO plan is, in effect, a nonqualified deferred compensation plan for ERISA purposes.

4. IRC Section 2036; Rev. Rul. 76-304, 1976-2 CB 269.

5. IRC Section 2037; *Est. of Fried v. Comm.*, 54 TC 805 (1970), aff'd 445 F.2d 979 (2nd Cir. 1971), cert. denied, 404 U.S. 1016 (1972); Rev. Rul. 78-15, 1978-1 CB 289.

6. IRC Section 2038.

7. *Est. of Levin v. Comm.*, 90 TC 723 (1988). The IRS' position in this case was a reversal of an earlier private ruling, TAM 8701003.

8. IRC Section 2039; *Est. of Fusz v. Comm.*, 46 TC 214 (1966).

9. IRC Section 2041.

10. IRC Section 2042.

11. *Edith L. Courtney v. U.S.*, 84-2 USTC ¶13580 (N.D. Ohio 1984).

Chapter 31

DEPENDENT CARE ASSISTANCE PLAN

WHAT IS IT?

A dependent care assistance plan reimburses employees for day-care and other dependent care expenses or provides an actual day-care center or similar arrangement. If the program is properly structured the day-care expenses are deductible to the employer under Code section 162 and non-taxable to the employee under Code section 129. The dependent care plan can be funded using employee salary reductions under a flexible spending account (FSA) described in Chapter 33.

WHEN IS IT INDICATED?

1. When the employer wants to attract and keep employees who need help in caring for small children or other dependents during working hours.

2. To provide an attractive tax benefit to all employees who have dependent care expenses.

ADVANTAGES

1. The plan can be helpful in recruiting and keeping relatively low-paid employees who have dependent care needs.

2. The employer gets more benefit for each dollar spent on this form of compensation as opposed to cash compensation since benefits paid under a properly structured dependent care assistance program are tax-free to the employees.

3. The plan can be funded partially or entirely through FSA salary reductions.

DISADVANTAGES

1. A fully-subsidized day-care or other dependent care program can be expensive while a partially-subsidized program may not be helpful in attracting and keeping employees.

2. A substantial day-care program may be seen by nonparticipating employees as discriminatory in favor of participating employees.

DESIGN FEATURES

1. Dependent care can be provided in kind.[1] For example, the employer can provide a day-care and after-school center for employees' children right on the business premises or contract with a nearby center to provide day-care.

2. Alternatively, the benefit can be provided through full or partial reimbursement of qualifying employee expenses for dependent care. This is the approach usually taken when the plan is funded through employee salary reductions as part of an FSA plan.

TAX IMPLICATIONS

1. The costs of the plan are deductible to the employer as employee compensation.

2. If the plan meets the requirements of Code section 129, the benefits are non-taxable to participating employees.

3. Section 129(d) imposes a variety of nondiscrimination rules summarized as follows:

   • Contributions or benefits must not discriminate in favor of highly compensated employees, as defined in Code section 414(q) (see Chapter 23).

   • The plan must cover a group that the IRS finds nondiscriminatory. The following may be excluded:

     —employees who have not completed 1 year of service, or attained age 21

     —employees in a collective bargaining unit if there has been good faith bargaining on dependent care

   • Benefits for all employees who own more than 5 percent of the employer, and their spouses and dependents, cannot be more than 25 percent of the total benefits each year.

   • The average benefits provided to employees who are not highly compensated must be at least 55 percent of the average benefits provided to highly compensated employees. In applying this benefit test the employer can elect to exclude employees earning less than $25,000 (or a lower specified amount) if the plan is funded through salary reductions.

Failure to meet these rules makes plan benefits taxable, but only to "highly compensated" participants.[2]

4. Dependent care assistance eligible under Section 129 can be provided only to (a) a child under 13 for whom the employee-taxpayer is entitled to take a dependency deduction on the income tax return or (b) a taxpayer's dependent or spouse who is physically or mentally unable to care for himself.[3]

5. The amount of benefits excluded annually by the employee—the value of the services provided directly plus any employer reimbursements of expenses paid by the employee—cannot be more than the employee's earned income or, if the employee is married, the lesser of the employee's or spouse's earned income. Furthermore, the total amount excluded by the employee is limited to $5,000 annually, or $2,500 if the employee is married and files a separate return.[4]

6. Qualifying expenses must be for care alone, not for education above the kindergarten level. Following are items that qualify as care:[5]

• full preschool and kindergarten expenses (full tuition and fees for these programs)

• after-school programs for children under 13

• summer camp for children under 13 (however, expenses for overnight summer camp do not qualify)

• cost of a housekeeper/sitter for children or other dependents cared for at home. (However, payments to a child under 19 or to a child that the employee is entitled to a personal exemption for do not qualify.)

7. A dependent care assistance plan must be in writing.[6]

8. In order to claim the exclusion for dependent care assistance benefits under Section 129 the taxpayer must report the correct name, address and taxpayer identification number of the care provider on his tax return.[7]

ERISA AND OTHER REQUIREMENTS

The plan is considered a "welfare benefit plan" for ERISA purposes. This requires a written plan document, a summary plan description (SPD) explaining the plan that is provided to

employees, a designated plan administrator and a formal claims procedure. (Appendix A details these requirements more fully.) Further, Section 129 requires that the employer provide each employee with an annual statement of the expenses incurred in providing the prior year's benefits by January 31 of each year.[8]

ALTERNATIVES

One alternative to dependent care assistance programs is the informal coverage of these expenses for selected employees through extra compensation or bonuses. However, this extra compensation is fully taxable to the employee.

HOW TO INSTALL A PLAN

ERISA and the Code require a written plan and an SPD but no governmental approval. Some employers may want to obtain an IRS ruling stating that the plan complies with Section 129 if there are plan features, such as liberal benefits or limited employee eligibility, that raise compliance questions.

WHERE CAN I FIND OUT MORE ABOUT IT?

1. IRS Publication 503, *Child and Dependent Care Expenses*, (annual IRS publication available at local IRS office).

2. IRS Publication 334, *Tax Guide for Small Business* (annual IRS publication available at local IRS office).

3. Beam, Burton T., Jr. and John J. McFadden, *Employee Benefits*, 3rd ed. Chicago, IL: Dearborn Financial Publishing, Inc., 1992.

QUESTIONS AND ANSWERS

Question — Can an unincorporated business have a dependent care plan covering partners or proprietors as well as regular employees?

Answer — Yes. Section 129 allows self-employed individuals—partners or proprietors—to be treated as employees under the plan.[9] As with regular employees, dependent care benefits are excluded from the income of partners or proprietors who are covered by the plan.

Question — Can employees who receive tax-free benefits under a dependent care plan also use the dependent care tax credit of Code section 21?

Answer — Only if the employee receives benefits from the plan that are taxable to the employee or makes additional expenditures not paid for by the plan. Tax-free benefits from an employer dependent care plan are not eligible for the Section 21 tax credit. Additionally, the amount of expenses eligible for the dependent care credit must be offset dollar for dollar by the amount of expenses that the taxpayer excludes from income under the dependent care plan. For example, if a taxpayer has $2,400 of eligible dependent care expenses during the year and the employer's plan reimbursed him for $1,000 of the expenses only the remaining $1,400 would be eligible for the dependent care credit.[10]

Question — How can an employee decide between using the employer's dependent care assistance plan and using the dependent care tax credit (Section 21)?

Answer — In the past, employees could get a tax break on as much as $9,800 of child care expenses by combining the child care credit with a company's dependent care assistance plan. However, current law prohibits "double dipping" by taxpayers who pay child care expenses qualifying for the child care credit and who participate in a company sponsored dependent care assistance program.[11]

An employee's tax benefit from the child care credit is reduced to the extent he or she uses a company plan to cover expenses. Specifically, the maximum amount of qualifying expenses ($2,400 for one child; $4,800 for two or more children) a taxpayer may use for the child care credit is reduced dollar-for-dollar by amounts paid through a company plan. For example, if a company plan reimburses an employee with two children $4,000 for child care expenses, only $800 ($4,800 - $4,000) of additional child care expenses paid by the employee will qualify for the child care credit.

As a result, all employees who have child care expenses exceeding $4,800 and who may participate in a company sponsored dependent care assistance program must choose between the company plan and the child care credit.

The choice depends on the employee's tax rate and whether or not amounts that would otherwise be allocated to child care under the company plan can be allocated to other benefits. For example, if the company dependent care assistance plan is part of a cafeteria plan or FSA salary-reduction plan where the employees can choose to allocate the amount that would otherwise go to child care expenses to fund other benefits such as medical expenses, health insurance premiums, or life insurance, the employees will generally be better off if they elect benefits other than child

care reimbursements from their company plan. In this way they still get the full benefit of the company plan and may take the child care credit for the child care expenses they pay with after-tax dollars separately from the plan.

However, if the company plan does not allow the employees to use the amount that would otherwise go to child care expenses to fund other benefits, or for those employees who cannot fully use the other benefits that may be elected, the choice between the company plan and the child care credit depends on their tax rate (taxable income), filing status, and adjusted gross income.

The child care credit is equal to 30 percent of qualified expenses for persons with adjusted gross income (AGI) of $10,000 or less. The credit is reduced by one percentage point for each $2,000 of AGI above $10,000 with a floor of 20 percent for persons with income over $28,000.[12] Therefore, for each dollar of qualifying child care expenses the tax savings range from 30 cents to 20 cents for AGIs ranging from $10,000 to $28,000 and above.

In contrast, if child care expenses are reimbursed through a company salary-reduction plan, the tax savings will depend on the person's tax rate, which depends on his or her taxable income and filing status. Employees whose taxable income falls in the 15 percent tax bracket will save only 15 cents on each qualifying dollar of child care expenses reimbursed through a company plan. Consequently, they should clearly opt out of the company plan and use the child care credit since they will save between 5 and 15 cents on the dollar. However, if taxable income falls in the 28 percent or 33 percent bracket, the employees will save either 28 cents or 33 cents on each qualifying dollar of child care expenses reimbursed through the company plan. For these levels of taxable income the tax savings with the company plan will always equal or exceed the tax savings from the child care credit.

FOOTNOTES

1. IRC Sections 129(a)(1), 129(e)(8).
2. IRC Section 129(d)(1).
3. IRC Sections 129(e)(1), 21(b).
4. IRC Sections 129(a)(2), 129(b)(1).
5. IRC Sections 21(b)(1). 21(b)(2), 129(c).
6. IRC Section 129(d)(1).
7. IRC Section 129(e)(9).
8. IRC Section 129(d)(7).
9. IRC Sections 129(e)(3), 129(e)(4).
10. IRC Sections 21(c), 129(e)(7).
11. IRC Section 21(c).
12. IRC Section 21(a).

Chapter 32

EDUCATIONAL ASSISTANCE PLAN

WHAT IS IT?

An employer's educational assistance plan pays or reimburses employees for expenses incurred in educational programs aimed at improving job skills. Some broader plans provide assistance for education even if not job-related, or for education for children or dependents of employees.

ADVANTAGES

1. Employers benefit from improvement in employee skills through education that the employee might not be able to afford otherwise.

2. Properly structured job-related educational benefits are not taxable income to employees.

DISADVANTAGES

1. A program that is too broad may simply train an employee for a job with another employer.

2. Educational benefits beyond certain limits are taxable as compensation to the employee.

TAX IMPLICATIONS

1. An individual can deduct educational expenses—including not only tuition but incidental expenses such as transportation, books, and supplies, if the education:

   (a) maintains or improves a skill required in the individual's employment, or

   (b) is expressly required by the individual's employer as a condition of keeping the individual's job.

   Educational expenses are not deductible if they do not meet these requirements. The IRS specifies that the costs for two types of education are not deductible: (a) education required to meet the minimum qualification requirements for an individual's present employment and (b) education that qualifies the individual for a new trade or business (see Figure 32.1).[1]

Some examples will illustrate this:

   • Suppose an individual who has not completed a law degree begins working with a law firm on the understanding that the degree will be completed. Expenses for completing the law degree are nondeductible, because they are incurred simply to meet the minimum qualification requirements of the individual's current job.

   • For a tax accountant in an accounting firm, law school expenses could be deductible if the accountant can prove to the IRS that the education will maintain or improve the accountant's skills as a tax expert.

   • For an English teacher, expenses for law school probably would not be deductible since they would not maintain or improve skills in the teacher's existing job and would be seen as training to qualify in a new trade or business.

2. An individual can claim these deductions only as employee business expenses, so (1) they are available only if the individual itemizes deductions and (2) they are subject to the 2%-of-adjusted-gross-income "floor" on total miscellaneous deductions.[2]

3. Expenses for travel are not deductible as educational expenses.[3]

4. Employer reimbursements to employees for educational expenses are deductible by the employer as compensation.[4]

5. To the extent that the employer's deduction for reimbursements is matched by a corresponding deduction at the employee level, the educational assistance plan provides the employee with a form of tax-free income.

   Usually an employer's educational assistance plans are designed to reimburse only the deductible expenses, both to provide the tax benefit and because the deductible expenses will be the ones that the employer will be most interested in subsidizing. For example, it does not make sense for an employer to pay for education that qualifies an employee for a career with a different company.

6. Section 127 of the Code allows an employer to provide a broader range of educational reimbursements to employ-

Figure 32.1

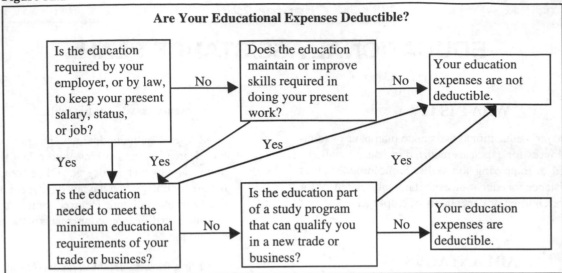

Are Your Educational Expenses Deductible?

Is the education required by your employer, or by law, to keep your present salary, status, or job? — No → Does the education maintain or improve skills required in doing your present work? — No → Your education expenses are not deductible.

Is the education needed to meet the minimum educational requirements of your trade or business? — No → Is the education part of a study program that can qualify you in a new trade or business? — No → Your education expenses are deductible.

ees on a tax-free basis. Congress has allowed Section 127 to expire several times in the past, then revived it. Currently, it is in effect for taxable years beginning on or before June 30, 1992.

Section 127 plans- "qualified educational assistance plans"- currently have the following characteristics:

• Under the plan, an employer can make payments up to a maximum of $5,250 annually for tuition, fees, books, supplies, and equipment for educational programs for an employee. Payments under the plan are deductible by the employer and excluded from the employee's gross income. The employer may pay these expenses directly, provide the education directly, or reimburse employees for expenditures they make.

• Courses taken by employees and covered under the plan need not be job related. However, course benefits may not involve sports, games, or hobbies unless they relate to the employer's business.

• Section 127 provides no tax benefits for tools or supplies retained by the employee after completion of the course or for meals, lodging, or transportation.

• A Section 127 plan must be in writing. However, it need not be funded in advance and does not have to be approved in advance by the IRS.

• A Section 127 plan must not discriminate in coverage in favor of highly compensated employees. In addition, there is a nondiscrimination rule for benefits: not more than five percent of the total amount

paid or incurred annually by the employer for educational assistance under the plan may be provided for employees who are shareholders or owners of at least five percent of the business.

• Eligible employees must be notified of the program.

7. Employer reimbursements of employee expenses for educating children or other dependents are taxable income to the employee and deductible as compensation by the employer. For a highly compensated employee, such payments may create a question as to whether the overall compensation meets the reasonableness of compensation test for deductibility. This test is discussed in Chapter 28.

ERISA REQUIREMENTS

An employer's educational assistance plan may be considered a "welfare benefit plan" for ERISA purposes, which means that the plan should be in writing, with a written claims procedure, and a Summary Plan Description (SPD) must be furnished to employees. If the plan is funded (most plans are not) additional requirements may apply. The ERISA rules are summarized in Appendix A.

HOW TO INSTALL A PLAN

There should be a written plan, especially if the plan covers more than a few employees, but the document can be a simple one. An SPD should be drafted and distributed to meet ERISA requirements. No government approval is required, nor is it usually recommended. A request for an IRS ruling can be made if there are any tax questions.

WHERE CAN I FIND OUT MORE ABOUT IT?

1. IRS Publications 17, *Your Federal Income Tax*, and 508, *Educational Expenses*, cover the deduction for educational expenses. They are revised annually and available from the IRS.

2. Beam, Burton T., Jr. and John J. McFadden, *Employee Benefits*, 3rd ed. Chicago, IL: Dearborn Financial Publishing, Inc., 1992.

QUESTIONS AND ANSWERS

Question — What is an "educational benefit trust" and how is it used?

Answer — An educational benefit trust is an arrangement under which an employer creates a trust fund to pay educational expenses for dependents of employees cov-ered under the plan. Typically, this is used as an executive benefit, but it can also be provided to a larger group of employees or all employees.

As a result of changes in the tax law, there is little, if any, tax advantage to this type of plan. The employer can deduct amounts paid into the trust fund for plan purposes. However, under Code Section 419, the deduction is limited to the amount of benefits provided during the year. In other words, the employer cannot accelerate deductions by setting up the trust fund rather than paying benefits directly.

To the employee, benefits are taxable when they are paid to dependents for educational expenses. The amount paid to an employee's dependent is considered additional compensation income to the employee.

FOOTNOTES

1. Reg. §1.162-5.
2. IRC Section 67.
3. IRC Section 274(m)(2).
4. Reg. §1.162-10.

Chapter 33

FLEXIBLE SPENDING ACCOUNT

WHAT IS IT?

A flexible spending account, or FSA, is a cafeteria plan—a plan under which employees can choose between cash and specified benefits—that is funded through salary reductions elected by employees each year.

WHEN IS IT INDICATED?

1. When an employer wants to expand employee benefit choices without significant extra out-of-pocket costs (or possibly realize some actual dollar savings). Some situations where benefit choices are desirable:

    • Where many employees have employed spouses with duplicate medical coverage

    • Where employees contribute to health insurance costs

    • Where the employer's medical plans have large deductibles or coinsurance (co-pay) provisions

    • Where employees are nonunion (collective bargaining units prefer uniform benefit packages)

    • Where there is a need for benefits that are difficult to provide on a group basis, such as dependent care.

2. Where costs of an employee benefit plan such as health insurance have increased and the employer must impose additional employee cost sharing in the form of (a) increased employee contributions, (b) deductibles, or (c) coinsurance, the FSA approach minimizes employee outlay since the FSA converts after-tax employee expenditures to before tax expenditures.

3. The FSA provides a tax benefit for employees (tax exclusion for various benefits) that is not available through any other plan.

4. Because of administrative costs, FSAs are usually impractical for businesses with only a few employees. Most FSAs involve employers with 25 or more employees, but the plan could be considered for as few as 10 employees.

5. FSA benefits cannot be provided to self-employed persons—partners or sole proprietors.

ADVANTAGES

1. Since it is a type of cafeteria plan, the plan provides employees some degree of choice as to whether to receive compensation in cash or benefits, and what form the benefits will take.

2. The FSA is funded through employee salary reductions, which requires no extra outlay by the employer, except for administrative costs.

3. The plan may result in a reduction in some employment taxes paid by the employer, since taxable payroll is reduced.

4. Salary reductions elected by employees to fund nontaxable benefits under the plan are not subject to federal income taxes.

5. The list of potential nontaxable benefits available from the plan is large and includes many benefits that employers might not otherwise provide to employees—for example, dependent care.

DISADVANTAGES

1. An FSA must meet all of the complex nondiscrimination requirements for cafeteria plans (see Chapter 27). Monitoring compliance with these rules raises administrative costs. Also, particularly in some closely held corporations, there could be a loss of tax benefits to highly compensated employees if the nondiscrimination rules are not met.

2. FSAs require employees to evaluate their personal and family benefit situations and file a timely election form every year. They must estimate—at the end of each year—the amount that will be required for covered expenses in the following year. This is sometimes both confusing and difficult, and some employees may not fully utilize the plan because of the perceived complexity or paperwork involved. Others may not want to risk the forfeiture required of any funds left in the account at the end of the year (see number 6 in the discussion below).

3. The plan could result in "adverse selection" that would ultimately raise benefit costs. For example, dental plan

options might be selected primarily by employees who know that they will soon undergo a regime of expensive dental procedures. This will tend to raise the cost of dental insurance made available by the employer to fund dental benefits.

4. Administrative costs are greater than in a fixed benefit plan.

5. As discussed in the "Questions and Answers," below, IRS proposed regulations require an employer to be "at risk" regarding the total annual amount an employee elects to allocate to health benefits under his or her FSA.

HOW IT WORKS—AND AN EXAMPLE

These are the basic features of an FSA plan:

1. The employer decides what benefits are to be provided in the FSA and adopts written plans to provide these benefits, if the plans are not already in place. (The design of these individual plans is generally covered in separate chapters of this book.) For example, the employer might decide that the FSA will allow employee salary reductions to be applied to

• the employee's share of health insurance premiums

• medical expenses not covered under the health insurance plan (this requires the employer to adopt a medical reimbursement plan)

• expenses of dependent care (the employer must adopt a dependent care assistance plan)

2. The employer advises employees to review their benefit needs toward the end of each year and estimate their next year's expenses for items covered in the plan.

3. Before the end of the calendar year, employees file with the employer a written election to reduce salary by the amount they choose (the amount they estimate they will spend on covered benefits) and allocate it among the benefits in the plan. A sample enrollment form is reproduced in Figure 33.1 at the end of this chapter. The chosen salary reduction goes into a "benefit account." The benefit account is a book account—it is not actually funded by the employer in most cases.

4. Each employee keeps a record of expenses in each benefit category and makes a claim on the plan for reimbursement. Claims are usually made on a quarterly basis for administrative convenience. (The employee does not have to make a written claim for expenses that would otherwise be a payroll deduction, such as the employee share of health insurance. Such claims are handled automatically by the plan.) A sample claim form appears in Figure 33.2 at the end of this chapter.

5. The employer issues checks to employees for reimbursement. These reimbursements are free of income tax.

6. At the end of the year, if anything is left in the employee's benefit account, it is forfeited. It cannot be carried over to the next year. This feature requires careful planning by the employee.

As an example, suppose employee Patella earns $40,000 per year and is covered under an FSA having the features noted in this discussion. On December 31, 1993, having reviewed his probable benefit needs for 1994, he files an FSA election with his employer to reduce his 1994 salary by $2,000. The $2,000 will go into his FSA benefit account and he elects to allocate it as follows:

• $600 ($50 per month) to cover his share of health insurance premiums

• $1,000 for medical expenses covered under the medical reimbursement plan but not the health insurance (Patella anticipates orthodontic expenses during 1994 for his daughter Rubella)

• $400 for expenses under the dependent care plan (Patella plans to send his daughter, age 11, to summer day camp costing about $400)

If Patella's expenses run as expected, the FSA will have turned $2,000 of nondeductible after-tax expenditures into before-tax payments, saving Patella the federal income tax on $2,000, and saving the employer the employment taxes on $2,000 of compensation paid.

If Patella's covered expenses are higher, he will simply lose the tax benefits that would have been available if he had made a larger salary reduction election.

However, if Patella's expenses are less than predicted, he will actually forfeit the amount remaining in his FSA benefit account at the end of the year. The amount forfeited in effect reverts to the employer, since it represents compensation that will not have to be paid.

DESIGN FEATURES

1. An FSA is a cafeteria plan under Code section 125, and it must meet all the complex rules prohibiting discrimina-

tion in favor of highly compensated employees and prohibiting a concentration of benefits among the key employees. These rules are discussed in detail in Chapter 27, Cafeteria Plan.

In general, these rules will be satisfied if all employees are allowed to participate and if benefits, as a percentage of compensation, are approximately equal for all employees. If the employer wants more selective coverage and benefits compliance with the nondiscrimination rules must be carefully analyzed.

The cost of noncompliance with the rules is not disqualification of the plan as a whole. What happens is that tax benefits for highly compensated employees—only—are lost.

2. What benefits can be provided in the plan? These are the same as for cafeteria plans in general. Thus, employers can include the following types of benefits in an FSA arrangement:

• Health insurance (the FSA can be used to cover the employee-paid portion or even the entire cost of the insurance).

• Medical reimbursement, including anything not covered in the health insurance plan—dental care, eyeglasses, hearing aids, etc. The potentially wide range of this option is discussed further in Chapter 44 of this book.

• Group term life insurance on the employee's life. Insurance on the employee's life up to $50,000 is a tax-free option. Additional insurance on the employee is generally a taxable option.

• Disability insurance premiums under an employer group arrangement (disability *benefits* under such a plan are taxable—see Chapter 43).

• Legal services provided under a group legal services plan

• Contributions to a Section 401(k) plan

• Extra vacation days (but unused days cannot be cashed out or carried over to a subsequent year).

Some benefits are specifically prohibited by the Code for an FSA or other cafeteria plan. These are—

— scholarships and fellowships under Code section 117

— educational assistance provided under a plan governed by Code section 127

— employee discounts (for example, those for department store employees), no-additional-cost services (for example, standby airline travel for airline employees) and other fringe benefits provided under Code section 132[1]

—deferred compensation, other than under a Section 401(k) plan[2]

3. On the practical side, the critical design feature is *adequate employee communication* so that employees use the plan and the employer's efforts in instituting the plan pay off in employee appreciation.

TAX IMPLICATIONS

1. Employee salary reductions applied to nontaxable benefits are not subject to income tax. Highly compensated employees may be taxed on these benefits if the plan is discriminatory. Further, key employees may lose the tax benefits of an FSA if the percentage of benefits going to them is too large. See Chapter 27, Cafeteria Plan, for more detail.

   Salary reductions, to be effective for tax purposes, must be made before the compensation is earned. IRS regulations require FSA elections to be made annually before the beginning of the calendar year for which the salary reduction is to be effective.[3]

2. The employer gets a tax deduction for the amounts it pays to reimburse employees for covered expenditures.

3. The employer's payroll subject to payroll taxes is reduced by the amount of any employee salary reductions under an FSA.[4] Payroll taxes include:

   (a) FICA (social security),

   (b) FUTA (federal unemployment tax),

   (c) state unemployment taxes, and

   (d) workers' compensation.

   This potential reduction in payroll taxes is subject to two cautionary notes. First, state laws relating to unemployment taxes and workers' compensation may vary and should be checked. Second, FICA and FUTA may be payable on amounts that are contributed to a Section 401(k) plan as part of an FSA arrangement.[5]

ERISA REQUIREMENTS

The ERISA requirements are those applicable to the various individual plans—health insurance, dependent care, etc.—that are part of the FSA arrangement. Generally, these plans are exempt from any requirement of advance funding and follow the rules applicable to welfare benefit plans under ERISA (see Appendix A). Written plans, a summary plan description, and a formal claims procedure are required under ERISA.

HOW TO INSTALL A PLAN

Suppose an FSA plan is to be effective January 1, 1993. The essential step before this date is to obtain effective employee salary reduction elections. Thus, the plan must be designed, communicated to employees, and the salary reduction forms must be designed and furnished to employees before January 1, 1993. (See enrollment form in Figure 33.1 at the end of this chapter.)

Formal plan documents for the FSA and for each plan included in the FSA—medical reimbursement, dependent care, etc. must be drafted and adopted by the employer. (All these can be incorporated in a single document but separate documents are often convenient.) To be effective January 1, 1993, a corporation would have to formally adopt these documents, with a written resolution of the board of directors, before the end of the corporation's taxable year in which the effective date—January 1, 1993—falls. For example, a calendar-year corporation would have to formally adopt these plans no later than December 31, 1993.

WHERE CAN I FIND OUT MORE ABOUT IT?

Fundamentals of Employee Benefit Programs, 3rd ed. Washington, DC: Employee Benefit Research Institute, 1987.

QUESTIONS AND ANSWERS

Question — Is an employee "locked-in" for a full year to his or her FSA salary reduction amount and benefit allocation, or can it be changed during the year?

Answer — Changes are not generally allowed unless there are major life events that affect benefit needs. The regula-

tions list marriage, divorce, death of a spouse or child, birth of a child or addition of a dependent, and loss of a spouse's job as some of the permitted qualifying events.[6]

Question — Since FSA salary reductions eliminate Social Security taxes on the salary reduction, are Social Security benefits also affected?

Answer — If an FSA salary reduction reduces an employee's wages below the taxable wage base for the year ($57,600 for 1993), then Social Security benefit credit for that year will also be reduced. This probably will not reduce an employee's ultimate Social Security retirement benefit by very much, but it may deter FSA participation by lower-paid employees. It is advisable for employers to investigate exactly how much effect this will have and communicate it to employees to allay any unreasonable fears they may have. Also, for a relatively low cost, employers can provide an insurance or annuity benefit to compensate employees for this loss.

Question — Are FSA salary reductions recognized for state or local income tax purposes?

Answer — If state or local income taxes are based on federal taxable income—as most are—then salary reductions are generally effective for state tax purposes. However, state and local laws vary. For example, as of 1993 the state income tax laws of Alabama, Arkansas, New Jersey, and Pennsylvania do not recognize salary reduction elections.

Question — Is there a dollar limit on annual salary reductions in an FSA plan?

Answer — There is no dollar limit applicable to FSA salary reductions as such. However, the separate employee benefit plans that are part of an FSA program may have their own dollar limits. For example, there is a $5,000 annual limit for dependent care plans (see Chapter 31). Also, employers often limit salary reductions to a relatively small amount in order to meet the nondiscrimination rules of Section 125. If the plan permits large salary reductions, highly compensated employees are likely to use the plan disproportionately. Regulations require the plan to specify a maximum dollar limit or a maximum percentage of compensation.[7] For further discussion see Baxendale and Coppage, "Choosing Between the Child Care Credit and Flexible Accounts," *Taxation for Accountants*, May, 1993.

Question — If an employee uses up his or her benefit account allocated to one form of benefit, can amounts allocated to another form of benefit be reallocated?

Answer — The IRS takes the position that there can be no such "crossover" of benefit allocations during the year.[8] This emphasizes the importance (and difficulty) of careful employee planning in making the annual salary reduction election and allocation of the benefit account.

Question — What are the implications of the IRS position that an employer must be "at risk" with respect to health benefits in an FSA?

Answer — Proposed regulations issued in 1989 state that health care reimbursements under an FSA will not be tax free if the plan eliminates all "risk of loss" to an employer.[9] In effect, this forces the employer to be a health insurer with respect to the health care reimbursement aspect of the FSA.

For example, suppose a law firm's FSA plan covers employee Ben DeLaws. Ben elects in December 1993 to reduce his 1994 salary by $100 per month (a total of $1,200 for 1994) and use the salary reduction amount for health benefits under the FSA plan. In February, 1994, Ben's daughter incurs orthodontia expenses of $1,000 which are covered under the plan. Can the plan reimburse Ben in March 1994 only the $200 that he has contributed so far, and reimburse the remaining $800 as Ben makes further salary reduction FSA contributions over the rest of 1994? The IRS says no; Ben is entitled to reimbursement of the entire $1,000 (at the subsequent claims period under the plan). If Ben quits his job and goes to work for another firm in June, 1994, he will never have contributed enough to the FSA to cover this reimbursement and his prior employer will have to cover the difference. This is what the IRS means by "risk of loss."

The IRS view is questionable and probably will be litigated eventually. Since this regulation is a proposed regulation, taxpayers who do not follow it are not subject to criminal or negligence penalties. However, if it is made permanent the IRS will undoubtedly enforce it retroactively. It appears advisable for employers to recognize the rights of employees to receive full current reimbursement of FSA claims even before their FSA accounts have accumulated enough to pay the claim, but the employer may not have to pay the full amount in one installment unless the employee specifically requests immediate full payment.

FOOTNOTES

1. IRC Section 125(f).
2. IRC Section 125(d)(2).
3. Prop. Reg. §1.125-1, Q&A 6, Q&A 15.
4. IRC Sections 3121(a)(5)(G), 3306(b)(5)(G). Note that there is no exception for salary reductions under cafeteria plans as there is for 401(k) and 403(b) salary reductions.
5. IRC Sections 3121(v)(1)(A), 3306(r)(1)(A).
6. Prop. Reg. §1.125-2, Q&A 6.
7. Prop. Reg. §1.125-2, Q&A 3.
8. See Prop. Reg. §1.125-1, Q&A 17.
9. Prop. Reg. §1.125-2, Q&A 7.

Figure 33.1

(Name of Employer)
FLEXIBLE SPENDING ACCOUNT (FSA)
ENROLLMENT - 1994

Each employee must complete this form before December 31, 1993 and return it to the employer.

Name: _____   Social Security No. _____

( )NO, I do not wish to enroll in the FSA for 1994. I understand that I cannot enroll at any other time during the 1994 Plan Year. I also understand that since I am not enrolling in the FSA, my premium contribution for medical and dental coverages will continue to be deducted from my pay on an after-tax basis.

( )YES, I elect to enroll in the FSA, effective January 1, 1994, and authorize the employer to reduce my pay by the following amount(s):

*my premium(s) for health insurance coverage .... $_____
*an allocation for anticipated health expenses .... $_____
*an allocation for dependent care expenses (not to exceed $5,000) .... $_____

Total (Not to exceed $[0,000]) .... $_____

I understand that by electing to pay for my health insurance coverage through the FSA, my premiums will automatically be deducted from my pay on a before-tax basis. I authorize the employer to process these premium contributions as an automatic FSA reimbursement throughout the 1994 Plan Year.

I understand that the salary reduction I have elected for health expenses are recorded separately from the salary reduction for dependent care costs. If there is money recorded in one account at the end of the year, it is not transferable to meet expenses in the other category.

I understand that I cannot suspend, increase or decrease my salary reductions during the 1994 Plan Year unless I experience a major "life event" as described in federal regulations.

I understand that any money remaining in my Flexible Spending Account at the end of the 1994 Plan Year will be forfeited by me.

I have received a written explanation of the Flexible Spending Account. I understand that the employer cannot be responsible for any tax liabilities which may subsequently occur as a result of my FSA participation.

_____   _____
Your signature   Date

Flexible Spending Account

Figure 33.2

(Name of Employer)
FLEXIBLE SPENDING ACCOUNT (FSA)
EMPLOYEE REIMBURSEMENT REQUEST

INSTRUCTIONS:

When to file a reimbursement request form:

1. You need not submit a reimbursement request form for your portion, if any, of medical and dental insurance premiums that are subject to payroll withholding.

2. This form is to be filed every time you request reimbursement under the FSA for *eligible health expenses* or for *dependent care expenses*. Please submit your *original* bills or cancelled checks with this form. Legible photocopies are acceptable.

HEALTH EXPENSES

I authorize reimbursement of the health expenses indicated below through my FSA. I certify that, to the best of my knowledge, the expenses I am submitting would qualify as tax deductible medical expenses. I further certify that these expenses are not reimbursable under any other plan, including a plan of another employer that covers me, my spouse or another member of my family.

(1) DESCRIPTION OF ELIGIBLE EXPENSES	(2) DATE INCURRED	(3) TOTAL AMOUNT OF BILL	(4) AMOUNT PAID BY ANY OTHER PLAN

(5) FSA Col. (3) - Col. (4)	(6) EXPENSES FOR: NAME (If dependent, relationship and date of birth)

Figure 33.2 (continued)

DEPENDENT CARE EXPENSES

I authorize reimbursement of the expenses indicated below through my FSA. I certify that, to the best of my knowledge, the expenses I am submitting meet the requirements of employment-related dependent care expenses. If married, I further certify that these expenses, together with any other dependent day care expenses already reimbursed through FSA, do not exceed the lesser of my earned income or the earned income of my spouse. I also certify that my spouse was employed on the date these expenses were incurred.

(1)	(2)	(3)	(4)
NAME OF INDIVIDUAL OR ORGANIZATION PROVIDING DEPENDENT CARE SERVICE	PROVIDER SOCIAL SECURITY OR I.D. NUMBER	DATE INCURRED	TOTAL AMOUNT OF BILL
_____	_____	_____	_____
_____	_____	_____	_____
_____	_____	_____	_____
_____	_____	_____	_____

(5)	(6)
FSA CLAIM	EXPENSES FOR CARE OF: (Name, relationship, age)
_____	_____
_____	_____
_____	_____
_____	_____

Employee Name: _____ Social Security No. _____

_____

Employee Signature   Date

Plan
Administrator _____   Date _____

Chapter 34

"FRINGE" BENEFITS (SECTION 132)

WHAT ARE THEY?

Fringe benefits are noncash compensation benefits to employees. Most miscellaneous fringe benefits not discussed in other chapters of this book are governed by Code section 132, which determines whether the benefits are taxable to employees. This chapter covers:

- employee discounts

- no-additional-cost services

- company cafeterias and meal plans

- parking

- gyms and athletic facilities

- "working condition fringes"

- "de minimis fringes"

EMPLOYEE DISCOUNTS

Employers in the retailing business often provide employees with discounts on merchandise sold in the employer's stores. For example, a department store may provide a 10% discount on clothing purchased by employees.

Advantages

1. Discounts on merchandise are almost as valuable as cash to employees, but are very inexpensive for the employer because the employer can still make a profit on the items sold (or at least recover their cost) but does not have to bear the full cost of marketing and selling the items to the public.

2. In the retail fashion industry, discounts serve the retailer's interest in promoting its products by allowing sales employees to wear the retailer's fashion items (which they otherwise could not afford) on the job.

Tax Implications

Employee discounts are not includable in the employee's taxable income if the following conditions are met.

1. For a "highly compensated" employee (see definition below), the discount is excludable from income only if the discount is available on substantially the same terms to each member of a classification of employees which does not discriminate in favor of highly compensated employees. For example, if a department store provided discounts only to its executives, most of whom fell under the "highly compensated" definition, the discounts would be taxable income, but only to those executives who were highly compensated.

2. The discount does not exceed the employer's "gross profit percentage" on the item. Gross profit percentage is the percentage of the ordinary retail price equal to

$$\frac{\text{sales price less cost for all such items}^{1}}{\text{sales price for all such items}}$$

3. The items discounted must be property offered for sale to customers in the ordinary course of the line of business of the employer in which the employee is working.[2] However, real estate or investments are not available for employee discount programs, even if the employer is in the business of selling real estate or investment products.

Employee discounts can be offered not only to active employees but also to (1) retired and disabled employees, (2) a widow or widower of an employee of the business, or (3) a spouse or dependent child of an employee. Dependent child includes either an actual dependent for tax purposes or a child under age 25 both of whose parents are deceased.[3]

NO-ADDITIONAL-COST SERVICES

Service businesses can provide discounted services to employees at low cost, but with considerable perceived value to the employees. Probably the best-known example of this type of fringe benefit is the free or discounted "standby" air travel available to some airline employees.

Advantages

1. Free or discounted services to employees may be almost as valuable to them as cash, but they can be provided at almost no marginal cost to the employer if they primarily

involve excess capacity that provides no revenue to the employer.

Tax Implications

Services provided free or discounted to employees are not includable in the employee's taxable income if the following conditions are met:

1. For a highly compensated employee (see definition below), the value of the services used is excludable from income only if the services are available on substantially the same terms to each member of a classification of employees which does not discriminate in favor of highly compensated employees. For example, if an airline provided free standby air travel only to its executives, most of whom fell under the "highly compensated" definition, the value of any trips taken by highly compensated employees would be taxable income to them. Trips taken by nonhighly compensated employees would not be taxable.

2. Either of the following two conditions must be satisfied:

   • The employer must incur no substantial cost (including foregone revenues) in providing such service to the employee (determined without regard to any amount paid by the employee). For example, providing hotel employees free hotel accommodations on a standby basis—that is, where the rooms are not otherwise booked—would meet this condition, because there would be no foregone revenue, and no substantial additional cost to the employer. However, providing free hotel room reservations, thus "bumping" paying customers, would not meet this condition.[4]

   • Alternatively, if services are discounted to employees, the discount cannot be more than 20 percent of the price at which the services are offered by the employer to regular customers.[5]

3. The services must be those offered for sale to customers in the ordinary course of the line of business of the employer in which the employee is working.[6] For example, if a corporation operates both a hotel and an airline, employees of the hotel business can be provided with free standby hotel rooms in the employer's hotel, but not standby air transportation.

   Unrelated employers in the same line of business—for example, two unrelated airlines—can enter into reciprocal written agreements under which employees of both can obtain nontaxable services from either one of the employers.[7]

No-additional-cost services can be offered not only to active employees but also to (1) retired and disabled employees, (2) a widow or widower of an employee of the business, or (3) a spouse or dependent child of an employee. Dependent child includes either an actual dependent for tax purposes or a child under age 25 both of whose parents are deceased.[8] In addition, for air travel, the parent of an employee can be included in the plan.[9]

COMPANY CAFETERIAS AND MEAL PLANS

Employers often provide cafeterias or dining rooms for employees for various business reasons: (1) time is saved by having employees eat on the premises rather than travel to outside restaurants; (2) nearby restaurants may be too expensive for many employees; (3) the work environment is enhanced by providing company dining facilities; (4) employees may even talk business at lunch and trade ideas or make business decisions.

Employers can almost always deduct the cost of these facilities as business expenses. The significant tax question is—are the meals taxable to employees? The rules are surprisingly complicated.

There are two types of cafeteria/dining room/meal plans provided by an employer for employees that do not result in extra taxable income to employees: (1) a Section 119 "on-premises" plan and (2) a Section 132 (e)(2) "on or near" plan.[10]

Any *other* meals or meal plans, other than these two types, that are furnished to employees working at their regular workplace will constitute taxable income to the employee to the extent of the fair market value of the meal. However, meals and lodging furnished to employees who are working away from home are not taxable to the employees.[11]

Section 119 on-premises plan. If an employer furnishes meals for employees, or their spouses or dependents, the value of the meals is excluded from the employee's income if

   • the meals are for the "convenience of the employer" and

   • the meals are furnished on the business premises of the employer.[12]

The issue of whether the plan serves the convenience of the employer is a factual one, with guidelines set out in the regulations under Section 119.

There is no requirement that the meals must be furnished for all employees or a broad or nondiscriminatory classification of employees.

The tax treatment of the plan is the same whether or not employees must pay for the meals, in full or in part. The amount the employee pays for individual meals is not tax-deductible by the employee. However, if the plan is structured so that the employee is *required* to pay a fixed periodic charge for the plan (not on a per-meal basis), then the fixed periodic charge is excluded from the employee's income for tax purposes.[13]

Section 132(e) on or near plan. If an employer operates an eating facility for employees, the value of meals is not taxable to employees if the following conditions are met:[14]

- the eating facility is located on or near the business premises of the employer;

- revenue derived from the facility normally equals or exceeds the "direct operating costs" of the facility. The direct operating costs are the costs of food and beverages and labor performed directly at the eating facility.[15]

- if the employee is "highly compensated" (see definition below) the meal is taxable unless access to the eating facility is available on substantially the same terms to each member of a group of employees that is defined in a nondiscriminatory way.

In other words, an "executives only" dining room (including even a separate, posh dining room next to the employee mess[16]) can result in taxation of the meal's value to the executive, unless the plan meets the requirements of a Section 119 "on-premises" plan.[17]

PARKING

Although many employees probably do not think of parking as an employee benefit, particularly if they work in suburban locations, the value of parking to employees can be considerable.

Under the tax law, parking provided to employees is excludable from their taxable income up to $155 per month (as adjusted for inflation).[18] To qualify, the employer must provide the parking arrangement on or near the employer's place of business or near a location from which the employee can board some type of commuter vehicle.[19]

There are no nondiscrimination requirements—parking can be provided tax-free (up to the $155 per month limit) even

if it is provided only to selected executives. Planners of executive compensation programs for executives, particularly those working in downtown office buildings, should make note of the compensation opportunity provided by this tax exemption.

GYMS AND ATHLETIC FACILITIES

An athletic facility available to employees is tax free to them if

1. it is located on the premises of the employer (but this can be somewhere other than the employer's *business* premises and can be either owned or leased[20]),

2. it is operated by the employer, and

3. substantially all of the facility's use is by employees, their spouses, and their dependent children.[21]

There are no nondiscrimination requirements for this provision. That is, an athletic facility that is provided only for selected executives is tax-free to the executives if it meets the three requirements listed above.[22]

WORKING CONDITION FRINGES

Code section 132 contains a general provision that if an employer provides property or services to an employee, the value of these is not taxable to the employee if, had the employee paid for them himself, that payment would be allowable as an employee business expense deduction.[23] Such employer-provided property or services are referred to as "working condition fringes."

For example, if an employee is driven to an away-from-home work location in the company limousine, the value of that transportation is not taxable to the employee. This is because if the employee himself paid for travelling to a work location away from home, such costs would be deductible to him.

In the case of company cars and car expense reimbursement plans, the IRS has woven a vast web of regulation out of this seemingly simple provision, as discussed in Chapter 29.

DE MINIMIS FRINGE

A final general rule in the fringe benefit area is a provision of Section 132 that property or services provided to the employee are not taxable to him if their value is so small as to

Figure 34.1

NOT TAXABLE	
Transit passes for employees worth $21 or less per month	Occasional cocktail parties, group meals, picnics
Occasional money for meals or local transportation, not provided on a regular or routine basis	Traditional noncash birthday or holiday gifts with a "low" fair market value
Taxi fare for commute outside of normal work hours to or from unsafe area (employee must include only first $1.50 per trip in income but highly compensated must include full fare)	Occasional theater or sports tickets
	Coffee, doughnuts, or soft drinks
Occasional typing of personal letters by company secretary	Local telephone calls
Occasional personal use of copying machine (machine must be used 85 percent for business)	Flowers, gifts for illness, reward, family crisis

TAXABLE	
Season theater or sports tickets	Group-term life insurance on spouse or child
Commuting use of company car more than one day per month	Use of company apartment, lodge, etc. for weekend
Membership in private club	

make accounting for them "unreasonable or administratively impractical."[24] Such benefits are referred to as "de minimis fringes" after the legal term *de minimis* which means "among the small things (that can be ignored)."

Unfortunately, employers and employees still have to worry whether the IRS will agree that a "small" thing is small enough to be ignored. While the IRS is apparently not yet concerned about used pencils that employees take home from the office, there are many doubtful areas. Some current guidelines from the IRS regulations appear in Figure 34.1.[25]

DEFINITION OF HIGHLY COMPENSATED

For purposes of the fringe benefit rules that include nondiscrimination provisions, the definition of highly compensated employee is the same one used for qualified pension and profit sharing plans.[26]

A highly compensated employee is any employee who, during the year or the preceding year

1. was at any time an owner of *more* than 5 percent of the business;

2. received compensation from the employer in excess of $75,000 (as indexed; $96,368 for 1993);

3. received compensation from the employer in excess of $50,000 (as indexed; $64,245 for 1993) and was in the "top-paid group" (top 20 percent) for the year; or

4. was at any time an officer and received compensation greater than 50 percent of the defined benefit plan dollar limit in effect for that year (50% of $115,641 for 1993, or $57,820.50).

FOOTNOTES

1. IRC Section 132(c)(2)(B). Regulations provide details for calculating this percentage.
2. IRC Section 132(c)(4).
3. IRC Section 132(g).

4. IRC Section 132(b).
5. IRC Section 132(c)(1)(B).
6. IRC Section 132(b)(1). For airlines, certain affiliated airlines are deemed to be in the same line of business. IRC Section 132(i)(5).
7. IRC Section 132(h).
8. IRC Section 132(g).
9. IRC Section 132(g)(3).
10. The two Code sections dealing with meals for employees, 119 and 132, were enacted at different times and are not coordinated. The only provision dealing with the overlap is Section 132(j), and it is not explicit and subject to differing interpretations. The interpretation adopted in this chapter is that meals are tax-free to employees if they meet *either* of these two Code provisions.
11. See IRS Publication 463.
12. IRC Section 119(a).
13. IRC Section 119(b)(3).
14. IRC Section 132(e)(2).
15. Reg. §1.132-7(b).
16. Reg. §1.132-7(a)(1)(ii).
17. See footnote 10 as to whether Sections 119 and 132 are alternatives. A discriminatory executives-only dining facility could meet the requirements of Section 119, but it should be noted that the "convenience of the employer" test in the latter section must then be met; it has no counterpart in Section 132.
18. IRC Sections 132(f)(2)(B), 132(f)(6).
19. IRC Section 132(f)(5)(C).
20. Reg. §1.132-1(e)(2).
21. IRC Section 132(i)(4).
22. Reg. §1.132-1(e)(5).
23. IRC Section 132(d). The two-percent floor on itemized deductions is not considered. Reg. §1.132-5(a)(1)(vi).
24. IRC Section 132(e).
25. Reg. §1.132-6.
26. IRC Section 414(q).

Chapter 35

GOLDEN PARACHUTE PLAN

WHAT IS IT?

A golden parachute plan is a compensation arrangement that provides special severance benefits to executives in the event that the corporation changes ownership and the covered executives are terminated.

An executive who accepts employment with a company that is a potential target for acquisition often will insist on a parachute-type compensation arrangement as a matter of self protection. Within limits, such agreements are an acceptable compensation practice.

Compensation arrangements of this type have a potential for abuse: inefficient managers could potentially grant themselves large parachute payments that would act merely as a financial obstacle to acquisition, or would unduly burden successor management. Therefore, Congress added provisions to the Internal Revenue Code that limit corporate deductions for these payments and impose a penalty on the recipient for payments beyond specified limits. These provisions do *not* generally apply, however, to closely held corporations (see below).

See also Chapter 47, Severance Pay Plan, for further general considerations in the design of severance pay arrangements.

TAX IMPLICATIONS

1. An amount that is characterized as an "excess parachute payment" is subject to two tax sanctions:

   • no employer deduction is allowed[1] and

   • the person receiving the payment is subject to a penalty tax equal to 20 percent of the excess parachute payment.[2]

2. An excess parachute payment is (1) the amount of any "parachute payment" less (2) the portion of the "base amount" that is allocated to the payment. The formula to calculate the amount of a parachute payment considered to be excess is:

$$\begin{matrix} \text{Excess} \\ \text{Parachute} \\ \text{Payment} \end{matrix} = \begin{matrix} \text{Parachute} \\ \text{Payment} \end{matrix} - \frac{\begin{matrix} \text{Present value} \\ \text{of the} \\ \text{parachute} \\ \text{payment} \end{matrix}}{\begin{matrix} \text{present value} \\ \text{of all} \\ \text{parachute} \\ \text{payments} \\ \text{expected} \end{matrix}} \times \text{base amount}$$

Definition of parachute payment. A parachute payment is any compensatory payment to an employee or independent contractor who is an officer, shareholder, or highly compensated individual (defined as one of the highest paid 1% of company employees, up to 250 employees[3]) that meets the following criteria[4]:

(a) the payment is contingent on a change (i) in the ownership or effective control of the corporation or (ii) in the ownership of a substantial portion of the assets of the corporation, and

(b) the aggregate present value of the payments equals or exceeds 3 times the base amount.

Also included in the definition of a parachute payment is any payment made under an agreement that violates securities laws.[5]

If an agreement is made within one year of the ownership change, the presumption (which is rebuttable) is that the payment is contingent on an ownership change.[6]

Any amount that the taxpayer can prove is "reasonable compensation" for personal services rendered before the takeover will not be treated as a parachute payment. Reasonable compensation is determined by reference to either the executive's historic compensation, or amounts paid by the employer or comparable employers to executives performing comparable services.[7]

Definition of base amount. The base amount means the recipient individual's annualized includable (taxable) compensation for the "base period," which is the most recent 5 taxable years ending before the date on which the change of ownership or control occurs.[8]

Example 1: Roger Flabb, CEO of Wimpp Industries, Inc., has had annualized compensation of $700,000 annually for the past five years. His severance agreement provides a lump sum severance payment of $2,800,000 in the event he is fired after a corporate takeover. [Assume that $2,100,000, but not more than that, would be reasonable compensation as a severance payment.] Octopus, Inc. acquires Wimpp in 1993 and Roger is terminated and paid the $2,800,000 in 1993. Of that amount, $700,000 is an excess parachute payment (the excess of the total of $2,800,000 over three times the base amount, 3 x $700,000 = $2,100,000. Octopus (or whatever corporation pays the amount and is eligible to deduct compensation paid to Roger) is denied a deduction for the $700,000 excess parachute payment. The remaining $2,100,000 of the severance payment to Roger is deductible as a compensation payment. Roger must pay income tax on the entire $2,800,000 payment *plus* a 20% penalty tax on the excess parachute payment (20% of $700,000 or $140,000).

Example 2: Brenda Flabb, Vice President of Wimpp Industries, Inc., earned $20,000 each of the prior five years. She is entitled to two golden parachute payments, one of $200,000 at the time of her termination and a second payment of $400,000 at a future date. Assume that the present value of the second payment is $300,000. Applying the formula above, the portion of the base amount allocated to the first payment would be $40,000 ($200,000/$500,000 x $100,000) with $60,000 ($300,000/$500,000 x $100,000) allocated to the second payment. Therefore, the amount of the first excess payment is $160,000 ($200,000 - $40,000) and the second excess payment is $340,000 ($400,000 - $60,000).

3. The parachute rules do not apply to corporations that have no stock that is readily tradable on an established securities market, provided that the payments are approved by a majority of shareholders who, immediately before the change in control, owned more than 75% of the voting power of all outstanding stock following disclosure to them of all material facts.[9] Further, the parachute rules do not apply to payments from small business corporations (S corporations) or generally to payments from qualified retirement plans, tax sheltered annuities and simplified employee pension plans.[10]

WHERE CAN I FIND OUT MORE ABOUT IT?

Hevener, Mary B. "Golden Parachutes: Proposed Regulations," *Tax Management Compensation Planning Journal* 17/8, August 4, 1989.

Feldmon, "A Bird's-Eye View of Golden Parachutes," *Journal of Pension Planning and Compliance*, Spring, 1993.

FOOTNOTES

1. IRC Section 280G(a).
2. IRC Section 4999.
3. IRC Section 280G(c).
4. IRC Section 280G(b)(2).
5. IRC Section 280G(b)(2)(B).
6. IRC Section 280G(b)(2)(C).
7. IRC Section 280G(b)(4); Prop. Reg. §1.280G-1, Q&A 40, 42(a).
8. IRC Sections 280G(b)(3)(A), 280G(d)(2).
9. IRC Sections 280G(b)(5)(A)(ii), 280G(b)(5)(B); Prop. Reg. §1.280G-1, Q&A 6(a)(2), 7(a).
10. IRC Sections 280G(b)(5)(A)(i), 280G(b)(6).

Chapter 36

GROUP-TERM LIFE INSURANCE

WHAT IS IT?

A group-term life insurance plan provides insurance for a group of employees under a group insurance contract held by the employer. If the plan qualifies under Code section 79, the cost of the first $50,000 of insurance is tax-free to employees.

WHEN IS IT INDICATED?

Since virtually all employees have at least some basic need for life insurance, and since there are few other ways to obtain tax-free life insurance, most employers would find it difficult to find reasons not to provide a group-term plan, at least at levels up to the $50,000 tax-free limit.

At levels above $50,000, group-term plans may be a cost effective way to provide a life insurance benefit, both for employer and employee. However, group-term coverage may have costs and other disadvantages for coverage of amounts over $50,000; these disadvantages have led planners to investigate the "carve-out" concept discussed below.

DESIGN FEATURES

Nondiscrimination Requirements

Code section 79 prescribes rules to prevent discrimination in favor of "key employees" (key employee is defined under the top-heavy rules of Code section 416(i)—see Chapter 23). The nondiscrimination requirements do not apply to plans of churches, synagogues, or certain related organizations.

If these rules are not met, key employees lose the tax exclusion for the first $50,000 of coverage. Since coverage above $50,000 is included in taxable income, key employees must include the cost of the entire amount of coverage at the greater of Table I rates (see below) or the actual cost.

Coverage Rules

The plan must:

- benefit at least 70 percent of all employees; or

- benefit a group of which at least 85 percent are not key employees; or

- benefit a nondiscriminatory classification of employees, as determined by the IRS; or

- in a cafeteria (Section 125) plan, meet the Section 125 nondiscrimination rules (see Chapter 27).[1]

Benefit Rules

1. Benefits must not discriminate in favor of key employees.

2. All benefits available to key employees must be available to other plan participants.[2]

3. Life insurance coverage equal to the same percentage of compensation for all participants will not violate the benefit nondiscrimination rule. There is no dollar limit on the amount of compensation that can be taken into account for this purpose.[3]

Who Can Be Excluded

In applying the percentage tests, the following may be excluded:

- employees who have not completed 3 years of service;

- part-time or seasonal employees; and

- employees not included in the plan who are part of a collective bargaining unit that has engaged in good faith bargaining on the issue of death benefits.

Requirements of Section 79 Regulations

The regulations for Code section 79[4] require group-term insurance to have the following characteristics in order to obtain the $50,000 exclusion:

1. It must provide a *general death benefit*. Accident and health insurance, including double indemnity riders, or travel accident insurance are not considered part of the

Section 79 plan. Also, life insurance as an incidental benefit in a qualified pension or profit-sharing plan is not considered part of the Section 79 plan.

2. It must be provided to a *group of employees* as compensation for services. The group can be all employees or a group defined in terms of employment-related factors—union membership, duties performed, etc.—or a group restricted solely on the basis of age or marital status. (Nondiscriminatory coverage requirements also apply, as discussed below.) The plan cannot cover company shareholders who are not employees, or a group consisting only of shareholder-employees.

3. The insurance policy must be *carried directly or indirectly by the employer*. This requirement is met if the employer pays any part of the cost of the plan.

4. Insurance amounts for employees must be determined under a *formula that precludes individual selection*. The formula must be based on factors such as age, years of service, compensation, or position in the company.

The plan can, however, provide a given level of coverage to persons in a position defined such that only a few (but at least more than one) highly compensated employees are in that category. (However, note the nondiscrimination rules discussed above.)

Group Life Insurance Carve-out for Executives

The Carve-out Concept

An executive now covered under a company's group-term life insurance plan (Section 79 plan) can often obtain a better benefit if the executive is taken out of the group plan and given a separate individual policy plan provided by the employer. A group of selected executives can be similarly treated. Removing these executives does not affect the qualified status of the group-term plan for the remaining employees.

Advantages of Carve-Out Coverage Over Group-Term

1. Executives can be provided with more insurance than would be available under a group-term plan. A group-term plan requires the same multiple of salary for all employees while the carve-out plan formula can be selective and discriminatory.

2. The plan can provide cash growth which is a "portable" benefit for the executive. In a group-term plan, coverage

after retirement can be provided only by an expensive policy conversion or purchasing new individual coverage.

3. Cost to the employer can be favorable.

4. Carving out the discriminatory benefits in a group-term plan can save an otherwise discriminatory plan.

How To Structure the Carve-Out Coverage

All of the methods used to finance executive life insurance are generally available for carved-out benefits; that is —

• bonus or "Section 162" plans

• split dollar plans

• death benefit only plans

For a comparison of carve-out with regular group-term coverage, see Figure 36.3 at the end of this chapter.

TAX IMPLICATIONS

1. The cost of the first $50,000 of group-term insurance provided for each employee is tax-free to the employee. Key employees may lose this benefit if the plan does not meet the Section 79 nondiscrimination rules discussed above. The cost of any discriminatory coverage (including any coverage over $50,000) is included in the key employee's income at the greater of the Table I rates (see below) or the actual cost.[5]

2. For the cost of nondiscriminatory coverage above $50,000, the amount taxable to the employee is determined on a monthly basis.[6] The amount of coverage in excess of $50,000 is multiplied by the "Table I" rates[7] (see below). The annual taxable amount is the sum of the monthly amounts, less any premiums paid by the employee.

"TABLE I" RATES FOR GROUP TERM INSURANCE

5-year age bracket	Cost per $1,000 of insurance for 1-month period
Under 30	$ .08
30 to 34	.09
35 to 39	.11
40 to 44	.17
45 to 49	.29
50 to 54	.48
55 to 59	.75
60 to 64	1.17
65 to 69	2.10
70 and above	3.76

Figure 36.1

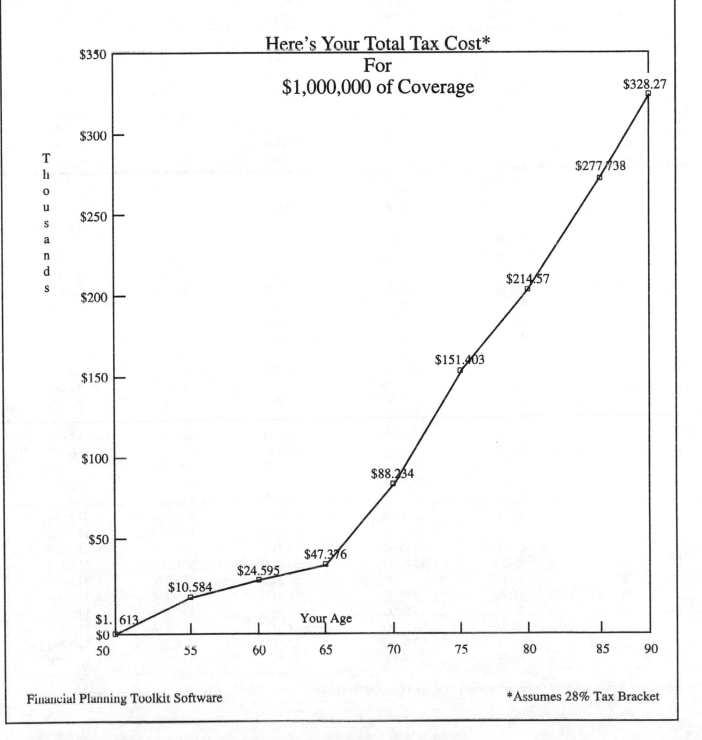

SKYROCKETING COSTS OF GROUP TERM LIFE

Do You Know What It Will Cost <u>You</u>?

Figure 36.2

SKYROCKETING GROUP TERM TAX COSTS

Age 43
Amount of Taxable Coverage $100,000
Tax Bracket 0.28

Age	Cost per $1,000 Per Month	Monthly Table I Income	Annual Table I Income	Cumulative Table I Income	Total Tax
43	$0.17	$17.00	$204	$204	$57
44	$0.17	$17.00	$204	$408	$114
45	$0.29	$29.00	$348	$756	$212
46	$0.29	$29.00	$348	$1,104	$309
47	$0.29	$29.00	$348	$1,452	$407
48	$0.29	$29.00	$348	$1,800	$504
49	$0.29	$29.00	$348	$2,148	$601
50	$0.48	$48.00	$576	$2,724	$763
51	$0.48	$48.00	$576	$3,300	$924
52	$0.48	$48.00	$576	$3,876	$1,085
53	$0.48	$48.00	$576	$4,452	$1,247
54	$0.48	$48.00	$576	$5,028	$1,408
55	$0.75	$75.00	$900	$5,928	$1,660
56	$0.75	$75.00	$900	$6,828	$1,912
57	$0.75	$75.00	$900	$7,728	$2,164
58	$0.75	$75.00	$900	$8,628	$2,416
59	$0.75	$75.00	$900	$9,528	$2,668
60	$1.17	$117.00	$1,404	$10,932	$3,061
61	$1.17	$117.00	$1,404	$12,336	$3,454
62	$1.17	$117.00	$1,404	$13,740	$3,847
63	$1.17	$117.00	$1,404	$15,144	$4,240
64	$1.17	$117.00	$1,404	$16,548	$4,633
65	$2.10	$210.00	$2,520	$19,068	$5,339
66	$2.10	$210.00	$2,520	$21,588	$6,045
67	$2.10	$210.00	$2,520	$24,108	$6,750
68	$2.10	$210.00	$2,520	$26,628	$7,456
69	$2.10	$210.00	$2,520	$29,148	$8,161
70	$3.76	$376.00	$4,512	$33,660	$9,425
71	$3.76	$376.00	$4,512	$38,172	$10,688
72	$3.76	$376.00	$4,512	$42,684	$11,952
73	$3.76	$376.00	$4,512	$47,196	$13,215
74	$3.76	$376.00	$4,512	$51,708	$14,478
75	$3.76	$376.00	$4,512	$56,220	$15,742
76	$3.76	$376.00	$4,512	$60,732	$17,005
77	$3.76	$376.00	$4,512	$65,244	$18,268
78	$3.76	$376.00	$4,512	$69,756	$19,532
79	$3.76	$376.00	$4,512	$74,268	$20,795
80	$3.76	$376.00	$4,512	$78,780	$22,058

Source: FINANCIAL PLANNING TOOLKIT SOFTWARE

NOTES

1. Age of the employee is attained age on the last day of the employee's taxable year.

2. If the employee is older than 64: before 1989, he or she was treated as if in the 60 to 64 age bracket; for tax years beginning after 1988, the above table is used.

For example, suppose an employee age 32 was covered under a group-term plan providing insurance of $100,000 for all twelve months of the year, and the employee paid $30 for this coverage for the year. The amount of coverage in excess of the $50,000 tax-free level is $50,000 ($100,000 - $50,000). Using Table I, 50 times $0.09 equals $4.50 of monthly cost, which multiplied by 12 (for 12 months) equals $54. The employee paid $30, and the difference between $54 and $30, $24, is taxable income for the year.

Figures 36.1 and 36.2 illustrate the rapid rise in taxable income at older ages under a group-term plan.

3. The death benefit from the insurance is tax-free to the beneficiary, just as if the insurance was personally-owned.

4. Premiums paid by the employer for group-term life insurance of employees are deductible business expenses.

5. The employer must pay employment taxes on the extra compensation that each employee includes in income as a result of plan coverage with insurance amounts over $50,000 or any coverage or benefits included by reason of the nondiscrimination rules.[8] Employment taxes include FICA (social security) and FUTA (federal unemployment tax). State unemployment and workers' compensation taxes may apply in some states—state laws vary and should be checked in each case.

ERISA AND OTHER REQUIREMENTS

A group-term plan is a "welfare benefit plan" subject to the ERISA requirements discussed in Appendix A.

ALTERNATIVES

1. Life insurance in a qualified plan

2. Split dollar life insurance

3. Death benefit only (employer death benefit)

4. Personally-owned insurance

HOW TO INSTALL A PLAN

In addition to group insurance contracts, it is also advisable to adopt a written plan meeting the Section 79 requirements listed above.

WHERE CAN I FIND OUT MORE ABOUT IT?

1. *Tax Facts 1*, Cincinnati, OH: The National Underwriter Co., (revised annually).

2. *Fundamentals of Employee Benefit Programs*, 3rd ed. Washington, DC: Employee Benefit Research Institute, 1987.

3. Cady, Donald F., *Field Guide to Estate Planning, Business Planning, & Employee Benefits*, Cincinnati, OH: The National Underwriter Co., (revised annually).

QUESTIONS AND ANSWERS

Question — Can group-term insurance be provided for self-employed persons or S corporation shareholders?

Answer — The exclusion from taxable income of the cost of the first $50,000 of group-term insurance under Code section 79 is not available to self-employed persons—partners or proprietors—or to shareholders of S corporations who own more than 2% of the corporation. (These more-than-2% shareholders are treated as partners for employee benefit purposes.)

However, self-employed persons and more-than-2% shareholders of S corporations can be included in the insured group for purposes of determining group coverage and premiums. The full cost of such insurance is taxable to the individual covered. (See Chapter 5.)

Question — How small a group can be covered under group-term insurance and are there any special rules for small groups?

Answer — Under the Section 79 Regulations,[9] group insurance for fewer than 10 employees qualifies for the tax exclusion under Section 79 if

—it is provided for all full-time employees, and

—the amount of protection is computed either as a uniform percentage of compensation, or on the basis of coverage brackets established by the insurer under which no bracket exceeds 2½ times the next lower bracket and the lowest bracket is at least 10 percent of the highest bracket.

For example, a plan dividing employees into four classes with insurance amounts according to the following brackets would meet the test in the regulations:

Class A:	$ 10,000
Class B:	25,000
Class C:	50,000
Class D:	100,000

Eligibility and amount of coverage may be based on evidence of insurability but this must be determined solely on the basis of a medical questionnaire completed by the employee and not by requiring a physical examination.

Meeting the under-10 employee regulations described in this answer is no guarantee that the plan will also be deemed nondiscriminatory. An under-10 employee plan must also meet the Section 79 nondiscrimination requirements.

Question — Can insurance providing a permanent benefit be used in a group-term life insurance plan?

Answer — Yes, under certain conditions. A policy is considered to provide a permanent benefit if it provides an economic value extending beyond one policy year. For example, a policy with a cash surrender value would be considered to provide a permanent benefit.

A policy with a permanent benefit may be treated as part of a group-term plan if

—the amount of death benefit considered part of the group-term plan is specified in writing, and

—the group-term portion of the death benefit each year complies with a formula in the regulations.

If permanent insurance is used in a group-term plan, the cost of the permanent benefit, less any amount contributed by the employee towards that permanent benefit, is included in the employee's taxable income for the year. The regulations contain a formula for computing the annual cost of permanent benefits.[10]

Question — Can "group universal life insurance programs" (sometimes referred to as "GULP") be used in a Section 79 group-term plan?

Answer—Group universal life programs are universal life insurance arrangements for a group of employees. These programs provide covered employees with (a) the advantages of universal life coverage—variation in the timing and amount of premiums, and cash values with attractive rates of investment return—as well as (b) the advantages of group underwriting—convenience for employees, reduced costs, and coverage without evidence of insurability, within limits.

Group universal life contracts can be used as part of a plan of group-term insurance meeting the requirements of Section 79 and the regulations. However, application of this Code section to a GULP plan does not produce a good tax result due to the rules for taxing "permanent" insurance benefits contained in Section 79. Thus, most GULP plans are designed specifically to *avoid* the application of Section 79. This can be done by using an employee-pay-all arrangement and structuring coverage through a third party (such as a trustee) so that the policy is not deemed to be "carried directly or indirectly by the employer" as required under Section 79. Planning requires close adherence to technical requirements and must be done with the advice of an expert.

It is possible to provide Section 79 group-term insurance up to the tax-free level, and also provide the GULP benefit as a (non-Section 79) supplement to the Section 79 plan, if adequate coverage for group underwriting can be obtained.

Question — Do the Section 79 nondiscrimination rules require, in effect, that the plan must cover practically all employees of an employer and provide all of them with insurance equal to the same multiple of salary?

Answer — Do all employees of the company have to receive life coverage equal to the same percentage of compensation? Not necessarily. The company can set up two or more plans, having different benefit formulas, as long as *each* plan meets the coverage rules.

Example: Employer has 600 employees; 500 are non-union hourly employees and 100 are salaried; of the 100 salaried, 10 are key employees. Plan 1 provides group insurance equal to 1X compensation for all hourly employees. Plan 2 provides group insurance equal to 2X compensation for all salaried employees. Both plans meet the coverage requirements (Plan 1: 100% of participants are not key employees; Plan 2: 90% of participants are not key employees; both percentages are greater than 85%.)

Question — Should dependent coverage be included in a group-term plan?

Answer — A small amount of dependent coverage in a group-term plan is treated favorably for tax purposes. Dependent coverage is regarded as a "de minimis fringe" that is not included in income (see Chapter 34) if the face amount of employer-provided group-term life insurance payable on the death of a spouse or dependent of an employee does not exceed $2,000.[11] Additional dependent coverage can be provided by the employee on an after-tax basis, without affecting the nontaxability of the employer-paid $2,000 of insurance.

FOOTNOTES

1. IRC Section 79(d)(3).
2. IRC Section 79(d)(2).
3. IRC Section 79(d)(5). Prior to its repeal by P. L. 101-140, Section 89 included a $200,000 (indexed) limit on the amount of compensation that

could be taken into account. P. L. 101-140 also includes a provision that even if Section 79 coverage is provided through a Section 501(c)(9) VEBA (see Chapter 51), the $200,000 limit applicable to VEBAs in general under Code section 505(b)(7) does not apply in determining whether the requirements of Section 79 are met. P. L. 101-140, Sec. 204(c).
4. Reg. §1.79-1.
5. IRC Section 79(d)(1).
6. Reg. §1.79-3.
7. Reg. §1.79-3(d)(2).
8. IRC Section 3121(a)(2)(C); See IRS Notice 88-82, 1988-2 CB 398 for current FICA reporting rules.
9. Reg. §1.79-1(c).
10. Regs. §§1.79-1(b), 1.79-1(d).
11. IRS Notice 89-110, 1989-2 CB 447.

Figure 36.3

GROUP-TERM VS. CARVE-OUT

	Group-term	Carve-out
Income tax to employee	1. First $50,000 is income tax free.	1. All coverage is taxable (except for DBO arrangement).
	2. Coverage over $50,000 is taxed at Table I rates (cannot use insurer's lower term rate).	2. Coverage is taxed at lower of PS 58 rates or insurer's term rate.
Premium deductibility to corporation	Fully deductible	Varies; bonus-type plan is fully deductible, nondeductible if corporation is beneficiary
Cost to corporation	Rises if group ages; experience-rated (rises if group mortality or incidence of policy conversion at 65 increases).	Most plans involve level-premium insurance contracts with guaranteed premium.
Nondiscrimination coverage requirements	Section 79 coverage requirements apply; if not met, key employees lose the $50,000 exemption	None
Benefit nondiscrimination requirements	Section 79 requirements apply; generally benefits must be uniform percentage of compensation for all participants.	None; coverage can vary from executive to executive
Underwriting	Group, with guaranteed issue	Generally individual
Treatment at retirement	Coverage usually terminates or is reduced sharply because of increasing employer cost; also, higher Table I rates past age 64 increase cost to employee	Can be continued beyond retirement with no increased employer cost; employee cost is PS 58 or lower term cost
Use of cash value or permanent insurance	May result in unfavorable taxation to covered employee	Enhances planning flexibility

Chapter 37

HEALTH INSURANCE

WHAT IS IT?

Health insurance is the most widespread employee benefit, covering more than 75 million employees in the United States. It is widespread as an employee benefit not only because it meets a critical employee need, but also because it receives almost unique tax benefits: the entire cost is deductible to employers, but nothing is includable in employees' taxable income as a result of plan coverage or payment of plan benefits, if the plan meets the rules discussed below. Thus health insurance is a completely tax-free form of employee compensation.

There are two main types of health insurance plans:

- prepaid plans, in which health care providers are paid in advance of providing services

- postpaid plans, which pay health care providers for services rendered, or reimburse employees for payments to providers.

The principal form of prepaid plans is the Health Maintenance Organization, or HMO. HMOs are discussed separately in Chapter 38. This chapter will focus primarily on postpaid plans, which are the traditional form of health insurance.

The federal government and may state governments are currently considering legislation that may greatly change the way in which employers provide health insurance as an employee benefit after 1993. This chapter reflects the law in effect in June, 1993.

PLAN DESIGN

Health insurance plans provided by employers are usually complicated and may even be "customized" to some degree, particularly for larger employers. However, three fundamental types of plan design are usually identified—the "basic" plan, the "major medical" plan, and the "comprehensive" plan.

Basic Plan. A basic plan primarily provides health care services that are connected with hospitalization. The types of benefits provided in a basic plan are:

(1) Inpatient hospital charges, such as room and board, nursing care, supplies, and other hospital expenses.

(2) In-hospital visits by physicians. Home or office visits are not covered in a basic plan.

(3) Surgical fees, including surgeons' fees as well as anesthesiologists' and other surgical assistants' fees. These plans often cover fees for surgical procedures performed in a doctor's office or at an outpatient facility—not just those performed on patients admitted to a hospital.

Major Medical Plan. A major medical plan covers medical services excluded from basic plans. For this reason it is sometimes referred to as a "supplemental major medical plan." Although the objective of the plan is to fill gaps in basic coverage, few plans cover all medical expenses. Routine doctors' office visits are usually excluded. Also, most plans do not cover dental, vision, and hearing care, although employers often provide these through separate plans.

Comprehensive Plan. The comprehensive type of plan combines the coverage of basic and major medical plans in one single plan. This is currently the dominant type of plan. Many employers have replaced basic/major medical plans with comprehensive plans.

BENEFIT STRUCTURE

Many health plans do not pay the full cost of covered benefits. Major medical and comprehensive plans in particular, but also some basic plans, use "deductibles" and "coinsurance" to reduce plan costs by requiring employees to share benefit costs. The plan also usually has a per-individual maximum coverage limit on covered expenses.

Deductibles. A deductible is an amount of initial expense specified in the plan that is paid by the employee toward covered benefits. For example, if the plan has a $200 deductible, the participant pays the first $200 of covered expenses and the plan covers the rest up to a specified limit. Deductibles generally range from $100 to $500.

Deductibles are usually computed annually. For example, if the deductible is $500 and a covered individual incurs $400 of doctors' bills covered under the plan between January and November, the plan does not pay anything. However, if the same individual incurs an additional covered medical expense of $200 in December, the $500 deductible will have been satisfied and the plan will pay the $100 in excess of the deductible. Some plans have carryover provisions to avoid an unfair impact of the deductible. For example, with a three-month carryover provision, medical bills incurred during the last three months of the year can be used toward the next year's deductible. Thus, if an individual has a serious illness in December and incurs a $1,000 medical expense, subsequent bills in January and thereafter will not be subject to another deductible.

Most deductibles are *all-causes* deductibles—that is, the deductible is cumulative over the year or other period even though the medical bills may reflect many different illnesses or medical conditions. However, some plans have *per-cause* deductibles. Under a per-cause deductible, the deductible amount must be satisfied for each separate illness or other medical condition.

Most employee plans use a *per-family* deductible as well as individual deductibles to minimize the payment burden for families. For example, the plan may have a $200 per individual deductible, but also a provision under which the plan pays for all covered expenses in full when total expenses for all family members exceed $500.

Coinsurance. Under a coinsurance provision, the plan participant is responsible for a specified percentage, usually 20 percent, of covered expenses. For example, if a plan has a $100 deductible, and a participant incurs expenses of $1100 during the year, the plan pays $800 of these and the participant pays the rest (the $100 deductible plus 20% of the remaining $1,000 of expenses).

The participant's 20% share can become burdensome quickly in the event of a major illness, so good plan design requires an upper dollar limit on the participant's share. The participant's costs are usually limited to several thousand dollars on an annual basis.

Maximum Coverage Limits. To limit the plan's ultimate liability, there is usually an upper "lifetime limit" on the amount the plan will pay for any one individual's medical expenses. This limit should be high enough so that only the rarest of medical events will cause it to be exceeded. Limits of $500,000 to $1 million are commonly used. If the limit is too low, the plan violates the basic principle of insurance, which is to share catastrophic losses that no one individual can bear. Also, extending the upper limit substantially is usually not expensive because of the rarity of medical catastrophes. It is best to obtain coverage of $1 million, or unlimited coverage, whenever possible.

PLAN FUNDING

Employers fund postpaid-type health plans in one or a combination of three ways:

(1) commercial insurance company contracts

(2) Blue Cross/Blue Shield contracts

(3) "self-funding" or self insurance (without an insurance contract)

Commercial Insurers. A health insurance contract from a commercial insurance company usually provides reimbursement to employees for their expenses for covered medical procedures. Some insurers may pay health care providers directly, however. Reimbursement is usually limited to the "usual, customary, and reasonable" (UCR) charges for a given procedure in the employee's geographical area. Thus, an employee may not receive full reimbursement for a medical claim if the insurer's claims department considers the amount charged to be greater than the UCR amount.

Premiums for commercial health insurance contracts reflect six elements:

(1) expected benefit payments

(2) administrative expenses

(3) commissions

(4) state premium taxes

(5) risk charges; and

(6) return on the insurer's capital allocated to the contract (profit).

For groups of 50 employees or more, premiums are usually "experience rated." That is, the insurer keeps separate records for the employer group and adjusts charges to reflect above or below-average benefit utilization by the group itself.

Blue Cross/Blue Shield. Blue Cross and Blue Shield plans were originally designed by organizations of hospitals and physicians in order to facilitate the payment of hospital and doctor bills. Blue Cross and Blue Shield plans generally provide direct payment in full to "participating" hospitals and doctors for medical benefits provided to covered employees. A participating hospital or doctor is one that agrees to preestablished rates and billing schedules with Blue Cross or Blue Shield. If an employee is admitted to a hospital or uses a doctor that is not participating, the Blue Cross or Blue Shield plan pays or reimburses on a UCR basis.

Blue Cross and Blue Shield plans can be obtained by individuals as well as by employers. A basic principle of the "Blues" is to offer coverage to any individual who requests it and to provide terminating employees under an employer plan the ability to convert to an individual product.

Blue Cross (for hospital bills) and Blue Shield (for doctors' bills) are nonprofit organizations operating within a given geographical area. However, they must meet standards prescribed by their national associations. Recently, federal tax law was changed to provide income taxation of these organizations on a basis similar to insurance companies.

Self-Funding. With self-funding (self insurance), the employer pays claims and other costs directly, either on a pay-as-you-go basis (that is, the employer pays claims out of current operating revenues as they are incurred by covered employees), or out of a reserve fund accumulated in advance. (However, as indicated below, the employer can accelerate its tax deductions for health and accident plans only to a limited extent even if a fund is accumulated in advance.)

Self-funding can be combined with an insurance contract that provides "administrative services only" (an ASO contract). Also, the employer can obtain a "stop-loss" insurance contract under which plan claims above a stated level are assumed by the insurer. This protects the employer against large unanticipated losses.

A self-funded plan can be referred to as a "medical reimbursement" plan. However, the term medical expense reimbursement plan (MERP) is usually reserved for a plan designed to supplement existing insured health plans and to provide special tax benefits. These plans are discussed in Chapter 44.

ELIGIBILITY AND COVERAGE

Employer health insurance plans generally cover all employees. Employees are usually covered immediately upon being hired, or after a brief waiting period for coverage such as three months. Some employers maintain separate plans for collective bargaining unit employees or some other identifiable group.

COBRA Continuation of Coverage

Many employers have plans that continue health insurance coverage for employees and their dependents for a period of time after termination of employment. Some methods of funding continued coverage after retirement are discussed below.

Employer flexibility in this area is significantly limited since passage of the Consolidated Omnibus Budget Reconciliation Act of 1985 (COBRA).[1] The COBRA continuation provisions apply for a given year if the employer had 20 or more employees on a typical business day in the preceding year. (Government and church plans are exempt.) COBRA *requires* continuation of coverage for former employees and their dependents in several situations.

In general, under COBRA the employer must provide the option to continue an employee's existing health plan coverage (including dependent coverage) for 36 months after the following "qualifying events":

(1) death of the employee

(2) divorce or legal separation of the covered employee (coverage continues for the former spouse and dependents)

(3) the employee's entitlement to Medicare benefits

(4) a bankruptcy proceeding under the United States Code where the employee retired from the employer

(5) a child ceasing to be a dependent for plan purposes

Health plan coverage must be continued for 18 months after termination of employment or reduction in hours of employment. If termination is due to disability, coverage must be continued for 29 months.

Continuation coverage can be terminated before the 36, 29, or 18 month period if

- the employer terminates its health plan for all employees

- the employee or beneficiary fails to pay his or her share of the premium

- the employee or beneficiary becomes covered under any other plan providing medical care. However, if the new plan excludes a pre-existing condition, the employee must be allowed to continue coverage under the prior plan for the full COBRA period.

The employer can require the former employee or beneficiary to pay part of the cost of continuation coverage. However, this former employee or beneficiary's share cannot be more than 102% of the cost to the plan of coverage for similarly situated beneficiaries with respect to whom a qualifying event has not occurred (whether the cost is paid by the employer or employee). The premium for an employee disabled at the time of his termination or reduction in hours may be as much as 150% of the plan cost after the eighteenth month of continuation coverage.

Employees and beneficiaries must be notified of their right to continuing coverage when a qualifying event occurs. A sample notification form is reproduced in Figure 37.1. Similar information must be provided in the plan's Summary Plan Description (SPD).

The penalty for noncompliance with the benefit continuation requirements is, generally, a tax of $100 a day during the period that any failure with respect to a qualified beneficiary continues.

Continuing Health Coverage For Retirees

Many employers want to continue company-paid health benefits for retirees, either for all employees or for a selected group. Rising costs as well as new developments in the tax and accounting treatment of such plans will require many of these plans to be redesigned.

The key issue is the method of funding or financing the plan. There is no one best way to design these plans, so the planner must weigh the advantages and disadvantages of each approach and fit it with the employer's unique situation. Currently, the alternatives are:

1. *Pay as you go.* With this alternative there is no advance funding or financing; health insurance premiums are simply paid each year after the covered employee retires. This alternative is simple and offers the lowest initial cost. There are no nondiscrimination requirements if the plan is insured[2] so the plan can be offered only to selected executives. However, costs of such plans can rise unpredictably and burden future cash flow of the company. Under FAS 106 (see Appendix E) a current accrual must nonetheless be made, so current earnings are reduced. Also, the employer's tax deduction for the payment is deferred to the year in which the premiums are actually paid.

2. *Earmarked corporate assets.* Under this approach, the plan is essentially a pay-as-you-go arrangement, but to provide a better indication of responsible financial management the corporation sets aside specified assets to offset the additional liability that the FASB rules would impose.

3. *Corporate-owned life insurance.* This is again a variation on the pay-as-you-go approach, but with a dedicated corporate asset reserve in the form of corporate-owned life insurance. The insurance is maintained on the life of each covered employee, with the corporation as owner and beneficiary. The tax-free cash buildup of the policy is used to pay the after-tax cost of health insurance premiums for retired employees. When the insured employee dies, the tax-free death benefit allows the company to recover part or all of its costs for the plan.

4. *Increase pension benefits.* Under this alternative, there is no formal health insurance continuation plan for retirees (except for the required COBRA coverage), but pension benefits are increased to provide employees with additional money to pay insurance premiums. This alternative allows a current deduction to the employer for the extra costs and tax-free accumulation of investment returns, but the pension nondiscrimination rules require that the increased benefits be provided to all employees covered under the pension plan. Also, the employee must pay taxes on the increased pension benefit, so the potentially tax-free nature of the health insurance benefit is lost. Also, there is no certainty or even reasonable expectation that the increased benefits will, in fact, cover health insurance costs incurred many years after retirement.

5. *Incidental benefit in qualified plan.* Under this approach, continued health insurance coverage is provided as an incidental benefit under a qualified pension or profit sharing plan. The health insurance coverage is funded as part of the plan cost. Under Code section 401(h), the fund for health insurance must be kept in a separate account for each participant. Neither health insurance costs nor benefit payments are taxable income to the employee,[3] which means that the 401(h) alternative has the same tax benefit as direct health insurance coverage. See the Questions and Answers for some limitations applicable to "key employees." Incidental benefits in a qualified plan are limited to 25% of the aggregate contributions to the plan after establishment of the 401(h) account,[4] and many actuaries consider this limit inadequate for funding the full potential liability. Also see "Questions and Answers," below.

6. *VEBA or other trust fund.* Here assets are set aside to meet the future insurance liability in a separate trust fund. A VEBA is a tax-exempt arrangement that can be used for this purpose. (VEBAs are discussed in detail in Chapter 51.) The approach is similar to using a Section 401(h) account, but the limits on contributions are not subject to the 25% incidental benefit rule, but rather to the rules for prefunded welfare benefits under Sections 419 and 419A. Although a VEBA is generally tax exempt, the rules for "unrelated business taxable income" as applied to a VEBA in this situation would generally tax most of the VEBA's income.[5] VEBAs must meet nondiscrimination

Figure 37.1

ABC Corporation
Employees' Medical Benefit Plan
Continuation of Coverage

NOTICE OF RIGHT TO CONTINUE COVERAGE

Your coverage under the Employees' Medical Benefit Plan terminates as of [date of qualifying event]. If you [and your covered dependents] are not covered under any other group health care plan, you may continue [health care] coverage without interruption under the Plan for up to [18] [29] [36] months.

You have 60 days from [later of the date notice is received or date of qualifying event] to elect to continue coverage.

COST OF CONTINUED COVERAGE

If you elect to continue coverage under the Plan, you must pay $ [amount equal to 102 percent or 150 percent (disability) of the total monthly cost of coverage for any similarly situated person covered by the Plan] on the first day of each month for which coverage is to be continued, in advance. Failure to pay this amount by the first of any month will result in loss of coverage.

WHEN CONTINUED COVERAGE CEASES

The continued coverage will cease for any person when:

    (a) the cost of continued coverage is not paid on or before the date it is due; or
    (b) that person becomes eligible for Medicare; or
    (c) that person becomes covered under another health care plan; or
    (d) the Plan terminates for all employees.

CONVERSION RIGHTS

Once continued coverage ceases for any person, that person may obtain a personal health care policy without evidence of insurability, as provided under the terms of the Plan. [Such a conversion right is not available for dental, vision care, or prescription drug coverages.]

HOW TO ELECT CONTINUED COVERAGE

Complete the request for continued coverage below. Return it together with your check or money order payable to [ABC Corporation] for $ [one month's cost] to the address shown within 45 days after you elect continued coverage. You will be billed separately for any amount due for the period between [the date shown above] and the date your payment is made.

Complete one form for each electing employee or beneficiary.

I elect continuing coverage under the ABC Corporation Employees' Medical Benefit Plan.

Name	Social Security No.	Date of Birth

Address

Signature	Date

rules[6] similar to those for qualified plans, so the benefits cannot be provided just to a selected group of executives.

The chart in Figure 37.2 summarizes the advantages and disadvantages of these approaches to preretirement financing of retiree medical benefits. For an extensive discussion see Hutchinson, "Prefunding Retiree Health Benefits," *BNA Pension Reporter*, Vol. 18, No. 51, pp. 2299-2308 (Dec. 23, 1991).

TAX IMPLICATIONS

1. The employer may deduct the cost of health insurance premiums in an insured plan or benefits paid in an uninsured plan as a general business expense. Plan administrative expenses are also deductible.

2. Deductions for prefunding medical benefits (that is, setting funds aside and deducting amounts for medical benefits to be paid in future years) are limited under rules set out in Code sections 419 and 419A. Generally, for a given year an employer can deduct expenditures for medical benefits up to a limit equal to the total of (a) the direct costs of the plan for the year—claims paid plus administrative costs, plus (b) contributions to an asset account up to 35 percent of the preceding year's direct costs.

3. The employee does not have taxable income when (a) the employer pays insurance premiums, (b) when benefits are paid, or (c) when the plan reimburses the employee for covered expenses (unless the employee is considered highly compensated and the plan is a discriminatory noninsured medical expense reimbursement plan).[7]

4. The employee is eligible for an itemized medical expense deduction under Code section 213 for (a) any portion of health insurance premiums paid by the employee, (b) unreimbursed out-of-pocket costs resulting from deductibles or coinsurance, and (c) any other medical expenses eligible for a Section 213 deduction. The Section 213 deduction is available only if the taxpayer itemizes deductions on the tax return. The deduction is limited to the amount by which the total of all eligible medical expenses exceeds 7.5% of the taxpayer's adjusted gross income.

ERISA AND OTHER REQUIREMENTS

An employer's health and accident plan is a "welfare benefit plan" subject to the ERISA requirements discussed in Appendix A.[8]

WHERE CAN I FIND OUT MORE ABOUT IT?

1. Beam, Burton T., Jr. and John J. McFadden, *Employee Benefits*, 3rd ed. Chicago, IL: Dearborn Financial Publishing, Inc., 1992.

2. *Tax Facts 1*, Cincinnati, OH: The National Underwriter Co., (revised annually).

3. Cady, Donald F., *Field Guide to Estate Planning, Business Planning, & Employee Benefits*, Cincinnati, OH: The National Underwriter Co., (revised annually).

QUESTIONS AND ANSWERS

Question — How do employer health and accident benefits fit into a cafeteria or FSA plan?

Answer — Since employees have varying needs for health benefits (some may prefer lower deductibles, others may want broader coverage such as dental expense coverage, etc.), the plan can be made attractive to employees by offering a number of optional plans under a "cafeteria" arrangement. Cafeteria plans are discussed further in Chapter 27.

The flexible spending account (FSA) or salary reduction type of cafeteria plan offers another attractive possibility in the health care area. An FSA makes possible the conversion of after-tax employee expenditures in a health plan to nontaxable expenditures. Such expenditures include the employee share of health insurance, deductibles, coinsurance payments, and medical expenses not covered by the plan. These expenditures are technically deductible as itemized medical deductions under Code section 213, but because of the 7.5% of adjusted gross income floor, few employees will be able to deduct them. The FSA approach in effect allows these items to be excluded from taxable income without any floor limit. FSA plans are discussed in detail in Chapter 33.

Question — Can a self-employed person (sole proprietor or partner in an unincorporated business) or S corporation shareholder-employee be covered under his business's health insurance plan and obtain any tax advantage?

Answer — A self-employed person or S corporation shareholder-employee can be covered under a business's health insurance plan. This may provide a more economical means of obtaining health benefits than individual insurance because of the group underwriting of an insured employer plan.

Figure 37.2

FINANCING OF
RETIREE MEDICAL BENEFITS

	Advantages	Disadvantages
Pay-As-You-Go	• low initial cash flow • simplicity • no nondiscrimination requirements	• FASB standards require liability • increasing cash flow requirements • burdens future management/shareholders
Earmarked Corporate Assets	• demonstrates responsible financial management • money managers can manage portfolio like pension fund • no nondiscrimination requirements	• no tax deduction until benefits are paid • investment income taxable • rate of return could be inadequate
Corporate-Owned Life Insurance	• offset to balance sheet liability • tax-free investment accumulation • policy loan interest deductible (up to $50,000 loan) • death benefits tax-free • potentially high rate of return • no nondiscrimination requirements	• high initial cash requirements • no tax deduction until benefits are paid
Increased Pension Benefits	• no FASB balance sheet liability except for increased pension • tax-free accumulation • deductibility of contributions	• nondiscrimination requirements • benefits taxable to employees • Sec. 415 limits for higher paid
Incidental Qualified Plan Benefit (401(h))	• deductibility of contributions • tax-free accumulation	• nondiscrimination requirements • contributions cannot exceed 25 percent of pension plan contributions • reduces maximum pension • tax deductions do not reflect future medical cost inflation
VEBA	• deductibility of contributions	• tax deductions do not reflect future medical cost inflation under Sec. 419-419A • nondiscrimination requirements • earnings in excess of current claims subject to UBIT (Unrelated Business Income Tax)

The cost of health insurance for a self-employed individual or a more than 2 percent shareholder-employee in an S corporation would ordinarily not be a deductible expense to the business because the self-employed individual is not considered an employee (and a more than 2 percent S corporation shareholder-employee is treated as a partner for fringe benefit purposes). However, a special provision, Code section 162(l), permits a limited special deduction in order to partially equalize the treatment of incorporated and unincorporated businesses in this regard. Under Section 162(l), a self-employed individual is entitled to a business expense deduction equal to 25 percent of the amount paid for health insurance. The deduction cannot exceed the self-employed individual's earned income for the year from the trade or business with respect to which the plan is established. The deduction cannot be used to reduce self-employment income subject to self-employment tax. Rules are provided to prevent duplication of deductions for other medical insurance covering the taxpayer or itemized medical expense deductions. This special deduction provision is scheduled to expire for taxable years beginning after June 30, 1992. This expiration has been extended several times in the past and it is expected to be further extended.

Question — Do the COBRA requirements for continuing health benefits apply if the employer's plan is not health insurance?

Answer — The COBRA continuation requirements apply to any kind of group health care coverage, including HMOs and self-funded or noninsured plans. However, the covered employee has the right only to continue the kind of coverage that existed during employment. For example, the employer must offer continuing HMO coverage to an employee covered under an HMO, but the employer need not offer alternative health insurance, although the employer can do so if it wishes. Note, however, that an employee on continued COBRA coverage should be given the same rights to switch coverage during an "open enrollment" period that is available to an active employee.

Question — Does COBRA's continuing coverage requirement preempt state law in states that require more generous continuing coverage in certain situations?

Answer — No; unlike ERISA, COBRA does not contain a preemption of state law. Therefore planners must continue to be aware of state continuation requirements applicable to their clients.

Question — Is the 401(h) "incidental benefit" account an advantageous method of funding postretirement benefits for key employees?

Answer — Coverage of key employees in a Section 401(h) arrangement adds some extra complexities that have led some planners to recommend against covering key employees in 401(h)-type plans. First, there must be separate, individual 401(h) accounts for each key employee.[9] In addition, the total amount allocated to a key employee for pension plus incidental medical or other benefits is subject to the $30,000 (as indexed) annual additions limitation under Section 415 of the code, which may limit the ability to prefund medical benefits for key employees in some cases. However, the 25% of compensation limit of Section 415(c) does not apply to medical-benefit contributions.[10] The definition of "key employee" in these rules is that used for purposes of the top-heavy rules, Code Section 416(i). (See Chapter 23.)

Question — Can an employer use the excess assets in an "overfunded" pension plan to fund retiree medical benefits?

Answer — An employer with an overfunded pension plan can amend the plan to add postretirement health insurance as an additional incidental benefit. The amount allocated to all incidental benefits cannot exceed 25% of the aggregate plan contributions after establishment of the 401(h) account.[11] If a plan is at the "full funding limit" it is not allowed to make any further actual contributions for pension purposes, so (since 25% of zero is zero) no additional deductible contributions for medical benefits can be made. The IRS initially attempted to provide some relief from this result.[12] However, Congress amended Section 401(h) in late 1989 to add the "actual contribution" language to Section 401(h), thus nullifying the IRS' proposed relief procedure.

Section 420, a temporary Code provision effective through 1995, allows an employer to make a transfer of excess pension assets to a Section 401(h) account without the employer having to pay either regular income tax or the pension reversion excise tax on the amount transferred. This provision, however, includes complex restrictions and regulatory requirements. Also, transferred assets may not be used for postretirement health benefits for key employees as defined in Code section 416(i).

It also appears unfeasible to withdraw excess funding from a qualified plan and transfer it to a VEBA to fund retiree benefits. The IRS apparently views this withdrawal as a "pension reversion" to the employer which is fully income taxable to the employer and is also subject to the 15% pension reversion penalty tax under Code section 4980.

Question — How is health plan coverage for retirees reflected by the employer for accounting purposes?

Answer — The accounting profession's Financial Accounting Standards Board (FASB) recently adopted a standard for accounting treatment of postretirement benefits other than pensions (FAS 106). This standard would require employers to reflect the promise of future benefits on an accrual basis—that is, as benefits are earned rather than when they are ultimately paid out. Accounting requirements for benefit plans are discussed further in Appendix E.

Question — May an employer drop retiree health insurance coverage after an employee has retired?

Answer — This is a complex issue involving both federal law (ERISA) and the interpretation of the retiree's employment contract. Many cases are now in litigation; see for example Goldsmith, "Courts Split on Employer's Right to Change Retiree Health Benefits," *Benefits Law Journal*, Spring, 1992.

As a practical matter, the best way for an employer to maintain flexibility is to have a clear "reservation of rights" clause in its collective bargaining agreements and other employment agreements, as well as its ERISA-required Summary Plan Descriptions (SPDs). This clause should clearly state that the employer reserves the right to change or withdraw the benefit at any time, both before and after the retirement of any covered employee. Although this may not prevent lawsuits by aggrieved employees, it will put the employer in the best possible position if these benefits must be revoked at some time in the future.

FOOTNOTES

1. The COBRA rules, which are found currently in Section 4980B, were originally enacted in 1986 as Code section 162(k). Effective for years after 1988, Code section 4980B imposes a $100 per day penalty tax for noncompliance.
2. IRC Section 105(h).
3. See Let. Rul. 8747069.
4. IRC Section 401(h), last paragraph.
5. IRC Sections 512(a)(3)(E)(iii) and 419A(c)(2).
6. IRC Section 505.
7. IRC Sections 105 and 106.
8. Labor Reg. §2510.3-1.
9. IRC Sections 401(h)(6), 415(l); Reg. §1.401-14(c)(2).
10. IRC Sections 415(l)(1), 415(c)(1)(B).
11. IRC Section 401(h), last paragraph; Reg. §1.401-14(c)(1)(i).
12. See Let. Ruls. 8924079, 8924080, 8924081. These rulings would have allowed the 25% limit to be based on actuarial "cost" of the plan rather than the actual contributions.

Chapter 38

HEALTH MAINTENANCE ORGANIZATION (HMO)

WHAT IS IT?

A Health Maintenance Organization, or HMO, is an organization of physicians or other health care providers that provides a broad and nearly complete range of health care services on a prepaid basis. An HMO is an alternative to traditional health insurance.

WHEN IS IT INDICATED?

1. As an alternative to traditional health insurance, HMOs are attractive to younger employees and employees with many dependents because the HMO typically covers all medical expenses without significant deductibles or co-pay provisions. Where such employees are predominant in an employer's work force, the employer may get the most perceived value for its benefit dollar by offering an HMO, or choice of HMOs, as its health benefit plan.

2. In certain circumstances, employers *must* offer HMO coverage to employees as an alternative; see the discussion below.

ADVANTAGES

1. HMOs typically cover more health care services than traditional health insurance, with fewer deductibles. Typically there is no co-payment provision.

2. HMOs are said to emphasize preventive medicine, and thus control overall costs better than plans that pay only when employees are hospitalized or sick.

DISADVANTAGES

1. An HMO subscriber generally must receive care from a doctor or other service provider who is part of the HMO. Except for certain emergencies, the HMO will not pay for services of non-HMO providers.

2. The cost advantage, if any, of HMOs may be due to the fact that they enroll younger and healthier participants than traditional health insurance plans, which emphasize coverage for major medical procedures. In time, therefore, it is argued that the cost advantage of HMOs will diminish.

HMO BENEFIT STRUCTURE

Conventional health insurance reimburses employees for expenses or pays providers for health care as required by covered employees. By contrast, an HMO either employs the providers or contracts directly with providers (see the discussion below on types of HMOs). The providers agree to provide medical services to HMO subscribers when required, in return for an annual payment determined *in advance*. Each subscriber to the HMO (or employer who sponsors the plan) pays a fee based on the HMO's projected annual cost.

As a result of this arrangement, the HMO assumes the risk that services required will cost more than the annual payment. In other words, the HMO has an incentive to hold down the costs of health care to subscribers. In theory, these reduced costs will be passed along in the form of reduced costs to the HMO subscribers or to employers who pay for the plan.

HMO subscribers generally must use physicians and other health care providers who are part of the HMO contractual arrangement. Exceptions are usually allowed for emergency services out of the HMO's geographic area, and for medical specialties not available within the HMO, if referred by the primary HMO physician. In return for this reduction in freedom of choice, HMO plans provide for almost all health care services, including routine physician visits. (The HMO must provide broad coverage in order to become *federally qualified* as discussed below.) Usually there are no deductibles. There may be a small co-payment fee for some services. For example, subscribers may be required to pay $2 for each visit to a doctor's office and $2.50 for each prescription.

A comparison of one employer's insured health plan with two alternative HMOs is included in Figure 38.1 at the end of this chapter to give some idea of the benefits provided under typical HMO plans and how they differ from insured plans.

TYPES OF HMOs

HMOs are organized in one of three ways:

(1) the *staff model* HMO is an HMO organization that directly employs doctors and other health care providers who provide the HMO's services to subscribers.

(2) the *group practice* or medical group model involves contracts between the HMO and a medical group or

groups that provide services to subscribers. The individual doctors and other providers are not directly employed by the HMO as an entity.

Both staff model and group practice HMOs are sometimes referred to as *closed panel* plans, because subscribers must use doctors and other providers who are employed by the HMO or under contract to the HMO.

(3) the *individual practice association* or IPA plan, under which the HMO is an association of individual doctors or medical groups that practice in their own offices. Most see non-HMO as well as HMO patients. These plans are often referred to as *open panel* plans, since HMO subscribers can choose any doctor who is part of the IPA. In some areas, many doctors participate in these plans, giving HMO subscribers a wide range of choice.

The structure of an HMO is relevant to an employer's benefit planning in that different types of HMOs may have varying attractiveness to employees. Many employees may be reluctant to give up their own doctors in order to sign up with an unfamiliar closed-panel type of HMO. On the other hand, the choice of doctors in a large IPA plan may be appealing. The IPA may even include some employees' own doctors already. So, an HMO affiliation may effectively change nothing from some employees' viewpoints except to drastically lower the cost of their doctor bills.

The appeal of HMOs in a given geographical area depends in large part on the local medical community's support of the HMO concept. If local doctors and hospitals, particularly the most prestigious ones, are in favor of HMOs, then many local health care providers will join HMOs. HMO subscribers will then have almost the same amount of choice as they would in a conventional insured plan.

FEDERAL HMO ACT REQUIREMENTS

Congress enacted the Health Maintenance Organization Act of 1973 to encourage HMOs as a way of keeping down health care costs. Under this Act, an employer may be required to offer HMO coverage to employees as an alternative to Blue Cross/Blue Shield coverage or conventional insurance. This is referred to as the "dual choice" option. (Under current legislation, the dual choice option is scheduled to expire in 1995.) The dual choice option is required if all of the following conditions exist:

(a) The employer is subject to the minimum wage requirements of the Fair Labor Standards Act.

(b) The employer has 25 or more employees, counting both full and part time employees.

(c) The employer has a health care plan for which the employer pays part or all.

(d) The employer has received a request from an HMO to make coverage available to its employees. The HMO must be *federally qualified* and at least 25 of the employer's employees must reside in the HMO's geographically defined operating area.

An HMO must meet various requirements of the HMO Act and accompanying federal regulations in order to be federally qualified. In addition, the employer may not financially discriminate against employees who elect the HMO.

The most important of the requirements for a federally qualified HMO lists the minimum basic benefits the HMO must provide to subscribers in return for the prepaid annual fee. These services must be provided at no additional cost or for a nominal co-payment fee. The required services are:

- Physicians' services, including specialist consultant and referral services

- Inpatient and outpatient hospital services

- Emergency health services

- Outpatient mental health services up to 20 visits

- Medical care for alcohol or drug addiction

- Laboratory and radiological (x-ray) diagnostic services

- Home health services

- Preventive services (immunizations, physical examinations, family planning, well-baby care)

- Medical social services (education in health or medical care)

Many HMOs provide services in addition to those required for federal qualification; for example dental or vision care services, prescription drugs (usually for a small co-payment), additional mental health services, or nursing and rehabilitation facilities.

TAX IMPLICATIONS

The tax treatment of payments to HMOs and benefits received is the same as that for health insurance, described in Chapter 37.

WHERE CAN I FIND OUT MORE ABOUT IT?

1. Beam, Burton T., Jr. and John J. McFadden, *Employee Benefits*, 3rd ed. Chicago, IL: Dearborn Financial Publishing, Inc., 1992.

2. Pictrick, "Legal Issues in Attempting to Influence Adverse Selection by Employers and HMOs," *Benefits Law Journal*, Summer, 1990.

QUESTIONS AND ANSWERS

Question — If a federally qualified HMO makes a request for coverage to an employer, is the employer obligated to offer that particular HMO to employees?

Answer — The dual choice provision requires only that the employer make an HMO available to employees in the particular geographical region where the requesting HMO operates. The HMO made available does not have to be the one making the request. The employer may choose which HMOs to make available.

Figure 38.1

| | EMPLOYER, INC.
Comparison of Health Care Benefits | | |
	Insured Plan	Health Maintenance Organization A	Health Maintenance Organization B
TYPE OF PLAN	Health insurance plan covering full or partial cost of medical services after they are provided	Prepaid Individual Practice Association — HMO A contracts with private physicians' offices located in the community.	Prepaid Group Practice Plan — a team of physicians and medical professionals practice together to provide members preventive, comprehensive care for a fixed, advanced payment
CHOICE OF PHYSICIAN	Member may select any licensed physician or surgeon.	Member selects a physician from one of the 230 primary medical offices. All types of specialists are available by referral.	Member selects a personal physician from the Health America medical group who coordinates and directs all health care needs including referrals to specialists.
WHERE PRIMARY AND SPECIALITY CARE IS AVAILABLE	Care provided in physician's office or outpatient facility.	Care provided in HMO-A participating private physician's offices	Care provided at 5 multi-specialty centers
CHOICE OF HOSPITALS	Member may select any accredited hospital. Choice depends on where physician has admitting privileges.	Member goes to hospital where physician has admitting privileges.	Selection among HMO-B participating hospitals (see brochure for locations).
DEDUCTIBLE AND COINSURANCE	Annual deductible; $200 individual, $500 Family. 10% or 50% coinsurance on covered charges after satisfying deductible. Selected procedures/care covered in full, no deductible. No coinsurance on covered services after $4,000, individual $10,000 Family annual expense incurred.	No deductible. No coinsurance (except small co-payments for office visits, home visits, prescriptions and outpatient mental health and other deductibles as noted in the comparison).	No deductible. No coinsurance except small co-payments for outpatient mental health.
MAXIMUM BENEFIT	No lifetime maximum.	No overall maximum limit.	No overall maximum limit.

Health Maintenance Organization (HMO)

Figure 38.1 (continued)

	Insured Plan	Health Maintenance Organization A	Health Maintenance Organization B
PREVENTIVE CARE			
Routine Physicians	Not covered.	Covered in full.	Covered in full.
Well Baby Care	Covered at 90%.	Covered in full.	Covered in full.
Pap Smears	Routine exams not covered.	Covered in full.	Covered in full; care provided by Gynecologist.
Immunizations	Not covered.	Covered in full.	Covered in full.
Eye Exam	Not covered.	Covered in full and $35 allowance for eyeglasses or contact lenses	Covered in full including written prescriptions for lenses.
Hearing Exam	Not covered.	Covered in full.	Covered in full.
Health Education	Available through some physicians' offices.	Weight watchers programs, YMCA physical fitness program, other programs offered periodically.	Periodic classes held on diet, prenatal care and physical fitness, smoking cessation, stress management, etc. Discount programs at many Nautilus clubs and health spas.
PHYSICIAN CARE			
Surgery	Outpatient—covered at 100% no deductible. (Charges for hospital, surgicenter or miscellaneous physician's expense connected to outpatient surgery covered at 90% after deductible.) Inpatient-covered at 90% after deductible. Specified elective procedures require 2nd opinion to insure unreduced benefits.	Covered in full.	Covered in full.
Inpatient Visits	Covered at 90% after satisfying deductible.	Covered in full.	Covered in full.
Office and Home	Covered at 90% after satisfying deductible.	Office visits covered with $2 co-pay at primary office. Physician home visits covered with $5 co-pay. No co-pay for specialist visits.	Office visits covered in full. Home visits covered in full.
X-rays and Lab	Pre-Admission status—covered at 100% with no deductible. Other instances covered at 90% after satisfying deductible when deemed medically necessary	Covered in full.	Covered in full.

Figure 38.1 (continued)

	Insured Plan	Health Maintenance Organization A	Health Maintenance Organization B
HOSPITAL SERVICES			
Room and Board	Covered at 90% for unlimited days after satisfying deductible.	Covered in full for unlimited days in semiprivate room. (Private room covered in full when medically necessary.)	Covered in full for unlimited days in semiprivate room. (Private room covered in full when medically necessary.)
Supplies, Tests, Medication, etc.	Covered at 90% after satisfying deductible. In hospital charges in connection with a scheduled surgical procedure incurred more than 24 hours prior are not covered.	Covered in full.	Covered in full.
Private Duty Nurse	Covered at 90% after satisfying deductible up to a maximum of $1,000 a year.	Covered in full when medically necessary.	Covered in full when medically necessary.
EMERGENCY CARE	Covered at 100% with no deductible if rendered in physician's office or an emergency care center within 48 hours of accidental injury. Hospital emergency room service covered at 90% after the deductible.	Covered with $15 co-pay at hospital and $5 co-pay at doctor's office.	Covered in full for around-the-clock emergency care by HMO-B physicians and in participating hospitals. Emergency care by non-HMO-B physicians or hospitals also covered when obtaining HMO-B care is not reasonable because of distance and urgency.
Ambulance Service	Covered at 90% for local transportation after satisfying deductible when medically necessary.	Covered in full when medically necessary.	Covered in full.
MATERNITY CARE			
Hospital	Co-pays and deductibles apply. See Hospital Services.	Covered in full.	Covered in full.
Physician	Co-pay and deductibles apply. See Physician Care.	Covered in full.	Covered in full.
Waiting Period	No waiting period — limitation of pre-existing conditions apply.	No waiting period.	No waiting period.

Figure 38.1 (continued)

	Insured Plan	Health Maintenance Organization A	Health Maintenance Organization B
MENTAL HEALTH CARE			
Hospital	Co-pays and deductibles apply. See Hospital Services.	Covered in full for 35 days per year.	Covered in full for 45 days per 12 months.
Inpatient Physician	Co-pays and deductibles apply. See Physician Care.	Covered in full 35 days per year.	Covered in full for 45 days per 12 months.
Outpatient Physician	Covered at 50% up to $40 per visit and $1,000 per year.	Covered for 20 visits per year. First 2 visits covered in full. Next 8 visits you pay $10 per visit. Next 10 visits, you pay $25 per visit. Member charge never exceeds 50% of fee.	Covered for 30 visits per 12 months. First 3 visits covered in full. Next 27 visits you pay $10 per visit.
Alcohol and Drug Addiction	Covered as other mental health services.	Covered in full for acute phase of alcohol or drug abuse.	No special limits. Covered as other medical and mental health services. Detoxification covered for acute phase only.
DENTAL CARE			
Hospital	Separate Dental option offered to all employees — Contact Personnel for details.	Covered for: hospital costs when confinement is necessary for dental care due to covered medical problem; treatment of accidental injury to natural teeth occurring while insured; impacted wisdom teeth, partially, or totally covered by bone.	Covered for: hospital costs when confinement is necessary for dental care; and treatment of accidental injury to natural teeth occurring while insured; and certain oral surgical procedures, e.g., impacted wisdom teeth partially or totally covered by bone.
Office visits	Separate Dental option offered to all employees.	Oral hygiene exams for children under 12, including cleaning and scaling to teeth, instruction and fluoride treatment.	Covered for: 2 checkups and 1 cleaning per year, 20% discount on other dental services including speciality areas and orthodontia at participating dental offices.
OUTPATIENT MEDICATION			
Prescription Drug	Covered at 90% after deductible.	Covered w/$2.50 Co-pay.	Covered w/$2 Co-pay.
Injections	Covered at 90% after deductible.	Covered in full.	Covered in full.

Health Maintenance Organization (HMO)

Figure 38.1 (continued)

	Insured Plan	Health Maintenance Organization A	Health Maintenance Organization B
PRESCRIBED HOME HEALTH SERVICES	Home Health Extension Services paid at 100% with no deductible if recommended by discharging hospital.	Covered in full except for travel.	Covered in full.
ALLERGY CARE	Covered at 90% after deductible.	Covered in full.	Covered in full.
ELIGIBILITY	Spouse; and unmarried dependent children to age 19 or age 23 if a full time student.	Spouse; and unmarried dependent children to age 19 or age 23 if a full time student.	Spouse; and unmarried dependent children to age 19 or age 23 if a full time student.
MEDICARE	Regular plan coverage continued coordinated with Medicare.	Medicare plan available.	Medicare coordinated benefit available.
CONVERSION	Conversion to individual coverage available.	Conversion to HMO-PA Non-Group coverage available. RX is not available to for conversion.	Conversion to HSP Non-Group coverage available.

NOTE: This comparison is not a contract. It is intended to highlight some of the principal differences between the plans. For a more detailed description of benefits, refer to the benefits brochures of each plan.

The Tools and Techniques of Employee Benefit and Retirement Planning

Chapter 39

INCENTIVE STOCK OPTION (ISO)

WHAT IS IT?

An incentive stock option (ISO) plan is a tax-favored plan for compensating executives by granting options to buy company stock. Unlike regular stock options, ISOs generally do not result in taxable income to executives either at time of the grant or the time of the exercise of the option. If the ISO meets the requirements of Internal Revenue Code section 422, the executive is taxed only when stock purchased under the ISO is sold. (Regular or "nonstatutory" stock options are discussed in Chapter 50. Also, see Appendix D for a comprehensive outline of stock option and similar plans used for compensating executives, particularly in large corporations.)

WHEN IS IT INDICATED?

ISOs are primarily used by larger corporations to compensate executives. ISOs are generally not suitable for closely held corporations because (a) ISOs are valuable to executives only when stock can be sold, and there is usually no ready market for closely held stock, and (b) shareholders of closely held corporations often do not want unrelated outsiders to become shareholders of the company.

ADVANTAGES

1. The ISO provides greater deferral of taxes to the executive than a nonstatutory stock option (see Chapter 50).

2. The ISO is a form of compensation with little or no out-of-pocket cost to the company. The real cost of stock options is that the company forgoes the opportunity to sell the same stock on the market and realize its proceeds for company purposes.

DISADVANTAGES

1. The corporation granting an ISO option does not ordinarily receive a tax deduction for it at any time.

2. The plan must meet complex technical requirements of Code section 422 and related provisions.

3. The exercise price of ISO options must be at least equal to the fair market value of the stock when the option is granted. There is no similar restriction on nonstatutory options.

4. Income from the sale of the ISO may be eligible for preferential capital gain treatment, enhancing the value of the tax deferral.

5. n executive may incur an alternative minimum tax (AMT) liability when an ISO option is granted or exercised.

TAX IMPLICATIONS

1. The executive is not subject to federal income tax on an ISO either at the time the option is granted or at the time he exercises the option (i.e., when he buys the stock). Tax consequences are deferred until the time of disposition of the stock.[1]

2. An order to obtain this tax treatment for incentive stock options, Section 422 prescribes the following rules:

   - the options must be granted under a written plan specifying the number of shares to be issued and the class of employees covered under the plan. There are no nondiscrimination rules; the plan can cover key executives only.

   - only the first $100,000 worth of ISO stock granted any one employee, which becomes exercisable for the first time during any one year, is entitled to the favorable ISO treatment; to the extent that the value of the stock exceeds $100,000, this amount is treated as a non-statutory (regular) stock option.

   - no option, by its terms, may be exercisable more than ten years from the date of grant.

   - the person receiving the option must be employed by the company granting the option at all times between the grant of the option and three months before the date of exercise (twelve months in the case of permanent and total disability, and no limit in the event of death).

   - stock acquired by an employee under the ISO must be held for at least two years after the grant of the option and one year from the date stock is transferred to the employee. (This requirement is waived upon the employee's death.)

- no options may be issued more than ten years from the date the ISO plan is adopted or approved, whichever occurs first.

- the option must not be transferable (except by will or descent and distribution) and must be exercisable only by the person receiving it.

- corporate stockholders must approve the ISO plan within twelve months of the time it is adopted by the company's board of directors.

- the exercise price of the option must be at least equal to the fair market value of the stock on the date the option is granted.

- ISOs may not be granted to any employee who owns, directly or indirectly, more than 10% of the corporation unless the term of the option is limited to not more than five years and the exercise price is at least 110% of the fair market value of the stock on the date of the grant.

3. Although there is no regular income tax to the executive when an ISO is exercised, the alternative minimum tax (AMT) may have an impact. The excess of the stock's fair market value over the option price at the time of exercise is included in the individual's alternative minimum taxable income. (However, if the individual is subject to the alternative minimum tax, his basis in the stock for alternative minimum tax purposes will be increased by the amount included in income.)[2]

4. If the executive holds the stock for the periods specified above, (two years after grant and one year after exercise) the gain on any sale is taxed at preferential long term capital gain rates.

5. If the stock is sold before the two year/one year holding periods specified above, the excess of the fair market value of the shares at the time of exercise over the exercise price is treated as compensation income to the executive in the year the stock is sold, depriving the executive of preferential capital gain treatment.[3]

Example: Executive Flo Through is covered under her company's ISO plan. Under the plan, Flo is granted an option in 1993 to purchase company stock for $100 per share. In January, 1995, Flo exercises this option and purchases 100 shares for a total of $10,000. The fair market value of the 100 shares in January, 1995, is $14,000. In October, 1995, Flo sells the 100 shares for $16,000. Flo's taxable gain is $6,000 ($16,000 amount realized less $10,000 cost). Of this amount, $4,000 (fair market value of $14,000 less $10,000 exercise price) is treated as compensation income for the year 1992. The remaining $2,000 is capital gain.

6. The corporation does not get a tax deduction for granting an ISO. Nor does it get a deduction when an executive exercises an option or sells stock acquired under an ISO plan.[4] However, the corporation *does* get a deduction for the compensation income element that an executive must recognize if stock is sold before the two year/one year holding period, as described in paragraph 5 above.

WHERE CAN I FIND OUT MORE ABOUT IT?

1. Graduate Course: Executive Compensation (GS 842), The American College, Bryn Mawr, PA.

2. *Tax Facts On Investments (Tax Facts 2)* (Cincinnati, The National Underwriter Company).

FOOTNOTES

1. IRC Section 421(a).
2. IRC Section 56(b)(3).
3. IRC Section 421(b).
4. IRC Section 421(a)(2), (b).

Chapter 40

KEY EMPLOYEE LIFE INSURANCE

WHAT IS IT?

Key employee life insurance is insurance on a key employee's life owned by the employer, with the death benefit payable to the employer. Technically, key employee insurance is designed to compensate the employer for the loss of a key employee and is not an employee benefit for the key employee. However, in closely held corporations, key employee insurance can be used to indirectly benefit shareholder-employees by providing a source of liquid assets in the corporation. Key employee policies make assets available from policy cash values during the employee's lifetime and from the policy proceeds on the death of the employee. These assets can be used to finance the employer's obligation under one or more employee benefit plans.

WHEN IS IT INDICATED?

1. When a corporation will incur an obligation to pay a specified beneficiary or class of beneficiaries at an employee's death under a death benefit only (DBO) plan—see Chapter 30.

2. When an employer has a nonqualified deferred compensation arrangement with one or more key executives or other employees and needs a way to finance its obligation upon the death of the employee. For example, such a plan might provide a benefit of $50,000 a year for 10 years if the employee lives to retirement or $50,000 a year for 10 years to a designated beneficiary if the employee dies either before or after retirement—see Chapter 16.

3. When a closely held corporation anticipates a need for liquid assets upon the death of a key employee to stabilize the corporation financially and enable it to continue contributing to employee benefit plans for surviving employees.

4. When a shareholder-employee expects the corporation to buy stock from his or her estate as part of an estate plan and the corporation needs additional liquid assets to carry out such a purchase.

TAX IMPLICATIONS

To the Employee

1. There is no income tax to a key employee or the key employee's estate when the corporation owns the policy, pays the premiums, and receives death proceeds from key employee life insurance.

2. Corporate-owned key employee life insurance may have some effect on the federal estate tax payable by the deceased key employee's estate.

   • The value of corporate stock held by a decedent at death is included in the decedent's gross estate for federal estate tax purposes. If the corporation held life insurance on the decedent's life, the insurance proceeds increase the value of the corporation, and therefore can be included in the value of the stock held by the decedent. The general rule for key employee life insurance, where the corporation is the beneficiary, is that the insurance proceeds are taken into account in valuing the decedent's stock, but not necessarily included in the decedent's estate dollar for dollar.[1] However, in many situations the IRS attempts to increase the value of the stock as much as possible where the corporation held key employee life insurance.

   • If the insured key employee was a majority shareholder (more than 50%), the tax law provides that policy proceeds, to the extent payable to or for the benefit of a party other than the corporation or its creditors, will be taxed in the insured key employee's estate as life insurance.[2] For this reason, policy proceeds of corporate-owned life insurance should generally be payable only to the corporation or its creditors.

To the Corporation

1. Corporate-paid premiums on life insurance on the life of a key employee, where the corporation is the owner and beneficiary of the life insurance contract, are not deductible for federal income tax purposes.[3]

2. The death proceeds of key employee life insurance are tax-free when paid to the corporation, except for the potential application of the alternative minimum tax (AMT) discussed below.[4]

3. If the corporation has accumulated earnings of more than $250,000 ($150,000 for certain service corporations) then the further accumulation of income to pay life insurance premiums for key employee insurance potentially exposes the corporation to the accumulated earnings tax. There are, however, many exceptions to the application of this tax. The purchase of life insurance to cover the potential loss of a bona fide key employee should not result in a significant risk of accumulated earnings tax exposure in most cases.

4. Key employee life insurance involves some potential corporate exposure to the corporate alternative minimum tax (AMT). The purpose of the AMT is to require corporations to pay a minimum level of income tax on actual economic income, even if taxable income has been reduced by significant amounts of tax-exempt or tax-preferred income. The AMT is a tax computed on a base of reported income plus certain "tax preferences." Generally, a corporation must pay the larger of its regular tax or the AMT.[5]

The AMT is imposed on a base of "adjusted minimum taxable income" or AMTI. The AMTI includes regular income plus tax preferences. In addition, there is included in the AMTI an amount equal to 75% of the excess of corporate "adjusted current earnings" over the AMTI (computed without regard to the adjustment for current earnings), with various adjustments.[6]

Adjusted current earnings includes amounts that are income for accounting purposes and treated as "earnings and profits" under tax law (Code section 312) but are not included in taxable income. IRS regulations indicate that both death proceeds (in excess of the taxpayer's basis) and the annual increases in cash value are part of adjusted current earnings.[7]

The corporate AMT is equal to 20% of AMTI reduced by a $40,000 exemption which is phased out at the rate of 25% of AMTI exceeding $150,000 (in other words, the exemption disappears for AMTI that is equal to or greater than $310,000 ($310,000 exceeds $150,000 by $160,000 and 25% of $160,000 is $40,000)).

A simple example will illustrate the impact of AMT on corporate-owned life insurance:

Example. Professional Services, Inc. (PSI) has regular taxable income of $200,000. Also, PSI receives $300,000 of net death proceeds from corporate-owned term life insurance. PSI's regular income tax is 34% of $200,000 or $68,000. The AMT is computed as follows:

Taxable income		$200,000
AMTI without adjustment for current earnings		200,000
Current earnings	$500,000	
Less AMTI w/o adjustment	-200,000	
	$300,000	
75% of 300,000		$225,000
AMTI		425,000
Exemption amount		0
AMTI less exemption		425,000
AMT (20% of AMTI less exemption)		85,000
Less regular tax		-68,000
Additional tax		17,000

This example shows an additional tax of $17,000, which is 5.7% of the insurance proceeds of $300,000. In general, the maximum tax that can be imposed on death proceeds is 20% of 75% of the death proceeds, or 15%.

Although the AMT is unfavorable to corporate-owned life insurance, its maximum impact is not extreme. Furthermore, the best way to avoid the impact of the AMT is to purchase additional life insurance, to insure that the corporation receives the full amount expected, after AMT.

ALTERNATIVES

Personally-owned insurance can provide estate liquidity and funds to meet the needs of beneficiaries. Corporate funds can be used indirectly by paying extra compensation to the employee as discussed in Chapter 26. This extra compensation is deductible so long as it meets the reasonableness test discussed in Chapter 28. In a situation where the corporation's marginal income tax bracket is higher than the employee's, personally-owned insurance may provide a better tax result.

WHERE CAN I FIND OUT MORE ABOUT IT?

1. Leimberg, Stephan R., et al., *The Tools and Techniques of Estate Planning*, 9th ed. Cincinnati, OH: The National Underwriter Co., 1992.

2. CLU/ChFC Course: Planning for Business Owners and Professionals (HS 331), The American College, Bryn Mawr, PA.

3. Graduate Courses: Business Tax Planning (GS 845) and Advanced Estate Planning (GS 815 and 816), The American College, Bryn Mawr, PA.

4. Stoeber, "Corporate Ownership of Life Insurance — Complexities Abound," *Journal of the American Society of CLU & ChFC*, May, 1991, p. 32.

FOOTNOTES

1. Reg. §20.2031-2(f).
2. Reg. §20.2042-1(c)(6).
3. IRC Section 264(a)(1).
4. IRC Section 101(a)(1).
5. IRC Sections 55, 56.
6. IRC Section 56(g).
7. Reg. §1.56(g)-1(c)(5).

Chapter 41

LEGAL SERVICES PLAN

WHAT IS IT?

A legal services plan (sometimes referred to as a "prepaid legal services plan") is an employer-funded plan that makes legal services available to employees when needed. The expenses of the plan are deductible to the employer and if the plan meets qualification rules under Code section 120, as described below, neither the employer's payments to cover costs of the plan nor the legal services provided are taxable income to employees. Code section 120 has been extended several times. It currently expires for taxable years beginning after June 30, 1992 and is likely to be extended again.

WHEN IS IT INDICATED?

In theory, any group of employees can benefit from the advantages of these plans. However, in practice they are used primarily by larger employers for employees in collective bargaining units. Such plans are usually funded through multiemployer trusteeships sponsored by labor unions. Group insurance for funding these plans is also available but is not yet widely used.

ADVANTAGES

1. A legal services plan that meets the standards of Code section 120 provides a tax-free form of compensation income for employees.

2. Many employees, particularly middle and lower income employees, are not well-served by the traditional fee-for-service system of delivering legal services and, as a result, often do without a lawyer when they really need one. For example, many middle income people do not have adequate legal advice in tax and domestic matters. A legal services plan provides these services without additional employee expenditure.

3. Legal expenses such as the cost of a criminal trial can be the kind of catastrophic expense that is best provided through an insurance-type or group benefit program such as a legal services plan.

DISADVANTAGES

1. Since most employees rarely need a lawyer, or rarely perceive the need for one, a legal services plan may not be fully appreciated by employees compared with other forms of employee compensation.

2. Funding and administering a legal services plan is difficult in light of the limited availability of group legal insurance or multiemployer arrangements.

3. Some employers fear that a legal services plan will make it more likely that employees will sue the employer in the event of a dispute. However, legal services for actions by employees against the employer can be (and usually are) excluded from the plan.

4. If the standards of Code section 120 are not met by a legal services plan, either employer expenditures for the plan or the value of legal services provided will be taxable income to covered employees.

DESIGN FEATURES

1. Eligibility must be nondiscriminatory in order to meet the Code section 120 standards discussed below. If this is not a factor, any group of employees can be covered.

2. Benefits are usually provided on either a *scheduled* or a *comprehensive* basis.

    With a scheduled plan only those benefits listed in the plan are provided. Most plans provide at least the following benefits:

    - legal consultations and advice on any matter

    - preparation of wills, deeds, powers-of-attorney and other routine legal documents

    - personal bankruptcy

    - adoption proceedings

    - defense of civil and criminal matters

    - juvenile proceedings

    - divorce, separation, child custody, and other domestic matters.

    A plan that provides comprehensive benefits pays for all legal services, with specified exclusions. The most common exclusions include:

- audits by the IRS

- actions against the employer, the plan, or a labor union sponsoring the plan

- contingent fee cases or class action suits

- actions arising out of the employee's separate business transactions

3. Some plans provide benefits on an indemnity basis, that is, by reimbursing the employee for covered expenditures. In that case, benefits are usually limited to a flat amount for a given legal service or a maximum hourly rate. There may also be a maximum annual benefit such as $1,000.

   Prepayment-type plans are more common than indemnity plans. In a prepayment plan there is no direct expenditure by employees. In a *closed-panel* prepayment plan, the most common type, employees must obtain covered services from specified groups of lawyers who are either employed by or under contract with the plan (similar to an HMO—see Chapter 38). In an *open-panel* prepayment plan employees can choose their own lawyer or choose a lawyer from an approved list. The lawyer must agree in advance to a fee schedule set by the legal services plan. A plan can combine both the closed panel and open panel approaches, allowing occasional use of top legal specialists for serious matters, while routine matters are handled by the closed panel.

TAX IMPLICATIONS

1. Costs of a legal services plan, whether or not it meets the standards of Code section 120, are deductible to the employer,[1] with certain limitations:

    (a) as with all deductions for employee compensation, the overall compensation of each employee must meet the "reasonableness" test discussed in Chapter 28;

    (b) if the plan is funded in advance, the amount of deductible advance funding is limited to approximately the benefits provided during the taxable year plus administrative expenses.[2]

2. If the plan does not meet the requirements of Code section 120[3]:

    (a) if the plan is prefunded by the employer—for example, if the employer pays a group legal insurance premium to an insurance company—the employee is taxed on his or her share of the premium at the time the employer pays it, if the employee is fully vested in the benefit (legally entitled at that time to receive benefits under the plan).

    (b) if the employer pays for benefits out of current revenues as employees receive benefits the employee is taxed on the value of benefits as they are received.

3. If the plan meets the requirements of Code section 120, neither employer payments for funding the plan nor benefits received from the plan are taxable income to the employee. Code section 120 has been allowed to expire several times and subsequently been revived by Congress. Currently, Section 120 expires for taxable years beginning after June 30, 1992 and is expected to be extended again. Section 120 imposes the following requirements:

- Contributions or benefits must not discriminate in favor of "highly compensated" employees. For the definition of highly compensated, see Chapter 23.

- Eligibility must be based on a nondiscriminatory classification. Employees in collective bargaining units that have bargained separately on legal services benefits may be excluded.

- Not more than 25 percent of the amounts contributed under the plan can be for employees who own more than 5 percent of the employer.

- The IRS must be notified in accordance with regulations that the employer has adopted a qualified legal services plan.

- Employer contributions for the plan can be paid only to an insurance company, a special type of tax-exempt trust set up under Code section 501(c)(20) to fund legal services plans, a nonprofit organization such as a labor union or state bar organization that funds prepaid legal services plans, or providers of legal services, as prepayments. Any combination of these four methods of funding may be used.

- Coverage above a $70 annual premium value is taxable to the employee.

- The plan must be in writing and must be for the exclusive benefit of employees or their spouses or dependents.

A Section 120 plan can provide benefits to employees and also to their spouses or dependents. Section 120 does not restrict the types of legal benefits that can be provided or require any specific legal benefits to be included.

HOW TO INSTALL A PLAN

For a plan intended to qualify under Section 120, the formal requirements listed above must be complied with and notice given to the IRS. For a non-Section 120 plan, the procedure can be more informal, but a written document is advisable in any case.

WHERE CAN I FIND OUT MORE ABOUT IT?

Beam, Burton T., Jr. and John J. McFadden, *Employee Benefits*, 3rd ed. Chicago IL: Dearborn Financial Publishing, Inc., 1992.

FOOTNOTES

1. IRC Section 162(a)(1).
2. See generally IRC Section 419.
3. The rules discussed here are the general rules for inclusion under Code sections 61 and 83; there are no specific rules for these benefits other than Section 120.

Chapter 42

LOANS TO EXECUTIVES

Many employers make loans available to executives, usually restricted to loans for specified purposes. Typically such loans are interest-free or made at a favorable interest rate. Current tax law reduces, but does not eliminate the advantages of such loans.

WHEN IS IT INDICATED?

Employers rarely act as an unrestricted "bank" for executives. However, loan programs can be extremely attractive as a compensation supplement to help executives meet cash needs in special situations. Loans are typically offered for the following:

- Mortgage or "bridge" loan to help in the purchase of a home, where the employee is moving from one of the employer's business locations to another.

- College or private school tuition for members of the executive's family.

- Purchase of stock of the employer through a company stock purchase plan or otherwise.

- Meeting extraordinary medical needs, tax bills, or other personal or family emergency such as divorce settlement costs.

- Purchase of life insurance.

- Purchase of a car, vacation home, or other expensive item.

ADVANTAGES

1. Although the tax rules discussed under "TAX IMPLICATIONS," below, provide no great tax advantage to executive loans, such loans still provide a valuable benefit by (a) making cash available where regular bank loans might be difficult to obtain and (b) providing loans at a favorable rate of interest.

2. Certain types of loans are generally exempt from the complex tax rules for "below-market" loans:

- mortgage and "bridge" loans made in connection with an employment-connected relocation,

- 'de minimis" loans aggregating less than $10,000 (see below), and

- low interest loans without "significant tax effect" on the lender or borrower.

3. The cost of a loan program to the employer is only the administrative cost plus the loss of interest on the loan, if any, compared to what the employer could have obtained by another type of investment or investment in the business itself.

4. There are no nondiscrimination rules for executive loan programs. Loans can be provided to selected groups of executives or even a single executive. The terms, amounts, and conditions of executive loans can be varied from one executive to another as the employer wishes.

DISADVANTAGES

1. The tax rules for "below-market" loans are complicated and confusing, which increases the administrative cost of the loan program for both employer and employee.

2. The tax treatment of term loans (as opposed to demand loans) is unfavorable—the employee must include a substantial portion of the loan in income immediately in some cases.

3. The employer must bear the cost of administering the loan, (for example, determining whether the loan should be granted, monitoring the payback, and advising the executive as to the tax consequences), and also must bear the risk of default (either losing the money altogether or the costs of foreclosure on a house or other asset used as collateral).

TAX IMPLICATIONS

1. The following tax rules apply if a loan is

(a) a "below-market"[1] loan,

(b) "compensation-related,"[2] and

(c) a "demand" loan—a loan payable in full at any time upon demand of the lender. A "demand" loan also includes any loan (1) where the interest arrangements are conditioned on the future services of the employee, and (2) of which the interest benefits are not transferable by the employee.[3]

Most executive loan programs involve loans that meet these definitions. Term loans—those payable at a specified time in the future—are discussed in the "Questions and Answers" at the end of this chapter.

For federal income tax purposes, interest on a loan meeting conditions (a), (b), and (c) is treated as three transactions combined—the actual transaction plus two "deemed" transactions:

(1) interest *actually* paid by the executive borrower is taxable income to the company (lender) and that interest payment is deductible by the borrower, subject to the usual limitations on interest deductions. For example, if the loan qualifies as a home mortgage loan, the interest is fully deductible, but if it is a personal loan not secured by a home mortgage it is nondeductible.

(2) the employer is treated as if it paid additional compensation to the employee in the amount of the difference between the actual rate of interest and the "applicable federal rate" (see below).[4] This additional compensation income is deductible by the employer (within the usual "reasonable compensation" limits) and is taxable to the executive.

The applicable federal rate (AFR) is published monthly by the IRS as a Revenue Ruling (which appears in the monthly Internal Revenue Bulletin). For demand loans the AFR is the short-term semiannual rate. For a term loan, the AFR is the short-term, mid-term, or long-term rate in effect as of the day the loan was made, also compounded semiannually. Both figures can be found in Table 1 of each month's Revenue Ruling establishing the AFR. If the loan is of a fixed principal amount that remains outstanding for the entire calendar year, the "blended annual rate" (published in July of each year) is the AFR.

(3) the executive is treated as if he paid the amount in (2) above to the employer. This amount is additional taxable income to the employer. The amount is deductible by the executive borrower, again under the usual limitations on interest deductibility.

Example: Executive Flint borrows $100,000 from her employer. Assume that interest at the applicable federal rate for Year 1 would be $12,000, but actual interest under the loan agreement is only $5,000. This loan results in additional taxable compensation income to Flint for Year 1 of $7,000 ($12,000 less $5,000). If interest is deductible (for example, if the loan qualifies as a home mortgage loan), Flint can deduct $12,000 (the actual $5,000 plus the deemed $7,000) as an interest payment. Flint's employer can deduct $12,000 as compensation paid to Flint for Year 1, regardless of whether Flint can deduct any of the interest.

Are these loans advantageous to the employee in light of these rules? Yes, because with a low interest loan it still costs the employee less to borrow money even if it results in additional taxable income. For example, suppose that in the example above executive Flint had not been able to deduct any interest on the loan. Then, in this "worst-case" scenario, Flint would have had additional taxable income of $7,000, resulting in additional tax at a 31% rate of $2,170. The total cost of borrowing for Year 1 therefore would be the actual interest paid ($5,000) plus the additional tax ($2,170), or a total of $7,170. By comparison, a loan at the applicable federal rate (which presumably is close to the actual market rate) would have cost Flint $12,000 in Year 1.

2. *Exceptions.*

Mortgage and bridge loans. The rules described above do not apply to certain mortgage and bridge loans used to help an employee purchase a house in connection with the employee's transfer to a new principal place of work. In other words, such loans are treated for tax purposes by the employer and employee just as they are actually negotiated, without any "deemed" transactions.

The following requirements must be met in order to qualify for the mortgage loan exception:[5]

(a) the loan is compensation-related and is a demand loan, as defined earlier;

(b) the new principal residence is acquired in connection with the transfer of the employee to a new principal place of work (which meets the distance and time requirements for a moving expense deduction under Code section 217—see Chapter 45);

(c) the executive certifies to the employer that he or she reasonably expects to be entitled to and will itemize deductions while the loan is outstanding;

(d) under the loan agreement, loan proceeds may be used only to buy the executive's new principal residence; and

(e) the loan is secured by a mortgage on the new principal residence of the employee.

A bridge loan must satisfy the requirements above, as well as the following additional requirements:

(a) the loan must be payable in full in 15 days after the old principal residence is sold;

(b) the aggregate principal of all bridge loans must not exceed the employer's reasonable estimate of the equity of the executive and his spouse in the old residence; and

(c) the old residence must not be converted to business or investment use.

De minimis loans. The below-market rules do not apply to a compensation-related loan for any day on which aggregate loans outstanding between the company and the executive do not exceed $10,000, provided that tax avoidance is not one of the principal purposes of the interest arrangements.[6] A husband and wife are treated as one borrower for this purpose.[7]

No tax effect. A loan is exempt from the below-market rules if the taxpayer can show that the interest arrangements will have no significant effect on any federal tax liability of the lender or borrower.[8] In making this determination the IRS will consider

- whether items of income and deduction generated by the loan offset each other;

- the amount of such items;

- the cost to the taxpayer of complying with the below-market loan rules; and

- any non-tax reasons for structuring the transaction as a below-market loan.[9]

ERISA AND OTHER REGULATORY IMPLICATIONS

An executive loan program does not appear to fall within the definition of either a "welfare benefit plan" or a "pension plan" for ERISA purposes. Therefore, ERISA requirements should not apply and a Form 5500 need not be filed.

Federal "Truth in Lending"[10] requirements may conceivably apply.

Employers should investigate the Truth in Lending requirements if they extend more than 25 loans (or more than 5 loans secured by dwellings) in a calendar year. The Truth in Lending requirements primarily involve additional paperwork, but failure to meet them could result in penalties.

ALTERNATIVES

Because of the administrative cost and complexity of loan programs, employers may wish to investigate alternatives that would provide substantially the same benefits to executives. These could include:

- loans by the employer at full market rates, but "bonus" the interest cost to the executive as additional compensation.

- guarantees by the employer of regular bank loans taken out by executives. This works best where the bank is one with which the employer has an established business relationship.

QUESTIONS AND ANSWERS

Question — How is a term loan to an executive treated for tax purposes?

Answer — A term loan is defined in the below-market loan rules as any loan that is not a demand loan.[11] Generally, a term loan is one with a fixed payment date such as five years—that is, a loan that does not by its terms have to be paid back until a specified date in the future.

A term loan is deemed to be below-market if the amount loaned is more than the present value of all payments due under the loan.[12] The present value is determined with a discount rate based on the applicable federal rate (AFR).

If a below-market compensation-related loan is made, the executive (borrower) is treated as if he immediately received an amount equal to the excess of (a) the amount of the loan, over (b) the present value of all payments required to be made under the loan.[13]

For example, suppose employer Rocks, Inc. lends executive Rubble $40,000, interest-free, payable in 5 years. Assume that based on the AFR for the first year of the loan, the present value of the loan is $22,000. Rubble is treated as having received additional compensation income of $18,000 ($40,000 less $22,000) in the first year of the loan. Rocks, Inc. can deduct this $18,000 as additional compensation paid (subject to the reasonable compensation rules). Over the five-year period of the loan, Rubble is also treated as paying interest to Rocks, Inc. at the applicable federal rate on the deemed "unpaid amount" of $22,000, and Rocks, Inc. must include this interest in income.

The $10,000 de minimis rule for term loans is similar to the one for demand loans; however, once a term loan has exceeded $10,000, it continues to be subject to the below-market loan rules, even if the balance later falls below $10,000.[14]

FOOTNOTES

1. IRC Section 7872(e)(1) defines below-market loans; a demand loan is a below-market loan if interest is payable on it at a rate less than the "applicable federal rate" in effect for the loan period.
2. IRC Section 7872(c)(1)(B) provides that a below-market loan is compensation-related if it is directly or indirectly between (1) an employer and an employee, or (2) an independent contractor and the person for whom the independent contractor provides services.
3. IRC Section 7872(f)(5). The IRS is given authority to issue regulations treating any loan with an indefinite maturity as a demand loan.
4. The actual calculation is complicated; the rules are given in detail in the proposed and temporary regulations under Code section 7872.
5. Temp. Reg. §1.7872-5T(c)(1).
6. IRC Section 7872(c)(3).
7. IRC Section 7872(f)(7).
8. Temp. Reg. §1.7872-5T(b)(14).
9. Temp. Reg. §1.7872-5T(c)(3).
10. Title I of the Consumer Protection Act, as amended, 15 U.S.C. 1601 *et seq.*
11. IRC Section 7872(f)(6).
12. IRC Section 7872(e)(1)(B).
13. IRC Section 7872(b)(1).
14. IRC Section 7872(f)(10).

Chapter 43

LONG TERM DISABILITY INSURANCE

WHAT IS IT?

Long term disability insurance is an employer-sponsored program to provide disability income to employees who are disabled (unable to work) beyond a period specified in the plan, usually six months. Such plans are designed to supplement the Social Security disability coverage available to almost all employees. Disability income under an employer plan usually continues for the duration of the disability, or until death. The plan is usually funded through an insurance contract, particularly for smaller employers.

WHEN IS IT INDICATED?

1   When employees have a need for income to provide for themselves and their families in the event of long term disability.

Unfortunately, disability is a common event. It is more likely that an employee will become disabled before age 65 than that he or she will die before 65. Social Security disability benefits are available only for severe disabilities. Social Security benefit levels are not adequate for highly paid employees to maintain their standard of living. Disability income plans are very common as employee benefits because of the great perceived need for them. They would be even more common, or more generous, if it were not for their high cost to employers. The question employers face is not so much whether there is a need for these programs, but rather how they can be financed.

2. When an employer wants to provide a special benefit for executives, if the company has no regular long term disability program for all employees, or if the regular program provides limited benefits. Under current law, employers can provide disability plans on a discriminatory basis—that is, special plans can be provided for selected executives only. The employer is free to choose (1) who will be covered, (2) the amounts of coverage provided (amounts can vary from employee to employee) and (3) the terms and conditions of coverage.

DESIGN FEATURES

Eligibility

Since long term disability plans provided by employers are not subject to nondiscrimination rules, the employer has great flexibility in deciding who is covered under the plan. Many plans cover only full-time salaried employees, or only a select group of executive employees. This reduces plan costs not only because fewer employees are covered, but also because experience in many firms indicates that disability claims are more frequent among non-salaried employees. Some plans simply use the approach of covering only employees above a specified salary level. Exclusions like these in an employer plan are not necessarily grossly inequitable to lower paid employees because Social Security disability benefit levels—income replacement ratios—are relatively satisfactory for lower paid employees.

Most long term disability plans require a waiting period of three months to a year before an eligible employee becomes covered.

Definition of Disability

The plan's definition of disability is very important in establishing its cost to the employer. The definition can be strict or liberal, or somewhere in between. Three common definitions will illustrate the range of options:

* the "Social Security" or "total and permanent" definition—disability is defined as a condition under which the individual "is unable to engage in any substantial gainful activity by reason of any medically determinable physical or mental impairment which can be expected to result in death or which has lasted or can be expected to last for a continuous period of not less than 12 months." This is the strictest (i.e., least favorable to the employee) definition that is commonly used.

* the "qualified for" definition—disability is defined as "the total and continuous inability of the employee to engage in any and every gainful occupation for which he or she is qualified or shall reasonably become qualified by reason of training, education, or experi-

ence." This definition is more liberal than the Social Security definition since it does not require the disabled employee to be incapable of any gainful employment, only employment for which the employee is qualified. This definition, or some variation of it, is commonly used in employer long term disability plans.

- the "regular occupation" or "own occupation" definition—disability is defined as the "total and continuous inability of the employee to perform any and every duty of his or her regular occupation." Although this definition is often used in short term disability plans (see Chapter 48), it is generally too liberal for an employer's long term plan. However, if the plan is designed purely as an extra benefit for a selected group of executives, a liberal definition might be used. Most individual disability policies also use a liberal definition since individuals, for themselves, tend to define disability in terms of inability to do their current job.

As these definitions indicate, most long term disability plans require total disability in order to receive benefits. However, some plans provide payments for partial disabilities, particularly if the partial disability is preceded by a total disability. This may encourage rehabilitation and return to gainful employment, which is desirable for both employer and employee.

Disability plans usually contain specific exclusions under which benefits will not be paid even if the definition of disability is otherwise met. Common exclusions are (1) disabilities during periods when the employee is not under a physician's care; (2) disabilities caused by an intentionally self-inflicted injury; and (3) disabilities beginning before the employee became eligible for plan coverage.

Benefit Formulas

Long term plans generally do not provide 100 percent of pre-disability income. The principal reason for this, from the employer's viewpoint, is to avoid disincentives to return to work. Insurers generally do not underwrite plans providing too high a replacement ratio. Disability income amounts of 50 to 70 percent of pre-disability income are typical.

Benefits are usually "integrated" with disability benefits from other plans. For example, a plan's benefit formula might provide that the disability benefit from the employer is 70 percent of the employee's pre-disability compensation, less disability benefits from specified other sources. This provides the employee with the desired 70 percent disability income level but the employer only pays whatever additional amount is required after other sources are taken into account. Typical

sources of disability benefits, other than the disability plan itself, include (1) Social Security; (2) workers' compensation; (3) qualified or nonqualified retirement plans; (4) other insurance; or (5) earnings from other employment.

Integration with other plans can use either a full (dollar for dollar) offset of the disability benefit by the other income sources, or an integration formula of some kind can be used under which benefits from the employer plan are reduced by something less than a dollar for each dollar of other disability benefits. There are no federal tax law restrictions on integration similar to those applicable to qualified retirement plans. This means that the employer is free to design any kind of integration formula that meets its cost limits and other objectives for the plan.

TAX IMPLICATIONS

1. Employer contributions to disability income plans, either insurance premium payments or direct benefit payments under an uninsured plan, are deductible as employee compensation. Like all compensation deductions, they are subject to the "reasonableness" requirement described in Chapter 28.

2. In some plans, employees pay part of the cost of the plan, usually through payroll deductions. These payments are not deductible by the employee.

3. Employer payments of premiums under an insured disability plan do not result in taxable income to the employee.[1]

4. Benefit payments under an employer plan are fully taxable to the employee (subject to the credit described below) if the plan was fully paid for by the employer. If the employer paid part of the cost, only a corresponding part of the benefit is taxable, again subject to credit. For example, if the employer paid 75 percent of the disability insurance premiums and the employee paid the remaining 25 percent, only 75 percent of the disability benefit received by the employee is taxable.[2]

   IRS regulations specify the time over which the employer and employee percentages are to be measured for this purpose. For group disability insurance, generally, payments over the three year period prior to the disability are taken into account in determining the percentages paid by employer and employee.[3]

5. If an employee receiving benefits meets the "total and permanent" disability definition described earlier, a limited tax credit reduces the tax impact of disability payments for lower-income recipients.[4]

Generally, the disability credit is calculated by taking the maximum amount subject to the credit (see below) and subtracting ½ of the amount by which the taxpayer's adjusted gross income exceeds the AGI limits (see below). The credit is equal to 15 percent of this amount. Thus, the maximum annual tax credit is $1,125 for a joint return, as indicated below. The chart below shows the maximum amounts eligible for the credit, the maximum credit that may be obtained, and the limitations to adjusted gross income (AGI):

MAXIMUM AMOUNT SUBJECT TO CREDIT

Single Person	$5,000
Joint Return (where one spouse is a qualified individual)	$5,000
Joint Return (where both spouses are qualified individuals)'	$7,500
Married Filing Separately	$3,750

MAXIMUM CREDIT

Single Person	$750
Joint Return (where one spouse is a qualified individual)	$750
Joint Return (where both spouses are qualified individuals)	$1,125
Married Filing Separately	$562.50

ADJUSTED GROSS INCOME LIMITS

Single Person	$7,500
Married Filing Jointly	$10,000
Married Filing Separately	$5,000

For example, if a disabled employee has adjusted gross income (from all sources, including taxable disability income) of $14,000, and is married, filing jointly, the amount on which his disability tax credit is calculated would be $5,000 (the maximum amount for a joint return where only one spouse receives disability income payments) less $2,000 (½ of the amount by which the taxpayer's AGI exceeds $10,000). In short, this is $5,000 - $2,000, or $3,000. The taxpayer's credit is equal to 15 percent of $3,000, or $450. Accordingly, the employee's income tax bill for the year is reduced by $450. Note that to receive this credit the employee must meet the Social Security total and permanent definition of disability. An employee might receive benefits under some employer plans without meeting this strict definition of disability, as discussed above.

This tax credit is even further reduced by 15 percent of any tax-free income received by the employee from a pension, annuity, or disability benefit, including Social Security. Since most disability plans are integrated with Social Security benefits, this further reduction makes the credit even less valuable.

In view of all the reductions applicable to this credit, and the extremely low AGI limits on full availability, the credit has become a minor factor in the design of disability benefits.

6. Disability insurance premiums paid by the employer under the plan are not considered wages subject to employment taxes (FICA—Social Security—and FUTA—federal unemployment).[5] Generally disability insurance premiums are not subject to state employment taxes either, but individual state laws should be consulted.

7. Disability benefits are subject to federal income tax withholding if paid directly by the employer. If paid by a third party such as an insurance company, withholding is required only if the employee requests it.[6]

8. Disability benefits attributable to employer contributions are subject to Social Security taxes for a limited period (six months generally) at the beginning of a disability. Thereafter, they are not considered wages subject to Social Security tax.[7]

ERISA REQUIREMENTS

A disability income plan is considered a welfare benefit plan under ERISA (see Appendix A). Such plans require a written summary plan description, the naming of a plan administrator, and a formal written claims procedure by which employees can make benefit claims and appeal denials. The plan is not subject to the eligibility, vesting, or funding requirements of ERISA. The plan administrator must provide plan participants with a summary plan description (SPD).

WHERE CAN I FIND OUT MORE ABOUT IT?

1. Beam, Burton T., Jr. and John J. McFadden, *Employee Benefits,* 3rd ed. Chicago, IL: Dearborn Financial Publishing, Inc., 1992.

2. *Tax Facts 1*, Cincinnati, OH: The National Underwriter Company. Revised annually.

QUESTIONS AND ANSWERS

Question What are the alternatives to the classic employer-paid long term disability plan?

Answer — When an employer considers providing a disability income to an executive or group of executives, the advantages and disadvantages of an employer-paid plan versus individual disability insurance must be weighed.

The employer plan results in no current taxable income to the employee, and thus provides deferral of taxes. Disability benefits are, however, fully taxable, except for a credit which benefits only low-income employees. This raises some planning issues. First, the amount of disability benefit for a particular employee may be, and in fact usually is, much more than what the employer paid for it. Thus, the total tax bill to the employee is usually larger if the employee does in fact become disabled. Second, many authorities believe that current tax rates are lower than they will be in the future. So, each dollar of taxable disability income may be subject to more tax in the future than the value of a dollar's worth of current tax exclusion (ignoring the time value of money).

These factors may make individual disability income policies, or a group policy paid for totally by the employee, more attractive to some executives than an employer-paid long term disability plan. An employee-paid policy results in no current tax deduction, but benefits are free of tax. The cost of the policy to the executive can be minimized or eliminated if the employer pays additional compensation or an annual bonus in the amount of the employee's cost for the coverage, plus the income tax on the bonus itself—a so-called "double bonus" plan.

Question — Is there any type of disability plan that provides *both* employer payment of deductible premiums and non-taxation of benefits to the employee?

Answer — Under section 105(c) of the Code, disability benefits are tax-free if the amount of benefit is (a) based on permanent loss of use of a member or function of the body and (b) is computed by reference to the nature of the injury and not to the period the employee is absent from work. This Code provision is intended primarily to cover plans such as accidental death and dismemberment (AD&D) plans that pay a lump sum for loss of a leg, eye, etc. However, some planners have made use of this exclusion as a substitute for traditional disability insurance. This is done by designing a plan that pays a stated amount for a heart attack, for arthritis, or for other specified conditions, with benefits based on a schedule in the plan and not specifically on the employee's compensation. These benefits can be paid by the employer directly, or in some cases can be paid out of a qualified pension or profit-sharing plan.

Another approach—one with less validity—that is sometimes used in order to get the best of both worlds is to design a plan under which the decision as to whether the employer or the employee pays premiums is postponed to the last possible time each year. This permits an employee to opt for employee payment if he or she becomes disabled during the year. However, if all the facts about such a plan were known to the IRS, it would probably be viewed as a sham—that is, treated as an employer-paid plan if an employee becomes disabled.

FOOTNOTES

1. IRC Section 106.
2. IRC Sections 104(a)(3), 105(a); Reg. §1.105-1(d).
3. Regs. §§1.105-1(d), 1.105-1(e).
4. IRC Section 22.
5. IRC Sections 3121(a)(2), 3306(b)(2).
6. IRC Section 3402(o).
7. IRC Section 3121(a)(4).

Chapter 44

MEDICAL EXPENSE REIMBURSEMENT PLAN (MERP)

WHAT IS IT?

Under a medical expense reimbursement plan, or MERP, an employer reimburses covered employees for specified medical (health and accident) expenses. These reimbursements come directly from corporate funds rather than from a third party insurer.

A MERP is used (1) as a substitute for health insurance (see Chapter 37), (2) as a supplement to provide payments for medical expenses not covered under the company's health insurance plan (such as dental expenses or cosmetic surgery), or (3) to pay for medical expenses in excess of the limits in the company's health insurance plan. The tax objective of the plan is to provide tax-free benefits to the covered employees and obtain a corresponding employer tax deduction for the benefits paid.

MERPs were often used in the past to provide extra benefits for selected groups of executives. However, current tax law denies tax benefits to highly compensated employees if a "self-insured" plan does not meet the nondiscrimination tests of Code section 105(h), as described below.

WHEN IS IT INDICATED?

1. Where a corporation is closely held and shareholders and their family members are the primary or only employees.

2. In a professional corporation where the only employee is a professional in a high income tax bracket or where there are few other employees.

3. Where an employer would like to provide employees with medical benefits beyond those provided by the basic medical coverage already in force.

DESIGN FEATURES

Basically, a MERP is simple. The company adopts a plan by corporate resolution specifying (1) the group of employees covered, (2) the types of medical expenses that will be reimbursed, and (3) any limits or conditions on payment by the company. When an employee incurs medical expenses subject to reimbursement the employee submits a claim to the employer. The employer reimburses the employee if the claim is covered under the plan.

The plan's objective is to provide tax-free benefits to employees. Benefits will be tax free if (1) they qualify as medical expenses under the Code, and (2) (for a highly compensated employee) the plan is nondiscriminatory under Code section 105(h), as discussed below under "Tax Implications."

A broad range of expenses can qualify as medical expenses under a MERP. This is one of the advantages of these plans—the plan can cover expenses often not available under health insurance plans. For example, a MERP can cover cosmetic surgery, full dental expenses including orthodontia, and even items such as swimming pools prescribed by a physician for treatment of a condition such as arthritis. Any expense that could be deducted by an individual as an itemized medical expense under Code section 213 is eligible for tax free reimbursement under a MERP. See Figure 44.1 at the end of this chapter for a partial list of items that have been approved for deduction under Section 213 and, thus, are eligible for tax free reimbursement under a MERP.

The plan can be fully funded and administered by the employer or the employer can obtain an insurance contract to provide one or more features. Insurance contracts can help to make plans more workable by providing (1) administrative services, (2) claims evaluation, or (3) insurance against large claims—known as "stop loss" coverage.

Stop loss coverage is generally very important if the employer is small and the MERP could become potentially liable for a large medical expense. For example, suppose Mullions, P.C., an architectural firm, has a MERP for its sole shareholder-employee Ornate Mullions and its two employees. The reimbursement plan supplements the company's health insurance. In some years there have been no claims at all against the plan. However, in 1991 suppose an employee has cosmetic surgery that results in complications and $90,000 in hospital and doctors' bills. Such a payment could bankrupt a small company.

An insurance stop loss contract could be obtained that would prevent this disaster by limiting the company's exposure in any one year to some specified amount that the company considers within its means. The premiums for stop loss coverage are usually relatively low because medical catastrophes are rare events.

TAX IMPLICATIONS

1. The employer may deduct 100 percent of the cost of benefits paid to employees under the plan. Plan administrative expenses, and the cost of any insured stop loss coverage, are also fully deductible.[1]

2. Deductions for prefunding medical benefits (that is, setting funds aside and deducting amounts for medical benefits to be paid in future years) are limited under rules set out in Code sections 419 and 419A. Generally, for a given year an employer can deduct expenditures for medical benefits up to a limit equal to the total of (a) the direct costs of the plan for the year—claims paid plus administrative costs, plus (b) contributions to an asset account up to 35% of the preceding year's direct costs.

3. The employee does not have taxable income when benefits are paid. Benefits are tax free when medical expenses are paid directly to doctors or hospitals or when the plan reimburses the employee for covered expenses.[2] Highly compensated employees may have to pay taxes on the reimbursements to the extent the plan is discriminatory under the Section 105(h) rules described below. See the "Questions and Answers" for further discussion.

4. The employee is eligible for an itemized medical expense deduction under Code section 213 for any medical expenses not covered by the MERP or an employer health insurance plan. The Section 213 deduction is available only if the taxpayer itemizes deductions on the tax return. The deduction is limited to the amount by which the total of all eligible medical expenses exceeds 7.5% of the taxpayer's adjusted gross income.

Nondiscrimination Rules

Medical reimbursement plans that are funded on a "pay as you go" basis are generally considered "self insured" for tax purposes and therefore are governed by nondiscrimination rules found in Code section 105(h). Failure to comply with these rules means that plan benefits will be taxable to "highly compensated" employees. Code section 105(h) defines a highly compensated employee as one who is one of the five highest paid officers, is a shareholder who owns more than 10 percent of the company's stock or is among the highest paid 25 percent of all employees. Nonhighly compensated employees receive benefits tax-free even in a discriminatory plan. The nondiscrimination rules are as follows:

Coverage Test

The plan must:

- benefit 70 percent or more of all employees;

- benefit 80 percent or more of all employees who are eligible to participate in the plan if at least 70 percent of all employees are eligible to participate; or

- benefit a classification of employees set up by the employer that does not discriminate in favor of highly compensated employees.

Benefits Test

All benefits provided for highly compensated employees under the plan must be provided for all plan participants.

Who Can Be Excluded

In applying the coverage tests, the following can be excluded:

- employees who have not completed 3 years of service

- employees who have not attained age 25

- part-time or seasonal employees

- employees in a collective bargaining unit if there has been good faith bargaining on the health plan issue

- nonresident alien employees who received no U.S. income

Continuation of Coverage

An employer's adoption of any kind of health plan for employees results in an additional and typically unexpected cost due to certain provisions in the Consolidated Omnibus Budget Reconciliation Act of 1985 (COBRA), under which the employer is subject to penalties unless the plan makes available continuation of health plan benefits for certain employees and their dependents after termination of employment and certain other qualifying events.[3] There is an exemption for small employers—the COBRA continuation provisions apply for a given year only if the employer had 20 or more employees on a typical business day in the preceding year. Government and church plans are also exempt.

In general, under COBRA the employer must provide the option to continue an employee's existing health plan coverage (including dependent coverage) for 36 months after the following qualifying events:

- death of the employee

- divorce or legal separation of the covered employee (coverage continues for the former spouse and dependents)

- the employee's entitlement to Medicare benefits

- a bankruptcy proceeding under the United States Code where the employee retired from the employer

- a child ceasing to be a dependent for plan purposes

Health plan coverage must be continued for 18 months after termination of employment or reduction in hours of employment. If termination is for disability, coverage must be continued for 29 months.

Continuation coverage can be terminated before the 36, 29, or 18 month period if

- the employer terminates its health plan for all employees

- the beneficiary fails to pay his or her share of the premium

- the beneficiary becomes covered under any other plan providing medical care. However, if the new plan excludes a pre-existing condition, the employee must be allowed to continue coverage for the full COBRA period.

The employer can require the former employee or beneficiary to pay part of the cost of continuation coverage. However, this former employee or beneficiary's share cannot be more than 102% of the cost to the plan of coverage for similarly situated beneficiaries with respect to whom a qualifying event has not occurred. This is true whether the cost is paid by the employer or employee. The premium for an employee disabled at the time of his termination or reduction in hours may be as much as 150% of the plan cost after the 18th month of continuation coverage.

The penalty for noncompliance with these requirements is, generally, a tax of $100 a day during the period that any failure with respect to a qualified beneficiary continues.

The COBRA continuation requirements are discussed further in Chapter 37.

ERISA AND OTHER REQUIREMENTS

An employer's MERP is a "welfare benefit plan" subject to the ERISA requirements discussed in Appendix A.

WHERE CAN I FIND OUT MORE ABOUT IT?

1. Beam, Burton T., Jr. and John J. McFadden, *Employee Benefits,* 3rd ed. Chicago, IL: Dearborn Financial Publishing, Inc., 1992.

2. *Tax Facts 1*, Cincinnati, OH: The National Underwriter Co. (revised annually).

3. Leimberg, Stephan R., et al., *The Tools and Techniques of Estate Planning,* 9th ed. Cincinnati, OH: The National Underwriter Co., 1992.

4. Cady, Donald F., *Field Guide to Estate Planning, Business Planning, & Employee Benefits*, Cincinnati, OH: The National Underwriter Co., (revised annually).

QUESTIONS AND ANSWERS

Question — Is it possible to design a MERP that excludes rank and file employees by funding the MERP with a health insurance contract?

Answer — Yes. Insured MERPs are exempt from the nondiscrimination requirements of Code section 105(h). However, a plan is not considered insured just because an insurance company is somehow involved by paying claims or providing administrative services. There must be an actual "shifting of risk" for the payment of health benefits from the employer to the insurance company.[4]

Question — Is there ever any advantage in designing a MERP that discriminates by covering only specific executives?

Answer — The consequence of not meeting the nondiscrimination requirements is only that

(1) part or all of plan reimbursements (the excess reimbursements, as computed under the complex Section 105(h) rules) are taxable to highly compensated employees;

(2) taxable excess reimbursements must be reported by the employer on the employee's Form W-2.

The employer does not lose any part of its deduction for a discriminatory plan.

The excess reimbursement in a discriminatory plan is either:

(1) if the plan provides a benefit to a highly compensated employee but not to other participants, the excess reimbursement is the amount of such benefit that is reimbursed; or

(2) if the benefit is provided to both nonhighly and highly compensated employees but on a discriminatory basis, the excess reimbursement is the amount reimbursed to the highly compensated participant multiplied by the total amount reimbursed to all highly compensated participants for the year over the total amount reimbursed to all employees for the year.[5]

For example, supposed that a plan provides eligibility for medical reimbursement immediately upon hire to Hal Gall, a highly compensated executive, but under the plan all other employees must be employed for 4 years before they are covered. In 1993, Hal is reimbursed $6,000 for hospital and surgical expenses for his knee surgery. In 1993, amounts reimbursed under the plan to all highly compensated participants totaled $30,000 out of a total of $90,000 of reimbursements. Hal's excess reimbursement for 1993 is

$$\$6,000 \quad X \quad \frac{\$30,000}{\$90,000} \quad = \quad \$2,000$$

Thus, for 1993 Hal must report $2,000 of the $6,000 reimbursement as additional taxable income. The remaining $4,000 of the reimbursement is tax free.

If there is a case where these consequences are not objectionable, a discriminatory plan may be useful. The consequences of a discriminatory plan can be alleviated by paying bonuses to highly compensated employees—taxable to employees and deductible to the employer—to cover the amount of tax generated by "excess reimbursements" taxed to the employee. Such a plan may still provide some tax advantage, if the employer's outlay exceeds the employee's tax cost. And the cost may be substantially less than providing the benefit on a nondiscriminatory basis.

FOOTNOTES

1. Reg. §1.162-10(a).
2. IRC Section 105(b).
3. IRC Section 4980B.
4. Reg. §1.105-11.
5. IRC Section 105(h)(7).

Medical Expense Reimbursement Plan (MERP)

Figure 44.1
(pg. 1)

The following is a partial list of items which the IRS or the courts have held to constitute deductible medical expenses. Items traditionally covered under health insurance plans (physicians, dentists, hospitals, etc.) are also deductible even if not included specifically on this list.

- **Professional Services of**
  - Christian Science Practitioner
  - Oculist
  - Unlicensed practitioner if the type and quality of his services are not illegal
- **Equipment and Supplies**
  - Abdominal supports
  - Air conditioner where necessary for relief from an allergy or for relieving difficulty in breathing
  - Arches
  - Autoette (auto device for handicapped person), but not if used to travel to job or business
  - Back supports
  - Contact lenses
  - Cost of installing stair-seat elevator for person with heart condition
  - Elastic hosiery
  - Eyeglasses
  - Fluoridation unit in home
- **Medical Treatments**
  - Acupuncture
  - Cosmetic Surgery
  - Diatheray
  - Healing services
  - Hydrotherapy (water treatments)
- **Medicines**
  - Drugs
  - Patient medicines
- **Miscellaneous**
  - Birth control pills or other birth control
  - Braille books — excess cost of braille books over cost of regular editions
  - Clarinet lessons advised by dentist for treatment of tooth defects
  - Convalescent home — for medical treatment only
  - Face lifting operation, even if not recommended by doctor
  - Fees paid to health institute where the exercises, rubdowns, etc., taken there are prescribed by a physician as treatments necessary to alleviate a physical or mental defect or illness

- Hair transplant operation
- Practical or other non-professional nurse for medical services only; not for care of a healthy person or a small child who is not ill
- Costs for medical care of elderly person, unable to get about, or person subject to spells
- Hearing aide
- Heating devices
- Invalid chair
- Orthopedic shoes
- Reclining chair if prescribed by doctor
- Repair of special telephone equipment for the deaf
- Sacroiliac belt
- Special mattress and plywood bed boards for relief of arthritis of spine
- Truss
- Wig advised by doctor as essential to mental health of person who lost all hair from disease
- Navajo healing ceremonies ("sings")
- Sterilization
- Vasectomy
- Whirlpool baths
- Vitamins, tonics, etc., prescribed by doctor — but not if taken as food supplement or to preserve your general health
- Kidney donor's or possible kidney donor's expenses
- Legal fees for guardianship of mentally ill spouse where commitment was necessary for medical treatment
- Nurse's board and wages, including social security taxes you pay on wages
- Remedial reading for child suffering from dyslexia
- Sanitarium and similar institutions
- "Seeing-eye" dog and its maintenance
- Special school costs for physically and mentally handicapped children
- Wages of guide for a blind person
- Telephone-teletype costs and television adapter for closed caption service for deaf person

Figure 44.1
(pg. 2)

The following is a list of expenses which have been held *not* deductible.

- Antiseptic diaper service
- Athletic club expenses to keep physically fit
- Babysitting fees to enable you to make doctor's visits
- Boarding school fees paid for healthy child while parent is recuperating from illness. It makes no difference that this was done on a doctor's advice
- Bottled water bought to avoid drinking fluoridated city water
- Cost of divorce recommended by psychiatrist
- Cost of hotel room suggested for sex therapy
- Cost of trips for a "change of environment" to boost morale of ailing person. That doctor prescribed the trip is immaterial
- Dance lessons advised by doctors as physical and mental therapy or for the alleviation of varicose veins or arthritis; however, the cost of a clarinet and lessons for the instrument were allowed as deduction when advised as therapy for a tooth defect
- Deductions from your wages for a sickness insurance under state law
- Domestic help — even if recommended by doctor because of spouse's illness. But part of cost attributed to any nursing duties performed by the domestic is deductible
- Funeral, cremation or burial, cemetery plot, monument, mausoleum
- Health programs offered by resort hotels, health clubs and gyms
- Illegal operation and drugs
- Marriage counseling fees
- Maternity clothes
- Premiums, in connection with life insurance policies, paid for disability, double indemnity or for waiver of premium in event of total and permanent disability or policies providing for reimbursement of loss of earnings or a guarantee of a specific amount in the event of hospitalization
- Scientology fees
- Special food or beverage substitutes — but excess cost of chemically uncontaminated foods over what would have ordinarily been spent on normal food was deductible for allergy patients
- Toothpaste
- Transportation costs of a disabled person to and from work
- Traveling costs to look for a new place to live on doctor's advice
- Travel costs to favorable climate when you can live there permanently
- Tuition and travel expenses to send a problem child to a particular school for a beneficial change in environment
- Veterinary fees for pet; pet is not a dependent
- Weight reduction or stop smoking programs undertaken for general health, not for specific ailments
- Your divorced spouse's medical bills. You may be able to deduct them as alimony

The Tools and Techniques of Employee Benefit and Retirement Planning

Chapter 45

MOVING EXPENSE REIMBURSEMENT

WHAT IS IT?

Many companies reimburse employees' moving expenses connected with changes in job location. While the reimbursements are taxable income to the employee, the moving expenses are deductible within limits, if the employee itemizes deductions. Moving expense reimbursement therefore not only helps employees bear a major expense but can be a form of tax-free compensation for employees.

WHEN IS IT INDICATED?

Because of the major benefits of moving expense reimbursement to employees, employers should consider it whenever it is consistent with their recruitment and staffing needs.

ADVANTAGES

1. A company may have to recruit executives and employees from a wide geographical area; reimbursing moving expenses can help induce the employee to change jobs.

2. Larger companies with more than one geographical location can encourage mobility of their employees among company locations by adopting a moving expense reimbursement policy.

3. Moving expense reimbursement can be a tax-free form of compensation for employees if they itemize deductions.

4. Employers are completely flexible in designing moving reimbursement plans. Reimbursement can be offered only to selected employees or even a single employee. Amounts and terms of reimbursement can be varied from employee to employee, and reimbursement can be offered as needs arise without having to adopt a formal plan in advance.

DISADVANTAGES

1. Expenses to move an employee's household a long distance can be considerable, but tax benefits are limited to specific dollar amounts. Amounts in excess of the deductible limits are taxable income to the employee.

2. If the employee does not itemize deductions, or does not meet certain requirements for taking the deduction, the entire amount of moving expense reimbursement is taxable income.

TAX IMPLICATIONS

Employer tax treatment

1. Moving expense reimbursements to employees or to third parties (moving companies, etc.) on behalf of employees are deductible by the employer as compensation expenses if, together with all other forms of compensation, the amount is reasonable (the "reasonable compensation" test).

2. Reimbursement amounts must be reported as compensation on the employee's Form W-2 for the year. The employer does not have to withhold taxes if it reasonably believes that the employee will be entitled to an offsetting deduction; however withholding is required on nondeductible moving expense reimbursements.[1]

   In addition, the employer must provide the employee with Form 4782 (reproduced at the end of this chapter), which itemizes the reimbursement amounts.

3. There are no coverage or nondiscrimination rules that limit employer and employee deductions for moving expenses to "nondiscriminatory" plans. Reimbursement can be provided for whatever employee the employer chooses, and in whatever amounts the employer considers appropriate.

Employee tax treatment

Employees can deduct moving expenses as an itemized deduction *without* any "floor" amount such as that applicable to medical expenses or employee business expenses. The deduction is subject to a variety of typically complex rules and limitations:

1. the *distance* test

2. the *time* test

3. limitations on the *types of expenses* that are deductible

4. limitations on *amounts* deductible.

Distance test. A move meets the distance test if the new main job location is at least 35 miles farther from the employee's former home than the old main job location was. For example, if the employee's old job location was 10 miles from his home, moving expenses are deductible if the new job location is at least 45 miles from the old home. Distances are measured by the shortest of the commonly traveled routes.[2]

Time test. To deduct moving expenses, the employee must work full time for at least 39 weeks during the first 12 months after arriving at the new job location. The regulations contain numerous complex exceptions to and variations on this rule.[3]

Types of expenses deductible. Deductible moving expenses include reasonable costs of the following[4]:

(A) (1) packing, crating, and moving household goods and personal effects (personal effects include a car and household pets; moving expenses include the costs of connecting and disconnecting utilities) and (2) storage and insurance within any consecutive 30-day period after moving out of the former home and before delivery to the new home;

(B) traveling to the new home (a 9 cents/mile allowance can be used for travel in the employee's own car[5]);

(C) house hunting trips after the employee gets the new job. Deductible expenses include transportation, lodging for employee and members of household, and 80% of meal costs;

(D) temporary housing (lodging and 80% of meals[6]) in the new area for a 30-day period after getting the new job and before moving into the new home;

(E) sale, purchase and lease expenses. These include expenses of:

(1) selling the former home and buying a new one, including real estate commissions, attorneys' fees, title fees, escrow fees, "points" or loan placement charges, state transfer taxes, and similar expenses; and

(2) settling an old lease and negotiating a new lease, including payments to the lessor for release from the old lease, attorneys' fees, real estate commissions, and expenses such as the difference between any rent the employee must continue to pay under an old lease and the rent received by the employee from a sublessee. Advance rent or security deposits for the new lease are *not* deductible.

Limitations of amounts deductible. The dollar limits for deductions, as well as certain other rules, are more generous for moves outside the United States than for moves within the United States.[7] The IRS chart in Figure 45.1 shows the dollar limits for deducting each type of moving expense on Form 3903 (moves within the U.S.) or Form 3903F (moves outside the U.S.). Househunting and temporary living expenses (within the limitations shown) are combined with sale, purchase and lease expenses for purposes of the limitations on the aggregate amount.

Nondeductible expenses. The following expenses are not deductible as moving expenses:[8]

- home improvements to help sell the old home

- loss on sale of the old home

- mortgage penalties

- forfeiture of club dues or entry fees

- any part of the purchase price of the new home

- real estate taxes

- car registration or driver's license fees

- reinstalling carpets or draperies

- storage charges other than as described earlier.

Reporting by Employee. An employee claiming a moving expense deduction, whether or not the employer provided any reimbursement, must file Form 3903 or Form 3903F; copies of these forms are reproduced at the end of this chapter.

ERISA AND OTHER IMPLICATIONS

A moving expense reimbursement plan does not appear to fall within the definition of either a pension or welfare benefit plan for ERISA purposes.[9] Consequently, there is no reporting requirement (so no Form 5500 needs to be filed), nor do any other ERISA provisions apply.

WHERE CAN I FIND OUT MORE ABOUT IT?

IRS Publication 521, *Moving Expenses*, is available without charge from the IRS.

Figure 45.1

Moving Expense Dollar Limits (1992)			
		Dollar Limits	
Type of Expense	**Marital Status**	**Form 3903**	**Form 3903F**
Household goods and personal effects (line 4, Form 3903 or line 3, Form 3903F)	Not applicable	No limit	No limit
Travel expenses (lines 5-8, Form 3903 or lines 4-7, Form 3903F)*	Not applicable	No limit	No limit
Househunting and temporary living expenses (lines 9-13, Form 3903 or lines 8-12, Form 3903F)*	Single	$1,500	$4,500
	Married filing jointly— 1) Spouses shared same new home by end of tax year 2) Both spouses began work at new job locations but lived apart	$1,500 $3,000 (limited to $1,500 each)	$4,500 $9,000 (limited to $4,500 each)
	Married filing separately— 1) Both spouses began work at new job locations and lived together 2) One working spouse 3) Both spouses began work at new job locations but lived apart	$750 each $1,500 $1,500 each	$2,250 each $4,500 $4,500 each
Househunting and temporary living expenses; and expenses of selling and buying home (lines 13, 14, and 15, Form 3903 or lines 12, 13, and 14, Form 3903F)*	Single	$3,000	$6,000
	Married filing jointly— 1) Spouses shared same new home by end of tax year 2) Both spouses began work at new job locations but lived apart	$3,000 $6,000 (limited to $3,000 each)	$6,000 $12,000 (limited to $6,000 each)
	Married filing separately— 1) Both spouses began work at new job locations and lived together 2) One working spouse 3) Both spouses began work at new job locations but lived apart	$1,500 each $3,000 $3,000 each	$3,000 each $6,000 $6,000 each
*Meals are subject to an 80% limit.			

QUESTIONS AND ANSWERS

Question — Suppose you change jobs to a more distant location and try commuting from your old home for several years, then decide it's too difficult and move closer to the new job. Are moving expenses deductible then?

Answer — The IRS's position is that moving expenses are not closely related to work at the new job location (and therefore not deductible) unless they are incurred within one year from the date the employee first reported to work at the new job. However, the expenses can be deducted if the employee can show that circumstances did not permit a move within one year, such as the need for children to complete high school in the old location. The IRS probably would not view the circumstances in the question as justifying a moving expense deduction.[10]

Question — Are self-employed persons (partners or proprietors) entitled to a moving expense deduction?

Answer — Yes. However, there are some rules reflecting the differences in the nature of the employment situation. Pre-move househunting and temporary living expenses are not deductible unless the proprietor or partner has made "substantial arrangements" to begin work at the new location. These include (1) leasing or buying a new business location; (2) purchasing inventory or supplies; (3) hiring of employees; and (4) making arrangements to advertise and contact customers.[11]

Question — If an employer wants to protect an employee against obtaining an inadequate price on the forced sale of a residence when moving, what is the best way to do it?

Answer — If the employer simply reimburses the employee for any reduction in house/sale proceeds, the reimbursement is taxable income to the employee and it is not offset by any moving expense or other tax deduction. (Capital losses on the sale of a personal residence by an individual are nondeductible.[12])

It is better from a tax standpoint for the employer to actually buy the house from the employee. Any capital gain that the employee realizes on the sale can be deferred under Code section 1034 if the employee purchases a new residence within 2 years. The sale price should be the fair market value as determined by an independent real estate appraiser. Although this price may legitimately be higher than a "forced sale" price, it should not exceed the fair market value, as any excess over fair market value could be deemed to be additional compensation income to the employee.

FOOTNOTES

1.   IRC Section 3401(a)(15).
2.   IRC Section 217(c). However, if the *new* home is farther from the new job location than the old home was, the moving expenses are not deductible on the ground that the move is not related to starting work. Reg. §1.217-2(a)(3). For example, suppose the old home was 5 miles from the old job. You change job locations to a location 40 miles from the old home. You then move to a new home 50 miles from the new job. The distance test is met because the new job location is at least 35 miles farther from your old home, but moving expenses are not deductible because the move actually produces a longer commute than if you had stayed put. However, you can deduct the moving expenses if you can show that the 50-mile commute takes less time and money than the 40-mile commute from your old home, or if you are required as a condition of employment to live in the new home.
3.   IRC Section 217(c)(2); see also, Reg. §1.217-2(c)(4).
4.   The list given here is a summary of the rules in IRC Section 217(b), Reg. §1.217-2(b), and IRS Pub. 521.
5.   Rev. Proc. 92-104, 1992-2 CB 583.
6.   Under IRC Section 274(n), tax deductions for meals in general are limited to 80 percent of the expense.
7.   See IRC Section 217(h).
8.   Reg. §1.217-2(b)(3); see also, IRS Pub. 521.
9.   See DOL Reg. §2510.3-1.
10. See Reg. §1.217-2(a)(3), Ex. (2).
11. IRC Section 217(f); Reg. §1.217-2(f)(2).
12. Reg. §1.165-9(a). If a corporation purchases the house from an employee and later sells it at a loss, the loss is treated by the corporation as a capital loss. *Azar Nut Co. v. Comm.*, 931 F.2d 314 (5th Cir. 1991).

Moving Expense Reimbursement

Form **3903**	**Moving Expenses**	OMB No. 1545-0062
Department of the Treasury Internal Revenue Service	▶ Attach to Form 1040. ▶ See separate instructions.	**1992** Attachment Sequence No. **62**

Name(s) shown on Form 1040	Your social security number

1	Enter the number of miles from your **old home** to your **new workplace**	**1**	
2	Enter the number of miles from your **old home** to your **old workplace**	**2**	
3	Subtract line 2 from line 1. Enter the result but not less than zero . . . . ▶	**3**	

If line 3 is 35 or more miles, complete the rest of this form. If line 3 is less than 35 miles, you may not deduct your moving expenses. This rule does not apply to members of the armed forces.

Caution: *If you are a member of the armed forces, see the instructions before continuing.*

Part I Moving Expenses

Note: *Any payments your employer made for any part of your move (including the value of any services furnished in kind) should be included on your W-2 form. Report that amount on* **Form 1040, line 7.** *See* **Reimbursements** *in the instructions.*

Section A—Transportation of Household Goods

4	Transportation and storage for household goods and personal effects	**4**	

Section B—Expenses of Moving From Old To New Home

5	Travel and lodging **not** including meals		**5**	
6	Total meals	**6**		
7	Multiply line 6 by 80% (.80)		**7**	
8	Add lines 5 and 7		**8**	

Section C—Pre-move Househunting Expenses and Temporary Quarters (for any 30 days in a row after getting your job)

9	Pre-move travel and lodging **not** including meals		**9**	
10	Temporary quarters expenses **not** including meals		**10**	
11	Total meal expenses for both pre-move househunting and temporary quarters	**11**		
12	Multiply line 11 by 80% (.80)		**12**	
13	Add lines 9, 10, and 12		**13**	

Section D—Qualified Real Estate Expenses

14	Expenses of (check one): **a** ☐ selling or exchanging your old home, or ⎫ **b** ☐ if renting, settling an unexpired lease. ⎭ .	**14**	
15	Expenses of (check one): **a** ☐ buying your new home, or ⎫ **b** ☐ if renting, getting a new lease. ⎭ . . .	**15**	

Part II Dollar Limits and Moving Expense Deduction

16	Enter the **smaller** of: • The amount on line 13, or • $1,500 ($750 if married filing a separate return and at the end of 1992 you lived with your spouse who also started work in 1992).	**16**	
17	Add lines 14, 15, and 16	**17**	
18	Enter the **smaller** of: • The amount on line 17, or • $3,000 ($1,500 if married filing a separate return and at the end of 1992 you lived with your spouse who also started work in 1992).	**18**	
19	Add lines 4, 8, and 18. Enter the total here and on Schedule A, line 18. This is your **moving expense deduction** . . . . ▶	**19**	

For Paperwork Reduction Act Notice, see separate instructions. Cat. No. 12490K Form **3903** (1992)

☆ U.S. GOVERNMENT PRINTING OFFICE: 1992 315-318

1992 Instructions for Form 3903

Department of the Treasury
Internal Revenue Service

Moving Expenses

General Instructions

Paperwork Reduction Act Notice

We ask for the information on this form to carry out the Internal Revenue laws of the United States. You are required to give us the information. We need it to ensure that you are complying with these laws and to allow us to figure and collect the right amount of tax.

The time needed to complete and file this form will vary depending on individual circumstances. The estimated average time is:

Recordkeeping	1 hr., 5 min.
Learning about the law or the form	7 min.
Preparing the form	31 min.
Copying, assembling, and sending the form to the IRS	20 min.

If you have comments concerning the accuracy of these time estimates or suggestions for making this form more simple, we would be happy to hear from you. You can write to both the IRS and the Office of Management and Budget at the addresses listed in the Instructions for Form 1040.

Purpose of Form

Use Form 3903 to figure your moving expense deduction if you moved to a new principal place of work (workplace) within the United States or its possessions.

Note: *Use Form 3903F, Foreign Moving Expenses, instead of this form if you are a U.S. citizen or resident alien who moved to a new principal workplace outside the United States or its possessions.*

Additional Information

For more details, get **Pub. 521, Moving Expenses.**

Who May Deduct Moving Expenses

If you moved to a different home because of a change in the location of your job, you may be able to deduct your moving expenses. You may be able to take the deduction whether you are self-employed or an employee. But you must meet certain tests explained next.

Distance Test.—Your new principal workplace must be at least 35 miles farther from your old home than your old workplace was. For example, if your old workplace was 3 miles from your old home, your new workplace must be at least 38 miles from that home. If you did not have an old workplace, your new workplace must be at least 35 miles from your old home. The distance between the two points is the shortest of the more commonly traveled routes between them.

Time Test.—If you are an employee, you must work full time in the general area of your new workplace for at least 39 weeks during the 12 months right after you move. If you are self-employed, you must work full time in the general area of your new workplace for at least 39 weeks during the first 12 months and a total of at least 78 weeks during the 24 months right after you move.

You may deduct your moving expenses for 1992 even if you have not met the time test before your 1992 return is due. You may do this if you expect to meet the 39-week test by the end of 1993 or the 78-week test by the end of 1994. If you have not met the test by then, you will have to do one of the following:

• Amend your 1992 tax return on which you deducted moving expenses. To do this, use **Form 1040X,** Amended U.S. Individual Income Tax Return; or

• In the year you cannot meet the test, report as income on your tax return the amount of your 1992 moving expense deduction that reduced your 1992 income tax. For more details, see **Time Test** in Pub. 521.

If you do not deduct your moving expenses on your 1992 return and you later meet the time test, you may take the deduction by filing an amended return for 1992. To do this, use Form 1040X.

Exceptions to the Distance and Time Tests.—You do not have to meet the time test in case of death, if your job ends because of disability, if you are transferred for your employer's benefit, or if you are laid off or discharged for a reason other than willful misconduct.

You do not have to meet the time test if you meet the requirements explained later for retirees or survivors living outside the United States.

If you are in the armed forces, you do not have to meet the distance and time tests if you meet the conditions explained below.

Members of the Armed Forces

If you are in the armed forces, you do not have to meet the **distance and time tests** if the move is due to a permanent change of station. A permanent change of station includes a move in connection with and within 1 year of retirement or other termination of active duty.

Note: *If the total reimbursements and allowances you received from the government in connection with the move are more than your actual moving expenses, include the excess in income on Form 1040, line 7. Do not complete Form 3903.*

How To Complete Form 3903.—If your reimbursements and allowances are less than your actual moving expenses, first complete Part I of Form 3903 using your actual expenses. Do not reduce your expenses by any reimbursements or allowances you received from the government in connection with the move. Also, do not include any expenses for moving services that were provided by the government. If you and your spouse and dependents are moved to or from different locations, treat the moves as a single move.

Next, complete lines 16 through 18 of Form 3903. Then, read the instructions for line 19 on the next page to figure your moving expense deduction.

Qualified Retirees or Survivors Living Outside the United States

If you are a retiree or survivor who moved to a home in the United States or its possessions and you meet the requirements below, you are treated as if you moved to a new workplace located in the United States. You are subject to the distance test and other limitations explained on Form 3903. Use this form instead of Form 3903F to figure your moving expense deductions.

Retirees.—You may deduct moving expenses for a move to a new home in the United States when you actually retire if both your old principal workplace and your old home were outside the United States.

Survivors.—You may deduct moving expenses for a move to a home in the United States if you are the spouse or dependent of a person whose principal workplace at the time of death was outside the United States. In addition, the expenses must be for a move (1) that begins within 6 months after the decedent's death, and (2) from a former home outside the United States that you

Cat. No. 64324D

lived in with the decedent at the time of death.

Deductible Moving Expenses

You may deduct most of the reasonable expenses you incur in moving your family and dependent household members. These include your costs to move to the new location (Part I, Sections A and B), pre-move househunting expenses and expenses of temporary quarters once you arrive in the new location (Section C), and certain qualified real estate expenses (Section D).

You MAY NOT deduct expenses of a loss on the sale of your home, mortgage penalties, refitting draperies and carpets, or canceling club memberships. Nor can you deduct expenses for employees such as a servant, governess, or nurse.

Reimbursements

You must include in gross income as compensation for services any reimbursement of, or payment for, moving expenses. If your employer paid for any part of your move, you must report that amount as income on **Form 1040, line 7.** Your employer should include the amount paid in your total income on Form W-2. However, if you are not sure that the reimbursements have been included in your Form W-2, check with your employer. Your employer must give you a statement showing a detailed breakdown of reimbursements or payments for moving expenses. Your employer may use **Form 4782**, Employee Moving Expense Information, or his or her own form.

You may choose to deduct moving expenses in the year you are reimbursed by your employer, even though you paid for the moving expenses in a different year. However, special rules apply. See **How To Report** in Pub. 521.

Meal Expenses

Only 80% of your meal expenses are deductible. This limit is figured on line 7 in Section B and on line 12 in Section C.

No Double Benefits

You may not take double benefits. For example, you may not use the moving expenses on line 14 that are part of your moving expense deduction to lower the amount of gain on the sale of your old home. In addition, you may not use the moving expenses on line 15 that are part of your moving expense deduction to add to the basis of your new home. Use **Form 2119**, Sale of Your Home, to figure the gain, if any, you must report on the sale of your old home and the adjusted basis of the new one.

Specific Instructions

Part I—Moving Expenses

Line 4.—Enter the actual cost to pack, crate, move, store in transit, and insure your household goods and personal effects.

Lines 5 and 6.—Enter the costs of travel from your old home to your new home. These include transportation, meals, and lodging on the way. Include costs for the day you arrive. Report the cost of transportation and lodging on line 5. Report your meal expenses separately on line 6. Although not all the members of your household have to travel together or at the same time, you may only include expenses for one trip per person.

If you use your own car, you may figure the expenses in either of the following two ways:

● Actual out-of-pocket expenses for gas and oil (keep records to verify the amounts), or

● At the rate of 9 cents a mile (keep records to verify your mileage).

You may add parking fees and tolls to the amount claimed under either method.

Lines 9 through 11.—Enter the costs of travel to look for a new home before you move and temporary quarters expenses after you move. Report pre-move househunting travel and lodging on line 9, temporary quarters expenses on line 10, and the combined cost of meals on line 11.

Pre-move househunting expenses are deductible only if:

● You took the trip after you got the job, **and**

● You returned to your old home after looking for a new one, **and**

● You traveled to the new work area primarily to look for a new home.

There is no limit on the number of househunting trips you may take and you do not have to be successful in finding a home to qualify for this deduction. If you used your own car, figure transportation costs as explained in the instructions for lines 9 through 11. If you are self-employed, you may deduct househunting costs only if you had already made substantial arrangements to begin work in the new location.

You may deduct the cost of meals and lodging while occupying temporary quarters in the area of your new workplace. Include the costs for any period of 30 days in a row after you get the job, but before you move into permanent quarters. If you are self-employed, you may count these expenses only if you had already made

substantial arrangements to begin work in the new location.

Lines 14 and 15.—Enter your qualified real estate expenses. You may include most of the costs to sell or buy a home or to settle or get a lease. Examples of expenses you MAY include are:

● Sales commissions.

● Advertising costs.

● Attorney's fees.

● Title and escrow fees.

● State transfer taxes.

● Costs to settle an unexpired lease or to get a new lease.

Examples of expenses you MAY NOT include are:

● Costs to improve your home to help it sell.

● Charges for payment or prepayment of interest.

● Payments or prepayments of rent.

Check the appropriate box, **a** or **b**, on lines 14 and 15 when you enter the amounts for these two lines.

Part II—Dollar Limits and Moving Expense Deductions

Lines 16 and 18.—The dollar limits on these lines apply to the total expenses **per move** even though you may claim expenses related to the same move in more than one year. For more details, see **How To Report** in Pub. 521.

If both you and your spouse began work at new workplaces and shared the same new home at the end of 1992, you must treat this as one move rather than two. If you file separate returns, each of you is limited to a total of $750 on line 16, and to a total of $1,500 on line 18.

If both you and your spouse began work at new workplaces but each of you moved to separate new homes, this is treated as two separate moves. If you file a joint return, line 16 is limited to a total of $3,000, and line 18 is limited to a total of $6,000. If you file separate returns, each of you is limited to a total of $1,500 on line 16, and a total of $3,000 on line 18.

Note: If you checked box a on line 14, any amount on line 14 that you cannot deduct because of the dollar limit should be used on Form 2119 to decrease the gain on the sale of your old home. If you checked box a on line 15, use any amount on line 15 that you cannot deduct because of the dollar limit to increase the basis of your new home.

Line 19.—If you are a member of the armed forces, add the amounts on lines 4, 8, and 18. From that total, subtract the total reimbursements and allowances you received from the government in connection with the move. If the result is more than zero, enter the result on line 19 and on Schedule A, line 18.

Form **3903F** Department of the Treasury Internal Revenue Service	**Foreign Moving Expenses** ▶ **Attach to Form 1040.** ▶ **See separate instructions.**	OMB No. 1545-0062 19**92** Attachment Sequence No. **63**
Name(s) shown on Form 1040		Your social security number

1 City and country in which your **old** workplace was located ▶ ....

2 City and country in which your **new** workplace is located ▶ ....
   Caution: *If you are a member of the armed forces, see the instructions before continuing.*

Part I   Moving Expenses

Note: *Any payments your employer made for any part of your move (including the value of any services furnished in kind) should be included on your W-2 form. Report that amount on* **Form 1040, line 7.** *See* **Reimbursements** *in the instructions.*

Section A—Transportation of Household Goods

3 Transportation and storage for household goods and personal effects . . . . | **3** |

Section B—Expenses of Moving From Old To New Home

4 Travel and lodging **not** including meals . . . . | **4** |

5 Total meals . . . . | **5** |

6 Multiply line 5 by 80% (.80) . . . . | **6** |

7 Add lines 4 and 6 . . . . | **7** |

Section C—Pre-move Househunting Expenses and Temporary Quarters
(for any 90 days in a row after getting your job)

8 Pre-move travel and lodging **not** including meals . . . . | **8** |

9 Temporary quarters expenses **not** including meals . . . . | **9** |

10 Total meal expenses for both pre-move househunting
   and temporary quarters . . . . | **10** |

11 Multiply line 10 by 80% (.80) . . . . | **11** |

12 Add lines 8, 9, and 11 . . . . | **12** |

Section D—Qualified Real Estate Expenses

13 Expenses of (check one): **a** ☐ selling or exchanging your old home, or ⎱
   b ☐ if renting, settling an unexpired lease. ⎰ | **13** |

14 Expenses of (check one): **a** ☐ buying your new home, or ⎱ . . .
   b ☐ if renting, getting a new lease. ⎰ | **14** |

Part II   Dollar Limits and Moving Expense Deduction

15 Enter the **smaller** of:
   ● The amount on line 12, or
   ● $4,500 ($2,250 if married filing a separate return and at the end of ⎱ . .
   1992 you lived with your spouse who also started work in 1992). ⎰ | **15** |

16 Add lines 13, 14, and 15 . . . . | **16** |

17 Enter the **smaller** of:
   ● The amount on line 16, or
   ● $6,000 ($3,000 if married filing a separate return and at the end of 1992 you lived with ⎱ . . .
   your spouse who also started work in 1992). ⎰ | **17** |

18 Add lines 3, 7, and 17 . . . . | **18** |

19 Amount of expenses allocable to excluded income or housing costs (see instructions) . . . . . | **19** |

20 Subtract line 19 from line 18. Enter the result here and on Schedule A, line 18. This is your **moving expense deduction** . . . . ▶ | **20** |

For Paperwork Reduction Act Notice, see separate instructions.   Cat. No. 12493R   Form **3903F** (1992)
★U.S.GPO:1992-0-315-321

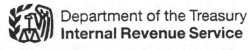

1992

**Department of the Treasury
Internal Revenue Service**

Instructions for Form 3903F
Foreign Moving Expenses

General Instructions

Paperwork Reduction Act Notice

We ask for the information on this form to carry out the Internal Revenue laws of the United States. You are required to give us the information. We need it to ensure that you are complying with these laws and to allow us to figure and collect the right amount of tax.

The time needed to complete and file this form will vary depending on individual circumstances. The estimated average time is:

Recordkeeping	52 min.
Learning about the law or the form	7 min.
Preparing the form	29 min.
Copying, assembling, and sending the form to the IRS	20 min.

If you have comments concerning the accuracy of these time estimates or suggestions for making this form more simple, we would be happy to hear from you. You can write to both the IRS and the Office of Management and Budget at the addresses listed in the Instructions for Form 1040.

Purpose of Form

Use Form 3903F to figure your moving expense deduction if you are a U.S. citizen or resident alien who moved to a new principal place of work (workplace) outside the United States or its possessions.

Note: *Use Form 3903, Moving Expenses, instead of this form if you moved from a foreign country to the United States or its possessions because of a change in the location of your job. Form 3903 should also be used by retirees and survivors who qualify to deduct their expenses for moving from a foreign country to the United States or its possessions.*

Additional Information

For more details, get **Pub. 521,** Moving Expenses. Retirees and survivors should also get Pub. 521 for an explanation of the requirements that must be met to deduct moving expenses.

Who May Deduct Moving Expenses

If you moved to a different home because you began work at a new workplace outside the United States or its possessions, you may be able to deduct your moving expenses. You may be able to take the deduction whether you are self-employed or an employee. But you must meet certain tests explained next.

Distance Test.—Your new principal workplace must be at least 35 miles farther from your old home than your old workplace was. For example, if your old workplace was 3 miles from your old home, your new workplace must be at least 38 miles from that home. If you did not have an old workplace, your new workplace must be at least 35 miles from your old home. The distance between the two points is the shortest of the more commonly traveled routes between them.

Time Test.—If you are an employee, you must work full time in the general area of your new workplace for at least 39 weeks during the 12 months right after you move. If you are self-employed, you must work full time in the general area of your new workplace for at least 39 weeks during the first 12 months and a total of at least 78 weeks during the 24 months right after you move.

You may deduct your moving expenses for 1992 even if you have not met the time test before your 1992 tax return is due. You may do this if you expect to meet the 39-week test by the end of 1993 or the 70-week test by the end of 1994. If you have not met the test by then, you will have to do one of the following:

● Amend your 1992 tax return on which you deducted moving expenses. To do this, use **Form 1040X,** Amended U.S. Individual Income Tax Return; or

● In the year you cannot meet the test, report as income on your tax return the amount of your 1992 moving expense deduction that reduced your 1992 income tax. For more details, see **Time Test** in Pub. 521.

If you do not deduct your moving expenses on your 1992 return and you later meet the time test, you may take the deduction by filing an amended return for 1992. To do this, use Form 1040X.

Exception to the Time Test.—You do not have to meet the time test in case of death, if your job ends because of disability, if you are transferred for your employer's benefit, or if you are laid off or discharged for a reason other than willful misconduct.

Members of the Armed Forces

If you are in the armed forces, you do not have to meet the **distance and time tests** if the move is due to a permanent change of station. A permanent change of station includes a move in connection with and within 1 year of retirement or other termination of active duty.

Note: *If the total reimbursements and allowances you received from the government in connection with the move are more than your actual moving expenses, include the excess in income on Form 1040, line 7.* **Do not complete Form 3903F.**

How To Complete Form 3903F.—If your total reimbursements and allowances are less than your actual moving expenses, first complete Form 3903F using your actual expenses. **Do not** reduce your expenses by any reimbursements or allowances you received from the government in connection with the move. Also, do not include any expenses for moving services that were provided by the government. If you and your spouse and dependents are moved to or from different locations, treat the moves as a single move.

Next, complete lines 15 through 17 of Form 3903F. Then, read the instructions for line 18 on the next page.

Deductible Moving Expenses

You may deduct most of the reasonable expenses you incur in moving your family and dependent household members. These include your costs to move to the new location (Part I, Sections A and B), pre-move househunting expenses and expenses of temporary quarters once you arrive in the new location (Section C), and certain qualified real estate expenses (Section D).

You MAY NOT deduct expenses of a loss on the sale of your home, mortgage penalties, refitting draperies and carpets, or canceling club memberships. Nor can you deduct expenses for employees such as a servant, governess, or nurse.

Reimbursements

You must include in gross income as compensation for services any reimbursement of, or payment for, moving expenses. If your employer paid for any part of your move, you must report that amount as income on **Form 1040, line 7.** Your employer should include the amount paid in your total income on Form W-2. However, if you are not sure that the reimbursements have been included in your Form W-2, check with your employer. Your employer must give you a statement showing a detailed breakdown of reimbursements or payments for moving expenses. Your employer may use **Form 4782,** Employee Moving Expense Information, or his or her own form.

You may choose to deduct moving expenses in the year you are reimbursed by your employer, even though you paid for the moving expenses in a different year. However, special rules apply. See **How To Report** in Pub. 521.

Meal Expenses

Only 80% of your meal expenses are deductible. This limit is figured on line 6 in Section B and on line 11 in Section C.

No Double Benefits

You may not take double benefits. For example, you may not use the moving expenses on line 13 that are part of your moving expense deduction to lower the amount of gain on the sale of your old home.

Cat. No. 64387M

In addition, you may not use the moving expenses on line 14 that are part of your moving expense deduction to add to the basis of your new home. Use **Form 2119,** Sale of Your Home, to figure the gain, if any, you must report on the sale of your old home and the adjusted basis of the new one.

If you file **Form 2555,** Foreign Earned Income, to exclude any of your income or housing costs, you may not deduct the part of your moving expenses that is allocable to the excluded income. See the instructions for line 19 and **Pub. 54,** Tax Guide for U.S. Citizens and Resident Aliens Abroad, for information on how to figure the part of your moving expenses that is allocable to the excluded income and how to report this amount.

Specific Instructions

Part I—Moving Expenses

Line 3.—Enter the actual cost to pack, crate, move, store, and insure your household goods and personal effects. Also, include moving your possessions to and from storage and storing them for all or part of the time the new workplace continues to be your principal workplace.

Note: *If you moved in an earlier year and are claiming only storage fees during your absence from the United States, you do not have to complete this form. Enter the net amount (after the reduction for the part that is allocable to excluded income) on Schedule A (Form 1040), line 18. Next to the amount, write "Storage Fees."*

Lines 4 and 5.—Enter the costs of travel from your old home to your new home. These include transportation, meals, and lodging on the way. Include costs for the day you arrive. Report the cost of transporation and lodging on line 4. Report your meal expenses separately on line 5. Although not all the members of your household have to travel together or at the same time, you may only include expenses for one trip per person.

If you use your own car, you may figure the expenses in either of the following two ways:

• Actual out-of-pocket expenses for gas and oil (keep records to verify the amounts), or

• At the rate of 9 cents a mile (keep records to verify your mileage).

You may add parking fees and tolls to the amount claimed under either method.

Lines 8 through 10.—Enter the costs of travel to look for a new home before you move and temporary quarters expenses after you move. Report pre-move househunting travel and lodging on line 8, temporary quarters expenses on line 9, and the combined cost of meals on line 10.

Pre-move househunting expenses are deductible only if:

• You took the trip after you got the job, **and**

• You returned to your old home after looking for a new one, **and**

• You traveled to the general location of the new workplace primarily to look for a new home.

There is no limit on the number of househunting trips you may take and you do not have to be successful in finding a home to qualify for this deduction. If you used your own car, figure transportation costs as explained in the instructions for lines 4 and 5. If you are self-employed, you may deduct househunting costs only if you had already made substantial arrangements to begin work in the new location.

You may deduct the costs of meals and lodging while occupying temporary quarters in the area of your new workplace. Include these costs for any period of 90 days in a row after you get the job but before you move into permanent quarters. If you are self-employed, you may count these expenses only if you had already made substantial arrangements to begin work in the new location.

Lines 13 and 14.—Enter your qualified real estate expenses. You may include most of the costs to sell or buy a home or to settle or get a lease. Examples of expenses you MAY include are:

• Sales commissions.

• Advertising costs.

• Attorney's fees.

• Title and escrow fees.

• State transfer taxes.

• Costs to settle an unexpired lease or to get a new lease.

Examples of expenses you MAY NOT include are:

• Costs to improve your home to help it sell.

• Charges for payment or prepayment of interest.

• Payments or prepayments of rent.

Check the appropriate box, **a** or **b,** on lines 13 and 14 when you enter the amounts for these two lines.

Part II—Dollar Limits and Moving Expense Deduction

Lines 15 and 17.—The dollar limits on these lines apply to the total expenses **per move** even though you may claim expenses related to the same move in more than one year. For more details, see **How To Report** in Pub. 521.

If both you and your spouse began work at new workplaces and shared the same new home at the end of 1992, you must treat this as one move rather than two. If you file separate returns, each of you is limited to a total of $2,250 on line 15, and to a total of $3,000 on line 17.

If both you and your spouse began work at new workplaces but each of you moved to separate new homes, this is treated as two separate moves. If you file a joint return, line 15 is limited to a total of $9,000, and line 17 is limited to a total of $12,000. If you file separate returns, each of you is limited to a total of $4,500 on line 15, and a total of $6,000 on line 17.

Note: *If you checked box a on line 13, any amount on line 13 that you cannot deduct because of the dollar limit should be used on Form 2119 to decrease the gain on the sale of your old home. If you checked box a on*

line 14, use any amount on line 14 that you cannot deduct because of the dollar limit to increase the basis of your new home.

Line 18.—If you are a member of the armed forces, add the amounts on lines 3, 7, and 17. From that total, subtract the total reimbursements and allowances you received from the government in connection with the move. If the result is more than zero, enter the result on line 18 and complete the rest of the form to figure the amount to enter on Schedule A, line 18.

Line 19.—If you file Form 2555 and your period of bona fide residence or physical presence in the year of your move is 120 days or more, the moving expense is connected with earning the income at the foreign location in the year of your move. Figure the unallowable part of the moving expenses by multiplying the amount on line 18 by a fraction. The numerator of the fraction is the excluded income and the denominator is total foreign earned income. Enter the result on line 19. Attach a statement to your return showing how you figured this amount.

If your period of bona fide residence or physical presence in the year of your move is **less** than 120 days, the moving expense (except storage expense) is connected with earning the income at the foreign location in the year of the move **and** the year following the move. Figure the unallowable part of the moving expense by multiplying the amount on line 18 by a fraction. The numerator of the fraction is the income excluded in both years and the denominator is the total foreign earned income in both years. Enter the result on line 19. Attach a statement to your return showing how you figured this amount.

Recapture of Moving Expense Deduction.— If your moving expense deduction is attributable to your foreign earnings in 2 years (the year of the move and the following year), you should preferably request an extension of time to file your return for the year of the move until after the end of the following year. You would then have all the information needed to properly figure the moving expense deduction.

If you do not request an extension, you should provisionally figure the part of the entire moving expense deduction that is disallowed by multiplying the moving expense by a fraction. The numerator of the fraction is your excluded foreign earned income for the year of the move and the denominator is your total foreign earned income for the year of the move. Then, when you know your foreign earnings and exclusion for the following year, you must adjust the moving expense deduction by filing an amended return for the year of the move, or by recapturing any additional unallowable amount as income on your return for the following year. If after you make the final computation you have an additional amount of allowable moving expense deduction, you may claim this only on an amended return for the year of the move; you may not claim it on the return for the second year.

Page 2

Form **4782** (Rev. October 1992) Department of the Treasury Internal Revenue Service	**Employee Moving Expense Information** Payments made during the calendar year 19 .... ▶ See instructions on back.	OMB No. 1545-0182 Expires 9-30-95 **Do not file. Keep for your records.**
Name of employee		Social security number

Moving Expense Payments		**(a)** Amount paid to employee		**(b)** Amount paid to a third party for employee's benefit and value of services furnished in kind		**(c)** Total (Add columns (a) and (b).)
Section A—Transportation of Household Goods						
1 Transportation and storage of household goods and personal effects	**1**					
Section B—Expenses of Moving From Old To New Home						
2 Travel and lodging payments **not** including meals	**2**					
3 Meal payments for travel	**3**					
Section C—Pre-move Househunting Expenses and Temporary Quarters for any 30 Days in a Row After Obtaining Employment (90 Days for a Foreign Move)						
4 Pre-move travel and lodging payments **not** including meals	**4**					
5 Temporary quarters payments **not** including meals	**5**					
6 Total meal payments for both pre-move househunting and temporary quarters . . .	**6**					
Section D—Qualified Real Estate Expenses						
7 Qualified expenses of selling, buying, or renting a home	**7**					
Section E—Miscellaneous Payments						
8 List all other payments (specify) ▶	**8**					
9 Total moving expense payments. Add the amounts in column (c) of lines 1 through 8 . . . ▶	**9**					

Note: *The amount on line 9* **must** *be included in the employee's income.*

For Paperwork Reduction Act Notice, see back of form.   Cat. No. 13079T   Form **4782** (Rev. 10-92)

Instructions for Employer

Paperwork Reduction Act Notice

We ask for the information on this form to carry out the Internal Revenue laws of the United States. You are required to give us the information. We need it to ensure that taxpayers are complying with these laws and to allow us to figure and collect the right amount of tax.

The time needed to complete this form will vary depending on individual circumstances. The estimated average time is: 7 hours and 3 minutes.

If you have comments concerning the accuracy of this time estimate or suggestions for making this form more simple, we would be happy to hear from you. You can write to both the **Internal Revenue Service,** Washington, DC 20224, Attention: IRS Reports Clearance Officer, T:FP; and the **Office of Management and Budget,** Paperwork Reduction Project (1545-0182), Washington, DC 20503. **DO NOT** send this form to either of these offices. Instead, give it to your employee.

Purpose of Form

You are required to give your employees a statement showing a detailed breakdown of reimbursements or payments of moving expenses. Form 4782 may be used for this purpose or you may use your own form as long as it provides the same information as Form 4782. A separate form is required for each move made by an employee for which reimbursement or payment is made.

Form W-2

Any payments you made for an employee's move (including the value of any services furnished in kind) must be included in box 10, "Wages, tips, other compensation," on the employee's Form W-2.

Payments for moving expenses that **are** deductible by your employee **are not** subject to withholding.

Payments for moving expenses that **are not** deductible by your employee are subject to withholding.

When To Give the Information

You must give Form 4782 (or your own form) to your employee by January 31 following the calendar year in which the employee received the reimbursement or payment. However, if the employee stops working for you before December 31 and submits a written request to receive the form earlier, you must give the completed form to the former employee within 30 days after you receive the request if the 30-day period ends before the regular January 31 deadline.

Penalty for Not Providing the Information or Providing Incorrect Information

If you fail to give Form 4782 (or your own form) to your employee by the due date or fail to include correct information on the form, you may be subject to a penalty. The penalty is $50 for each failure.

Additional Information

For more details on withholding requirements, get **Pub. 15,** Circular E, Employer's Tax Guide. For assistance in determining what moving expenses would be deductible by your employee, get **Form 3903,** Moving Expenses, and its instructions; **Form 3903F,** Foreign Moving Expenses, and its instructions; or **Pub. 521,** Moving Expenses.

General Information for Employees

Purpose of Form

This form is furnished by your employer to give you the information you need to figure your moving expense deduction. The form shows the amount of any reimbursement made to you, payments made to a third party for your benefit, and the value of services furnished in kind for moving expenses. You should receive a separate form for each move you made during the calendar year for which you receive any reimbursement or during which payment is made for your benefit.

Caution: *Do not use this form as verification of your moving expenses. It reports only amounts your employer included in your income for moving expenses, which may be different than the amounts you actually spent.*

Who May Deduct Moving Expenses

If you file Form 1040 and itemize your deductions, you may deduct the reasonable expenses you paid or incurred during the tax year to move to a new principal place of work (workplace). But you must generally meet the "distance" and "time" tests explained below. If you incurred expenses shown on this form and they qualify as deductible moving expenses, you may include them in figuring your moving expense deduction.

For moves within or to the United States, use **Form 3903,** Moving Expenses, to figure your deduction. If you moved outside the United States or its possessions, use **Form 3903F,** Foreign Moving Expenses, to figure your deduction.

Distance Test. Your new workplace must be at least 35 miles farther from your old home than your old workplace was.

Time Test. If you are an employee, you must work full time in the general area of your new workplace for at least 39 weeks during the 12 months right after you move.

Additional Information

See the form instructions and **Pub. 521,** Moving Expenses, for detailed moving expense information, including which expenses qualify and what are reasonable expenses.

Chapter 46

RESTRICTED STOCK PLAN

WHAT IS IT?

A restricted stock plan is an arrangement to compensate executives by giving them shares of stock subject to certain restrictions or limitations. Usually the stock used in such plans is stock of the employer corporation or its subsidiary.

Company stock is attractive to executives as an element of compensation because it allows sharing in company growth. To the employer, the use of stock is attractive as a "double incentive" plan for executives, because the terms of the plan can be based on executive performance and, in addition, increases in the value of the stock may reflect to some extent the executive's performance.

Employers often adopt stock plans with restrictions designed to help retain employees or discourage conduct the employer deems undesirable, such as going to work for a competitor. These restrictions can also serve the employee's interest by postponing taxability of compensation to the employee.

For an outline of some advanced types of stock and other plans used for compensating executives, particularly in large corporations, see Appendix D.

WHEN IS IT INDICATED?

1. When the employer is willing to create new shareholders of the company. Shareholders of a closely held corporation often do not want to share company stock and potential control of the business outside of the existing group of shareholders.

2. When a corporation wants to provide an executive with an incentive-based form of compensation. In restricted stock plans, the ultimate amount the executive receives generally depends on the value of the stock. If the plan is well designed, the value of company stock will reflect the executive's performance at least to some extent.

3. When an employer wants to use a compensation arrangement as a way of discouraging certain specified conduct such as leaving employment within a short time or going to work for a competitor.

4. When an executive wants an "equity-based" form of compensation—that is, compensation based on the value of the company's stock. Equity-based compensation allows an executive to share in the upside potential of a company's growth. This type of compensation is particularly useful in the startup phase of a high technology company where growth can be very significant.

ADVANTAGES

1. Restricted stock plans can allow deferral of taxation to the employee until the year in which the restricted stock becomes "substantially vested." Essentially this means nonforfeitable, as discussed below under "Tax Implications."

2. A stock plan allows employees an interest in the increase in value of a company's stock. This type of payment, especially when coupled with deferral of taxation, can be much more valuable than straight compensation.

3. A restricted stock plan allows an employer to grant an executive an equity interest in the company but withdraw it if the executive leaves prematurely or goes to work for a competitor.

4. For non-tax purposes, an executive has all the advantages of stock ownership, such as voting rights, dividends, and appreciation potential, but is not taxed on receipt of the stock to the extent it is not substantially vested.

DISADVANTAGES

1. The employer does not receive a tax deduction for a restricted stock plan until the year in which the property becomes substantially vested and therefore taxable to the executive (unless the executive elects to be taxed earlier under Section 83(b), as discussed under "Tax Implications," below).

2. The possibility of a Section 83(b) election by the executive means that the employer may not have control of the amount or timing of its tax deduction.

3. S corporations must be certain that the restrictions do not create a second class of stock, which would violate the S

corporation one-class-of-stock rule. An S corporation that violates this rule will terminate its S election, thus subjecting all corporate income to taxation at ordinary corporate rates.

Generally, an S corporation will not be treated as having more than one class of shares so long as all shares confer identical rights to liquidation and distribution proceeds. Thus, guaranteed distributions following a vesting period may violate the rule unless all shares enjoy the same guaranteed distributions. Ordinary contractual arrangements, such as employment agreements, will not be deemed to affect distribution and liquidation proceeds unless a principal purpose of the arrangement is to circumvent the one-class rule.

4. Issuing new shares of restricted stock tends to dilute ownership of the corporation. This may be particularly undesirable for closely held corporations. Shareholders of these corporations seldom want to share control or profits, or share company assets on sale or liquidation of the business.

5. If the change (up or down) in value of the stock is not consistent with the executive's performance, this can be disadvantageous to both employer and executive. If the stock goes up with little or no effort by the executive, other shareholders will be resentful. If the stock drops in value in spite of excellent executive performance, the incentive element of the plan is lost or diminished.

WHAT CAN BE ACCOMPLISHED WITH RESTRICTIONS ON STOCK

The types of restrictions used in restricted stock plans can be tailored to meet employer and employee objectives.

Employee Retention

Employers often use stock plans to tie key employees to the company. With this type of objective, for example, stock might be transferred to an employee subject to a restriction that it cannot be sold or otherwise transferred by the employee during a specified period—such as 5 years. If the employee quits before this time, the stock must be returned to the company. This simple form of restriction can also be used as a way of keeping retirees tied to the company and providing them with some useful deferral of income. The stock can be transferred to an executive retiree subject to a provision that the retiree remain available for consulting services to the employer during a specified time, such as 5 years.

Discouraging Misconduct

Restrictions can also be associated with specific employee conduct that the company wants to discourage. For example, a restricted stock plan might provide that stock must be returned to the employer if during a period of 5 years the employee is discharged by the company for cause, or discharged for some specific reason such as embezzlement or disclosure of trade or marketing information. In certain industries, typically high technology industries, stock in restricted stock plans is forfeitable if the employee engages in competition with the employer—for example, starts a competitive business or goes to work for a competitor.

From a contractual point of view, restrictions involving noncompetition agreements may be unenforceable in the courts if they go beyond reasonable limits. However, the courts generally will enforce a noncompetition provision if it is *reasonable* as to (a) the geographic area to which it applies, and (b) the period of time for which it applies.

For example, suppose Apex Industries operates a plumbing fixture business only on the east coast and has no plans to expand geographically. Apex's restricted stock agreement with employee Hank, aged 35, provides a forfeiture of stock if Hank works in a competing business anywhere in the country. Hank quits and starts a plumbing fixture business in California. If Apex tries to enforce the noncompetition provision, the courts are likely to deem it unreasonable and unenforceable because it goes beyond a reasonably broad geographic area. The same result would probably apply if the plan restricted Hank from competing in the immediate geographic area "for the rest of his life."

Incentives

Restricted stock plans can be designed as incentive plans similar to bonus plans. For example, a restricted stock plan might give an executive 1,000 shares of company stock subject to a forfeiture if gross sales in the executive's division do not increase by at least 20 percent within 5 years. When sales reach the targeted level, the forfeitability restrictions would end. The stock would then belong to the executive without restriction. The advantage of this arrangement over a cash bonus is simply that it increases the security of the benefit to the employee compared with the mere promise by the company to pay a cash bonus. However, there are some risks from the employee's point of view compared with the stated contingent bonus amount, because the value of the stock could very well go down even though the employee works effectively and meets or exceeds the designated target sales level.

TAX IMPLICATIONS

1. Under Section 83 of the Internal Revenue Code, an employee is not subject to tax on the value of restricted property received as compensation from the employer until the year in which the property becomes "substantially vested" (unless the employee makes a "Section 83(b) election" to include it in income in the year received, as discussed in section 2 below).

   The definition of substantial vesting in Code section 83 and the regulations thereunder is of great significance in designing restricted stock plans. These plans are obviously much less attractive to employees if they are not carefully designed to provide tax deferral within the rules of Section 83.

   For example, if an employee receives restricted stock in 1993 that is deemed (for tax purposes) to be substantially vested in 1993, the employee will pay tax in that year even if under state law the employee does not completely own the stock (and the corporation will get a corresponding deduction; see below). In spite of the taxability to the employee, the restrictions on the stock received may still be legally effective under state property law so that the employee cannot sell the stock in 1993 and realize any cash at that time.

   Substantial vesting. Under Section 83, property is not considered substantially vested so long as it is subject to a "substantial risk of forfeiture" and is not transferable by an employee to a third party free of this risk of forfeiture.

   The question of whether a substantial risk of forfeiture exists depends on the facts and circumstances in each case. The regulations under Section 83 contain various examples and guidelines.

   • Generally, a substantial risk of forfeiture is considered to exist if the employee must return the property unless a specified period of service for the employer is completed.[1]

   • A forfeiture only as a result of some event that is relatively unlikely generally would not constitute a substantial risk of forfeiture. For example, the plan might provide that an employee must return the stock if he commits embezzlement within a specified period of time. This unlikely event, which furthermore is within the control of the employee, probably would not constitute a substantial risk of forfeiture.[2] (The executive would therefore be taxed immediately upon receipt of the stock.)

   • A forfeiture as a result of failing to meet certain incentive targets, such as a certain level of sales, generally is a substantial risk of forfeiture.[3]

   • A forfeiture resulting from going to work for a competitor constitutes a substantial risk if the employee has scarce skills in an active job market.[4]

   Where an employee is an owner or major shareholder in a company, forfeiture provisions of almost any type are likely to be challenged by the IRS as being insubstantial, because the employee's control or influence over the company can render them relatively ineffective.[5]

   As indicated above, property will not be considered subject to a substantial risk of forfeiture if it can be transferred by the employee to another person or entity who takes the stock free of the risk of forfeiture. When employer stock is used in a restricted stock plan, this requirement is usually met by a "legend" or statement imprinted on share certificates indicating that transfer and ownership of the shares are subject to a restricted property plan. This notifies any prospective buyer or other recipient that the employee is not free to sell, give away, or otherwise transfer the shares without restrictions.

2. Under Code section 83(b), an executive can elect to recognize income as of the date of receipt of the restricted property, rather than waiting until it becomes substantially vested. This election must be made within thirty days of receiving the property and must comply with requirements in the IRS regulations.

   The amount included in income under this Section 83(b) election is the excess, if any, of the fair market value of the property at the time of transfer (determined without regard to any restrictions other than "non-lapse" restrictions—see below) over any amount the executive paid for the property. For example, if the stock is worth $60 per share at the time of receipt and the executive pays nothing for it, under a Section 83(b) election the executive would report ordinary income of $60 per share in the year of receipt.

   Why would an executive make a Section 83(b) election? If a Section 83(b) election is made, any subsequent appreciation in value of the property is treated as capital gain and taxed at lower capital gain rates. That gain is not subject to tax until the stock is sold. This can be a major consideration in deciding whether to make a Section 83(b) election. Section 83(b) elections may also be advantageous in special situations; for example, where the executive wants to maximize taxable income in a particular year in order to offset deductible losses.

When an executive includes an amount in income under a Section 83(b) election, the employer gets a tax deduction at that time for the same amount. The employer gets no further tax deduction if the property subsequently increases in value in the hands of the executive, whether or not the executive sells the property. Another disadvantage of the Section 83(b) election is that if the stock is forfeited for any reason, no deduction is allowed to the executive for the loss.

The executive making a Section 83(b) election is therefore gambling that the stock will increase substantially in value from the date of the election and that the stock will not be forfeited before the executive is able to sell or dispose of it without restriction.

3. Sometimes the stock received does not have a forfeiture provision as such but rather a restriction that reduces the value of the stock to the employee. In that case, the value of the stock is includable in income when received. But the amount includable is less than the full market value.

For example, a plan may provide an employee with a fully vested interest in the stock, but with a provision that the employee cannot resell the stock without first offering it back to the company at a specified price. In that case, because of the "first offer" provision, the value of the stock in the hands of the executive would not be its unfettered market value, but rather a reduced value reflecting the restriction.

A restriction will be taken into account for valuation purposes only if it is a "non-lapse restriction"—a restriction that by its terms will never lapse.[6] The first offer requirement of the type described in the above example would probably qualify as a non-lapse restriction. The issue of whether a restriction constitutes a non-lapse restriction is one of facts and circumstances. The IRS takes a restrictive view in its regulations and rulings, so non-lapse restrictions are difficult to design.

4. When an employee has become substantially vested in restricted property, its value is taxed in that year as compensation income.[7] Gain on any subsequent sale of the property is generally taxed as capital gain, as in the case of similar property acquired by any other means.

5. The employer's tax deduction for compensation income to the executive under a restricted stock plan is deferred until the year in which the employee is substantially vested and includes the amount in income. Technically, the employer's tax deduction occurs in the employer's taxable year in which, or with which, ends the taxable year of the employee in which the amount is includable in

the employee's income.[8] This is the usual rule for the timing of an employer's deduction for deferred compensation payments as discussed in Chapter 28. As with other types of compensation, the employer is required to withhold and pay tax. Withholding is particularly important here because the employer's deduction is, under the regulations, conditioned on the employer's actually withholding and paying tax.[9]

WHERE CAN I FIND OUT MORE ABOUT IT?

1. Leimberg, Stephan R. et al., *The Federal Income Tax Law*. Warren, Gorham, and Lamont, 1989.

2. Graduate Course: Executive Compensation (GS 842), The American College, Bryn Mawr, PA.

QUESTIONS AND ANSWERS

Question — How does a restricted stock plan affect an employer's accounting statements?

Answer — If stock is issued with restrictions based only on continued employment, the excess of the stock's fair market value when issued over the amount paid for it by the executive is a compensation expense for accounting purposes and is charged to earnings on a systematic basis over the related period of employment—the period during which the restrictions are in effect. If restrictions are based on contingent factors such as executive or company performance, the charge to expense can be delayed until the result is known for certain. These rules are set out in the currently effective official accounting statement, APB 25. The accounting profession is currently reconsidering the treatment of many executive compensation arrangements and some changes may appear in the future.

Question — Do federal securities laws apply to restricted stock, and what is their effect?

Answer — Federal securities registration is not generally required if stock is issued without cost, because no "sale" is deemed to occur for securities law purposes. However, the SEC (Securities Exchange Commission) views stock issued to executives as compensation to have been bargained for and thus sold, so the securities laws may apply. Many restricted stock arrangements qualify for one or more of the exemptions from securities registration, typically the "private placement" exemption whereby registration is not required where securities are issued to a limited number of persons.

Planners must also determine whether executives are restricted under the federal securities laws from reselling stock acquired under the plan. SEC Rule 144 includes conditions under which such stock can be resold freely. Executives holding stock in a restricted stock plan may also be subject to the anti-fraud provisions of the securities law such as the insider trading restrictions.

FOOTNOTES

1. Reg. §1.83-3(c)(1).
2. Reg. §1.83-3(c)(2).
3. Ibid.
4. Ibid.
5. Reg. §1.83-3(c)(3).
6. Regs. §§1.83-5(a), 1.83-3(h).
7. IRC Section 83(a).
8. Reg. §1.83-6(a)(1).
9. Reg. §1.83-6(a)(2).

Chapter 47

SEVERANCE PAY PLAN

WHAT IS IT?

A severance pay plan is an agreement between employer and employee to make payments after the employee's termination of employment.

Severance pay arrangements are almost completely flexible if characterization as an ERISA pension plan is avoided (see below). If ERISA's pension plan rules do not apply, the plan can cover any group of employees or even a single employee, on any terms and conditions the employer considers appropriate. For example, severance pay can be withheld if severance is for misconduct, if ERISA's pension plan rules do not apply. Severance agreements can and often are negotiated individually with executives.

For a discussion of additional considerations where severance pay is contingent upon a change in corporate ownership, see Chapter 35, Golden Parachute Plan. See also Chapter 51, Welfare Benefit Trusts and VEBAs, for plans that pay severance benefits from prefunded trust arrangements.

TAX IMPLICATIONS

1. Severance payments are deductible by the employer if (a) the payments are compensation for services previously rendered by the employee and (b) the payments are reasonable in amount.[1]

    Severance payments pursuant to a written plan or agreement entered into while the employee is still actively at work should be considered compensation for services in most cases. The promised severance benefits in this case are considered part of the employer's pay/benefit package that compensate the employee for services. However, if there is no written plan or agreement in place prior to termination of employment, the IRS could argue that the payment is something other than compensation—such as a gift, a dividend, a "buy out" payment for the employee's interest in the business, or whatever other characterization might square with the particular facts of the situation. Planners should counsel clients to try to avoid this by adopting formal severance plans, policies, or agreements.

The "reasonableness" test is the same that applies to all forms of compensation payments. (See the discussion in Chapter 28, Cash Compensation Planning.)

2. Severance payments are taxable to the recipient as compensation income in the year actually or constructively received.[2]

    The constructive receipt issue concerning severance payments is one to be aware of. For example, suppose employee Bob Cratchit is terminated on December 24, 1993 and is entitled to an immediate severance benefit of $350 (two weeks' pay). Bob asks his employer to give him a tax break by paying the severance benefit on January 2, 1994, and the employer does so. Technically, Bob has run afoul of the constructive receipt doctrine (see Chapter 16 for discussion); he should report the $350 severance benefit in 1993 because he had an unrestricted right to receive the payments in 1993.

    While the IRS may sometimes overlook small "constructive receipt" issues in situations like the Cratchit example, they will be alert to constructive receipt where substantial amounts are involved. For example, suppose an executive severance pay plan provides a severance benefit of 1½ years' salary, payable over a two-year period. If the executive has no option but the two-year payment, the payments will be included in income as they are received. However, if the executive can choose, at the time of or after severance, to accelerate the payments into one year (without risk of forfeiting the benefit), then the entire amount must be reported in that one year even if the executive chooses to actually receive it over a two-year period. Careful drafting of the agreement is essential to avoid such unexpected tax results.

3. If the severance payment is characterized as a "parachute payment," the employer's deduction may be limited and the employee may be subject to penalty. In general, parachute payments are severance payments that take effect upon changes in business ownership. The parachute rules are discussed in Chapter 35.

4. In general, the tax consequences of a severance pay plan (whether or not it is governed by ERISA as discussed below) are similar to those of a nonqualified deferred compensation plan. Refer to Chapter 16 for a discussion of further tax considerations.

5. The Social Security tax treatment of severance payments is not entirely clear. If severance pay is characterized as "deferred compensation" under Code section 3121(v)(2), then the Social Security tax is payable in the later of the year when services are performed or when there is no substantial risk of forfeiture of the rights to the payment. However, it has been reported that the IRS is considering regulations that would exempt severance pay from this provision, resulting in Social Security taxation in the year the payments are actually made.

ERISA IMPLICATIONS

1. Labor Department regulations provide that a severance pay plan will not be considered a "pension plan" for ERISA purposes if the following requirements are met:[3]

   • Payments are not contingent, directly or indirectly, upon retirement;

   • The total payments do not exceed twice the employee's annual compensation during the year immediately preceding the termination of employment; and

   • All payments are completed within 24 months after termination of employment (or, in the case of a "limited program of terminations," within the later of 24 months after termination or 24 months after the employee reaches normal retirement age).

   If these conditions are met, the plan will be considered a "welfare benefit plan" for ERISA purposes. See Appendix A for the reporting requirements applicable to welfare plans.

2. If a severance pay plan does not meet the ERISA "pension plan" exemption described above, it will be treated essentially as a nonqualified deferred compensation plan for ERISA purposes. Unfunded plans for a select group of executives may be eligible for the "top hat" ERISA limited exemption, as discussed in Chapter 16.

3. If the plan covers only a single person and was individually negotiated, some courts have found that ERISA is not applicable.[4] Therefore, for example, there would be no reporting requirements. However, many employers might want to file "protective" ERISA filings to avoid possible penalties.

FOOTNOTES

1. Reg. §1.162-7.
2. Reg. §1.61-2(a).
3. Labor Reg. §2510.3-2(b).
4. See, e.g., *Motel 6, Inc. v. Superior Court*, No. B025972 (Cal. App. Nov. 5, 1987).

Chapter 48

SICK PAY (SHORT TERM DISABILITY)

WHAT IS IT?

A sick pay or short term disability plan is a plan that continues employees' salary or wages during periods of illness or other disability for a limited time. Generally, sick pay or short term disability payments do not extend beyond about six months. Programs covering disabilities lasting more than six months are considered long term disability programs and are discussed in Chapter 43.

WHEN IS IT INDICATED?

1. Almost all employers have a broad based program providing some sick pay for short absences from work. This is a "high visibility" benefit that employees count on and appreciate.

2. An employer may want to provide special favorable short term disability programs for selected executives. Under current law, such plans can be provided on a discriminatory basis. That is, the employer can choose (1) who will be covered, (2) the level of benefits, which can vary from employee to employee, and (3) the terms and conditions of coverage.

DESIGN FEATURES

Most planners divide short term coverage into two types of plans: (1) sick pay and (2) short term disability plans. Although there is some overlap in these concepts, *sick pay* generally refers to uninsured continuation of salary or wages (usually 100% replacement) for a short period of time beginning on the first day of illness or disability. A *short term disability plan* is one that goes into effect when the employee's sick pay benefits run out and extends until the six month limit has been reached, when the employer's long term plan (if any) and Social Security disability go into effect. Short term plans, as defined this way, can be and often are insured.

Sick Pay

Sick pay benefits are usually provided for a broad group of employees. However, an employer can have a plan for se-

lected executives only or a plan with more favorable benefits for executives.

Usually only full-time employees are covered under sick pay plans. The employer can define the term "full-time" for this purpose in any reasonable manner; the 1,000 hour "year of service" definition applicable to qualified plans does not apply.

The duration of sick pay benefits is often tied to the length of an employee's service. For example, there may be no benefits until an employee has three months of service, then the plan will provide full benefits. Or, duration of benefits can be graded based on service. For example, employees may be entitled to 20 days of sick pay annually after 10 years of service, with the number of days of sick pay reduced for shorter service. One danger in providing increasingly generous sick pay as a "benefit" is that employees may come to believe that they are expected to take advantage of such sick days and abuse the benefit.

Some sick pay plans allow "carryover" of unused benefits. For example, if an employee is entitled to 10 days of sick pay in 1993 and uses only 5 of them, then the plan could allow the employee to carry over these 5 days to 1994, thus having 15 days of sick pay available in 1994. Plans allowing carryovers usually provide some maximum limit on the sick pay available for any one year. Usually no more than six months of sick pay can be accumulated.

If long periods of sick pay are allowed, benefits are often reduced below 100% of salary after a specified period of time (such as 30 days). This reduces employer costs and helps to "phase in" the long term benefits available, which usually do not provide 100% salary replacement.

Preventing sick pay abuse is a major management problem in many organizations. Some employers require a physician's certificate to obtain sick pay, particularly if the employee's absence is longer than one week. In some organizations management simply accepts the idea that employees will take whatever "sick days" are available and limits them accordingly. Generally speaking, absenteeism is a symptom of management problems that cannot be solved simply by the design of employee benefit programs.

Short Term Disability Plans

A short term disability plan fills the gap between sick pay and the employer's long term disability plan, if any. These plans are often insured, particularly for smaller employers, since the employer's liability to continue a disabled employee's salary for six months or so can be a considerable burden.

The design of short term plans, particularly if they are insured, is similar to the long term plans discussed in Chapter 43. However, there are some significant differences:

- Short term plans often have broader coverage than long term plans. An employer's long term plan may be limited to selected executives.

- Short term plans often require less service for coverage. Long term plans may be reserved for career employees, such as those with five or more years of service.

- The definition of disability is typically more generous (i.e., easier to meet) in a short term plan than in a long term plan. Usually the "regular occupation" definition is used. That is, disability in a short term plan is typically defined as "the total and continuous inability of the employee to perform any and every duty of his or her regular occupation."

Coverage exclusions in insured short term plans are similar to those in long term plans, as discussed in Chapter 43. As with long term plans, the Civil Rights Act of 1964 prohibits exclusion of pregnancy-related disabilities if the employer has 15 or more employees. (State civil rights laws may apply even to smaller employers.)

TAX IMPLICATIONS

1. The employer can deduct payments made directly to employees under a sick pay or short term disability plan, as compensation to employees. The employer can also deduct premium payments made under an insured plan. Like all compensation deductions, these payments are subject to the "reasonableness" requirement described in Chapter 28.

2. In some insured plans, employees pay part of the cost of the plan, usually through payroll deductions. These payments are not tax deductible by the employee.

3. Employer payments of premiums under an insured disability plan do not result in taxable income to the employee.[1]

4. Benefit payments under an employer-paid plan are fully taxable to the employee as received (subject to the credit described below) if the plan was fully paid for by the employer. If the employer paid only part of the cost, only a corresponding part of the benefit is taxable, again subject to credit. For example, if the employer paid 75 percent of the disability insurance premiums and the employee paid the remaining 25 percent, only 75 percent of the disability benefit received by the employee would be taxable.[2]

IRS regulations specify the time over which the employer and employee percentages are to be measured for this purpose. For group disability insurance, generally, payments over the three year period prior to the disability are taken into account in determining the percentages paid by employer and employee.[3]

5. *Disability credit.* If an employee receiving benefits meets the "total and permanent" disability definition, a limited tax credit reduces the tax impact of disability payments for lower-income recipients.[4] Because of this definition, the credit has little or no impact on most employees receiving sick pay or short term benefits, but it may come into effect for more serious or long term conditions.

"Total and permanent disability" (the Social Security definition) means a condition under which the individual "is unable to engage in any substantial gainful activity by reason of any medically determinable physical or mental impairment which can be expected to result in death or which has lasted or can be expected to last for a continuous period of not less than 12 months."[5] This is the strictest disability definition that is commonly used for any purpose.

Generally, the disability credit is calculated by taking the maximum amount subject to the credit (see below) and subtracting ½ of the amount by which the taxpayer's adjusted gross income exceeds the AGI limits (see below). The credit is equal to 15 percent of this amount. Thus, the maximum annual tax credit is $1,125 for a joint return as indicated below. The chart below shows the maximum amounts eligible for the credit, the maximum credit that may be obtained and the limitations to adjusted gross income (AGI):

MAXIMUM AMOUNT SUBJECT TO CREDIT

Single Person	$5,000
Joint Return (where one spouse is a qualified individual)	$5,000
Joint Return (where both spouses are qualified individuals)	$7,500
Married Filing Separately	$3,750

MAXIMUM CREDIT

Single Person	$750
Joint Return (where one spouse is a qualified individual)	$750
Joint Return (where both spouses are qualified individuals)	$1,125
Married Filing Separately	$562.50

ADJUSTED GROSS INCOME LIMITS

Single Person	$7,500
Married Filing Jointly	$10,000
Married Filing Separately	$5,000

For example, if a disabled employee has adjusted gross income (from all sources, including taxable disability income) of $14,000, and is married, filing jointly, the amount on which his disability tax credit is calculated would be $5,000 (the maximum amount for a joint return where only one spouse receives disability income payments) less $2,000 (½ of the amount by which the taxpayer's AGI exceeds $10,000). In short, this is $5,000 - $2,000, or $3,000. The taxpayer's credit is equal to 15 percent of $3,000, or $450. Accordingly, the employee's income tax bill for the year is reduced by $450. Note that to receive this credit the employee must meet the Social Security total and permanent definition of disability. An employee might receive benefits under some employer plans without meeting this strict definition of disability, as discussed above.

This tax credit is even further reduced by 15 percent of any tax-free income received by the employee from a pension, annuity, or disability benefit, including Social Security. Since most disability plans are integrated with Social Security benefits, this further reduction makes the credit even less valuable.

In view of all the reductions applicable to this credit, and the extremely low AGI limits on full availability, the credit is a minor factor in the design of disability benefits, and plays practically no part in designing benefits for executives.

6. Disability insurance premiums paid by the employer under the plan are not considered wages subject to em-

ployment taxes (FICA—Social Security—and FUTA—federal unemployment).[6] Generally disability insurance premiums are not subject to state employment taxes either, but individual state laws should be consulted.

7. Disability benefits are subject to federal income tax withholding if paid directly by the employer. If paid by a third party such as an insurance company, withholding is required only if the employee requests it.[7]

8. Disability benefits attributable to employer contributions are subject to Social Security taxes for a limited period at the beginning of a disability. Thereafter, they are not considered wages subject to Social Security tax.[8]

ERISA REQUIREMENTS

A sick pay or short term disability income plan is considered a welfare benefit plan under ERISA (see Appendix A). Such plans require a written summary plan description, the naming of a plan administrator, and a formal written claims procedure by which employees can make benefit claims and appeal denials. The plan is not subject to the eligibility, vesting, or funding requirements of ERISA. The plan administrator must provide plan participants with a summary plan description (SPD).

WHERE CAN I FIND OUT MORE ABOUT IT?

1. Beam, Burton T., Jr. and John J. McFadden, *Employee Benefits*, 3rd ed. Chicago, IL: Dearborn Financial Publishing, Inc., 1992.

2. *Tax Facts 1*. Cincinnati, OH: The National Underwriter Company. Revised annually.

FOOTNOTES

1. IRC Section 106.
2. IRC Sections 104(a)(3), 105(a); Reg. §1.105-1(d).
3. Regs. §§1.105-1(d), 1.105-1(e).
4. IRC Section 22.
5. IRC Section 22(e)(3).
6. IRC Sections 3121(a)(2), 3306(b)(2).
7. IRC Section 3402(o).
8. IRC Section 3121(a)(4).

Chapter 49

SPLIT DOLLAR LIFE INSURANCE

WHAT IS IT?

Split dollar life insurance is an arrangement, typically between an employer and an employee, in which there is a sharing of the costs and benefits of the life insurance policy. (Split dollar plans can also be adopted for purposes other than providing an employee benefit—for example between parent corporation and subsidiary, or between a parent and a child or in-law.) Usually split dollar plans involve a splitting of premiums, death benefits, and/or cash values, but they may also involve the splitting of dividends or ownership.

Under the classic approach, the employer corporation pays that part of the annual premium which equals the current year's increase in the cash surrender value of the policy. The employee pays the balance, if any, of the premium. In the long run this provides a low outlay protection incentive for selected employees to stay with the employer. If the insured employee dies, the corporation recovers its outlay (an amount equal to the cumulative cash value) and the balance of the policy proceeds is paid to the beneficiary chosen by the employee.

There are an almost infinite number of variations on the "splitting of dollars" theme, limited only by the needs and premium paying abilities of the parties and the creativity of the planner.

WHEN IS IT INDICATED?

1. When an employer wishes to provide an executive with a life insurance benefit at low cost and low outlay to the executive. Split dollar plans are best suited for executives in their 30's, 40's, and early 50's since the plan requires a reasonable duration in order to build up adequate policy cash values and the cost to the executive (the P.S. 58 cost—see below) can be excessive at later ages.

2. When a preretirement death benefit for an employee is a major objective, split dollar can be used as an alternative to an insurance-financed nonqualified deferred compensation plan.

3. When an employer is seeking a totally selective executive fringe benefit. An employer can reward or provide incentives for employees on a "pick and choose" basis. Neither the coverage, amounts, nor the terms of the split dollar arrangement need to meet nondiscrimination rules that add cost and complexity to many other benefit plans.

4. When an employer wants to make it easier for shareholder-employees to finance a buyout of stock under a cross purchase buy-sell agreement or make it possible for non-stockholding employees to effect a one way stock purchase at an existing shareholder's death. This helps establish a market for what otherwise might be unmarketable stock while providing an incentive for bright, creative, productive employees to remain with the company and increase profits.

ADVANTAGES

1. A split dollar plan allows an executive to receive a benefit of current value (life insurance coverage) using employer funds, with minimal or no tax cost to the executive.

2. In most types of split dollar plans, the employer's outlay is at all times fully secured. At the employee's death or termination of employment, the employer is reimbursed from policy proceeds for its premium outlay. The net cost to the employer for the plan is merely the loss of the net after-tax income the funds could have earned while the plan was in effect.

3. Many types of split dollar design are possible so the plan can be customized to meet employer and employee objectives and premium paying abilities.

DISADVANTAGES

1. The employer receives no tax deduction for its share of premium payments under the split dollar plan.

2. The employee must pay income taxes each year on the current "P.S. 58 cost" (less any premiums paid by the employee) of life insurance protection under the plan.

3. The plan must remain in effect for a reasonably long time—10 to 20 years—in order for policy cash values to rise to a level sufficient to maximize plan benefits.

4. The plan must generally be terminated at approximately age 65, since the employee's tax cost for the plan, the P.S. 58 cost, rises sharply at later ages.

DESIGN FEATURES

In a split dollar arrangement between employer and employee, at least three aspects of the policy can be subject to different types of "split": (1) the premium cost, (2) the cash value, and (3) the policy ownership. Following is a brief discussion of these variations, their advantages and disadvantages, and when they are used.

Premium Cost Split

There are four major categories of premium split:

(a) the classic or "*standard*" split dollar plan under which the employer pays a portion of the premiums equal to the increase in cash surrender value of the policy for the year, or the net premium due, if lower. (See Figure 49.1.) The employee pays the remainder of the premium.

Advantages of this approach are that the employer's risk is minimized (since the cash value is enough to fully reimburse its outlay even if the plan is terminated in the early years) and the plan is (arguably) simple to design and explain.

The principal disadvantages are that the employee's outlay is very high in the initial years of the plan, when cash values increase slowly, and the tax benefits available are not maximized under this option, as discussed in "Tax Implications," below.

(b) the "*level premium*" plan, under which the employee's premium share is leveled over an initial period of years, such as 5 or 10. (See Figure 49.2.) This alleviates the large initial premium share required of the employee under the standard arrangement. If the plan stays in existence long enough the employee and employer ultimately pay nearly the same total amount as under the standard arrangement.

The disadvantage of the level premium plan is that if the plan is terminated in the early years, the policy cash value is not sufficient to fully reimburse the employer for its total premium outlay. This possibility should be considered in drafting the split dollar agreement.

(c) the "*employer pay all*" arrangements, with the employer paying the entire premium and the employee paying nothing. (See Figure 49.3.) This arrangement is used when the employee's funds to pay for the plan are severely limited. The employee's cost in this arrangement is limited to the "P.S. 58" cost of pure insurance coverage that must be reported by the employee as taxable income, as discussed below under "Tax Implications."

As with the level premium plan, if the plan is terminated early, the policy cash value will not fully reimburse the employer outlay; again, the agreement between the employer and employee should address this problem.

(d) the "*P.S. 58 offset*" plan, under which the employee pays an amount equal to the P.S. 58 cost for the coverage (or if less, the net premium due) each year. The employer pays the balance of the premium. (See Figure 49.4.) The purpose of this arrangement is to "zero out" the employee's income tax cost for the plan, as discussed below.

As a further refinement, the employer can reduce the employee's out-of-pocket cost for this arrangement by paying a tax deductible "bonus" to the employee equal to the employee's payment under the split dollar plan. The employer might want to go a step further and pay an additional amount equal to the tax on the first bonus as a "double bonus."

The P.S. 58 offset arrangement is an advantageous one that is commonly used. However, as with most variations on the standard plan, the employer remains exposed to some risk if the plan is terminated early, since the cash value will be less than the employer's outlay in some cases. The split dollar agreement should deal with this issue.

Cash Value and Death Proceeds Split

The purpose of the split of cash value or death proceeds is to reimburse the employer, in whole or in part, for its share of the premium outlay, in the event of the employee's death or termination of the plan.

At the employee's death, any policy proceeds not used to reimburse the employer go to the employee's designated beneficiary. This provides a significant death benefit in the early years of the plan, one of the principal objectives of a split dollar plan.

Most plans are designed to provide cash value growth sufficient to reimburse the employer after a number of years. The excess cash value can also benefit the employee, by allowing the plan to provide an attractive investment element (in a sense, a "deferred compensation" or "pension" element)

Figure 49.1

"STANDARD" PLAN

WHOLE LIFE
FACE AMOUNT: $100,000
DIVIDENDS APPLIED TO BUY ONE-YEAR TERM INSURANCE,
REMAINDER TO REDUCE PREMIUM
MALE AGE: 40
FIRST-YEAR PREMIUM = $2,298.00

Year	Guar. Cash Value	Premium Split Paid By Employer	Premium Split Paid By Employee	Payment on Death To Employer	Payment on Death To Employee's Beneficiary
1	0	0	2,298	0	100,000
2	1,700	1,700	598	1,700	98,300
3	3,600	1,900	219	3,600	100,000
4	5,500	1,900	189	5,500	100,000
5	7,500	2,000	60	7,500	100,000
6	9,500	2,000	32	9,500	100,000
7	11,500	2,000	0	11,500	100,000
8	13,600	1,974	0	13,474	100,126
9	15,700	1,948	0	15,421	100,279
10	17,800	1,926	0	17,347	100,453
Total		17,347	3,396		
Average		1,735	340		
11	20,000	1,905	0	19,252	100,748
12	22,200	1,888	0	21,141	101,059
13	24,400	1,864	0	23,004	101,396
14	26,700	1,869	0	24,874	101,826
15	29,000	1,866	0	26,740	102,260
Total		26,740	3,396		
Average		1,783	226		
16	31,300	1,870	0	28,609	102,691
17	33,700	1,879	0	30,488	103,212
18	36,000	1,895	0	32,383	103,617
19	38,400	1,926	0	34,309	104,091
20	40,900	1,969	0	36,278	104,622
Total		36,278	3,396		
Average		1,814	170		

Figure 49.2

"LEVEL PREMIUM" PLAN

WHOLE LIFE
FACE AMOUNT: $100,000
DIVIDENDS APPLIED TO BUY ONE-YEAR TERM INSURANCE,
REMAINDER TO REDUCE PREMIUM
MALE AGE: 40
FIRST-YEAR PREMIUM = $2,298.00

Year	Guar. Cash Value	Premium Split Paid By Employer	Premium Split Paid By Employee	Payment on Death To Employer	Payment on Death To Employee's Beneficiary
1	0	2,004	294	2,004	97,996
2	1,700	2,004	294	4,008	95,993
3	3,600	1,824	294	5,832	97,768
4	5,500	1,795	294	7,626	97,874
5	7,500	1,766	294	9,392	98,108
6	9,500	1,738	294	11,130	98,370
7	11,500	1,706	294	12,836	98,664
8	13,600	1,680	294	14,515	99,085
9	15,700	1,653	294	16,169	99,531
10	17,800	1,631	294	17,800	100,000
Total		17,800	2,943		
Average		1,780	294		
11	20,000	1,905	0	19,705	100,295
12	22,200	1,888	0	21,594	100,606
13	24,400	1,864	0	23,457	100,943
14	26,700	1,869	0	25,327	101,373
15	29,000	1,866	0	27,193	101,870
Total		27,193	2,943		
Average		1,813	196		
16	31,300	1,870	0	29,062	102,238
17	33,700	1,879	0	30,941	102,759
18	36,000	1,895	0	32,836	103,164
19	38,400	1,926	0	34,762	103,638
20	40,900	1,969	0	36,731	104,169
Total		36,731	2,943		
Average		1,837	147		

Figure 49.3

"EMPLOYER PAY ALL" PLAN

WHOLE LIFE
FACE AMOUNT: $100,000
DIVIDENDS APPLIED TO BUY ONE-YEAR TERM INSURANCE,
REMAINDER TO REDUCE PREMIUM
MALE AGE: 40
FIRST-YEAR PREMIUM = $2,298.00

Year	Guar. Cash Value	Premium Split		Payment on Death	
		Paid By Employer	Paid By Employee	To Employer	To Employee's Beneficiary
1	0	2,298	0	2,298	97,702
2	1,700	2,298	0	4,596	95,404
3	3,600	2,119	0	6,715	96,885
4	5,500	2,089	0	8,804	96,696
5	7,500	2,060	0	10,864	96,636
6	9,500	2,032	0	12,896	96,604
7	11,500	2,000	0	14,896	96,604
8	13,600	1,974	0	16,870	96,730
9	15,700	1,948	0	18,817	96,883
10	17,800	1,926	0	20,743	97,057
Total		20,743	0		
Average		2,074	0		
11	20,000	1,905	0	22,649	97,351
12	22,200	1,888	0	24,537	97,663
13	24,400	1,864	0	26,400	98,000
14	26,700	1,869	0	28,270	98,430
15	29,000	1,866	0	30,136	98,864
Total		30,136	0		
Average		2,009	0		
16	31,300	1,870	0	32,005	99,295
17	33,700	1,879	0	33,884	99,816
18	36,000	1,895	0	35,779	100,221
19	38,400	1,926	0	37,705	100,695
20	40,900	1,969	0	39,674	101,226
Total		36,674	0		
Average		1,984	0		

Figure 49.4

"P.S. 58 OFFSET" PLAN

WHOLE LIFE
FACE AMOUNT: $100,000
DIVIDENDS APPLIED TO BUY ONE-YEAR TERM INSURANCE,
REMAINDER TO REDUCE PREMIUM
MALE AGE: 40
FIRST-YEAR PREMIUM = $2,298.00

Year	Guar. Cash Value	Premium Split Paid By Employer	Premium Split Paid By Employee	Payment on Death To Employer	Payment on Death To Employee's Beneficiary
1	0	1,864	434	1,864	98,136
2	1,700	1,842	456	3,706	96,294
3	3,600	1,628	490	5,334	98,266
4	5,500	1,565	524	6,899	98,601
5	7,500	1,499	561	8,398	99,102
6	9,500	1,420	612	9,818	99,682
7	11,500	1,344	656	11,500	100,000
8	13,600	1,268	706	13,600	100,100
9	15,700	1,188	760	15,700	100,000
10	17,800	1,106	820	17,800	100,000
Total		14,724	6,019		
Average		1,472	602		
11	20,000	1,022	883	20,000	100,000
12	22,200	936	952	22,200	100,000
13	24,400	848	1,015	24,400	100,000
14	26,700	759	1,110	26,700	100,000
15	29,000	665	1,201	29,000	100,000
Total		18,956	11,180		
Average		1,264	745		
16	31,300	570	1,300	31,300	100,000
17	33,700	470	1,408	33,700	100,000
18	36,000	367	1,527	36,000	100,000
19	38,400	268	1,658	38,400	100,000
20	40,900	167	1,802	40,900	100,000
Total		20,799	18,875		
Average		1,040	943		

in addition to the death benefit. Some plans are designed primarily to maximize this element. The "equity" type plan, described below, is one example.

The following are commonly used cash value/death proceeds split arrangements:

(a) the employer's share is the *greater* of (i) the aggregate premiums it has paid or (ii) the policy's cash value;

(b) the employer can recover only up to the amount of its aggregate premiums paid (a feature of the "equity" split dollar plan described below); or

(c) the employer is entitled to the entire cash value.

If a plan terminates early—usually when the employee terminates employment before the plan has matured—the cash value of the policy may not be sufficient to fully reimburse the employer for the aggregate premium payments it has made. The plan can provide that the employee is personally responsible to reimburse the employer in that event. As a practical matter, however, it may be difficult to enforce such a requirement, particularly if the amount is insufficient to justify the costs of a lawsuit. (A practical suggestion is to make sure that the company's severance pay arrangement, if any, allows recovery of any such amount out of severance pay otherwise due.)

Policy Ownership

There are two methods of arranging policy ownership under a split dollar plan: the "endorsement method" and the "collateral assignment method."

Under the *endorsement* method, the employer owns the policy and is primarily responsible to the insurance company for paying the entire premium. The beneficiary designation provides for the employer to receive a portion of the death benefit equal to its premium outlay (or some alternative share), with the remainder of the death proceeds going to the employee's designated beneficiary. An endorsement to the policy is filed with the insurance company under which payment to the employee's beneficiary cannot be changed without consent of the employee (or, in some cases, a designated third person where the employee wishes to avoid incidents of ownership for estate tax purposes).

Advantages of the endorsement method are:

(1) greater control by the employer over the policy.

(2) simpler installation and administration; the only documentation required (except for possible ERISA re-

quirements described below) is the policy and endorsement.

(3) avoidance of any formal arrangement that might be deemed to constitute a "loan" for purposes of state laws prohibiting corporate loans to officers and directors.

(4) if the company owns an existing key employee policy on the employee, it can be used directly in the split dollar plan without change of ownership. (Using an existing policy may be important if the employee has developed health problems since the policy was issued.)

Under the *collateral assignment* method, the employee (or a third party) is the owner of the policy and is responsible for premium payments. The employer then makes what are in effect (but not for tax law purposes) interest free "loans" of the amount of the premium the employer has agreed to pay under the split dollar plan. To secure these "loans" the policy is assigned as collateral to the employer. At the employee's death, the employer recovers its aggregate premium payments from the policy proceeds, as collateral assignee. The remainder of the policy proceeds is paid to the employee's designated beneficiary. If the plan terminates before the employee's death, the employer has the right to be reimbursed out of policy cash values; the employee continues as the owner of the policy.

Some advantages of the collateral assignment method are:

(1) it arguably gives more protection to the employee and the employee's beneficiary.

(2) it is easier to implement using existing insurance policies owned by the employee.

Policy Dividends

If the plan uses a participating life insurance policy, policy dividends can be used in various ways; this significantly increases flexibility in plan design. (See Figure 49.7.) A method of applying dividends should be chosen at the plan's inception.

SPLIT DOLLAR PLAN VARIATIONS

In recent years, changes in the tax law have resulted in a need for new kinds of tax planning. Because of the inherent flexibility of the split dollar concept, planners have been able to devise variations on these plans that meet tax and financial objectives for executives in the changing investment and tax climate. Following is a brief description of some of these variations.

Equity Split Dollar

In the equity split dollar arrangement the employer's interest in the policy cash value is limited at all times to the aggregate premiums it has paid. Thus, after the policy cash value reaches the level of the aggregate employer premium payments, the employee begins receiving a gradually-increasing interest in the investment build-up in the policy.

The tax treatment of these plans has not been definitely settled by the courts or the IRS. Consequently, there is a risk to the employee of premature taxation of some of the benefits of the plan. The IRS may argue that the plan constitutes a transfer of property from the corporation to the employee subject to restrictions—a "restricted property" plan. As such, it would be taxed under section 83 of the Code. This means that the employee's share of the policy cash value would be taxable to the employee in the earliest year in which there was no substantial risk of forfeiture. In most split dollar arrangements, there is no risk that the employee will forfeit benefits, thus any cash value increases belonging to the employee would be taxed immediately if Section 83 applies. The meaning of the "substantial risk of forfeiture" test and other aspects of Section 83 are discussed in detail in Chapter 46.

There are a number of arguments as to why Section 83 does not apply to equity split dollar plans. However, planners should be aware of the tax risk involved. It is possible to include provisions in the plan to create a "substantial risk of forfeiture" that would avoid current taxation but for obvious reasons most employees do not favor such provisions.

To avoid an IRS argument that the employer has "transferred" the policy to the employee (and thus Section 83 applies), many planners believe that only the collateral assignment method of policy ownership should be used in an equity split dollar plan. With collateral assignment there is no "transfer" of property from employer to employee—the employee always owns the policy.

Split Dollar Rollout

The "rollout" type of plan was designed to take advantage of pre-1986 tax law that allowed individuals to deduct personal interest. Interest on a policy loan was deductible to the individual so long as premiums on the policy had been paid without borrowed funds in at least four of the first seven years of the policy's existence. In a rollout arrangement, therefore,

the employer paid premiums during the seven year period. Then the policy was "rolled out" (sold) to the employee or a third party. The employee's out-of-pocket cost for the policy could be recovered by making a policy loan. Premiums after the rollout were paid by the employee or third party in part or entirely through policy loans, on which interest was deductible.

Under current law, most policy loans would be classified as nondeductible personal interest. In addition, the MEC (modified endowment contract) rules of current law limit the use of policy loans and other policy distributions for rollout purposes.[1] However, even though earlier rollout techniques are less advantageous, rollout may still be useful in certain planning situations.

For example, if a split dollar policy is held for a long time, the P.S. 58 costs can reach a substantial level. If the employee is reporting costs on the basis of the insurance company's term rates, there may be no available term rate past age 75, so the cost can then jump to the high P.S. 58 rate at that age. Thus, it may be desirable to roll out the policy before these costs reach high levels. Also, a rollout may be advantageous where the employee is terminating employment because of disability, making him uninsurable at standard rates, and he may wish to continue the policy as personally-held insurance.

Rollout essentially means terminating the split dollar arrangement by having the covered employee "pay off" the corporation — that is, terminate the corporation's policy rights. This automatically terminates the economic benefit and thus the further P.S. 58 costs. Three ways to pay off the employer can be identified:

1. At rollout, the employee simply buys out the employer's policy rights for cash. The cash can come from any source, including a policy loan. (For policy loans, the employee should be policyowner — the collateral assignment method of ownership). The purchase by the employee is not income-taxable to the employee, but any gain to the employer (proceeds in excess of the employer's basis) is taxable to the employer.

2. At rollout, the employer provides, as additional deductible compensation, a relinquishment to the employee of the employer's rights in the policy. This results in taxable income to employee in the amount of the employer's relinquished rights. Funds for the employee to pay the resulting income tax can come out of policy cash values.

3. The split dollar plan provides for gradual buyout of the employer's rights by using policy dividends for this purpose. Dividends so used appear to be taxable

Figure 49.5

REVERSE SPLIT DOLLAR PLAN

The following is a simplified illustration of a reverse split dollar policy of $100,000 on the life of a male executive aged 45, with a $1,650 annual premium.

Year	Corporate Premium	Executive Premium	Corporate Net Death Benefit	Executive Net Death Benefit
1	635	1,015	100,739	227
2	689	961	101,676	545
3	744	906	101,693	2,066
4	801	849	101,528	4,050
5	866	784	101,476	6,206
6	936	714	101,526	8,548
7	1,014	636	101,677	11,087
8	1,100	550	101,930	13,843

[In later years, the premium "vanishes;" the executive makes no further payment, and the employer pays only the P.S. 58 cost, which "zeros out" its taxable income. In year 20 the corporate net death benefit is $71,584 and the executive's benefit is $37,324.]

income to the employee as they are so used. At some point, the employer's rights are fully paid off and the employee is full owner of the policy.

Reverse Split Dollar

A "reverse split dollar" plan is one in which the *employee* has the right to policy cash values up to the aggregate of his or her premium payments. The employer is beneficiary of the death proceeds in excess of the employee's share. In other words, as its name implies, a reverse split dollar plan is the reverse of the usual arrangement. (Figure 49.5 is a simplified illustration of a reverse split dollar plan.)

The purpose of this reversal is to maximize the investment benefit of the plan to the employee. Policy cash values provide a substantial investment return over the years as they build up free of tax. At retirement or when the plan terminates the cash value is substantial and the policy is generally substantially funded. In the closely held corporation reverse split dollar can be used to fund a stock redemption buy-sell agreement with the employee paying part of the cost with personal funds.

The disadvantage to the employee of a reverse split dollar arrangement is that the death benefit for the employee's beneficiaries is very low in the early years, since the corporation, not the employee, is the beneficiary of the "amount at risk" (pure term life insurance element) of the arrangement.

The premium is split so that the executive pays a share equal to the cash value build-up, while the corporation pays the remainder of the premium. Most tax planners advise that the corporation should include something in income to reflect the economic benefit of the "amount at risk" or insurance coverage that will benefit the corporation if the employee dies. Although the IRS has not ruled on how this is determined, most advisers assume that the corporation's economic benefit is computed the same as the employee's would be under a conventional split dollar plan. That is, the corporation reports as income the P.S. 58 cost of the amount at risk, less the amount contributed to the plan by the corporation.

The reverse split dollar plan raises unresolved questions concerning the employee's possible taxation under Section 83, as with the equity split dollar plan discussed earlier. In addition, if the employee is a majority shareholder, there is a risk of federal estate tax inclusion, as discussed below under "Tax Implications."

Leveraged Split Dollar

Current law denies corporate deductions for interest paid on indebtedness over $50,000 with respect to a life insurance policy covering an officer, employee or other person financially interested in the taxpayer's business. (However, certain existing policies are "grandfathered.")[2] This has had an adverse impact on split dollar plans based on the corporation borrowing large amounts to pay for the plan.

The "leveraged split dollar plan" is designed specifically to fully exploit the tax benefits that still remain. The basic concept is for the corporation to borrow $50,000 from the insurance company at the inception of the plan and immediately contribute this amount back as an advance deposit of premiums. The initial $50,000 deposit covers the regular or "scheduled" premiums for a number of years. The corporation's only annual payments to the insurance company are interest payments which fully deductible as paid. Under the insurance contract all interest paid by the corporation is credited to the cash value of the insurance. The plan participant collaterally assigns the insurance to the corporation to secure the total payment made by the corporation.

This arrangement provides two advantages to the employer corporation:

(1) The corporation's contribution to the plan is tax deductible since it consists only of interest on the $50,000 loan;

(2) On the participant's death or termination of employment, the policy cash value is always adequate to reimburse the corporation for its aggregate outlay. The leveraged split dollar plan also has the usual advantages to employer and employee of a regular split dollar plan.

The IRS has not ruled on the tax consequences of leveraged plans; the problem area is whether the loan will be considered a bona fide loan under the circumstances.

TAX IMPLICATIONS

1. The IRS has ruled (in Rev. Rul. 64-328)[3] that the tax consequences of a split dollar plan are the same regardless of whether the collateral assignment or the endorsement arrangement is used. In effect this ruling holds that the transaction will not be treated as an "interest free loan" to the employee. The tax consequences are:

(a) The employee is considered to be in receipt each year of an amount of taxable "economic benefit." This taxable amount for the basic insurance coverage is equal to the "P.S. 58" rate for the insurance protection under the plan less the premium amount paid by the employee. As an alternative, the annual renewable term insurance rates of the company issuing the split dollar policy may be substituted for the P.S. 58 rates in calculating the employee's reportable economic benefit if the term rates are lower than the P.S. 58 rates.[4]

For example, how much is included in the employee's income in the second year of the policy in

Figure 49.2? The amount of the death benefit in the second year is $95,993. At age 41, the P.S. 58 rate from Figure 49.6 is $4.73 per thousand, or $454.05 ($4.73 times 95.993) for $95,993 of insurance protection. The employee paid $294 as his premium share in the second year. The taxable income is $454.05 less $294, or $160.05.

The application of policy dividends further affects the employee's income tax consequences. Figure 49.7 shows the available options for dividends and their income tax consequences.

Figure 49.8 is an illustration of how the P.S. 58 computation is made.

(b) The employer cannot deduct any portion of its premium contribution. The IRS does not allow a deduction even for the part of the employer's contribution that results in taxable compensation income to the employee.[5]

(c) If the employee's share of the premium is greater than the P.S. 58 cost of the insurance protection, the employee cannot carry over any of the excess to future years. In effect, this excess goes to waste. This situation generally occurs in the early years of the "conventional" split dollar plan as illustrated in Figure 49.1. This waste of a potential tax benefit is one of the reasons why other types of split dollar plans have been developed. In particular, the "P.S. 58 offset" design of Figure 49.4 is intended to maximize the use of the P.S. 58 cost.

(d) No extra income tax results to an employee who is a "rated" insured. The same P.S. 58 rates that apply to standard risks are used to determine the reportable income of employees with insurance ratings.

2. Death benefits from a split dollar plan—both the employer's share and the employee's beneficiary's share—are generally income tax free.[6]

The tax-free nature of the death proceeds is lost if the policy has been "transferred for value" in certain situations. The transfer for value trap should be carefully avoided in designing split dollar plans.[7]

The following transfers of insurance policies are exempt from the transfer for value rules—in other words, they will not cause the loss of the death proceed's tax-free nature:

(a) a transfer of the policy to the insured;

Figure 49.6

"P.S. 58" RATES

The following rates are used in computing the "cost" of pure life insurance protection that is taxable to the employee under qualified pension and profit sharing plans, split dollar plans, and tax-sheltered annuities. Rev. Rul. 55-747, 1955-2 CB 228; Rev. Rul. 66-110, 1966-1 CB 12.

One Year Term Premiums for $1,000 of
Life Insurance Protection

Age	Premium	Age	Premium	Age	Premium
15	$ 1.27	37	$ 3.63	59	$ 19.08
16	1.38	38	3.87	60	20.73
17	1.48	39	4.14	61	22.53
18	1.52	40	4.42	62	24.50
19	1.56	41	4.73	63	26.63
20	1.61	42	5.07	64	28.98
21	1.67	43	5.44	65	31.51
22	1.73	44	5.85	66	34.28
23	1.79	45	6.30	67	37.31
24	1.86	46	6.78	68	40.59
25	1.93	47	7.32	69	44.17
26	2.02	48	7.89	70	48.06
27	2.11	49	8.53	71	52.29
28	2.20	50	9.22	72	56.89
29	2.31	51	9.97	73	61.89
30	2.43	52	10.79	74	67.33
31	2.57	53	11.69	75	73.23
32	2.70	54	12.67	76	79.63
33	2.86	55	13.74	77	86.57
34	3.02	56	14.91	78	94.09
35	3.21	57	16.18	79	102.23
36	3.41	58	17.56	80	111.04
				81	120.57

(b) a transfer to a partner of the insured or to a partnership of which the insured is a partner;

(c) a transfer to a corporation of which the insured is a shareholder or officer; and

(d) a transfer in which the transferee's basis is determined in whole or in part by reference to the transferor's basis (i.e., a "substituted" or "carryover" basis).

Some examples of potential transfer for value situations to be avoided in split dollar plans are:

• Do not initiate the plan by transferring an existing corporate-owned key employee policy to a third party beneficiary;

• Do not start the plan by transferring an employee-owned policy to the corporation unless the employee is a shareholder or officer;

• At termination of the plan, do not transfer the corporation's interest in the policy to a third party beneficiary, although there are some arguments that this presents no problem, it is better to make such a transfer to the insured.

Figure 49.7

TAX RESULTS OF DIVIDEND OPTIONS

Dividend option	Income tax results to employee	Income tax results to employer
Cash to employee	Dividend is taxable income	No deduction
Cash to employer	None	Not taxable
Reduce employee's premium share	Dividend is taxable income	No deduction
Reduces employer's premium share	None	Not taxable
Deposit at interest for employee	Dividend is taxable income - interest taxable in year earned	No deduction
Deposit at interest for employer	None	Dividend not taxable - interest taxable in year earned
Paid up additions - cash value and death benefit controlled by employee	Dividend is taxable income	No deduction
Paid up additions - cash value controlled by employer and death benefit in excess of cash value controlled by employee	P.S. 58 cost of insurance protection provided by dividend is taxable income	No deduction
One year term insurance (5th dividend option) with death benefit controlled by employee	Dividend is taxable income	No deduction
One year term insurance (5th dividend option) with death benefit controlled by employer	None	Not taxable

Figure 49.8

P.S. 58 COMPUTATION

(INSERT CO'S. STANDARD INDIVIDUAL 1 YR. TERM RATES AT B1 IF LOWER)
PART A

Input:	Employee's Age	45
Input:	Face Amount of Death Benefit	$100,000
Input:	Cash Value to Employer	- $40,000
	Net Amount at Risk	$60,000
	P.S. 58 Charge	$6.30
	Gross Amount Includible	$378.00
Input:	Employee's Contribution	$.00

PART B

Input:	Amount of Dividend Paid in Cash to Employee	$.00
Input:	Amount of Dividend to Reduce EE's Premium Contribution	$.00
Input:	Amount of Dividend Held at Interest for Employee	$.00
Input:	Amount of Dividend - If Cash Value & Death Benefit of Paid Up Additions are Controlled By Employee	$.00
Input:	Amount of Dividend - If Dividends Were Used to Buy One Year Term Insurance for the Employee	$.00
Input:	P.S. 58 Cost or, If Lower, Published Yearly Renewable Term Cost - If Employer Gets Cash Value of Paid Up Additional Insurance and Employee's Beneficiary Receives Any Balance	$.00
	Reportable P.S. 58 Cost	$378.00

Source: NumberCruncher Software

3. If the employee had no "incidents of ownership" in the policy, the death benefit is not includable in the employee's estate for federal estate tax purposes unless the policy proceeds are payable to the employee's estate.[8] If an employee is potentially faced with a federal estate tax liability, all incidents of ownership in the policy should therefore be assigned irrevocably to a third party—a beneficiary or a trust. Proceeds generally should be payable to a named personal beneficiary and not to the employee's estate.

    If the employee is a controlling shareholder (more than 50 percent) in the employer corporation, the *corporation's* incidents of ownership in the policy will be attributed to the majority shareholder. The current IRS position is that even if the corporation has only the right to make policy loans against its share of the cash value, this is an incident of ownership that will be attributed to the controlling shareholder and cause estate tax inclusion of the policy death proceeds.[9]

    For a majority shareholder, the only way to avoid estate tax inclusion is for not only the employee but also the employer to get rid of the incidents of ownership. The corporation can avoid such incidents by retaining no rights of ownership in the policy, including any policy contract provisions or riders relating to the split dollar agreement. One procedure for accomplishing this is for the employee's personal beneficiary to be the original purchaser of the policy, and the beneficiary to enter into the split dollar agreement with the corporation on a collateral assignment basis.

4. There may be federal gift tax consequences if a person other than the employee owns the insurance policy used in a split dollar plan. The transfer of the policy from the employee to another party is a gift subject to tax. In addition, there is a continuing annual gift if the employee pays premiums. There is also a continuing annual gift by the employee if the *employer* pays premiums, because this employer payment represents compensation earned by the employee that is indirectly transferred to the policyowner.[10] Such potentially taxable gifts may avoid taxation if they qualify for the $10,000 annual gift tax exclusion. Gifts made directly to beneficiaries generally qualify, while gifts to insurance trusts may be considered "future interests" that do not qualify for the $10,000 exclusion.

ERISA REQUIREMENTS

A split dollar plan is considered an "employee welfare benefit plan" and is subject to the ERISA rules applicable to such plans, as discussed in Appendix A.

A welfare plan can escape the ERISA reporting and disclosure requirements, including the Form 5500 filing and the summary plan description (SPD) requirement, if it is an "insured" plan maintained for "a select group of management or highly compensated employees."[11] Most split dollar plans qualify for this exception. If the plan covers more than a select group, it must provide SPDs to participants. (If the plan covers fewer than 100 participants, the SPD need not be filed with the DOL.[12])

ERISA further requires a written document, a "named fiduciary," and a formal claims procedure for split dollar plans.[13]

WHERE CAN I FIND OUT MORE ABOUT IT?

1. Graduate Course: Executive Compensation (GS 842), The American College, Bryn Mawr, PA.

2. Floridis, Ronald, *Comprehensive Split Dollar*, 3rd ed., Cincinnati, OH, National Underwriter Company, 1992.

3. Cady, Donald F., *Field Guide to Estate Planning, Business Planning, & Employee Benefits*, Cincinnati, OH: The National Underwriter Co., (revised annually).

QUESTIONS AND ANSWERS

Question — What is the impact of a split dollar plan on corporate earnings for accounting purposes?

Answer — Many corporate managers, particularly in publicly held corporations, are concerned that adoption of various executive compensation plans may cause a charge to corporate earnings for financial reporting purposes. The tendency in the accounting profession is toward requiring charges to earnings for most types of executive compensation, and the official Financial Accounting Standards Board (FASB) is currently considering new accounting rules in this area.

Under the rules currently in effect, however, there would not be a charge to earnings under a "standard" split dollar plan such as that in Figure 49.1, because the corporation controls the cash value of the policy and the premium outlay is always balanced by a cash value increase owned by the corporation.

Question — Is a split dollar plan subject to the "below market loan" provision of the tax law?

Answer — Code section 7872 provides a set of rules by which no-interest or low-interest loans are recharacterized for tax purposes by treating the transaction as if interest at the market rate is involved.

At one time, the IRS took the position that some split dollar plans were in fact interest-free loans, but then in 1964 it revised its views and issued Revenue Ruling 64-328 which set out the tax rules for all split dollar plans that are summarized in "Tax Implications," above.

Code section 7872 was enacted much later than Revenue Ruling 64-328 was issued. It appears that Section 7872 gives the IRS adequate statutory authority to rule that split dollar plans involve interest-free loans governed by the rules of Section 7872. However, at this writing the IRS has not so ruled nor has it rescinded Revenue Ruling 64-328. Since there generally would be no additional tax revenue to the government resulting from the application of Section 7872 rather than Revenue Ruling 64-328 to split dollar plans, the IRS may have little reason to change the rules in this area.

Question — Is split dollar a useful compensation technique for a partner, proprietor, or shareholder employee of an S corporation?

Answer — Generally, split dollar does not work as a way of using "corporate dollars" for owners of S corporations or other unincorporated entities. For example, suppose an S corporation earns $50,000 after paying a $100,000 salary to its sole shareholder-employee Lionel. The corporation proposes to pay $10,000 of this as premiums for a split dollar insurance program for Lionel. Lionel's taxable income *with* the split dollar plan: $150,000 (plus possible P.S. 58 costs, although it is not clear that double taxation is required). *Without* the split dollar plan, Lionel's taxable income is also $150,000. At best, the split dollar plan risks taxation on the premium plus the P.S. 58 costs, and using the corporation in this manner provides no advantage over holding the insurance personally.

More generally, with an S corporation split dollar plan on several shareholder-employees, the effect is to reallocate the cost of the plan toward the majority shareholder. Most majority shareholders will not be interested in such an arrangement. The results are generally the same for partners and proprietors.

Split dollar can sometimes work in unincorporated businesses. First, it does work for key (non-shareholder) employees of an S corporation or unincorporated business, since they are not subject to the income pass-through that applies to owners.

Split dollar may also work for owners where an S corporation's taxable income is reduced to zero through carryovers, depreciation, etc. Then the use of corporate funds for split dollar insurance for a shareholder-employee does not affect taxable income.

Another possible use for split dollar for a shareholder in an S corporation applies where saving gift taxes, not income taxes, is the object. For example, suppose an S corporation shareholder-employee wants to set up an irrevocable insurance trust for his children. He will make gifts to the trust to pay premiums, which puts the entire premium into his gift tax base and to the extent the annual exclusion is exceeded, this will reduce his lifetime exclusion or result in gift taxes. If, however, the plan is set up as a split dollar arrangement between the trust and the S corporation, the shareholder-employee's annual gift will be equal only to his P.S. 58 costs or other term premium. This will be below the annual exclusion ceiling for considerable amounts of insurance for many years in some cases.

FOOTNOTES

1. IRC Sections 7702A, 72(v). A modified endowment contract is basically a life insurance policy for which the premium payments exceed a certain limit during the first seven years. Taxable distributions from such a policy are subject to a 10 percent penalty, with certain exceptions.
2. IRC Section 264(a)(4).
3. Rev. Rul. 64-328, 1964-2 CB 11.
4. Rev. Rul. 66-110, 1966-1 CB 12.
5. IRC Section 264(a)(1).
6. IRC Section 101(a)(1).
7. IRC Section 101(a)(2).
8. IRC Section 2042.
9. Rev. Rul. 82-145, 1982-2 CB 213.
10. Rev. Rul. 78-420, 1978-2 CB 67.
11. Labor Reg. §2520.104-24.
12. Labor Reg. §2520.104-20.
13. ERISA Section 402(a).

Chapter 50

STOCK OPTION

WHAT IS IT?

A stock option is a formal written offer to sell stock at a specified price within specified time limits. Employers often use stock options for compensating executives. Such options are generally for stock of the employer company or a subsidiary.

Options are typically granted to an employee as additional compensation at a favorable price either below or near the current market value, with an expectation that the value of the stock will rise, making the option price a bargain beneficial to the executive. Options typically remain outstanding for a period of ten years. If the price of the stock goes down, the executive will not purchase the stock, so the executive does not risk any out-of-pocket loss.

The executive is generally not taxed upon the grant of an option; taxation is deferred to the time the stock is purchased or later. Thus, stock options are a form of deferred compensation with the amount of compensation based on increases in the value of the company's stock. This "equity" form of compensation is popular with executives because it gives them some of the advantages of business ownership.

There are two main types of stock option plans used for compensating executives: (1) incentive stock option (ISO) plans and (2) nonstatutory stock options. ISOs are a form of stock option plan with special tax benefits; these are discussed in Chapter 39. Nonstatutory stock options will be discussed here.

For an outline of some advanced types of stock option and other plans used for compensating executives, particularly in large corporations, see Appendix D of this book.

WHEN IS IT INDICATED?

1. When an employer is willing to compensate employees with shares of company stock. Many family corporations or other closely-held corporations do not want to share ownership of the business in this manner. Option plans are most often used by corporations whose ownership is relatively broadly held, and are common in large corporations whose stock is publicly traded.

2. Where an employer wishes to reward executive performance by providing equity-type compensation—that is,

compensation that increases in value as the employer stock increases in value.

ADVANTAGES

1. Nonstatutory stock option plans can be designed in virtually any manner suitable to an executive or to the employer. There are few tax or other government regulatory constraints. For example, a stock option plan can be provided for any group of executives or even a single executive. Benefits can vary from one executive to another without restriction. There are no nondiscrimination coverage or benefit rules.

2. Stock options are a form of compensation with little or no out-of-pocket cost to the company. The real cost of stock options is that the company forgoes the opportunity to sell the same stock on the market and realize its proceeds for company purposes.

3. Stock options are a form of compensation on which tax to the employee is deferred. As discussed under "Tax Implications," below, tax is generally not payable at the time a stock option is granted to the executive.

DISADVANTAGES

1. The executive bears the market risk of this kind of compensation. If the market value of stock goes below the option price while the option is outstanding, the employee does not have any actual out-of-pocket loss; however, since the executive will not purchase the stock, there is no additional compensation received. And, after an option is "exercised" (i.e., company stock is purchased by the executive), the executive bears the full market risk of holding company stock.

2. The executive must have a source of funds to purchase the stock (and pay taxes due in the year of exercise) in order to benefit from the plan. Executives often borrow money with the anticipation that dividends from the stock purchased, plus immediate resales of some stock, will be sufficient to pay part or all of the interest on the borrowed funds. However, investment interest in excess of investment income is not deductible.

3. Fluctuation in the market value of the stock may have little or no relation to executive performance. This factor weakens the value of a stock option plan as a performance incentive.

4. As discussed under "Tax Implications," below, the employer's tax deduction is generally delayed until the executive exercises the option and purchases stock. Furthermore, the employer generally gets no further deduction even if the executive realizes substantial capital gains thereafter.

TAX IMPLICATIONS

1. If an option has no readily ascertainable fair market value (see below) at the time it is "granted" (i.e., transferred to the executive), there is no taxable income to the executive at the date of the grant.[1]

2. The employee has taxable compensation income (ordinary income) in the year when shares are actually purchased under the option. The amount of taxable income to the employee is the "bargain element"—the difference between the fair market value of the shares at the date of purchase and the option price (the amount the executive actually pays for these shares).[2] The employer must withhold and pay federal income tax with respect to this compensation income.

3. The employer does not get a tax deduction at the time an option is granted. The employer receives a tax deduction in the same year in which the employee has taxable income as a result of exercising the option and purchasing shares. The amount of the deduction is the same as the amount of income the employee must include.[3]

An example will illustrate this tax treatment.

> *Example*: Executive Lee was given an option in 1991 to purchase 1,000 shares of Employer Company stock at $100 per share, the 1991 market price. The option can be exercised by Lee at any time over the next 5 years. In 1993, Lee purchases 400 shares for a total of $40,000. If the fair market value of the shares in 1993 is $60,000, Lee has $20,000 of ordinary income in 1993. Employer Company gets a tax deduction of $20,000 in 1993 (assuming that Lee's total compensation meets the reasonableness test), which is the same amount as Lee's compensation income. If Lee resells this stock at a gain in a later year, he has capital gain income. Employer Company gets no

further tax deduction even though Lee realizes and reports capital gain income from selling the stock.

4. The executive's basis in shares acquired under a stock option plan is equal to the amount paid for the stock, plus the amount of taxable income reported by the executive at the time the option was exercised.[4] In the example in paragraph 3 above, Lee's basis for the 400 shares purchased in 1993 is $60,000—the $40,000 that Lee paid, plus the $20,000 of ordinary income that he reported in 1993. Therefore if Lee sells the 400 shares in 1994 for $90,000, he must report $30,000 of capital gain in 1994 (the selling price of $90,000 less his basis of $60,000). Employer Company gets no additional tax deduction in 1994.

5. If the option has a readily ascertainable fair market value at the time of the grant, paragraphs (1) through (4) above do not apply. An option will be deemed to have a readily ascertainable fair market value if (a) the option has a value that is determinable as of the time of the grant, *and* (b) the option can be traded on an established market.[5]

The tax rules that apply are:

(a) If an option meets these rules, it is taxed at the time of the grant and the employer receives a corresponding tax deduction at that time.

(b) The employee has no further taxable compensation income when the option is later exercised.

If the employer stock is expected to increase in value substantially, there is an advantage in designing an option plan so that it is taxed at the time of the grant. However, this approach can be used only where options can be traded on an established market.

WHERE CAN I FIND OUT MORE ABOUT IT?

1. Leimberg, Stephan R., et al., *The Federal Income Tax Law*, Warren, Gorham, and Lamont, 1993.

2. Graduate Course: Executive Compensation (GS 842), The American College, Bryn Mawr, PA.

QUESTIONS AND ANSWERS

Question — What is the effect of federal securities laws on stock option plans?

Answer — From the employer viewpoint, it is necessary to determine if the stock is subject to the registration requirements of federal securities law. Various exemptions from registration may apply to stock provided only to selected executives for compensation purposes, but the existence of such an exemption must be verified. State securities laws may also apply.

Advisers to the executive must determine if any of the resale restrictions of federal securities law apply to the sale of stock acquired under the plan. In addition, the executive may be considered an "insider" and subject to the insider trading restrictions on resale of stock.

FOOTNOTES

1. IRC Section 83(e)(3).
2. IRC Section 83(a).
3. IRC Section 83(h).
4. Reg. §§1.61-2(d)(2); 1.83-4(b).
5. Reg. §1.83-7(b).

Chapter 51

WELFARE BENEFIT TRUSTS AND VEBAs

WHAT ARE THEY?

Welfare benefit trusts and VEBAs are not employee benefit plans as such. They are types of welfare benefit funds into which employers make deposits that will be used to provide specified employee benefits in the future. Benefit plans commonly using this approach include life insurance (death benefit) and severance pay plans.

In some cases, using a welfare benefit fund (including a VEBA) allows the employer's tax deduction for contributions to the fund to be accelerated—that is, taken in a year prior to the year in which benefits are paid.

Maximum acceleration of tax deductions is available if the fund is part of a "10 or more employer plan" under Code section 419A(f)(6). Such plans are sometimes referred to as "419A(f)(6)" plans, or, in the case of benefits funded through a trust, a "multiple employer trust."

Two types of welfare benefit funds are frequently used for this purpose:

1. A *taxable* trust, sometimes referred to as a welfare benefit trust (WBT).

TERMINOLOGY NOTE: There is no settled terminology in this area. The term "welfare benefit trust" can be used to refer to both taxable trusts and nontaxable VEBAs. For purposes of this chapter, the term *WBT* will be used to refer to a *taxable* welfare benefit trust.

2. A *nontaxable* trust that is a VEBA (the initials stand for voluntary employees' beneficiary association). A VEBA is a kind of organization (it can be either a trust or a corporation) that is set up by an employer or through collective bargaining to hold funds used to pay benefits under an employee benefit plan.[1] Income of the VEBA is exempt from regular income tax if the VEBA meets the requirements of Code section 501(c)(9).

WHEN IS IT INDICATED?

1. When an owner of a professional corporation or closely held business wants to increase the level of prefunded, tax-deferred benefits beyond the levels allowed under qualified plans. Recent changes in the qualified plan law have reduced or even eliminated further contributions to defined benefit plans for certain highly compensated employees. The WBT or VEBA approach allows additional benefits to be prefunded on a tax-deductible basis.

2. When an employer wants to provide benefit security for all covered employees by placing funding amounts in trust, for the exclusive benefit of employees and beyond the reach of corporate creditors.

ADVANTAGES

1. The use of a VEBA or WBT can permit the employer's tax deduction for welfare benefits to be accelerated. In designs using a Section 419A(f)(6) multiple employer trust, the amount of acceleration can be considerable.

2. The IRS has approved the use of employer funded whole life insurance policies meeting certain guidelines to fund a death benefit in a VEBA.[2] However, the Department of Labor (DOL) has recently been challenging the propriety of using whole life insurance for such purposes.

3. Benefit security for individual employees is enhanced by using a WBT or VEBA, since there is an irrevocable trust for the exclusive benefit of employees and protection against reversion of funds to the employer.

DISADVANTAGES

1. Installing and administering a WBT or VEBA is complex and costly. Smaller employers will find these plans feasible only if they use a vendor of "package" plans provided to groups of employers.

2. Unresolved tax issues exist, particularly with respect to the amount of employer deductions allowable. While the 10 or more employer plan is theoretically sound, there is a possibility of IRS attack or changes in the Code affecting these programs.

3. Use of a multiple-employer plan, which is often the only feasible approach, means that the employer loses some degree of control over the plan's design, investments, and even, to some extent, the tax consequences of the plan

(since maintenance of the "multiple employer" nature of the plan is not within the individual employer's control).

4. A reversion of assets to the employer is effectively prohibited[3] (by contrast to qualified pension and profit-sharing plans, where reversions are allowed subject to a penalty). This means that the plan must be carefully designed to avoid overfunding and potential losses of funding intended for owner-employees.

HOW IT WORKS—AN EXAMPLE

To get a general idea of how a 10 or more employer plan works, let's take a look at a hypothetical VEBA program for a typical small professional corporation. (This example is not meant to suggest that all VEBAs or WBTs have to be designed like the following.) The employee census of G. Crown D.D.S., P.C., looks like this:

	Age	Years of Service	Compensation
Dr. Crown	56	20	$150,000
Frieda Hand	40	5	20,000
Laura Sweet	21	2	15,000

Crown, P.C., has had for several years a qualified defined benefit plan and a health insurance plan covering all employees. The qualified plan currently provides maximum benefits for Dr. Crown. The employer now adopts the following additional benefit arrangements to be funded through the multiple employer trust:

- A severance pay plan for all employees equal to two years' salary, accruing at the rate of 10 percent per year of service (e.g., an employee with five years of service accrues a benefit of one year of service, etc. Dr. Crown's 2-year benefit is already fully accrued). Severance benefits are forfeited if death occurs before termination of employment.

- A preretirement death benefit equal to ten times compensation.

The VEBA is maintained by a vendor of financial products for a group of more than 10 participating employers, and the vendor provides the actuarial, investment, and most administrative services in return for an initial setup and documentation fee and an annual administrative fee. Fund investments include life insurance policies that provide insured death benefits and cash values that can be used to fund the severance benefit.

The level of annual contributions to the VEBA in order to fund these benefits is determined actuarially. This amount is paid annually or in more frequent installments if the employer desires, and is fully deductible to the employer for the year in which each contribution is made.

> NOTE: In the most aggressively-designed plans, the severance benefit is funded almost entirely in the first year of the plan, which provides substantial tax deferral. The reason for this is that the employee could potentially sever employment at any time and the fund must be adequate for this contingency. A Tax Court case, *Wade L. Moser v. Comm.*,[4] approved a deduction under Code section 162[5] for a $200,000 initial contribution to a VEBA, which contribution the court believed was no greater than necessary to fully fund the severance benefits to which the employees were then entitled ($198,200) and to generate sufficient income to pay premiums on insurance that would fund the plan's other benefits (the first year's insurance premiums were calculated to be $20,411), even though over 90% of the contribution was for benefits attributable to two (2) owner-employees.

Employees report no current income tax on the severance pay benefit. Severance benefits are fully taxable to employees when paid. For the death benefit provided by the plan, employees report the current pure insurance or "P.S. 58" cost each year as taxable income. Death benefits payable by the insurer to beneficiaries may be tax free as proceeds of life insurance (see discussion under "Tax Implications," below).

CHOOSING BETWEEN WBTs AND VEBAs

Prefunding of employee benefits through either a WBT or a VEBA is theoretically a sound technique. There are favorable Code provisions, IRS rulings, and court cases on various issues involving WBTs and VEBAs.

However, there are also numerous other issues about which neither the IRS nor the courts have specifically issued favorable conclusions. On these issues, clients can have only the comfort of a tax attorney's favorable opinion letter.

Any client entering into a WBT or VEBA arrangement has to (1) determine the magnitude of the possible "downside" risks and (2) make a business decision whether these risks are worth the extra tax benefits available from the WBT or VEBA.

In the current climate it is difficult for many businesses to deal with these issues. Because of the potentially large amounts of money to be invested, vendors of WBTs and VEBAs are aggressively advertising the advantages of their particular arrangement over competing arrangements, and there are few neutral sources of advice available. It is generally quite expensive for an individual business client to obtain a detailed legal opinion on the proposed arrangement from the client's own attorney, since the issues are complex. But the client may be reluctant to rely solely on a legal opinion provided by the vendor of VEBA or WBT investment products. Thus, many clients who otherwise might benefit from WBTs and VEBAs are avoiding them because they do not feel they can obtain enough information to provide a sound basis for a business judgment.

The following is a summary of some of the important issues involved in adopting a WBT or VEBA, with an indication of the differences, if any, between the two approaches.

Deductibility of Contributions

Deductibility is the key issue. The WBT or VEBA associated with a 10 or more employer plan involves a large upfront contribution, and the advantages of the arrangement require that deductibility of these accelerated contributions be sustained. For maximum deductibility, both WBTs and VEBAs must get over two major hurdles:

Hurdle No. 1: the "10 or more employer" exception. The *general* rules for accelerated deductions in welfare benefit funds, Code sections 419 and 419A, are very restrictive and provide little, if any, tax advantage over conventional insurance or pay-as-you-go funding of employee benefits.[6] The key to success with WBTs and VEBAs is to qualify for the *exception* to these rules.

The exception is Code section 419A(f)(6): If a WBT or VEBA is part of a "10 or more employer plan," the limits of Sections 419 and 419A (discussed in "Questions and Answers," below) do not apply. Employer contributions to the VEBA or WBT to fund benefits are deductible when made and the deductibility may be without limit as to amount except for the "reasonable compensation" limitation that applies to all forms of employee compensation.

A 10 or more employer plan means a plan (1) to which more than one employer contributes, (2) to which no employer contributes more than 10 percent of the total contributions, and (3) which does not maintain experience rating for individual employers.[7]

Multiple-employer plans currently being marketed are designed carefully to make use of this exception; however, there are few official IRS or other legal guidelines for doing so.

Hurdle No. 2: is it a welfare benefit plan—or a plan for deferred compensation? If the plan funded through a WBT or VEBA is deemed to be a plan for "deferred compensation" rather than a "welfare benefit plan," its tax advantages are doomed, because the employer's deduction for nonqualified deferred compensation cannot be taken until the year in which the employee includes it in income.[8]

On this issue, there are some useful guidelines. In particular, *Greensboro Pathology Associates v. United States*,[9] an important court case, contains in effect a definition of "welfare benefit plan." Also, the IRS issued a favorable opinion that certain benefits in a small-company VEBA were *not* deferred compensation.[10]

Based on these authorities primarily,[11] WBTs and VEBAs generally should reflect the following to help insure that they will not be considered to provide "deferred compensation":

- Funding for the benefit should be within actuarial limits[12] so that any excess funds available (to remaining employees) after all beneficiaries have been paid their benefits will be due merely to actuarial discrepancies rather than a deliberate attempt to provide deferred compensation to the remaining employees.

- Although the sponsoring corporation may retain the right to terminate the plan, no benefits should revert back to the corporation; all funds remaining after termination should be allocated to remaining participants. This is effectively required by the VEBA regulations,[13] but it should also be provided in a WBT to help meet the "welfare benefit plan" criteria.[14]

- Plans typically provide preretirement death benefits but no postretirement death benefits, because preretirement death benefits are less likely to be characterized as deferred compensation.[15]

- The business should be one with more than one employee.[16]

- A broad group of employees should be covered. VEBAs have specific coverage requirements (see below) but most planners believe that WBTs should also have broad coverage in order to be considered a bona fide employee welfare benefit plan. Some planners recommend covering *all* employees.

Who Must Be Covered?

VEBAs. It is possible to design VEBA-funded plans that do not cover all employees, but excluding employees brings the planner into a fearsome thicket of overlapping, complex, and unclear rules designed to prevent discrimination. In summary, these are:

- Provisions in the Section 501(c)(9) regulations that result in a loss of the VEBA's tax exemption if violated.[17]

- A separate Code section providing specific nondiscrimination rules for VEBA-funded plans.[18] Full regulations under this section have not yet been issued by the IRS.

- Nondiscrimination provisions in the Code applicable to each separate benefit plan included in the VEBA. For example, a group term life insurance plan funded through a VEBA must meet the provisions of Section 79.

In many cases these rules require such broad coverage that relatively few employees can be excluded from VEBA plans. Because the savings to be gained through excluding employees often do not outweigh the tax risks and expense of compliance with these rules, many VEBA plans simply cover all employees.

The direct result of failing to meet these rules is loss of tax exemption of the VEBA, which may not be a severe sanction if the VEBA has relatively little taxable income (by having invested in life insurance or tax-free bonds, for example). However, the underlying problem is that a plan with too little coverage may also fail to qualify as a welfare benefit plan, as discussed above. The result of that is a loss of all or a substantial part of the employer's tax deduction.

WBTs. There are no specific coverage requirements in the Code or elsewhere in the tax law for WBTs. However, as with VEBAs each separate benefit must meet whatever coverage rules are provided in the Code—for example, the nondiscrimination rules under Section 79 for group insurance must be met if the WBT includes a Section 79 plan (most do not).

As indicated earlier, WBTs should have broad employee coverage of some kind in order for the plan to be characterized as a welfare benefit plan rather than as a plan for deferred compensation. Planners generally recommend coverage at least as broad as that required under the VEBA rules, and preferably coverage of all employees.

The lack of specific coverage requirements for WBTs has been argued to be an advantage and a disadvantage, depending on who is making the argument. WBT advocates point out that under the VEBA rules generally a plan providing a disproportionate share of benefits to owner-employees will not be tax-exempt,[19] while WBTs, being taxable, do not have this problem. On the other hand, VEBA advocates argue that it is better to have a set of coverage rules to comply with than to have to guess what those rules should be.

What Kinds of Benefits Can Be Provided?

VEBAs. The VEBA regulations list the following as permitted VEBA benefits:[20]

- Life insurance before and after retirement

- Other survivor benefits

- Sick and accident benefits

- Other benefits including vacation and recreation benefits, severance benefits paid through a severance pay plan discussed below, unemployment and job training benefits, disaster benefits, and legal service payments or credits

The following are specifically *prohibited* as VEBA benefits: savings, retirement, or deferred compensation plans, coverage of expenses such as commuting expenses, accident or homeowners' insurance covering damage to property, or other items unrelated to maintenance of the employee's earning power.[21]

In practice, severance and preretirement death benefits are those most frequently used in VEBAs, since the VEBA funding approach allows deductible advance funding, while such funding of these programs would not be possible without a VEBA or WBT.

VEBAs are also subject to the benefit nondiscrimination rules of Code section 505. In particular, Section 505(b)(7) limits compensation used in the plan's benefit formula to $200,000 annually (as indexed, $235,840 for 1993). For example, if a plan provided a death benefit of 2 times compensation for all employees, the death benefit for an employee earning $300,000 would be limited to $471,680 (1993) rather than $600,000.

WBTs. For WBTs, there are no specific guidelines as to types of plan permitted. Since the plan must qualify as a welfare benefit plan, planners look to the general definition of welfare plan under the Department of Labor regulations.[22] In practice, the types of benefits under WBTs are generally the same as those provided by a VEBA.

WBTs are not subject to the $200,000 limitation of Code section 505, which makes it easier to provide particularly good benefits for highly compensated employees. This is clearly an advantage of WBTs. On the other hand, it could also be said to make WBTs more vulnerable to IRS attack or to the enactment of unfavorable new Code provisions.

Severance benefits. In designing a severance pay plan for a WBT or VEBA, care must be taken to distinguish the severance plan from a pension plan. Characterization as a pension plan eliminates the availability of accelerated deductions[23] and in the case of a VEBA results in the loss of tax-exemption.[24] In addition, if the plan is deemed a pension plan, ERISA pension plan requirements apply (funding, vesting, etc.—see Chapter 23). A severance pay plan will not be a pension plan if it satisfies the following requirements:

- Payments must not be directly or indirectly contingent on retirement,

- The total amount of payments must not exceed twice the employee's annual compensation in his or her last year, and

- Generally, payments must be completed within 24 months of termination.[25]

TAX IMPLICATIONS

Taxation of Employees

Benefits payable to employees or beneficiaries are, in general, subject to the same income tax treatment as if they were paid directly by the employer.

Life insurance. The value of life insurance protection would be taxable (measured either by the P.S. 58 table or some other measure, as applicable—see Chapter 14). If coverage is provided by group term insurance, the cost of the first $50,000 of protection is tax-free to the employees.

Life insurance proceeds paid directly by a commercial insurer to a beneficiary on group term policies held by a VEBA or WBT are income tax free to beneficiaries.[26] It is unclear whether proceeds paid under a whole life policy are entirely income tax free or are taxed similarly to life insurance proceeds received under a qualified plan (see Chapter 14).

For federal estate tax purposes, life insurance held by a VEBA or WBT can be kept out of the participant's estate by avoiding incidents of ownership, just as with personally-owned insurance. If an irrevocable beneficiary designation is made at least three years before death, the policy proceeds will not be includable in the estate.

Severance benefits. Funded severance benefits appear to be governed by Section 83 of the Code. Under that section, benefits will be taxable in the first year in which they are "not subject to a substantial risk of forfeiture." Accordingly, in order to defer taxation on these benefits, the plan must impose risks of forfeiture on the employee-participant.

Forfeiture provisions commonly used in severance plans include (1) a provision that benefits will be lost upon death prior to termination of employment; (2) loss of benefits if the employee is discharged by the employer for cause; and (3) a graduated vesting schedule (the vesting schedule in itself would only defer taxation until the employee is vested).

For a controlling shareholder-employee, the IRS scrutinizes forfeiture provisions very closely, since where the employee controls the corporation there is some doubt as to whether forfeiture provisions would actually be enforced.[27] However, a provision requiring forfeiture upon death should be effective even for a controlling shareholder-employee.

For federal estate tax purposes, if death occurs before termination of employment, a severance benefit that is forfeited upon death should not be includable in the estate, since at death the benefit ceases to exist.

Taxation of the WBT or VEBA

VEBA. Income of a VEBA is exempt from regular income tax if all the requirements of Sections 501(c)(9) and 505 are met, as discussed above.

An organization will not be treated as a tax-exempt VEBA unless it notifies the IRS.[28] This is generally accomplished by filing within 15 months from the end of the month in which the VEBA was organized an application for recognition of exempt status (Form 1024).[29]

Generally, VEBA income set aside (to provide for appropriate benefits and reasonable costs of administering those benefits) in excess of the Section 419A account limits (calculated without reference to any reserve for postretirement medical benefits) is subject to taxation as "unrelated business taxable income (UBTI)" under Code sections 511 and 512. (Any VEBA income derived from an unrelated trade or business regularly carried on by the VEBA is also subject to such taxation.) This is true even if the VEBA is part of a 10 or more employer plan under Section 419A(f)(6).[30] Since maximum tax deduction benefits derive from funding such 10 or more employer plans far in excess of the Section 419 and 419A limits (discussed below in the "Questions and Answers"), to some extent this UBTI exposure nullifies the advantage of the tax-exempt status of the VEBA. Funding with life insurance or tax-free investment vehicles can eliminate or minimize UBT exposure.

WBT. Income of a WBT is generally subject to tax. The WBT is generally designed to be a "grantor trust," which means that its income, deductions, and credits are reported directly on the employer's tax returns.[31]

Income of a WBT that would be UBTI if the trust were a VEBA may also be reportable by the employer.[32]

ERISA AND OTHER REQUIREMENTS

ERISA treatment of benefits funded through a VEBA or WBT is the same as the treatment of any individual benefit plan funded by any other means. The use of a VEBA or WBT does not create or remove any reporting and disclosure, fiduciary, or other requirement otherwise applicable to the benefit plan.

However, a VEBA is subject to the filing requirement discussed in "Taxation of the WBT or VEBA," above. There is no such initial filing requirement for a WBT.

WHERE CAN I FIND OUT MORE ABOUT IT?

1. Amoroso, "Computing Deduction Limits for Contributions to Welfare Benefit Plans," *Journal of Taxation*, September 1992.

2. Katz, "Funded Severance Pay Plans—The New Boy on the Block," *Tax Management Compensation Planning Journal*, August 2, 1991.

3. Stiefel and Roth, "VEBAs Revisited as Funding Mechanisms—After DEFRA," *Benefits Law Journal*, Winter 1989/1990.

4. Weiss, "The Multiple Employer Welfare Benefit Trust," *Journal of the American Society of CLU & ChFC*, March 1990.

QUESTIONS AND ANSWERS

Question — What amounts are deductible if a VEBA or WBT does *not* qualify under the "10 or more employer" exception of Section 419A(f)(6)?

Answer — If the VEBA or WBT is not part of a 10 or more employer plan, deductible contributions are severely limited.

If the contributions would be deductible under provisions of the Code in the absence of Sections 419 and 419A, then they are deductible when made, but subject to the "deduction acceleration" limits of Code sections 419 and 419A.

In summary, the employer's deduction for the taxable year is limited to the "qualified cost" for each plan for the taxable year of the fund that ends with or within the taxable year of the employer.[33] The qualified cost is calculated through the following formula:

- The "qualified direct cost"—the amount that would be allowed as a deduction if the employer paid benefits directly and used the cash method of accounting; plus

- The amount that can be added to the "qualified asset account" for the taxable year (the "qualified asset account" is an account with assets set aside to provide for the payment of: (1) disability benefits; (2) medical benefits; (3) supplemental unemployment or severance benefits; or (4) life insurance benefits); minus

- The after tax income of the fund.[34]

Question — Can whole life or other cash value life insurance product be used to fund a death benefit in a WBT or VEBA?

Answer — The IRS has approved the use of whole life insurance by a VEBA to fund a death benefit plan for employees.[35] The premium schedule under the insurance policies apparently provides an actuarially sound method of funding the death benefit. The same result should apply for a WBT. However, the Department of Labor has recently been challenging the use of whole life insurance to fund death benefits.

Question — Can an employer recover excess assets in a VEBA or WBT when it terminates after paying out all benefits due to participants?

Answer — The VEBA regulations effectively provide that when a VEBA is terminated, all excess assets must be paid out to covered employees.[36] Also, under Code section 4976, there is generally a 100 percent penalty tax imposed when a portion of a welfare benefit fund reverts to an employer. What this means in practice is that an employer must avoid overfunding a plan funded through a VEBA or WBT.

Question — How are VEBA or WBT assets allocated when a plan terminates?

Answer — As indicated in the preceding question, plan assets cannot revert back to the employer. The plan must include a nondiscriminatory formula under which excess assets are allocated to plan participants.[37] For example, assets could be allocated under a formula as follows:

$$\text{Participant's share} = \frac{\text{Participant's compensation during period of participation}}{\text{Total compensation of all participants for all plan years}}$$

X Excess plan assets.

Since this formula would tend to increase the share of long-term key employees, consideration should be given to restricting the number of years of participation used in the numerator—to five years, for example.

Question — If a plan participant dies and forfeits a severance benefit, what happens to the plan assets that have been set aside to fund this benefit?

Answer — These assets revert to the VEBA or WBT and are used to fund benefits for remaining plan participants. Excess funds are allocated to remaining participants when the trust eventually terminates, as discussed in the preceding questions. Clients considering VEBAs or WBTs should be sure this result is acceptable. In particular, if there is only one key employee whose severance benefit is responsible for most of the funding, death of that employee could result in an undesired windfall for remaining employees.

Question — Can plan participants borrow from a VEBA or WBT?

Answer — Loans from VEBAs are not permitted except in times of "distress," which appears to be strictly interpreted by the IRS.[38]

Loans from WBTs are not specifically prohibited, but some advisers recommend against them since they may cause the IRS to assert that the plan is not bona fide.

FOOTNOTES

1. See Reg. §1.501(c)(9)-2(a)(1).
2. GCM 39440 (1985).
3. Generally, an organization will not be a tax-exempt VEBA if the written instrument creating the organization provides for the distribution of its assets upon dissolution to the contributing employers or if state law (in the state in which the organization was created) provides for such distribution. Reg. §1.501(c)(9)-4(d). Additionally, Code section 4976 generally imposes a 100% penalty tax when a portion of a welfare benefit fund reverts to an employer.
4. TC Memo 1989-142, *aff'd*, 90-2 USTC ¶50,498 (8th Cir. 1990). *Joel A. Schneider, M.D., S.C. v. Comm.*, TC Memo 1992-24, is a similar case.
5. Although the Moser case was decided recently, the tax year in issue was 1982; thus Code sections 419 and 419A did not need to be considered in determining the deductibility of the contribution.

6. See "Questions and Answers" at the end of this chapter for a discussion of the Section 419 and 419A rules. See also the Amoroso article listed above in "Where Can I Find Out More About It?"
7. IRC Sec. 419A(f)(6).
8. See Chapter 16.
9. 83-1 USTC ¶9112 (Fed. Cir. 1982).
10. GCM 39300 (1984).
11. Other important authorities to consult include *Lima Surgical Associates, Inc., Voluntary Employees' Beneficiary Association Plan Trust v. U.S.*, 90-1 USTC ¶50,329 (Cl. Ct. 1990), *aff'd*, 944 F.2d 885, 91-2 USTC ¶50,473 (Fed. Cir. 1991) (severance benefits based on length of service and level of compensation and payable upon retirement are deferred compensation); *Harry A. Wellons, Jr., M.D., S.C. v. Comm.*, TC Memo 1992-704 (severance benefits are deferred compensation where five years of service must be given before benefits accrue and benefit amount is linked to level of compensation and length of service).
12. See Rev. Rul. 73-599, 1973-2 CB 40, modified on other grounds by Rev. Rul. 77-92, 1977-1 CB 41. But see *Lima Surgical*, note 11 above, (the fact that the employer's contributions to a trust were actuarially determined was considered to be an indication that the plan was a plan for deferred compensation rather than a VEBA).
13. See Reg. §1.501(c)(9)-4(d).
14. Note Code section 4976, under which, generally, "any portion of a welfare benefit fund reverting to the benefit of the employer" is subject to a penalty tax equal to 100% of the reverted amount.
15. The Conference Committee Report to the Deficit Reduction Act of 1984 provides that a plan providing life insurance benefits exclusively for retirees would be considered a deferred compensation plan rather than a welfare benefit plan. H.R. Conf. Rep. 861, 98th Cong., 2d Sess. 1157, *reprinted in* 1984-3 CB (vol. 2) 411. Note also that an employer will generally be subject to a tax of 100% of (1) any postretirement medical or death benefit provided to a key employee other than from a separate account (if a separate account was required), or (2) any postretirement medical or death benefit provided with respect to a highly compensated individual unless the plan is nondiscriminatory. IRC Sec. 4976(b)(1)(A) and (B).
16. Relevant parts of the Code's definition of a welfare benefit fund are written in the plural: a welfare benefit fund is, in part, a fund providing welfare benefits to "employe*es* or *their* beneficiaries." Language describing VEBAs in a similarly plural fashion has been held to require that a VEBA provide benefits to more than one employee. IRC Section 419(e)(1)(b). See also Rev. Rul. 85-199, 1985-2 CB 163.
17. See Reg. §1.501(c)(9)-2(a)(2).
18. IRC Sec. 505(b)(1)(A).
19. Reg. §1.501(c)(9)-2(a)(2). See also GCMs 39818 (1990), 39801 (1989).
20. Reg. §1.501(c)(9)-3.
21. Reg. §1.501(c)(9)-3(f).
22. Labor Regs. §§2510.3-1, 2510.3-2.
23. See IRC Sec. 419(e)(2)(B).
24. See Reg. §1.501(c)(9)-3(f). See also *Lima Surgical*, note 11 above.
25. Labor Reg. §2510.3-2(h)
26. See, e.g., Let. Ruls. 8534048, 8332022, 8035066, and 8025100.
27. See discussion in Chapter 46, Restricted Stock Plan.

28. IRC Sec. 505(c).

29. Reg. §1.505(c)-1T, Q&A-3, Q&A-4, Q&A-5, and Q&A-6.

30. IRC Sec. 512(a)(3)(E)(i); Temp. Reg. §1.512(a)-5T, Q&A-3

31. See generally IRC Secs. 671-677.

32. See IRC Secs. 419A(g)(1), 419A(g)(2), 419A(f)(6)(A).

33. IRC Sec. 419(b); Temp. Reg. §1.419-1T, Q&A-4. See also the Amoroso article listed above in "Where Can I Find Out More About It?"

34. IRC Secs. 419(c), 419A(a).

35. GCM 39440 (1985).

36. See Reg. §1.501(c)(9)-4(d).

37. See Reg. §1.501(c)(9)-4(d).

38. Reg. §1.501(c)(9)-3(f). This regulation provides that permissible VEBA benefits do not include "the provision of loans to members except in times of distress (as permitted by §1.501(c)(9)-3(e))." That regulation provides examples of acceptable VEBA benefits, but only explicitly mentions loans once: stating that VEBAs may provide "temporary living expense loans...at times of disaster (such as fire or flood)...." Reg. §1.501(c)(9)-3(e).

APPENDICES

Appendix A

ERISA REPORTING AND DISCLOSURE FOR PENSION AND WELFARE PLANS

The Employee Retirement Income Security Act of 1974—ERISA—imposed extensive reporting and disclosure requirements on a broad range of employee benefit plans.

These provisions require various forms and information to be disclosed to plan participants and/or filed with the IRS or the Department of Labor.

Under ERISA, employee benefit plans are divided into two types—pension plans and welfare plans. These terms are defined broadly enough that it generally makes sense to think of them in terms of their exceptions rather than their definitions. That is, an employee benefit plan should be considered covered by the provisions of ERISA unless there is a specific exemption in ERISA or the regulations interpreting ERISA.

PLANS EXEMPT FROM ERISA

ERISA Section 4(b) contains an exemption from most or all ERISA provisions, including the reporting and disclosure requirements, for certain types of employer plans (both pension and welfare plans). These ERISA-exempt employer plans are:

- plans of state, federal, or local governments or governmental organizations.

- plans of churches, synagogues, or related organizations. (These plans, however, can elect to be covered under ERISA.)

- plans maintained outside the United States for nonresident aliens.

- unfunded excess benefit plans. (These are one type of nonqualified deferred compensation plan, as described in Chapter 16.)

- plans maintained solely to comply with workers' compensation, unemployment compensation, or disability insurance laws.

"PENSION PLANS" UNDER ERISA

ERISA Section 3(2) defines an "employee pension benefit plan" and "pension plan" as any plan, fund, or program which is established or maintained by an employer or by an employee organization (such as a labor union), or by both, to the extent that by its express terms or as a result of surrounding circumstances such plan, fund, or program (1) provides retirement income to employees, or (2) results in a deferral of income by employees for periods extending to the termination of covered employment or beyond, regardless of the method of calculating the contributions made to the plan, the method of calculating the benefits under the plan, or the method of distributing benefits from the plan.

This definition includes all qualified pension, profit-sharing, stock bonus, and similar qualified plans. It also includes some nonqualified deferred compensation plans. (These may, however, be eligible for exemption from ERISA's strict reporting and disclosure requirements—see Chapter 16, at "ERISA REQUIREMENTS".) In general, an ERISA pension plan is any employee benefit plan that involves deferral of an employee's compensation to his or her retirement date or later.

Regulatory Exemptions

In addition to these exemptions in ERISA itself, Section 2510.3-2 of the Labor regulations gives partial exemption or special treatment to a number of other types of plans. These special regulatory exemptions include the following:

- A *severance pay plan* is not treated as a pension plan if

    (1) payments do not depend directly or indirectly on the employee's retiring;

    (2) total payments under the plan do not exceed twice the employee's annual compensation during the year immediately preceding the separation from service; and

(3) all payments to any employee are generally completed within 24 months of separation from service.

A severance pay plan meeting these criteria need not comply with the reporting and disclosure requirements for pension plans, but must meet the more limited reporting and disclosure requirements for welfare plans discussed below. For example, welfare plans with fewer than 100 participants need not file an annual report (Form 5500 series) if benefits are fully insured or are paid by the employer out of its general assets.

- *Supplemental payment plans* that provide extra benefits to retirees to counteract inflation are exempt from numerous ERISA requirements under Department of Labor regulations.

- *Employer-sponsored IRAs, simplified employee pensions (SEPs), and Section 403(b) TDA plans* are subject to reduced ERISA reporting and disclosure requirements in some cases.[1] For details, see the chapters in the main text relating to these plans.

Reporting and Disclosure

Pension plans must meet the reporting and disclosure requirements described in the chart at the end of this Appendix, with certain exceptions.

At the end of this Appendix is a compliance chart indicating the major reporting and disclosure requirements of ERISA and the timetables for filing or reporting. Copies of the Form 5500 annual report forms and instructions are also included.

The following brief explanation of the most important of these reporting and disclosure requirements for pension plans should be helpful in interpreting the significance of these requirements. The major elements of reporting and disclosure are as follows:

1. *The Summary Plan Description (SPD)*. The SPD is intended to describe the major provisions of the plan to participants in plain language. An SPD must be furnished automatically to participants within 120 days after the plan is established or 90 days after a new participant enters an existing plan.[2] The SPD must also be filed with the Department of Labor within 120 days after a new plan is adopted.[3] If plan provisions change, supplements to the SPD generally must be provided to

participants and the DOL. The contents of the SPD are prescribed by Labor Department regulations, but there is no government form for SPDs.

2. *The Annual Report (Form 5500 series)*. This annual financial reporting form must be filed with the IRS each year by the end of the seventh month after the plan year ends.[4] In addition to balance sheets and income statements, an actuary's report (Schedule B, Form 5500) must be included if the plan is a defined benefit plan, and information about any insurance contracts held by the plan must be included on Schedule A, Form 5500.

The annual report forms are simpler for plans covering fewer than 100 participants. These plans file the simplified Form 5500-C/R, which provides a further simplified filing in two out of every three years.

3. *Summary Annual Report*. The summary annual report is a brief summary of financial information from the Annual Report (Form 5500 series) that must be provided to plan participants each year within nine months of the end of the plan year.[5] Labor regulations have essentially reduced this report to a formality. Participants have a right to see the full Annual Report if they need information about the plan's financial status.

4. *Individual Accrued Benefit Statement*. If a plan participant requests a statement of his or her individual benefits under the plan, the plan administrator must provide it within 30 days. Only one such statement each year needs to be provided to a participant.[6] However, it is good policy to provide an annual individual benefit statement to plan participants, since this helps to communicate the plan's benefits and give them greater impact.

"WELFARE PLANS" UNDER ERISA

A welfare plan (also called a "welfare benefit plan") is defined in Section 3(1) of ERISA as any plan, fund, or program established or maintained by an employer or by an employee organization, or by both, for the purpose of providing for its participants or their beneficiaries, through the purchase of insurance or otherwise, medical, surgical, or hospital care or benefits, or benefits in the event of sickness, accident, disability, death or unemployment, or vacation benefits, apprenticeship or other training programs, or day care centers, scholarship funds, or prepaid legal services. Certain other plans described in federal labor law are also included.

Regulatory Exemptions

For welfare plans, Section 2510.3-1 of the Labor regulations provides exemptions and limitations from the applicability of ERISA. The following employment practices and benefits are among those that have been declared by regulation to be exempt from the ERISA reporting and disclosure requirements:

- overtime pay, shift pay, holiday premiums, and similar compensation paid for work done other than under normal circumstances.

- compensation for absence from work due to sickness, vacation, holidays, military duty, jury duty, or sabbatical leave or training programs, if paid out of the general assets of the employer (i.e., not funded in advance).

- recreational or dining facilities or first aid centers on the employer's premises.

- holiday gifts.

- group insurance programs offered to employees by an insurer under which no contribution is made by the employer, participation is voluntary, and the program is not actively sponsored by the employer.

- unfunded tuition reimbursement or scholarship programs (other than Section 127 educational assistance plans—see Chapter 32) that are paid out of the employer's general assets.

Reporting and Disclosure

All other welfare plans are subject to ERISA reporting and disclosure requirements. However, in general, these are less onerous than those applicable to pension plans.

Small welfare plan exemption. Welfare plans with fewer than 100 participants need not file an annual report (Form 5500 series) if they are fully insured or are paid out of the general assets of the employer on a pay-as-you-go basis. These plans also do not need to file a Summary Plan Description.[7]

At the end of this Appendix there is a compliance chart indicating major forms that must be filed with the IRS or Department of Labor or disclosed to participants. Copies of the current government forms of the 5500 series are also included. Current versions of these forms may be obtained from the local IRS office.

Additional IRS Reporting

In addition to having reporting obligations under ERISA, certain welfare plans (Section 79 group-term life insurance plans, Section 105/106 medical plans, and Section 129 dependent care plans) are subject to a reporting requirement under Section 6039D of the Internal Revenue Code. This would apparently have required these plans to file the Form 5500 series of annual reports even though they are eligible for an ERISA exemption such as that for "under-100" insured plans (see below). However, the IRS has postponed the effectiveness of this provision.[8] Eventually, it is expected that Section 6039D will be modified or repealed in connection with future employee benefit legislation.

FOOTNOTES

1. See also Labor Regs. §§2520.104-48, 2520.104-49 (SEPs).
2. ERISA Section 104(b)(1).
3. ERISA Section 104(a)(1)(C).
4. ERISA Sections 103(a)(1)(A), 104(a)(1)(A); IRC Section 6058(a).
5. Labor Reg. §2520.104b-10(c).
6. ERISA Section 105.
7. Labor Reg. §2520.104-20.
8. IRS Notice 90-24, 1990-1 CB 335.

Figure A.1

MAJOR REPORTING AND DISCLOSURE REQUIREMENTS FOR PENSION PLANS

I. Government Filings

Form	Description	Who Must File	When to File	Where to File
5500	Annual Return/Report of Employee Benefit Plan (with 100 or more participants at beginning of plan year).	Plan administrator.	On or before last day of seventh month after close of plan year. (2½ month extension available — file Form 5558).	IRS Service center indicated in instructions to Form 5500.
5500-C/R	Return/Report of Employee Benefit Plan (with fewer than 100 participants at beginning of plan year).	Plan administrator. (Simplified filing in 2 out of 3 years).	Same as Form 5500.	Same as Form 5500.
5500EZ	Annual Return of One-Participant (Owners and Their Spouses) Plans.	May be filed for plans that cover only an individual or an individual and spouse who are the owners of a business. May also be filed for partnership plans that cover only partners or partners and their spouses.	Same as Form 5500.	Same as Form 5500.
Schedule A (Form 5500 Series)	Insurance Information.	Plan administrator, where any plan benefits are provided by an insurance company or similar organization.	Attachment to Form 5500 series.	Same as Form 5500.
Schedule B (Form 5500 Series)	Actuarial Information.	Plan administrator of defined benefit plan subject to minimum funding standards.	Attachment to Form 5500 series.	Same as Form 5500.
Schedule C (Form 5500 Series)	Service Provider and Trustee Information.	Plan administrator.	Attachment to Form 5500 series.	Same as Form 5500.
Schedule P (Form 5500 Series)	Annual Return of Fiduciary of Employee Benefit Trust.	Trustee or custodian of qualified trust or custodial account. (Begins running of statute of limitations.)	Attachment to Form 5500 series.	Same as Form 5500.
Schedule SSA (Form 5500 Series)	Annual Registration Statement Identifying Separated Participants with Deferred Vested Benefits.	Plan administrator, if plan had participants who separated with deferred vested benefits during the plan year.	Attachment to Form 5500 Series.	Same as Form 5500.

Figure A.1 (continued)

Form	Description	Who Must File	When to File	Where to File
PBGC Form 1-ES	Estimated Premium Payment (Base premiums for plans with 500 or more participants).	Plan administrator or sponsor of defined benefit plan (with more than 500 participants) subject to PBGC provisions.	Within two months after the end of the prior plan year.	Pension Benefit Guaranty Corporation P.O. Box 105655 Atlanta, GA 30348-5655
PBGC Form 1	Annual Premium Payment.	Plan administrator or sponsor of defined benefit plan subject to PBGC provisions.	Within 8½ months after the end of the prior plan year.	Pension Benefit Guaranty Corporation P.O. Box 105655 Atlanta, GA 30348-5655
Summary Plan Description	Summary of the provisions of the plan in plain language; includes statement of ERISA rights.	Plan administrator.	Within 120 days after the plan is adopted. New SPD must be filed once every 5 years after the initial filing date if the plan is amended; otherwise, must be filed every 10 years.	SPD, Room N-5644 Pension and Welfare Benefits Administration U.S. Department of Labor 200 Constitution Ave. NW Washington, DC 20210
Summary of Material Modifications	Summary of any material modification to the plan and any change in information required to be in summary plan description.	Plan administrator.	Within 210 days after the close of the plan year in which the modification was adopted unless changes or modifications are described in timely filed summary plan description.	SMM, Room N-5644 Pension and Welfare Benefits Administration U.S. Department of Labor 200 Constitution Ave. NW Washington, DC 20210

II. Disclosure to Pension Plan Participants

Item	Description	Who Must Provide	When Provided
Summary Plan Description	Summary of the provisions of the plan in plain language; includes statement of ERISA rights.	Plan administrator.	New plans: within 120 days after effective date. Updated SPD must be furnished within 210 days of every fifth plan year for plans that have been amended; otherwise SPD must be redistributed every 10 years. New participants: within 90 days after becoming a participant or benefits commence (in the case of beneficiaries).
Summary of Material Modification	Summary of any material modification to the plan and any change in information required to be in summary plan description.	Plan administrator.	Within 210 days after the close of the plan year in which the modification was adopted unless changes or modifications are described in a timely distributed summary plan description.

Figure A.1 (continued)

Item	Description	Who Must Provide	When Provided
Summary Annual Report	Summary of annual report Form 5500 series. (Form 5500-C/R may be distributed for plans filing that form.)	Plan administrator.	Nine months after end of plan year, or within two months after close of extension period for filing annual report, if applicable.
Notice of Preretirement Survivor Benefit	Written explanation of preretirement survivor annuity, participant's right to make an election (or revoke election) to waive the annuity, spouse's rights, and effect of election or revocation.	Plan administrator of plan required to provide (see Chapter 24).	Within period beginning on first day of plan year in which participant attains age 32 and ending with close of plan year in which participant attains age 34. Election must be made within the period beginning on the first day of the plan year in which the participant attains age 35 and ending with the participant's death. For individuals who become participants after age 32, plan must provide explanation within three years of first day of plan year they become participants.
Notice of Joint and Survivor Benefit	Written explanation of joint and survivor annuity, right to make election to waive the annuity, right to revoke waiver, effect of election or revocation, and rights of the spouse.	Plan administrator of plan required to provide (see Chapter 24).	Within reasonable period before annuity starting date. Election must be made no sooner than 90 days before the annuity starting date.
Notice to Terminated Vested Participants	Same information as provided to IRS on Schedule SSA (Form 5500 series) concerning participant's accrued benefit. Statement must include notice if certain benefits may be forfeited if the participant dies before a particular date.	Plan administrator.	No later than due date for filing Schedule SSA (Form 5500 series).
Individual Accrued Benefit Statement	Statement of participant's benefit accrued to date based on the latest available data. Statement must include notice if certain benefits may be forfeited if the participant dies before a particular date.	Plan administrator.	Within 30 days of participant's request. Need not be provided more than once in a 12-month period.

Figure A.2

MAJOR REPORTING AND DISCLOSURE REQUIREMENTS FOR WELFARE PLANS

I. Government Filings

Form	Description	Who Must File	When to File	Where to File
5500	Annual Return/Report of Employee Benefit plan (with 100 or more participants at beginning of plan year)	Plan administrator.	On or before the last day of the seventh month after the close of the plan year. (2½ month extension available — file Form 5558.)	IRS service center indicated in instructions to Form 5500.
5500-C/R	Return/Report of Employee Benefit Plan (with fewer than 100 participants at beginning of plan year).	Plan administrator. Need not file if plan benefits paid solely from the general assets of the plan sponsor, or if plan is fully insured.	Same as Form 5500.	Same as Form 5500.
Schedule A (Form 5500 series)	Insurance information.	Plan administrator, where any benefits under the plan are provided by insurance company or similar organization.	Attachment to Form 5000 series.	Same as Form 5500.
Summary Plan Description	Summary of the provisions of the plan in plain language; includes statement of ERISA rights.	Plan administrator of a welfare plan except for unfunded or fully insured welfare plans with fewer than 100 participants.	Within 120 days after the plan is adopted. A new SPD must be filed once every five years after the initial filing date if the plan is amended; otherwise, must be filed every 10 years.	SPD, Room N-5644 Pension and Welfare Benefits Administration U.S. Department of Labor 200 Constitution Ave. NW Washington, DC 20210
Summary of Material Modifications	Summary of any material modification to the plan and any change in summary plan description.	Plan administrator of a welfare plan except for unfunded or fully insured welfare plans with fewer than 100 participants.	Within 210 days after the close of the plan year in which the modification was adopted unless changes or modifications are described in a timely filed summary plan description.	SMM, Room N-5644 Pension and Welfare Benefits Administration U.S. Department of Labor 200 Constitution Ave. NW Washington, DC 20210

Figure A.2 (continued)

II. Disclosure to Welfare Plan Participants and Beneficiaries

Item	Description	Who Must Provide	When Provided
Summary Plan Description	Summary of the provisions of the plan in plain language; includes statement of ERISA rights.	Plan administrator.	New plans: within 120 days after effective date. Updated SPD must be furnished within 210 days of every fifth plan year for plans that have been amended. Otherwise, SPDs must be redistributed every 10 years. New participants: within 90 days after becoming a participant or benefits commence (in the case of beneficiaries).
Summary of Material Modifications	Summary of any material modification to the plan and any change in information required to be in summary plan description.	Plan administrator.	Within 210 days after the close of the plan year in which the modification was adopted unless changes or modifications are described in a timely distributed summary plan description.
Summary Annual Report	Summary of annual report Form 5500 or 5500-C/R.	Plan administrator.	Nine months after end of plan year or within two months after close of extension period for filing annual report, if applicable.

| Form **5500**
Department of the Treasury
Internal Revenue Service

Department of Labor
Pension and Welfare Benefits
Administration
Pension Benefit Guaranty Corporation | **Annual Return/Report of Employee Benefit Plan**
(With 100 or more participants)
This form is required to be filed under sections 104 and 4065 of the
Employee Retirement Income Security Act of 1974 and sections 6039D,
6057(b), and 6058(a) of the Internal Revenue Code, referred to as the Code.
► See separate instructions. | OMB No. 1210-0016
19**92**
This Form Is Open to
Public Inspection. |

For the calendar plan year 1992 or fiscal plan year beginning , 1992, and ending , 19

A If *(1)* through *(4)* do not apply to this year's return/report, leave the boxes unmarked. This return/report is:

(1) ☐ the first return/report filed for the plan;

(2) ☐ an amended return/report;

(3) ☐ the final return/report filed for the plan; or

(4) ☐ a short plan year return/report (less than 12 months).

For IRS Use Only
EP–ID

If the preprinted information in 1a through 6d is incorrect, please correct it; if any information is missing, please add it. Be sure to include this page with your completed return/report.

B IF YOU CORRECT ANY OF THE PREPRINTED INFORMATION OR ADD MISSING INFORMATION IN 1a THROUGH 6d, CHECK HERE . . . . . ► ☐

C If your plan year changed since the last return/report, check here . . . . ► ☐

D If you filed for an extension of time to file this return/report, check here and attach a copy of the approved extension . . . . ► ☐

1a Name and address of plan sponsor (employer, if for a single-employer plan)
(address should include room or suite no.)

1b Employer identification number

1c Sponsor's telephone number

1d Business code (see instructions, page 23)

1e CUSIP issuer number

2a Name and address of plan administrator (if same as plan sponsor, enter "Same")

2b Administrator's employer identification no.

2c Administrator's telephone number

3 If you are filing this page without the preprinted historical plan information and the name, address and EIN of the plan sponsor or plan administrator has changed since the last return/report filed for this plan, enter the information from the last return/report in **3a** and/or **3b** and complete **3c**.

a Sponsor .... EIN .... Plan number...........

b Administrator .... EIN ....

c If 3a indicates a change in the sponsor's name, address, and EIN, is this a change in sponsorship only? (See instruction 3c on page 9 for the definition of sponsorship.) Enter "Yes" or "No." ► ....

4 **ENTITY CODE.** (If not shown, enter the applicable code from page 9 of the instructions.) ►

5a Name of plan ► ....
....

5b Effective date of plan (mo., day, yr.)

5c Three-digit plan number ►

6 All filers must complete 6a through 6d, as applicable.

a ☐ Welfare benefit plan **b** ☐ Pension benefit plan
(If the correct codes are not preprinted below, enter the applicable codes from page 9 and 10 of the instructions in the boxes.)

c Pension plan features. (If the correct codes are not preprinted below, enter the applicable pension plan feature codes from page 10 of the instructions in the boxes.)

d ☐ Fringe benefit plan. Attach Schedule F (Form 5500). See instructions.

Caution: *A penalty for the late or incomplete filing of this return/report will be assessed unless reasonable cause is established.*

Under penalties of perjury and other penalties set forth in the instructions, I declare that I have examined this return/report, including accompanying schedules and statements, and to the best of my knowledge and belief, it is true, correct, and complete.

Signature of employer/plan sponsor ►.. Date ►...........................

Type or print name of individual signing for the employer/plan sponsor...

Signature of plan administrator ►.. Date ►...........................

Type or print name of individual signing for the plan administrator

For Paperwork Reduction Act Notice, see page 1 of the instructions.   Cat. No. 13500F   Form **5500** (1992)

Form 5500 (1992)   Page **2**

6e Check all applicable investment arrangements below (see instructions):

(1) ☐ Master trust   *(2)* ☐ 103-12 investment entity

(3) ☐ Common/collective trust   *(4)* ☐ Pooled separate account

....

....

....

....

f Single-employer plans enter the tax year end of the employer in which this plan year ends ► Month .... Day .... Year ....

g Is any part of this plan funded by an insurance contract described in Code section 412*(i)* . . . . ☐ Yes ☐ No

h If 6g is "Yes," was the part subject to the minimum funding standards for either of the prior two plan years? . . . . ☐ Yes ☐ No

7 Number of participants as of the end of the plan year (welfare plans complete only 7a(4), 7b, 7c, and 7d):

a Active participants: *(1)*   Number fully vested . . . . **a(1)** _____

                     (2)   Number partially vested . . . . **a(2)** _____

                     (3)   Number nonvested. . . . . **a(3)** _____

                     (4)   Total . . . . **a(4)** _____

b Retired or separated participants receiving benefits . . . . **b** _____

c Retired or separated participants entitled to future benefits . . . . **c** _____

d Subtotal (add 7a(4), 7b, and 7c) . . . . **d** _____

e Deceased participants whose beneficiaries are receiving or are entitled to receive benefits . . . . . **e** _____

f Total (add 7d and 7e). . . . . **f** _____

g Number of participants with account balances (Defined benefit plans do not complete this line item.) . . . **g** _____

h Number of participants that terminated employment during the plan year with accrued benefits that were less than 100% vested. . . . . **h** _____

i *(1)*   Was any participant(s) separated from service with a deferred vested benefit for which a Schedule SSA (Form 5500) is required to be attached? (See instructions.) . . . . **i(1)** | Yes | No

     (2)   If "Yes," enter the number of separated participants required to be reported ►

8a Was this plan ever amended since its effective date? If "Yes," complete 8b . . . . **8a** | Yes | No

If the amendment was adopted in this plan year, complete 8c through 8e.

b If 8a is "Yes," enter the date the most recent amendment was adopted ►   Month .... Day .... Year ....

c Did any amendment during the current plan year result in the retroactive reduction of accrued benefits for any participants? **c**

d During this plan year did any amendment change the information contained in the latest summary plan descriptions or summary description of modifications available at the time of amendment?. . . . . **d**

e If 8d is "Yes," has a summary plan description or summary description of modifications that reflects the plan amendments referred to in 8d been both furnished to participants and filed with the Department of Labor? . . . . **e**

9a Was this plan terminated during this plan year or any prior plan year? If "Yes," enter the year ► **9a**

b Were all the plan assets either distributed to participants or beneficiaries, transferred to another plan, or brought under the control of PBGC?. . . . . **b**

c Was a resolution to terminate this plan adopted during this plan year or any prior plan year? . . . . **c**

d If 9a or 9c is "Yes," have you received a favorable determination letter from the IRS for the termination?. . . . **d**

e If 9d is "No," has a determination letter been requested from the IRS? . . . . **e**

f If 9a or 9c is "Yes," have participants and beneficiaries been notified of the termination or the proposed termination? **f**

g If 9a is "Yes" and the plan is covered by PBGC, is the plan continuing to file a PBGC Form 1 and pay premiums until the end of the plan year in which assets are distributed or brought under the control of PBGC? . . . . **g**

h During this plan year, did any trust assets revert to the employer for which the Code section 4980 excise tax is due? **h**

i If 9h is "Yes," enter the amount of tax paid with Form 5330 ► $

10a In this plan year, was this plan merged or consolidated into another plan(s), or were assets or liabilities transferred to another plan(s)? If "Yes," complete 10b through 10e, and see the instructions for 9a to complete item 9 if the plan was terminated ☐ Yes ☐ No

If "Yes," identify the other plan(s)   **c** Employer identification number(s)   **d** Plan number(s)

b Name of plan(s) ► .... | .... | ....

e If required, has a Form 5310-A been filed? . . . . ☐ Yes ☐ No

11 Enter the plan funding arrangement code from page 12 of the instructions . . . . ► | **12** Enter the plan benefit arrangement code from page 12 of the instructions ► | Yes | No

13a Is this a plan established or maintained pursuant to one or more collective bargaining agreements? **13a**

b If 13a is "Yes," enter the appropriate six-digit LM number(s) of the sponsoring labor organization(s) (see instructions):

(1)   *(2)*   *(3)*

14 If any benefits are provided by an insurance company, insurance service, or similar organization, enter the number of **Schedules A (Form 5500)**, Insurance Information, attached. If none, enter "-0-." ►

Welfare Plans Do Not Complete Items 15 Through 24. Go To Item 25.

			Yes	No
15a	If this is a defined benefit plan subject to the minimum funding standards for this plan year, is **Schedule B** (Form 5500) required to be attached? (If this is a defined contribution plan leave blank.)	**15a**		
b	If this is a defined contribution plan (i.e., money purchase or target benefit), is it subject to the minimum funding standards? (If a waiver was granted, see instructions.) (If this is a defined benefit plan leave blank.)	**b**		

If "Yes," complete (1), (2), and (3) below:

(1)	Amount of employer contribution required for the plan year under Code section 412	**b(1)**	$
(2)	Amount of contribution paid by the employer for the plan year	**b(2)**	$
	Enter date of last payment by employer ▶ Month.......... Day........ Year......		
(3)	If (1) is greater than (2), subtract (2) from (1) and enter the funding deficiency here; otherwise, enter -0-. (If you have a funding deficiency, file Form 5330.)	**b(3)**	$

			Yes	No
16	Has the annual compensation of each participant taken into account under the current plan year been limited to $228,860?	**16**		
17a (1)	Did the plan distribute any annuity contracts this year? (See instructions.)	**a(1)**		
(2)	If (1) is "Yes," did these contracts contain a requirement that the spouse consent before any distributions under the contract are made in a form other than a qualified joint and survivor annuity?	**a(2)**		
b	Did the plan make distributions to participants or spouses in a form other than a qualified joint and survivor annuity (a life annuity if a single person) or a qualified preretirement survivor annuity (exclude deferred annuity contracts)? . . .	**b**		
c	Did the plan make distributions or loans to married participants and beneficiaries without the required consent of the participant's spouse?	**c**		
d	Upon plan amendment or termination, do the accrued benefits of every participant include the subsidized benefits that the participant may become entitled to receive subsequent to the plan amendment or termination?	**d**		
18	Were distributions, if any, made in accordance with the requirements under Code sections 411(a)(11) and 417(e)?	**18**		
19	Have any contributions been made or benefits accrued in excess of the Code section 415 limits, as amended by the Tax Reform Act of 1986?	**19**		
20	Has the plan made the required distributions in 1992 under Code section 401(a)(9)? (See instructions.)	**20**		

21 Check if you are applying either of the following in completing items 21a through 21o (see instructions):

 (i) ☐ Reasonable, good faith interpretation of the nondiscrimination provisions.

 (ii) ☐ Substantiation guidelines.

 If you checked 21(ii), enter the first day of the plan year for which data is being submitted ▶ Month ....Day .... Year ....

			Yes	No
a	Does the employer apply the separate line of business rules of Code section 414(r) when testing this plan for the coverage and discrimination tests of Code sections 410(b) and 401(a)(4)?	**21a**		
b	If 21a is "Yes," enter the total number of separate lines of business claimed by the employer ▶ .... If more than one separate line of business, see instructions for additional information to attach.			
c	Does the employer apply the mandatory disaggregation rules under Income Tax Regulations section 1.410(b)-7(c)? If "Yes," see instructions for additional information to attach.	**c**		
d	In testing whether this plan satisfies the coverage and discrimination tests of Code sections 410(b) and 401(a), does the employer aggregate plans?	**d**		
e	Does the employer restructure the plan into component plans to satisfy the coverage and discrimination tests of Code sections 410(b) and 401(a)(4)?	**e**		

f If you meet either of the following exceptions, check the applicable box to tell us which exception you meet and do NOT complete the rest of question **21:**

 (1) ☐ No highly compensated employee benefited under the plan at any time during the plan year;

 (2) ☐ This is a collectively bargained plan that benefits only collectively bargained employees, no more than 2% of whom are professional employees.

			Yes	No
g	Did any leased employee perform services for the employer at any time during the plan year?	**g**		

			Number
h	Enter the total number of employees of the employer. Employer includes entities aggregated with the employer under Code section 414(b), (c), or (m). Include leased employees and self-employed individuals.	**h**	
i	Enter the total number of employees excludable because of: (1) failure to meet requirements for minimum age and years of service; (2) collectively bargained employees; (3) nonresident aliens who receive no earned income from U.S. sources; and (4) minimum hours of service/last day rule	**i**	
j	Enter the number of nonexcludable employees (subtract line 21i from line 21h)	**j**	

k Do 100% of the nonexcludable employees entered on line 21j benefit under the plan? . . . . . ☐ Yes ☐ No

 If line 21k is "Yes," do NOT complete lines 21l through 21o.

l	Enter the number of nonexcludable employees (line 21j) who are highly compensated employees	**l**	
m	Enter the number of nonexcludable employees (line 21j) who benefit under the plan	**m**	
n	Enter the number of employees entered on line 21m who are highly compensated employees	**n**	

o This plan satisfies the coverage requirements on the basis of (check one):

 (1) ☐ The average benefits test (2) ☐ The ratio percentage test—Enter value ▶

Form 5500 (1992)   Page **4**

		Yes	No

22a Is it or was it ever intended that this plan qualify under Code section 401(a)? If "Yes." complete **22b** and **22c** . . .   **22a**

b Enter the date of the most recent IRS determination letter . . . . ▶ Month . . . . Year . . . .

c Is a determination letter request pending with the IRS? . . . .   **c**

23a Does the plan hold any assets that have a fair market value that is not readily determinable on an established market?
(If "Yes," answer **23b**) **23a**

b Were all the assets referred to in **23a** valued during the 1992 plan year by an independent third-party appraiser? . .   **b**

c If **23b** is "No," enter the value of the assets that were not valued by an independent third-party appraiser during the
1992 plan year. ▶ _____

d Enter the date the assets in **23c** were valued by an independent third-party appraiser. (If more than one date, enter the
earliest date.) ▶ -

(If this plan does not have ESOP features leave **23e** blank and go to item 24.)

e If dividends paid on employer securities held by the ESOP were used to make payments
on ESOP loans, enter the amount of the dividends used to make the payments . . . | **23e** |

24 Does the employer/sponsor listed in **1a** of this form maintain other qualified pension benefit plans? **24**
If "Yes," enter the total number of plans, including this plan ▶

25a Did any person who rendered services to the plan receive directly or indirectly $5,000 or more in compensation from
the plan during the plan year (except for employees of the plan who were paid less than $1,000 in each month)? . .   **25a**
If "Yes," complete Part I of **Schedule C** (Form 5500).

b Did the plan have any trustees who must be listed in Part II of **Schedule C** (Form 5500)? . . . .   **b**

c Has there been a termination in the appointment of any person listed in 25d below? . . . .   **c**

d If **25c** is "Yes," check the appropriate box(es), answer **25e** and **25f**, and complete Part III of **Schedule C** (Form 5500):
   (1) ☐ Accountant   *(2)* ☐ Enrolled actuary   *(3)* ☐ Insurance carrier   *(4)* ☐ Custodian
   (5) ☐ Administrator   *(6)* ☐ Investment manager   *(7)* ☐ Trustee

e Have there been any outstanding material disputes or matters of disagreement concerning the above termination?. . .   **e**

f If an accountant or enrolled actuary has been terminated during the plan year, has the terminated accountant/actuary
been provided a copy of the explanation required by Part III of **Schedule C** (Form 5500) with a notice advising them of
their opportunity to submit comments on the explanation directly to the DOL?. . . . .   **f**

g Enter the number of **Schedules C** (Form 5500) that are attached. If none, enter -0- ▶

26a Is this plan exempt from the requirement to engage an independent qualified public accountant? (see instructions). .   **26a**

b If **26a** is "No," attach the accountant's opinion to this return/report and check the appropriate box. This opinion is:
   (1) ☐ Unqualified
   (2) ☐ Qualified/disclaimer per Department of Labor Regulations 29 CFR 2520.103-8 and/or 2520.103-12(d)
   (3) ☐ Qualified/disclaimer other   *(4)* ☐ Adverse   *(5)* ☐ Other (explain) -
- -

c If **26a** is "No," does the accountant's report, including the financial statements and/or notes required to be attached to this return/report
disclose (1) errors or irregularities; (2) illegal acts; (3) material internal control weaknesses; (4) a loss contingency indicating that assets
are impaired or a liability incurred; (5) significant real estate or other transactions in which the plan and (A) the sponsor, (B) the plan
administrator, (C) the employer(s), or (D) the employee organization(s) jointly involved; (6) that the plan has participated in any related
party transactions; or (7) any unusual or infrequent events or transactions occurring subsequent to the plan year end that might significantly
affect the usefulness of the financial statements in assessing the plan's present or future ability to pay benefits? . . . .   **c**

d If **26c** is "Yes," provide the total amount involved in such disclosure ▶

27 If **26a** is "No," complete the following questions. (You may NOT use "N/A" in response to item 27):
If **27a, 27b, 27c, 27d, 27e,** or **27f** is checked "Yes," schedules of these items in the format set forth in the instructions
are required to be attached to this return/report. Schedule G (Form 5500) may be used as specified in the instructions.
During the plan year:

a Did the plan have assets held for investment? **27a**

b Were any loans by the plan or fixed income obligations due the plan in default as of the close of the plan year or classified
during the year as uncollectible? . . . .   **b**

c Were any leases to which the plan was a party in default or classified during the year as uncollectible? . . . . .   **c**

d Were any plan transactions or series of transactions in excess of 5% of the current value of plan assets? . . . . .   **d**

e Do the notes to the financial statements accompanying the accountant's opinion disclose any nonexempt transactions
with parties-in-interest? . . . .   **e**

f Did the plan engage in any nonexempt transactions with parties-in-interest not reported in **27e**? . . . .   **f**

g Did the plan hold qualifying employer securities that are not publicly traded? . . . .   **g**

h Did the plan purchase or receive any nonpublicly traded securities that were not appraised in writing by an unrelated
third party within 3 months prior to their receipt? . . . .   **h**

i Did any person manage plan assets who had a financial interest worth more than 10% in any party providing services
to the plan or receive anything of value from any party providing services to the plan? . . . .   **i**

★U.S.GPO:1993-0-315-357

         The Tools and Techniques of Employee Benefit and Retirement Planning

Form 5500 (1992)

		Yes	No
28	Did the plan acquire individual whole life insurance contracts during the plan year?	**28**	
29	During the plan year:		
a (1)	Was this plan covered by a fidelity bond? If "Yes," complete 29a(2) and 29a(3)	**29a(1)**	
(2)	Enter amount of bond ▶ $		
(3)	Enter the name of the surety company ▶		
b (1)	Was there any loss to the plan, whether or not reimbursed, caused by fraud or dishonesty?	**b(1)**	
(2)	If **29b(1)** is "Yes," enter amount of loss ▶ $		

30a Is the plan covered under the Pension Benefit Guaranty Corporation termination insurance program?

☐ Yes ☐ No ☐ Not determined

b If **30a** is "Yes" or "Not determined," enter the employer identification number and the plan number used to identify it.

Employer identification number ▶   Plan number ▶

31 Current value of plan assets and liabilities at the beginning and end of the plan year. Combine the value of plan assets held in more than one trust. Allocate the value of the plan's interest in a commingled trust containing the assets of more than one plan on a line-by-line basis unless the trust meets one of the specific exceptions described in the instructions. Do not enter the value of that portion of an insurance contract which guarantees, during this plan year, to pay a specific dollar benefit at a future date. **Round off amounts to the nearest dollar; any other amounts are subject to rejection.** Plans with no assets at the beginning and the end of the plan year, enter -0- on line 31f.

Assets

			(a) Beginning of year	(b) End of Year
a	Total noninterest-bearing cash	**a**		
b	Receivables: **(1)** Employer contributions	**b(1)**		
	(2) Participant contributions	**(2)**		
	(3) Income	**(3)**		
	(4) Other	**(4)**		
	(5) Less allowance for doubtful accounts	**(5)**		
	(6) Total. Add b(1) through (4) and subtract (5) . . . . . . ▶	**(6)**		
c	General Investments: **(1)** Interest-bearing cash (including money market funds) . .	**c(1)**		
	(2) Certificates of deposit	**(2)**		
	(3) U.S. Government securities	**(3)**		
	(4) Corporate debt instruments: **(A)** Preferred	**(4)(A)**		
	(B) All other.	**(4)(B)**		
	(5) Corporate stocks: **(A)** Preferred	**(5)(A)**		
	(B) Common	**(5)(B)**		
	(6) Partnership/joint venture interests	**(6)**		
	(7) Real estate: **(A)** Income-producing	**(7)(A)**		
	(B) Nonincome-producing	**(7)(B)**		
	(8) Loans (other than to participants) secured by mortgages: **(A)** Residential . .	**(8)(A)**		
	(B) Commercial	**(8)(B)**		
	(9) Loans to participants: **(A)** Mortgages	**(9)(A)**		
	(B) Other	**(9)(B)**		
	(10) Other loans	**(10)**		
	(11) Value of interest in common/collective trusts	**(11)**		
	(12) Value of interest in pooled separate accounts	**(12)**		
	(13) Value of interest in master trusts	**(13)**		
	(14) Value of interest in 103-12 investment entities	**(14)**		
	(15) Value of interest in registered investment companies	**(15)**		
	(16) Value of funds held in insurance company general account (unallocated contracts) .	**(16)**		
	(17) Other ▶............	**(17)**		
	(18) Total. Add c(1) through c(17) . . . . . . ▶	**(18)**		
d	Employer-related investments: **(1)** Employer securities	**d(1)**		
	(2) Employer real property	**(2)**		
e	Buildings and other property used in plan operation	**e**		
f	**Total** assets. Add a, b(6), c(18), d(1), d(2), and e . . . . ▶	**f**		

Liabilities

g	Benefit claims payable	**g**		
h	Operating payables	**h**		
i	Acquisition indebtedness	**i**		
j	Other liabilities	**j**		
k	**Total** liabilities. Add g through j . . . . ▶	**k**		

Net Assets

l	Line f minus line k . . . . ▶	**l**		

The Tools and Techniques of Employee Benefit and Retirement Planning

Form 5500 (1992)   Page **6**

32 Plan income. expenses. and changes in net assets for the plan year. *Include all income and expenses of the plan, including any trust(s) or separately maintained fund(s), and any payments/receipts to/from insurance carriers.* **Round off amounts to the nearest dollar; any other amounts are subject to rejection.**

Income

		(a) Amount	(b) Total
a **Contributions:**			
(1) Received or receivable from:			
(A) Employers	a(1)(A)		
(B) Participants	(B)		
(C) Others	(C)		
(2) Noncash contributions	(2)		
(3) Total contributions. Add a(1)(A), (B), (C) and a(2). ►	(3)		
b **Earnings on investments:**			
(1) Interest			
(A) Interest-bearing cash (including money market funds)	b(1)(A)		
(B) Certificates of deposit	(B)		
(C) U.S. Government securities	(C)		
(D) Corporate debt instruments	(D)		
(E) Mortgage loans	(E)		
(F) Other loans	(F)		
(G) Other interest	(G)		
(H) Total interest. Add b(1)(A) through (G) ►	(H)		
(2) Dividends: (A) Preferred stock	b(2)(A)		
(B) Common stock	(B)		
(C) Total dividends. Add b(2)(A) and (B) ►	(C)		
(3) Rents	(3)		
(4) Net gain (loss) on sale of assets: (A) Aggregate proceeds	(4)(A)		
(B) Aggregate carrying amount (see instructions)	(B)		
(C) Subtract (B) from (A) and enter result	(C)		
(5) Unrealized appreciation (depreciation) of assets	(5)		
(6) Net investment gain (loss) from common/collective trusts	(6)		
(7) Net investment gain (loss) from pooled separate accounts	(7)		
(8) Net investment gain (loss) from master trusts	(8)		
(9) Net investment gain (loss) from 103-12 investment entities	(9)		
(10) Net investment gain (loss) from registered investment companies	(10)		
c Other income	c		
d Total income. Add all amounts in column (b) and enter total ►	d		

Expenses

		(a) Amount	(b) Total
e Benefit payment and payments to provide benefits:			
(1) Directly to participants or beneficiaries	e(1)		
(2) To insurance carriers for the provision of benefits	(2)		
(3) Other	(3)		
(4) Total payments. Add e(1) through (3) ►	(4)		
f Interest expense	f		
g Administrative expenses: (1) Salaries and allowances	g(1)		
(2) Accounting fees	(2)		
(3) Actuarial fees	(3)		
(4) Contract administrator fees	(4)		
(5) Investment advisory and management fees	(5)		
(6) Legal fees	(6)		
(7) Valuation/appraisal fees	(7)		
(8) Trustees fees/expenses (including travel, seminars, meetings, etc.)	(8)		
(9) Other	(9)		
(10) Total administrative expenses. Add g(1) through (9)	(10)		
h Total expenses. Add e(4), f, and g(10) ►	h		
i Net income (loss). Subtract h from d ►	i		
j Transfers to (from) the plan (see instructions)	j		
k Net assets at beginning of year (Item 31, line l, column (a))	k		
l Net assets at end of year (Item 31, line l, column (b)) ►	l		

	Yes	No
33 Did any employer sponsoring the plan pay any of the administrative expenses of the plan that were not reported in line 32g?		

SCHEDULE A (Form 5500)	Insurance Information	OMB No. 1210-0016

SCHEDULE A
(Form 5500)
Department of the Treasury
Internal Revenue Service

Department of Labor
Pension and Welfare Benefits Administration

Pension Benefit Guaranty Corporation

Insurance Information

This schedule is required to be filed under section 104 of the Employee Retirement Income Security Act of 1974.

▶ **File as an Attachment to Form 5500 or 5500-C/R.**

▶ Insurance companies are required to provide this information as per ERISA section 103(a)(2).

OMB No. 1210-0016

1992

This Form Is Open to Public Inspection

For calendar year 1992 or fiscal plan year beginning _____, 1992 and ending _____, 19 __ .

▶ Part I must be completed for all plans required to file this schedule.
▶ Part II must be completed for all insured pension plans.
▶ Part III must be completed for all insured welfare plans.

▶ Enter master trust or 103-12 IE name in place of "sponsor" and specify investment account or 103-12 IE in place of "plan" if filing with DOL for a master trust or 103-12 IE.

Name of plan sponsor as shown on line 1a of Form 5500 or 5500-C/R	Employer identification number
Name of plan	Enter three-digit plan number ▶

Part I   Summary of All Insurance Contracts Included in Parts II and III
Group all contracts in the same manner as in Parts II and III.

1   Check appropriate box: a ☐ Welfare plan   b ☐ Pension plan   c ☐ Combination pension and welfare plan

2 Coverage: (a) Name of insurance carrier	(b) Contract or identification number	(c) Approximate number of persons covered at end of policy or contract year	Policy or contract year	
			(d) From	(e) To

3 Insurance fees and commissions paid to agents and brokers: (a) Contract or identification number	(b) Name and address of the agents or brokers to whom commissions or fees were paid	(c) Amount of commissions paid	(d) Fees paid	
			Amount	Purpose
Total				

4   Premiums due and unpaid at end of the plan year ▶ $ _____ : Contract or identification number ▶ _____

Part II   Insured Pension Plans Provide information for each contract on a separate Part II. Where individual contracts are provided, the entire group of such individual contracts with each carrier may be treated as a unit for purposes of this report.

▶   Contract or identification number ▶ _____

5   Contracts with allocated funds, for example, individual policies or group deferred annuity contracts:
a   State the basis of premium rates ▶ ....
b   Total premiums paid to carrier . . . .
c   If the carrier, service, or other organization incurred any specific costs in connection with the acquisition or retention of the contract or policy, other than reported in 3 above, enter amount . . . .
    Specify nature of costs ▶

6   Contracts with unallocated funds, for example, deposit administration or immediate participation guarantee contracts. Do not include portions of these contracts maintained in separate accounts:
a   Balance at the end of the previous policy year . . . .
b   Additions: (i) Contributions deposited during year . . . .
    (ii)   Dividends and credits . . . .
    (iii)   Interest credited during the year . . . .
    (iv)   Transferred from separate account . . . .
    (v)   Other (specify) ▶
    (vi)   Total additions . . . .
c   Total of balance and additions (add a and b(vi)) . . . .
d   Deductions:
    (i)   Disbursed from fund to pay benefits or purchase annuities during year . . . . .
    (ii)   Administration charge made by carrier . . . .
    (iii)   Transferred to separate account . . . .
    (iv)   Other (specify) ▶
    (v)   Total deductions . . . .
e   Balance at end of current policy year (subtract d(v) from c) . . . .
7   Separate accounts: Current value of plan's interest in separate accounts at year end . . . .

For Paperwork Reduction Act Notice, see page 1 of the Instructions for Form 5500 or 5500-C/R.   Cat. No. 13505I   Schedule A (Form 5500) 1992

Schedule A (Form 5500) 1992
Page **2**

Part III — Insured Welfare Plans

Provide information for each contract on a separate Part III. If more than one contract covers the same group of employees of the same employer(s) or members of the same employee organization(s), the information may be combined for reporting purposes if such contracts are experience-rated as a unit. Where individual contracts are provided, the entire group of such individual contracts with each carrier may be treated as a unit for purposes of this report.

8	(a) Contract or identification number	(b) Type of benefit	(c) List gross premium for each contract	(d) Premium rate or subscription charge

9 Experience-rated contracts: **a** Premiums: *(i)* Amount received . . . .

   (ii) Increase (decrease) in amount due but unpaid . . . .

   (iii) Increase (decrease) in unearned premium reserve . . . .

   (iv) Premiums earned, add *(i)* and *(ii)*, and subtract *(iii)* . . . .

 b Benefit charges: *(i)* Claims paid . . . .

   (ii) Increase (decrease) in claim reserves . . . .

   (iii) Incurred claims (add *(i)* and *(ii)*) . . . .

   (iv) Claims charged . . . .

 c Remainder of premium: *(i)* Retention charges (on an accrual basis)—

   (A) Commissions . . . .

   (B) Administrative service or other fees . . . .

   (C) Other specific acquisition costs . . . .

   (D) Other expenses . . . .

   (E) Taxes . . . .

   (F) Charges for risks or contingencies . . . .

   (G) Other retention charges . . . .

   (H) Total retention . . . .

  (ii) Dividends or retroactive rate refunds. (These amounts were ☐ paid in cash, or ☐ credited.) . .

 d Status of policyholder reserves at end of year: *(i)* Amount held to provide benefits after retirement . .

  (ii) Claim reserves . . . .

  (iii) Other reserves . . . .

 e Dividends or retroactive rate refunds due. (Do not include amount entered in **c***(ii)*.) . . .

10 Nonexperience-rated contracts: **a** Total premiums or subscription charges paid to carrier . . . . .

 b If the carrier, service, or other organization incurred any specific costs in connection with the acquisition or retention of the contract or policy, other than reported in 3 above, report amount . . . .

Specify nature of costs ▶ ....

....

....

If additional space is required for any item, attach additional sheets the same size as this form.

General Instructions

This schedule must be attached to Form 5500 or 5500-C/R for every defined benefit, defined contribution, and welfare benefit plan where any benefits under the plan are provided by an insurance company, insurance service, or other similar organization.

Specific Instructions

(References are to the line items on the form.)

Information entered on Schedule A (Form 5500) should pertain to contracts with policy or contract years ending with or within the plan year (for reporting purposes, a year cannot exceed 12 months). **Exception:** If the insurance company maintains records on the basis of a plan year rather than a policy or contract year, the information entered on Schedule A (Form 5500) may pertain to the plan year instead of the policy or contract year.

Include only the contracts issued to the plan for which this return/report is being filed.

Plans Participating in Master Trust(s) and 103-12 IEs—See the Form 5500 or Form 5500-C/R instructions for "Reporting Requirements for Investment Arrangements Filing With DOL."

Line 2(c).—Since the plan coverage may fluctuate during the year, the administrator should estimate the number of persons that were covered by the plan at the end of the policy or contract year.

Where contracts covering individual employees are grouped, entries should be determined as of the end of the plan year.

Lines 2(d) and (e).—Enter the beginning and ending dates of the policy year for each contract listed under column (b). Enter "N/A" in column (d) if separate contracts covering individual employees are grouped.

Line 3.—Report all sales commissions in column (c) regardless of the identity of the recipient. Do not report override commissions, salaries, bonuses, etc., paid to a general agent or manager for managing an agency, or for performing other administrative functions.

Fees to be reported in column (d) represent payments by insurance carriers to agents and brokers for items other than commissions (e.g., service fees, consulting fees, and finders fees).

Note: *For purposes of this item, commissions and fees include amounts paid by an insurance company on the basis of the aggregate value (e.g., policy amounts, premiums) of contracts or policies (or classes thereof) placed or retained. The amount (or pro rata share of the total) of such commissions or fees attributable to the contract or policy placed with or retained by the plan must be reported in column (c) or (d), as appropriate.*

Fees paid by insurance carriers to persons other than agents and brokers should be reported in Parts II and III on Schedule A (Form 5500) as acquisition costs, administrative charges, etc., as appropriate. For plans with 100 or more participants, fees paid by employee benefit plans to agents, brokers, and other persons are to be reported on Schedule C (Form 5500).

Line 5a.—The rate information called for here may be furnished by attachment of appropriate schedules of current rates filed with appropriate state insurance departments or by a statement as to the basis of the rates.

Line 6.—Show deposit fund amounts rather than experience credit records when both are maintained.

Line 8(d).—The rate information called for here may be furnished by attachment of the appropriate schedules of current rates or by a statement as to the basis of the rates.

SCHEDULE B
(Form 5500)
Department of the Treasury
Internal Revenue Service
Department of Labor
Pension and Welfare Benefits Administration
Pension Benefit Guaranty Corporation

Actuarial Information

This schedule is required to be filed under section 104 of the Employee Retirement Income Security Act of 1974, referred to as ERISA, and section 6059(a) of the Internal Revenue Code, referred to as the Code.

▶ **Attach to Form 5500, 5500-C/R, or 5500EZ if applicable.**
▶ **See separate instructions.**

OMB No. 1210-0016

1992

This Form is Open to Public Inspection

For calendar plan year 1992 or fiscal plan year beginning _____ , 1992, and ending _____ , 19____

▶ **Read the specific instructions** before attempting to complete this form.

▶ **Please complete every item on this form. If an item does not apply, enter "N/A."** ▶ **Round off amounts to nearest dollar.**

▶ **Caution:** *A penalty of $1,000 will be assessed for late filing of this report unless reasonable cause is established.*

Name of plan sponsor as shown on line 1a of Form 5500, 5500-C/R, or 5500EZ	Employer identification number

Name of plan	Enter three-digit plan number ▶	Yes	No

1 Has a waiver of a funding deficiency for this plan year been approved by the IRS? . . . .
If "Yes," attach a copy of the IRS approval letter.

2 Is a waived funding deficiency of a prior plan year being amortized in this plan year? . . . .

3 Have any of the periods of amortization for charges described in Code section 412(b)(2)(B) been extended by IRS?
If "Yes," attach a copy of the IRS approval letter.

4a Was the shortfall funding method the basis for this plan year's funding standard account computations?. . .

b Is this plan a multiemployer plan which is, for this plan year, in reorganization as described in Code section 418 or ERISA section 4241?. . . . .
If "Yes," you are required to attach the information described in the instructions.

5 Has a change been made in funding method for this plan year? . . . .
If "Yes," attach either a copy of the letter showing IRS approval or state the applicable Revenue Procedure authorizing approval if used.

6 Operational information:

a Enter the most recent actuarial valuation date ▶ ....

b Has any pre-participation service been excluded in current liability calculations? . . . . , ☐ Yes ☐ No

c Current value of the assets accumulated in the plan as of the beginning of this plan year . . . . . .

d Current liability as of beginning of plan year:

	(1) No. of Persons	(2) Vested Benefits	(3) Total Benefits
(i) For retired participants and beneficiaries receiving payments			
(ii) For terminated vested participants			
(iii) For active participants			
(iv) Total			

e Expected current liability increase as of mo. ....day ....yr. .... attributable to benefits accruing during the plan year . . . .

f Expected benefit payments. . . . .

7 Contributions made to the plan for the plan year by employer(s) and employees:

(a) Month Day Year	(b) Amount paid by employer	(c) Amount paid by employees	(a) Month Day Year	(b) Amount paid by employer	(c) Amount paid by employees
			Total		

Statement by Enrolled Actuary (see instructions before signing):

To the best of my knowledge, the information supplied in this schedule and on the accompanying statements, if any, is complete and accurate, and in my opinion each assumption used in combination, represents my best estimate of anticipated experience under the plan. Furthermore, in the case of a plan other than a multiemployer plan, each assumption used (a) is reasonable (taking into account the experience of the plan and reasonable expectations) or (b) would, in the aggregate, result in a total contribution equivalent to that which would be determined if each such assumption were reasonable. In the case of a multiemployer plan, the assumptions used, in the aggregate, are reasonable (taking into account the experience of the plan and reasonable expectations).

_____
Signature of actuary

_____
Date

_____
Print or type name of actuary

_____
Most recent enrollment number

_____
Firm name and address

_____
Telephone number (including area code)

For Paperwork Reduction Act Notice, see the instructions for Form 5500

Cat. No. 13507E

Schedule B (Form 5500) 1992

Schedule B (Form 5500) 1992 — Page **2**

8 Funding standard account and other information:

a Accrued liability as determined for funding standard account as of (enter date) ▶ ....

b Value of assets as determined for funding standard account as of (enter date) ▶ ....

c Unfunded liability for spread-gain methods with bases as of (enter date) ▶ ....

d *(i)* Actuarial gains or (losses) for period ending ▶ ....

(ii) Shortfall gains or (losses) for period ending ▶ ....

e Amount of contribution certified by the actuary as necessary to reduce the funding deficiency to zero, from **9o** or **10h** (or the attachment for **4b** if required).

9 Funding standard account statement for this plan year ending ▶ ....

Charges to funding standard account:

a Prior year funding deficiency, if any

b Employer's normal cost for plan year as of mo. .... day .... yr. ....

c Amortization charges: Balance

   (i) Funding waivers (outstanding balance as of mo. ...... day .... yr. .... ▶ $.................)

   (ii) Other than waivers (outstanding balance as of mo. ... day ... yr. ... ▶ $.................)

d Interest as applicable on **a**, **b**, and **c**

e Additional funding charge, if applicable (see line 13, page 3)

f Additional interest charge due to late quarterly contributions

g Total charges (add **a** through **f**)

Credits to funding standard account:

h Prior year credit balance, if any

i Employer contributions (total from column (b) of item 7)

j Amortization credits (outstanding balance as of mo. ...... day .... yr. .... ▶ $.................)

k Interest as applicable to end of plan year on **h**, **i**, and **j**

l Miscellaneous credits:

   (i) FFL credit before reflecting 150% of current liability component

   (ii) Additional credit due to 150% of current liability component

   (iii) Waived funding deficiency

   (iv) Total

m Total credits (add **h** through **l**)

Balance:

n Credit balance: if **m** is greater than **g**, enter the difference.

o Funding deficiency: if **g** is greater than **m**, enter the difference

Reconciliation:

p Current year's accumulated reconciliation account:

   (i) Due to additional funding charge as of the beginning of the plan year

   (ii) Due to additional interest charges as of the beginning of the plan year

   (iii) Due to waived funding deficiency:

      (a) Reconciliation outstanding balance as of mo. ...... day ...... yr. .....

      (b) Reconciliation amount (9c(i) balance minus 9p(iii)(a))

   (iv) Total as of mo. .... day ...... yr. ....

10 Alternative minimum funding standard account (omit if not used):

a Was the entry age normal cost method used to determine entries in line 9, above. ☐ Yes ☐ No

If "No," do not complete **b** through **h**.

b Prior year alternate funding deficiency, if any

c Normal cost

d Excess, if any, of value of accrued benefits over market value of assets

e Interest on **b**, **c**, and **d**.

f Employer contributions (total from columns (b) of item 7)

g Interest on **f**

h Funding deficiency: if the sum of **b** through **e** is greater than the sum of **f** and **g**, enter difference

11 Actuarial cost method used as the basis for this plan year's funding standard account computation:

- **a** ☐ Attained age normal   **b** ☐ Entry age normal   **c** ☐ Accrued benefit (unit credit)
- **d** ☐ Aggregate   **e** ☐ Frozen initial liability   **f** ☐ Individual level premium
- **g** ☐ Other (specify) ▶

12 Checklist of certain actuarial assumptions:

	Pre-retirement		Post-retirement	
	☐ Yes	☐ No	☐ Yes	☐ No
a Rates specified in insurance or annuity contracts	/////	/////	/////	/////
b Mortality table code:				
(i) Males				
(ii) Females				
c Interest rate:	/////	/////	/////	/////
(i) Current liability		%		%
(ii) All other calculated values		%		%
d Retirement age			/////	/////
e Expense loading		%		%

	Male	Female	
f Annual withdrawal rate:			/////
(i) Age 25	%	%	/////
(ii) Age 40	%	%	/////
(iii) Age 55	%	%	/////
g Ratio of salary at normal retirement to salary at:	/////	/////	/////
(i) Age 25	%	%	/////
(ii) Age 40	%	%	/////
(iii) Age 55	%	%	/////

h Estimated investment return on actuarial value of plan assets for the year ending on the valuation date .... %

13 Additional Required Funding Charge—Multiemployer plans or plans with NO unfunded current liability or plans with 100 or fewer participants check the box at the right and do not complete **a** through **r** below ☐

- **a** Current liability as of valuation date ....
- **b** Adjusted value of assets as of valuation date (subtract line 9h from line 8b) ....
- **c** Funded current liability percentage (**b** divided by **a**) .... %
- **d** Unfunded current liability as of valuation date (subtract **b** from **a**) ....
- **e** Outstanding balance of unfunded old liability as of valuation date ....
- **f** Liability attributable to any unpredictable contingent event benefit ....
- **g** Unfunded new liability (subtract **e** and **f** from **d**) ....
- **h** Unfunded new liability amount (_____ % of **g**) ....
- **i** Unfunded old liability amount ....
- **j** Deficit reduction contribution (add **h** and **i**) ....
- **k** Net amortization charge for certain bases ....
- **l** Unpredictable contingent event amount:
    - *(i)* Benefits paid during year attributable to unpredictable contingent event .
    - *(ii)* Unfunded current liability percentage (subtract the percentage on **13c** from 100%) .... %
    - *(iii)* Transition percentage .... %
    - *(iv)* Enter the product of lines *(i)*, *(ii)*, and *(iii)* ....
    - *(v)* Amortization of all unpredictable contingent event liabilities ......
    - *(vi)* Enter the greater of line *iv* or line *v* ....
- **m** Additional funding charge as of valuation date (excess of **j** over **k** (if any) plus **l***(vi)*) ......
- **n** Assets needed to increase current liability percentage to 100% (line **d**) ....
- **o** Lesser of **m** or **n** ....
- **p** Interest adjustment ....
- **q** Additional funding charge (add **o** and **p**) ....
- **r** Adjustment for plans with more than 100 but less than 150 participants (_____ % of **q**) ......

14 Has this form been prepared and signed subject to the qualification under Income Tax Regulations section 301.6059-1(d)(5)? (See instructions.) .... ☐ Yes ☐ No

SCHEDULE C
(Form 5500)

Department of the Treasury
Internal Revenue Service

Department of Labor
Pension and Welfare Benefits Administration

Pension Benefit Guaranty Corporation

Service Provider and Trustee Information

This schedule is required to be filed under section 104 of the Employee Retirement Income Security Act of 1974.

▶ File as an attachment to Form 5500.

Additional Schedules C (Form 5500) may be used, if needed, to provide additional information for Parts I, II, and/or III.

OMB No. 1210-0016

1992

This Form is
Open to Public
Inspection

For the calendar year 1992 or fiscal plan year beginning	, 1992, and ending	, 19

Name of plan sponsor as shown on line 1a of Form 5500	Employer identification number

Name of plan	Enter three-digit plan number ▶

Part I Service Provider Information (see instructions)

1 Enter the total dollar amount of compensation paid by the plan to all persons receiving less than $5,000 during the plan year . . . . | 1 |

2 (a) Name	(b) Employer identification number (see instructions)	(c) Official plan position	(d) Relationship to employer, employee organization, or person known to be a party-in-interest	(e) Gross salary or allowances paid by plan	(f) Fees and commissions paid by plan	(g) Nature of service code (see instructions)
(1)		Contract administrator				12
(2)						
(3)						
(4)						
(5)						
(6)						
(7)						
(8)						
(9)						
(10)						
(11)						
(12)						
(13)						
(14)						
(15)						
(16)						
(17)						
(18)						
(19)						
(20)						
(21)						
(22)						
(23)						
(24)						
(25)						
(26)						
(27)						
(28)						
(29)						
(30)						
(31)						
(32)						
(33)						
(34)						
(35)						
(36)						
(37)						
(38)						
(39)						
(40)						

For Paperwork Reduction Act Notice, see page 1 of the Instructions for Form 5500.   Cat. No. 13515E   Schedule C (Form 5500) 1992

Schedule C (Form 5500) 1992   Page **2**

Part II   **Trustee Information**   Enter the name and address of all trustees who served during the plan year. If more space is required to supply this information, attach additional Schedules C (Form 5500).

Name ....   Name ....
Address ....   Address ....

Name ....   Name ....
Address ....   Address ....

Name ....   Name ....
Address ....   Address ....

Name ....   Name ....
Address ....   Address ....

Name ....   Name ....
Address ....   Address ....

Name ....   Name ....
Address ....   Address ....

Name ....   Name ....
Address ....   Address ....

Name ....   Name ....
Address ....   Address ....

Part III   Termination Information (see instructions)

(a) Name	(b) EIN	(c) Position	(d) Address	(e) Telephone No.

(1)   Explanation: ....
....
....
....
....
....

(a) Name	(b) EIN	(c) Position	(d) Address	(e) Telephone No.

(2)   Explanation: ....
....
....
....
....
....

(a) Name	(b) EIN	(c) Position	(d) Address	(e) Telephone No.

(3)   Explanation: ....
....
....
....
....
....

Appendix A

Part I— Service Provider Information

General Instructions

Item 1 of Part I must be completed by all Form 5500 filers required to complete item 2.

Item 2 of Part I must be completed to report all persons receiving, directly or indirectly, $5,000 or more in compensation for all services rendered to the plan during the plan year except:

1. employees of the plan whose only compensation in relation to the plan was less than $1,000 for each month of employment during the plan year,

2. employees of the plan sponsor who received no direct or indirect compensation from the plan,

3. employees of a business entity (e.g., corporation, partnership, etc.), other than the plan sponsor, who provided services to the plan, or

4. persons whose only compensation in relation to the plan consists of insurance fees and commissions listed in Schedule A (Form 5500).

Generally, indirect compensation would not include compensation that would have been received had the service not been rendered and that cannot be reasonably allocated to the services performed. Indirect compensation includes, among other things, the payment of "finders' fees" or other fees and commissions by a service provider to an independent agent or employee for a transaction or service involving the plan.

Note: *The compensation listed should only reflect the amount of compensation received by the service provider from the plan filing the Schedule C (Form 5500), not the aggregate amount received by the service provider for providing services to several plans.*

Specific Instructions

In item 1, enter the total dollar amount of compensation received by all persons who provided services to the plan who are not listed in item 2 (except for those persons described in **2, 3,** or **4** above in the General Instructions).

Example: A plan had four service providers, A, B, C, and D, who received $12,000, $6,000, $4,500, and $430 respectively from the plan. Service providers A and B must be identified on separate lines in item 2 by name, EIN, official plan position, etc. As service providers C and D each received less than $5,000, the amounts they received must be combined and $4,930 entered in item 1.

In item 2, line (1), include any individual, trade or business, whether incorporated or unincorporated, responsible for managing the clerical operations (e.g., handling membership rosters, claims payments, maintaining books and records) of the plan on a contractual basis that is required to be reported in item 2 except for salaried staff or employees of the plan or banks or insurance carriers.

On the remaining lines ((2) through (40)) and additional Schedules C (Form 5500) if needed, list all other persons required to be reported in item 2 who provided services to the plan in the order of compensation received, starting with the most highly compensated and ending with the lowest compensated.

Column (b).—An EIN must be entered in column (b). If an individual is listed in column (a), the EIN to be entered in column (b) should be the EIN of the individual's employer.

Column (c).—For example, employee, trustee, accountant, attorney, etc.

Column (d).—For example, employee, vice-president, union president, etc.

Columns (c) and (f).—Include the plan's share of amounts of compensation for services paid during the year to a master trust or 103-12 IE trustee, and to persons providing services to the master trust or 103-12 IE, if such compensation is not subtracted from the gross income of the master trust or 103-12 IE in determining the net investment gain (or loss). Amounts of compensation subtracted from gross income in determining the net investment gain (or loss) of the master trust or 103-12 IE must be included as part of the report of the master trust or 103-12 IE filed with DOL.

Include brokerage commissions or fees only if the broker is granted some discretion (see 29 CFR 2510.3-21, paragraph (d) regarding "discretion"). Include all other commissions and fees on investments, whether or not they are capitalized as investment costs.

Column (g).—From the list below, select the code that best describes the nature of services provided to the plan, and enter the number. If more than one service was provided, enter only the code of the primary service.

Code	Service
10	Accounting (including auditing)
11	Actuarial
12	Contract administrator
13	Administration
14	Brokerage (real estate)
15	Brokerage (stocks, bonds, commodities)
16	Computing, tabulating, ADP, etc.
17	Consulting (general)
18	Custodial (securities)
19	Insurance agents and brokers
20	Investment advisory
21	Investment management
22	Legal
23	Printing and duplicating
24	Recordkeeping
25	Trustee (individual)
26	Trustee (corporate)
27	Pension insurance adviser
28	Valuation services (appraisals, asset valuations, etc.)
29	Investment evaluations
30	Medical
31	Legal services to participants
99	Other (specify)

Note: *Do not list PBGC as a service provider on Part I of Schedule C (Form 5500).*

Part III—Termination Information

Explain the reason for the change in appointment and provide the name, EIN, position, address, and telephone number of the person(s) listed in item 25d of Form 5500 whose appointment has been terminated. List them in the order of the boxes that are checked in item 25d, (i.e., accountants first, enrolled actuaries next, etc.). Include in this explanation a description of any disagreement for which item 25e of the Form 5500 is marked "Yes," even if the disagreement was resolved prior to the termination. If an individual is listed, the EIN to be entered should be the EIN of the individual's employer.

Use additional Schedules C (Form 5500) if needed, to list additional persons.

SCHEDULE P
(Form 5500)

Department of the Treasury
Internal Revenue Service

Annual Return of Fiduciary
of Employee Benefit Trust

► File as an attachment to Form 5500, 5500-C/R, or 5500EZ.
► For the Paperwork Reduction Notice, see page 1 of the Form 5500 instructions.

OMB No. 1210-0016

1991

For trust calendar year 1991 or fiscal year beginning _____ , 1991, and ending _____ , 19 ____

Please type or print

1a Name of trustee or custodian

b Number, street, and room or suite no. (If a P.O. box, see the instructions for Form 5500, 5500-C/R, or 5500EZ.)

c City or town, state, and ZIP code

2 Name of trust

3 Name of plan if different from name of trust

4 Have you furnished the participating employee benefit plan(s) with the trust financial information required to be reported by the plan(s)? . . . . □ Yes □ No

5 Enter the plan sponsor's employer identification number as shown on Form 5500, 5500-C/R, or 5500EZ . . . . ►

Under penalties of perjury, I declare that I have examined this schedule, and to the best of my knowledge and belief it is true, correct, and complete.

Signature of fiduciary ►

Date ►

Instructions

(Section references are to the Internal Revenue Code.)

A. Purpose of Form

You may use this schedule to satisfy the requirements under section 6033(a) for an annual information return from every section 401(a) organization exempt from tax under section 501(a).

Filing this form will start the running of the statute of limitations under section 6501(a) for any trust described in section 401(a), which is exempt from tax under section 501(a).

B. Who May File

(1) Every trustee of a trust created as part of an employee benefit plan as described in section 401(a).

(2) Every custodian of a custodial account described in section 401(f).

C. How To File

File Schedule P (Form 5500) for the trust year ending with or within any participating plan's plan year. Attach it to the Form 5500, 5500-C/R, or 5500EZ filed by the plan for that plan year.

Schedule P (Form 5500) must be filed only as an attachment to a Form 5500, 5500-C/R, or 5500EZ. A separately filed Schedule P (Form 5500) will not be accepted.

If the trust or custodial account is used by more than one plan, file one Schedule P (Form 5500). File it as an attachment to one of the participating plan's returns/reports. If a plan uses more than one trust or custodial account for its funds, file one Schedule P (Form 5500) for each trust or custodial account.

D. Signature

The fiduciary (trustee or custodian) must sign this schedule. If there is more than one fiduciary, one of them, authorized by the others, may sign.

E. Other Returns and Forms That May Be Required

(1) Form 990-T.—For trusts described in section 401(a), a tax is imposed on income derived from business that is unrelated to the purpose for which the trust received a tax exemption. Report such income and tax on **Form 990-T,** Exempt Organization Business Income Tax Return. (See sections 511 through 514 and the related regulations.)

(2) Form 1099-R.—If you made payments or distributions to individual beneficiaries of a plan, report these payments on Form 1099-R. (See sections 6041 and 6047 and the related regulations.)

(3) Forms 941 or 941E.—If you made payments or distributions to individual beneficiaries of a plan, you are required to withhold income tax from those payments unless the payee elects not to have the tax withheld. Report any withholding tax on Form 941 or 941E. (See Form 941 or 941E, and Circular E, Pub. 15.)

SCHEDULE SSA (Form 5500)

Annual Registration Statement Identifying Separated Participants With Deferred Vested Benefits

Under Section 6057(a) of the Internal Revenue Code

▶ File as an attachment to Form 5500 or 5500-C/R.

▶ For Paperwork Reduction Act Notice, see page 1 of the instructions for Form 5500 or 5500-C/R.

Department of the Treasury
Internal Revenue Service

OMB No. 1210-0016

1992

This Form Is NOT Open to Public Inspection

For the calendar year 1992 or fiscal plan year beginning _____ , 1992, and ending _____ , 19___

▶ This schedule must be filed for each plan year in which one or more participants with deferred vested benefit rights separated from the service covered by the plan. See instructions on when to report a separated employee.

▶ Type or print in ink all entries on this schedule. File the originals.

▶ All attachments to this schedule should have entries only on the front of the page.

1a Name of sponsor (employer if for a single employer plan)

1b Sponsor's employer identification number

Number, street, and room or suite no. (If a P.O. box, see the instructions for 1a.)

City or town, state, and ZIP code

1c Is this a plan to which more than one employer contributes? ☐ Yes ☐ No

2a Name of plan administrator (if other than sponsor)

2b Administrator's employer identification no.

Number, street, and room or suite no. (If a P.O. box, see the instructions for 1a.)

City or town, state, and ZIP code

3a Name of plan

3b Plan number. ▶

4 Have you notified each separated participant of his or her deferred benefit? . . . . ▶ ☐ Yes ☐ No

5 Separated participants with deferred vested benefits (if additional space is required, see instruction, "What To File"):

(a) Social security number	(b) Name of participant	Enter code for nature and form of benefit		Amount of vested benefit			(h) Plan year in which participant separated
		(c) Type of annuity	(d) Payment frequency	(e) Defined benefit plan—periodic payment	(f) Units or shares	(g) Total value of account	

The Following Information Is Optional (See Specific Instruction 6.)

6 Use this item to report: (i) separated participants with deferred vested benefits who were previously reported on Schedule SSA (Form 5500) and who have received part or all of their vested benefits or who have forfeited their benefits during the plan year for which this schedule is being filed, and (ii) to delete participants erroneously reported on a prior Schedule SSA (Form 5500).

Note: Participants listed in this item, because they have received part of their vested benefits, must also be reported in item 5 above listing their remaining vested benefits.

(a) Social security number	(b) Name of participant	Enter code for nature and form of benefit		Amount of vested benefit			(h) Plan year in which participant separated
		(c) Type of annuity	(d) Payment frequency	(e) Defined benefit plan—periodic payment	(f) Units or shares	(g) Total value of account	

Under penalties of perjury, I declare that I have examined this report, and to the best of my knowledge and belief, it is true, correct, and complete.

Signature of plan administrator ▶ _____ Date ▶ _____

Cat. No. 10506T

Schedule SSA (Form 5500) (1992)

General Instructions

Note: *Please type or print all information and submit original copy only.*

Who Must File.—The plan administrator must file this schedule for any plan year for which a separated plan participant is reported under "When To Report a Separated Participant," below.

What To File.—File this schedule and complete all items. If you need more space, use either: **(1)** additional copies of Schedule SSA, completing only items 1, 3, 5, and 6 of the additional copies, or **(2)** additional sheets the same size as the schedule containing the information asked for in items 1, 3, 5, and 6. The information required in items 5 and 6 should be listed in the same format as items 5 and 6 on Schedule SSA. Enter information on the front of the attachment only.

You may send a machine-generated computer listing showing the information required in items 5 and 6 in lieu of completing items 5 and 6 on the schedule. Complete items 1 through 4 on Schedule SSA and enter in items 5 and 6 a statement that a list is attached. On each page of the computer listing, enter the name of the sponsor, the EIN, the plan name, and the plan number. Use the same format as items 5 and 6 on Schedule SSA.

How To File.—File as an attachment to Form 5500 or 5500-C/R.

When To Report a Separated Participant.—

In general, *for a plan to which only one employer contributes,* a participant must be reported on Schedule SSA if:

1. The participant separates from service covered by the plan in a plan year, and

2. The participant is entitled to a deferred vested benefit under the plan.

The separated participant must be reported no later than on the Schedule SSA filed for the plan year following the plan year in which separation occurred. The participant may be reported earlier (i.e., on the Schedule SSA filed for the plan year in which separation occurred). Once separated participants have been reported on a Schedule SSA, they should not be reported on a subsequent year's Schedule SSA.

However, a participant is not required to be reported on Schedule SSA if, before the date the Schedule SSA is required to be filed (including any extension of time for filing), the participant:

1. Is paid some or all of the deferred vested retirement benefit,

2. Returns to service covered by the plan, or

3. Forfeits all of the deferred vested retirement benefit.

In general, *for a plan to which more than one employer contributes,* a participant must be reported on Schedule SSA if:

1. The participant incurs two successive one-year breaks in service (as defined in the plan for vesting purposes) in service computation periods, and

2. The participant is (or may be) entitled to a deferred vested benefit under the plan.

The participant must be reported no later than on the Schedule SSA filed for the plan year in which the participant completed the second of the two consecutive one-year breaks in service. The participant may be reported earlier (i.e., on the Schedule SSA filed for the plan year in which he or she separated from service or completed the first one-year break in service).

However, a participant is not required to be reported on Schedule SSA if, before the date the Schedule SSA is required to be filed (including any extension of time for filing), the participant:

1. Is paid some or all of the deferred vested retirement benefit,

2. Accrues additional retirement benefits under the plan, or

3. Forfeits all of the deferred vested retirement benefit.

Cessation of Payment of Benefits.—As described above in "When To Report a Separated Participant," a participant is not required to be reported on Schedule SSA if, before the date the Schedule SSA is required to be filed (including any extension of time for filing), some of the deferred vested benefit to which the participant is entitled is paid to the participant. If payment of the deferred vested benefit ceases before all of the benefit is paid to the participant, the benefit to which the participant remains entitled must be reported on the Schedule SSA filed for the plan year following the last plan year within which any of the benefit was paid to the participant. However, a participant is not required to be reported on Schedule SSA on account of a cessation of payment of benefits if, before the date the schedule is required to be filed (including any extension of time for filing), the participant:

1. Returns to service covered by the plan,

2. Accrues additional retirement benefits under the plan, or

3. Forfeits the remaining benefit.

Separation of a Re-employed Employee.—The deferred vested benefit reported on the current Schedule SSA for a re-employed employee who is again separated from service must include only the benefit not previously reported in or for prior years. Generally, the benefit to be shown on the current filing will be the benefit earned during the re-employment period.

Caution: *A penalty may be assessed if Schedule SSA (Form 5500) is not timely filed.*

Specific Instructions

1a.—If the Post Office does not deliver mail to the street address and you have a P.O. box, enter the P.O. box number instead of the street address.

4.—Check "Yes" if you have complied with the requirements of Code section 6057(e). The notification to each participant must include the information set forth on this schedule and the information about any contributions made by the participant and not withdrawn by the end of the plan year. Any benefits that are forfeitable if the participant dies before a certain date must be shown on the statement.

5(a).—Enter the exact social security number of each participant listed.

If the participant is a foreign national employed outside of the United States who does not have a social security number, enter the participant's nationality.

5(b).—Enter each participant's name exactly as it appears on the participant's social security card or the employer's payroll records for purposes of reporting to the Social Security Administration.

5(c).—From the following list, select the code that describes the type of annuity that will be provided for the participant. Enter the type of annuity that normally accrues under the plan at the time of the participant's separation from service covered by the plan (or for a plan to which more than one employer contributes at the time the participant incurs the second consecutive one-year break in service under the plan).

a. A single sum

b. Annuity payable over fixed number of years

c. Life annuity

d. Life annuity with period certain

e. Cash refund life annuity

f. Modified cash refund life annuity

g. Joint and last survivor life annuity

m. Other

5(d).—From the following list, select the code that describes the benefit payment frequency during a 12-month period.

a. Lump sum

b. Annually

c. Semiannually

d. Quarterly

e. Monthly

m. Other

5(e).—For a defined benefit plan, enter the amount of the periodic payment that a participant would normally be entitled to receive under 5(c), commencing at normal retirement age. However, if it is more expedient to show the amount of periodic payment the participant would be entitled to receive at early retirement date, enter that amount.

For a plan to which more than one employer contributes, if the amount of the periodic payment cannot be accurately determined because the plan administrator does not maintain complete records of covered service, enter an estimated amount and add the letter "X" in column 5(c) in addition to the annuity code to indicate that it is an estimate. If, from records maintained by the plan administrator, it cannot be determined whether the participant is entitled to any deferred vested benefit, but there is reason to believe he or she may be entitled, leave column 5(e) blank and enter "Y" in column 5(c) in addition to the annuity code.

5(f).—For a defined contribution plan, if the plan states that a participant's share of the fund will be determined on the basis of units, enter the number of units credited to the participant.

If, under the plan, participation is determined on the basis of shares of stock of the employer, enter the number of shares and add the letter "S" to indicate shares. A number without the "S" will be interpreted to mean units.

5(g).—For defined contribution plans, enter the value of the participant's account at the time of separation.

6.—If, after a participant has been reported on Schedule SSA, the participant:

(i) is paid some or all of the deferred vested retirement benefit, or

(ii) forfeits all of the deferred vested retirement benefit,

the plan administrator may, at its option, request that the participant's deferred vested benefit be deleted from Social Security Administration's records. Information reported in item 6, columns (a) through (g), must be the exact information previously reported on Schedule SSA for the participant.

If this option is chosen because the participant is paid some of the deferred vested benefit, the reporting requirements described in "Cessation of Payment of Benefits" above apply if payment of the benefit ceases before all of the benefit is paid to the participant.

Also, if a person was erroneously reported on a prior Schedule SSA, use item 6 to delete this information from Social Security Administration's records.

Signature.—This form must be signed by the plan administrator. If more than one Schedule SSA is filed for one plan, only page one should be signed.

Appendix A

Form **5500-C/R**

Department of the Treasury
Internal Revenue Service

Department of Labor
Pension and Welfare Benefits Administration

Pension Benefit Guaranty Corporation

Return/Report of Employee Benefit Plan
(With fewer than 100 participants)

This form is required to be filed under sections 104 and 4065 of the Employee Retirement Income Security Act of 1974 and sections 6039D, 6047(e), 6057(b), and 6058(a) of the Internal Revenue Code, referred to as the Code.

▶ See separate instructions.

OMB No. 1210-0016

1992

This Form Is Open to Public Inspection.

For the calendar plan year 1992 or fiscal plan year beginning , 1992, and ending , 19

You must check either box (5) or (6), whichever is applicable. See instructions.

A If (1) through (4) do not apply to this year's return/report, leave the boxes unmarked. This return/report is:

(1) ☐ the first return/report filed for the plan;
(2) ☐ an amended return/report;
(3) ☐ the final return/report filed for the plan; or
(4) ☐ a short plan year return/report (less than 12 months).

For IRS Use Only

EP–ID

(5) **Form 5500-C filer check here** ☐
(Complete only pages 1 and 3 through 6.) (Code section 6039D filers see instructions on page 6.)

(6) **Form 5500-R filer check here** ☐
(Complete only pages 1 and 2. Detach pages 3 through 6 before filing.) If you checked box (1) or (3), you must file a Form 5500-C. (See page 6 of the instructions.)

If the preprinted information in 1a through 6d is incorrect, please correct it; if any information is missing, please add it. Be sure to include this page with your completed return/report.

B IF YOU CORRECT ANY OF THE PREPRINTED INFORMATION OR ADD MISSING INFORMATION IN 1a THROUGH 6d, CHECK HERE ▶ ☐
C If your plan year changed since the last return/report, check here ▶ ☐
D If you filed for an extension of time to file this return/report, check here and attach a copy of the approved extension ▶ ☐

1a Name and address of plan sponsor (employer, if for a single-employer plan) (Address should include room or suite no.)

1b Employer identification number

1c Sponsor's telephone number

1d Business code (see instructions, page 19)

1e CUSIP issuer number

2a Name and address of plan administrator (if same as plan sponsor, enter "Same")

2b Administrator's employer identification no.

2c Administrator's telephone number

3 If you are filing this page without the preprinted historical plan information and the name, address, and EIN of the plan sponsor or plan administrator has changed since the last return/report filed for this plan, enter the information from the last return/report in 3a and/or 3b and complete 3c.

a Sponsor .... EIN .... Plan number ....
b Administrator .... EIN ....
c If 3a indicates a change in the sponsor's name, address, and EIN, is this a change in sponsorship only? (See instruction 3c on page 9 for the definition of sponsorship.) Enter "Yes" or "No." ▶ ....

4 **ENTITY CODE.** (If not shown, enter the applicable code from page 9 of the instructions.) ▶

5a Name of plan ▶ ....

5b Effective date of plan (mo., day, yr.)

5c Three-digit plan number ▶

All filers must complete 6a through 6d, as applicable.

6a ☐ Welfare benefit plan   6b ☐ Pension benefit plan
(If the correct codes are not preprinted below, enter the applicable codes from page 9 of the instructions in the boxes.)

6c Pension plan features. (If the correct codes are not preprinted below, enter the applicable pension plan feature codes from page 10 of the instructions in the boxes.)

6d ☐ Fringe benefit plan. Attach Schedule F (Form 5500). See instructions.

Under penalties of perjury and other penalties set forth in the instructions, I declare that I have examined this return/report, including accompanying schedules and statements, and to the best of my knowledge and belief, it is true, correct, and complete.

Signature of employer/plan sponsor ▶ .... Date ▶ ....
Type or print name of individual signing for employer/plan sponsor ....
Signature of plan administrator ▶ .... Date ▶ ....
Type or print name of individual signing for plan administrator ....

For Paperwork Reduction Act Notice, see page 1 of the instructions.   Cat. No. 10957K   Form **5500-C/R** (1992)

The Tools and Techniques of Employee Benefit and Retirement Planning

393

Form 5500-C R (1992)   **5500-R filers complete this page. 5500-C filers skip this page and complete pages 3 through 6.**   Page 2

		Yes	No
6e	Other plan features: **(1)** ☐ Master trust **(2)** ☐ Common/Collective trust **(3)** ☐ Pooled separate account		

7a Total participants: **(1)** At the beginning of plan year ▶ .... **(2)** At the end of plan year ▶ ....

b Enter number of participants with account balances at the end of the plan year (defined benefit plans do not complete this item) ▶ ....

c **(1)** Were any participants in the pension benefit plan separated from service with a deferred vested benefit for which a Schedule SSA (Form 5500) is required to be attached? (See instructions.) . . . . **7c(1)**

(2) If "Yes," enter the number of separated participants required to be reported ▶

8a Was this plan terminated during this plan year or any prior plan year? If "Yes," enter the year ▶ **8a**

b Were all the plan assets either distributed to participants or beneficiaries, transferred to another plan, or brought under the control of PBGC? **8b**

c If 8a is "Yes" and the plan is covered by PBGC, is the plan continuing to file PBGC Form 1 and pay premiums until the end of the plan year in which assets are distributed or brought under the control of PBGC? **8c**

9 Is this a plan established or maintained pursuant to one or more collective bargaining agreements? **9**

10 If any benefits are provided by an insurance company, insurance service, or similar organization, enter the number of Schedules A (Form 5500), Insurance Information, that are attached. If none, enter "-0-." ▶

11a **(1)** Were any plan amendments adopted during this plan year? If "No," complete (2) below and go to item 12a . . **11a(1)**

(2) Enter the date the most recent amendment was adopted . . . . ▶ mo.......day .....yr. .....

b If 11a is "Yes," did any amendment result in a retroactive reduction of accrued benefits for any participant? **11b**

c If 11a is "Yes," did any amendment change the information contained in the latest summary plan description or summary description of modifications available at the time of the amendment? **11c**

d If 11c is "Yes," has a summary plan description or summary description of modifications that reflects the plan amendments referred to in 11c been both furnished to participants and filed with the Department of Labor? **11d**

12a If this is a pension benefit plan subject to the minimum funding standards, has the plan experienced a funding deficiency for this plan year? Defined benefit plans must answer this question and attach Schedule B (Form 5500) **12a**

b If 12a is "Yes," have you filed Form 5330 to pay the excise tax? **12b**

13a Total plan assets as of the beginning .... and end .... of the plan year

b Total liabilities as of the beginning .... and end .... of the plan year

c Net assets as of the beginning .... and end .... of the plan year

14 For this plan year, enter: **a** Plan income .... **d** Plan contributions ....

b Expenses .... **e** Total benefits paid ....

c Net income (loss) **(subtract 14b from 14a)**

15 The following applies to item 15: (i) you may **NOT** use N/A in response to any line item, and (ii) if "Yes" is checked, you must enter a dollar amount in the amount column.

	During this plan year:		Yes	No	Amount
a	Was this plan covered by a fidelity bond?	**15a**			
b	If 15a is "Yes," enter the name of the surety company ▶				
c	Was there any loss to the plan, whether or not reimbursed, caused by fraud or dishonesty? . . .	**15c**			
d	Was there any sale, exchange, or lease of any property between the plan and the employer, any fiduciary, any of the five most highly paid employees of the employer, any owner of a 10% or more interest in the employer, or relatives of any such persons?	**15d**			
e	Was there any loan or extension of credit by the plan to the employer, any fiduciary, any of the five most highly paid employees of the employer, any owner of a 10% or more interest in the employer, or relatives of any such persons?	**15e**			
f	Did the plan acquire or hold any employer security or employer real property?	**15f**			
g	Has the plan granted an extension on any delinquent loan owed to the plan?	**15g**			
h	Has the employer owed contributions to the plan which are more than 3 months overdue? . . .	**15h**			
i	Were any loans by the plan or fixed income obligations due the plan classified as uncollectible or in default as of the close of the plan year?	**15i**			
j	Has any plan fiduciary had a financial interest in excess of 10% in any party providing services to the plan or received anything of value from any such party?	**15j**			
k	Did the plan at any time hold 20% or more of its assets in any single security, debt, mortgage, parcel of real estate, or partnership/joint venture interests?	**15k**			
l	Did the plan at any time engage in any transaction or series of related transactions involving 20% or more of the current value of plan assets?	**15l**			
m	Were there any noncash contributions made to the plan the value of which was set without an appraisal by an independent third party?	**15m**			
n	Were there any purchases of nonpublicly traded securities by the plan the value of which was set without an appraisal by an independent third party?	**15n**			
o	Has the plan reduced or failed to provide any benefit when due under the plan because of insufficient assets?	**15o**			

16a Is the plan covered under the Pension Benefit Guaranty Corporation termination insurance program? ☐ Yes ☐ No ☐ Not determined

b If 16a is "Yes" or "Not determined," enter the employer identification number and the plan number used to identify it.

Employer identification number ▶ ....   Plan number ▶

The Tools and Techniques of Employee Benefit and Retirement Planning

Form 5500-C/R (1992)   **5500-C filers complete this page and pages 4 through 6. (See instructions on page 13.)**   Page **3**

6e Check all applicable investment arrangements below (see instructions):

   (1) ☐ Master trust   **(2)** ☐ 103-12 investment entity

   (3) ☐ Common/collective trust   **(4)** ☐ Pooled separate account

....

....

....

....

  f Single-employer plans enter the tax year end of the employer in which this plan year ends ▶ Month .... Day .... Year ....

  g Is any part of this plan funded by an insurance contract described in Code section 412(i)? . . . . . .   ☐ Yes ☐ No

  h If 6g is "Yes," was the part subject to the minimum funding standards for either of the prior two plan years? . . .   ☐ Yes ☐ No

7a Total participants: **(1)** At the beginning of plan year ▶ .... **(2)** At the end of plan year ▶ ....

  b Enter number of participants with account balances at the end of the plan year. (Defined benefits plans do not complete this item.) ▶ ....

  c Number of participants that terminated employment during the plan year with accrued benefits that were less than 100% vested ▶ ....

		Yes	No
d (1) Were any participants in the pension benefit plan separated from service with a deferred vested benefit for which a Schedule SSA (Form 5500) is required to be attached?	**7d(1)**		
(2) If "Yes," enter the number of separated participants required to be reported ▶			
8a Was this plan ever amended since its effective date? If "Yes," complete 8b and, if the amendment was adopted in this plan year, complete 8c through 8e	**8a**		
b If 8a is "Yes," enter the date the most recent amendment was adopted ▶ Month .... Day .... Year			
c Did any amendment during the current plan year result in the retroactive reduction of accrued benefits for any participant?	**8c**		
d During this plan year, did any amendment change the information contained in the latest summary plan description or summary description of modifications available at the time of amendment?	**8d**		
e If 8d is "Yes," has a summary plan description or summary description of modifications that reflects the plan amendments referred to in 8d been both furnished to participants and filed with the Department of Labor?	**8e**		
9a Was this plan terminated during this plan year or any prior plan year? If "Yes," enter year ▶	**9a**		
b Were all plan assets either distributed to participants or beneficiaries, transferred to another plan, or brought under the control of PBGC?	**9b**		
c Was a resolution to terminate this plan adopted during this plan year or any prior plan year?	**9c**		
d If 9a or 9c is "Yes," have you received a favorable determination letter from the IRS for the termination?	**9d**		
e If 9d is "No," has a determination letter been requested from the IRS?	**9e**		
f If 9a or 9c is "Yes," have participants and beneficiaries been notified of the termination or the proposed termination? .	**9f**		
g If 9a is "Yes" and the plan is covered by PBGC, is the plan continuing to file a PBGC Form 1 and pay premiums until the end of the plan year in which assets are distributed or brought under the control of PBGC?	**9g**		
h During this plan year, did any trust assets revert to the employer for which the Code section 4980 excise tax is due? .	**9h**		
i If 9h is "Yes," enter the amount of tax paid with Form 5330 ▶ $			

10a Was this plan merged or consolidated into another plan(s), or were assets or liabilities transferred to another plan(s) since the end of the plan year covered by the last return/report Form 5500 or 5500-C which was filed for this plan (or during this plan year if this is the first return/report)? If "Yes," complete 10b through 10e, and see the instructions for 9a to complete item 9 if the plan was terminated **10a**

   If "Yes," identify the other plan(s):   **c** Employer identification number(s)   **d** Plan number(s)

  b Name of plan(s) ▶ ....

  e If required, has a Form 5310-A been filed? . . . .   ☐ Yes ☐ No

		Yes	No
11 Enter the plan funding arrangement code from page 14 of the instructions ▶	**12** Enter the plan benefit arrangement code from page 14 of the instructions ▶		
13 Is this a plan established or maintained pursuant to one or more collective bargaining agreements?	**13**		
14 If any benefits are provided by an insurance company, insurance service, or similar organization, enter the number of Schedules A (Form 5500), Insurance Information, that are attached. If none, enter "-0-." ▶			

Form 5500-C/R (1992)   Page **4**

Welfare Plans Do Not Complete Items 15 Through 25. Skip To Item 26.

			Yes	No
15a	If this is a defined benefit plan subject to the minimum funding standards for this plan year, is Schedule B (Form 5500) required to be attached? (If this is a defined contribution plan, leave blank.) . . . . If "Yes," attach Schedule B (Form 5500).	**15a**		
b	If this is a defined contribution plan (i.e., money purchase or target benefit), is it subject to the minimum funding standards (if a waiver was granted, see instructions)? (If this is a defined benefit plan, leave blank.) . . . . If "Yes," complete **(1)**, **(2)**, and **(3)** below:	**15b**		

    (1) Amount of employer contribution required for the plan year under Code section 412 **15b(1)** $

    (2) Amount of contribution paid by the employer for the plan year . . . . **15b(2)** $

    Enter date of last payment by employer ▶ Month ..... Day ...... Year ......

    (3) If **(1)** is greater than **(2)**, subtract **(2)** from **(1)** and enter the funding deficiency here. Otherwise, enter -0-. (If you have a funding deficiency, file Form 5330.) . . **15b(3)** $

			Yes	No
16	Has the annual compensation of each participant taken into account under the current plan year been limited to $228,860?	**16**		
17a (1)	Did the plan distribute any annuity contracts this year? (See instructions.)	**17a(1)**		
(2)	If **(1)** is "Yes," did these contracts contain a requirement that the spouse consent before any distributions under the contract are made in a form other than a qualified joint and survivor annuity?	**17a(2)**		
b	Did the plan make distributions to participants or beneficiaries in a form other than a qualified joint and survivor annuity (a life annuity if a single person) or a qualified preretirement survivor annuity (exclude deferred annuity contracts)? . . .	**17b**		
c	Did the plan make distributions or loans to married participants and beneficiaries without the required consent of the participant's spouse?	**17c**		
d	Upon plan amendment or termination, do the accrued benefits of every participant include the subsidized benefits that the participant may become entitled to receive subsequent to the plan amendment or termination?	**17d**		
18	Were distributions, if any, made in accordance with the requirements of Code sections 411(a)(11) and 417(e)? (See instructions.)	**18**		
19	Have any contributions been made or benefits accrued in excess of the Code section 415 limits, as amended by the Tax Reform Act of 1986?	**19**		
20	Has the plan made the required distributions in 1992 under Code section 401(a)(9)? (See instructions.)	**20**		

21 Check if you are applying either of the following in completing items **21a** through **21o** (see instructions):

    (i) ☐ Reasonable, good faith interpretation of the nondiscrimination provisions

    (ii) ☐ Substantiation guidelines

    If you checked **21(ii)**, enter the first day of the plan year for which data is being submitted ▶ mo. .. day .. yr. ....

			Yes	No
a	Does the employer apply the separate line of business rules of Code section 414(r) when testing this plan for the coverage and discrimination tests requirements of Code sections 410(b) and 401(a)(4)?	**21a**		
b	If **21a** is "Yes," enter the total number of separate lines of business claimed by the employer . . . ▶ .... If more than one separate line of business, see instructions for additional information to attach.			
c	Does the employer apply the mandatory disaggregation rules under Income Tax Regulations section 1.410(b)–7(c)? If "Yes," see instructions for additional information to attach	**21c**		
d	In testing whether this plan satisfies the coverage and discrimination tests of Code sections 410(b) and 401(a), does the employer aggregate plans?	**21d**		
e	Does the employer restructure the plan into component plans to satisfy the coverage and discrimination tests of Code sections 410(b) and 401(a)(4)?	**21e**		

    f If you meet either one of the following exceptions, check the applicable box to tell us which exception you meet and do NOT complete the rest of question 21:

        (1) ☐ No highly compensated employee benefited under the plan at any time during the plan year;

        (2) ☐ This is a collectively bargained plan that benefits only collectively bargained employees, no more than 2% of whom are professional employees.

			Yes	No
g	Did any leased employee perform services for the employer at any time during the plan year?	**21g**		

			Number
h	Enter the total number of employees of the employer. Employer includes entities aggregated with the employer under Code section 414(b), (c), or (m). Include leased employees and self-employed individuals	**21h**	
i	Enter the total number of employees excludable under the plan because of: *(1)* failure to meet requirements for minimum age and years of service; *(2)* collectively bargained employees; *(3)* nonresident aliens who receive no earned income from U.S. sources; and *(4)* minimum hours of service/last day rule?	**21i**	

Form 5500-C/R (1992)

Page **5**

		Number	

j Enter the number of nonexcludable employees (subtract line **21i** from line **21h**) . . . . | **21j** |

k Do 100% of the nonexcludable employees entered on line **21j** benefit under the plan? . . . ☐ Yes ☐ No

   If line **21k** is "Yes," do NOT complete lines **21l** through **21o**.

l Enter the number of nonexcludable employees (line **21j**) who are highly compensated employees . . . . . . | **21l** |

m Enter the number of nonexcludable employees who benefit under the plan . . . . | **21m** |

n Enter the number of employees entered on line **21m** who are highly compensated employees . . . . . . | **21n** |

o This plan satisfies the coverage requirements on the basis of (check one):

   (1) ☐ The average benefits test   (2) ☐ The ratio percentage test—enter value ▶

	Yes	No

22a Is it or was it ever intended that this plan qualify under Code section 401(a)? If "Yes," complete **22b** and **22c** . . . | **22a** |

  b Enter the date of the most recent IRS determination letter . . . . Month . . . . Year . . . .

  c Is a determination letter request pending with the IRS? | **22c** |

23a Does the plan hold any assets that have a fair market value that is not readily determinable on an established market? (If "Yes," answer **23b**.) . . . | **23a** |

  b Were all the assets referred to in **23a** valued during the 1992 plan year by an independent third-party appraiser? . . | **23b** |

  c If **23b** is "No," enter the value of the assets that were not valued by an independent third-party appraiser during the 1992 plan year . . . . ▶ | **23c** |

  d Enter the date the assets in **23c** were valued by an independent third-party appraiser. (If more than one date, enter the earliest date.) ▶ . . . .

   (If this plan has NO ESOP features, leave **23e** blank and go to **24**.)

  e If dividends paid on employer securities held by the ESOP were used to make payments on ESOP loans, enter the amount of the dividends used to make the payments . . ▶ | **23e** |

24 Does the employer/sponsor listed in **1a** of this form maintain other qualified pension benefit plans? . . . | **24** |

   If "Yes," enter the total number of plans, including this plan ▶

25a Is the plan covered under the Pension Benefit Guaranty Corporation termination insurance program? . . . . ☐ Yes ☐ No ☐ Not determined

  b If **25a** is "Yes" or "Not determined," enter the employer identification number and the plan number used to identify it.

   Employer identification number ▶   Plan number ▶

26 The following applies to item 26: (i) you may **NOT** use **N/A** in response to any line item, and (ii) if "Yes" is checked, you must enter a dollar amount in the amount column.

	Yes	No	Amount

   During this plan year:

a Was this plan covered by a fidelity bond? . . . . | **26a** |

b If **26a** is "Yes," enter the name of the surety company ▶ . . . .

c Was there any loss to the plan, whether or not reimbursed, caused by fraud or dishonesty? . . . | **26c** |

d Was there any sale, exchange, or lease of any property between the plan and the employer, any fiduciary, any of the five most highly paid employees of the employer, any owner of a 10% or more interest in the employer, or relatives of any such persons? . . . . | **26d** |

e Was there any loan or extension of credit by the plan to the employer, any fiduciary, any of the five most highly paid employees of the employer, any owner of a 10% or more interest in the employer, or relatives of any such persons? . . . . | **26e** |

f Did the plan acquire or hold any employer security or employer real property? . . . . . . | **26f** |

g Has the plan granted an extension on any delinquent loan owed to the plan? . . . . . . | **26g** |

h Has the employer owed contributions to the plan which are more than 3 months overdue? . . . | **26h** |

i Were any loans by the plan or fixed income obligations due the plan classified as uncollectible or in default as of the close of the plan year? . . . . . . | **26i** |

j Has any plan fiduciary had a financial interest in excess of 10% in any party providing services to the plan or received anything of value from any such party? . . . . | **26j** |

k Did the plan at any time hold 20% or more of its assets in any single security, debt, mortgage, parcel of real estate, or partnership/joint venture interests? . . . . | **26k** |

l Did the plan at any time engage in any transaction or series of related transactions involving 20% or more of the current value of plan assets? . . . . . . | **26l** |

m Were there any noncash contributions made to the plan whose value was set without an appraisal by an independent third party? . . . . | **26m** |

n Were there any purchases of nonpublicly traded securities by the plan whose value was set without an appraisal by an independent third party? . . . . . . | **26n** |

o Has the plan reduced or failed to provide any benefit when due under the terms of the plan because of insufficient assets? . . . . | **26o** |

Form 5500-C/R (1992)   Page **6**

27 Current value of plan assets and liabilities at the beginning and end of the plan year. Combine the value of plan assets held in more than one trust. Allocate the value of the plan's interest in a commingled trust containing the assets of more than one plan on a line-by-line basis unless the trust meets one of the specific exceptions described in the instructions. Do not enter the value of the portion of an insurance contract which guarantees during this plan year to pay a specific dollar benefit at a future date. **Round off amounts to the nearest dollar. Any other amounts are subject to rejection. Plans with no assets at the beginning and end of the plan year enter -0- on line 27f.**

Assets		(a) Beginning of year	(b) End of year
a	Cash	27a	
b	Receivables	27b	
c	Investments:		
	(1) U.S. Government securities	27c(1)	
	(2) Corporate debt and equity instruments	27c(2)	
	(3) Real estate and mortgages (other than to participants)	27c(3)	
	(4) Loans to participants:		
	A Mortgages	(4)A	
	B Other	(4)B	
	(5) Other	27c(5)	
	(6) Total investments (add (1) through (5)) ▶	27c(6)	
d	Buildings and other property used in plan operations	27d	
e	Other assets	27e	
f	Total assets (add a, b, c(6), d, and e) ▶	27f	
Liabilities			
g	Payables	27g	
h	Acquisition indebtedness	27h	
i	Other liabilities	27i	
j	Total liabilities (add g through i) ▶	27j	
k	Net assets (f minus j) ▶	27k	

28 Plan income, expenses, and changes in net assets for the plan year. Include all income and expenses of the plan including any trust(s) or separately maintained fund(s) and any payments/receipts to/from insurance carriers. **Round off amounts to the nearest dollar. Any other amounts are subject to rejection.**

Income		(a) Amount	(b) Total
a	Contributions received or receivable in cash from:		
	(1) Employer(s) (including contributions on behalf of self-employed individuals)	28a(1)	
	(2) Employees	28a(2)	
	(3) Others	28a(3)	
	(4) Add (1) through (3)	28a(4)	
b	Noncash contributions (enter total of a(4) and b in column (b))	28b	
c	Earnings from investments (interest, dividends, rents, royalties)	28c	
d	Net realized gain (loss) on sale or exchange of assets	28d	
e	Other income (specify) ▶	28e	
f	Total income (add b through e) ▶	28f	
Expenses			
g	Distribution of benefits and payments to provide benefits:		
	(1) Directly to participants or their beneficiaries	28g(1)	
	(2) Other	28g(2)	
	(3) Total distribution of benefits and payments to provide benefits	28g(3)	
h	Administrative expenses (salaries, fees, commissions, insurance premiums)	28h	
i	Other expenses (specify) ▶	28i	
j	Total expenses (add g through i) ▶	28j	
k	Net income (loss) (subtract j from f) ▶	28k	

*U.S. Government Printing Office: 1993 — 315-367

The Tools and Techniques of Employee Benefit and Retirement Planning

Appendix B

COMMON CONTROL RULES

COMMONLY CONTROLLED EMPLOYERS

In designing qualified plans and other employee benefit plans, the plan designer often deals with employer organizations (incorporated or unincorporated) that are owned or controlled in common with other such organizations. Plan coverage must then sometimes be coordinated among members of the commonly controlled group of employers.

Common control must be taken into account in identifying the "employer" in an employee benefit plan under a variety of complex rules in the Internal Revenue Code. The objective of these rules is to prevent a business owner from getting around the coverage and nondiscrimination requirements for qualified plans by artificially segregating employees to be benefited from a plan into one organization, with the remainder being employed by subsidiaries or organizations with lesser plan benefits or no plan at all. While this is still technically possible, the controlled group rules restrict this practice considerably.

Overview of Controlled Group Rules

The common control rules are inherently complicated, because the forms in which businesses can be owned are complicated. Complexity in the ownership structure of a business reflects many non-tax considerations such as capital structure and administrative needs; consequently these common control rules probably will always be complicated. There are four sets of these common control rules:

1. Under Code section 414(b), all employees of all corporations in a *controlled group* of corporations are treated as employed by a single employer for purposes of Sections 401, 408(k), 410, 411, 415, and 416. The major impact of this comes from the participation rules of Section 410, which, in effect, require the participation and coverage tests to be applied to the entire controlled group, rather than to any single corporation in the group. Code section 414(c) provides similar rules for commonly controlled partnerships and proprietorships.

2. Code section 414(m) provides that employees of an *affiliated service group* are treated as employed by a single employer. This requirement similarly has its major impact in determining participation in a qualified plan, but it applies to other employee benefit requirements as well.

3. A *leased employee* is treated as an employee of the lessor corporation under certain circumstances under Code section 414(n).

4. If a qualified plan covers a partner or proprietor who owns more than 50 percent of another business, then the plan or a comparable plan must provide contributions or benefits that are at least as favorable as those provided for the partner or proprietor for employees of the controlled business (Code section 401(d)).

Some examples will give a general idea of the impact of these provisions on plan design; these are discussed in detail later. *Note*: the common thread of these examples is that the related organization's employees must be *taken into account* in applying the participation rules. This does not mean that these employees must necessarily be covered.

Example: Alpha Corporation owns 80 percent of the stock of Beta Corporation. Alpha and Beta are members of a parent subsidiary-controlled group of corporations. In applying the participation and coverage rules of section 410 of the Code, Alpha and Beta must be considered as a single employer.

Example: Bert and Harry own stock as follows:

Owner	Corporation A	Corporation B
Bert	60%	60%
Harry	30	30
	90%	90%

Corporations A and B are a brother-sister controlled group. Thus, A and B must be considered as a single employer for purposes of Code section 410 and most other qualified plan rules.

Example: Medical Services, Inc., provides administrative and laboratory services for Dr. Sam and Dr. Joe, each of whom is an incorporated sole practitioner. Dr. Sam and Dr. Joe each own 50 percent of Medical Services, Inc. If either Dr. Sam or Dr. Joe adopts a qualified plan, employees of Medical Services, Inc., will have to be taken into account in determining if plan coverage is nondiscriminatory.

Example: Calculators Incorporated, an actuarial firm, contracts with Temporary Services, Inc., an employee-leasing firm, to lease employees on a substantially full-time basis. The leased employees will have to be taken into account in determining nondiscrimination in any qualified plan of Calculators, unless Temporary maintains a minimum (10 percent nonintegrated) money-purchase pension plan for the leased employees.

Example: Stan and Fran are partners in a construction business. Fran is also a 60 percent partner in a road paving business that has 50 employees. If Stan and Fran's partnership adopts a qualified plan covering Stan and Fran, then the plan must either cover the 50 employees of the road paving business or the road paving business must provide a plan with contributions and benefits comparable to that provided for Stan and Fran.

CONTROLLED GROUPS OF CORPORATIONS AND OTHER BUSINESS ORGANIZATIONS

Under sections 414(b) and (c) of the Code, all employees of members of a controlled group of corporations or controlled group of trades or businesses (whether or not incorporated) that are under common control are treated as employed by a single employer for purposes of Sections 401, 408(k), 410, 411, 415, and 416. This covers most provisions of the qualified plan law. The most important impact relates to the coverage requirements of Code section 410. Thus, all employees of employers in a controlled group must be taken into account when determining whether a qualified plan maintained by any employer in the controlled group satisfies the percentage participation tests or the discretionary tests.

The existence of a controlled group is determined by applying the rules of Code section 1563(a), a section originally designed to inhibit corporations from breaking up into smaller units to take advantage of the graduated corporate tax rates. Under this provision, there are three types of controlled groups: parent-subsidiary controlled groups, brother-sister controlled groups, and combined groups.

Parent-Subsidiary Controlled Group

A parent-subsidiary controlled group is one or more chains of corporations connected through stock ownership with a common parent corporation if, with respect to the stock of each corporation (except the parent corporation):

At least 80 percent of the total combined voting power of all classes of stock entitled to vote or at least 80 percent

of the total value of shares of all classes of stock is owned by one or more corporations in the group and the common parent corporation satisfies the same 80 percent test with at least one other corporation in the group. Stock owned directly by any other corporation in the group is excluded in determining the parent corporation's ownership.

In applying this test to unincorporated trades or businesses, the 80 percent test is applied to an interest in profits or to a capital interest.

Example: Suppose Alpha Corporation owns 80 percent of the total combined voting power of all classes of stock entitled to vote of Beta Corporation. Beta Corporation owns stock that possesses at least 80 percent of the total value of shares of all classes of stock of Gamma Corporation. Alpha is the common parent, and the parent-subsidiary controlled group consists of Alpha, Beta, and Gamma.

Brother-Sister Controlled Group

A brother-sister controlled group consists of two or more corporations in which five or fewer individuals, estates, or trusts own (with attribution, as described below) stock possessing:

At least 80 percent of the total combined voting power or value of all classes of stock (excluding nonvoting stock which is limited and preferred as to dividends) of each corporation, and more than 50 percent of the total combined voting power or value of all classes of stock (excluding nonvoting stock, which is limited and preferred as to dividends) of each corporation, taking into account the stock ownership of each owner only to the extent that the owner's interest is identical in each corporation.

Examples: Corporations M, N, and O have only one class of stock, which is owned by five unrelated individuals as follows:

Investor	M	Percentage of Ownership in N	O	Identical Ownership in MNO
Alex	20%	10%	20%	10%
Bartley	20	30	10	10
Clay	20	20	30	20
Davis	20	20	20	20
Ensley	20	20	20	20
Total	100%	100%	100%	80%

Corporations M, N, and O constitute a brother-sister controlled group.

Another example illustrates some further complexities. Three corporations, Q, S, and T are owned by four unrelated individuals as follows:

	Percentage of Ownership in			Identical Ownership in		
Investor	Q	S	T	Q-S	Q-T	S-T
Walt	50%	25%	25.5%	25%	25.5%	25.0%
Xavier	50	25	25.5	25	25.5	25.0
Yolanda	0	25	24.5	0	0.0	24.5
Zorba	0	25	24.5	0	0.0	24.5
Totals	100%	100%	100%	50%	51%	99%

Corporation Q and S do not constitute a brother-sister controlled group, because, although four individuals together own 100 percent of each, taking only identical ownership into account, there is only 50 percent common control. Although identical ownership in Q and T adds up to 51 percent, they are not a brother-sister group—see the next example. Finally, S and T constitute a brother-sister controlled group, with identical ownership adding up to a total of 99 percent.

At one time, the IRS included an example in the regulations which, somewhat simplified, went as follows:

	Percentage of Ownership in			Identical Ownership in		
Investor	A	B	C	AB	AC	BC
1	100 %	60 %	60 %	60 %	60 %	60 %
2	0	40	0	0	0	0
3	0	0	40	0	0	0
Total	100 %	100 %	100 %	60 %	60 %	60 %

*100 percent under prior regulations; 60 percent under current regulations. See below.

The regulations asserted that AB, AC, and BC constituted brother-sister controlled groups, even though some of the owners held no interest at all in A, B, or C. This interpretation was declared invalid by the U.S. Supreme Court in *U.S. v. Vogel Fertilizer Company*.[1] The regulations now reflect this by providing that each person whose stock ownership is taken into account for purposes of the 80 percent requirement also must be a person whose stock ownership is counted toward the 50 percent requirement.[2] Under this interpretation, there are no brother-sister groups in this situation.

Combined Group

A combined group is three or more corporations each of which is a member of a parent-subsidiary group or a brother-sister group and one of which is a common parent of a parent-subsidiary group and also is included in a brother-sister group.

Example: Ken, an individual, owns 80 percent of the total combined voting power of all classes of stock of Steel Corporation and Lint Corporation. Lint Corporation owns 80 percent of the total combined voting power of all classes of the stock of Octopus Corporation. Steel and Lint are members of a brother-sister controlled group. Lint and Octopus are members of a parent-subsidiary group. Lint is the common parent of the parent-subsidiary group and also a member of the brother-sister group. Therefore, Steel, Lint, and Octopus constitute a combined group.

Stock Not Taken into Account in Controlled Group Determination

Certain stock is excluded from consideration in computing the percentages in the controlled group tests.[3] In general, note that excluding stock from consideration makes it more likely that the tests will be met, because the target shareholder's stock will be a larger percentage of the amount outstanding. This is the purpose of these exclusionary rules; in general, they are designed to thwart attempts to get around controlled group tests by transferring stock to various trusts or other entities, as the rules indicate.

First of all, nonvoting preferred stock and treasury stock are not taken into account.

In addition, if the parent owns 50 percent or more of the total combined voting power or value of all classes of stock in the potential subsidiary corporation, the following are not taken into account in determining the existence of a parent-subsidiary controlled group:

Stock in a subsidiary held by a trust that is part of a plan of deferred compensation for the benefit of the employees of the parent or the subsidiary.

Stock in the subsidiary owned by an individual who is a principal shareholder (5 percent or more of voting power or total value) or an officer of the potential parent.

Stock in the subsidiary owned by an employee of the subsidiary, if the stock is subject to conditions that run in favor of the parent or subsidiary and which substantially restrict the right to dispose of such stock. Stock subject to the typical buy-sell agreement generally would fall within this provision.

Stock in the subsidiary owned by a tax-exempt organization that is controlled directly or indirectly by the parent or subsidiary or by an individual, estate, or trust that is a principal shareholder of the parent, by an officer of the potential parent, or by any combination of the above.[4]

For purposes of the brother-sister controlled group tests, the following stock is excluded whenever five or fewer potential common owners own at least 50 percent of the total combined voting power or value of all classes of stock:

Stock held for the benefit of the employees of the corporation by a qualified retirement plan trust.

Stock owned by an employee of the corporation, if the stock is subject to restrictions that run in favor of any of the common owners of the corporation and which substantially restrict the right to dispose of the stock (with an exception for a bona fide reciprocal stock-purchase agreement).

Stock owned by a tax-exempt organization that is controlled directly or indirectly by the corporation, by an individual, estate, or trust that is a principal shareholder of the corporation, by an officer of the corporation, or by any combination of these.[5]

Constructive Ownership (Attribution) Rules

In determining the existence of a controlled group, an individual may be deemed to own not only stock owned directly but also stock owned by certain related parties.[6]

The following rules apply for both parent-subsidiary and brother-sister determinations[7]:

An option to acquire stock causes the optionholder to be treated as owning the stock.

Stock owned directly or indirectly by or for a partnership is considered owned by any partner having an interest of 5 percent or more in capital or profits, in proportion to the partner's interest in capital or profits (whichever is greater).

Stock owned directly or indirectly by an estate or trust (excluding a qualified trust) is considered owned by a beneficiary who has an actuarial interest of 5 percent or more in such stock, to the extent of the actuarial interest.

Stock owned directly or indirectly by or for any portion of a grantor trust is considered owned by the grantor.

Further attribution rules apply in the brother-sister situation.[8] These are:

Stock owned directly by or for a corporation is considered owned by any person who owns 5 percent or more in value of its stock in proportion to the percentage of corporate value owned by the person.

An individual is considered to own stock in a corporation owned directly or indirectly by or for his spouse (if not legally separated under a decree of divorce or separate maintenance), unless the person's ownership satisfies certain standards of remoteness set out in Section 1563(e)(5).

A parent is deemed to own stock owned directly or indirectly by or for his children, including legally adopted children, who are less than 21 years of age, and an individual less than 21 years old is deemed to own stock owned directly or indirectly by or for his parents, including legally adoptive parents.

If an individual owns more than 50 percent of the total combined voting power or value of all classes of stock in a corporation, the individual is considered as owning stock in the corporation owned directly or indirectly by or for his parents, grandparents, grandchildren, and children who have attained age 21.

The above attribution rules all can be used to provide reattribution to another owner, except that stock attributed under the family attribution rules is not reattributed.[9] This can result in very complex attribution patterns, in some cases.

Consequences of Controlled Group Status

Once again, all employees of all corporations that are members of a controlled group of corporations are treated as employed by a single employer for various purposes, specified in Code section 414(b). Probably the most significant of these consequences is the application of the coverage tests of section 410 of the Code. All three tests will be applied to the group as a whole, except to the extent that the tests can be applied to a subgroup constituting a separate line of business under Code section 414(r). This does not necessarily mean that a plan cannot qualify if it involves employees of only one member of a controlled group. The plan for a single company in the controlled group could qualify if it meets one of the three tests, such as the average-benefit test in particular.

It is also possible that the controlled group aggregation rules can be applied to the advantage of the employer. For example, a plan for a controlled group might meet the average-benefit test, even though in a given corporation included in the group there might be only one or two participants, both among the highest-paid employees of that corporation. Considered separately, the plan for that corporation would fail to qualify.

AFFILIATED SERVICE GROUP

The purpose and effect of the affiliated service group rules of Code section 414(m) are best understood by looking at the loophole that this provision was designed to close. This loophole typically involved professional corporations or partnerships that desired to exclude rank-and-file employees from qualified plans maintained for the professional owners.

Example: Consider a situation in which two physicians enter into an equal partnership for the practice of medicine. A similar alternative practice was for each doctor to form a one-person professional corporation and then have the professional corporation enter into a partnership. The partnership could then form a separate support business to provide all support services for the medical practice, and the support business would become the employer of all the support employees. Each of the doctors would own just 50 percent of the support organization. Under all the other aggregation rules discussed here, except for the affiliated service group rules, the doctors could each adopt a qualified plan covering only themselves and none of the regular employees. The affiliated service group rules basically eliminate this type of planning or restrict it severely.

The affiliated service group provisions provide complex rules under which the employees of an *affiliated service group* must be included in any qualified plans that benefit the owners. An affiliated service group includes the *service organization* and the professional organization itself. For purposes of most of the pension provisions, including the coverage and nondiscrimination rules, all employees of an affiliated service group are treated as being employed by a single employer.

An affiliated service group means a service organization and one or more organizations that meet one of the following two tests[10]:

1. A service organization that is a shareholder or partner in the first organization and regularly performs services for the first organization or is regularly associated with the first organization in performing services for third persons.

2. An organization in which a significant portion of its business is the performance of services of a type historically performed for the first organization or for

a service organization that is the shareholder or partner in the first organization. However, this applies only if 10 percent or more of the organization is owned by highly compensated employees (as defined in Chapter 23) of the first organization or any service organization that is a shareholder or partner in the first organization.

Under the proposed regulations, the rules apply primarily to service organizations of the type that provide professional services in the field of health, law, engineering, architecture, accounting, actuarial science, performing arts, consulting, or insurance. However, this list can be further expanded through regulations.[11]

Example: As an example of the operation of the affiliated service group rules, suppose Dr. VanDerslice incorporates and the corporation becomes a partner with the professional corporations of other doctors. Doctor VanDerslice's corporation regularly associates with the other professional corporations in performing services for a third person—individual patients, a hospital, and the like. Each corporation and the partnership of these corporations constitutes an affiliated service group, because the corporation is a service organization that is a partner with the others and is regularly associated with the partnership in performing services for third persons.

As is readily apparent, the affiliated service group rules go considerably beyond the loophole they were initially intended to close. Furthermore, the complexity of these rules is such that it is often difficult to determine whether they apply. Furthermore, many of the affiliated service group provisions involve a degree of subjective judgment—that is, ultimately they are up to the discretion of the IRS—unlike the controlled group rules which, though complex, are relatively mechanical. Thus, in doubtful cases, it is advisable to obtain a ruling from the IRS about whether an organization is a member of an affiliated service group.[12]

Employee Leasing

The leased employee provisions of Code section 414(n)[13] were designed to reduce the discrimination potential from an employer's choosing to lease employees from an independent employee leasing organization, rather than employ them directly. The purpose of this practice is to keep the employees technically off the payroll of the lessee business and, thus, outside the coverage of its qualified plans.

This practice is limited under current law. A leased employee is considered an employee of the lessee organization for which the services are performed if:

The employee has performed services on a substantially full-time basis for at least one year, and the services are of a type "historically performed, in the business field of the recipient, by employees."

This rule does not apply if the leasing organization itself maintains a "safe-harbor" plan for the leased employees meeting certain minimum requirements:

The plan must be a nonintegrated money-purchase plan with an employer contribution rate of at least 10 percent of compensation, and the plan must provide immediate participation and full and immediate vesting; and

All employees of the leasing organization with compensation of $1,000 or more over the past four years must be covered.

The safe-harbor exemption may not be used if leased employees constitute more than 20 percent to the recipient's (lessor's) nonhighly compensated work force.

Since 10 percent is a relatively modest plan contribution level, many leasing organizations are adopting this approach. Thus, employee leasing remains a viable method for minimizing plan benefits and contributions for low-level employees, even with the restrictions of Code section 414(n).

Because of the one-year requirement, the leasing provision has no impact on most short-term temporary help. Attempts to technically avoid this requirement by rotating leased employees may not be effective, because the one-year requirement is determined on the basis of cumulative service for the recipient. The requirement of treating the leased employee as an employee of the recipient does not begin until the leased employee has met the one-year service requirement.

Because of the relatively low safe-harbor provision, some employers might be tempted to convert all their employees to leased employees through some arrangement with a leasing organization. However, the IRS has taken the position that the Code provision applies only to bona fide employee leases. If the lease is not deemed bona fide, the employees will be treated for qualified plan purposes as if they were employed directly.

FOOTNOTES

1. 102 S. Ct. 821 (1982).
2. Reg. §1.1563-1(a)(3).
3. IRC Section 1563(c).
4. IRC Section 1563(c)(2)(A).
5. IRC Section 1563(c)(2)(B).
6. IRC Section 1563(e)(1).
7. IRC Section 1563(d).
8. IRC Section 1563(d)(2).
9. IRC Section 1563(f)(2).
10. Proposed regulations on "management-type" affiliated service groups have been withdrawn by the IRS. See CO-53-92, 1993-21 IRB 9.
11. IRC Section 414(m)(2).
12. A ruling can be obtained pursuant to Rev. Proc. 85-43, 1985-2 CB 501, as modified by Rev. Proc. 91-10, 1991-1 CB 439, Section 14.
13. Proposed regulations under Code section 414(n) have been withdrawn by the IRS. See CO-53-92, 1993-21 IRB 9.

APP FORM 101

RETIREMENT PLAN DATA AND ABSTRACT FORM

Prepared for _____

By _____

Date _____

SECTION I — RETIREMENT PLAN DATA

PART A — CLIENT PROFILE

A-1.   Legal Name _____

        Address _____

        _____ Zip _____

        Telephone Number _____

        Contact _____

A-2.   Employer (Taxpayer) Identification Number _____

A-3.   Nature of Enterprise (Check Appropriate Line)

        3.1 _____ Sole proprietorship   3.6 _____ Municipal corp. or government agency

        3.2 _____ Partnership   3.7 _____ Professional corporation

        3.3 _____ Business corporation   3.8 _____ Business or real estate trust

        3.4 _____ S corporation   3.9 _____ Other: specify

        3.5 _____ Exempt org. (Sec. _____)   _____

A-4.   Nature of Business (Principal Business Activity)0

        _____

        _____

        IRS business code number _____

A-5.   Accounting Method (Check One)

        _____ Cash   _____ Accrual

A-6.   Fiscal Year Ends _____
                                 (Month)   (Day)

A-7.   Date of Incorporation or Establishment

        _____ (Month and Year)

A-8.   State of Incorporation or Domicile _____

A-9.   Related Corporation or Unincorporated Entities, including Affiliated Service Groups (Names, Nature of Enterprises, Ownership Percentages of Related Enterprises)

        _____

        _____

        _____

        _____

        _____

A-10.   Predecessor Entities

    10.1 Name _____

    10.2 Nature of Entity _____

    10.3 Date of Establishment_____

    10.4 Date of Transfer_____

A-11.   What is the Approximate Rate of Employee Turnover as a Percent of the Active Group for the Past Five Years?

                19____   _____%

                19____   _____%

                19____   _____%

                19____   _____%

                19____   _____%

A-12.   Client Motives (For a New Benefit Program)

    _____

    _____

    _____

A-13.   Employee Groups under Consideration (For a New Benefit Program)

    13.1 _____ Salaried Employees

    13.2 _____ Hourly Employees

    13.3 _____ Collective-Bargaining Unit Employees

    13.4 _____ Leased Employees

    13.5 _____ Other

A-14.   Competitors in Industry (Details as to Their Compensation Programs)

    _____

    _____

    _____

A-15.   Local Nonindustry Employers (Details as to Their Compensation Programs)

    _____

    _____

    _____

    _____

PART B — FINANCIAL DATA

B-1.   Attach Balance Sheets (Last Two or Three Years) and Summarize

_____

_____

B-2.   Attach Profit and Loss Statements and Summarize

_____

_____

_____

_____

_____

_____

_____

B-3.   Summarize Earnings Projections

_____

_____

B-4.   What Type of Cost Commitment Can Be considered for a Pension or a Profit-Sharing Plan or Both?

4.1   _____% of payroll

4.2   _____% of profit

4.3   _____% of profit in excess of $_____

4.4 $_____ Flat dollar amount

4.5   Other _____

_____

PART C — CLIENT'S OTHER BENEFIT PROGRAMS

C-1. Nonqualified Retirement Plans

    1.1 Plans of general application _____

_____

_____

_____

    1.2 Personal plans (for individuals) _____

_____

_____

_____

C-2. Group Life Insurance

    2.1 How much _____

    2.2 Who is covered _____

    2.3 Beneficiary _____

    2.4 Premiums paid by

        (a) _____ Employer

        (b) _____ Employee

            _____ Payroll deduction

            _____ Other (specify) _____

    2.5 Carrier _____

C-3. Accidental Death and Dismemberment

    3.1 How much _____

    3.2 Who is covered _____

    3.3 Beneficiary _____

    3.4 Premiums paid by

        (a) _____ Employer

        (b) _____ Employee

            _____ Payroll deduction

            _____ Other (specify) _____

    3.5 Carrier _____

    3.6 Workmen's compensation offset

        _____ Yes   _____ No   Explain _____

3.7 All accidents covered

_____ Yes _____ No Explain _____

C-4. Long-Term Disability Coverage

4.1 How much _____ How long _____

4.2 Who is covered _____ Waiting period _____

4.3 Premiums paid by

_____ Employer

_____ Employee

_____ Payroll deduction

_____ Other (specify) _____

4.4 Carrier _____

4.5 All causes

_____ Yes _____ No Explain _____

4.6 Offsets
_____ Yes _____ No Explain _____

4.7 Definition of disability _____

_____

_____

C-5. Existing Qualified Retirement Plans (list the following for each plan—use additional sheets if necessary)

5.1 Name of plan _____

5.2 Circle type of plan: Defined-Benefit Money-Purchase Target Profit-Sharing

5.3 a. Collectively bargained plan?_____No _____Yes (attach relevant portions of collective bargaining agreement)

b. Multiemployer plan? _____No _____Yes

5.4 Eligibility: a. age _____ b. Waiting period _____ c. employee classification _____

5.5 Contribution rate: By employer _____ By employee _____

5.6 Benefit structure_____

5.7 Normal retirement benefit _____ At Age _____

5.8 Early retirement benefit _____ At Age _____

5.9 Death benefit _____

5.10 Disability benefit _____

Definition of disability _____

5.11 Vesting rate _____

5.12 Number of employees covered _____

5.13 Are there any employees who are covered by this plan to be covered by new plan? _____

If so, are there to be offset provisions? _____

PART D — EMPLOYEE CENSUS DATA

| Name | Sex | Date of Birth (or Age) | Date Hired (or Years of Service) | Position | Highly Compensated (HC) or Key (K) Employee? | Percent of Voting Stock | Annual Nondeferred Compensation |||| Social Security Number |
							Basic	Bonus	Overtime	Total	

Appendix C

SECTION II — RETIREMENT PLAN ABSTRACT

PART E — PLAN CHARACTERISTICS AND PROVISIONS

E-1.   Name of Plan _____

E-2.   Type of Plan

    2.1 _____ Defined-benefit: _____ Unit-benefit _____ Flat-benefit _____ Fixed-benefit

    2.2 _____ Defined-contribution money purchase

    2.3 _____ Target (assumed-benefit)

    2.4 _____ Profit-sharing

    2.5 _____ Thrift (savings)

    2.6 _____ Section 401(k)

    2.7 _____ Stock bonus

    2.8 _____ ESOP

    2.9 _____ Tax-deferred annuity (Section 403(b))

    2.10 _____ Other or combination of types (specify) _____

    _____

    _____

E-3.   Effective Date _____

E-4.   Anniversary Date _____

E-5.   Formal Name of Plan _____

E-6.   Eligibility Requirements

    6.1 Minimum age _____

    6.2 Waiting period _____

    6.3 Entry dates (explain) _____

    6.4 Employee classification _____

    _____

6.5   Other (specify) _____

_____

_____

E-7.   Past Service: Is Past Service with Prior Employer(s) to Count as Service with Company for Eligibility Purposes?

_____

For benefit computation purposes? _____

If yes, name prior employer(s) _____

_____

_____

_____

E-8.   Integration

8.1   _____   Nonintegrated

8.2   _____   Social security (OASDI)

8.3   _____   Railroad retirement act

E-9.   Type of Integration

9.1   _____   Excess (stepped up)

9.2   _____   Offset

E-10.   Integration Level

10.1   _____   Uniform integration break point $_____

10.2   _____   Covered compensation table I

10.3   _____   Covered compensation table II

10.4   _____   Other _____

_____

E-11.   Integration Benefit Formula _____

_____

_____

_____

E-12.   Other Offsets: Indicate the Contributions to or Benefits from Other Plans Which Are to be Used as Offsets to This Plan and Whether or Not Such Other Plans Are Qualified Plans under the Internal Revenue Code.

_____

_____

_____

_____

E-13.   Normal Retirement Benefit

    13.1   Formula

    13.2   Age _____

    13.3   Minimum years of service _____

    13.4   Minimum years of plan participation _____

    13.5   Other _____

E-14.   Early Retirement Benefit

    14.1   Formula

    14.2   Age _____

    14.3   Minimum years of service _____

    14.4   Minimum years of plan participation _____

    14.5   Other _____

E-15.   Deferred Retirement Benefit

    15.1   Formula

    15.2   Maximum age _____

    15.3   Minimum years of service _____

    15.4   Minimum years of plan participation _____

    15.5   Other _____

E-16. Disability Retirement

    16.1 Formula

    16.2 Minimum age _____

    16.3 Minimum years of service _____

    16.4 Minimum years of plan participation _____

    16.5 Benefit commencement date _____

    16.6 Definition of disability _____

        (a) _____ Disability for social security purposes

        (b) _____ Other (specify) _____

            _____

            _____

            _____

E-17. Death Benefits

    17.1 Preretirement _____

            _____

            _____

    17.2 Postretirement _____

            _____

            _____

E-18. Emergency Distributions _____

        _____

        _____

E-19. Describe Deferral or Salary Reduction Option (Section 401(k) Plan) _____

        _____

        _____

E-20. Withdrawal of Participant Contributions

    20.1 When _____

    20.2 How much _____

    20.3 Earnings on contributions _____

20.4 Penalty _____

20.5 Notice requirement _____

E-21. Loans to participants

21.1 Maximum (if other than §72(p) limit ($50,000, ½ vested benefit, $10,000)) _____

21.2 Minimum _____

21.3 Interest rate _____

21.4 Duration _____

E-22. Other Benefits (specify) _____ _____

_____

_____

E-23. Contributions

23.1 Rate of employer contributions

(a) _____ Discretionary

(b) _____ As actuarially determined

(c) _____ Formula (state formula)

23.2 Rate of Participant Contributions

(a) _____ Voluntary

Minimum _____

Maximum _____

(b) _____ Required

Amount of rate _____

Method of collection

_____ Payroll withholding

_____ Other (specify) _____

_____

23.3 Employer Contributions To Be In

(a) _____ Cash

(b) _____ Stock

(c) _____ Other

E-24. Use of Forfeitures (If Any)

    24.1   _____ To reduce subsequent employer contributions

    24.2   _____ Reallocated among plan participants (defined-contribution only) state reallocation basis: _____

_____

E-25. Employer Contribution Allocation Formula

    25.1   _____ None. Unallocated funding

    25.2   _____ Prorate according to compensation

    25.3   _____ Prorate according to service

    25.4   _____ Prorate according to compensation and service

    25.5   _____ According to amounts contributed by employees

    25.6   _____ Other (specify) _____

_____

E-26. Vesting Schedule (Employer Contributions, Amounts Attributable to Employer Contributions, or Benefits Purchased with Employer Contributions)

    26.1 5-year vesting _____

    26.2 3- to 7-year vesting _____

    26.3 100% vesting with 2-year eligibility period _____

    26.4 Other basis (specify) _____

_____

    26.5 Set forth the vesting schedule in space below

_____

_____

_____

_____

_____

_____

E-27. Full and Immediate Vesting Is Required for Amounts, Earnings, and Benefits Derived from Employee Contributions.

E-28.   Special Provisions Relating to Vesting in Individual Insurance Contracts _____

_____

_____

_____

_____

E-29.   Definition of "Compensation" and "Hour of Service" for Plan Purposes (Indicate Status of Commissions, Bonuses, Overtime, etc., and for Defined-Benefit Plan Indicate Career Average, Final Average, or Other Basis for Determining Benefits)

_____

_____

_____

_____

E-30.   Definition of "Net Income" or "Net Profits" for Plan Purposes (If Applicable)

30.1   _____   Profits for federal income tax purposes, but prior to reduction for contributions under (a) _____ this plan or (b) _____ qualified plans including this plan, but excluding

_____

(state plans to be excluded) sponsored by employer

30.2   _____   Other (specify) _____

_____

E-31.   Beneficiary Designations

31.1   _____   None

31.2   _____   Automatic to spouse, if surviving, otherwise to estate of (a) _____ deceased participant or (b) _____ deceased spouse

31.3   _____   Automatic to estate of deceased participant

31.4   _____   As per designation by employee

E-32.   Earmarking of Contributions (Directed Investments)

32.1   _____   Yes

32.2   _____   No

If yes, indicate investment options and limitations _____

_____

_____

_____

E-33.   Mode of Distribution of Benefits (Normal Retirement)

    33.1 _____ Joint life, participant and spouse (at least 50% to spouse)

    33.2 _____ Full range of options (see below)

    33.3 _____ Limited range of options (indicate which options are available below)

    33.4 _____ Range of options

        (a) _____ Life of participant only

        (b) _____ Life of participant, 5 years certain

        (c) _____ Life of participant, 10 years certain

        (d) _____ Joint life, participant and spouse (at least 50% to spouse)

        (e) _____ Joint life, participant and dependent

        (f) _____ Joint life, participant and designated joint annuitant

        (g) _____ Installments for 3 years

        (h) _____ Installments for 5 years

        (i) _____ Installments for 10 years

        (j) _____ Installments for 15 years

        (k) _____ Lump sum

        (l) _____ Other (specify) _____

        _____

    33.5 Method of determining actuarial equivalence _____

    _____

    _____

    33.6 How options are elected _____

    _____

E-34.   Timing of Distribution of Benefits

    34.1 Normal retirement benefits

        (a) _____ First day of month following normal retirement date

        (b _____ Other (specify) _____

        _____

    34.2 Early Retirement Benefits

        (a) _____ First day of month following early retirement date

        (b) _____ First day of month following normal retirement date

        (c) _____ First day of any month after early retirement date but not later than first day of month following normal retirement date

        (d) _____ Combination of (b) & (c) above at employee's option

34.3 Disability benefits

(a) _____ First day of month following disability

(b) _____ First day of month following normal retirement date

(c) _____ First day of month following early retirement date after disability and before normal retirement date

(d) _____ Other (specify) _____

_____

(e) _____ Combination of (b) & (c) above at

_____ Employee's option

34.4 Preretirement death benefits

(a) _____ As promptly as practicable following death

(b) _____ Other (specify) _____

_____

34.5 Postretirement death benefits

(a) _____ As promptly as practicable following death

(b) _____ Pursuant to mode of retirement benefit election

(c) _____ Other (specify) _____

_____

34.6 Severance benefits

(a) _____ As promptly as practicable following termination of employment
(not later than 60th day after close of plan year)

(b) _____ At normal retirement date

(c) _____ 10 years after plan participation

(d) _____ (a) or (c) at option of plan participant

E-35. Plan Administration

35.1 Plan administrator _____ Employer _____ Other (specify) _____

_____

35.2 Plan administrator to have investment power? _____ Yes _____ No

E-36. Insurance Provision and Restrictions _____

_____

_____

_____

E-37.   Should There be Provisions in Plan and Trust Specifying That Insurance Company is Not a Party?

_____ Yes   _____ No

E-38.   Other Special Features and Notes as to Plan Provisions (Attach Additional Sheets if Necessary)

_____

_____

_____

_____

_____

Appendix C

PART F — PLAN CENSUS DATA

Data for test under Section 410(b)(1) of the Internal Revenue Code

F-0. Is this data being provided for a separate line of business under Code Sec. 414(r)?
    ☐ Yes, eligible (describe)   _____
    ☐ No, not eligible
    ☐ No separate line of business

F-1. Total number of employees   _____

F-2. Number of employees in collective-bargaining unit
(retirement benefits were subject to good faith bargaining)
(Code Sec. 410(b)(3)(A))   _____

F-3. Number of employees who have not yet satisfied
proposed plan eligibility waiting period* and
minimum age requirements (Code Sec. 410(b)(4))   _____

F-4. Number of employees excluded under Code Secs. 410(b)(3)(B)-(C)   _____

F-5. Total Lines F-2 through F-4   _____

F-6. Difference = Line F-1 minus Line F-5   _____

F-6.1. Number of employees included in F-6 who are highly compensated
(Code Sec. 414(q))   _____

    *NOTE: *If plan excludes part-time or seasonal employees, defined as other than employment for fewer than
1,000 hours per year, indicate here the definition used in the plan*

_____

_____

F-7. Employees excluded from coverage*

    7.1   Ineligible due to being salaried   _____

    7.2   Ineligible due to being hourly paid   _____

    7.3   Ineligible due to job classification   _____

    7.4   Ineligible due to being covered in another
           qualified plan   _____

    7.5   Ineligible due to geographic location   _____

    7.6   Ineligible for other reasons (specify)   _____

                                       _____

    _____   _____

    _____   _____

    7.8   Total excluded under F-7   _____

    NOTE: No excluded employee should be counted in more than one category above.

F-8. Number of employees presently eligible to participate in plan
(F-6 minus F-7.8)   _____

F-9. Number of employees actually participating in plan   _____

F-10. Number of plan participants who are highly compensated   _____

Percentage test

F-11. Percentage of non-highly compensated employees participating—100 times

$$\left(\frac{\text{line F-9 minus line F-10}}{\text{line F-6 minus line F-6.1}} \right)$$

_____%*

Ratio test

F-12. Percentage of highly compensated employees participating—100 times
(line F-10 divided by F-6.1)

_____%

F-13. 0.7 times line F-11

_____%

F-14. Percentage of non-highly compensated employees participating—100 times

$$\left(\frac{\text{line F-9 minus line F-10}}{\text{line F-6 minus line F-6.1}} \right)$$

_____%**

Average Benefits Test

F-15. Describe nondiscriminatory classification of employees _____

F-16. Average benefit percentage _____

_____

*   If F-11 is 70 or greater, the plan's coverage meets the percentage test and no further computation is required.
**   If F-14 is equal to or greater than F-13, the plan meets the ratio test and no further compensation is required.

Appendix C

PART G — FUNDING

G-1. Type of Instrument

    1.1 _____ Self-administered trust

    1.2 _____ Group DA

    1.3 _____ Group IPG

    1.4 _____ Group annuity

    1.5 _____ Individual policy (fully insured)

    1.6 _____ Individual policy and investment fund

    1.7 _____ Other (specify) _____

    _____

G-2. Actuarial Assumptions and Cost Method

    2.1 Actuarial assumptions

        (a) _____ Interest _____

        (b) _____ Turnover _____

        (c) _____ Annuity form to be funded _____

        (d) _____ Annuity purchase rate (dollar amount needed to purchase benefit of $10.00 per month at normal retirement)

        Male _____   Female _____

                    or

        (Dollar amount of monthly retirement income that can be purchased at normal retirement by $1,000)

        Male _____   Female _____

        (e) _____ Preretirement mortality _____

        (f) _____ Salary scale _____

        (g) _____ Other (specify) _____

        _____

    2.2 Actuarial cost method _____

    _____

G-3. Type of Fiduciary Arrangement

    3.1 _____ Bank trustee

    3.2 _____ Individual trustee(s)

    3.3 _____ Insurance or annuity contracts

    3.4 _____ Custodial account

    3.5 _____ U.S. retirement bonds

    3.6 _____ Other (specify) _____

G-4. Annual Asset Valuation Date _____

G-5. Trust (or Other) Fiscal Year_____

G-6. Fund (Trust, Custodial Account, Annuity Plan) Identification Number _____

G-7. SS-4 Needed? _____ Yes _____ No

G-8. Full Name and Address of Trustee or Other Fiduciary (Named Fiduciary) _____

_____

_____

_____

G-9. Is Trustee or Other Fiduciary Subject to Instruction by or Consent of Plan Committee, Advisor, or Other Party as to Acquisition, Retention, or Disposition of Investment Assets?_____

If so, specify name and address of party whose consent is needed and acts for which consent is needed.

_____

_____

_____

G-10. Situs of Trust

G-11. Who Will Prepare and File Plan/Trust Returns and Reports with Internal Revenue Service and Department of Labor?

11.1 Form 5500 (or 5500-C or 5500-R—indicate which)_____

11.2 Schedule A Form 5500 _____

11.3 Schedule B Form 5500 _____

11.4 Other reports _____

_____

_____

_____

G-12. Unusual Trust Agreement Provisions (Or Unusual Provisions to Be Included in Agreements Used in Lieu of or in Addition to Trust Agreement) _____

_____

_____

_____

G-13. Fiduciary Employer (Taxpayer) Identification Number _____

G-14. Plan Administrator (If Other Than Employer) Identification Number_____

PART H — AGENCY FILING RECORDS

H-1.   Internal Revenue Service

1.1   Who will file for "Letter of Determination" _____

_____

_____

_____

1.2   Indicate forms needed and date filed*

	Needed	Form No.	Date Filed	Response Received
(a)	_____	SS-4 (Employer)	_____	_____
(b)	_____	SS-4 (Plan Administrator	_____	_____
(c)	_____	2848 or 2848-D	_____	_____
(d)	_____	5300	_____	_____
(e)	_____	5302	_____	_____
(f)	_____	5303	_____	_____
(g)	_____	5307	_____	_____
(h)	_____	5309	_____	_____
(i)	_____	5310	_____	_____

*Form Index:

(a)/(b)   SS-4—Application for employer (taxpayer) or plan administrator identification number

(c)   2848 or 2848-D—Power of attorney or authorization and declaration

(d)   Form 5300—Application for determination

(e)   5302—Employee census

(f)   Form 5303—Application for determination for collectively bargained plan

(g)   Form 5307—Short form application for determination for employee benefit plan

(h)   Form 5309—Application for determination of employee stock ownership plan

(i)   5310—Application for determination upon termination—notice of merger, consolidation or transfer of plan assets or liabilities

Where Letters of Determination are issued, indicate date of issuance and symbols in "response received" column.

H-2.   State Government Filings (Preempted by Federal Law in Most Cases)

Filings Required	Forms to Be Submitted	Parties to Do Filing	Dates of Filing	Responses Received

H-3.   Securities and Exchange Commission _____

_____

_____

_____

H-4.   Other _____

_____

_____

Appendix C

PART I — OTHER PROFESSIONALS

(Insert names, addresses, telephone numbers, and tax numbers)

I-1.   Company's Accountant _____
_____
_____
_____

I-2.   Company's Counsel _____
_____
_____
_____

I-3.   Actuary _____
_____
_____
_____

I-4.   Consultant _____
_____
_____
_____

I-5.   Fiduciary _____
_____
_____
_____

I-6.   Insurance Consultants (Indicate Lines of Coverage) _____
_____
_____
_____

I-7.   Union Representatives _____
_____
_____
_____

I-8.   Others (Specify) _____

_____

_____

_____

Long-Term Incentives: A Comparative Analysis

Non-Qualified Stock Options (NQSOs) Public Companies

Description & Common Features

Option to purchase shares of company stock at a stated price ("option price") over a given period of time, frequently ten years.

Option price normally equals 100% of the stock's fair market value on date of grant, but may be set below or above this level (i.e., "discount" or "premium").

NQSOs may be exercised by cash payment or by tendering previously owned shares of stock, depending on plan terms. NQSOs may be granted in tandem with stock appreciation rights or other devices.

Incentive Stock Options (ISOs) — Public Companies

Description & Common Features

Option to purchase shares of company stock at 100% (or more) of stock's fair market value on date of grant ("option price") for a period of up to ten years, and designed to meet various other statutory requirements to qualify for ISO tax treatment, for example:

• $100,000 annual vesting limitation

• holding period (i.e., stock cannot be sold until two years after option grant and one year after exercise)

• limit on post-termination exercise (e.g., one year after disability terminations, three months after other terminations except for death).

ISOs may be exercised by cash payment or by tendering previously owned shares of stock, depending on plan terms. ISOs may be granted in tandem with stock appreciation rights that have identical terms.

Phantom Stock — Public Companies

Description & Common Features

Units analogous to company shares, with a value generally equal to appreciation in the value of the underlying stock.

Phantom stock is valued at a fixed date, typically, at retirement or five to fifteen years after grant. Essentially, it is like an SAR with a fixed exercise time.

Payment may be in cash and/or stock.

Note: The term "phantom stock" is used in other contexts (e.g., formula or appraised value stock for non-public companies or divisions).

Restricted Stock — Public Companies

Description & Common Features

An award of stock with no or nominal cost to executives that is non-transferable and subject to a substantial risk of forfeiture. As owners of the shares, executives normally have voting and dividend rights even while shares are subject to restrictions. These restrictions typically lapse over a period of three to five years.

Performance Units/Performance Cash Public Companies

Performance Shares — Public Companies

Description & Common Features

A grant of a contingent number of units or a contingent cash award. Units may have a fixed dollar value, with the *number* earned varying with performance. Alternatively, a fixed number of units may be granted, with the *value* varying on the basis of performance.

Duration of performance cycle varies, but is typically three to five years. Financial objectives may relate to such items as cumulative growth in earnings or improvements in rates of return.

At end of cycle, awards are paid in cash and/or stock according to the plan's earnout provisions and actual company performance.

Description & Common Features

A contingent grant of a fixed number of common shares at the beginning of a performance cycle, with the *number* of shares payable at the end of the cycle dependent on how well performance objectives are achieved. The ultimate *value* of the performance shares depends on both the number of shares earned and their market value at the end of the cycle.

Duration of performance cycles varies, but is typically three to five years. Financial objectives may relate to such items as cumulative growth in earnings or improvements in rates of return.

At end of cycle, awards are paid in cash and/or stock according to the plan's earnout provisions and actual company performance.

Stock Appreciation Rights (SARs) — Public Companies

Limited Stock Appreciation Rights (LSARs) — Public Companies

Description & Common Features

Description & Common Features

Rights, normally granted in tandem with stock options, that permit the executive to receive a payment equal to the excess of the stock's value at exercise over the option price, in lieu of exercising the underlying stock option. Once exercisable, participants control when to exercise outstanding SARs during the SARs' term

SARs may be attached to incentive stock options or nonqualified stock options or may be granted on a "freestanding" or "independent" basis without a tandem option.

Payment may be in cash, and/or stock.

Rights granted in tandem with stock options designed for use in the event of a change in the company's ownership or control. LSARs permit the executive to receive a payment equal to the excess of the stock's value at exercise over the option price, rather than exercising the underlying stock option.

Normally, such rights are granted only to SEC insiders who are prohibited from selling shares within six months of a share purchase — even in the midst of a tender offer or other change in control. Some plans permit insiders to exercise an LSAR (as opposed to the underlying stock option) only if there was another share purchase in the preceding six months that would preclude an immediate share sale upon exercise. LSARs usually remain in effect only for a limited period of time, such as 90 days from the change in control or other defined plan triggering event.

LSARs under some plans provide more favorable computational terms than might otherwise be achieved with a regular stock option. For example, LSAR payments might reflect the *highest* gain the executive could realize by exercising the option *at any time* during the three month period following the change in control, rather than the gain on any specific date.

Payment is almost always in cash.

Appendix E

ACCOUNTING FOR BENEFIT PLANS

Accounting rules, including those affecting employee benefit plans, are promulgated by the Financial Accounting Standards Board (FASB). The FASB is a private organization designated by the accounting profession to promulgate general principles, practices and standards for accounting and financial disclosure. These FASB rules do not have the force of law as such, but they represent, de facto, the standards expected by shareholders, investors, and the government in financial reports of businesses, and they are generally followed by independent accountants for purposes of certifying financial statements. They are, therefore, quasi-regulatory in effect and should be considered along with state and federal government regulations in the design of executive benefit plans.

PENSION PLANS

The accounting rules for deferred compensation make no distinction between qualified and nonqualified plans as such. Instead, the applicable accounting rule depends on whether the plan constitutes one or more "individual deferred compensation contracts" on the one hand, or a "pension plan" on the other. While the balance sheet result is about the same either way, individual deferred compensation contracts are governed by the older Accounting Principles Board (APB) Opinion No. 12, as amended by FAS 106. Pension plans, however, are governed by FAS 87.

Whether a plan is one or the other is to some extent a matter of the accountant's discretion. In general, if one or only a few executives are covered, APB No. 12 would be applied, while if the plan is a defined benefit plan or a pension plan as defined in ERISA, FAS 87 would apply.[1]

Under APB No. 12, the benefits accrued under a deferred compensation contract are charged to expense and spread ratably over the period of the executive's service. As amended by FAS 106, the period of service to be used is the period between the time the contract is entered into and the first year in which the executive is eligible for benefit payments (even if the executive might choose to further defer actual payment). Accrued benefits are charged to expense at their present value; the discount rate is not specified in APB No. 12 but accountants are likely to use current rates of return on high quality fixed-income investments. No funding method is specified in APB No. 12, but apparently either a level funding or accrued benefit approach can be used.

FAS 87, "Employers' Accounting for Pensions," was put in final form in 1985. Highlights of FAS 87 are:

1. Annual pension cost—the periodic cost charged against earnings, referred to as the "net periodic pension cost"—is determined under a uniform method prescribed by FAS 87. The employer may not simply charge the amount actually contributed to the plan to expense for the accounting year.

2. Generally, the unit credit (accrued benefit) method is used in determining the net periodic pension cost, regardless of the actuarial method used by the plan.

3. If the net periodic pension cost differs from the employer's actual plan contribution for the year, the difference will be shown as an asset or liability on the balance sheet.

4. If the plan's past service costs (accumulated benefit obligation) exceed the fair market value of plan assets, a liability referred to as the *unfunded accumulated-benefit obligation* must be reflected on the balance sheet. This liability is balanced by an intangible asset on the balance sheet.

5. A specific format is prescribed for various financial statement footnotes relating to the pension plan, such as the fair market value of plan assets and any unamortized prior service costs.

For a plan that is terminating during the year, FAS 88, "Employers' Accounting for Settlements and Curtailments of Defined Benefit Pension Plans and Termination Benefits," provides rules for dealing with special accounting problems in plan termination.

Nonqualified and qualified plans must be reported separately by employers, since assets of qualified and nonqualified plans cannot be mingled. If a nonqualified plan is informally funded or financed—as such plans usually are (see Chapter 16)—the plan is considered to have no assets for accounting purposes, a fact which will increase the magnitude of the reported liabilities. The assets used for informal financing are corporate assets, not plan assets.

These accounting rules increase the balance sheet "visibility" of nonqualified plans, as compared with qualified plans, because of the fact that the liability will generally rise steadily in a plan that is not formally funded. Planners can generally mitigate this disadvantage by using an informal funding mechanism that produces a steadily increasing corporate asset, such as the cash value of an insurance policy; this asset can be pointed to as evidence of the company's financial responsibility with regard to the nonqualified plan liability.

CORPORATE-OWNED LIFE INSURANCE

Corporate-owned life insurance, whether held as an informal financing asset for a nonqualified pension plan (see above) or for other corporate or employee benefit purposes, is accounted for in accordance with FASB Technical Bulletin 85-4. The charge to corporate earnings is the premium less the cash value increase. Generally, this produces a charge to earnings only in the first few years of the policy, after which there is a profit. The policy's cash value appears as an asset on the balance sheet.

FASB Statement No. 109 (1992), superseding FAS 96 (1987), requires corporations to create a balance sheet liability to reflect taxes anticipated to be payable in the future (deferred taxes). If the corporation holds property with unrealized gain, it must generally show a liability for taxes on that gain, even if the gain is not realized during the accounting year. This rule potentially has an impact on corporate-owned life insurance, such as that held in a split-dollar plan, informally funded deferred compensation plan, or other plan. If the corporation's share of the cash value exceeds the corporation's basis, there is a potentially taxable gain. However, in the great majority of plans using corporate-owned life insurance, the corporation intends to hold the policy until the insured dies, at which point the corporations's realized gain will be nontaxable, except for possible alternative minimum tax liability.

FASB's previous statement on accounting for income taxes, FAS 96, stated the requirement of creating a tax liability in an inflexible way that appeared to apply to all insurance policies, regardless of whether the policy was likely to actually generate taxable income. However, FAS 109, which supersedes FAS 96, states that the difference between basis and cash value of a corporate-owned policy does not create a reportable liability if "the asset is expected to be recovered without tax consequence upon the death of the insured (there will be no taxable amount if the insurance policy is held until the death of the insured)."

FAS 109 does not directly discuss whether possible AMT on the death proceeds must be reflected as a balance sheet liability. However, it can be argued that the principles of the FAS would require the potential AMT to be so reported. As discussed in Chapter 40, the receipt of a death benefit, even though regular income-tax free, can result in an AMT liability.

HEALTH AND OTHER WELFARE BENEFIT PLANS

Health and life insurance benefit plans generally involve no significant accounting issues so long as the plans provide simply the usual year-to-year benefit and premium payment obligations. However, where employers provide benefits after employees retire, the FASB has recognized that there is a question as to how this obligation should be recognized for accounting purposes. The issue has become more important in light of recent court cases that restrict an employer's right to unilaterally modify or rescind benefits provided to retirees.

The FASB in 1989 issued an "exposure draft" of rules in this area, which was formalized as FAS 106, effective generally for fiscal years beginning after December 15, 1992, with a later date for certain small (under 500) nonpublic plans.

FAS 106 is based on the premise that post-retirement benefits of all types are, like pension benefits, a form of deferred compensation that is earned year by year by employees while they are actively working for the employer. Accordingly, FAS 106 requires an accrual of such benefits as they are earned, rather than as they are paid. This accrual will create a charge to earnings, and unfunded accrued benefits will create a growing balance sheet liability.

FAS 106 covers medical and life insurance, tuition assistance, day care, legal services, and housing subsidies, as well as other benefits provided during retirement in return for prior employment services. Retiree medical benefits have by far the greatest potential financial impact. FAS 106 includes specific guidelines for valuing post-retirement medical benefits.

This potential balance sheet liability will cause employers to seek to provide either funded plans or asset reserves or other financing assets such as life insurance contracts to cover the liabilities created by post-retirement benefits.

Under FAS 106, if assets are not segregated into a trust specifically for the purpose of funding the post-retirement benefits, they are not "plan assets" that directly reduce the balance sheet liability for post-retirement benefits. Thus, typical corporate-owned life insurance policies or asset reserves would not qualify as plan assets, nor would a Section 501(c)(9) trust (VEBA) if the VEBA included assets to fund benefits for active employees. However, Section 401(h) medical accounts (see Chapter 37) probably would qualify.

Although informal financing of retiree benefits will not reduce the balance sheet liability, the existence of assets can help to demonstrate the corporation's financial responsibility in planning to meet the projected liability. Corporate-owned life insurance can be used favorably for this purpose. Methods of financing retiree medical benefits are discussed further in Chapter 37.

FOOTNOTES

1. See *Tax Management Portfolio 393-2nd,* "Accounting for Pensions and Deferred Compensation," Bureau of National Affairs, Inc., Washington, D.C., (1991), page A-6 for authors' views on how this distinction is made. According to their rationale, it would appear that most accountants would not apply FAS 87 to an unfunded plan, but this is not clear from FAS 87 itself.

THE UNAUTHORIZED PRACTICE OF LAW IN THE EMPLOYEE BENEFIT AREA

It is often difficult to draw the boundaries of professional responsibility in areas as complex, sophisticated, and rapidly changing as employee benefit and retirement planning. Special skills and learning are necessary prerequisites—not only to the attorney but also to the CPA, CLU, CFP, ChFC, or any other individual serving a client in an advisory capacity.

WHY ONLY ATTORNEYS?

Yet it is clear that regardless of how knowledgeable an advisor is, only the attorney may "practice law." This regulation and limitation on the practice of law is in the public interest and is intended to provide reasonable protection for the clients advised. Among the specific reasons for the prohibition are these:

(1) The public needs and deserves protection against advice by self-styled advisors who have not been trained, examined, or licensed by a recognized and accredited educational body or by governmental authorities.

(2) Even a non-lawyer who is highly skilled in specific areas of tax law may lack the broader viewpoint and depth provided by a good law school.

(3) The lawyer-client relationship is one of confidentiality, relative objectivity, and impartiality. It is impossible for the non-lawyer to match the protection afforded by the law to the "attorney-client" relationship. Although no professional is completely objective (attorneys and accountants sell their time and expertise), the attorney is generally in a position to be more objective than a professional selling a product. Certainly, when the time comes to make a choice between competing vendors or competing products, the attorney is more likely to be impartial (although not necessarily more knowledgeable) than either of the parties selling the products.

THE ROLE OF THE SPECIALIST

None of these points, however, imply that the non-attorney has no viable or vital part in the planning process. Much to the contrary, the employee benefit and retirement planning specialist can add immensely to the end result. In fact, it is often the non-attorney specialist who introduces the tool or technique to the client, motivates the client, and follows through to make sure the employee benefit or retirement plan is fully implemented.

If moving the process along were the only role and utility of the non-attorney, that alone would be enough to warrant a place on the planning team. But the non-attorney specialist does so much more. Few attorneys are expert in employee benefit and retirement planning. But even those that are can learn a great deal from the specialist about the available products, the actuarial assumptions and implications, and how these factors interact with each other and can be best utilized in meeting the client's objectives.

NO ONE PROFESSION (OR PROFESSIONAL) IS ENOUGH

The key point is that no single professional is competent to know everything or single-handedly complete the entire employee benefit or retirement planning process. Each member of the planning team should serve the client with his or her own essential and very special skills. If any member of the team usurps the rightful province of another, it is the client who loses. Stated in a more positive way, the client is best served if the attorney and non-attorney specialists work together to formulate, implement, qualify, and maintain a plan which best meets the client's needs.

THE UNAUTHORIZED PRACTICE OF LAW—WHAT IS IT NOT?

There is consensus that certain activities are not the unauthorized practice of law. Even the most conservative authorities[1] generally agree that the following would not be considered the unauthorized practice of law in the field of employee benefit and retirement planning:

(1) Promoting, marketing, and selling the plan. This assumes the specialist does not hold himself out as an attorney or as a provider of services which constitute the practice of law.

(2) Explaining alternatives generally available to the public. This means the planner can safely:

A. review the different types of tools or techniques available,

B. describe which classes of employees are required to be covered under federal and state law,

C. explain the costs of benefits provided to employees,

D. illustrate the amounts of contributions to the plan and

E. discuss general legal principles.

(3) Gather client data. A non-attorney can:

A. assemble employee census data,

B. obtain information on the employer's resources and objectives,

C. ascertain the costs and liabilities associated with the plan's operation and various plan options.

(4) Perform certain form completion. A non-attorney can:

A. complete the annual returns and reports for the plan.

B. complete and file the SPD (Summary Plan Description).

C. decide upon the elections, consents, and waivers to be used in the administration of the plan—to the extent federal rules and regulations specifically state that such can be completed by a non-lawyer.

D. present a plan to the IRS for "qualification"—if a federal law or regulation specifically authorizes such an action.

E. administer a plan and deal with regulators—if, when a situation arises which requires legal advice, the administrator advises the client to seek legal advice.

If an employee benefits/retirement planning firm hires an attorney as an employee, that attorney can draft a master or prototype plan for the employer. Upon the request of the client's attorney (an attorney independently selected by the client) he or she may also assist that attorney in drafting plan documents.

THE UNAUTHORIZED PRACTICE OF LAW—WHAT IT IS (MAYBE)

Almost everyone will agree that the actual drafting of a specific employer's plan document, the preparation of the instruments and contracts by which legal rights are secured, is the practice of law. The odds are very high that he who drafts such documents is practicing law.

Beyond this point, however (and in the minds of some, even at this point) things become hazy. Each state has the right to decide independently from all others what is meant by "unauthorized practice of law."

Will the following constitute the unauthorized practice of law?

You review a plan document and advise a client that—in their particular circumstance—that document will—or will not—have specific legal implications or that the instrument in question is "right" or "not right" for them.

After analyzing client information, you decide on the type of plan the client should have and select the specific provisions that should be inserted into the plan documents.

You make "bottom line recommendations" as to which format and plan provisions would be most suitable to a client's needs.

The employer has decided to adopt a master or prototype plan. You advise the employer as to which plan options would best meet the firm's needs and objectives.

You draft amendments to an already existing plan or to corporate documents adopting the plan.

You do the initial draft of a plan document but submit it for review, approval, and adoption by the client's lawyers.

You apply to the IRS, on behalf of the employer, for qualification of the plan.

The employer wants to terminate a plan. You prepare all papers and submit them to the IRS.

You give advice regarding the tax laws and other laws on the plan and its participants.

If these actions are the unauthorized practice of law, is the client denied the benefit of receiving advice from accountants, actuaries, and plan specialists who are experts in their fields? Would prohibiting such actions by these experts amount to a questionable restraint on interdisciplinary competition? Is it not only possible but highly likely that the non-attorney expert is better suited than the attorney in matters such as product choice and design? Would thwarting the non-attorney from performing these vital roles significantly increase the cost of plan creation and administration (or further discourage the use of plans vital to the security of millions of employees)?

A strong working knowledge of law is essential to professionals in the employee benefits and retirement planning field. Generally, the protection of the public can be achieved without hampering or unduly burdening professionals with impractical and technical restrictions which have no reasonable justification. To say that non-attorneys cannot discuss any pertinent legal principles with a client would be so unreasonable and narrow as to be absurd.

THEORIES AND MYTHS

Where are the bounds? In most states they are decided on a case by case basis. Here are some guidelines that will provide a continuum of risk, if not answers:

The General-Specific Test: Where a statute or legal interpretation has become so well known and settled that no further legal issue is involved, there should be no problem in suggesting its simple application on a general basis. No violation should arise from the sharing of legal knowledge which is either generally informative or, if specific, so obvious as to be common knowledge. But it is when the advice moves from the general and obvious to the specific and uncertain that the line is approached. Providing advice involving the application of legal principals to a specific fact situation is clearly the "practice of law" under the "general-specific" test.

The "Complexity" theory: This theory states that the non-attorney should not answer "difficult" or "complex" questions of law. One court said that an issue is "difficult" or "complex" when the advice that is given or the service that is rendered requires the use of any degree of legal knowledge or skill. Perhaps a "judgment" theory should be applied instead. Rather than focus on difficulty or complexity, the focus should be on the extent to which legal judgment is required with respect to controversial or uncertain questions of law in an actual case.

The "Expert/Specialist" theory: No safety can be found in proving that the non-lawyer is both a specialist and an acknowledged expert in the field. The rationale for this seemingly harsh stand is that the interest of the public is not protected by narrow specialization of a person who lacks the broad perspective and orientation of a state licensed attorney. That dimension of skill and knowledge comes only from a thorough understanding of legal concepts, processes, and the interaction of all the branches

of law. In other words, according to this theory, the rules may have been learned by the non-lawyer but often the full meaning and import of the rule and its components—and the impact of that rule on other seemingly unrelated rules—may not be fully understood by even a highly competent specialist who is an expert in his or her field but who is not a state licensed attorney.

The "No Fee" theory: A study of the unauthorized practice cases shows that a non-attorney is not protected by merely refraining from charging fees for legal advice. Most courts had little trouble finding violations where clients relied on advice or were provided with legal services regardless of whether or not fees were charged.

The "Practices of the Past" theory: Custom and tradition long acquiesced to by the local bar association will not make proscribed activities any less the practice of law. Practices of the past, therefore, provide little defense in the present.

THE BOTTOM LINE

TOOLS AND TECHNIQUES is not designed to help the non-lawyer eliminate the need for an attorney. To the contrary, it is a text (widely used by attorneys and in law schools throughout the country) designed for all the members of the employee benefit and retirement planning team to help delineate the large number of alternative solutions to general problem areas. Definitive solutions, the choice of which specific tools and techniques to use in a given case or the decisions as to how they should be used should be considered by the client, together with his or her attorney and plan specialists. The drafting or adopting of plan documents needed to execute the techniques or utilize the tools discussed in this text is exclusively the province of the lawyer.

Every member of the planning team is obligated to be aware of the alternative tools and techniques, to understand their limitations as well as their problem-solving potential, and to be knowledgeable enough to discuss them in general terms with clients and other advisors.

FOOTNOTES

1. The Florida Bar Association issued a proposed advisory opinion filed with the Florida Supreme Court (Case Number 74-479) that sought to restrict non-attorneys to a severe and unprecedented degree in connection with the design and installation of pension plans. The Florida Supreme Court rejected this proposal, however. In any event, most of the items listed here would be permissible for non-attorneys even under this restrictive advisory opinion.

ETHICS WHAT THE EMPLOYEE BENEFIT AND RETIREMENT PLANNER MUST KNOW
A Practical Guideline

WHY ETHICS?

Ethics are standards of an aspirational and inspirational nature reflecting commitments to model standards of exemplary professional conduct.[1] Every major profession[2] has adopted some form of "near law"—a Code, Canon, or set of guidelines to what the profession expects of its members.[3] This discussion is meant to provide a checklist for the practitioner in the employee benefit and retirement planning field. It is not intended to be anything more than what its title implies, a "practical guideline," a self-monitoring device to help employee benefit and retirement planners.

Why do professional organizations need such codes of conduct? Why do planners need a practical code of ethics?

First, ethics are a means of creating standards by which conduct can be measured both by the member and by the group itself. Second, ethics serve as a way to acknowledge an obligation to society, to the professional group, and to the client. Third, a code of ethics increases the likelihood that the profession will be governed by high standards. Fourth, ethics are a means of examining priorities and building a tradition based on integrity.

A fifth reason for ethics is as a limitation on power. It is the "power of the experts" that ethics help to control; the attorney, accountant, trust officer, the employee benefit and retirement planning expert all know things the client does not.[4] This special knowledge gives the professional a Kafkaesque power over a layman who must put great faith and trust in (and take great risk in the accuracy and appropriateness of) what he is told. The client cannot possibly know the full extent of the problems, possibilities, and consequences without the assistance of the planner.

The premise upon which practical ethics must be based is that power must be exercised in the interest of those for whose benefit it was entrusted rather than abused for the self aggrandizement of the planner. The limitations and restrictions on the planner must not, however, be so unenforceable, unrealistic, and impractical as to be counter productive. Practical ethics, therefore, must strike a balance. The questions that follow are designed to help the reader do just that.

Honesty: Have you engaged in any business or professional activity which involved an act (or omission) of a dishonest, deceitful, or fraudulent nature?

Have you used your license, degree, or designation to attribute to yourself a depth or scope of knowledge, skills, and professional capabilities you do not, in fact, possess?

Have you been fair and honest in your dealings with the IRS and in fostering confidence in the system?[5]

Competency: Do you have the requisite legal knowledge, practical skill, and have you exercised thoroughness?

Have you undertaken a role which entails responsibilities in addition to that inherent to your profession—and if so—are you properly trained and equipped (and willing and otherwise able) to perform them in a competent and efficient manner?

Have you done the proper preparation? In other words, are you qualified to perform the services requested and do you know enough to perform the services required beyond those requested?

What have you done to understand the specific facts and circumstances of the client, the company, its employees, and their needs and objectives?[6]

Do you keep abreast of changing economic and legislative conditions which may affect the client's plan?[7]

Representation: Have you established the boundaries of your relationship so that the client knows what you will or will not do?

Have you specified those limits in writing for all parties concerned?

Have you—in any way—denied the client the benefit of the knowledge and skill of another professional who could assist in serving the client?

Diligence: Did you do what was required in a reasonably prompt manner?

If you are responsible for preparing IRS forms, documents, affidavits, or other papers for the client, did you do so in a timely manner?

Did you advise a client promptly of any noncompliance, error, or omission having to do with a state or federal tax return or other document the client was required by law to complete?

Communication: Did you return phone calls or answer letters promptly? Do you keep the client (and other professionals) informed on a regular basis of economic and legal changes that may impact upon the client's plans?[8]

Confidentiality: Did you keep client information confidential (except to the extent specifically authorized by the client to disclose it)?[9]

Fees: Did you charge fees which were reasonable based on (a) the amount of work performed or the number of hours it took to do the work, (b) the difficulty and judgment involved in the problems that had to be solved, (c) the importance of the problem, and (d) your professional expertise, skill, and standing?

Did you communicate, in writing, the formula by which fees or other charges would be based?

Have you billed only after performing services in a satisfactory manner?

Have you refunded any advance fee which has not been fully earned?

Conflict of Interest:[10] Did you inform the parties you are representing of their respective rights and the pros and cons of the proposed action (or inaction) on each party?

Have you used the special knowledge you have in any manner which would operate to the detriment of the client?[11]

Do you represent two parties who have or are likely to have conflicting interests? (This problem is known as "simultaneous representation"). If so, are you satisfied that you can represent both parties adequately and have you made full disclosure to and obtained consent from both parties?

Have you, in any way, allowed the pursuit of financial gain or any other personal benefit to interfere with the exercise of sound professional judgment and skills?[12]

Have you made full disclosure of any conflicts of interest in writing to your client?

Disclosure: Have you, in any other way, breached your duty of loyalty to your client (or your associates, partners, or employer) by failing to disclose information?

Have you withheld information from another professional or governmental official that it is important and appropriate for that person to know?

Have you misrepresented the benefits, costs, or limitations of any employee benefit and retirement planning tool or technique or failed to fully explain the advantages and disadvantages of viable alternatives?[13]

Direct Relations: Have you obtained information directly from the client or did you obtain it second or third hand from another party or advisor acting as a conduit?[14]

Courtesy: Has your courtesy extended, not only to your client, but also to the other professionals who seek to serve that person?[15]

Public Regard: Have you followed the laws applicable to your business and professional activities?[16]

Have you done what you can to raise the level of integrity and professionalism and avoided activities which detract from the opinion the public places on your profession?

Have you impaired the reputation of another practitioner?

Have you competed unfairly?

Have you used your degree or designation in less than a responsible or dignified or appropriate manner?

Do you avoid associating with those who are not ethical?[17]

Have you provided the public with useful and objective information concerning potential problems, possible solutions, and impartial advisory opinions?

Have you attempted—in all your dealings with the public—to avoid the appearance of impropriety?

Mentoring: Have you helped others enter the profession? Have you helped them attain and retain competence?[18]

Have you encouraged and assisted others in obtaining higher levels of professional competence?

It is not enough merely to avoid advocating, sanctioning, participating in, or carrying out an unethical act. Professional ethics forbid condoning the unethical act of another and require taking positive action to maintain an exemplary level of conduct. For instance, the *Code of Ethics of the International Association for Financial Planning* directs its members to

"Oppose those who are deficient in moral character or professional competence, whose actions may cause financial harm to their clients."

Ethics are a reminder that the client sees the professional in this area as much of a counselor as an advocate, more of an advisor than a scholar. Ethics reinforce the importance of the role of all the members of the planning team as intermediaries and protectors who look out for the overall best interests of the business in recommending a course of action.

Ethical standards do not demand absolute, unreasoning, and undivided loyalty to a single client nor do they demand saint-like perfection in any other area. But being ethical has its (generally quite affordable) price; professional honesty, integrity, and competence compatible with the realities of modern practice. In fact the increased pride and respect gained from others (and oneself) is well worth the price. Can any planner afford not to pay it?

FOOTNOTES

1. See *Code of Professional Ethics of the American Institute for Property and Liability Underwriters.*
2. See "For the Long Term—Professional Ethics and The Life Underwriter," *Life Association News*, December 1985, for an excellent discussion on that subject. Dr. Clarence C. Walton, the author of that article, states that among the characteristics of a mature profession are:

    A. Primary commitment to the interest of the client,

    B. Possession of expert knowledge,

    C. Self regulation,

    D. Awareness of the long term consequences of his or her action

    Dr. Walton provides excellent guidelines for organizations that sincerely wish to promote and enforce a code of ethics.
3. Information on the Code of conduct for your profession should be obtained by writing to the appropriate national organization to which you belong. For information on The ABA's Model Rules of Professional Conduct, attorneys should write to Information Officer, Office of Professional Ethics, American Bar Association, Chicago, Ill.
4. See "Estate Planners: Where Do Your Ethics Lie?," *Trusts and Estates.*
5. The duties of a professional to the IRS are spelled out in IRS circular 230 which embraces, under a uniform standard, many of the traditional ethical and professional standards common to national professional organizations. See "Regulations Within The IRS," *Trusts and Estates*, April 1990, p. 30.
6. The *Code of Ethics of the American Society of CLU and ChFC* states, "The member must make a conscientious effort to ascertain and to understand all relevant circumstances surrounding the client."
7. The *Code of Ethics of The American Society of CLU and ChFC* states, "A member shall continue his education throughout his professional life." Interpretive comment adds, "A member must continue to maintain and to improve his professional abilities. Continuing education includes both the member adding to his knowledge of the practice of his profession; and, the member keeping abreast of changing economic and legislative conditions which may affect the financial plans of the insuring public."
8. The *Code of Ethics of the American Society of CLU and ChFC* states, "A member shall render continuing advice and service." Its interpretive comment provides, "Advice and service to be competent must be ongoing as the client's circumstances change and as these changes are made known to the member."
9. The *Code of Ethics of the American Society of CLU and ChFC* states, "A member shall respect the confidential relationship existing between client and member."
10. The *Code of Ethics of the International Association of Financial Planning* states, "The reliance of the public and the business community on sound financial planning and advice imposes on the financial planning profession an obligation to maintain high standards of technical competence, morality, and integrity. To this end, members of the International Association for Financial Planning, Inc. shall at all times maintain independence of thought and action..." The *Code of Ethics of the American Society of CLU and ChFC* states, "In a conflict of interest situation the interest of the client must be paramount."
11. The *Code of Ethics of the American Society of CLU and ChFC* states, "A member possessing a specific body of knowledge which is not possessed by the general public has an obligation to use that knowledge for the benefit of the client and to avoid taking advantage of that knowledge to the detriment of the client."
12. See the *Code of Professional Ethics of The American Institute for Property and Liability Underwriters.*
13. Each professional must ask himself or herself three questions:

    1. What are the pros and cons of the viable alternatives?
    2. Which alternatives offer the client the greatest financial security and the least overall cost?
    3. What if the client does nothing?

    Then these three issues must be shared with the client's other advisors and with the client.
14. Only through direct relations can a professional be sure that he or she has all of the relevant facts including an understanding of the client's objectives and fears and can make sure both parties fully understand each other.
15. The *Code of Ethics of the American Society of CLU and ChFC* states, "A member is to accord due courtesy and consideration to those engaged in related professions who are also serving the client."
16. The *Code of Ethics of the American Society of CLU and ChFC* states, "A member has a legal obligation to obey all laws applicable to his business and professional activities. The placement of this Guide within the Code raises this obligation to the level of an ethical obligation."
17. The *Code of Ethics of the International Association for Financial Planning* states, "Avoid association with anyone who does not comply with the spirit of these principles."
18. The *Code of Ethics of the American Society of CLU and ChFC* states, "Encouraging others who might be qualified to enter into a practice is one hallmark of a professional."

MALPRACTICE IN COMPENSATION PLANNING HOW TO AVOID IT — AND THE LAWSUIT THAT COMES WITH IT

Errors in pension and employee benefit design and administration are an increasingly common source of malpractice claims.

Reducing the risk of a malpractice suit and enhancing available defenses is the subject of this discussion.

"TARGET OF OPPORTUNITY" — WHY ME?

Those professionals wise enough to know that malpractice is a disease that may attack anyone do not ask the question, "Why Me?" Instead, they ask, "When?" Malpractice claims are made uncomfortably often against those who—out of ignorance, arrogance, or incompetence—thought it could not happen to them. Suits are also brought against planners with fine reputations who honestly thought they had done everything right. It is a dangerous misconception to think that only those who are clearly sloppy and unethical encounter malpractice claims.[1]

Mere good faith and honest intent will not protect the practitioner who has caused a client loss. It may be true that a planner will not be held liable for the failure to foresee the ultimate resolution of a debatable point of law or for an error in judgment if he acts in good faith and in an honest belief that his advice and acts are well founded and in the best interest of his clients.[2] But such a planner can still be sued and still incur most of the costs of someone who in fact is guilty of malpractice.

Who are likely "targets of opportunity"?

"DEEP POCKETS." When clients sue, they sue everyone in sight. But the bulk of the litigation effort is understandably against those from whom recovery is most likely. The appearance of success is a magnet.

INSURANCE. Certainly one contributing factor is the common knowledge that professionals carry insurance for malpractice. Some plaintiffs feel they are not suing the professional; they are suing the insurer.

TOUTED EXPERIENCE, SKILL, AND KNOWLEDGE. In general, professionals who obtain or retain clients by holding themselves out as possessing a higher level of skill than other practitioners will be held to that higher level. If an advisor's business card says, "Compensation Planner" or "Tax Specialist" or he has an advanced degree or a CFP, CLU, ChFC or otherwise advertises greater expertise or skill than an ordinary practitioner, he is expected to exercise that expertise or skill.[3]

IMPERSONAL. It is far easier to sue a party perceived as a "giant institution guided by computers rather than people" than to sue a long time advisor who has served with warmth, openness, compassion and has provided substantial personal attention in a respectful manner. This public image of banks, insurance companies, large law firms, and other institutions as impersonal money machines can best be changed from the top down by an insistence on courtesy and attention to the client from everyone in the firm.

BIG GUY vs LITTLE GUY. There is a feeling in this country, right or wrong, that the "Big Guys" are using their weight to beat up the "Little Guys." So when the little guy gets into the judicial system a jury may feel sympathetic and tend to punish the big guy with an angry vengeance.

FRUSTRATION WITH THE LAW(S). The potential for malpractice increases in proportion to the complexity, speed of change, and labyrinthine interrelationship of various federal and state corporate, tax, labor, and securities laws—and to clients' confusion and frustration. From the planner's point of view, the combination is a nightmare. If the planner feels this way, think of how angry clients must be when told that last year's law is now out and substantial time, money, and emotional energy must be invested all over again. Consider, for example, that a compensation planner for a client having employees in many states may have to consider variations in benefit plans to meet each state's requirements. Furthermore, a malpractice claim might be converted into an unfair trade practice claim in order to gain the advantage of a longer statute of limitations.[4]

TO WHOM IS ONE LIABLE?

This question is not always as easy to answer as it sounds. The simple answer is, one is liable to those who employ him. The general rule is that a duty is only to the person with whom he contracts, his client. But liability may extend to others as well.[5]

An advisor is not liable—even for an act of negligence—to someone to whom he owes no duty.[6] The legal term is "privity." But the defense that there is no privity, no duty to an injured party, can easily be forfeited and is currently being eroded in the courts.[7]

This six-pronged test may be used to determine privity[8]:

1. To what extent is the transaction intended to benefit the third person?

2. Can harm to that third person be foreseen?

3. How likely is it that the third person will suffer real injury?

4. How close is the connection between the advisor's conduct and the injury that the third party could suffer?

5. How "morally wrong" is the advisor's action?

6. Would future harm to this or some other client be served by finding privity here?

At least one state will grant "standing" (the right to sue) to a narrow class of third party beneficiaries where it is clear that the client intended to benefit that party and the client is unable to enforce the contract.[9] Generally, for a third party to collect, written evidence must show that the client's intent must be frustrated and the client's loss must be a direct result of the planner's negligence.

WHAT CAN GET THE ADVISOR INTO TROUBLE?

IF HE SAYS HE KNOWS, HE'D BETTER. Compensation and retirement planning is too complex to be a sideline. Failure to exercise reasonable care and skill in performing duties for a person induced to rely on an advisor because of his professed skills, knowledge, or experience ("John Jones, Benefit Consultant") can result in liability for loss incurred.[10] If one holds himself out as an expert and directly or indirectly promises to provide a product or service to serve a specific purpose or accomplish a particular objective, he assumes the liability for the achievement of that purpose or objective.[11] The skill, knowledge, diligence, and care used must equal or exceed that standard ordinarily exercised by others in the same profession.[12] In short, if one calls himself a professional (or by action or inaction allows others to rely on him as such), he

must assume the responsibilities and duties generally associated with such a status—or be held liable for the client's loss.

NOT KNOWING WHO THE CLIENT IS. Is the client the employer or an executive negotiating for benefits and compensation? If there is any question or inherent conflict in their positions, separate advisors for each may be best.

There are many cases where the planner never or seldom meets the client. For instance, suppose that a benefit advisor prepares a form and explanatory material for a wife to waive spousal benefits under a pension plan. If the advisor never met the wife, how can it be argued that she has been properly advised or that she understood what she signed? The situation is a "lack of informed consent" case in the making.

IF HE SAYS HE WILL, HE'D BETTER. An advisor should never create false expectations by making promises he has no intention of keeping or by promising results he does not know he can deliver. He may be held liable to clients if he promises to keep them informed of significant developments and then does not.[13] He has an obligation to finish substantially the task he has begun for a client, decline the appointment, or, with the client's consent, accept the employment and associate a lawyer who is competent. He must also prepare adequately for, and give appropriate attention to, the work he has accepted.

OVERNIGHT EXPRESS. Clients often want various plans implemented almost overnight—just before government filing deadlines or when they are about to leave on an extended vacation or business trip. This means there is insufficient time to collect, analyze, and act upon complete information. One should refuse to be rushed (but be prepared to work quickly).

HOW DOES ONE STAY OUT OF TROUBLE?

"HIRING—AND FIRING—THE CLIENT." The advisor should ask why the client has chosen him. It's flattering to think one has been selected because of one's expertise or reputation, but the reason may be that another practitioner decided not to represent the client. One should obtain as much information about the client's background with other professionals as possible before agreeing to work with the client. The first interview should be considered a primary opportunity to screen and qualify the client. Perhaps the potential client should be discarded if he seems to be a perfectionist, unrealistic, hurried, angry, overly optimistic, overly fee-conscious, or if he wants services one is not positive he can provide cost effectively.[14] One should beware of clients who are wealthy but in constant cash flow difficulty, seem immature, refuse to accept responsibility for their own actions, or appear constantly ambivalent.[15] These personality types are likely to present a future litigation problem.

Trust instincts. One should turn down a client who requests something that is not quite right. If a client has outgrown the advisor's capacity, he should either recommend another firm or bring a specialist in to work with the client. If an advisor feels the client can not be trusted, he should refuse to work with the client.

RISK TAKING PROPENSITY. One of the biggest causes of claims is that the professional misjudges or never considers or does not reevaluate the risk taking propensity of the client as his circumstances change. The solution is constant communication.

EXPERTISE BOUNDARIES. The advisor should do only those things he is competent (and licensed) to do—and do those things competently. Should a life insurance agent review a pension plan? Should an attorney or accountant judge the adequacy or appropriateness of a client's life insurance portfolio? Should a trust company review documents? Should a financial planner serve as trustee?[16]

Document examination exposure is real. Should one disclaim any liability for review of document viability or efficacy? Incompetent, inconsistent, and informal review is a formula for disaster. If the task is undertaken, it should be done by a person with the appropriate training, expertise, and time to do the job competently and enthusiastically. "You assume an obligation to your client to undertake reasonable research in an effort to ascertain relevant legal principals and to make an informed decision as to a course of action based on an intelligent assessment of the problem."[17]

Furthermore, the planner has a duty either to avoid involving a client in "murky" areas of the law if there are viable alternative tools or techniques that are available, or to inform the client of the risks and let the client make the decision.[18]

Lack of specialized investment knowledge on the part of the planner or fiduciary often results in investment problems. Numerous trust funds are managed by individuals who adopt a passive and simplistic approach. The need for professional investment management and the complexity of modern portfolio theory is ignored or overlooked and too little time is spent in making investment decisions or addressing overall investment policy and asset allocation.[19]

RESOURCE LIMITS. The advisor should not accept engagements that will require resources beyond what he can cost effectively deliver. For example, if his operation does not have the backup personnel to properly service a high number of clients, he should not agree to do deferred compensation and benefit planning for a firm's top 100 executives.

OUTSIDE EXPERTS. An advisor should seek help before it is needed. When appropriate, he should recommend that another professional be used, either in his place or together with him. If he makes a specific recommendation, he may be held liable for the actions of that professional. One way to protect himself is by giving out the names of at least three qualified professionals (make sure the criteria for "qualified" extend beyond mere reputation), or stay involved with the representation.

THE "ENGAGEMENT LETTER"

The engagement letter is the first and primary step in insulating yourself from a successful malpractice suit. An engagement letter should be obtained in every client relationship at the first possible time. The letter spells out the extent and limits of the services to be performed. The following are critical elements of such a letter:

Scope of services and description of work product;

Period of time covered;

Responsibilities undertaken;

Responsibilities the client is expected to assume;

Fee arrangements—amount, terms, and frequency of billing;

Arrangements for update and extension of service;

List of parties represented - and exclusion of those not represented;

Intended use and potential distribution (or restriction) of the advisor's work product[20]; and

Client's acceptance signature and date.

PUT IT (ALL) IN WRITING

Protecting one's self means meticulous record keeping starting at the onset of the relationship. Changes in risk taking propensity or attitude of the client or his family, comments at meetings, phone conversations, and other special instructions should be noted. The advisor's files should clearly reflect and support his recollection of events and should be dictated and transcribed as soon as possible after the occurrence (preferably, contemporaneous with the events). The more complete and organized the files, the more likely the judge, jury, or board of arbitrators will consider the advisor's word persuasive (assuming, of course, the files corroborate what he is now saying).

Whenever possible, quote the client's exact words.[21] This is particularly important whenever a client—or one of his other advisors—decides to pursue an aggressive tax policy or take an investment risk (and doubly important if you have advised against that course of action). For instance, if an attorney tells a client that the business does not need all of the life insurance the agent is suggesting, the agent should attempt to take down as accurately as possible the exact words of the attorney. The attorney should do the same.

Contemporaneous and near verbatim notes should also be taken if the client asks that the advisor not do a service (or anything) he would normally do or if the client asks him to attempt a service that he ordinarily would not do.

Detailed notes are particularly important if the client seems uncooperative or unwilling to provide the information or documents that are necessary to do the job properly.

FEES. Fees should not be set at levels that will require cutting corners or operating at a loss for this engagement. The fee must be large enough to justify internally the time that should be invested in a case—or the case should be turned down. Fees should include the costs that will be incurred to meet high ethical standards and avoid malpractice by implementation of systematic quality control and other appropriate courses of action.

A fee dispute which results in litigation with a client may trigger a malpractice case. The solution is to secure a written agreement as to fees and billing procedures at the onset of the relationship with the client. One should think carefully about the wisdom of suing the client and the likelihood and expense of a malpractice lawsuit by the client. It is wise to communicate clearly the basis or rate of fee or other method of compensation to a new client in writing before or as soon as possible after the relationship begins. The client should be billed periodically and provided detailed information about the services rendered and the time invested.

DATA FORMS. Many times the error or omission of the planner is due to an incomplete or incorrect understanding of the facts. The advisor should obtain comprehensive and accurate data by developing a data gathering system (see Appendix C). Some planners feel they can gather data without forms or checklists but inevitably forget to ask basic questions. One must be sure to confirm with the client the facts gathered—before acting upon them.

A client's existing compensation arrangements should be verified from the documents themselves. It is astounding how often otherwise competent attorneys draft plans that do not match the facts. One needs to check benefit plan documents, insurance contracts, and employee benefit booklets and summary plan descriptions rather than rely on the client's memory. Current insurance policy information should be confirmed by writing to the insurer.

LIMITS OF THE RELATIONSHIP

The client's instructions must be followed—correctly. This entails first truly understanding what those instructions are. Then it requires a written memorandum (preferably signed by the client). Meticulous records of all conversations should be made and kept. If investments are or will be involved in the relationship, an investment policy should document agreed-upon investment objectives, risk parameters, return targets, volatility tolerance, and asset allocation ranges.

A written consent should be obtained for actions outside the scope of the relationship as contained in the engagement letter.

RECORDS AND SYSTEMS

THE RIGHT STUFF. Keep research documents that indicate decisions were made in a methodical and logical manner and that a deliberate investigation preceded and supported each suggestion. Retain documents which illustrate the tax law as it existed at the time tax decisions were made.[22] Memos to the file, prepared contemporaneously with conversations with a client and decision making, are highly useful in establishing the background and intent at the time an action was taken. Make controversial decisions only with the informed knowledge and written consent of the client. Document any oral advice immediately.

Develop and use a presentation system that will prove that regular discussions covering all of the important areas of benefit planning with a client took place.[23] A checklist should be incorporated into that system in order to demonstrate that these issues have been discussed with the client and reflect the client's circumstances and objectives.

A retrieval system should be established to locate documents or plans that need updating for specific changes. For example, all qualified plans, active or inactive, must be regularly amended to reflect changes in the law.

"TRIGGER SYSTEM." A checklist of follow-up procedures should be developed so time-sensitive responsibilities will be met by the appropriate parties and unreasonable delays in the preparation and implementation of the plan can be avoided. Set deadlines, establish priorities, and specify responsibilities. Create a "tickler file (docketing system) to meet all deadlines, statutes of limitations, and filing and payment deadlines. Set up a centralized system to personally remind the party responsible for action and review at given times or events. Incorporate into the system a series of client reminders (e.g., "Major new tax law changes suggest we should review your qualified plans as soon as possible.")

QUALITY CONTROL

An advisor is responsible for the errors or omissions of his partners, associates, and employees. Quality control is therefore not a luxury. It is a business necessity.

UNDERSTANDING OF ETHICAL ISSUES. The planner should discuss with colleagues the danger when a breach of ethics is coupled with an angry or disgruntled client or family member.

WHO IS THE "QUARTERBACK?" In any operation larger than a one-person firm, it is essential that the activities of the entire staff be co-ordinated by a "quarterback" who accepts responsibility. This person must be sure that all staff members are kept informed and that there is a logical and automatic flow of necessary information, that no tasks have been overlooked, and that no efforts are duplicated. He must also be sure that information received by staff members is properly recorded and relayed to him and to the central file on each client.

INDEPENDENT REVIEW. An effective method of quality control is to have the final product reviewed by a well qualified associate before it is shared with a client.

REVIEW OF STAFF COMPETENCE, EXPERIENCE, QUALIFICATION. Compensation planning, almost by definition, requires the input of many professionals. Most planners not only must cooperate with other planners outside their offices but must also rely on associates within their offices. Staff members must be currently competent, and they must be well trained in and conform to standardized office procedures, policies, and proper file management techniques. Appropriate supervision for all levels of staff should be built in. Continuing education should be a part of any firm's ongoing business plan.

EXTERNAL COMMUNICATIONS

Almost every authority who speaks and every article that is written on malpractice states that many lawsuits could probably have been avoided by a simple solution: "Communicate, Communicate, Communicate!"[24]

Many, or even most, of the grievance complaints and malpractice actions can be headed off if the advisor will:

MAKE IT CLEAR AND MAKE IT OFTEN. The planner should avoid technical jargon. He should not assume lay persons understand what he means by such terms as "A qualified plan," a "QDRO," or "an ESOP." He can use word pictures, graphs, flow charts, or diagrams to illustrate his points - and give the clients copies to take home.[25]

He should continually inform clients of all actions he and his staff have taken (or not taken); forward to clients copies of documents he sends to other professionals; provide the client with periodic written reports even if a particular report merely explains why no progress has been made since the last report; and confirm in writing all transactions, expenses, fees, income, or other events of importance.

He should inform the client of any changes in the relationship or responsibilities of the parties; make sure reports are understandable; and use graphs, charts, and checklists to show the progress he has made.

He should confirm through a series of scheduled meetings among the client and other advisors objectives, responsibilities, and timetables.

A newsletter is a good way to keep in touch with clients on a regular basis.

The advisor should schedule regular reviews and give special emphasis to contacting clients from whom he has not heard or had contact with in a given period of time; and document his attempt to contact those who do not respond.

He should keep copies of all correspondence and conversations with other professionals who are working with his client.

He should study the client's verbal and body language to be sure he is understood and encourage the client to call or write to him after the meeting to ask questions if "he has not made himself understood."

AVOID CASUAL OR INFORMAL ADVICE. The advisor should not give advice at cocktail parties or other social events.[26] Liability can be imposed even though no fee has been charged for services if a client relies on information he has been provided.

CALL BACK—PROMPTLY. A careful advisor will return telephone calls promptly. If this is impossible, his secretary or an associate should do it for him so the client does not feel ignored.

AVOID "HEEL COOLING." A planner should not keep clients waiting on the phone or in his office. He should be sure he receives messages promptly—and accurately. He should not allow a phone call to interrupt a meeting with a client. It is a good idea to reward staff members for being extra polite. In short, give the client respect and common courtesy.

AVOIDING (OR NEUTRALIZING) CONFLICT OF INTEREST PROBLEMS

CONFLICTS WITH EXISTING CLIENTS.[27] The duty of loyalty requires any planner to be extremely cautious about serving a client in more than one capacity. For instance, the client of an attorney or CPA may want that person to serve as an executor or trustee—while at the same time desiring that person to continue to provide planning advice and other services to various family members. Can the advice be disinterested and objective. Can the professional ethically charge fees for both services? Can those fees honestly be set at "arms' length"?

Although there is no legal prohibition against representing more than one client in a single transaction, planners should be particularly alert for situations in which there is an obvious or potential difference in their interests. For instance, a defined benefit plan typically favors older long service employees while profit-sharing and defined contribution pension plans usually are to the benefit of younger employees.

Another conflict of interest problem that often occurs where more than one person is represented is the disclosure of confidential information. Can a planner freely tell a wife what her husband has disclosed? Can a planner share information from one shareholder with others? The planner needs to inform all parties that information may not be privileged or confidential as to other members of the group unless specific direction is given.

Any possible conflicts of interest should be disclosed—in writing—to the client as quickly as possible or the planner should withdraw without disclosure if confidential information is involved. Recognition of disclosure and acceptance of its consequent risks should be acknowledged in any instrument signed by the client.

The planner should avoid or treat extremely carefully any financial involvement in a client's business or in a business venture.

CONFLICTS WITH FUTURE CLIENTS. A planner should ask himself whether acceptance of a client will create a conflict with respect to more desirable work with another client in the future?[28]

RED FLAG PROCEDURES. It is important for the planner to train himself and his staff to recognize "red flags." A procedure for identifying problems and quickly dealing with them is essential.

DEALING WITH PROBLEMS. The planner must routinely review and deal with problems promptly. If a problem occurs, he must call or write the client immediately and explain the problem and the potential consequences and alternatives. If a client is angry or dissatisfied, he ought to take immediate action—talk to the client and resolve the problem. He cannot safely assume the problem will go away or that the client will forget it.

THE PROBLEM TEAM. A good idea is to create a "Problem Team" in the firm which meets immediately every time the potential for a dissatisfied client is recognized. That team should not only review the file in the case in point but also any other procedures, activities, omissions, or oversights which may trigger future problems that could develop into litigation.

EARLY ACTIVE REMEDIAL CONCILIATORY EFFORTS. The quicker an attempt is made to resolve the problem to the client's satisfaction, the less likely there will be litigation. Providing a large apology might avoid writing a small check. Writing a small check might avoid defending a large lawsuit. One litigation attorney put it this way: "The good will that can be generated by such an act and accompanying attitudes might be much cheaper and better in the long run than paying expensive attorneys for years of litigation with an uncertain outcome."[29] Sometimes, assigning a new person to speak to the client will serve to quell the objection.

ABOUT MALPRACTICE INSURANCE

SUFFICIENT LEVELS OF COVERAGE. The first step in evaluating current insurance is to see if there is enough insurance to cover any likely risk. But this is only a first step.

"CLAIMS MADE" POLICIES. Most malpractice coverage is sold on a "claims made" basis. This means the policy covers only claims which are first asserted and reported to the insurer within the policy year.

"PRIOR ACTS" COVERAGE. The action alleging malpractice often does not occur until years after the alleged negligence occurred. If the policy has a "prior acts" coverage, it covers a claim asserted during a policy year even though the negligence giving rise to the claim occurred in some prior year.[30] If a policy lacks or excludes prior acts or limits prior acts coverage, it is likely that there will be a "coverage gap." There will be no coverage under the policy in effect when the alleged negligence occurred because the claim was not made in that policy year. The current policy will not cover the alleged negligence because negligence alleged to have occurred before the present policy year is excluded or omitted from the coverage.

THE "TAIL." A tail is an extended reporting option somewhat related to prior acts coverage. If one purchases a tail, he is permitted (usually at the end of each policy year or earlier if the policy is canceled during the term) to convert "claims made" coverage to "occurrence" coverage for any negligence allegedly committed—but not yet reported—up to the end of that policy year. The extended reporting of claims option available through a tail is expensive. The premium is a multiple of the regular annual premium. Tails should be considered by retiring planners who will no longer keep their full malpractice coverage in force or by attorneys who are forced to switch malpractice insurance carriers because of a cancellation or a refusal of a carrier to renew coverage (typically due to claims made) if the new carrier refuses to provide prior acts coverage. Tails are "cut off" after some period of time unless the tail is unlimited. Under an unlimited tail, the insurer remains liable for negligence occurring before the policy period expires regardless of when the claim is asserted.

THE DEDUCTIBLE. Most planners opt for a higher deductible in order to reduce the premium outlay. But one should check to see if legal costs he would incur in a malpractice suit apply against his share of the deductible. Does the deductible apply "per claim" or "per policy year"? Where there is more than one claim in a given policy year, a per claim deductible becomes a hidden cost: a second deductible must be satisfied in the event of a second claim within a year. A per year deductible means the deductible amount need be paid only once in a given year regardless of the number of claims. Because when it rains, it pours, a per claim provision might prove quite costly.

SETTLEMENT. Some policies give the insurer the right to limit its exposure through a provision entitled "Settlement." This means the insurer can force a settlement with the plaintiff (regardless of the insured's wishes) because of the cost. Some settlement provisions state that if one does not wish to settle under specified terms, the insurer will limit its payment to the amount specified in a settlement agreement at which point all other exposure (including defense cost) becomes the insured's obligation. Why might an insured not want to settle—even though economically it might make sense? The psychological cost of admitting wrongdoing or malpractice—coupled with the loss in reputation—are strong reasons why he may want to maintain the right to say "NO" to a settlement. One should be

sure that right does not expose him to a loss of coverage above the limits in the proposed settlement.

DUTY TO DEFEND vs DUTY TO INDEMNIFY. A "duty to defend" policy requires the insurer to appoint defense counsel and pay that attorney's fee as billed. An "indemnification" policy allows the insured to select counsel but he must fund his defense unless he can reach an interim fee agreement.[31] He will not be reimbursed for defense costs until the case is concluded. Obviously, interim funding can be a problem.

DEFINITION OF "DAMAGES." The way covered damages is defined is crucial. One may be exposed to fines, penalties, and punitive, or even treble, damages. Check with the insurance agent to clarify how broadly or narrowly the policy construes the term "damages."

INNOCENT PARTNER COVERAGE. Does the policy provide coverage for the defalcations of another member of the firm? One is liable for his partner's embezzlement even if he has not benefited by it. The insurer will deny a claim based on the partner's fraud and/or criminal activity unless there is "innocent partner" coverage.

OTHER KEY PROVISIONS. A malpractice policy ideally will provide coverage for the defense costs if it is claimed the insured is guilty of intentional conduct (even though the policy does not indemnify the costs of the intentional conduct). Does the policy cover libel or slander or defense of RICO claims?

INSURER'S STABILITY. It is important to check the financial stability of the insurer and to be sure the insurer has a solid reputation for integrity and responsiveness. It is worth finding out if the insurer itself has been involved in litigation with its own insureds. The lowest premium will not compensate for the aggravation and other costs of suing the carrier to get it to defend properly a malpractice case.

HANDLING A CLAIM. A detailed discussion of malpractice claims procedures is beyond the scope of this article. However, the following steps will help in the defense of a malpractice suit:

1. Notify the insurer immediately no matter how small the suit is.

2. Once the insured has been notified formally that he is being sued, say as little as necessary to the suing client.

3. Secure all work product immediately.

4. Inform the entire staff of the problem and the action game plan.

5. Do whatever is necessary to assist in the defense of the case.

THE TOTAL COST

The frequency of malpractice actions in the 1990s can be expected to increase many times what it was in the 1980s. No profession in the compensation planning team will escape unscathed. There are no conclusive signs that this trend is reversing.[32]

DIRECT COSTS. Malpractice premiums are in the highest classification—along with corporate securities work—for a very good reason. The dollars at risk are big.

LOSS OF REPUTATION. The cost of a malpractice suit can not be measured merely in terms of the court judgment or out of court settlement or the cost of attorneys. The cost to a professional's reputation (win or lose) may be staggering. For instance, it would be difficult to attract new partners or new associates if one has been successfully sued for malpractice.

LOSS OF STANDING WITH PEERS. Compensation planning is a process based partially on knowledge and largely on trust. A malpractice suit calls into question competence which in turn destroys confidence, not only of current and potential clients but also the confidence of other members of the planning team with whom one must deal.

THE PSYCHOLOGICAL TRAUMA. A planner who becomes a defendant in a lawsuit must deal with the incredible pressure and emotional trauma of being sued.[33] Often, the planner (and perhaps office associates, partners, and friends) will see the action taken by the client as an attack on his professional ability, integrity, or judgment. This can not help the practitioner's morale and will probably result in adverse fallout on other projects. This psychological strain is compounded by time; the legal process is typically long and drawn out over a period of years even if the claim is unfounded.

HIDDEN ECONOMIC COSTS. Colleagues from whom the practitioner received referrals and the general public may hear about the lawsuit. This will cause almost certain financial damage. Furthermore, the planner is required to participate in his own defense whether or not he is adequately insured. This, in turn, translates into dozens, sometimes hundreds, of unbillable hours spent gathering facts and records and recreating the facts, giving depositions, briefing defense attorneys, and testifying at trial.

CUT AND RUN? If it appears a matter can not be resolved by the procedures discussed above, it may be prudent to consider "discharging the client." Obviously, this is a last resort but it should not be overlooked in a "heads they win—tails we lose situation."

SUMMARY

Creating and maintaining a successful compensation planning practice requires a methodical, systematic approach to risk management. Planners are vulnerable to litigation no matter how careful they are. But the risk of a claim and the potential for a successful claim can be substantially reduced through continuing a vigorous and systematized policy of internal and external positive communication, common sense courtesy, quality control, and a strong emphasis on high quality continuing education of every member of the firm.

A planner should check that he has:

- Established and improved client relationships.
- Controlled the management of client relationships.
- Improved office practices.
- Identified problem areas.
- Corrected problems before they occur.

Looking at everything in this discussion positively, the "action suggestions" described here can be thought of not only as defensive but as the blueprint for a vigorous office organizing and client market building campaign.

FOOTNOTES

1. Cf. "Avoiding Malpractice Suits: Some Sound Advice," *Trusts and Estates*, April 1990, p. 12.
2. This is called the "best judgment" or "good faith" defense.
3. Cf. *Killey Trust*, 457 Pa. 474 (1974). Large corporate planners such as banks and trust companies will likely be held to a higher level of competence than others because of their access to information and expertise.

   On the other hand, the sophistication, education, and expertise of the client is not a defense. See *Blankenheim v. E.F. Hutton and Co. Inc.*, 217 Cal. App. 3d 1463 (1990), which held that the relationship between a stockbroker and his customer is fiduciary in nature, imposing on the former the duty to act in the highest good faith toward his customer. The court held that the plaintiff's concession that they were experts in the accounting and taxation area and any experience the plaintiff may have acquired following his investment was irrelevant to reliance on the broker's representations at the time of the sale.

4. In one case the attorney drafted a trust that failed to qualify for the marital deduction. This action was barred by a 3 year statute of limitations. So the plaintiff also sued for a violation of the state's Unfair Trade Practices Act which had a much longer statute of limitations and allowed a suit by "any person who purchases or leases goods, services, or property." The estate successfully alleged that the will draftsman had engaged in an unfair and deceptive act and practice by holding himself out as an attorney reasonably skilled in the preparation and drafting of last wills and testaments and in his ability to comply with the decedent's wishes and to minimize the tax obligations of her estate.

5. See "Court Decisions Reinforce the Idea That An Insurance Agent Who Holds Himself Out To Have Great Expertise Will Be Bound To the Exercise of it," *Trusts and Estates*, Oct. 1988, p. 55.

6. Cf. *Bell v. Manning*, 613 S. W.2nd 335 (1981).

7. *Lucas v. Hamm*, 15 Cal. Rptr 821 (1961).

8. The California Supreme Court used this test in *Biakanja v. Irving*, 49 Cal. App. 2nd 647, 320 P.2nd 16 (1958).

Although there is a trend toward relaxing the requirement of privity, New York and Texas are staunch supporters of the rule. See *Victor v. Goldman*, 344 N.Y.S.2nd 672 (1973) and *Dickey v. Jansen*, 731 S.W.2nd 581 (1987).

9. Pennsylvania Supreme Court in *Guy v. Liederbach*, 459 A.2nd 744 (1983).

10. See *Bogley v. Middletown Tavern, Inc.*, 288 Md. 645, 421 A.2nd 444 (1984). Of course, the knee jerk defense is, "The insurance was purchased in an arms' length transaction involving no confidential or fiduciary relationship between the insured and the agent." This tactic might work if the agent never professed to be anything other than a salesperson. See *Lazovick v. Sun Life Ins. Co. of America*, 586 F. Supp. 918 (E.D. Pa. 1984). This defense probably would not hold up for most readers of this text who typically hold themselves out as having significantly greater expertise than the average life insurance agent.

11. *Wright Body Works v. Columbus Interstate Insurance*, 233 Ga. 268, 210 S.E. 2nd 801 (1974).

12. *State Farm Life v. Fort Wayne National Bank*, 474 N.E. 2nd 524 (Ind 1985).

13. *Morales v. Field, DeGoff, Huppert and MacGown*, 99 Cal. App. 3d 307 (1979).

14. See "Does This Prospect Mean Trouble?," *Practical Financial Planning*, Oct/Nov. 1988, p. 23.

15. See "Reducing the Risk of Estate Planning Malpractice," *Tax Management Estates, Gifts, and Trusts Journal*, (BNA) March-April 1984, p. 36.

16. See "How Not To Be A Trustee," *Financial Planning*, May 1990, p. 69.

17. *Horne v. Peckham*, 97 Cal. App. 3rd 404 (1979).

18. Where there is reasonable doubt among well informed practitioners, there should be no liability. But this assumes a diligent quest for answers was made. Failure to research an issue or fully understand the facts will result in a denial of the "unsettled law" defense. See *Martin v. Burns*, 429 P.2nd 660 (1967).

19. See "Steps To Protect The Fiduciary From Liability For Investment Decisions," *Estate Planning*, July/August, 1989, p. 228.

20. In "Taming The Liability Monster," *L&H Perspective*, V. 15, No. 1/1989, p. 38 the author states that "A nightmare for the professional is reliance by unknown third parties on their work product."

21. As one attorney was interviewing a couple, he would pause from time to time to "capsulize" their thoughts into a dictaphone. Before he did, he would remind them each time, "Be sure to stop me if this isn't exactly what you want or if I've misunderstood what you've just said."

22. You may have to prove that, at the time you were making the decision, the available information was much different from what it is at the time litigation occurs. See "How To Manage A Growing Tax Practice," *The Practical Accountant*, May 1990, p. 27.

23. See "Avoiding and Handling Malpractice Claims Against Estate Planners," *Estate Planning*, Sept/Oct. 1989, p. 267.

24. Cf. "Coping With Administrative Problems: There's More To Life and Death Than Taxes," 21 U. of Miami Institute on Estate Planning, Chapter 17 (1987).

25. Some attorneys use commercially written brochures to make their points or to give clients something to take home that will help them understand more complex concepts. A number of highly useful client oriented brochures are available from Financial Data Corporation, P.O. Box 1332, Bryn Mawr, Pa. 19010 (215-525-6957).

26. See *Newton Estate*, T.C. Memo 1990-208, April 24, 1990 for an example of the damage a well intended but offhand remark can do. The executor's reliance on the statement of an attorney as to the filing deadline did not constitute reasonable cause for the filing delay where the attorney admittedly had not been retained to render advice on federal estate tax matters, was not paid any fee for the advice, did not normally practice in that area of the law, and had advised the executor to verify any information with a tax practitioner. The "offhand remark" may not result in a malpractice case for this attorney — but it certainly would not result in a good relationship with the client either.

27. Consider an index which includes data on clients and other parties to transactions with which the firm is involved. Include a procedure through which the system automatically updates the files to add the names of new family members, business associates, or others related to the client.

28. Obtain a "Waiver of Conflict" letter with respect to one time consulting arrangements. Obtain advance written consent to future simultaneous adverse representation on any matter not substantially related to the matter undertaken for a new client.

29. "Protecting the Corporate Fiduciary's Tender Backside," *Trusts and Estates*, Feb. 1988, p. 72.

30. See "About Your Malpractice," *Lawyer's Digest*, Pa., May 1988, p. 11.

31. "How the Accountant/Financial Planner Can Reduce Exposure to Liability Claims," *The Practical Accountant*, Feb. 1990, p. 15.

32. See "Taming the Liability Monster," *L&H Perspective*, Vol. 15/No. 1, 1989, p. 37.

33. See "Strategies to Avoid Malpractice," *Practical Financial Planning*, Vol. 2, No. 3, April/May 1989, p. 29.

Appendix I

AGE AND SEX DISCRIMINATION

I. AGE DISCRIMINATION

A. Pension Plans

Age Discrimination in Employment Act

The federal Age Discrimination in Employment Act (ADEA), as amended in 1978, 1986, and 1990, provides that it is unlawful for an employer

(1) to fail or refuse to hire or to discharge any individual or otherwise discriminate against any individual with respect to his compensation, terms, conditions, or privileges of employment, because of such individual's age;

(2) to limit, segregate, or classify his employees in any way which would deprive or tend to deprive any individual of employment opportunities or otherwise adversely affect his status as an employee, because of such individual's age; or

(3) to reduce the wage rate of any employee in order to comply with [ADEA].[1]

ADEA applies to workers and managers of any business that engages in interstate commerce (which the courts have defined very broadly) and employs at least 20 persons during the year.[2]

State laws are not preempted by ADEA. Therefore it is possible that benefit discrimination allowed under ADEA might be prohibited under applicable state law.

The primary impact of ADEA on pension plans is that the language quoted above prohibits mandatory retirement at any age. However, mandatory retirement at age 65 is specifically permitted for an individual who has been in a "bona fide executive or high policy making position" for at least two years before retirement and who is entitled to a minimum fully vested pension of $44,000 annually calculated as a straight life annuity.[3]

Beyond the issue of compulsory retirement, the language of ADEA is general and does not provide specific guidance regarding its application to pension plans, qualified or nonqualified. The Equal Employment Opportunities Commission (EEOC) has issued some regulations in this area, but in light of the *Betts* case discussed below, the current validity of prior ADEA interpretations may be questionable.

For qualified plans, there are specific age discrimination provisions in the Internal Revenue Code, as discussed below, that are not affected by any controversy regarding ADEA.

IRC Age Discrimination Provisions for Qualified Plans

Under Code section 411(b)(2), a *defined contribution* plan cannot reduce allocations (or the rate of allocations) of employer contributions, forfeitures, or income, gains or losses, in a participant's account because of the participant's age. However, the plan can have a "cap" on the number of years during which employer contributions and forfeitures will be allocated, or the total amount of contributions of forfeitures, provided that it is not based on age as such. For example, a plan can provide that employer contributions and forfeitures will be allocated only over the participant's first 25 years of service. Few plans use this approach.

Correspondingly, under Code section 411(b)(1)(H), in a *defined benefit* plan, the benefit formula cannot cutoff accruals at a specified age, but it can provide that benefits are accrued fully after a specified number of years of service, such as 25. Plans can continue to use age 65 as the "normal retirement age" for funding and benefit accrual purposes. If employees work past age 65, the Regulations provide alternative methods for benefit payment and/or accrual.[4]

B. Welfare Benefit Plans

Prior to the *Betts* case discussed below, in applying ADEA to benefit plans, an "equal cost" approach was developed in court cases and in EEOC regulations. That is, an employer was not required to provide exactly the same benefits to older as to younger employees, but rather to provide benefits having the same cost level. Thus, for example, amounts of life insurance coverage (amounts of death benefit) could be reduced for older employees to reflect the increasing premium cost. EEOC regulations allowed the use of up to 5-year age brackets for computing benefit costs. Costs were to be determined on a benefit by benefit basis under the EEOC regulations.[5]

ADEA contains a provision allowing an employer to "observe the terms of a bona fide....employee benefit plan....which is not a subterfuge to evade the purposes of [ADEA]."[6] For many years the courts and the regulatory agencies have interpreted this as an authorization for adopting rules such as the EEOC regulations.

However, in 1989 the U. S. Supreme Court decided *Public Employees Retirement System of Ohio v. Betts*.[7] Specifically, the *Betts* case involved a disability retirement benefit that was not available to employees who retired after age 59. While the Court found that this benefit did not violate ADEA, it also ruled broadly that ADEA exempts all provisions of bona fide employee benefit plans, unless the plan is a subterfuge for discrimination in non-fringe benefit aspects of the employment relationship. In so holding, the Supreme Court invalidated the EEOC's "equal cost" regulation referred to above.

After the decision in the *Betts* case, Congress took up the age discrimination issue fairly quickly, and in 1990 passed corrective legislation that essentially restores and codifies the DOL's "equal benefit or equal cost" rule. Age Discrimination in Employment Act, PL 101-433. Highlights of this legislation include:

1. The equal benefit or equal cost principle under prior EEOC regulations discussed above has now been adopted legislatively.

2. The law establishes minimum standards for employee waivers of rights under limited early retirement "window" provisions in which employees must decide whether or not to accept the program during a limited time period. If an employer adopts an early retirement incentive plan to encourage older employees to retire, employees must be given at least three weeks to decide if they want to accept the plan and must be advised in writing to consult a lawyer before accepting.

3. The new law does not apply retroactively.

4. Like the original Age Discrimination in Employment Act, the amended Act applies to businesses that employ at least 20 persons during the year.

5. All current and proposed employee benefit plans must be reviewed. Private employers had 180 days after the effective date (October 16, 1990) to amend existing plans to comply with the new law. (There is a longer phase-in period for collective bargaining employees).

II. SEX DISCRIMINATION

Sex discrimination in employee benefit plans is governed primarily by the federal Civil Rights Act of 1964, which provides as follows:

(a) It shall be an unlawful employment practice for an employer—

(1) to fail or refuse to hire or to discharge any individual, or otherwise to discriminate against any individual with respect to his compensation, terms, conditions, or privileges of employment, because of such individual's race, color, religion, sex, or national origin; or

(2) to limit, segregate, or classify his employees or applicants for employment in any way which would deprive or tend to deprive any individual of employment opportunities or otherwise adversely affect his status as an employee, because of such individual's race, color, religion, sex, or national origin.[8]

The Civil Rights Act covers all employers in interstate commerce who have at least 15 employees for each working day in at least 20 calendar weeks in the current or preceding calendar year.[9]

There are no provisions in the Internal Revenue Code or ERISA directly dealing with sex discrimination, so court decisions and regulations under the Civil Rights Act are the primary source of authority in the benefits area.[10]

In the area of wage and benefit discrimination, the Civil Rights Act provisions overlap with another federal statute, the Equal Pay Act of 1963.[11] For most benefit purposes, it is adequate to discuss only the Civil Rights Act, since there are few, if any, benefit practices permitted by the Civil Rights Act that are prohibited by the Equal Pay Act. However, there is an important difference that affects smaller employers: the Equal Pay Act has *no small employer exception*.[12]

Sex discrimination raises obvious issues in employee benefits because so many common benefits involve actuarial differences in cost between men and women—life insurance, annuities (pensions), and health insurance, particularly with regard to coverage for pregnancy. The issues involved have been fought over in the courts and the regulatory agencies; the history will not be rehashed here, but instead the result—the state of current law—will be summarized as well as possible.

Pension plans. Pension plans raise the issue of whether the law requires employers to make equal *contributions* or provide equal *benefits*. The court cases on this issue are not entirely clear, but the weight of Supreme Court decisions has convinced most commentators that an equal-benefit approach is required.[13] Specifically,

- A defined benefit plan should offer the same benefit for men and women retirees similarly situated (most always have done so).

- Employers with defined benefit plans can use sex-based actuarial assumptions for funding purposes, since this does not affect employees' benefits.

- If a retirement plan includes an incidental life insurance benefit, the same amount of life insurance must be provided to men and women employees with the same retirement benefits. If the plan is contributory, contributions must be based on unisex tables.

- If a defined contribution plan offers an annuity form of payout, either exclusively or as an option, unisex annuity rates must be used within the plan itself. (This will not prevent male retirees from taking a lump sum distribution and using the money to purchase a sex-based annuity providing higher monthly payments from an insurance company.)

Life insurance. The same Supreme Court cases cited for pension plans have convinced most commentators that the courts will uphold prohibitions against sex-based life insurance benefits.[14] Therefore, any life insurance plan should provide the same amount of insurance to any participant, male or female, who is otherwise similarly situated (same compensation, same job classification, etc.). If plan participants must contribute to the plan (as in supplemental group coverage, for example) unisex premium rates must be used.

Health insurance. In the area of health insurance, certain controversies have been settled only by federal legislation. Congress in 1978 added Section 701(k) to the Civil Rights Act to indicate that distinctions among employee benefits based on pregnancy or childbirth are considered sex-related. EEOC interpretive guidelines based on this act[15] require pregnancy and childbirth-related medical expenses of employees to be treated the same as other medical expenses. Also, the EEOC guidelines require pregnancy benefits to be provided to spouses of male employees if spouses of female employees also receive health benefits.

Other EEOC regulations prohibit restricting spousal and family benefits to employees who are deemed "head of household" and also prohibit plans that provide benefits to spouses of male employees that are not available to female employees.[16]

FOOTNOTES

1. ADEA, §4(a); 29 USC §623(a).
2. 29 USC §630(b).
3. ADEA, §12(c)(1), 29 USC §631(a)(1); 29 CFR (EEOC Reg.) §1627.17.
4. Prop. Reg. §1.411(b)-2(b)(4).
5. 29 CFR (EEOC Reg.) §1625.10.
6. ADEA, §4(f)(2), 29 USC §623(f)(2). This exception does not permit involuntary retirement because of age or failure to hire because of age.
7. *Public Employees Retirement System of Ohio v. Betts*, 492 U.S. 158, 109 S. Ct. 2854, 57 USLW 4931 (June 23, 1989).
8. Civil Rights Act of 1964, §703(a), 42 USC §2000e-2(a).
9. 42 USC §2000e(b).
10. Some commentators have theorized that the fiduciary provisions of ERISA require impartial dealing with plan participants.
11. 29 USC §206.
12. Certain types of business are excepted, however, such as retail sales, fishing, agriculture, and newspaper publishing. 29 USC §§203(s), 213(a).
13. *Los Angeles Department of Water and Power v. Manhart*, 435 U.S. 702 (1978) involved a contributory pension plan of a municipality. The Court held that the plan could not require women to pay higher contributions than men to receive equal periodic benefits upon retirement. *Arizona Governing Committee v. Norris*, 103 S. Ct. 3492 (1983) involved a Section 457 deferred compensation plan (see Chapter 11) of a municipality. The plan provided a sex-based annuity table for retirees, so that for a given account balance, a female participant received a smaller monthly retirement payment. In both these cases, the Supreme Court found a violation of the Civil Rights Act.
14. Existing EEOC regulations prohibit sex discrimination in all fringe benefits, 29 CFR §§1604.9(b), 1620.4, 1604.9(e), 1620.5(e).
15. 44 Federal Register 23804 (April 20, 1979). The provision of these guidelines requiring pregnancy benefits to spouses of male employees was upheld by the Supreme Court in *Newport News Shipbuilding and Dry Dock Co. v. EEOC*, 103 S. Ct. 2622 (1983).
16. 29 CFR §§1604.9(c), 1604.9(d), 1620.5(c), 1620.5(d) (prop.).

INDEX

Index

OBRA '93 SUPPLEMENT
to
THE TOOLS AND TECHNIQUES OF EMPLOYEE BENEFIT AND RETIREMENT PLANNING
Third Edition

COMPENSATION LIMIT FOR QUALIFIED PLANS, TDAs, SEPs, AND VEBAs REDUCED

The amount of annual compensation that can be taken into account under a qualified plan, a tax deferred annuity, a SEP, or a VEBA has been reduced to $150,000 for plan years beginning after 1993. The limit will no longer be indexed annually but will be indexed in increments of $10,000. For calendar years beginning after 1994, the $150,000 limit will not be indexed until the cost-of-living adjustment (relative to this limit) equals or exceeds $10,000. For example, cumulative cost-of-living increases totaling 6.67% ($150,000 × .0667 = $10,005) would increase the limit to $160,000 ($150,000 + $10,005 = $160,005, rounded to the next lowest multiple of $10,000). OBRA '93, Sec. 13212. *Chapters affected: Chapter 9, Defined Benefit Plan; Chapter 10, ESOP/Stock Bonus Plan; Chapter 15, Money Purchase Pension Plan; Chapter 17, Profit-Sharing Plan; Chapter 20, Simplified Employee Pension (SEP); Chapter 21, Target/Age-Weighted Plan; Chapter 22, Tax Deferred Annuity; Chapter 23, Qualified Plans: Rules for Qualification; Chapter 51, Welfare Benefit Trusts and VEBAs.*

EDUCATIONAL ASSISTANCE PLANS EXTENDED

The expiration date of Section 127 relating to Educational Assistance Programs has been extended by OBRA '93. Section 127 will now be in effect for taxable years which begin on or before December 31, 1994. Prior to OBRA '93, Section 127 was scheduled to be in effect only for taxable years beginning on or before June 30, 1992. OBRA '93, Sec. 13101(a). *Chapters affected: Chapter 32, Educational Assistance Plan.*

HEALTH INSURANCE DEDUCTION FOR SELF-EMPLOYED PERSONS EXTENDED

The availability of the deduction for 25% of health insurance premiums paid by self-employed persons has been extended. OBRA '93 amends Code section 162(l) to make this deduction available for taxable years beginning on or before December 31, 1993. Generally, sole proprietors, partners and S corporation shareholders owning more than two percent of the S corporation's shares may take advantage of this deduction. OBRA '93, Sec. 13174(a). *Chapters affected: Chapter 5, Benefit Plans for S Corporations, Partnerships and Proprietorships; Chapter 37, Health Insurance.*

INCREASE IN CORPORATE INCOME TAX RATES

For tax years beginning on or after January 1, 1993, the top marginal income tax rate has been increased from 34% to 35% for corporations with taxable incomes exceeding $10,000,000. Corporations with taxable incomes exceeding $15,000,000 pay an additional amount equal to the lesser of 3% of such excess or $100,000. Personal service corporations are now taxed at a flat 35% rate rather than at a flat 34% rate. From a planning perspective this change will effect most employee benefit plans which involve an income tax deduction for the corporation. OBRA '93, Sec. 13211. *Chapters affected: Chapter 16, Non-qualified Deferred Compensation; Chapter 26, Bonus Plan; Chapter 28, Cash Compensation Planning; Chapter 30, Death Benefit Only (DBO) Plan; and Chapter 49, Split Dollar Life Insurance.*

LEGAL SERVICES PLANS NOT EXTENDED

Although it was expected to, OBRA '93 did not extend the date applicable to Legal Services Plans governed by Code section 120. As of August, 1993, Section 120 is not available for taxable years beginning after June 30, 1992. *Chapters affected: Chapter 41, Legal Services Plans.*

LIMIT ON DEDUCTIBILITY OF EXECUTIVE COMPENSATION

OBRA '93 places an upper limitation on the amount of compensation paid to certain executives that may be deducted by a corporation. Effective for taxable years beginning on or after January 1, 1994, no deduction will be permitted for compensation in excess of $1,000,000 paid to any covered employee by any publicly-held corporation. Generally, a "covered employee" is the corporation's chief executive officer or any employee who is one of the 4 highest compensated officers of the company (other than the chief executive officer). This new provision, which is now reflected in Code section 162(m), provides exceptions from the $1,000,000 limitation for commission payments, certain performance-based payments and amounts paid under a binding contract in effect on February 17, 1993. Also included is a provision which coordinates the deduction limitation with the golden parachute provisions. OBRA '93, Sec. 13211. *Chapters affected: Chapter 28, Cash Compensation Planning; Chapter 35, Golden Parachute Plans.*

MOVING EXPENSE DEDUCTION MODIFIED

The availability of the deduction for moving expenses incurred in connection with the commencement of work by a taxpayer at a new place of work has been restricted by OBRA '93. No longer does the definition of "moving expenses" provided by Code section 217 include meals taken during travel incident to the move. In addition, in order for moving expenses to be deductible, the taxpayer's new place of work must now be at least 50 miles farther from his former residence than was his former place of work or, if he had no former place of work, at least 50 miles from his former residence. (Under prior law, the distance threshold was 35 miles.) However, OBRA '93 has converted the moving expense deduction to an "above-the-line" deduction (i.e., a deduction allowed in computing adjusted gross income). These changes are effective for expenses incurred after December 31, 1993. OBRA '93, Sec. 13213. *Chapters affected: Chapter 45, Moving Expense Reimbursement.*

IN GENERAL

Income Tax Rates

The tax rate tables have been amended by OBRA '93 retroactively to tax years beginning after December 31, 1992. The amendments include an increase in the top marginal tax rate to be applied to income earned by individual taxpayers. The tax rates are 15%, 28%, 31%, and 36%, as well as a surtax on high income taxpayers in the form of a 39.6% tax rate. OBRA '93 also includes a provision that creates an election to pay in installments any additional 1993 income taxes due because of the new top marginal rate. OBRA '93, Secs. 13201, 13202.

Alternative Minimum Tax

The alternative minimum tax (AMT) rate for individuals has been changed so that a rate of 26% applies to alternative minimum taxable income (AMTI) above applicable exemption amounts but below $175,001, while a rate of 28% applies to AMTI above the exemption amounts and exceeding $175,000. The applicable exemption amounts used to determine an individual's AMT liability have been increased as well. OBRA '93, Sec. 13203.

Estate, Gift and Generation-Skipping Tax Rate

The top estate and gift tax rate has been made permanent at 55 percent (a 5 percent additional tax designed to recapture the benefit of the lower tax brackets and the unified credit on estates exceeding $10 million can, in effect, push the marginal estate and gift tax rate to 60 percent, although the average rate will never exceed 55 percent). Correspondingly, the generation-skipping transfer tax (GSTT) rate is a flat 55 percent. The scheduled reduction in the top estate and gift tax rate and the GSTT rate to 50 percent in 1993 has been retroactively repealed. OBRA '93, Sec. 13208.

Medicare Hospital Insurance Tax

The dollar limit on wages and self-employment income subject to the Medicare Hospital Insurance (HI) tax has been repealed for 1994 and later calendar years. For wages paid in 1993, the HI tax rate of 1.45% for both employers and employees applies to the first $135,000 of wages. For self-employed individuals, the HI tax rate of 2.90% applies to the first $135,000 of self-employment income. For 1994 and later, all income will be subject to the HI tax. OBRA '93, Section 13207.

Complete Your
LEIMBERG
TOOLS AND TECHNIQUES
LIBRARY

Use this handy postage-paid form to order additional copies of *The Tools and Techniques of Employee Benefit and Retirement Planning*—3rd edition or copies of

❏ *The Tools and Techniques of Financial Planning*—4th edition

❏ *The Tools and Techniques of Estate Planning*—9th edition

or call

1-800-543-0874

and ask for Operator BD,
or FAX: 1-800-874-1916

Prices*

The Tools and Techniques of Employee Benefit & Retirement Planning

Single copy	$35.00
5 copies, ea.	33.25
10 copies, ea.	31.50
25 copies, ea.	30.00

The Tools and Techniques of Financial Planning

Single copy	$37.50
5 copies, ea.	35.60
10 copies, ea.	33.75
25 copies, ea.	32.15

The Tools and Techniques of Estate Planning

Single copy	$39.95
5 copies, ea.	37.95
10 copies, ea.	35.95
25 copies, ea.	34.25

Special Package Prices—
Order two different titles for $62.00 or all three for $90.00.

PAYMENT INFORMATION

* Add shipping & handling charges to all orders as follows. If your order exceeds total amount listed in chart, call 1-800-543-0874 for shipping & handling charge. Any order of 10 or more items or over $250.00 will be billed by actual weight, plus a handling fee. Unconditional 30 day guarantee.

ORDER TOTAL	SHIPPING & HANDLING
$20.00 - 39.99	$5.00
40.00 - 59.99	6.00
60.00 - 79.99	8.00
80.00 - 109.00	9.00
110.00 - 149.99	11.00

NATIONAL UNDERWRITER

The National Underwriter Co.
Customer Service Department #2-BD
505 Gest Street
Cincinnati, OH 45203-1716

2-BD

Please send me the following:

_____ copies of *The Tools & Techniques of Employee Benefit and Retirement Planning* (#271)
_____ copies of *The Tools & Techniques of Financial Planning* (#277)
_____ copies of *The Tools & Techniques of Estate Planning* (#285)

❏ Check enclosed made payable to the National Underwriter Co.*
❏ Charge My VISA/MC (circle one)   ❏ Bill me

Card #_____ Exp.Date_____ Signature_____
Name_____ Title_____
Company_____
Address_____
City_____ State_____ Zip+4_____
Business Phone_____

Residents of the following, please add appropriate sales tax: CA, DC, FL, GA, IL, NJ, NY, OH, PA. Offer expires 12/31/94.

NATIONAL UNDERWRITER

The National Underwriter Co.
Customer Service Department #2-BD
505 Gest Street
Cincinnati, OH 45203-1716

2-BD

Please send me the following:

_____ copies of *The Tools & Techniques of Employee Benefit and Retirement Planning* (#271)
_____ copies of *The Tools & Techniques of Financial Planning* (#277)
_____ copies of *The Tools & Techniques of Estate Planning* (#285)

❏ Check enclosed made payable to the National Underwriter Co.*
❏ Charge My VISA/MC (circle one)   ❏ Bill me

Card #_____ Exp.Date_____ Signature_____
Name_____ Title_____
Company_____
Address_____
City_____ State_____ Zip+4_____
Business Phone_____

Residents of the following, please add appropriate sales tax: CA, DC, FL, GA, IL, NJ, NY, OH, PA. Offer expires 12/31/94.

NATIONAL UNDERWRITER

The National Underwriter Co.
Customer Service Department #2-BD
505 Gest Street
Cincinnati, OH 45203-1716

2-BD

Please send me the following:

_____ copies of *The Tools & Techniques of Employee Benefit and Retirement Planning* (#271)
_____ copies of *The Tools & Techniques of Financial Planning* (#277)
_____ copies of *The Tools & Techniques of Estate Planning* (#285)

❏ Check enclosed made payable to the National Underwriter Co.*
❏ Charge My VISA/MC (circle one)   ❏ Bill me

Card #_____ Exp.Date_____ Signature_____
Name_____ Title_____
Company_____
Address_____
City_____ State_____ Zip+4_____
Business Phone_____

Residents of the following, please add appropriate sales tax: CA, DC, FL, GA, IL, NJ, NY, OH, PA. Offer expires 12/31/94.

**NO POSTAGE
NECESSARY
IF MAILED
IN THE
UNITED STATES**

BUSINESS REPLY MAIL
FIRST CLASS MAIL   PERMIT NO. 68   CINCINNATI, OH

POSTAGE WILL BE PAID BY ADDRESSEE

THE   NATIONAL   UNDERWRITER   CO.
CUSTOMER   SERVICE   DEPT   #2-BD
505   GEST   STREET
CINCINNATI   OH   45203-9928

**NO POSTAGE
NECESSARY
IF MAILED
IN THE
UNITED STATES**

BUSINESS REPLY MAIL
FIRST CLASS MAIL   PERMIT NO. 68   CINCINNATI, OH

POSTAGE WILL BE PAID BY ADDRESSEE

THE   NATIONAL   UNDERWRITER   CO.
CUSTOMER   SERVICE   DEPT   #2-BD
505   GEST   STREET
CINCINNATI   OH   45203-9928

**NO POSTAGE
NECESSARY
IF MAILED
IN THE
UNITED STATES**

BUSINESS REPLY MAIL
FIRST CLASS MAIL   PERMIT NO. 68   CINCINNATI, OH

POSTAGE WILL BE PAID BY ADDRESSEE

THE   NATIONAL   UNDERWRITER   CO.
CUSTOMER   SERVICE   DEPT   #2-BD
505   GEST   STREET
CINCINNATI   OH   45203-9928